PREACHING THROUGH THE BIBLE

BY
JOSEPH PARKER

VOL. 21

MARK-LUKE

BAKER BOOK HOUSE
Grand Rapids, Michigan

Standard Book Number: 8010-6884-3

Library of Congress Catalog Card Number: 59-10860

Reprinted 1971 by
Baker Book House Company

Originally printed
under the title,
The People's Bible

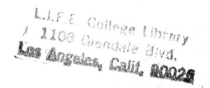

CONTENTS.

THE GOSPEL ACCORDING TO ST. MARK.

THE GOSPEL ACCORDING TO ST. LUKE.

GOSPEL ACCORDING TO MARK.

Chapter i. 1-8.

1. The beginning of the gospel of Jesus Christ, the Son of God;

2. As it is written in the prophets, Behold, I send my messenger before thy face, which shall prepare thy way before thee.

3. The voice of one crying in the wilderness, Prepare ye the way of the Lord, make his paths straight.

4. John did baptize in the wilderness, and preach the baptism of repentance for the remission of sins.

5. And there went out unto him all the land of Judæa, and they of Jerusalem, and were all baptized of him in the river of Jordan, confessing their sins.

6. And John was clothed with camel's hair, and with a girdle of skin about his loins; and he did eat locusts and wild honey

7. And preached, saying, There cometh one mightie than I after me, the latchet of whose shoes I am not worthy to stoop down and unloose.

8. I indeed have baptized you with water: but he shall baptize you with the Holy Ghost.

THE THREEFOLD BEGINNING OF THE GOSPEL.

THE gospel may be said to have three beginnings, and yet it is perfectly correct to say that each beginning has a speciality and completeness of its own. The beginning of the gospel is, of course, to be found in the thought and love of God. We may cast our lines back as far as we can through the ages of eternity, and we shall never be able to find the point at which God's concern for the welfare of the universe that was to be first began, and yet the Lamb of God is said to have been slain from before the foundation of the world. The sacrifice of Christ was not an afterthought on the part of the Divine Being; it was, so to speak, part of himself, an element of his very Godhead and of his very existence. So that, if we are really to go back to what may be termed the beginning of beginnings, we shall have to search the depths of the divine existence, and follow all the wonderful and infinite course of the divine thinking and purpose and love.   There, of course, we are lost.   Our hearts can only point, as it were, towards that great solemn mystery. Explanation we have none.   Special indication is entirely beyond our power.   We are lost in wonder, and our wonder is lost in speechlessness.

But there was what may be termed a second beginning of the gospel, and it is to that event that the gospel before us relates. The second beginning of the gospel of Jesus Christ, the Son of God, is found in the incarnation of God's Son.   We begin the next time at Bethlehem.   We were lost when it was a mere question of unuttered and in speech unutterable love.   We only begin to think and to feel and to understand in part God's meaning, when he utters his love not in speech, but in the person, the flesh and blood of God's dear Son.   We can begin there—little children can begin at that point; our love can commence its study at the cradle of our Lord Jesus Christ.   Creatures like ourselves need alphabets, beginnings, sharp lines, visibilities. We are not all mind; we cannot dwell upon the abstract, the unconditioned, the absolute, the infinite, in matters of this kind. We need some one to look at, to speak to, to go up to quite closely, and to hear speak the language of the love of God.   This is what may be termed the second beginning of the gospel of Jesus Christ.

But Jesus Christ himself went away.   That beginning was, so to speak, taken from us.   Where, then, are we to look for the third beginning of the gospel of Jesus Christ, the Son of God? We look for it in the Church.   As he was, so are we to be in the world.   We are to be "living epistles, known and read of all men."   When men ask, "Where is Christ?" we are to show them Christianity.   And when they ask, "What is Christianity?" we are to show them the Church—meanwhile, indeed, an incomplete representation of the truth, yet Jesus Christ himself claims it, and upon the Church devolves the responsibility not only of bearing his name by exemplifying his life, but of interpreting his doctrine and living upon his love. So, then, we do not treat the Church as a mere accident; we do not regard even the visible Church as something that is of the nature of an ordinary human association. It is more than a society; it is more than a club; more than a confraternity based upon kindred social sympathies. It is the embodied doctrine and love of Christ; and in so far as it falls short of that embodiment, it has yet to be crucified, purged with fire, and searched by the light of God. Is it not the same with all great sublime far-reaching life? Yonder is a man sitting alone with closed eyes, yet the vision of his soul is fastened upon a wondrous picture. He is looking at a great poem built in stone, at a piece of wondrous thinking, having great foundations, far-ascending and glittering pinnacles or majestic domes. It is all in his mind. At present it is nothing but a thought. He is an architect. He has a cathedral in his brain, and he sees it, every line—sees the great gaping places dug out for the foundations, sees the courses of great rough unpolished stone— sees the building rising into shape, into presence, into meaning, into awfulness—petrified poesy. But that is not enough for him. Now he draws his plan. He gives the thought visibility; he interprets it to duller brains; he calls in what may be termed, without offence, a secondary order of intellect—not the dreaming and poetic intellect, that creates new heavens and new earths and lives in continued newness of beauty,—he calls in the power that can give expression and visibleness to great ideas, and he is not content until he sees this thought of his built up in all its grandeur and completeness; and even then, if he be a true artist, if the divine fire of art be really in him, he wants something more. He does not content himself with looking at the great stone-work; he wants to see the purpose for which that stone-work was put up carried out, in so far as he himself is a complete man and works upon complete ideas. There is to be an inner cathedral, a human cathedral, a cathedral of praises, a cathedral of living worshippers. Probably he does not in all cases reach that third idea, but that third idea ought to be consequential upon the other two; and is, in the up-building of the great cathedral which God himself is to inhabit—first, his own great speechless, silent, infinite, universe-encompassing love, and then his visible Son, and then his redeemed Church, and then the Cathedral of Praise which the Holy One of Israel is to inhabit throughout eternity.

As it is written in the prophets, " Behold, I send my messenger before thy face which shall prepare thy way before thee. The voice of one crying in the wilderness, Prepare ye the way of the Lord, make his paths straight." The divine dispensations have all been progressive. You cannot point to a single backward step in the divine thinking, in the divine movement. This Book, the book of inspiration, the Book of God, goes right forward. There is progress, but not progress by correction—progress by development, by natural expansion—the tree coming out of the seed, and the seed only lost when the tree has reached the fulness of the divine intent. This is a legitimate test of all truth, a legitimate test of every ministry and a legitimate test of every Christian life. The question which may be fairly put about the Bible and about all life, all ministries and all churches, is this, " What of their progressiveness ? " If a man is the same to-day that he was twenty years ago, he is growing downwards, and is really not the same man that he was twenty years ago. A man must be double the man he was twenty years ago, or there is something wrong in him. If you say he preaches exactly as he did a quarter of a century since, then he was a poor preacher to begin with, and he has become worse and worse as the years have rolled away. I fasten this inquiry upon the Book of God, and I will stake great results upon it. What of its progressiveness ? How did divine revelation begin ? How has it proceeded ? How did it culminate ? Is the culmination of the divine truth of the same nature and quality as the beginning, or is there disjunction, is there vital separation ? And everything will depend upon the answer that can be returned to these inquiries. We claim on a Christian basis, and for Christian purposes, that all the dispensations have been progressive and culminative and climacteric, and the last point of the series is of the same quality as the first. This is a great mystery, but it is an unanswerable argument. Here you have the prophets living their tumultuous, exciting, bewildering life—great men to-day by reason of special divine visitation, by reason of having been called away suddenly by the Spirit of God, shown wondrous sights, and having their ears opened to wondrous sounds—and to-morrow, weak as common men, if not weaker, by reason of the terrible reaction—thrown down, shattered, unable to make anything of the world or of their strange life. God then, in the first instance, has his prophets in the world—men that lived less in the present than in the future, men, therefore, who were continually being subjected to tests of a capricious and arbitrary kind, but never responding to such demands—men who by reason of living in the future were subjected to continual misjudgment and misapprehension. Oh! but theirs was a sad life at times. To have little or no connection with the men that are round about you, to have a heart that cannot understand or thinks it unworthy of understanding the little things that go to make up the present dying hour; to be in existence to-day, and yet to be breathing the atmosphere of centuries to come,—that was a test of life that was almost a divine judgment upon those strange men the prophets.

Then after the prophets we have a voice of one crying in the wilderness, "Prepare." We have John the Baptist, and of John the Baptist it is said that he was sent before the face of the Redeemer,—"Behold, I send my messenger before thy face.' He was next to the face, the presence, of the coming One. The prophets were centuries away from him, but this man was all but a transparent veil; they could almost see the coming God through him. He went immediately before the face. If he stood aside but for a moment there was the One that was to come. And oh! what a burden he carried who had the breath of the predicted One breathed upon him as he was going through his introductory ministry. Now the question is, how to get from Malachi to Matthew? Almighty God has so trained the world by prophecy, by type, by figure, by ritualism, by manifold discipline, that he has made the world very impatient for the next step. How to get from the Old Testament into the New?—that is the great question; how to get from the one dispensation in its final phase, into another dispensation that shall satisfy an impatient, necessitous world. Where is your human genius there? Shut up this New Testament and deal with the Old Testament alone, and I say, now how are you to write a testament that shall be New, and yet of the nature of the Old, that shall answer all the questions suggested by the Old, and satisfy the impatience which has been wrought in the hungry heart of man by the manifold system of training which the Divine Being has adopted ? Unfortunately for this point of the inquiry, we know how the New Testament opens, and our familiarity with it becomes our weakness. Forget if you can for one moment how the New Testament opens. Read from Genesis to Malachi, and then ask yourselves this question : Now what can be done that shall not throw us back ; that shall make the best possible use of the elements we have gathered ; that shall move not on a side, not upon a tangential line, but that shall move upon some straight line, and carry it forward to a natural and satisfactory climax ? Will men put their genius to the torment that will impose upon them—how to write a testament, when for so many centuries we have got an old one ? We have got almost tired of writing now. Almighty God hath wrought us up almost into an angry mood. We are now jealous, impatient, strained to the highest tension, and if we step one point backwards, it is to us atheism, defiance, and hell if need be. What will he do ? We have had prophecy, we have had great temples, we saw the procession of the priests, we have watched the sacrifices, always beginning, never ending, or ending only to begin again ; but we are tired of that now, and we in this excited, strained, impatient, anxious, wondering temper say, "How will God go on next ? " Oh, I dare hardly turn the page over; it seems that in the turning of this page our destiny is being turned, is being settled for good or evil. What can come after prophets and minstrels and priests, mighty but insufficient interpreters of the divine purpose ? Now I turn the page and I find this solution—"Emmanuel, God with us," and the artist that is in me, the idealist that is in me, as well as the sinner that is in me, says, "It is enough ! " My Lord and my God ! Yes, we could not have written in mere words a New Testament. The world could not have borne that ; but when the New Testament was written in the flesh and blood of God himself, and the man that spoke to us was Emmanuel, a man that could stoop like a mother and look like a God—It is enough !

And John said, "I indeed have baptised you with water : but

he shall baptise you with the Holy Ghost." The crowning dispensation must be spiritual. "He shall baptise you with the Holy Ghost." There cometh a time in all study when we want to get clear of mere formulæ. and mere lines and laborious and intricate processes, and we want to have that mental dominance which brings us into constant recognition and appreciation of the truth. We get tired of looking, we get tired of using powers that were intended to be merely temporary. The Divine Being comes to us, and turns our religion from a process of looking and inquiry and hard service into spiritual life, spiritual love, until we know what it is to have the power of instantly going to God, and of holding, as it were, face-to-face communion and fellowship with him. That is, if we be baptised with the Holy Ghost, the Holy Ghost takes hold of the highest faculties of our nature and works with these alone. The body falls off. All that was instrumental and of the nature of agency fades and drops away, and we come into mind-power, moral power, spiritual mastery; and things which aforetime were difficult, and almost impossible to us, become easy and natural, and communion with God becomes the very breath of our souls.

What, then, of the subject as it has thus been hinted at? If we have in any degree laid hold of its meaning, it is evident that the subject addresses a word in the first place to students. Here is a revelation to be studied, and we shall only be wise masters in this art in proportion as we have a grasp of the whole. Our theology must not be angular but circular; it must not be beautiful in one or two places, it must be complete. We must understand every dispensation by itself and in its relation to the succeeding order of things; otherwise we shall be thrown about by everybody who chooses to play legerdemain with us. We shall have questions put to us that we cannot answer, and difficulties which we might otherwise count as trifles will be mountainous and insuperable. We must get into that state of mind that sees the beginning and that sees the end, and grasps the extremes, so far as it is possible for limited life so to grasp them. There are many men who are very clever at certain points, but take them away from those points, and they are shorn Samsons—any child can trifle with them. No, we must, if we are to be successful and useful students and ministers of these holy mysteries, have something like a grasp of the whole; and though we may not be able to answer special difficulties and peculiar inquiries, yet, as in the spiritual life so in the intellectual regions, we shall bring the power of the endless to bear upon the difficulties that are momentary. I confess, after having done my best to study this Book, that I am most impressed by its unity, its completeness, by the inter-relation of part to part, so that if I touch one point I break up its completeness, I impair and injure its wondrous beauty. There are points where I am dumb—mysteries that I cannot shed any light upon, and from which I cannot extract one explanatory word—but when I look at the whole, the complete dispensations of God, I find their very completeness one of the most convincing and determining arguments.

Here is a lesson to Churches. "Have ye received the Holy Ghost?" It was reserved for you specially to be baptised by the Holy Spirit. Are you still lingering among the prophets? You are not in Christ if so be ye have not received the Holy Ghost. Do you tell me you are busy gathering what you may from the lightning-scarred slopes of Sinai? I say Sinai! A fragment of the past! It is now, What of Calvary and what of Olivet and what of the Church, the temple into which the Holy Ghost came as baptising fire? No man is at liberty to live backwards. If the prophets underwent misjudgment and torment by reason of having to live in the future, what shall be said of those poor rickety creatures who are always trying to go back into the dim past, to exhume the prophets, and to live three or four centuries behind their privileges? The whole judgment now is a judgment of the Holy Ghost, not what questions can we answer, nor what histories have we considered and mastered? but what about the inward baptism, the baptism of fire, the baptism of life, the gift of the spirit of interpretation and the spirit of purity? These are the searching questions which become to us terrible as the judgment of Almighty God.

Here is a lesson to pioneers. John was a herald, and John knew the position to which he was called, and he never trespassed the limits of his vocation. When he spoke he did not speak in his own name, he did not draw attention to himself; he always spoke of the One mightier than he, who was immediately coming. And what are we, whether we be ministers or teachers or parents or churches, what are we really so far as our service goes but pioneers, those who shall prepare for and point out the One mightier than ourselves? If for a moment John had supposed himself to be the Messiah, what a shock and what terrible results would have followed! Men must know their power, men must know their calling, and when a man knows his limitations it is surprising how mighty a weak man is. Keep him within his own province, bind him to his own mission, and within his proper boundaries, he is a prince and a son of God; but let him get beyond that line, and he is captured as an intruder or is slain as a spy. Let us know what is meant by our position as pioneers. If the frame-maker should ever take it into his head that he is the artist, what an anti-climax would be perpetrated! If April should ever take it into its head that it can do the work of August, what a block there would be in the process of the year!

We are called to different positions in the Church. God hath set some in the Church pastors, prophets, evangelists, teachers, helps, governors, every one as it pleaseth him. What then? We are not to devour one another, we are not to envy one another, we are not to say hard, cruel, unkind, depreciatory words about one another; a man must find out what God intended him to be in the course of his dispensation, and if he be that, however humble the position, he will have resting upon him the ever-sustaining and ever-comforting blessing of God. Are you an evangelist? I glorify God in you; do not try to be anything else. Have you in you the consciousness that you can be something else, something that you think higher? First of all I do not know that it is higher—I do not know that there is anything higher in the Church than being an evangelist, one who preaches the Gospel here and there and wheresoever opportunity is given him, or he himself can make opportunity for the proclamation of it. But if it has got into you that you can do something higher, be careful, make it a matter of profound religious inquiry before you step out of the position you are now in. Are you a pastor? I glorify God in you; I long for, I almost covet your powers. You have such a way of dropping your voice so that the dullest can hear you, and the weakest are made glad by your presence; you can put so much truth into so few words, that one covets, with a godly covetousness, your rich and most fruitful gifts. Do not try to be anything else, merely for the sake of change. If there be in you another calling, God in his own time and in his own way will make it quite clear to you. Are you labouring in a village, and does it ever enter into your head that you would like to labour in London? You had better not; you had better not entertain that notion; it hath driven some men almost crazy, and it is a very perilous thing to play with—a notion of that kind, that a man is adapted to Metropolitan life when probably he is adapted to nothing of the sort. "To fill up the sphere we have" should be our duty and our joy. "It is only a nutshell." Well, then, it will take less filling. "It is only a little village." Well, then, you will make your work the more manifest and the more speedy. I do not say that every man is to ab de just where he is—nothing of the kind; but whilst he is there he is bound by every consideration than can stir a true man's heart and strength to make the very best of his position.

Here is a lesson to inquirers. If I have read this Book aright, I find that it is a shut volume; it is now complete; there is nothing more to be written. If you are waiting for something else, I feel it incumbent upon me, as the result of my own studies, to say in my own name that the vision is closed, and there is nothing more to come. What more can you possibly want? The prophets have been here, flaming men, men with voices like trumpets and thunder—they have been here. The minstrels, men of poesy, dreaming men, men who had eyes that could see visions in the night-time—they have been here. They are gone. Priests have been here, men who shed blood, and who explained the meaning of the blood which they shed, who built the altars and officiated at those altars—they have been here, and they have gone. And John the Baptist, the pre-liminary man, the man who went immediately before the Face—he has been here and gone. And Emmanuel has been here—"God with us." And the Holy Ghost is come to us. What more can there be to wait for? If this cannot satisfy us, then what will appease our hunger? He must be a bold man that can elbow and cleave and force his way to hell through prophets and priests and psalmists and Baptists, and God's Son and God the Holy Ghost, and then say, as he takes the last plunge, "There was not enough given me; I was waiting for something else, and that something. else never came." Will you risk that? Have you made the best of what has been given? Are you really masters of the Book of God, able to understand its scope and its meaning? Oh, see to it, that there is not some little or great pebble of selfishness over which you are just going to topple into darkness and ruin and death. O thou, who madest the eyes of the heart, anoint the eyes of our love, that we may see thee, and be fascinated by thy beauty for ever. Amen.

NOTE.

"Mark, who, besides his Latin name of *Marcus*, appears to have had the Hebrew name of *John*, was the son of Mary, a pious woman at Jerusalem, who received in her house the assemblies of the primitive church, and welcomed the Apostle Peter after his deliverance out of prison by the angel (Acts xii. 12). Mark was the nephew of Barnabas, Paul's companion in his travels (Col. iv. 10). These two, being at Jerusalem about the time of Peter's deliverance, took Mark with them upon their mission (Acts xii. 25). He accompanied them to Antioch; and thence, on their first journey, as far as Perga in Pamphylia; where he left them, and returned to Jerusalem (Acts xiii. 5, 13). We afterwards find him at Antioch, with Paul and Barnabas, desiring to accompany them on a second journey; but Paul, regarding him as unfit for the work, since he had left them on the former occasion, was unwilling to take him. This decision caused a warm dispute and a temporary separation between the two apostles; and Barnabas, influenced probably by his affection for his kinsman, 'took Mark, and sailed unto Cyprus.' There can be no doubt that Mark afterwards acknowledged his error, whatever it was—whether he was wanting in the courageous self-denial of the missionary, or had misgivings on the extension of the gospel to the heathen—for the Apostle Paul appears to have given him his confidence and affection, and commends him to the church. See Col. iv. 10; 2 Tim. iv. 11 ; Philem. 24.

"To these notices, gathered from the sacred writers, others add that Mark afterwards went to Egypt; and, having planted a church at Alexandria, died there."—ANGUS's *Bible Handbook.*

Chapter i. 9-45.

SPIRITUAL REPARATION.

[An Analysis.]

9. And it came to pass in those days, that Jesus came from Nazareth of Galilee, and was baptized of John in Jordan.

(1) JOHN'S dispensation was thus shown to be of divine appointment. Notice the beauty of John's work in relation both to the past and to the future : it was a baptism unto repentance ; a baptism, and so connected with the ceremonial past ;—a baptism unto repentance, and so introductory to a new and more intensely spiritual state of things.

(2) But why should Jesus Christ identify himself with a baptism which was unto repentance ? His identification with that baptism was not for the purpose of personal confession, but for the purpose of official absorption. He took up the dispensation, and ended it by the introduction of a better. So, when he took upon himself the nature of mankind, he did not degrade and enfeeble God, he elevated and glorified man.

10. And straightway coming up out of the water, he saw the heavens opened, and the Spirit like a dove descending upon him.

11. And there came a voice from heaven, saying, Thou art my beloved Son, in whom I am well pleased.

Whatever is done in the divine name and for the divine glory is succeeded by increasing evidence of divine favour. What Jesus saw on coming out of the water, we should all see on returning from every act of homage and obedience. (1) The Spirit is a heavenly gift, not a natural grace. (2) Sonship is not generic; it is specific—thou. (3) Sonship is not left a mystery; it is declared and confirmed to the individual heart.

12. And immediately the Spirit driveth him into the wilderness.

13. And he was there in the wilderness forty days, tempted of Satan ; and was with the wild beasts ; and the angels ministered unto him.

(1) Sonship does not exempt from temptation. (2) Temptation does not invalidate sonship. (3) Temptation, rightly answered, makes sonship a life and power. We are not to be content with nominal sonship. We are to be proved men. Contrast Matthew's account of the Temptation with Mark's. The one is minute and elaborate ; the other is compendious. What history may be put into a sentence ! There are experiences which cannot be put into words—they can only be hinted at. Some men have not the power of spiritual analysis ; they cannot follow a temptation through its changing assaults and attitudes. Mark was probably not equal to Matthew in this particular. As with temptation, so with conversion. Some men can only say that they are converted ; explanation and discussion are beyond their power. " And the angels ministered unto him." The darkest temptation has some light to relieve it. When we feel the devil we should look for the angels.

14. Now after that John was put in prison, **Jesus came into Galilee,** preaching the gospel of the kingdom of God.

15. And saying, The time is fulfilled, and the **kingdom of God is at** hand : repent ye, and believe the gospel.

(1) The imprisonment of the servant does not hinder the progress of the Master. (2) Ill-treatment of the messenger may actually help the divinity of the message : (*a*) it tests sincerity, (*b*) it tests the sustaining power of the doctrine that is preached.

The 15th verse shows Jesus Christ in three aspects : (1) as the interpreter of time ; (2) as the revealer of the divine kingdom ; (3) as a spiritual regenerator. Under these heads note—

Time : The preparative process ; the development of opportunity ; the moral import of special times.

Kingdom : Not a transient erection; not a subordinate arrangement ; not a human ambition—the kingdom of God.

Regeneration : Vital ; progressive ; spiritual. Vital—Repent, destroy the past, humble yourselves on account of sin. Progressive—after humiliation is to come trust, the broken heart is to be the believing heart. Spiritual—not a change of mere attitudes and relations, but a change of life.

It is to be specially noted that Jesus Christ preached the kingdom of God as a gospel : rightly understood, it is not a despotism, it is not a terror ; it is the supremacy of light, of truth, of love.

16. Now as he walked by the sea of Galilee, he saw Simon and Andrew his brother casting a net into the sea : for they were fishers.

17. And Jesus said unto them, Come ye after me, and I will make you to become fishers of men.

18. And straightway they forsook their nets, and followed him.

19. And when he had gone a little farther thence, he saw James the son of Zebedee, and John his brother, who also were in the ship mending their nets.

20. And straightway he called them : and they left their father Zebedee in the ship with the hired servants, and went after him.

(1) Christ is the preparer of his servants—"I will make you": how much was involved in that promise! (a) Authority; (b) qualification. (2) Small beginnings compatible with sublime results. (3) The claims of God over-ride all other claims—the sons left their father. (4) The discharge of common duties the best preparation for higher calls—two were casting the net into the sea, and two were mending their nets. The transition from one duty to another need not be abrupt. The humblest duty may be very near the highest honour. (5) The place of the servant is after the Master—"Come ye after me": they are not invited to equal terms—they must walk in the King's shadow.

Some hearts respond to Christ instantly—some linger long, and yield, as it were, with reluctance.

"They left their father Zebedee in the ship": fathers should never keep back their sons from Christ's service.

21. And they went into Capernaum: and straightway on the sabbath day he entered into the synagogue, and taught.

22. And they were astonished at his doctrine: for he taught them as one that had authority, and not as the scribes.

(1) Men will teach well only as they teach under Christ. (2) Authority is impossible apart from association with the Master. (3) Authority of tone must come from intensity of conviction. (4) Hearers know the voice of authority. (5) The Christian teacher is to show his supremacy over all other teachers.

23. And there was in their synagogue a man with an unclean spirit; and he cried out,

24. Saying Let us alone; what have we to do with thee, thou Jesus of Nazareth? art thou come to destroy us? I know thee who thou art, the Holy One of God.

25. And Jesus rebuked him, saying, Hold thy peace, and come out of him.

26. And when the unclean spirit had torn him, and cried with a loud voice, he came out of him.

27. And they were all amazed, insomuch that they questioned among themselves, saying, What thing is this? what new doctrine is this? foɪ with authority commandeth he even the unclean spirits, and they do obey him.

28. And immediately his fame spread abroad throughout all the region round about Galilee.

(1) Wickedness always afraid of purity. (2) Wickedness having no favour to ask of purity, except to be let alone. (3) Wickedness can always identify the presence of the spirit of Jesus Christ. (4) For this reason, the Church is a constant judgment upon all unclean spirits. (5) The completeness of Jesus Christ's authority—his authority in doctrine, and his authority in work. (6) Fulness of spiritual life is the guarantee of fulness of spiritual power. Jesus Christ came to this work after the most complete and severe preparation. He had received the Holy Ghost; he had undergone special and long-continued temptation in the wilderness, and had returned to preach the Gospel of the kingdom of God; and after all this he encountered with perfect power the unclean spirits that were in men. This opens the whole subject of Spiritual Preparation. Christians have also to meet unclean spirits in society. What if these unclean spirits should baffle the imperfect strength of Jesus Christ's followers? Christians are not at liberty to let unclean spirits alone; they are called to a life-long contention; their preparation must be intensely and increasingly spiritual. (7) That is the highest fame which is associated with beneficent deeds. Jesus Christ became famous because he had destroyed the dominion of a wicked spirit. The fame of evil is infamous; the fame of selfish cunning is mere notoriety; the fame of good doing is immortal and blessed renown.

This paragraph may be used as the basis of a discourse upon First Efforts in Christian service. (1) Those efforts are often forced upon Christians—it was so in this case; the wicked spirit challenged the attention of Christ. (2) Christians are to seek opportunities of putting forth such efforts; they are not to wait for the challenge, they have also to give it.

29. And forthwith, when they were come out of the synagogue, they entered into the house of Simon and Andrew, with James and John.

30. But Simon's wife's mother lay sick of a fever, and anon they tell him of her.

31. And he came and took her by the hand, and lifted her up; and immediately the fever left her, and she ministered unto them.

Jesus Christ exercised both a public and a private ministry; he worked in the synagogue, he worked also in the domestic circle. Here is Simon's wife's mother sick of the fever, and instantly Jesus Christ addressed himself to the difficulty, showing that the Christian ministry may be exercised with great advantage alike in public and in private. Learn from it : (1) That the individual case, as well as the case of the multitude, should be regarded as worthy of attention. (2) That bodily diseases as well as spiritual ailments are within the sphere of our solicitude; we are to be philanthropic as well as spiritually-minded. (3) We are to put ourselves in personal contact with those who suffer. "Jesus took her by the hand, and lifted her up." We can do little by proxy. We must work with our own hand, as though everything depended on it. It is true that what is distinctly known as miraculous power has ceased in the Church, yet there is a higher power than that which works physical miracles. It is still possible for the entrance of a good man into any house to be as the coming in of the light and life of heaven. Christians have it in their power to do a great work in the sick chamber. The raising of the man towards heaven is a greater work than healing him of mere bodily disease. We should never leave a home without blessing it. When Jesus Christ entered into a house it was known that he was there; his were not mere visits of courtesy, or attention to the claims of routine; wherever he went he took with him healing and manifold spiritual blessings. We are to do the same thing according to our capacity. In this case we see the servants standing behind the Master; Simon and Andrew and James and John were all there, but Jesus alone did the work. In our case, if we are the public figures in any work of mercy, it is only because our Master is concealed from the common vision. He is still there, still first; and it is only as we realise his presence and position that we can bless men.

The immediateness of Christ's cures ought to have some moral suggestion in it. Simon's wife's mother did not gradually recover from her affliction; she was cured instantly, and showed the extent of her recovery by immediately ministering to those who were in her house. In the spiritual world, why should not Jesus Christ heal men as suddenly as in the physical world? When men are spiritually healed, how long should they be before they make an attempt to serve others? It is quite true that there may be precipitancy in this matter of spiritual ministry; at the same time it should be remembered that every healed soul should prove its life by seeking to do some good thing for those who are round about. Here, as in everything else, the law holds good—By their fruits ye shall know them. Jesus Christ did not require that any body of men should examine the case to which he had just devoted himself, in order to procure a testimonial of efficiency; the service which the healed sufferer rendered was itself testimonial enough. We know that men have been with Christ when they are doing Christ's work: all other signs are inadequate; this is the absolute standard.

32. And at even, when the sun did set, they brought unto him all that were diseased, and them that were possessed with devils.
33. And all the city was gathered together at the door.
34. And he healed many that were sick of divers diseases, and cast out many devils; and suffered not the devils to speak, because they knew him.

The natural sun set, but the Sun of righteousness arose upon all those people with healing in his wings. In the evening, as well as in the morning, Jesus Christ was at work. Men come to Jesus Christ according to the urgency of their want. These people felt that urgency in their physical nature rather than in their souls, consequently they approached Christ with a request that they might be healed. It is well if men can feel their want of Christ at any point. If men did but know it, they would find in their hunger and thirst, in their suffering and loss, grounds of appeal to Jesus Christ. It is not easy to work from the highest point of nature: men may not be conscious of great spiritual necessities, yet may feel wants of a lower kind; they begin with the lower and ascend to the higher; they who eat of the loaves and fishes should not leave Christ until they have eaten of the bread from heaven.

We are not to consider all this pressure upon Jesus Christ as
an illustration of mere selfishness on the part of the sufferers
and their friends.   That would entirely depend upon their spirit;
in the act of their coming to Christ there was nothing necessarily
selfish.   Men may come to Christ for spiritual advantages, and
yet may charge themselves with selfish motives; at all events,
the devil will not be slow to suggest that in coming to Christ for
salvation men merely act upon a selfish instinct.   Such an
unclean spirit is to be resisted, and to bring down upon itself the
admonition of holy anger.   The selfishness will be seen afterwards if it really exists; to go to Christ that we should be healed
ourselves, and then to say nothing about his gracious power to
others, is to exhibit the intensest selfishness; but to go ourselves,
and then make our own healing testimony in his favour, is to
preach the Gospel, is to approach the benevolence of God himself.

By so much then may men test their own spirit; if they are
content to enjoy what they term spiritual advantages without
publishing the Saviour to others, they are justly chargeable with
the most criminal selfishness.   Gratitude will always make
eloquent preachers.

The fact that Jesus Christ did not suffer the devils to speak
shows his perfect dominion over the spiritual region.   All devils
are weak in the presence of the Saviour.   They are mighty and
terrible to us, because of our many infirmities ; but in the presence
of the bold man who is clothed with perfect holiness, all devils
are infinitely weak.   The lesson is evident : we are mighty only
as we are in Christ.

35. And in the morning, rising up a great while before day, he went out,
and departed into a solitary place, and there prayed.

There is something very touchingly illustrative of our Saviour's
humanity in this verse: he could have prayed upon his couch ;
none might have known how close was his intercourse with God
as he continued in the house; yet as he worked after the sun was
set, so he departed to pray before the sun had risen !   If the Master
required to pray, can the servants live without communion with
God ?   The subject suggested by this verse may be called Morning
Devotion.   To begin the day with God is the only method of
setting one's self above all its events, and triumphing over them

with perfect mastery.   Our life will be poor if there be in it no solitary places where we pray.   True life can never be developed among throngs and noises ; we must betake ourselves into desert places; in a word, we must get away from men, and view life from such a distance as may be realised by intimate divine fellowship.   As it is necessary for the artist to stand back from his work in order that he may see how it is shaping itself, so it is often necessary for us who are doing Christ's work to retire into solitary places that we may look at it from the altar of worship or perhaps from the valley of humiliation.   How rapidly Christ lived !   How he consumed himself in his ministry !   This should be an appeal to Christians, calling them to enthusiasm and to vehemence in work.   Jesus Christ did not remain in solitary places; he went to the sacred fountain that he might prepare himself to return to society, and do the work of the common day. A discourse might be founded upon these words, showing the religious uses of time.   (1) Social service such as we have seen in the life of Christ.   (2) Public ministry, in which crowds might enjoy our Christian teaching.   (3) Sacred devotion, in which the soul will hold close intercourse with God.

These uses should not be separated one from the other ; the teacher should show that all these uses really make up one true ministry.   The incident may also be used to show the place of prayer in the earnest life.   There is a sentimentalism which says work is prayer; so it is ; and yet if we work without praying, our work will be powerless.   Work is only prayer in so far as it is done in a prayerful spirit.   He who works must pray, and he who truly prays must also work.   In this verse the narrator uses a summary expression ; he could only say that Jesus Christ prayed : what he says in his prayers, what entreaties he breathed on behalf of himself and his work, never can be known.   There are also passages in our own life which can never be written ; we ourselves have offered prayers which it is impossible to recall, so intense was their agony, so comprehensive their desire ; yet, though unable to recall the intercession in detail, yet are strong in the memory that they were offered : the individual petitions have been forgotten, but the great exercise has strengthened, and the great answer nourished, the soul.

36. And Simon and they that were with him followed after him.

37. And when they had found him, they said unto him, All men seek for thee.

38. And he said unto them, Let us go into the next towns, that I may preach there also; for therefore came I forth.

39. And he preached in their synagogues throughout all Galilee, and cast out devils.

The true disciple always knows where to find the Master : the disciples knew the habits of their Lord : they knew that in some hidden place he could be found in the early hours of the day; at all events they knew that Jesus Christ would be found in the path of usefulness or preparation for usefulness. Do men know where they can find us? Are our Christian habits so distinct and unchangeable that our friends can with certainty explain our position?

The picture in the 37th verse is most impressive; viz., the picture of all men seeking for Jesus. What the disciples said in their wondering delight shall one day be literally true—all men will be in search of the Saviour of the world. In the first instance the Saviour sought all men, and in the second all men will seek the Saviour. "We love him because he first loved us." Instant response to the desire of the world, as shown in Christ's readiness still further to preach the Gospel. His object in life was un-divided, and its unity was its omnipotence. We are only strong in proportion to the concentration of our powers. Wherever we are we ought to be within the sphere of our ministry; and it ought to be an easy transition from one department of duty to another : Jesus Christ knew wherefore he had come forth, and it is incumbent upon us that we too should know our mission in life. No man can work mightily and constantly except in so far as he has a distinct and worthy object before him : the object must stir his whole nature, and move him by an importunate compulsion amounting in fact to inspiration. When a man begins to question the utility or practicability of his object in life, he enfeebles himself. There are many questionable objects which men set before themselves; and it is our delight as Christian observers to mark how they break down, and how those who were pursuing them abandon them with sorrow and disgust. We have to set before all men an object sufficiently simple to

engage the affections of the feeblest, and sufficiently sublime to
absorb the energies of the strongest. Jesus Christ preached, and
he called his servants to the same work. Preaching can never
fail to be one of the mightiest instruments in stirring the human
mind, and in moulding human society. Individual preachers
may become feeble; even distinguished ministers may cool in the
enthusiasm with which they undertook their great work; but
preaching, as instituted by Jesus Christ, and exemplified in his
own ministry, can never cease to be one of the most effective
agencies in human education and progress. Preaching will be
powerless except in proportion as it relates to Christ. We have
a distinct Gospel to unfold; and if we are faithful to our calling,
that Gospel will be found more than sufficient to supply our
own want as preachers, and to meet all the necessities of the
world. Jesus Christ preached and cast out devils, and we have
to do the same thing. We may not meet the devil in the same
form as that in which he presented himself during the personal
ministry of Jesus Christ, but we have to meet him in all the
subtlety, the insidiousness, and the terribleness of his unchanging
and unchangeable nature. The preacher must make up his mind
that there are still devils to be cast out; every man carries within
him his own devil, some indeed carry legion. The only exorcist
is the Saviour, and we are called to tell this fact, and to persuade men to avail themselves of his delivering power.

Under these verses might be shown the positive and the negative work of the Christian ministry; the positive work being to
preach the Gospel, the negative to cast out devils. Great service
would be done to humanity by fully developing the idea that all
evil purposes and dispositions are to be associated distinctly with
the name of the devil. We are to tell men, not merely that we
seek to make them better by conducting them into the knowledge
of new doctrines, but we are to take our stand before them as
men who have come to deliver them from the personal power of
the devil. There is hope of a man when he realises that he has
actually been under Satanic dominion. So long as he looks upon
his life as being blemished here and there, it is possible that he
may have most inadequate ideas of the mission of Jesus Christ;
but when he realises that he has actually been the habitation of the

very devil, he may be led to cry out for the deliverance which the Gospel has come to effect. The realisation on the part of the minister that he has to counteract and destroy the devil will stimulate him to use his utmost endeavours to make full proof of his ministry. He has not only to cope with wrong notions, but with a diabolic personality; and if this conviction thoroughly possess him, he will of necessity cultivate ever-deepening fellowship with Jesus Christ, who alone has the power to break up the kingdom of Satan.

40. And there came a leper to him, beseeching him, and kneeling down to him, and saying unto him, If thou wilt, thou canst make me clean.

41. And Jesus, moved with compassion, put forth his hand, and touched him, and said unto him, I will; be thou clean.

42. And as soon as he had spoken, immediately the leprosy departed from him, and he was cleansed.

43. And he straitly charged him, and forthwith sent him away;

44. And saith unto him, See thou say nothing to any man: but go thy way, show thyself to the priest, and offer for thy cleansing those things which Moses commanded, for a testimony unto them.

45. But he went out, and began to publish it much, and to blaze abroad the matter, insomuch that Jesus could no more openly enter into the city, but was without in desert places: and they came to him from every quarter.

In the 27th verse we found men putting questions regarding Jesus Christ's power; in the 40th verse we find a poor sufferer seeking to avail himself of Jesus Christ's curative energy. This marks the great difference between various classes of society in relation to the work of the Saviour. One class is content with looking, wondering, and perhaps admiring; another class may test his power in direct personal experience. Let it be distinctly pointed out that it is not sufficient to wonder at the ministry of Jesus Christ. In this chapter we have seen some who were brought to the Saviour; in the 40th verse we find a man who came to Jesus. Point out the blessedness of those who have others to conduct them to Jesus Christ; also point out the opportunity which each man has of making his own case known to Jesus Christ. This incident shows the trust which the ministry of the Saviour had inspired in the minds of sufferers, especially so in the case of the leper; the leper lived under the most terrible restrictions, yet his heart rose to the point of trust and love when he heard of the wonderful works of this new man. Others would have turned him away or would have run eagerly beyond his reach ; but Jesus Christ, the undefiled and undefiling Man, touched him, and recovered him of his leprosy.   Regarding this incident as illustrative of the method of spiritual salvation, it should be distinctly shown that the leper put himself un- reservedly, without any suggestion or wishes of his own, into the hands of the Healer.   He did not wish to be a party to the active work of healing himself; he was content to be passive, to wait his Lord's will.   It should also be shown that Jesus Christ instantly gave practical expression to his own deep pity and mercy; he delights in immediately answering prayer.   When we appeal to his justice, his righteousness, his sovereignty, we may be held a long time waiting, that we may know more fully what is meant by these high terms ; but when we come in weak- ness and poverty, crying to his compassion, his heart instantly moves towards us.   The humble desire of suffering soon moves the heart of Jesus Christ.   The third point that may be dwelt upon is the completeness of Christ's cure : immediately the leprosy departed from the man, and he was cleansed.   Is our Christian state one of complete pardon and hope ?   It is not asked whether it is one of complete sanctification, that is a progressive work ; but the work of pardon will bring with it an instantaneous assurance that the burden of guilt has been removed.   The impossibility of silence under the influence of great blessing is here most vividly illustrated.   The joy of thankfulness cannot always be controlled.   Christians must speak.   The explanation of a true ministry is found in this incident.   When we have received the highest blessings from the hands of Christ, we feel an insatiable desire to tell others of the great results of our having met the Saviour.   The 45th verse shows how much can be done by the energy of one man. So much did the recovered leper publish his restoration, that Jesus Christ could no more openly enter into the city by reason of the multitude that thronged upon him, and by reason of the sensation which so great a miracle had created.   Is there not in this incident an illustration of what we may do by being faithful to our convictions and impulses regarding the Son of God ? Have we been healed without publishing the fact?   Have we mentioned the fact of our conversion even to our dearest friend ? Learn from the leper the possibility of so exciting a whole neighbourhood about personal recovery as to extend the name and bring blessings upon the gracious power of Jesus Christ.

The 44th verse may be used for the purpose of showing how Jesus Christ brings men into the established laws and relations of his own government, even under circumstances which might seem to justify an exception to the usual course of things. In our highest moments of inspiration and delight we ought to be controlled by law. Even our ecstasy should be regulated where it might endanger the constancy and faithfulness of our life. Jesus Christ never dissociates the ministry from the preceding dispensations; he always heightens and consummates, he never destroys except by fulfilment, as the fruit destroys the blossom. The whole chapter might be used for the purpose of showing how possible it is for our Christian life to be sublime from the very beginning. This is the very first chapter in the Gospel of Jesus Christ, yet it is full of light; it might have been the last chapter, so crowded is it with incidents and good works. There are Christian people who are afraid of doing too much at the beginning; such people cannot have entered very deeply into the spirit of their Lord's enthusiasm and self-sacrifice. Youthful Christians should be encouraged to work from the very moment of the beginning of their new life. The earnest man does not care about the artistic graduation of his services, he does not even consider such a possibility; instantly that Jesus Christ takes possession of his heart his whole life becomes consecrated to the service of true doctrine and practical philanthropy. This chapter gives a most terrible rebuke to the notion that men should come only gradually into high Christian engagements; no renewed heart can too soon begin to do the good works and bear the blessed fruits of Christian regeneration. On the other hand, it should be pointed out for the encouragement of such as have few opportunities for the development of Christian vocation, that they will be judged not by the more public services which their brethren may render, but by the position in life which they have been called providentially to occupy.

Chapter ii.

CHRIST UNDER CRITICISM.

[An Analysis.]

1. And again he entered into Capernaum after some **days, and it was** noised that he was in the house.

THE importance of having the names of towns and other places associated with religious services. Capernaum was thus associated with the name of Christ. Show what it is to have bad associations with places, how tormenting to the memory, and how enfeebling in the matter of enterprise.

2. And straightway many were gathered together, insomuch that there **was** no room to receive them, no, not so much as about the door: and he preached the word unto them.

The Gospel has a word to crowds as well as individual men. The Gospel is universal in its doctrines, and hence can be preached to all classes at all times and in all places. It is also particular in its application of truth, so that it can be addressed to any single human being. When Jesus Christ saw crowds, his business was to preach the word to them. Christians should endeavour to get Jesus Christ's view of crowds of men. To the Christian heart a crowd is a most exciting scene. The histories, the passions, the purposes, the designs of a great crowd, who can tell but God! Yet the Gospel is adapted to all.

3. And they come unto him, bringing **one sick of the palsy, which was** borne of four.

4. And when they could not come nigh unto him for the press, they uncovered the roof where he was: and when they had broken it up, they let down the bed wherein the sick of the palsy lay.

5. When Jesus saw their faith, he said unto the sick of the palsy, Son, thy sins be forgiven thee.

6. But there were certain of the scribes sitting there, **and reasoning in** their hearts,

7. Why doth this man thus speak blasphemies ? who can forgive sins but God only ?

8. And immediately when Jesus perceived in his spirit that they so reasoned within themselves, he said unto them, Why reason ye these things in your hearts ?

9. Whether is it easier to say to the sick of the palsy, Thy sins be forgiven thee ; or to say, Arise, and take up thy bed, and walk ?

10. But that ye may know that the Son of man hath power on earth to forgive sins (he saith to the sick of the palsy),

11. I say unto thee, Arise, and take up thy bed, and go thy way into thine house.

12. And immediately he arose, took up the bed, and went forth before them all ; insomuch that they were all amazed, and glorified God, saying, We never saw it on this fashion.

(1) The helplessness of some men: all helplessness traceable to sin. (2) The social usefulness of other men ; we can all carry sufferers to Christ, even when we cannot heal them ourselves. To point a sinner to Jesus Christ is a good work, to carry a little child to the Saviour is to execute a most blessed mission. (3) The possibilities of earnestness ; these men uncovered the roof in their determination to approach the Healer. Some would have gone away, saying they would return on a more favourable occasion ; some would have given up the endeavour altogether ; these earnest men had an object in view, and were resolved on its accomplishment. All men can get to the Saviour if they so determine, however many be the apparent or real difficulties in their way. (4) The vigilance of Jesus Christ over human action. Notwithstanding the crowds, and his engagement in addressing them, Jesus Christ saw what was being done in this particular instance ; he knew the meaning of the extraordinary movement that was taking place, and the reward which he gave to the earnest men was great. (5) The censorious spirits of technical observers. The scribes accused the Saviour of blasphemy ; they could not understand his inspiration, and it is always a misfortune to be misunderstood. Whoever determines to live the highest life, determines also to expose himself to the heavy penalties of misinterpretation. Jesus Christ did not deny their inference regarding his claim to the Godhead ; he did not instantly disclaim any pretence to be as God ; on the contrary, he so asserted his power as to justify the astounding inference of the scribes. Particular notice should be taken of this as an incidental proof of

Jesus Christ's Godhead. To have allowed even tacitly the rightness of such inferences as were forced upon the scribes was, apart from his divinity, nothing short of a blasphemous assertion on his part. Jesus Christ works in much the same manner in relation to spiritual diseases. We can get no higher than himself; he is exalted to be a Prince and a Saviour, and he gives according to his sovereign will in response to human faith. The fulness of Jesus Christ's power is shown in the perfect ease with which he works his miracles. He speaks the recreating word, and yet there is within him no sign of exhaustion or insufficiency. Sinners should learn from this incident not to be discouraged because there are technical reasoners in their way, who are fertile in the suggestion of objections ; those who bore the sick of the palsy on this occasion did not listen to the reasonings or the objections of those by whom they were surrounded. If any man in going to Jesus Christ can be detained in the way to listen to the criticisms and counsels of those who are opposed to Christ, the probability is that he will never reach the Saviour. It is true that in this instance the scribes were reasoning in their hearts, and not openly so that they could be heard by a crowd ; it is also true in our own day that many reason aloud against the possibility of Jesus Christ's saving sinners ; those therefore who are conscious of sin ought to be put on their guard against subtle and persistent objectors. Had the man been unconscious of a deep and distressing want, he and his friends might have listened to captious reasoning ; but his necessity was so urgent that nothing less than a personal interview with Christ would satisfy him.

It is the same with the deadlier palsy of sin. If it be not to us the most terrible reality in our nature—if we do not so comprehend its horribleness as to loathe it unutterably—if we do not feel the moral agony which it inflicts until we cry out almost in despair—" What shall we do to be saved ? "—it is almost certain that we shall be turned aside by frivolous critics. The first thing to be done is to feel bitterly and inexpressibly the infinite abomination of sin. No progress in our approach to Jesus Christ can be made until we have come into this experience of the exceeding sinfulness of sin. In proportion as a man's estimate of sin is low will he be indisposed to find Jesus Christ ; when his sin fills his heart with sorrow and despair, he will be resolved to surmount all obstacles that would interrupt his course toward the Saviour. The great result of the cure wrought upon the palsied man will be repeated on a broader scale in the consummation of Jesus Christ's ministry. It is said that " The people were all amazed, and glorified God, saying, We never saw it on this fashion." So shall it be in the end of all things ; there will be one universal ascription of glory to him who has redeemed the human race from sin, and given it eternal life. Here is contention at the beginning ; men see things only in shadow and outline ; whilst the process is going on they are victimised by their own impatience, and oftentimes interrupt the Saviour, and show their utter want of self-control ; but when the whole work is finished, there will be throughout the universe a sense of thankful and glad amazement.

13. And he went forth again by the seaside ; and all the multitude resorted unto him, and he taught them.

14. And as he passed by, he saw Levi the son of Alphæus sitting at the receipt of custom, and said unto him, Follow me. And he arose and followed him.

The Saviour was not content with an occasional great effort, as we are apt to be. He is now found teaching the multitudes. Here is an illustration of the twofold ministry of Jesus Christ, namely, doing good to the bodies and also to the minds of men. We are left to infer what is meant by this word taught. It is clear from the whole course of Jesus Christ that he regarded all men as requiring teaching ; and it is also clear that he set himself forth as the Teacher who alone could reveal the highest truths of the universe. The Christian minister is to be emphatically a teacher ; he can only teach truly and successfully as he repeats the lessons which he finds in the life of the Saviour. Teaching is more difficult than preaching. In teaching there must be inquiry into the special circumstances of the learners, and an encountering of the particular difficulties of those who come to be taught. The preacher has to a large extent to deal with general truths, he has to make bold universal proclamations ; whereas the teacher may have to go into special adaptation of the divine truth to the distinctive circumstances of the individual case. The teacher requires to be not only thoroughly intelligent and intensely devoted to his work, but to be long-suffering in his

spirit and method of service. Men cannot be taught truth off-
handedly; their prejudices must be studied, their capacities must
be considered, and there must be such skilful balance in the
offering of truth as shall meet different degrees of culture and
sensibility.

In the 14th verse we turn once more to the individual case.
In the 13th verse we have a multitude receiving instruction; in
the 14th verse we have one man specially called. This is the
way Christian ministers and teachers must work. We cannot
all be like our Master, having equal facility in addressing crowds
and persuading individual hearers. Some men have a gift of
speaking so as to hold great multitudes under their dominion;
others, again, have a most useful talent in speaking to the
individual life and conscience. Levi was called from the receipt
of custom; the great point is to consider, not what a man is
called from, but what he is called to. We are all called from
sin; we look not so much to that as to the infinite glory which
is set before us as the outcome of Christian faith and love and
service.

The same verse might be used as showing what can be done
in the way of incidental work for Christ. We learn that Jesus
Christ " passed by," as if this circumstance occurred quite
casually, and not in the working out of a set purpose. It does
not seem to have been part of the plan; yet undoubtedly it was
so in the mind of Christ, to whom nothing could happen by
chance. There is, however, a lesson to us, that we are to be
always on the outlook for the good of men whom we are passing
by in the various ways of life. Wherever we see a man we see
an opportunity of speaking a word for Christ, and of calling men
to a higher life. Courage and prudence are equally required in
the discharge of these incidental services. There is a modesty
that is immodest, and there is a forwardness which is but the
courage of humility.

15. And it came to pass that as Jesus sat at meat in his house, many
publicans and sinners sat also together with Jesus and his disciples: for
there were many, and they followed him.

16. And when the scribes and Pharisees saw him eat with publicans and
sinners, they said unto his disciples, How is it that he eateth and drinketh
with publicans and sinners ?

These verses show that Jesus Christ lived under a constant

fire of criticism. This was not unnatural. If we have escaped criticism it may be because we have escaped Christianity.

Criticism will always be provoked by an intensely Christian spirit. Men are apt to think that Jesus Christ took upon himself all criticism, and so relieved his followers from the remarks of those who are now opposed to them. This should be shown to be a deadly error. Those who criticised Jesus Christ were men of good outward standing; yet they were destitute of moral purity: such men are always most forward in giving opinions about the conduct of other people. Where there is a high moral character there will be prolonged forbearance of other people's weaknesses; but where the outward habit is in excess of the inward principle there will be no lack of censorious criticism.

In the case of Jesus Christ it is clearly shown that where there is moral purity there is noble independence of public opinion. Jesus went boldly into such houses as he elected as his temporary residences, he sat openly with publicans and sinners; and the reason of what in other men would have been defiant bravado was the intense and incorruptible purity of his own heart. Men can only brave public criticism surely and serenely in proportion as they are right. Righteousness is peace.

17. When Jesus heard it, he saith unto them, They that are whole have no need of a physician, but they that are sick: I came not to call the righteous, but sinners to repentance.

Jesus hears all the objections that are urged against him. He sees all the objections that are in the heart before they are formed into words. Of him it may be said, " Thou knowest my thoughts afar off." Jesus Christ does not look upon one opinion as secret and another as public; to him the whole story of human life is an open page, on which the noonday sun is shining. Jesus Christ has an instant answer to all objections: witness the case in point. From this answer we may see—(1) Duty of doing good avowedly—not going about it in an indirect manner as if we were making an experiment, but boldly and distinctly, approaching it with a set purpose of spending our best energy upon it. (2) We may see it to be our duty to go to those who are least cared for. We are only working in the line of the Saviour's mission as we begin at the very lowest point in the social scale. We cannot do fundamental and permanent good by beginning at the top or in the middle; we must get down to springs and causes, we must begin at the very deepest point of human apostasy, and work our way steadily upward ; there is a temptation even in Christian work to stop short of the lowest depth of human necessity.   (3) Jesus Christ shows it to be our duty to associate with those whom we seek to save : he sat with them, he talked to them, he asked them questions, he made himself their personal friend, and so attained over them personal supremacy.   This practice levels a deadly blow at the theory of doing good by proxy.   It is comparatively easy to send other men on errands of mercy ; but we are only working in Christ's spirit in so far as we are prepared to go ourselves, and openly identify our whole influence with the cause of fallen men.   Where there is this intense personal consecration, there will, of course, be a disposition to engage as much co-operation as possible ; our duty is to see that we do not find in co-operation an excuse for personal negligence.   Jesus Christ answered his opponents almost invariably by laying down a great principle.   He did not trust to uncommon reasonings, or work according to the special mood of the day.   He had intense personal conviction, to which he constantly referred in explanation and defence of his ministry. Ministers are only strong up to the degree in which they know precisely what they have come to do ; Jesus Christ said he came for the express purpose of healing the sick and calling sinners to repentance.   Unity in this as in all other things is strength. When a man works with divided heart, his work ends in failure.

18. And the disciples of John and of the Pharisees used to fast: and they come and say unto him, Why do the disciples of John and of the Pharisees fast, but thy disciples fast not?

19. And Jesus said unto them, Can the children of the bridechamber fast, while the bridegroom is with them ? as long as they have the bridegroom with them they cannot fast.

20. But the days will come when the bridegroom shall be taken away from them, and then shall they fast in those days.

21. No man also seweth a piece of new cloth on an old garment : else the new piece that filled it up taketh away from the old, and the rent is made worse.

22. And no man putteth new wine into old bottles : else the new wine doth burst the bottles, and the wine is spilled, and the bottles will be marred : but new wine must be put into new bottles.

(1) There should be difference between Jesus Christ's disciples

and the disciples of all other men. It is noticeable how soon those differences were detected by the critics of the day. The differences should be as broadly marked now as they were in the days of Jesus Christ's visible ministry. (2) Those differences should find their explanation in Jesus Christ, not in the expression of the disciples themselves. Jesus Christ takes upon himself the responsibility of determining the public attitude of his disciples. They must be joyful or sad according to the spirit which he puts into them, or the temporary discipline to which he subjects them. There is a time when it is right for the disciples to be glad and triumphant, joyful as men who are at a wedding feast in the presence of the bridegroom ; there is also a time in which they must bow down their heads in pensiveness and sad wonder about the future. The difficulty in many cases is for the heart to realise that, alike in joy and in sorrow, it may be working out the beneficent purposes of the Saviour. (3) The illustration about pieces of cloth and the different wines shows the perfect uniqueness of Christianity : there is to be no patching, there is to be no compromising. Christianity is to have a distinctiveness and speciality of its own ; the ancient make and the modern variation are not to be put together as part and parcel of Christian truth ; Christianity is to stand out alone complete in its indivisible and perfect unity. In this case again we see how Jesus Christ throws himself back upon great principles, and finds in the simplicity of nature and the integrity of truth the surest defence of his Church.

23. And it came to pass, that he went through the corn fields on the sabbath day, and his disciples began, as they went, to pluck the ears of corn.

24. And the Pharisees said unto him, Behold, why do they on the sabbath day that which is not lawful ?

25. And he said unto them, Have ye never read what David did, when he had need, and was an hungered, he, and they that were with him ?

26. How he went into the house of God in the days of Abiathar the high priest, and did eat the shewbread, which is not lawful to eat, but for the priests, and gave also to them which were with him ?

27. And he said unto them, The sabbath was made for man, and not man for the sabbath :

28. Therefore the Son of man is Lord also of the sabbath.

Jesus is still living under the fire of criticism already referred to. In this particular interview it is made clear—(1) That all

critical inquiries are not to be condemned. This question on
the part of the Pharisees was not at all unnatural.   Men ought to
be called upon to give explanations of habits that are opposed to
the public sentiment and usages of their times.   Jesus Christ does
not resent the inquiry as if it proceeded from a wicked spirit.
Let it be inferred from this that there are right questions to be
put concerning the Christian religion and the practice of Christians.   There are questions that are bad in their spirit and bad
in their purpose ; there are also questions which come quite
naturally out of the extraordinary development of Christian conviction and impulse.   Jesus Christ shows by his answers that he
considered human life to be above all technical law.   The disciples were an hungered as they passed through the corn fields.
David was an hungered when he ate the shewbread ; there are
courses in human life when men are apparently or really lifted
above the current of law and usage, and when life becomes to
itself a determining law.   (2) The perfect and inalienable supremacy of Jesus Christ is asserted in the last verse.   He proclaims
himself Lord over time, over institutions, and over human
affairs.   This great claim is not to be overlooked in estimating
the dignity of Jesus Christ's personal ministry.   Could any mere
man have proclaimed his lordship over the Sabbath day ?   A man
cannot be Lord of the Sabbath without being Lord of something
beyond.   God does not distribute these lordships ; the Lord of
the Sabbath is also the Lord of hosts.

PRAYER.

JESUS, Son of David, have mercy upon us! Our hands are withered, the whole head is sick, the whole heart is faint: come to us in thy healing power, and make us young again. We would be born of water and of the Spirit; we would know in its effects the process of regeneration. Not by works of righteousness which we have done, for we can do none, but according to thy mercy must this washing of regeneration be effected. We know that thy purpose towards us is love; whatsoever the discipline may be, the end is our perfection; thou wilt have us in Christ Jesus, thou eternal Father, perfect, accepted, sanctified: may we, knowing the purpose and the end, even joyfully accept the process in all its painfulness. Thou dost not finish thy work to-day or to-morrow, but on the third day thou dost perfect thy purpose amongst men; then they see the topstone brought on, and hear the song of angels and the benediction of God; then hast thou rest and joy, and all thy people are filled with contentment. Jesus, never leave us, never withdraw from us even for one moment: only in thy presence are we safe; only under thy blessing can we grow in all holy progress; we are too weak to be left alone, the enemy is too strong for us, temptations are thick beyond all counting, and urgent with desperateness. Keep near us, abide with us, break bread to us in our hunger, and in the very manner of the breaking of the bread we shall see thee, and know thee to be the Lord. Help thy servants in the ministry to see thy will, to understand the meaning of thy kingdom, and to reveal what thou hast told them in all simplicity and sincerity, so that men may hear and fear, and turn unto the Lord in great multitudes. Help thy servants to bear all the difficulties, burdens, temptations of the ministry; and grant unto all thy Church in all its sections and departments a plentiful rain from heaven, that it may rejoice in the acknowledgment of thy blessing, in the recognition of thy love, and the bestowal of thine approval. Help us to read thy word aright, to receive it joyfully and gratefully, and to repeat it in consecrated and progressive lives. This our prayer we say at the Cross of Christ, the altar of the universe, the one way into heaven because the one way to pardon for guilty souls. At that Cross we tarry for God's great answer. Amen.

Chapter ii. 4.

"And when they could not come nigh unto him for the press, they uncovered the roof."

UNUSUAL METHODS.

THE idea is that if you want to get at Christ you can do so. That is all. If you do not want to get at Christ you can easily escape by excuse. That is true. We all know it: we

34

have been partakers of that shameful trick.   If you do not want
to go to church you can find pleas enough for not going—lions in
the way by the thousand: if you want to go the lions may be
ten thousand in number, but you will be there.   So we come
back upon a homely but expressive proverb which says, " Where
there's a will there's a way."   We can do very much what we
want to do.   This is true in all things.   See if the fault be not
in the will.   What a weak point is here; what a very fickle
constitution is there; what an irrational sensitiveness puts in
its plea at another point.   How selfishness plays a subtle but
decisive part in the tragedy or comedy of life !   Whoever knew
an earnest man permanently baffled ?   But how difficult to be
earnest about religion !   It is invisible, impalpable, imponderable; it is so largely distant, so truly spiritual; it cannot be
weighed, measured, looked at; it does not come within the range
of observation to any extent which appeals to a competitive
selfishness.   So men fail, and blame the devil; so men do not go
to Christ, and say they were fated to keep away; thus men tell
lies until they shut out the light of noonday by their shadow.
The men in question could not get easily at Christ: but what is
worth having that can be easily got at ?   When they could not
come nigh unto him for the press, they tore off the roof, they
broke it up.   They meant to succeed, we do not; they did
succeed, we fail; they ought to succeed, we ought to be defeated.
Shame upon the economy of the universe if the coward ever won
a battle, if the lazy man ever came back with a sheaf of corn !
Do we really want to get at Christ ?   Our answer will contain
everything that explains our success or our defeat.   Is it the
heart that wants to see the Saviour ? or is it some adventure of
the imagination that wants to catch his profile and then vanish,
because it is a profile that ought to be seen ?   Is it the soul that
says, " I will " ?   If so, the battle is half won; Christ himself
comes into vision when he hears that poignant cry.

For what purpose do we want to see Christ ?   Everything
will depend upon our reply to that inquiry.   Christ himself will
not come to some calls.   Herod expected to see some great
thing done by him, and Christ went into a cold stone, looked at
Herod as a corpse might have looked at him, answered him not

—not by look, or touch, or word, or sign—until Herod was afraid. There is a silence more awe-inspiring than speech can ever be. For what purpose, therefore, do we want to see Christ? Is it upon real business? He answers nothing to curiosity; he cannot stop to chaffer with speculation; he will stay all night with an earnest Nicodemus; he will keep the sun from going down or rising up if the soul really wants him to settle questions of guilt and pardon. Are we prepared to take the roof away rather than not see Christ? In other words, are we prepared to take unusual methods, peculiar and eccentric ways, rather than be baffled in our quest after the Son of God? If these men had taken off the roof without first going to the door, Jesus Christ would have rebuked them. We must not be eccentric merely for the sake of eccentricity. There is a defiance of conventional propriety which is itself nothing but a base vulgarity that ought to be frowned down. But the men went to the door, they tried the regular way, and when they could not enter by the door, because the throng was so great, then they must make a door. Everything depends upon our treatment of circumstances. We must not defy conventional propriety merely for the sake of defying it; but when conventional propriety is closing up the door so that we cannot get in, we must find admission by the roof. Conventional propriety is killing the Church. Infidelity is doing the Church no harm at all. It does not lie within the power of a blatant scoffer to touch the Cross of Christ; but its protectors may not be faithful to their responsibility; the professors of Christ have it in their power to crucify him every day, and put him to an open shame.

Let us try to get at Christ, and first try to get in by the door. There are several doors, let us try the first. How crowded it is; how long-bearded the men are who are filling up the opening; and there is intelligence in their eyes, there is earnestness in every wrinkle of their venerable faces; these are men who have sat up all night over many a weary problem; they are not foolish men, they are men of culture, reading, thought, study; they are inquisitive men, they do not read the books of yesterday, they read the records that are a thousand years old. But we cannot pass them, because we have not learned their letters. These are

the rabbis of the Church, and unless we can take their language
and swing with them over ten centuries, we cannot be allowed to
pass that way. Then let us try some other door. Here are
other men not wholly dissimilar; they, too, have marks of study
upon their faces; these eyes have been tried by many a midnight
lamp; but they talk long words, and hard words; we never
heard our mother use such language; every word is a word of
many syllables that requires a kind of verbal surgeon to take it
to pieces. Hear how they talk; though the words be very long,
yet they speak them glibly, with a fluency that itself is a mockery,
because we feel that we could not even stumble our way across
such stony paths. Who are they? They are the philosophers.
We cannot get in there; let us try another door. Here are men
looking one another in the face, and reasoning in high argument,
and proving and then disproving, reaching conclusions only to
shatter them; we shall make nothing out at that door. Who are
these men, who have weights and scales and measures, and who
will not admit anything that does not prove certainties? They
are the logicians, the controversialists, the men of open throat,
and eye of fire, and tongue like a stormy wind; they will argue.
What does it all come to? To blocking the way, to shutting up
the door. You and I, poor broken hearts, cannot find access
there. Shall we go home?

We came to see Christ, and we mean to remain until we do
see him. Then let us try another door. Who are these men
robed and certified, and who bear the image and aspect of officers?
They are skilled hands here. Evidently they keep no end of
keys; mayhap they may have the key we want. They are
burning incense, opening doors, ringing bells, performing ceremonies, almost dancing in their strange gesticulations. Who
are they? Ceremonialists. You never caught one of them ten
minutes late in the morning. They live by ceremony; they like
it, it suits them wholly. Who are they? They are ecclesiastics; men who have tailors to themselves. " Clerical tailors "
is a word you now see in brass letters on certain audacious
windows. We cannot get in there. Shall we go home?
No. We came out to find the Son of God, and we will find
him. Saviour, Son of David, have mercy upon us! What shall

we do? We must resort to unusual ways. They will not allow us to go to church, then let us meet on the seashore; they will not admit us without certain cards and certificates and endorsements: ruin be to all their mechanism! Let us, brother, fall down here on bare knees at an altar consecrated by the incarnation of the Son of God; mayhap he will see us without the piece of official paper; he may hear heart-prayer when we cannot have access to written form, couched in noble language, if anything too dignified for heaven.

Do you want to see Christ? There are men who say they would go in but they cannot find their way through the rabbis, or through the philosophers, or through the logicians, or through the ecclesiastics, and there they are. Shame on them! they are not earnest; they would not allow a friend to escape in that way. They do not want Christ. Nicodemus found a way. It was a long weary day that. He looked often at the clouds and at the sun, to see if he could steal forth. He was determined not to rest until he had spoken to this wondrous man. He waited for the night, and the night like a veiled friend came and took him to the Saviour, and they sat up all night; and that night the heaven trembled with stars, there was hardly room in all the firmament for the stars that wanted to glitter out their infinite secret upon the heart of this inquiring master in Israel; never did a night so starry bend over the earth. To have been there! Zacchæus found a way. He said, I am short, I cannot reach over the shoulders of these men, but I will climb up yonder sycamore tree. He never would have been chief among the publicans, and rich, if he had been afraid of climbing a tree; that explains the man's success in life. To have seen him otherwise you would have just seen a dapper little gentleman that never seemed to have touched anything with his fine fingers; but when he wanted to carry an object, then see how the dapper little gentleman changed into a fiery little furnace that meant to win, and up the tree he went, for Christ was to pass that way. Some men would never have seen the tree; some men certainly would not have climbed the sycamore; others would have said, "Perhaps on another occasion we may see him." But to earnestness there is no "other occasion"; there is only one day, and that is to-day.

There be indolent, leisurely, contemplative souls who play with time; they speak of "to-morrow" as if it were theirs; they speak of "another occasion" as if they had compromised with death, and staved the monster off for a settled series of years. Zacchæus has only one time, one opportunity; he lives in a burning now. There was a woman who found a way. They need not have called her a woman; she could not have concealed that fact; they might have told us the incident, and we should have fixed the sex. She said, If I might but touch the hem of his garment; if these poor fingers could but touch the craspedon, I shall be healed. She did it quietly, silently, but Jesus knew that she did it, for he said, "Who hath touched me?" and the vulgar disciples said, "Touched thee! Why, see how they throng thee, and sayest thou who touched thee? Why, we are all touching thee." "No," said Christ, "no; some finger has taken life out of me; whose finger was it? I am conscious that virtue has gone out of me." There is a rude touch that gets nothing; there is a sensitive touch that extracts lightning from God, virtue from the Cross. There is a hearing that gets nothing, because the hearer simply hears the noise, the succession of syllables, words, paragraphs; there is another hearing that catches a sound within the sound, music within the articulation; there is a hearing that only wants one word, it can supply all the rest; give it that one word, and see how it runs to tell its exultant joy. He that hath ears to hear, let him hear; he that hath fingers to touch, let him touch; he that hath eyes to see the invisible, let him look, and all heaven shall be full of angels. Do we want to see Christ? That is the urgent, recurrent, tremendous question.

There is a permissive violence—"They uncovered the roof . . . and when they had broken it up——" There are respectable persons who lock up their churches six days out of seven, lest by some accident some poor blunderer should scratch the paint. They say they are careful of the church. So they are, much too careful. But the church was made for man, not man for the church; the roof was made for man, not man for the roof. Were they going to let fifteen feet of canvas stand between them and the living Healer of the universe? Were they going to balance a dying man against a roof that a hand could tear off? They must be at Christ. There is an acceptable violence. When Jesus saw their faith, he said, "Son, thy sins be forgiven thee." That is his constant reply to earnestness. It is not stated that he had any conversation with the man. Some of us are blessed on the road to church; it cost us a great deal to get to church that day, and Jesus joined us on the road and gave us Sabbath before we got inside, so that when we came within the gates of the sanctuary the whole place glowed like a chamber let down from heaven. Jesus knows what it cost some people to get at him; he knows that they have to give up old acquaintances, bad ways of business, habits that had laid themselves with iron grip upon the heart, and before they have time to speak, he says, I know it all; thou shalt have the fatted calf, a ring for thy hand, and shoes for thy feet, and this shall be thy father's house; as for thy sins, they are in the sea, they have gathered themselves together and plunged into the deep. Son, stand up! There is a church-going that amounts to battle and victory in one supreme act. Unusual ways are permitted under certain circumstances; when there is real need they are permitted; where there is no alternative they are allowed.

This is where the Church has got wrong. It has its little methods, and its small plans, and its neat ways of doing things, and the devil never was afraid of neatness. That is an awful blemish anywhere. A "neat" sermon! Could you degrade that loftiest, noblest, grandest speech more than by calling it a neat sermon? We must get rid of a good many people in order to get at reality in all this matter of adaptation to the necessities of the case. We must part with all the cold hearts; they have occupied so much space in the church in what are called for some inscrutable reason "pews," and therefore we shall miss them, because they did weigh and measure so much arithmetically; but they are better gone! Personally I would turn every church to its most multifarious uses, if I could do good in that way which is impossible in any other way. Unusual ways have always been permitted. Once there was a man who was very hungry, and there was nothing to eat but the shewbread, the holy bread, and he took it ravenously and devoured it, and God said, "That is right." Hunger has a right to bread. No man should be punished for taking bread when after honest endeavour and strenuous service he has failed to get it otherwise. He is no thief who, being honest in his soul, has failed to get bread and is dying of hunger, and that openly says, "This is for man, and I solemnly, religiously take it." God never condemned such an action. I know how dangerous it is even to hint at this, because there be some mischievous minds that do not turn water into wine, but wine into water, and water into poison; there is a process of deterioration; if any such man should pervert my words so the blame be his, not mine. Once it was impossible to eat the passover in the regular way; circumstances so combined that a good deal of the prescribed mechanism had to be done away with; and we read in the historical books that they ate the passover, "otherwise than as it was written." Everything goes down under the agony of human need. Once there was a number of persons who assailed the Son of God because he healed a man on the Sabbath day ; and he said, "The Sabbath was made for man, not man for the Sabbath." If we do not find Christ, blame ourselves. Never does Christ blame himself because the people have not found him. That is a remarkable circumstance; consider it well ; in no instance does Jesus Christ say, "These people might have been saved if I had shown myself to them. But I kept out of the way purposely, therefore they are not saved." He declares the contrary to be the fact ; he says ; "I would, but ye would not ; ye will not come unto me that ye might have life." "O Jerusalem, Jerusalem, thou that killest the prophets, and stonest them which are sent unto thee ; how often would I have gathered thy children together, even as a hen gathereth her chickens under her wings, and ye would not !" He never says, "He would not." He lived to die ; he died to live ; he ascended to intercede.

It is never easy to get at Christ ; it ought not to be easy to get at him. It means battle, pressure, determination. "Strait is the gate, narrow is the way which leadeth unto life, and few there be that find it." The road is over a place called Calvary, and a voice says to those who attempt that way, "Except a man deny himself, and take up his cross, and follow me, he cannot be my disciple." To one man Jesus said, "Sell all that thou hast, and come"; to another he said, "Except a man hate his father and his mother [in comparison] he cannot be my disciple"; another who thought he was going on to riches and honour said he would go, and Jesus said, "The foxes have holes, and the birds of the air have nests, but the Son of man hath not where to lay his head." But the battle has a great victory. Small efforts end in small consequences. Again, therefore, the question recurs, Do we want to see Christ? Is it our heart that wants him, or our curiosity? Are we only asking the question of imagination, or are we propounding the inquiry of agony? To-day I set open the door of the kingdom of heaven in the name of Jesus. To weary men I would represent him saying, "Come unto me, all ye that labour and are heavy laden, and I will give you rest." "In the last day, that great day of the feast, Jesus stood and cried, saying, If any man thirst"—Lord, we all thirst; our hearts thirst, our souls have drunk rivers of water and still they thirst—"if any man thirst, let him come unto me, and drink." May we all go? "He, every one that thirsteth, come!" Who says so? The Spirit, the bride, and the Giver of the water, the First, and the Last. It is an awful thing to have heard this discourse. It puts us into a new relation. Cursed be the tempter that led me into this church! some soul may say, for without being here I should have bewildered myself and perplexed myself and excused myself; but this man has torn the roof off the house of my excuses, and laid my bad man's pleas open to the sun of heaven. Others may say, Blessed be God for this word, for we have heard to-day that if any man really desires to see the Son of God, him the Son of God will see.

PRAYER.

ALMIGHTY GOD, teach us that all things are naked and open to the eyes of
him with whom we have to do. The eyes of the Lord run to and fro
throughout the whole world; there is nothing hidden from the sight thereof.
Help each of us to say, Thou God seest me. In this fear and in this hope
may we live every day. We thank thee for the Son of God, who reads our
hearts, who knows our inward and unspoken reasoning, and who will judge
us accordingly. Behold, we stand before him to be judged; but do we not
first stand before his Cross to be saved? May we not there plead with
God, each saying for himself, God be merciful unto me a sinner? Then we
shall not fear the judgment-seat, for there shall we meet our Saviour, and he
will know the power and grace of his own priesthood. We would therefore
live in Jesus: we would be crucified with Christ, that we may rise with the
Son of God: we would know the fellowship of his sufferings, that we might
afterwards know the power of his resurrection. Help us to be true in soul,
pure in heart; then shall our lives be open, fearless, useful. Holy Spirit,
hear us when we humbly say, Dwell with us: continue thy ministry of light
and purification in our mind and heart until the sacred process is complete.
For all we know of light, for all we care for things divine and eternal, we
bless and magnify the grace of God. Once we were blind, now we see;
we have returned unto the Shepherd and Bishop of our souls: may we go
out no more for ever. May we abide in the tabernacle of the Most High,
and be sheltered evermore under the wings of the Almighty; may our
spirits grow in holy anger against all things wrong and mean, false and
selfish. Because thou knowest us altogether we will come to thee with
fearless childlike trust. Lord, undertake for us; show us the right way;
may we give no heed to our own vain imaginings, but look into the law and
to the testimony of wisdom and progress, and abide in the same, diligently
obeying the will of our Father in heaven. Pity us wherein we have been
wrong, and done wrong in instances countless, each aggravating the other.
The Lord shows us that where sin abounds grace doth much more abound;
that the Cross of Christ erects itself in welcoming love above all the tumult
and uproar of human sin. Keep us until the end, until the day of doom;
then, life's little journey done, may we stand, through the power of the everlasting Cross, among those who are arrayed in white garments, never more
to be spotted by the world. Amen.

Chapter ii. 8.

"Why reason ye these things in your hearts?"

UNSPOKEN OBJECTIONS TO CHRIST.

THEN there is an unspoken life. Then silence may be eloquence. This is mysterious, and this is alarming. Here are words found for our silence. We thought our silence was sacred; we said, Our words being spoken belong to us exclusively no more, they are common property, but our silence is our own; that never can become public property; we can have a heart-life quite solitary, and of that life we may be absolute monopolists. All this is broken in upon suddenly and ruthlessly by this new voice. There is now no secrecy; privacy is a term of very limited application. The new voice is very explicit; it says, Whatsoever is spoken in secret shall be proclaimed from the housetop. That which was supposed to have been done under the cover of darkness shall stand forth in the blaze of noonday. It will be well to take this fact into consideration in studying man's history and action. By neglecting this fact, who can tell how much we lose of intellectual reality and spiritual beneficence? By omitting this fact as an element of reality in the government of mind we may soon come to live a fool's poor life. We should be greater men, built on another scale, sustaining new and higher relations, if we realised the fact that there is nothing in our minds or hearts that is not perfectly and absolutely known. It will be difficult for some men to believe this; but it is difficult for some men to believe anything. The difficulty may arise from want of mental capacity and spiritual sensitiveness, or that general faculty which lays hold of things subtle and impalpable. Did you hear the tinkling of that bell? No. I did; that is the difference between you and me. Did you hear that footstep? I did not, but you did; I should have said there was no footstep, but you heard it. Ignorance must not stand in the way of wisdom; speculation about probability and improbability must not stand in the way of realised fact. Here is a piece of soft pensive music; listen: did you ever hear anything quite so exquisite? You say you cannot hear; why can you not hear? Because of the infirmity of deafness. Then is your deafness to be the measure of other people's sensitiveness of hearing, or is the sensitiveness of other people only to show you more clearly the reality and the pitiableness of your infirmity ?   Christian believers say—and you must ruin their character before you can destroy their evidence— that they see the unseen, endure as seeing the invisible, fasten their eyes upon things not seen and eternal, realise the nearness of spiritual intelligences and ministries ; and you want us in an age of advanced learning and culture to set up ignorance against wisdom, and to oppose insensateness to that sensitivity which hears the footfall of God in the wind.   That cannot be done. We are anxious to accommodate every capacity and degree, but we cannot allow boundless ignorance to urge its immensity as an argument for its acceptance.

Every man, then, is really two men.   He is, first, viewing him from an external point, a speaker ; then he is a thinker.   As a man thinketh in his heart so is he.   Not a word you have said is worthy of a moment's attention if it has not expressed the reality of your heart.   The smile upon your face is a lie if it express not a finer smile on the heart.   Here we are a perplexity and a mystery to ourselves.   Sometimes we hardly know whether we are on the one side or on the other ; so subtle is the whole action of life that there are points in consciousness when it is almost impossible to say whether we are leaning towards the reality or the semblance.   There are other times when we want to speak out everything that is in the heart and mind.   We are checked by fear.   We are disabled for want of language ; a hundred considerations instantaneously flash themselves upon the judgment, and want to be umpire over the conflicting processes of our own mind.   We carry things in the soul by majority.   One man is not one vote in any case of real intellectual and spiritual excitement ; nor is one mind one decision regarding many practical outgoings, reasons, and responsibilities of life.   In your own soul, the silent parliament of the spirit, you carry things by majorities.   You say, On the whole this is better than that ; taking a large view of the case, there are seven reasons why I should do it, and I can only discover four why I should not do it ; I will obey the indication of the larger number.   But whilst we are willing to grant that there are spheres and sections of life in which it is almost impossible to tell whether it is the thinker or the speaker that is about to act; yet there is difference enough amongst the sections of life to excite our spiritual jealousy, lest we should be telling lies to ourselves in the very act of speaking them so loudly as to delude the conscience into a belief in our sincerity. We have employed emphasis to cheat the conscience. Here is the mystery of man : what he thinks is one thing, what he says is another. Christ wants to bring these two hemispheres of mental action into unity, harmony, and identical expressiveness. He would make us so clean of heart that we cannot be foul of lip ; he would so exalt the soul in love of truth that it could not speak a lie. Any religion that proposes to work this miracle is a true religion, wherever its Author came from ; and its Author has a right to be heard by the moral grandeur of his purpose.

What is Christ's relation to this mysterious dual relation of man ? It is a relation of perfect knowledge. The scribes and others round about him were reasoning, saying, " Why doth this man thus speak blasphemies ? who can forgive sins but God only, and immediately when Jesus perceived in his spirit . . . ." "He needed not that any should testify of man, for he knew what was in man." How could he do otherwise ? He made man, he redeemed man ; he sends forth the Paraclete to sanctify man. He knows us therefore creatively, experimentally, sympathetically, and by every process that can possibly be applied to the knowledge of human nature. He hears our heart beat; he knows how the pulse stands; he writes down in his book the history of the day—not the history of the deceptive, often self-deceiving, hand, but the history of the heart, the soul, the mind, the spirit, which is the real man. The hand is but the glove of the soul. We must penetrate to inward realities before we can know how much Christ knows. He searches us through and through. This is the prerogative of God : he searches the heart and he tries the reins of the children of men. He knows our thought afar off. We speak of plasm, of things remote, small, microscopical, growing, accumulating upon themselves, ever rising in capacity and expressiveness of life; in talking so we talk according to fact. It is said therefore of God that he knows our thought before it is a thought; he knows the plasm of it, he knows it in its first, its earliest, its invisible conception. Before we know it he knows; before we dare find words for our thought he has written that thought fully down in heaven. Unless we stand in this consciousness—let me recur to an early point—we shall live a fool's life, quite lineal, superficial, without cubic measurement, depth, value, worth. And are we to live such a life when we can escape it? Are we to live externally when we can live metaphysically, internally, spiritually? Are we to be content with things on the surface when we may penetrate and bring up things from the very depths of the wisdom and grace of God? To this higher life we are called, and God the Holy Ghost is pledged to accomplish our education in this development if we will yield ourselves to his gracious ministry.

Christ sustains a position of fearlessness in regard to the whole internal economy of the human mind and human life generally and particularly. He need not have challenged these men. A false teacher would not have challenged them; he would have said, If they raise no objection I shall suggest none; they look very troubled and doubtful, but I shall not trouble them to express their trouble or their doubt; it is not for me to encourage men to express scepticism or unbelief; I will therefore close this subject, and swiftly turn to another. That is not Christ. Christ said, "Why?"—let us have nothing hidden about these mysteries; speak out your objection, give it word that we may consider it openly, and for the advantage of yourselves and others. This fearlessness of the Son of God is no small consideration in estimating the quality of his character. He will have nothing hidden away in the heart that can be brought out of it, and used helpfully in the Christian education of the soul. Preachers are sometimes blamed for raising doubts; whereas in reality they are only answering them. Let us beware of a self-considering and cowardly ministry that says in effect, If the people do not know these things I shall not tell them; if they do not express the doubts I will not answer them; in fact, I may flatter myself with the observation that perhaps I may raise more doubts than

I can settle. I may suggest more questions than I can answer;
I think, therefore, I will live on the sunny side of my work, and
do as little as possible towards encountering the unspoken tumult
and conflict of the human soul. It is perfectly true that we may
raise more doubts than we can settle, we may ask more questions
than we can answer; at the same time every ministry ought to
address itself to the realest part of the life. Do not address
mere fancy or taste or sentiment, but get at the unspoken heart-
thought. The people are quite content in numberless cases that
we should address their fancy : How lovely, how bird-like some of
the notes of the voice; how fascinating and enchanting altogether
in manner ! Some are perfectly content that we should address
their taste ; they say, How polished, how quiet, how very beautiful,
how classic; how vividly the speaker recalled the best of days
of Attic eloquence ! Away with this intolerable and indescribable
rubbish ! We meet in the house of God to talk reality, to get
at life in its inmost thought, to address not the decoration of the
face, but the disease of the heart. The Lord send us, if need be,
rough prophets, Elijahs and John the Baptists, who will speak out
thunderously and boldly, and sweep away from the debased pulpit
all attempts to please mere sentiment, and gratify pedantic and
therefore perverted taste. When we are revealed to ourselves
it may be found that we are altogether inverted, and that we have
been making a false impression upon society, if not actually upon
ourselves. The heart is deceitful above all things, and despe-
rately wicked, and therefore it is perfectly possible for a man to
be imposed upon by himself,—to be, in other words, his own
impostor. He wants to look well in his own eyes, and he is
willing to overlook a little here and overlook a little there, and
may promise himself concessions of divers kinds ; upon the
whole he will recommend himself to himself. Let us not fear
the scathing, searching process, the cruel analysis of Christ.
Then the matter may stand thus : For such and such reasons
I proceeded in this course. Then the Lord will say, You call
them reasons; now let me show you that they are all excuses.
You defrauded your own soul by talking euphemistically, by
speaking of reasons as if they were points wrought out by logic
and fact and a right connection of events properly interpreted ;
whereas in reality they are all excuses, vain pleas, selfish argu-

ments; you wanted to reach such and such a conclusion, and you laid the stepping-stones accordingly.

There is all the difference in the world between light and darkness, between reasons and excuses. We have degraded our life by processes of self-excusing. We would not go out because —then we told a lie in measured language to ourselves. We would have gone out ten times that night if we could have made a thousand pounds; and we know it, and we shall have to face that challenge some day. We were afraid; whereas the fear was a selfish fear and a miserable cravenness, and ought to have been eradicated and blown away as if by contemptuous winds. And thus would the process go on : namely, I endeavoured to be amiable and gentle, and to put a good appearance upon things. And the Lord will say, Amiability is your word— insincerity is mine; it was not light that was on your face, but sheen, glamour, a calculated and manufactured thing. Amiability you call it—hypocrisy I name it; you ought not to have been amiable; you ought to have been stern, resolute, unbending, judicial; you ought to have insisted on right being acknowledged, even if right was not done. And thus will the process advance, namely : I was tolerant of men's weaknesses, I was charitable in relation to their prejudices and their actions; I endeavoured to take a large and tolerant view. Christ will say, Thou wicked servant! it was not toleration, it was self-defence; you allowed a man to do something wrong that you might do something still more deeply evil; you tolerated vice in others that you might practise it yourself; you call that toleration—it was not toleration, it was false judgment, bad character, rottenness of heart and soul. Why did you not speak to yourselves words of fire? Why did you not criticise yourselves with the judgment of God? If you had then spoken out boldly, fearlessly, the very action of so speaking might have lifted you into a higher spiritual manhood, and then you would have displayed a true courage. Do not talk of reasons when they are excuses; do not speak of amiability when it is insincerity; do not set up toleration as a plea for self-indulgence : be true in your hearts that you may be true in your speech.

We are entitled to believe that there is no objection which Christ cannot answer. Personally, I never heard a single objection against Christ that could not be completely answered and satisfied. Let us beware lest we call objections what ought to be called quibbles. The quibbler will do nothing for you in the extremity of your life. He is a very clever wordmonger; he has a great skill in verbal legerdemain; he can twist the words wondrously, he can play with them like so many balls thrown up in the air, and kept there in rhythmic movement; but if he be only a quibbler he will do nothing for you when the rain falls and the wind blows and the earth shakes under your feet. Quibbling cannot cover all the need of life. Let it have its half-day's sunshine and holiday; let it practise its little gambols on some little greensward, but let it know that beyond that it cannot go. When night darkens and the storm roars and the foundations of things are out of course, and death—pale, grim, cruel death—comes for his dole and tax, the quibbler will not be within earshot in that dark time. If you have objections to Christ, state them, state them in the plainest, simplest, directest terms; and distinguish between an objection and a quibble, and especially distinguish between a reason and an excuse, and still further distinguish between a solid objection to Christianity and a secret love of sin that would get rid of the Cross, that it might get rid of self-accusation. Thus, thou Son of God, thou dost call us to reality, faithfulness, candour. A voice so calling is like a great and mighty wind from heaven. It is not earth-wind, full of dust; it is heaven's gentle tempest, charged with love.

Chapter iii.

HEALING THE WITHERED HAND.

[An Analysis.]

1. And he entered again into the synagogue; and there was **a man there** which had a withered hand.

2. And they watched him, whether he would heal him on the sabbath day : that they might accuse him.

3. And he saith unto the man which had the withered hand, Stand forth.

4. And he saith unto them, Is it lawful to do good on the sabbath **days,** or to do evil? to save life, or to kill? But they held their peace.

5. And when he had looked round about on them with **anger, being** grieved for the hardness of their hearts, he saith unto **the man, Stretch** forth thine hand. And he stretched it out, and his hand **was restored** whole as the other.

(1) CHRIST'S detection of human incompleteness. He instantly discovered that there was a man in the synagogue with a withered hand. The musician instantly detects a false note; the painter instantly detects an inartistic line; the complete Christ instantly detects the incomplete man. (2) Jesus Christ's power over partial disease. The man had only a withered hand. In some cases Christ had to heal thoroughly diseased men, in this case the disease was local; yet in both instances his power was the same. (3) Christ's inability to heal the obstinacy of his enemies. Here we come into the moral region, where all power is limited, and where omnipotence itself can work effectually only by the consent of the human will. A series of contrasts may be drawn in connection with this point. Christ could raise dead bodies; but dead souls had first to be willing to be raised. Christ could quell the storm on the sea, but he could not quiet the tumult of rebellious hearts. (4) Christ's moral indignation overcoming all outward obstacles. He was indignant with the men who valued the sacredness

of a day above the sacredness of a human life. Herein he
showed the intense benevolence of his mission. Everything
was to give way to the importunity of the wants of men. An
important point is involved in the question which Jesus Christ
puts in the fourth verse, viz., not to do good is actually to do
evil.

The instance shows Christ's carefulness over individual life.
There was only one man, yet Jesus Christ give that solitary
sufferer the full benefit of his omnipotence. The Gospel is a
revelation of God's love to individual men.

There are special moral deformities as well as special bodily
diseases. Some Christians have withered hands, or defective
vision, or one-sided sympathies, imperfect tempers, or faulty
habits. Christ alone can heal such diseases.

All kinds of sufferers ought to associate the synagogue, the
sanctuary, with their best hopes. It should be a place of healing,
and of instruction, and of all holy stimulus.

6. And the Pharisees went forth, and straightway took counsel with the
Herodians against him, how they might destroy him.

This verse shows the working of three determined and most
mischievous powers: (1) The power of prejudice; (2) The power
of technicality; (3) The power of ignorance. Prejudice as against
Christ; technicality as opposed to humanity; ignorance as forgetful of the fact that in morals as well as in physics the greater
includes the less. Sabbath-keeping is less than man-healing.

7. But Jesus withdrew himself with his disciples to the sea; and a great
multitude from Galilee followed him, and from Judæa,

8. And from Jerusalem, and from Idumæa, and from beyond Jordan; and
they about Tyre and Sidon, a great multitude, when they had heard what
great things he did, came unto him.

(1) There is a time to withdraw from opponents. (2) Withdrawment is not necessarily the result of cowardice. (3) Withdrawment from one sphere ought to be followed by entrance into
another.

Great things draw great multitudes. How did Christ exercise
his influence over great throngs? (1) He never lowered the
moral tone of his teaching; (2) He was never unequal to the
increasing demands made upon his power; (3) He never
requested the multitude to help him in any selfish endeavours.

No subject can draw such great multitudes as the Gospel. No subject can so deeply affect great multitudes as the Gospel. No subject can so profoundly and lastingly bless great multitudes as the Gospel.

9. And he spake to his disciples, that a small ship should wait on him because of the multitude, lest they should throng him.

10. For he had healed many: insomuch that they pressed upon him for to touch him, as many as had plagues.

11. And unclean spirits, when they saw him, fell down before him, and cried, saying, Thou art the Son of God.

12. And he straitly charged them that they should not make him known.

(1) Whoever has power to satisfy human necessities will never be in want of applicants. This is most obvious in the case of bodily suffering, but the principle holds good in reference to the deepest wants of human nature. (2) Unclean spirits may pay compliments to the good without changing their own disposition. (3) Unclean spirits are always commanded, as in this case, not to attempt the revelation of Christ. In the instance before us there was of course a special reason for the injunction ; but the principle is applicable to the whole subject of teaching and interpreting Christ and his doctrine.

13. And he goeth up into a mountain, and calleth unto him whom he would : and they came unto him.

14. And he ordained twelve, that they should be with him, and that he might send them forth to preach,

15. And to have power to heal sicknesses, and to cast out devils.

16. And Simon he surnamed Peter ;

17. And James the son of Zebedee, and John the brother of James; and he surnamed them Boanerges, which is, The sons of thunder :

18. And Andrew, and Philip, and Bartholomew, and Matthew, and Thomas, and James the son of Alphæus, and Thaddæus, and Simon the Canaanite,

19. And Judas Iscariot, which also betrayed him : and they went into an house.

20. And the multitude cometh together again, so that they could not so much as eat bread.

This paragraph may be used as showing the beginnings of the Christian Ministry. (1) The Christian ministry is an organization ; (2) the Christian ministry is divinely selected ; (a) a warning to pretenders ; (b) an encouragement to true servants ; (c) a guarantee of adaptation and success. (3) The Christian ministry is invested with special powers. The work of the ministry is to heal and bless mankind. This work can be fully sustained only by close communion with him who gave the power. Jesus Christ does not give even to ministers power for more than the immediate occasion. They must renew their appeals day by day. To them as to all the Church applies the admonition— " Pray without ceasing."

Amongst the general remarks which may be made upon the subject are the following: (1) Some ministers are marked by special characteristics, as, for example, Peter and James and John. (2) Some ministers are more prominent than others. One or two of the names in this list are prominent and illustrious; others are comparatively obscure. (3) The principal fact to determine is not a question of fame, but a question of vocation; whom Christ has called to the ministry he will also award appropriate honour.

On the 19th verse, remark (1) the possibility of debasing a divine position; (2) the impossibility of detaching the stigma of unfaithfulness. The name of Judas will always be associated with the betrayal, and the name of Simon Peter will always bring to memory his denial of his Lord.

21. And when his friends heard of it, they went out to lay hold on him: for they said, He is beside himself.

The abuses of friendship. (1) Friendship unable to follow the highest moods of the soul. (2) Friendship unable to see the spiritual meaning of outward circumstances. (3) Friendship seeking to interfere with spiritual usefulness. (4) Friendship seeking to reduce life to commonplace order. The sincere servant of Jesus Christ will take his law from the Master, and not from public opinion. The most complete detachment from worldly considerations and pursuits is necessary to sustain the soul when friendship itself becomes an assailant. The misinterpretation of our conduct by friendly critics often occasions the severest pain which is inflicted upon our spiritual life. The hand of enmity may be concealed within the glove of friendship.

22. And the scribes which came down from Jerusalem said, He hath Beelzebub, and by the prince of the devils casteth he out devils.

23. And he called them unto him, and said unto them in parables, How can Satan cast out Satan?

24. And if a kingdom be divided against itself, that kingdom cannot stand.

25. And if a house be divided against itself, that house cannot stand.

26. And if Satan rise up against himself, and be divided, he cannot stand, but hath an end.

Christ now encounters open hostility in addition to friendly, though mischievous, remonstrance. A theory of explanation was proposed by the scribes. Christ's answer to that theory shows (1) that opinions of leading minds may be entirely fallacious; and (2) that common-sense often suggests the best answer to fanciful theories respecting the work of Christ. Christ's whole answer turned upon the common-sense of his position. He does not plead authority; nor does he plead exemption from the ordinary laws of thought and service; he simply puts in the plea of common-sense. This fact supplies the basis for a discourse upon the relations of common-sense to the Gospel. The Gospel may in this respect be likened to Jacob's ladder, the foot of which was upon the earth. The Gospel has its peculiar mysteries, and its light too brilliant for the naked eye; at the same time it has aspects and bearings admitting of the most vivid illustration and defence within the region accessible to all minds. On the other hand the paragraph shows (1) the binding power of religious prejudice; and (2) the utter recklessness of religious bigotry. With regard to the suggestion of the scribes it should be remembered (1) that bold theories are not necessarily true; and (2) that the espousal of untrue theories will end in the confusion and humiliation of the theorists.

27. No man can enter into a strong man's house, and spoil his goods, except he will first bind the strong man; and then he will spoil his house.

Human life as affected by two different forces. (1) The strong enemy; (2) the strong friend. It is important to recognise the strength of the enemy, because it may be supposed that little or no effort is required to encounter his assaults. It should always be pointed out that Jesus Christ never speaks with hesitation as to the results of his repulse of the enemy. He never represents himself as clothed with more than sufficiency of power. In the text he is set forth as spoiling the strong man. It was prophesied that he should bruise the serpent's head.

Application: (1) Man must be under one or other of these forces,—the enemy or the friend. (2) Those who continue under the devil will share the ruin to which he is doomed. When Satan's head is bruised, all who are in his empire will be crushed.

28. Verily I say unto you, All sins shall be forgiven unto the sons of men, and blasphemies wherewith soever they shall blaspheme :

29. But he that shall blaspheme against the Holy Ghost hath never forgiveness, but is in danger of eternal damnation :

30. Because they said, He hath an unclean spirit.

Tischendorf reads the twenty-ninth verse "in danger of the eternal sin." Two aspects of human probation : (1) the pardonable, (2) the unpardonable. (1) The pardonable. (*a*) Its great extent, "all sins," etc.; (*b*) the implied greatness of the divine mercy. (2) The unpardonable : (*a*) its intense spirituality; (*b*) its perfect reasonableness. To sin against the Spirit is to cut away the only foundation on which the sinner can stand. Christianity is the appeal of God's Spirit to man's spirit; men may sin against the letter, the form, the dogma, and yet be within the pale of forgiveness; but when they revile and defy the very Spirit of God, they cut themselves off from the current of divine communion.

31. There came then his brethren and his mother, and, standing without, sent unto him, calling him.

32. And the multitude sat about him, and they said unto him, Behold, thy mother and thy brethren without seek for thee.

33. And he answered them, saying, Who is my mother, or my brethren ?

34. And he looked round about on them which sat about him, and said, Behold my mother and my brethren.

35. For whosoever shall do the will of God, the same is my brother, and my sister, and mother.

(1) The spirituality of Christ's relationships. The kinship of the body is held subordinate to the kinship of the spirit. (2) The true bond of communion with Christ : (*a*) not merely natural ; (*b*) not merely social. What is the true bond of communion with Christ ? Obedience to God's will. (*a*) There is but one infallible will ; (*b*) that will appeals for universal obedience,— " whosoever." (3) The privileges resulting from communion with Christ. (*a*) Intimate relationship,—mother, sister, brother ; (*b*) social communion : this is the family idea.

Among the general inferences which may be drawn from this passage are the following : (1) If men are to obey the Divine will, a great change must pass upon their natural dispositions. (2) If our communion with Christ is spiritual, it will be eternal. (3) If all the good are Christ's kindred, they are the kindred of one another, and ought therefore to live in the spirit of brotherhood.

PRAYER.

ALMIGHTY GOD, do thou take away the heart of unbelief, and put within us a believing spirit. Lord, we believe; help thou our unbelief. Thou canst do all things with him who believeth; all things are possible to him : but is not faith the gift of God ? Lord, increase our faith. Thou knowest how we are beset by the senses, how we are limited and tempted and urged by a thousand influences which only thine own strength can resist: come to our aid, stand by our side. Christ, thou Son of God, thou wast in all points tempted like as we are; thou knowest our frame, thou rememberest that we are dust, and thou wilt not suffer us to be tempted with any temptation that cannot be overcome. Our hope is in God; our confidence is in the Cross; we fly unto the Son of God as unto an eternal refuge. Save us, keep us, protect us, in all the hours of agony which make our life so deep a trouble. Thou knowest us altogether: the difficulties here and there, in the house, in the church, in the market, in the soul itself—that inner battlefield on which the great contests are urged and waged and finished. Lord, again and again we say, Come from thy Cross and save us; Christ, Thou Son of man, have mercy on us ! Lead us into the knowledge of thy truth; give us such a love of thyself and thy purpose that all other influences and impulses shall be shut out from our life, or sanctified and regulated by thy presence. Thou knowest our downsitting and our uprising, our going out and our coming in; there is not a word upon our tongue, there is not a thought in our heart, but lo, O Lord, thou knowest it altogether. This is our joy, and this is our terror; for wherein we would be right how blessed is thy smile; and wherein we would seek to deceive thee or evade thee, how awful is the penetration of thine eye. Regard us in all the relations of life, and make us strong in Christ and in his grace, hopeful because his kingdom is ever coming, and willing to work in the Lord's service, for in his labour there is rest. Help the good man to pray some bolder prayer; help the timid man to put out his soul in one act of faith; disappoint the bad man; when the cruel man is seeking his prey, let sudden darkness fall upon him and rest upon his eyes like a load. The Lord thus undertake for us, guide us, uphold us; give us wisdom, grace, purity, strength, and patience, and all the fruits of the Spirit. Let the Holy Ghost be our life, and light, and joy; quicken our spiritual discernment that we may see things that are not seen; so excite our highest sensibilities as to enable us to respond with instant and grateful love to all the appeals of thy truth. Thou alone canst renew human life, and establish it in everlasting blessedness. Truly thou workest in mystery, yet are the results of thy work beautiful and noble exceedingly. Thou hidest thyself in the chambers of our heart, so that none can see thee, and yet we know that thou art there by the flooding love which overflows our being, by the heavenward desires which stir our nature with blessed unrest, and by the lofty power with which we are enabled to do all the common work of life. Abide with us! When thou goest, our light is put out; when thou returnest, no shadow can be found upon us. In the light of thy mercy we see all our guilt; in the sweetness of thy love we feel the bitterness of our sin. Abide with us! By thy word we see the folly of our own wisdom; by thy Holy Spirit we know the wickedness of the devil. Abide with us! Where our sin abounds let thy grace much more abound. Shame us by the incessancy of thy love, rather than destroy us by thy great power. O loving One, patient, tender, abide with us! And to God who made us, and to God who redeemed us with an infinite price, to the Holy Ghost, the God who sanctifieth us, be the kingdom, and the power, and the glory, world without end. Amen.

Chapter iii. 7-9.

"And a great multitude from Galilee followed him. . . . A great multitude came unto him. . . . Because of the multitude."

CHRIST'S RELATION TO GREAT MULTITUDES.

WHY were these multitudes so urgent? Why was there any multitude at all? The man is simple, gracious, tender, sympathetic: why should there have been such a display of public interest in his ministry and action? He called his discourses "sayings," and he said they were his own—"these sayings of mine." Sometimes he spoke sharply, critically, with no mistake as to his moral purposes; the denunciation was explicit and tremendous; the beatitudes were tender, profound healing: why all this multitudinousness? We might have expected a few kindred hearts to follow such a ministry; but all the world went after him. There must be some explanation of this: what is that explanation? There are class preachers. We know the epithets which belong to them as of right; a superficial, transient, partly illegitimate right or claim; they are profound, polished, finished; exquisite, tasteful, brilliant, magnificent: but the world cares nothing about them, as a world —a grand, complete humanity. Those who do care for them care very much. The Gospel can fascinate classes; the Gospel can talk all languages, live in all climates, adapt itself to all circumstances; it can have an academy, it can go where people can neither read nor write; but the Gospel can do more than fascinate classes and sections of human nature. This is the explanation of Christ's ministry, in all its graciousness, in all its power of healing : he touched the universal heart.   There was strength in Christ's teaching for everybody, for that everybody which is manhood.   He did not speak to representatives, or recognise merely and exclusively aspects and phases of life ; he poured his wisdom and his love into the heart of the world, and that heart knew him ; if sometimes the testimony was reluctant, yet in the issue it was emphatic, fervent, overwhelming. There is a music which is for classes.   We know the epithets which belong to that partial music ; we know the illegitimate claims which are put in to understand it ; we know the simulated intelligence with which the most consummate ignorance listens to it ; it is classic music.   Poor music ! that it should ever be so debased as to accept an epithet.   Music needs no qualifying terms.   There is a music that belongs to the world ; the moment it is uttered the world's heart answers it ; it belongs to the child, the mother, the nurse, the shepherd on the mountains, the merchant in the city ; the moment the right notes are uttered the whole world takes up those notes, and everywhere they are heard expressing emotions of the moment, or hinting at emotions deep as life, lasting as duration.   So it is with the gospel of Jesus Christ.   You can minimise it ; you can found an academy with it ; you can so speak it that nobody will either understand it or feel it ; you can crucify the gospel as you crucified its Author.   There is a witchery and influence that cannot be explained.   You think you can unravel the mystery, and tell some brother man exactly how it is, and when you have completed your analysis you find you have simply mistaken the origin, and the drift, and the issue of your purpose.

What is, then, the influence that touches great multitudes ? It is an influence which often disregards, we need not say despises, classes.   Luther said, " I take no notice of the doctors who are present, of whom there may be twelve ; I preach to the young men and maidens, and the poor, of whom there are two thousand."   That was Christlike.   When Jesus did turn to the classes it was with a look of denunciation ; if any pity mingled with that denunciation it made but a painful irony.   Scribes, Pharisees, rich, proud, selfish people ; on all these he turned a face full of displeasure. He would not accept their patronage, he paid no attention either to their commendation or their flattery or their displeasure and repudiation; he was the Son of man,— in that title, in all its music, you have the explanation of these multitudes that followed him, and thronged him, and drew out of him all that he came to give the world. As a preacher you can have—that is to say, it lies within your power—the very selectest congregation that ever gathered. It lies within your power, sanctified by the Holy Ghost, to have the poor, and the young, and all kinds of men round about your pulpit, as thirsty men go where the fountain is, as hungry men flee with what strength is left to the house of bread. These multitudes are arguments. If they were mere mobs no heed need be paid to them. They are not mobs, they are illustrations, expositions; they tell on the human and needy side what Christ is telling on the divine and all-supplying side of this marvellous history. Men are not aware of all they are doing. To see men hastening to the house of prayer is, when properly understood and weighed, to see a new and exquisite aspect of Providence, to see a high and noble view of the human soul. Every man who so flies to the altar, hastes with the eagerness of hunger to God's house, condemns the world, in very deed tramples it under foot, and says by that very act of going into the sanctuary with a right purpose, The world cannot satisfy me: I pant for heaven as the hart panteth after the waterbrooks.

The great multitudes that thronged Christ were not to be re- garded only in a statistical way. They are rather to be interpreted as expressing a universal interest because a universal need. No subject can draw and permanently hold such great multitudes as the Gospel. Why? Curiosity has its momentary crowd, but the reason is assignable, and intelligible, and sometimes despic- able. Novelty of this kind or that has its transient success, but the Gospel has not only a momentary fascination, but an enduring influence and a growing power over all who come within the mystery of its touch. Look at a congregation gathered to see Christ, as revealed in his Word, and what a spectacle it is! All men are there, in type, in characteristic, in symbolic need, in representative energy; the old man is sure that there will be

some word for grey hairs, and leaning on the top of his staff he
waits for his portion of meat; and the little child is sure that
there will be some bright sentence, some parabolical outline;
maybe some pathetic story, briefly told, with the urgency of
earnestness, not with the elaborateness of mere artistic gift and
passion; the humblest soul says to itself, My word will come
presently; this preacher never neglects the humble, untaught, but
necessitous soul. Let him talk in his grandest sentences for a
while, he will not forget the poor : I wait. Broken hearts come
to Christ's congregation, or altar, or Cross, for healing. The
sanctuary that ignores broken hearts ignores the Cross whose
name it desecrates. The sanctuary was built for the broken
heart; not for the strong, mighty, gay, rich, flourishing, domineering, but for the shattered and the contrite, the lonely and
the sad, the self-convicted sinner who cries in the very silence of
agony, "What must I do to be saved ? " So long as men are
conscious of sin, and conscious of the need of salvation, the
multitude following Christ will be very large, yet it will increase
in number, and in expectancy and urgency; its very attitude
shall be a prayer, its earnestness shall be a prevailing plea. A
marvellous spectacle is any Christian congregation. The difficulty
of the preacher is that so few people recognise the diversity of
the congregation, and make allowance for a ministry that would
follow the scale of Christ's own method of meeting human need.
The selfishness of the congregation is seen in that every individual
himself wants all the service. He cannot have it. The Christ-
like preacher must follow the lines of Christ : how high he is
now, and anon how low down, walking amidst our very feet,
and looking at our footprints as if haply he might interpret them
into some attitude or direction that would betoken the state of
our spirit; how profound in simplicity, how generous in
concession, how condescending in taking up a little child and
hugging the dear creature, and how tremendous in rebuking the
men who have the patronage of the dead *ex cathedrâ*.

Christ had the multitudes because he spoke to the multitudes.
No subject can so deeply affect great multitudes as the Gospel.
It develops our humanity ; it reaches and strengthens the point
of fellowship. This Gospel handles the matter of individu-

ality very delicately, but very fully. For a time the man, individual, singular, is everything; he is talked to as if there were nobody else in the universe but himself and God; yet immediately he is put down, and made of the multitudes that constitute humanity; and then he feels himself in totally other and new and enlarging relations; his vanity is reproved, his self-sufficiency is rebuked, he feels that he needs a friend on the right hand, and the left, behind, before, and round about him : he realises God's conception of humanity. Out of that we have the Church, we have fellowship, the commonwealth, the interchange of relations, sympathies, and interests—that marvellous interaction which makes up society in its highest aspects. Hence we have had occasion to say in rebuke to some, that men cannot pray altogether and exclusively alone. Solitary prayer we must have. Secret communion is essential to the full development of the spiritual life; but there is a larger prayer, call it the common prayer, in which I may hear what my brother needs, and my brother may catch from my tones some hint of my sorrow and my necessity; and thus by commingling of supplication, and the common expression of desire, we realise the larger conception of prayer, and create an atmosphere favourable to the cultivation and the progress of our noblest life; "forsake not the assembling of yourselves together." Hence, too, we have had occasion to say that no man can read the Bible alone. The Bible is a public book. Whatever was meant for the world must be read by the world in one grand multitudinous voice, if all its music is to be elicited, if all its emphasis is to be delivered with the thunder that is worthy of such eloquence. Here is a verse for one soul, and there is an appeal addressed to the solitary heart, and if some other man were present to hear it part of the message would be lost. The Bible has its corners and sanctuaries and places into which individual souls can repair for special perusal of heaven's will; but taking the book as a whole it realises God's idea when it seizes the whole world, and makes every man hear in the tongue in which he was born the wonderful works of God. Every man has a tongue of his own—to speak of the English tongue is to speak vulgarly. The English tongue has to accommodate itself to every lip over which it falls; has to catch its accent from every tongue that uses it, and has to have suggestions

which can only be imported into it by the unutterable meaning
of the heart.

The Gospel thus affects great multitudes by dealing with fundamental questions. If we looked to the Gospel for aught else we
should be mistaken and disappointed. The Gospel is not a riddle
book ; the Gospel is not a series of conundrums which nobody
can answer but priests and preachers, ministers and office-
bearers : the Bible is the people's book, it belongs to the common
humanity; men who can barely spell can draw out of it living
water. If this Gospel were a mere exercise in grammar, then
only grammarians could be saved. When we rebuke grammarians they do not understand us ; but what did a grammarian
ever understand ? He says, We must have grammar. Certainly ; we must have vessels to hold the water ; but it is the water
that quenches the thirst. The meaning is beyond the letter, not
in any sense of despising the letter, but in the sense of having
a meaning to convey which the most significant symbols fail
adequately to typify. Hence Christ's need of the hereafter.
The present time was too small for him ; it caged and barred
him ; so he must needs often say :—Hereafter ye shall see :
hereafter ye shall know : what thou knowest not now thou shalt
know hereafter. Time would be a very small cage to live in if
it had not a door somewhere in it that opened on eternity : thus
we get content and rest and assurance of hope ; we say, This
time-day is not long enough for us, but it opens upon a day that
never darkens into night. So the Gospel affects great multitudes
variously and profoundly ; teaching patience to some, giving
hope to all, and blessing the soul with an assurance that by-and-
by we shall know as we are known ; see as we are seen, and
have access into the wider spaces, yea, into the infinite liberties
of God's eternal revelation, as a man might reveal himself face
to face with a friend he loved.

No subject can so lastingly bless the multitude as the Gospel.
It is not a sensation, an impression, it is in no sense a merely
momentary feeling ; it is a conviction, a persuasion, a regeneration, a new life. There are theories that are cheerful, vivacious
almost to impertinence and insolence, when everything is quiet

and bright and prosperous; but they have an ungrateful way of dropping off from the pilgrims' side when the road is very steep and the valley is very dark, or the wind is very cold. There are a thousand such theories lying dead at the mouth of the valley yonde ; go and pick them up if you have peculiar taste for gathering things that are dead and never can be revived. They were lovely for a time, quite blooming little impertinences, with a smart way of talking, and a glib way of criticising the universe, and a haughty way of pronouncing upon all things, from trinities down to insects. They are lying yonder, dead, a thousand thick ; go and make what you can of them. This Christ of God never leaves, never forsakes, the souls that put their trust in him ; he is most when we need him most, tenderest when we are sick ; and if a lamb is shorn he goes out to feel the wind before he lets the shorn lamb go out to full exposure. Gentle Jesus, gentle Shepherd, loving Lord, where we cannot understand the deity we can feel thy motherliness, and such motherliness means deity.

How did Christ exercise his influence ? He never lowered his moral tone. He never made the Ten Commandments into nine, or took away three of them to accommodate some rich young ruler that was willing to bestow a very dignified patronage upon the kingdom of God. He never said, You must not strive after academic justice ; it is well enough to hear ideal theorists talk about ideal righteousness, but you must do what you can, and above all things never make righteousness a discipline or a burden. No such speech did Christ ever teach to men ; he said, Unless a man take up his cross he cannot come ; except a man deny—not a habit or a custom, but—himself, he cannot be my disciple. Suicide begins regeneration. We have now an adaptable morality. We are tempted to say to the erring public, Dear friends, what do you want ? Jesus Christ never talked so to the multitude. He spake the Commandment, he delivered himself as a king ; he commanded, he uttered the decree ; yet when he came to deal with men how gracious he was, and meek and gentle, but always making his gentleness the conductor of his righteousness. His pity never conducted men past the law in any evasive sense ; rather did that pity

mysteriously fulfil the law, and show that where there is no
mercy there can be no justice. Never did Jesus Christ use his
influence with the multitudes to promote selfish objects. He
came to bless men, to save men, to do men good on every hand ;
he did "great things" according to this chapter,—"A great
multitude, when they had heard what great things he did, came
unto him." Whatever he did was great. The great man makes
great occasions. Even the simplest sayings of Christ root themselves in his deity. There are sentences we think we can understand, but when we come into close quarters with them we find
they go back syllable by syllable, up, up to the eternal throne.
There is no simplicity in Christ that can be interpreted as
meaning mere shallowness. Never did Jesus Christ do anything
that was not in the heart of it great ; when he did it, it might
look easy enough, but it was the King that did it. The heavens
look well shaped, but it was not man's clumsy hand that rounded
the sky ; the stars are all peaceable as if they were filled with a
spirit of content. How serene they are in their brightness ! It
looks quite easy to make these stars ; yet it was God that made
them, and Omnipotence makes all things easy ; but who, God
only excepted, has omnipotence ? When his popularity rolled
through the land, and when the people came to be healed, and
pressed upon him to be touched ; when men afflicted with plagues
and unclean spirits came before him, and cried out, "Thou art
the Son of God," he said, I do not want you to preach my doctrine.
For reasons we cannot understand, Christ might forbid even the
saintliest men to anticipate some of his revelations ; but by an
accommodation that could well vindicate itself we may learn from
such prohibitions as are given in this chapter that Christ will
not be revealed by unclean spirits. He says in effect, Do not
talk about my divine sonship, do not reveal my deity ; it is not
for your lips to use holy words. The bad man cannot reveal the
Son of God ; the hollow-hearted, self-seeking preacher cannot
preach Christ's Gospel ; he may preach about it, but he cannot
deliver the message that whosoever will may come and be saved,
and the chief of sinners is the chief guest at Christ's love-table, at
Christ's redeeming Cross.

A message of this kind should be uttered with the tears of

the heart, with the very agony of love, with a self-prostration which men cannot understand, but which adds ineffable value to every message that is delivered. If we would reveal the deity of Christ we must ourselves be divine men, in the sense of being pure of heart, lofty and incorruptible in purpose, unselfish in spirit, marked through and through, all over, not with the image, but with the meaning of the Cross. Do I speak to some man who has no multitude to talk to? I would not discourage him. Sometimes one man is a multitude. Do not be victimised by merely statistical lines and numbers. If Christ will come where there are two or three gathered together in his name we ought not to be ashamed to make such a convocation a great occasion. What Christ accepts surely it does not lie within our right to despise or reject. On the other hand, let us be careful lest we make the Gospel a message to a class, lest we be damned by respectability. Our message is to the whole world, and wherever there is a multitude that multitude belongs to the humblest minister amongst us. The preacher does not rule, so to say, morally and influentially over his own numerable congregation ; the humblest preacher that preaches Christ is in a sense the preacher to the greatest multitude that ever assembled. Let us hold not only the unity of the faith, but consequently the unity of the Church.

Chapter iv.

THE PARABLE OF THE SOWER.

[An Analysis.]

1. And he began again to teach by the sea side: and there was gathered unto him a great multitude, so that he entered into a ship, and sat in the sea; and the whole multitude was by the sea on the land.

2. And he taught them many things by parables, and said unto them in his doctrine,

3. Hearken; Behold, there went out a sower to sow:

4. And it came to pass, as he sowed, some fell by the way side, and the fowls of the air came and devoured it up.

5. And some fell on stony ground, where it had not much earth; and immediately it sprang up, because it had no depth of earth:

6. But when the sun was up, it was scorched; and because it had no root, it withered away.

7. And some fell among thorns, and the thorns grew up, and choked it, and it yielded no fruit.

8. And other fell on good ground, and did yield fruit that sprang up and increased; and brought forth, some thirty, and some sixty, and some an hundred.

9. And he said unto them, He that hath ears to hear, let him hear.

10. And when he was alone, they that were about him with the twelve asked of him the parable.

11. And he said unto them, Unto you it is given to know the mystery of the kingdom of God: but unto them that are without, all these things are done in parables:

12. That seeing they may see, and not perceive; and hearing they may hear, and not understand; lest at any time they should be converted, and their sins should be forgiven them.

13. And he said unto them, Know ye not this parable? and how then will ye know all parables?

14. The sower soweth the word.

15. And these are they by the way side, where the word is sown; but when they have heard, Satan cometh immediately, and taketh away the d that was sown in their hearts.

16. And these are they likewise which are sown on stony ground; who when they have heard the word, immediately receive it with gladness;

17. And have no root in themselves, and so endure but for a time: afterwards, when affliction or persecution ariseth for the word's sake, immediately they are offended.

18. And these are they which are sown among thorns; such as hear the word,

19. And the cares of this world, and the deceitfulness of riches, and the lusts of other things entering in, choke the word, and it becometh unfruitful.

20. And these are they which are sown on good ground; such as hear the word, and receive it, and bring forth fruit, some thirtyfold, some sixty, and some an hundred.

THE work of Christ and the general preaching of the Gospel are represented in this simple illustration. From it we learn—1. That a general proclamation is attended by particular results. This is notable, because one would have imagined that any declaration of God's will would have elicited an instantaneous, universal, and satisfactory response. The only difference which could have been supposed would be that each would be striving to excel the other in prompt and reverent obedience. 2. We learn, secondly, that those particular results are not to be attributed to any special arrangement on the part of the sower. The sower went forth to sow the whole field, at the same time, with the same seed, and with the same purpose; with entire impartiality he moved along the courses of the field, and scattered the grain on the right hand and on the left. Looking at the case from his point of view, we might have expected that his labours would have been productive of the most satisfactory results. Sowers cannot control harvests. They may sow well, and be mocked by a lean and withered harvest. This marks not only a limitation of power on the part of man, but on the part of God also in moral operations. No man can be compelled to bring forth fruit unto God. A man may receive the best seed and let it rot; he may live under the most fertilising influences, and yet be barren of all holy fruits. The startling practical reflection suggested by this circumstance is, that men are not saved by having opportunities, but by improving them. It is no light consideration that with God himself for a sower we may be disappointed in the fruitfulness and quality of the harvest. This refutes the sophism, that if the Gospel were properly proclaimed, men would yield to it. The fault is not in the instrumentality. The ministry of Jesus Christ was in certain aspects a failure; there were vast breadths of the field which he sowed with a

liberal hand, which bore no trace of his service. The world is
not perishing for lack of good preaching. Never was preaching
so excellent and so abundant as it is to-day, yet hardly one token
of harvest can be seen. We may learn—3. That hearers must
themselves supply the conditions of spiritual success. Look at
the particulars for illustration : The wayside hearer listens to
the word, but understandeth (regardeth) it not, and from want
of attention the enemy is suffered to " catch away that which
was sown in heart." The condition which this hearer should
have brought with him is meditation. The word touched him
only by the outside ; he gave it no lodgment in his heart, never
watered the seed, never protected the fences, never opened his
spirit to its power. The seed was good, the soil was bad ;
the sower was God, the enemy the devil. See how the case
stands : the sower is God, the field is the heart, the destroyer
is the devil ; and in order to disappoint the enemy, the heart
must co-operate with God. Take the stony-ground hearer. He
listens to the word with gladness. He thinks it a pleasant
sound, and while the music is in his ear, he resolves to profit
by the Holy Word. What condition is wanting in his case ? It
is well named " root in himself " ; no reality and depth of nature ;
empty, trifling, unreflecting ; easily moved, self-indulgent, pliable ;
all right in sunshine, but cowardly in darkness ; loving the
Gospel sound, but lacking courage to endure anything for the
Gospel's sake. Such a hearer brings much disappointment to
his minister. The starting tear, the responsive gleam, the ready
assent, are mistaken by being over-valued by the zealous preacher.
No man can live to much purpose who has " no root in himself,"
nothing upon which even God can work. Mark the possibility
of exhausting one's manhood ; throwing away, or allowing to die
out, the germ which was given to be cultured and expanded into
fruitfulness towards God ! Think of a man being dead at the
roots ! The thorny-ground hearer is represented in all congregations : the seed is good, the soil itself even may not be of the
worst quality ; the man is simply preoccupied ; his idea is that
life depends entirely upon his own exertions, and he consequently
works as if he had no spiritual sources to draw upon. Give him
a perpetual Sabbath, and he will be attentive, and perhaps
partly religious ; but as the working-week begins, the old

tyrannous mammon-spirit masters him. There is an influence which seems to be born, or at least revived, every Monday morning, which overpowers the partial religiousness of the Sabbath. It is not to be understood that religious men are exempt from the cares of this world, or even the deceitfulness of riches; they have them all, but the spirit that is in them is greater than the spirit that is in the world, and they thereby overcome.

[The expression—"the deceitfulness of riches," is an excellent text for a sermon to the busy. It may also be the foundation of a discourse to young merchants. The deceitfulness is shown in several ways, such, for example, as—"I am laying up for a rainy day"; "I care nothing for wealth, except to do good with it"; when I have realised a sufficient sum, I shall spend the remainder in works of benevolence." All these are sophisms. The rainy day may never come; the rich man seldom does as much good as he did when he was not half so wealthy; money likes money, and the difficulty is to know when a man has "sufficient." The subject might then be viewed in a graver aspect, viz. :—the power of riches to choke the divine word in man Think of a man selling his aspirations, his faculties, his capacities, selling his soul for gold! This love of money does not come upon a man all at once, but "deceitfully," until a nature which might have been open and generous becomes shrivelled and impenetrable.]

Each class of hearers may be specially treated—

Wayside : Opportunity given : Opportunity lost : A constantly watchful enemy.

Stony Ground : Impulsiveness : Shallowness : Want of conviction and fortitude.

Thorns : Mental pre-occupation : Thoughtlessness : Worldly-mindedness.

Good Ground : Moral preparation : Earnestness : Visible reward in fruitfulness, which reward is to constitute the most evident proof of the reality of the divine life in the soul.

The whole parable may be used as showing the operation of four powerful influences in human life. (1) The influence of the devil as seen in the wayside hearers. (2) The influence of frivolity as seen in the stony-ground hearers. (3) The influence of worldliness as seen in the thorny-ground hearers. (4) The influence of earnestness as seen in the good-ground hearers.

21. And he said unto them, Is a candle brought to be put under a bushel, or under a bed ? and not to be set on a candlestick ?

22. For there is nothing hid, which shall not be manifested ; neither was any thing kept secret, but that it should come abroad.

23. If any man have ears to hear, let him hear.

24. And he said unto them, Take heed what ye hear : with what measure ye mete, it shall be measured to you : and unto you that hear shall more be given.

25. For he that hath, to him shall be given : and he that hath not, from him shall be taken even that which he hath.

The subject is : Christian life viewed as a revelation, a responsibility, and a law.

I. As a revelation : (*a*) It is to be luminous ; (*b*) it is to be properly placed in the midst of society. The gospel is a great revealing power. In all truth there is power of exposure and judgment ; how much more in the highest truth of all !

II As a responsibility : (*a*) Stewardship in doctrine ; (*b*) stewardship in action.

III. As a law : (*a*) Usefulness is productiveness ; (*b*) indolence is ruin.

The kingdom of Christ is thus shown to be founded on law. Man never becomes more than a subject : Christ never less than a king.

26. And he said, So is the kingdom of God, as if a man should cast seed into the ground :

27. And should sleep, and rise night and day, and the seed should spring and grow up he knoweth not how.

28. For the earth bringeth forth fruit of herself ; first the blade, then the ear, after that the full corn in the ear.

29. But when the fruit is brought forth, immediately he putteth in the sickle, because the harvest is come.

(1) Though the sower sleep after his labour, yet the process of germination goes on night and day. (2) Simple beginnings and practical results may be connected by mysterious processes : " he knoweth not how." There is a point in Christian work where knowledge must yield to mystery. (3) As the work of the sower is assisted by natural processes (" the earth bringeth forth of itself," etc.), so the seed of truth is aided by the natural conscience and aspiration which God has given to all men. (4) The

mysteriousness of processes ought not to deter from reaping the harvest. The spiritual labourer may learn from the husbandman.

30. And he said, Whereunto shall we liken the kingdom of God ? or with what comparison shall we compare it ?

31. It is like a grain of mustard seed, which, when it is sown in the earth, is less than all the seeds that be in the earth :

32. But when it is sown, it groweth up, and becometh greater than all herbs, and shooteth out great branches ; so that the fowls of the air may lodge under the shadow of it.

(1) Small beginnings may have great endings. (*a*) This should encourage all holy labourers ; (*b*) this should alarm all wicked men. (2) Vitality more important than magnitude. (*a*) This applies to creeds ; (*b*) to church agencies and organisations ; (*c*) to a public profession of faith. (3) The least thing in nature a better illustration of divine truth than the greatest object in art. The least of all seeds more fitly represents the kingdom of heaven than the most elaborate of all statuary. The natural flower is a revelation of God, the artificial flower is a proof of the skill of man. It should be noticed that human art is never referred to in the Scripture as illustrating the divine nature and purposes, but continual reference is made to all the works of creation. God illustrates himself by himself.

33. And with many such parables spake he the word unto them, as they were able to hear it.

34. But without a parable spake he not unto them : and when they were alone, he expounded all things to his disciples.

This text may be used as supplying three lessons as to the duties of the Christian teacher. (1) He must adapt himself to his hearers. Are they young ? Are they educated ? Are they courageous ? Are they surrounded by any peculiar circumstances ? (2) He must consider his hearers rather than himself. This was Jesus Christ's method. The question should be not what pleases the preacher's taste, but what is most required by the spiritual condition of the people. (3) He must increase his communication of truth and light according to the progress of his scholars. Reticence is power. In teaching children the teacher does not dazzle them by the splendour of his attainments, he adapts the light to the strength of their mental vision. The preacher should always know more of divine truth than the hearer. Christ's method of imparting knowledge is, so far as we can infer, unchanged. He has yet more light to shed upon his word.

35. And the same day, when the even was come, he saith unto them, Let us pass over unto the other side.

36. And when they had sent away the multitude, they took him even as he was in the ship. And there were also with him other little ships.

37. And there arose a great storm of wind, and the waves beat into the ship, so that it was now full.

38. And he was in the hinder part of the ship, asleep on a pillow : and they awake him, and say unto him, Master, carest thou not that we perish ?

39. And he arose, and rebuked the wind, and said unto the sea, Peace, be still. And the wind ceased, and there was a great calm.

40. And he said unto them, Why are ye so fearful ? how is it that ye have no faith ?

41. And they feared exceedingly, and said one to another, What manner of man is this, that even the wind and the sea obey him ?

(1) The organised Church in peril,—Christ and his disciples were all in this tempest. (2) Dangers beset the Church even whilst it is carrying out the express commands of Christ,—Jesus himself bade them pass over unto the other side. (3) The spirit of Christ, not the body of Christ, must save the Church in all peril. The sleeping body was in the vessel, but it exercised no influence upon the storm. It is possible to have an embalmed Christ, and yet to have no Christianity. It is also possible to have the letter of Christ's word without the spirit and power of his truth. (4) Jesus Christ answering the personal appeal of the imperilled Church. The power of the servant is often exhausted, —exhausted power should betake itself to supplication. (5) All the perils of the Church may be successfully encountered by profound faith in God (v. 40).

Chapter iv. 41.

"What manner of man is this?"

THE UNKNOWN QUANTITY IN CHRIST.

THERE was, of course, no doubt upon the mind of the disciples that Jesus Christ was a man, yet there was something about him which very often made them look upon him with surprise and even bewilderment. For a time things would go on in an ordinary course, and then, quite suddenly, Jesus Christ would utter a tone unlike all other tones, and the disciples would be startled by the unusual music. For days together they would be able to look upon his face as the face of a gentle brother, pensive, indeed, and much worn, yet quite human, and most tender. Then, in an unexpected moment, there would come into that brother's face a look, unlike all other looks; a gleam of spiritual light,—a flush and colour showing that through his heart there had just passed a wave of more than mortal life, and he would look more like an angel than a man. He was a man; no doubt at all about that; yet there was something about him that there was about nobody else; even when he appeared to be but a common stranger, there was a power in his speech which made men's hearts burn. He was a man, but a man *plus*, to say the least of it. There was in him an unknown quantity, and it is about this unknown quantity that I propose now to say one or two things that may help our wonder to become reverent and loving homage.

We shall get a bolder and clearer aspect of the whole case if we begin on common ground, and look at it through one or two earthly parallels. Take, for example, a company of poor, uncultivated, unpretending men; let them all be of one sort, all thoroughly familiar with each other; they talk without restraint; all their remarks proceed upon the same low level; all their

74

language is marked by the same commonness or vulgarity. Into this company let a gentleman by some means be introduced; let that gentleman disguise himself by putting on the plainest possible clothing; let him adapt himself with the utmost care to his new circumstances; his one object is to resemble most closely the men whose society he has sought. His own familiar friend would not know him through the disguise he has assumed. Given such a case, that man, by one tone, by one movement of his hand, by one glance, may cause all eyes to be turned upon him in wonder, in suspicion, in anxiety! It is felt there is something about him that there is not about any of the others, —he looks plain enough, takes upon himself no airs, sits on a level with the whole company, yet a tone thrilled them, one remark shot through their murky conversation like lightning flashing through darkness. Instantly there is felt to be an unknown quantity among them; they cannot quite recover themselves; there is a stranger in the house,—to each other they would fain say, " What manner of man is this ? "

Take a very different scene. Here is a company of educated and most polished gentlemen. They speak various languages; they are at home upon every question of the day; their information, standard and current, is considered extensive and profound. Suppose that by some means they should be brought into contact with a man, clothed in the plainest garb, without pretence of bearing, or one outward sign of superiority, yet, when he speaks, he adds to the information of the most learned, to every discussion he contributes something unique, yet obviously pertinent; to the polish of learning he adds the vigour of originality. Precisely the same resul twould follow in this case as in the other. By so much as he was superior to others, and yet concealed his superiority under an exterior which denoted the utmost lowliness of condition, he would excite and justify the inquiry, " What manner of man is this ? "

Now we find that Jesus Christ was constantly puzzling and bewildering men by the action, sometimes subtle and remote, sometimes almost visible and approachable, of an unknown quantity in his nature. He was quite close at hand, yet he could separate himself from men by an immeasurable distance ; when familiarity seemed to be completing itself, one look would recall the old reverence and awe ; when equality was just about to be established, a single question would prove the depth of men's ignorance, and send them away to learn the merest alphabet of knowledge.

The argument which comes out of the unknown quantity in Christ may take some such shape as this : It was beneficent, and therefore not from beneath ; it was intensely spiritual, and therefore not of the earth, earthy ; it was wholly self-sacrificial, and therefore different from ordinary human policy and purpose ; it set aside canons, traditions, and standards established and valued by men, and therefore claimed a wisdom superior to the ripest wisdom of all human teachers. All this was the more obvious and impressive, because he was without form or comeliness ; he was as a root out of a dry ground ; he bore the form of a servant ; he made himself of no reputation,—yet out of him there went virtue which healed the incurable, and light which made the saddest lives take heart again. There was in him more than could be quite concealed. The disguise was most wonderful, yet not altogether complete. The cloud was vast and dense, yet it was pierced now and again by shafts of the supreme glory. What was the meaning of this ? We boast that no social humiliation can conceal a gentlemen,—through rags and poverty and weakness, there will come signs of gentle blood or noble spirit ; be it so, we rejoice in it as one of our most pleasant and gratifying social truths ; what if we carry our own reasoning one point higher, and inquire whether, as no disguise can conceal a gentleman, it is possible that any condescension can put God in total eclipse.

We have said that the unknown quantity in Christ was beneficent, and therefore not from beneath. The proof of this is open to any reader, " The Son of man is come to seek and to save that which was lost." " The Son of man is not come to destroy men's lives, but to save them." " I came not to judge the world, but to save the world." Look at the idea of saving the world ! Regard it in what light we may, there is no other idea which can compare with it in point of sublimity of goodness. If we had met with it in any heathen writer, we should have been constrained to point it out as the most marvellous conception of the human mind. The father says, Save the family; the citizen says, Save the city; the patriot says, Save the country. So far good: this is beneficent, this is noble; yet, when these voices have ceased, the Son of man says, Save the world! There is the unknown quantity—the subtle, mysterious, inexplicable something, which separates the man from all other men, and causes us to exclaim, "What manner of man is this?"

Observe, with special care, that it is not needful that we should even make a profession of religion in order to know somewhat of the value of this idea of saving a world. We take it merely as an idea; we take it as if we had found it written by an unknown hand in the obscurest of pagan books; we claim for it no sectarian interpretation; we put aside all sectarian interpretation; we put aside all Church mediums of vision as standards of measurement: there stands in its own simplicity the fact that some man, somewhere, at some time, proposed to save the world! To save it, and therefore his heart was full of mercy—to save the world, and therefore his mind was as comprehensive as his heart was generous. And this he proposed to do, not when great ideas had become familiar, but when exclusiveness was predominant, when lines hard and fast had mapped off the little provinces of human regard and trust. And more than this: he came into the world to save it; this was his original purpose: it did not gradually lay hold upon him: it was not something that grew imperceptibly, and at last was found to be a ruling passion. It was a complete thought from the first. Sometimes men surprise themselves by the greatness of their achievements: warriors conquer more provinces than they originally intended to attack; inquirers are led from little to much, in carrying out their great schemes; discoverers, travellers, and projectors of all kinds learn the possible from the actual, and by the help of the known grope their way to the unknown: but here is a man who came with a complete plan, who never amended his scheme, who owed nothing to human suggestion—a man who at the first said, "I came to save the world," and at the last commanded, "Preach

the Gospel to every creature"; and this in the face of opposition
the most relentless, and of death the most ignominious. What
manner of man is this?

We say that Alexander conquered the world, and then cried
because there was not another world to conquer. But Alexander's
notion of the world would now excite the smile of a schoolboy.
Alexander was as much surprised by his exaggerated successes
as were the soldiers whom he led; and lastly, his rapacity can
be accounted for on principles neither very profound nor very
creditable.

The unknown quantity in Christ was spiritual, and therefore
not of the earth, earthy: "My kingdom is not of this world."
"Ye are from beneath, I am from above; ye are of this world,
I am not of this world." "Except a man be born again, he
cannot see the kingdom of God." "They that worship God must
worship him in spirit and in truth." We feel that these words
are not earthly: they are ghostly; they are spiritual; they are
full of mystery, mystery which would affright us, but that the
speaker came to save the world. He reveals himself as a contradiction: he is here, yet he is not here; he is on the earth, yet he
is in heaven; he was alone, yet not alone; Mary was his mother,
yet before Abraham was, he was; he needed no sword, for more
than twelve legions of angels were within call; he revealed the
Father; he told men of heavenly things; he spoke of faith as
man's supreme power; he treated all earthly things as of less
than secondary consideration. How all this involves the presence
of an unknown quantity! Whence was this spiritual Christ?
How came he to have at his girdle keys which could open
invisible kingdoms? Whence his power to give men wider and
clearer vision in the empire of truth? How is it that Christ
always saw farther than the men who were around him? Why
should he have been more at home in the spiritual than in the
material? These questions are not to be treated carelessly. In
the consideration of so extraordinary a life as Jesus Christ's, they
are vital, and every honest student will linger upon their anxious
and reverent consideration. Jesus Christ's earthly course as a
public worker was intensely excited; yet every day was made

serene by "the power of an endless life." There is foam on the
stormy billow, but the earth itself flies in silent and tranquil
speed through its appointed course, though seas be tempest
driven. The volcano shakes with terrible agitation, but its
uproar never flutters the peace of the great globe. So in Christ,
there was a life within life—a mystery, a quantity unknown—
so that when the storm was angriest, through all the thunder
of men's vengeance, he breathed the peculiar benediction of
peace : "My peace I give unto you." What manner of man is
this ? The wonderful conjunction of unequalled trouble and
unspeakable peace, seen in the life of Jesus Christ, cannot be
figured except by the greatest works of the hand of God : as the
fierce wind desolates the forest, maddens the sea, and throws
down the fabrics of men, yet never arrests for a moment the
velocity of the earth, so the tempests of human opposition,
battering with incessant fury upon the life of Christ, never
touched the eternal calm of his infinite peace.

The unknown quantity in Christ was wholly self-sacrificial,
therefore different from ordinary human policy and purpose.
" I lay down my life for the sheep." " No man taketh it from me,
but I lay it down of myself." " From that time forth began Jesus
to show unto his disciples how that he must go unto Jerusalem,
and suffer many things of the elders and chief priests and scribes,
and be killed, and be raised again the third day." He constantly
moved towards the Cross. " The Son of man came not to be
ministered unto, but to minister, and to give his life a ransom for
many." "I am among you as he that serveth." "I came down
from heaven, not to do mine own will, but the will of him that
sent me." Thus we are taken out of ordinary motives, purposes,
and methods. This is altogether a new music. We cannot
follow this Man, except we take up a Cross. Herein we see the
deep truth of his word—"If any man will come after me, let him
deny himself, and take up his cross, and follow me." Never man
spoke thus before. Hear him : If you would gain your life, lose
it ! If you would lose your life, gain it ! If you would live, you
must die first ! If you would be crowned, you must be crucified !
What manner of man is this ? The severest of his critics has
never established a charge of selfishness against Jesus Christ. His

self-oblivion and self-expenditure have been left without explanation by the most determined of his opponents.   Never did he
accept such promotion as men could offer.   Never did he consult
his own ease at the expense of human suffering.   Never did he
turn aside that he might escape the Cross.   By speaking falsehood
he could have avoided humiliation ; hypocrisy would have saved
him many a frown; hesitation would have helped him out of
many a difficulty.   Our own selfishness wonders again and again
that he did not speak the word of flattery, or tamper with the
word of righteousness ; yet, though a sentence might have saved
him, he gave his back to the smiters, and his cheek to them that
plucked off the hair.   In a sense deeper than his revilers intended
to express, " He saved others,—himself he could not save " ; he
so loved as to be lost in self-forgetfulness !

> "O for this love, let rocks and hills
>   Their lasting silence break,
> And all harmonious human tongues
>   Their Saviour's praises speak."

The unknown quantity in Christ set aside canons, traditions,
and standards established and valued by men, and therefore
claimed a wisdom superior to the ripest wisdom of all human
teachers.   " It hath been said by them of old time ; but I say
unto you."   " Ye have heard that it hath been said ; but I say
unto you."   This was his tone throughout.   Nor was it a tone of
boastfulness.   Christ's word was not a word of mere antagonism
He never abrogated a truth except by fulfilment, by carrying it
to its widest and sublimest applications.   " All bare him witness,
and wondered at the gracious words which proceeded out of his
mouth.   And they said, Is not this Joseph's son ? "   Jesus taught
truth, rather than mere fact; principles, not mere rules; he
revealed the universal and the eternal, not merely the local and
temporary.

Now look at these suggestions in their unity.   The unknown
element is of the same quality, so to speak, throughout.   It
is beneficent, spiritual, self-sacrificial, independent.   Not only
socially and relatively beneficent, but beneficent up to the point
of salvation.   Not spiritual, in the limited sense of intellectual,
supersensuous, immaterial ; it searched the heart, it revealed the

invisible, it opened heaven. Not self-sacrificial in the spurious sense of well-calculated periods of self-assertion and self-withdrawment, but self-sacrificial even unto death—yea, the death of the cross. Not independent in the sense of defiant, self-sufficient, contemptuous, but in the sense of original, complete, omniscient.

Given such a character, to account for it ! Say it was a dream : the difficulty is increased rather than diminished by the suggestion. Where is the dreamer ? Who was he ? Where is the man who had heart enough to dream such beneficence, soul enough to dream such spirituality, will enough to dream such self-sacrifice, wisdom enough to dream such originality ? Find the dreamer ; name him ; account for his supremacy. Remember, you must find not only one dreamer, but many. You must find the dreamers of the most ancient prophecies, as well as of doctrines and theories historically Christian. You must, too, find dreamers whose dreams agree with each other, and dreamers who will unitedly, stubbornly, and lyingly avouch as facts what they know to be mere visions and eccentricities of fancy. Here we touch the moral nerve of the whole system. According to the dream theory, men told lies in order to reveal truth ; they divested themselves of all honesty in order to save the world ; they said, " Thus saith the Lord," when they knew that they were but relating a day-dream, or depicting a fancy ! The moral tone of revelation is the decisive answer to the mythical theory ; according to that theory, we are driven to the conclusion that the men who fabricated Christ and Christianity, not only dreamed the sublimest of poems, but the most splendid of falsehoods, and mistook those falsehoods as the very foundations of righteous and noble life. Not only so : they dreamed the lies, and then said to the world, If you believe this, you will suffer for it, you will have trials of cruel mockings and scourgings ; yea, moreover, of bonds and imprisonment ; you will be stoned, sawn asunder, slain with the sword : we tell you our dream as a fact, our falsehood as a truth,—believe, and your life shall be a daily crucifixion. Nay, more ! The dreamers themselves suffered for their dream ! They were fed with bread of affliction, and with water of affliction. They wandered about in sheep-skins and goat-skins, being destitute, afflicted, tormented ; they wandered in deserts, and in mountains, and in dens and caves of the earth. In every city bonds and afflictions awaited them. They were ready, not to be bound only, but also to die for the name of the Lord Jesus. And when host upon host of fiercest enemies pressed upon them, they exclaimed, " Who shall separate us from the love of Christ ? Shall tribulation, or distress, or persecution, or famine, or nakedness, or peril, or sword ? Nay, in all these things we are more than conquerors, through him that loved us." Such were not the men to suffer and die for a lying dream !

Say Jesus Christ was a good man, the best man, the man who realised most perfectly all that is meant by divine inspiration, yet after all was but a man. You aggravate the difficulty unspeakably. Not only have you to account for the most express claim of equality with God, and to explain language infinitely in excess of any inspiration which human capacity could realise or merely human excellence could justify—you have a harder task still to accomplish—you have a stupendous moral difficulty to overcome. If Jesus Christ was but a man, if there was nothing in him that may not in equal degree be in us, if he was only the perfect type of what any man may become—then God gave him an advantage which he has withheld from others, and the want of which occasions us sorrow intolerable, and apprehension the most agonising that can afflict the human mind. He made one perfect man, and left countless millions imperfect ; he gave one man inspiration enough to save him from sin, and by withholding that inspiration from others he necessitated their ruin ; he showed by one example what he could have made of all men, and yet has entailed upon all men the severest moral degradation and suffering, because something was lacking in the extent of their inspiration !

We find the only satisfactory explanation of the whole mystery of Christ in the facts of revelation. Those facts are many, unique, consistent, sublime. Jesus Christ was the only begotten of the Father : it pleased the Father that in him should all fulness dwell : by him were all things created that are in heaven, and that are in earth, visible and invisible, whether they be thrones, or dominions, or principalities, or powers : Jesus Christ, the same yesterday, to-day, and for ever: Alpha and Omega, the beginning and the ending, Son of God, God the Son, One with the Father, and heir of all things! Take this view of the case, and the solemn mystery becomes filled with light. Standing on this high ground, when men exclaim, " What manner of man is this ?" we can answer, Emmanuel! Wonderful! Counsellor! The mighty God! The everlasting Father! The Prince of Peace! There we answer the wonder of the finite with the wisdom of the infinite.

PRAYER.

ALMIGHTY GOD, thy riches are unsearchable. The hosts of heaven are thine, so are the gold and the silver and the cattle upon a thousand hills. The earth is the Lord's, and the fulness thereof. As for thy love it is boundless, and we will say with thy Church in all ages, Thy mercy endureth for ever. We would therefore come boldly unto the throne of grace that we may obtain mercy, and that we may find grace to help in time of need. Every time is a time of need. We humbly beseech thee therefore to dwell with us. Abide in our heart as in a redeemed and chosen house. Save us in the hour of temptation! Deliver us from all evil influences! Establish our hearts in the love of Christ, that we may never depart from the living God. Grant unto us now to know somewhat of the fulness of thy love, the infinitude of thy nature, the depths of thy heart, the tenderness of thy compassion! May we be filled with amazement, overwhelmed by visions of thy glory, encouraged and strengthened by assurances of thy goodness. We abide near the Cross ; we lay our hands upon the one Sacrifice for sin,—Jesus Christ, Son of man and Son of God. As we look upon him crucified, we say with all our heart, God be merciful unto us sinners! Shed upon us the light above the brightness of the sun. Assure us of thy nearness by the interpretation of thy blessed word to our anxious hearts and inquiring minds. May we see the Lord's beauty, and feel that the Lord's hand is upon us. Unto the Father and the Son and the Holy Ghost, whom we adore as one God, be the kingdom, and the power, and the glory, world without end. Amen.

Chapter V.

THE HUMAN AND THE DIVINE.

[An Analysis.]

1. And they came over unto the other side of the sea, in the country of the Gadarenes.

2. And when he was come out of the ship, immediately there met him out of the tombs a man with an unclean spirit,

3. Who had his dwelling among the tombs; and no man could bind him, no, not with chains;

4. Because that he had been often bound with fetters and chains, and the chains had been plucked asunder by him, and the fetters broken in pieces; neither could any man tame him.

5. And always, night and day, he was in the mountains and in the tombs, crying, and cutting himself with stones.

6. But when he saw Jesus afar off, he ran and worshipped him,

7. And cried, with a loud voice, and said, What have I to do with thee, Jesus, thou Son of the most high God? I adjure thee by God that thou torment me not.

8. For he said unto him, Come out of the man, thou unclean spirit.

9. And he asked him, What is thy name? And he answered, saying, My name is Legion, for we are many.

10. And he besought him much that he would not send them away out of the country.

11. Now there was there nigh unto the mountains a great herd of swine feeding.

12. And all the devils besought him, saying, Send us into the swine, that we may enter into them.

13. And forthwith Jesus gave them leave. And the unclean spirits went out, and entered into the swine: and the herd ran violently down a steep place into the sea (they were about two thousand); and were choked in the sea.

14. And they that fed the swine fled, and told it in the city, and in the country. And they went out to see what it was that was done.

15. And they come to Jesus, and see him that was possessed with the devil, and had the legion, sitting, and clothed, and in his right mind: and they were afraid.

16. And they that saw it told them how it befel to him that was possessed with the devil, and also concerning the swine.

17. And they began to pray him to depart out of their coasts.

THIS story may be viewed in four aspects :—I. The human; II. The Divine; III. The Diabolic; IV. The Social.

I. The Human. The human aspect is seen both in shadow

and in light :—(1) As seen in shadow : (*a*) man impure,—unclean spirit ; (*b*) man dis-socialised,—his dwelling was among the tombs ; (*c*) man unrestrained,—no man could tame him, no, not with chains ; (*d*) man self-tormented,—crying and cutting himself with stones. (2) As seen in light : (*a*) man tranquillised,— sitting ; (*b*) man civilised,—clothed ; (*c*) man intellectualised, —in his right mind.

II. The Divine. (1) Christ identified by his holiness ; (2) Christ feared for his power ; (3) Christ recognised in the realm of spirits.

III. The Diabolic. (1) As showing great resources,—" we are many " ; (2) as displaying subordination,—they besought Christ, etc. ; (3) as revealing destructiveness,—whatever they touch, man or beast, they destroy.

IV. The Social. (1) Society trembling under manifestations of spiritual power ; spiritual power is always more or less mysterious,—" they were afraid." (2) Society caring more for beasts than for men,—they prayed him to depart out of their coasts.

The prayer of the unclean spirits may be regarded as showing the intolerableness of life in hell. They wished to be sent anywhere but to the pit.

Or thus :—

The story may be used as showing at once the greatness and the weakness of man. (1) His greatness,—seen in the fact that many devils can enter into him. Show how men may be great in evil as well as in good,—tyrants, warriors, conspirators, hypocrites, etc. (2) His weakness,—seen in his yielding where he ought to have resisted ; in his helplessness when he had once admitted the power of evil into his heart,—seen also in his fear of the only power that could redeem him from its bondage. The last point should be urged as one of great importance,—showing how the tendency of sin is actually to destroy confidence, not only in God as Creator and Preserver, but actually as Redeemer. (*a*) It raises sceptical questions ; (*b*) it urges the doctrine of self-elevation.

Or thus :—

The story may be treated as showing some phases of Christ's ministry. (1) Christ caring for one man ; (2) Christ's rule over evil spirits; (3) Christ reconstructing manhood; (4) Christ showing himself the source of all blessings: (*a*) self-control,— "sitting"; (*b*) civilisation,—"clothed"; (*c*) mental restoration, —"in his right mind."

Christ's conduct in this case reveals the fearlessness of his spirit. (1) Holiness is fearless; (2) Philanthropy is fearless; (3) Trust in God is fearless. Show how fearlessness is required of all who follow Christ,—how it is necessary to beneficent activity,—and how it can only be sustained by ever-deepening communion with God. The whole subject may be treated as showing—(1) The Fearlessness; (2) the Aggressiveness; (3) the Beneficence of Christianity.

18. And when he was come into the ship, he that had been possessed with the devil prayed him that he might be with him.

19. Howbeit Jesus suffered him not, but saith unto him, Go home to thy friends, and tell them how great things the Lord hath done for thee, and hath had compassion on thee.

20. And he departed, and began to publish in Decapolis how great things Jesus had done for him: and all men did marvel.

21. And when Jesus was passed over again by ship unto the other side, much people gathered unto him: and he was nigh unto the sea.

(1) The recollection of our Christless state should beget a spirit of distrust in ourselves. The healed man was naturally anxious to remain at the side of his healer. (2) Show the possibility of being under the protection of Christ even though far from his physical presence. The healed man was as surely under the care of Christ when miles away as when within reach of his hand. Christ always pointed towards a spiritual reign, and both incidentally and directly discouraged trust in merely fleshly presence and power.

Christ's answer may be taken as showing how the gospel is to be propagated : (1) It is to be declared at home; (2) it is to be founded on personal experience; (3) it is to acknowledge the power and goodness of God alone.

Every Christian should himself be the chief argument in favour of Christianity. The Christian is not only to have an argument —he is himself to be an argument. The man whose sight was restored said to those who inquired concerning the process of restoration—"One thing I know, that whereas I was blind now I see." Had he allowed himself to be lured into a discussion about Moses or the supposed character of Christ, he might have been overcome by superiority of address on the part of his critics; but so long as he confined himself to his own case his position was invincible. The recovered man whose case is given in this chapter could always answer the quibbles of inquirers by a reference to his own experience. What has Christ done for us? What is our present state as compared with our former condition? What is our moral tone? What is our attitude in relation to the future? If we can answer these questions satisfactorily, we have a sufficient reply to all controversial difficulties and to all speculative scepticism.

22. And, behold, there cometh one of the rulers of the synagogue, Jairus by name; and when he saw him, he fell at his feet,

23. And besought him greatly, saying, My little daughter lieth at the point of death : I pray thee, come and lay thy hands on her, that she may be healed ; and she shall live.

24. And Jesus went with him; and much people followed him, and thronged him.

The case of the ruler may be treated as showing the instructiveness of domestic affliction. (1) It shows the helplessness even of the greatest men,—the applicant was a ruler, yet his rulership was of no avail in this case. All human influence is limited. (2) It shows the helplessness even of the kindest men, —the applicant was a father, yet all his yearning affection was unable to suggest a remedy for his afflicted child. (3) It shows the need of Christ in every life : looking over the whole chapter, we find a demoniac, a ruler, a child, and a woman who required the services of Jesus Christ.

25. And a certain woman, which had an issue of blood twelve years,

26. And had suffered many things of many physicians, and had spent all that she had, and was nothing better, but rather grew worse,

27. When she had heard of Jesus, came in the press behind, and touched his garment.

28. For she said, If I may touch but his clothes, I shall be whole.

29. And straightway the fountain of her blood was dried up ; and she felt in her body that she was healed of that plague.

30. And Jesus, immediately knowing in himself that virtue had gone out of him, turned him about in the press, and said, Who touched my clothes ?

31. And his disciples said unto him, Thou seest the multitude thronging thee, and sayest thou, Who touched me ?

32. And he looked round about to see her that had done this thing.

33. But the woman fearing and trembling, knowing what was done in her, came and fell down before him, and told him all the truth.

34. And he said unto her, Daughter, thy faith hath made thee whole; go in peace and be whole of thy plague.

(1) Human extremity,—the woman had suffered many years, and had spent all, and had become worse rather than better: she may be taken, therefore, as a picture of human extremity. (2) Human earnestness,—though much people thronged the Saviour, and she was weak, yet she found her way to the Healer. This may be taken as illustrative of the power of earnestness in seeking Christ. All of us have to go to Christ through a crowd, —a crowd of objectors, of indifferent persons, of apathetic professors, of quibbling critics, etc. : if we be in earnest, we shall find our way to Christ. (3) Divine sensitiveness. Jesus Christ knew the difference between mere pressure and the touch of loving faith. This shows that mere nearness to Christ is not enough. A man may be in the church, and yet far from the Saviour; a man may be looking at the Cross without seeing the Sacrifice. Expose all the pretences which are founded upon ancestry, nationality, the observance of religious rites, etc. (4) Public Confession. The poor woman drew near, and told him all the truth, and she told it in the hearing of the crowd. Thankfulness should always be courageous and explicit. Where there is a keen appreciation of the work of Christ in the soul, all timidity and hesitation will be overborne by the intensity of thankfulness and joy. This is the true explanation of Christian profession and testimony.

35. While yet he spake, there came from the ruler of the synagogue's house certain which said, Thy daughter is dead : why troublest thou the Master any further?

36. As soon as Jesus heard the word that was spoken, he saith unto the ruler of the synagogue, Be not afraid, only believe.

37. And he suffered no man to follow him, save Peter, and James, and John the brother of James.

38. And he cometh to the house of the ruler of the synagogue, and seeth the tumult, and them that wept and wailed greatly.

39. And when he was come in, he saith unto them, Why make ye this ado, and weep ? the damsel is not dead, but sleepeth.

40. And they laughed him to scorn. But when he had put them all out, he taketh the father and the mother of the damsel, and them that were with him, and entereth in where the damsel was lying.

41. And he took the damsel by the hand, and said unto her, Talitha cumi: which is, being interpreted, Damsel, I say unto thee, Arise.

42. And straightway the damsel arose, and walked; for she was of the age of twelve years. And they were astonished with a great astonishment.

43. And he charged them straitly that no man should know it; and commanded that something should be given her to eat.

This part of the incident shows how two views may be taken of the same case. (1) There is the human view,—the child is dead, trouble not the Master. Men see the outside; they deal with facts rather than with principles; they see the circumference, not the centre. (2) There is Christ's view,—only believe; man is called beyond facts, he is called into the sanctuary of God's secret. We often put the period where God himself puts only a comma : we say " dead " when God himself says " sleepeth." Jesus Christ was laughed to scorn when he put a new interpretation upon old facts. All who follow him must expect to hear Christian sentiments and predictions misunderstood and perhaps contemned.

The incident may be treated as showing three things :— (1) Christ not sent for until the last moment; (2) Christ misunderstood when sent for; (3) Christ never sent for in vain.

GENERAL NOTE ON THE WHOLE CHAPTER.

Look at the various instances of healing in this chapter :— Demoniac; woman; child; ruler. We train men to attempt the cure of special diseases, but Jesus Christ treated all afflictions alike of the mind and body, and never did his energy prove insufficient for the demands which were made upon it. What was the secret of the universality of his healing? It was that he infused life into all who came to him in their necessity. All other healing is but local and temporary. The gift of life alone can throw off all diseases, and recover the failing tone of the mind. Jesus Christ never displays surprise, or betrays hesitation, when the most extraordinary cases are brought under his attention. The calmness of his spirit and the perfect mastery of his working incidentally show the fulness of his Godhead. The cure of the demoniac alone would have made the reputation of any other man. In Christ's case it is written down as an ordinary event, so far as the exercise of his own power is concerned. The speciality is on the side of the sufferer, not on the side of the healer. Christ's interruption on his way to the ruler's house, and his cure of the poor woman, should show that his life is an unceasing ministration of good. He was going towards the house of suffering, yet on his way he healed a woman who had been given up by many physicians! The beneficent act was a kind of parenthesis. There is more history condensed into the very parentheses of Christ's life than can be found in all the volumes of other lives. The parenthetic characteristic of this cure may be dwelt on as showing that even in his movement towards a given point God may be interrupted by the appeal of human necessity.

Chapter v. 28.

"If I may but touch his clothes, I shall be whole."

THE SPIRITUAL VALUE OF THE NEAR AND VISIBLE.

[An Outline.]

APART from the general treatment which the incident invites, a practical turn may be given to the thought involved in this particular way of stating the case. The afflicted woman did not invoke the whole power of the Godhead; she said that a mere touch was enough. To her simple trust, God was close at hand. She believed that the divine element penetrated and vitalised the outward and visible covering, so much so that to touch the clothes was to touch God himself. The idea is that we need far less proof of God's existence and beneficence than we often demand. We may go too far. We may attempt too much. We seek to convince or silence the gainsayer by elaborate arguments respecting infinitude, immateriality, almightiness, and the like. Thus theology becomes a great intellectual effort. It strains men's thinking; it transcends and overwhelms all that is ordinary; it establishes itself in the secrecy of the clouds. There is something better than all this. God is accessible from a much lower point. He is nigh thee, O man; the shadow of his presence lies around thy whole life! Think not to lay a line upon the courses of his infinitude, or to gather into one thunderous note all the voices of his eternity. Do not strain thy poor strength or endanger thy feeble brain by long-continued and ambitious effort to find out God. Be simple in thy methods, be trustful in thy spirit. Pluck a spike of grass, a wild flower, a tender leaf of the spring—touch the hem of his garment, and thou shalt find health. There are great globes of fire; there are also little globes of water : begin with the latter,—thou wilt find God even in these frail crystal habitations.

Apply this thought (1) to spiritual existences. If I touch but
a grain of sand, I find the Mighty One. Who made it? Who
can destroy it? Who can send it away to some other world?
If I touch only a bud, I touch the King's garment. Who can
make one like it? Who can improve its beauty? Whose hand
is cunning enough to add one charm to its shape or one tint to
its colour? We need not dazzle the atheist's eyes with the light
of other worlds; we can show him God's signature in every
limb of his own body: in every hair of his own head. Apply
this thought (2) to the scheme of spiritual providence. Limit
the view to one life,—touch but the hem of the garment. Review
your own life from infancy, through youth, along the tortuous
paths of manifold experience, up to the vigour of full manhood.
What of extrication from difficulties? What of unexpected
turns and hair-breadth escapes? What of concessions yielded
without argument, of helps rendered by unlikely hands? The
theory of chance is a theory of difficulty, not to say a theory of
absurdity. Apply this thought (3) to the processes of spiritual
education. Some of us can never get beyond the hem of the
garment. Meanwhile, it is enough. Others are admitted to
high intercourse: they know the secret of the Lord: finding
their way far beyond the limitation of the mere letter, they see
the spiritual purpose of divine government, and enjoy the inexpressible communion of the Holy Ghost. It is possible that
the former may have as true and as efficient a faith as the latter.
May they not have even a stronger faith? Is it a great thing to
see God in heavens rich with systems of suns? Shall they be
praised for their faith who hear God in the thunder, or who say
of the lightning, Lo! this is the eye of the Lord? It is a
grander faith, surely, which can see God in a speck of dust, and
touch him in the hem of a garment. This was Christ's measurement of faith. It was ever the simplicity rather than the so-
called sublimity of faith which Christ praised. He ever sought
to train man's faith downwards as well as upwards. " Ye believe
in God ; believe also in me,"—in me, the human, visible, rejected
Christ,—believe in the lower as well as the higher manifestations
of God. " He that hath seen me hath seen the Father." Apply
this thought (4) to the uses of spiritual ordinances. The hymn,
the prayer, the lesson, the mere form itself, may do men good.

The commonest hearer who touches but the hem of the garment may be healed and comforted, as well as the student who can read deep things, and understand high counsels and purposes.

Application : The hand must touch Christ,—not an apostle, or minister, or an angel,—but God the Son, in whom alone there is redeeming life. He " only hath immortality." You may have " touched " many without benefit ; touch him, and you will live !

NOTES.

(*From the " Speaker's Commentary."*)

" I shall be whole " (ver. 28). " Literally, I shall be saved, *i.e.*, made whole." It was natural that expositors of Holy Scripture should see in this woman a type of the Jewish Church, bleeding to death, and tortured by superstitious, inefficacious, tedious, and costly treatment.

" And straightway," etc. (ver. 29). The immediate effect was the drying up of the source of her malady. This she felt inwardly, a sensation assuring her that the cure was complete. St. Mark gives details, such as St. Peter must have dwelt upon frequently, both for their significance and their resemblance to miraculous works wrought afterwards by himself in the name of Jesus. Cf. Acts iii. 6, 7 ; v. 15 ; ix. 34, 38.

" And Jesus . . . gone out of him " (ver. 30). Or, " *And immediately Jesus having perceived in himself* (or recognised inwardly) *that the virtue* (literally, the power) *had gone forth from him.*" This statement, taken from our Lord's own word (Luke viii. 46), throws some light on the nature of the miraculous effluence from the Person of our Saviour. It was physical in its operation—the woman felt the result in her body—but spiritual in its source and condition. Our Lord recognised the fact that the indwelling virtue had been drawn forth by an act of faith.

" And his disciples " (ver. 31). St. Luke notices that St. Peter was, as usual, the spokesman. The question was natural, but interesting as proving that no mere bodily sensation called the attention of Jesus to what was done.

" But the woman " (ver. 33). Each word indicates the inward struggle of the woman. She knew that what had been done in her was a result of her own act, without permission from Jesus, and she could scarcely hope that the faith which suggested it would be accepted as genuine ; hence the terror and trembling, the sudden prostration, and the full confession.

" And be whole " (ver. 34). A different word from that used in v. 28, giving an assurance of restoration to perfect health, such as was still needed by the woman. This is recorded expressly by St. Mark alone, but it is implied by other words of our Lord in St. Matthew and St. Luke,

Chapter vi.

HEROD AND HERODIAS.

[An Analysis.]

1. And he went out from thence, and came into his own country; and his disciples follow him.

2. And when the Sabbath day was come, he began to teach in the synagogue : and many hearing him were astonished, saying, From whence hath this man these things? and what wisdom is this which is given unto him, that even such mighty works are wrought by his hands?

3. Is not this the carpenter, the son of Mary, the brother of James, and Joses, and of Juda, and Simon? and are not his sisters here with us? And they were offended at him.

(1) CHRISTIAN doctrine applicable to all classes of men; (2) Christian doctrine calculated to excite the pro foundest surprise; (3) Christian doctrine always conveying the impression of unique power; (4) Christian doctrine showing the insignificance of the personality of its teachers. Even Christ himself, according to the flesh, seemed poor and inadequate when viewed in the light of the wondrous revelations which he made to the world.

The questions put by those who heard Jesus Christ show—(1) That even the greatest speakers cannot escape personal criticism. It is often suggested that earnest men succeed in drawing the attention of their hearers to the doctrine rather than to the speaker, but the life of Christ is a proof to the contrary; (2) that prejudiced hearers will sacrifice the truth because of the objectionableness of the instrument through which it is conveyed; (3) that such hearers actually dishonour God in their attempt to exalt him, because they deny his power to turn the humblest, poorest agency to the highest uses.

This incident may be treated as showing some of the difficulties of the Christian ministry: (1) The difficulty of locality,—Jesus was now in "his own country;" (2) the difficulty of personality,—ancestry, appearance, poverty, earnestness considered as

indicative of presumption ; all enter into this difficulty of personality.   There is a still deeper truth underlying this difficulty :—
Individuality of spirit, claim, manner, always provokes criticism.
The glory of the highest revelation of Christianity is that personality is superseded by spirituality.   The speaker is to be forgotten
in the speech.   When both personality and doctrine are to be
considered, the danger is that the former may be made to assume
undue prominence.   Instead of inquiring, What is said ? the
inquiry will be, Who said it ?   Personality is a mere question
of detail in comparison with the truths which nourish and save
the soul.

4. But Jesus said unto them, A prophet is not without honour, but in his
own country, and among his own kin, and in his own house.

(1) Jesus Christ taking his stand upon a great principle;
(2) Jesus Christ claiming his prophetic character in the face of
opposition.

This answer may be regarded as showing the true method
of encountering difficulties and dealing with opponents.   Jesus
Christ might have defended his relatives against the sneers of the
critics.   He might also have availed himself of the *tu quoque*
argument, and shown how little reason his censors had to make
remarks about his social connections.   Were the servants inspired with the spirit of the Master, they would show corresponding independence and courage.   It is remarkable that the
people should have so boldly condemned any part of Christ's
ministry when they daily saw how great was his power in
working miracles.   They never, so far as can be discovered
from the narrative, show any fear of his wonderful power.   They
appear to have treated him with as much freedom and insolence
as if he had never shown his almighty influence over the laws
of nature.

5. And he could there do no mighty work, save that he laid his hands
upon a few sick folk, and healed them.
6. And he marvelled because of their unbelief.   And he went round about
the villages, teaching.

This statement (1) refutes the notion that where there is a true
ministry there will be great success ; (2) shows the tremendous
difficulties which the human will can oppose to the highest purposes of God ; (3) justifies the true worker in leaving the sphere

in which he has been unsuccessful, to carry on his work under more favourable circumstances. The sphere has much to do with the development of the man. It is unreasonable to teach that a minister can be equally useful in all places. This remark must not be abused by the supposition that, because a man cannot get on where he is, he would infallibly get on somewhere else. Only in so far as Christ has called him to do his work will it be true of him that he will find a sphere in which he can work successfully.

7. And he called unto him the twelve, and began to send them forth by two and two; and gave them power over unclean spirits;

8. And commanded them that they should take nothing for their journey, save a staff only; no scrip, no bread, no money in their purse:

9. But be shod with sandals; and not put on two coats.

10. And he said unto them, In what place soever ye enter into an house, there abide till ye depart from that place.

(1) Christ the originator of missionary effort; (2) Christ the source of missionary power; (3) Christ the provider of missionary wants. There is no detail too minute to escape the notice of the Master. He does not teach carelessness,—he encourages dependence. It would be an abuse of the spirit of the text to insist that missionaries in our own day should go forth exactly according to these literal instructions. When the church is rich, the missionary should not be made an example of poverty. When the church is poor, the missionary who has Christ's spirit in him will not be deterred by a prospect of hard endurance. The one vital question relates not to the outward circumstances, but to the spirit in which missionary work is undertaken.

11. And whosoever shall not receive you, nor hear you, when ye depart thence, shake off the dust under your feet for a testimony against them. Verily I say unto you, It shall be more tolerable for Sodom and Gomorrha in the day of judgment, than for that city.

(1) The servant should always carry in his heart the words of his Master. Those words are wanted in times of darkness and trial. The riches of Christ are spiritual. They are hidden in the heart. Ideas, promises, divine assurances, are better than weapons of war. (2) The servant can only be identified with the Master by spiritual sympathy. The servant must not only do the Master's work, he must do it in the Master's spirit, and for the Master's

sake. (3) The tremendous responsibility of those who have gospel proposals made to them. If they reject them, " it shall be more tolerable for Sodom," etc. This is founded upon reason. It must be more criminal to shut out midday than to exclude dawn—to reject the Son, than to neglect a prophet. (4) The solemn and awe-inspiring fact that all ages are to culminate in a day of judgment ! Sodom, Capernaum, Egypt, England, shall confront each other at a common bar ! " From them to whom much has been given," etc. (5) The infinite comfort to the good man of knowing from Christ's own lips that there is to be a day of judgment. He remits his cause to that day. He is relieved as to the vindication of character and service, and feels at liberty to do his holy work.

12. And they went out, and preached that men should repent.
13. And they cast out many devils, and anointed with oil many that were sick, and healed them.

Their work was divided into three parts : it was moral, intellectual, and physical.

(1) It was moral. They preached that men should repent. This was fundamental. The apostles addressed themselves to the heart. No ministry can be permanently useful and successful which proceeds upon a superficial estimate of human depravity. The ministry goes down in power when it modifies its demands for human repentance.

(2) It was intellectual. They cast out devils. They restored the use of reasoning faculties. Of course, this might include a great moral work, but not necessarily. To expel a devil is one thing, to bring men to repentance is another. Restored reason does not involve the sanctification of the heart. In our ministry we may quicken mental power, we may enrich our hearers with many profound or brilliant ideas, we may elevate their thinking, and secure their highest admiration, yet may not lead them to repentance before God.

(3) It was physical. " They anointed with oil many that were sick, and healed them." They never treated death as a blessing. They valued every form of life. Christ's whole gospel is constructive. Christianity is still the greatest of healing powers. Keep its laws, and you will walk in life, or if disease come upon

you there will come also such views of God, of eternity, and truth, as will deliver from the dominion of death. Atheistic suffering is one thing, Christian suffering is another. If it is hard to suffer in the friendless desert, where no kind voice can speak one word of hope, what of suffering in the wilderness of atheism, and dying under unbroken gloom ?

Beautiful is the picture of men sent forth on such an errand. Observe, this is what Jesus Christ is daily doing,—seeking out men who warn, and teach, and heal. More : every man who feels that he is sent of Christ on this work will go to his Master for help, and rely upon his Master for success. Who sent me ? What is his name ? " I AM THAT I AM." It is enough ! It is Omnipotence !

14. And king Herod heard of him ; (for his name was spread abroad :) and he said, That John the Baptist was risen from the dead, and therefore mighty works do shew forth themselves in him.

King Herod is supposed to have been a Sadducee, and therefore to have discredited the doctrine of resurrection. Under the torment of conscience, however, he asserted the very doctrine which, as a speculator, he denied ! Learn that creeds should rest upon a moral, rather than upon an exclusively intellectual basis. In the long run conscience will put down all other voices.

15. Others said, That it is Elias. And others said, That it is a prophet, or as one of the prophets.

These men represent the speculators of society. Conscience is hardly concerned in their case. They give themselves to the consideration of mere problems or puzzles. They represent, too, the persons who can talk about religious subjects without having any religious feeling. Religion is to them only a topic of the day. It is something to be remarked upon, and then dropped in favour of something else. There are men around ourselves who suppose that to admire a preacher is to admire Christ, and that to be critical about sermons is to be concerned about truth.

16. But when Herod heard thereof, he said, It is John, whom I beheaded : he is risen from the dead.

Here is the reply of conscience to the suggestion of fancy. Herod was not to be soothed by guess-work. There is a profound truth here,—viz., that high moral excitement is beyond the control of merely intellectual skill. The gospel shows its divinity in the influence which it brings to bear upon the desires and sufferings of the self-accusing heart. Herod may be taken as the type of men who cannot be satisfied with fanciful theology or with flattering applications of partial truths. He wishes to get at realities, and to be faithful to himself, and to the facts which are around him. Earnest hearers make earnest preachers.

17. For Herod himself had sent forth, and laid hold upon John, and bound him in prison for Herodias' sake, his brother Philip's wife: for he had married her.

18. For John had said unto Herod, It is not lawful for thee to have thy brother's wife.

19. Therefore Herodias had a quarrel against him, and would have killed him; but she could not :

20. For Herod feared John, knowing that he was a just man and an holy, and observed him; and when he heard him, he did many things, and heard him gladly.

21. And when a convenient day was come, that Herod on his birthday made a supper to his lords, high captains, and chief estates of Galilee;

22. And when the daughter of the said Herodias came in, and danced and pleased Herod and them that sat with him, the king said unto the damsel, Ask of me whatsoever thou wilt, and I will give it thee.

23. And he sware unto her, Whatsoever thou shalt ask of me, I will give it thee, unto the half of my kingdom.

24. And she went forth, and said unto her mother, What shall I ask ? And she said, The head of John the Baptist.

25. And she came in straightway with haste unto the king, and asked, saying, I will that thou give me by and by in a charger the head of John the Baptist.

26. And the king was exceeding sorry; yet for his oath's sake, and for their sakes which sat with him, he would not reject her.

27. And immediately the king sent an executioner, and commanded his head to be brought: and he went and beheaded him in the prison,

28. And brought his head in a charger, and gave it to the damsel: and the damsel gave it to her mother.

29. And when his disciples heard of it, they came and took up his corpse, and laid it in a tomb.

Man may be slain, but truth cannot be annihilated. John was buried, but the gospel was still making way in the world. It has been thought that Herod Antipas (son of Herod the Great) was a Sadducee, and that this exclamation respecting Jesus testified in a remarkable manner to the power of conscience in relation to theological belief. The Sadducees denied the resurrection of the dead; yet conscience rebelled against the theory, and forced the superstitious tetrarch into this confession. Whether it be true or not that Herod was a Sadducee, it is certainly true that the moral nature does, on great occasions, clear its way through all fanciful theories and speculations, and become authoritative as the voice of God in the soul. Man overlays his spiritual constitution, so to speak, with creeds which flatter his vanity and give false peace to his conscience; but crises supervene which effect a moral resurrection, and give man to feel the discrepancy between the wants of his nature and the promises of false creeds. There is a great quickening and educational force in the exceptional circumstances of life. Crises make history. Man cannot tell what he is until some special event makes his soul quake with fear, or brings upon him the light of a great joy. As with individuals, so with nations; monotony would kill them; all enthusiasm would die out, and corruption would become universal. God has so arranged his government that monotony is broken up by startling events,—the thunderbolt, the pestilence, the mildew, come suddenly upon us,—death teaches life, and the grave calls to heaven. In all great crises, both in individual and national life, there is an instinctive movement of the soul towards God. The temporary creed is subordinated to the normal constitution; and it is most solemn to watch the soul in its resurrectional moods how impatient it is of mere speculation, and how anxious for positive doctrine and assurance. It then lives double life; with frightful energy it clears the field of false friends, and with startling rapidity passes over the chasms of the past, and brings up all the sins which have weakened and deformed itself. When Herod heard of the fame of Jesus a species of resurrection occurred. The night of Bacchanalian revel came back; the holy prophet's blood dripped upon the palace floor again; and the soul said, This Jesus is the man whom I murdered! There is, so to speak, a moral memory as well as a memory that is merely intellectual. Conscience writes in blood. She may brood in long silence, but she cannot forget. All the universe helps her recollection. Every leaf of the forest contains her indictments, and every voice of the air prompts her remembrance. The revel passed, the dancing demon-hearted daughter of Herodias went back to her

blood-thirsty mother, the lights were extinguished, and the palace
relapsed into its accustomed order ; but the prophet's blood cried
with a cry not to be stifled, and angels with swords of fire
watched the tetrarch night and day.   All men are watched.   The
sheltering wing of the unseen angel is close to every one of us.
The eye sees but an infinitesimal portion of what is around,—
we are hemmed in with God !   This great truth we forget; but
exceptional circumstances transpire which for a moment rend
the veil, and give us to see how public is our most secret life,
how the angels hear the throb of the heart, and God counts the
thoughts of the mind.

We see how behind all such feeling as Herod's there are
explanatory circumstances.   Such feeling can be accounted for.
Learn how life comes back upon a man, giving current events
unexpected and even tragical meanings, and forcing him to look
steadily at himself.   This doctrine has, of course, two bearings :
goodness will come up, as well as wickedness.   The paragraph
should be homiletically treated in its unity ; still, several verses
may afterwards be taken separately.   For example, the 17th
verse may be taken as the basis of a discourse upon the forcible
putting away of good influences.   A man can refuse to hear any
more preaching ; he can commit the printed Bible to the flames :
he can avoid every company in which the divine name is
honoured : and many other things he may do through sheer
force or by dogged obstinacy.   But the greatest things lie far
beyond the reach of mere force.

The 19th verse may show the impiety of social resentments :
showing (1) That social defiance does not necessarily arise from
social justice.   (2) That it is fallacious to suppose that in all
quarrels both sides are wrong.   Herodias had a quarrel with
John, yet Herodias alone was wrong, and John was the servant
of God.   (3) That in some quarrels there are the purposes of
murder.   Herodias would have killed John ; in effect, therefore,
she was guilty of murder.   Her heart had slain him, though
he was beyond the reach of her hand.

The 20th verse shows the good points in a bad character.
(1) Herod feared John ; had respect for his moral qualities.
(2) Herod recognised the excellences of John ; acknowledged
him to be " a just man and an holy."   (3) Herod was interested

in the ministry of John,—he heard him gladly. All this may be found where there is no saving grace in the heart, and in the case of Herod was found in connection with a most reproachable life ! Caress a mad dog, because of its silken hair; pet a murderer, because of his taste in dress; but never call him a saint whose morality is but an outward decoration.

30. And the apostles gathered themselves together unto Jesus, and told him all things, both what they had done, and what they had taught.

31. And he said unto them, Come ye yourselves apart into a desert place, and rest awhile : for there were many coming and going, and they had no leisure so much as to eat.

32. And they departed into a desert place by ship privately.

On the words "rest awhile," a sermon upon occasional rest might be founded. Look at the invitation (1) as given by Jesus Christ : he was careful even of men's physical energies; nothing escaped his attention; if we would trust him in physical and temporal matters he would do more for us. "Rest awhile" is a mother's gentle word; it is a sister's suggestion; it is most tenderly sympathetic. Look at the invitation (2) as relating to spiritual work. Great mistakes made about labour. Men may work without using their hands. Hardly any phrase is less correctly used than the expression "the working classes." Thought prostrates the thinker. Sympathy taxes every power. He who works with his hands has an easy life compared with him who works with his brain. He who gives ideas gives life. Look at the invitation (3) as limited as to time; rest awhile. It is not, Give up the work; abandon it in disgust; leave it to others; it is rest awhile. Rest should be a preparation for service. There is morality even in resting. Conscience should have something to do with holidays. It may be right to rest one hour, it may be immoral to rest two. There is morality in sleeping, in recreation, in all things.

33. And the people saw them departing, and many knew him, and ran afoot thither out of all cities, and outwent them, and came together unto him.

34. And Jesus, when he came out, saw much people, and was moved with compassion toward them, because they were as sheep not having a shepherd : and he began to teach them many things.

The great considerations which determine the conduct of Jesus Christ : (1) Earnestness on the part of people : they ran; they

outwent the evangelistic company. When Jesus sees faith he
never fails to reward it. (2) Destitution,—"because they were
as sheep not having a shepherd." Jesus proceeded upon the
principle that men could not live without instruction. A shepherd
is needed in all human societies. Men must be organised, taught,
disciplined. There are men divinely qualified to interpret truth;
they have insight, sympathy, and faculty of delicate and forcible
expression. There are other men who can only receive what
is given to them by God's ministry. They are as sheep, they
need a shepherd. Curious things are occasionally done by the
human flock : the sheep think themselves quite as good as the
shepherd; the sheep often tell the shepherd that they are tired
of him,—and sometimes they break his heart !

35. And when the day was now far spent, his disciples came unto him,
and said, This is a desert place, and now the time is far passed :
36. Send them away, that they may go into the country round about,
and into the villages, and buy themselves bread : for they have nothing
to eat.
37. He answered and said unto them, Give ye them to eat. And they
say unto him, Shall we go and buy two hundred pennyworth of bread, and
give them to eat ?
38. He saith unto them, How many loaves have ye ? go and see. And
when they knew, they say, Five, and two fishes.
39. And he commanded them to make all sit down by companies upon the
green grass.
40. And they sat down in ranks, by hundreds and by fifties.
41. And when he had taken the five loaves and the two fishes, he looked
up to heaven, and blessed, and brake the loaves, and gave them to his
disciples to set before them; and the two fishes divided he among them
all.
42. And they did all eat, and were filled.
43. And they took up twelve baskets full of the fragments, and of the
fishes.
44. And they that did eat of the loaves were about five thousand men.

Jesus Christ calls upon his followers not only to discover social
wants, but also to relieve them. Imagine the disciples coming
to Jesus to suggest something in the way of compassion ! The
disciples were exceedingly quick in finding out that the day was
waning, and that the place was not favourable to hospitality ; but
it never occurred to them that they themselves ought to feed the
multitude. Some men are remarkably sharp in finding out
difficulties, and pointing to external circumstances ; yet they never

dream that instead of merely indicating the want, they ought to supply it. They gave very cheap and easy advice to the Master; with sparkling neatness they said to him, " Send the multitude away." As if they cared more for the multitude than Jesus did ! There are many excellent statisticians in the Church; men who can strike averages, and add up three columns of figures at a time, and show the multitude how to get away. Such men may, by a condescending and inscrutable Providence, be made some use of in the world; but from a human point of view it is not easy to clear up the mystery of their birth. Let it be carefully observed that the disciples were called by Jesus to do what may be described as a secular work. They were told to give the people bread. This work they undertook at Christ's bidding. Here is a great lesson. The Church does even its outside work, its physical and philanthropic service, immediately under Jesus Christ's hand. The holy Master orders every department of the household. We keep the Church door, because we are appointed thereunto by the Master himself. The preacher and the distributor of bread are both Christ's servants. The Church is called upon to deal with all questions which affect the wellbeing of society : with education, with pauperism, with emigration, with sanitary arrangements, with amusements; in short, with every-thing that is needful for the healthy development of human life. Some men have an extraordinary way of dividing and distributing themselves. For example, they go to church as religious men, they go to the town council merely as citizens, they go to the school-board simply as educationalists; when they buy and sell, they have no Christian creed. When they sit at the board of health, they think it irreverent to name the name of Christ; and as for opening the meeting of the town council with prayer, they would think him a madman who proposed anything so monstrous. Yet these very men are most pious on Sunday, and severely critical in estimating the theological soundness of their respective pastors. When we are filled with Christ's spirit, we shall do everything in his name, and for his sake; the state will be swallowed up in the Church, and the secular will be glorified by the spiritual.

It should be pointed out that the poorest resources, when religiously used, are more than sufficient to meet all demands.

Look at the resources,—five loaves and two fishes ! Look at the demand,—five thousand men ! Look at the result,—" they did all eat, and were filled." Use what you have, and it will grow. Use it religiously, and it will be more than sufficient: this doctrine applies to mind, to strength, to time. You have more mind than you supposed. Use it, and you will be surprised how it answers your appeal. Your strength will go much further than it has yet gone. " Put on thy strength." Call thyself up to the highest point of power. Most of us are living within our strength. We are afraid of exhausting ourselves, forgetting that in Christ's service exhaustion is re-creation. As for time, make it ! Sleep less, eat less, talk less, and you will find time enough. Observe particularly—for this is the vital point of the argument —that all our resources are to be used religiously—" looking up to heaven, he blessed and brake." No man loses by the heaven-ward looks of his life. Some men say they have not time to pray. Nor have they time to die,—but they must find it.

The Church ought to be the one inclusive society—the sanctuary, the school, the hospital, the reformatory, the home of the whole world. " They need not go away : give ye them,"—that is the appeal of Christ to the Church.

45. And straightway he constrained his disciples to get into the ship, and to go to the other side before unto Bethsaida, while he sent away the people.

46. And when he had sent them away, he departed into a mountain to pray.

When he had worked, he prayed ! If the Master prayed, can the servant do without prayer ? Whilst yet upon earth, Jesus Christ prayed for others,—his intercession was not reserved for heaven. In this case, however, it is permissible to suppose that he prayed specially and exclusively for himself. We know from other sources that he did actually make his own circumstances the subject of repeated and most agonising prayer. All that he had done up to this time was indicative of the great thing which was yet to be done. It was in Christ's heart to bring to the maturity of the Cross all the germs of love and sacrifice which were present in his daily ministry. Have we not had experience of some such feeling as this : We have fed a multitude ; it is enough ; we may now be satisfied ; our work is finished ;—and so our life has been in danger of falling short of a higher purpose ?

A man may do many great works, and yet never do the greatest : he may feed a multitude, yet never go to Gethsemane : he may suffer many to touch him, and yet at last may shun the Cross ! So after every great work we should hasten to a mountain to pray,—that our ideal may be kept steadily and clearly before us, and that our main work should not be evaded through our incidental service, however beautiful and useful that service may be.

47. And when even was come, the ship was in the midst of the sea, and he alone on the land.

48. And he saw them toiling in rowing; for the wind was contrary unto them: and about the fourth watch of the night he cometh unto them, walking upon the sea, and would have passed by them.

49. But when they saw him walking upon the sea, they supposed it had been a spirit, and cried out:

50. For they all saw him, and were troubled. And immediately he talked with them, and saith unto them, Be of good cheer : it is I ; be not afraid.

51. And he went up unto them into the ship ; and the wind ceased : and they were sore amazed in themselves beyond measure, and wondered.

The subject may be regarded as showing the relation of Jesus Christ to the Church. (1) That relation sometimes appears to be very distant. In this case, for example, the ship was in the midst of the sea, and Jesus Christ was alone upon the land. There have been times when the Church has apparently drifted away from Christ ; there are also times when the alienation seems to have begun on the part of Christ. Is the separation real or is it merely apparent ? (2) That relation often discovers itself most substantially and pathetically under circumstances of trial and sorrow. See how this is proved in the incident : the circumstances were loneliness, danger, helplessness.

From this incident three things are clear : (1) That Christ himself may not be known by the Church ; (2) that some fears which distress the Church are not altogether unfounded ; (3) that a recovered sense of the presence of Christ brings with it complete and enduring calm and joy.

The incident may be regarded as showing some differences between Jesus Christ and his followers : (1) He was master of events ; they were slaves of circumstances. (2) He was ever calm ; they were often filled with fear. (3) He saw the whole of every case ; they saw but part of it. (4) He had power to approach them ; they had no power to move towards him.

52. For they considered not the miracle of the loaves: for their heart was hardened.

The miracles are to be considered in their connection and unity. The miracles are to have a cumulative value; as also are providences. Life is thus to help life; yesterday is to be the hope and defence of the heart in relation to to-morrow. The unity of the divine power is to be realised by the believer; it is one with God whether he quiet a storm or feed a multitude, heal the sick or raise the dead. In proportion as we realise this, we are delivered from the tyranny of mere circumstances or appearances; we live under the dominion of the divine, not under the fear of the external and transient.

The uselessness of miracles as moral agents is painfully demonstrated by this circumstance : " For their heart was hardened.' If any miracle could have softened the heart, a miracle of this particular nature would have done so ; it was the expression of a compassionate feeling on the part of Christ, as well as a display of supreme power; yet it was immediately forgotten, and the selfishness of human nature re-asserted itself. Some aspects of the divine nature can only be truly seen through the heart. We degrade life by making it into a merely intellectual puzzle; it is elevated when regarded as a development of the moral nature.

53. And when they had passed over, they came into the land of Gennesaret, and drew to the shore.

54. And when they were come out of the ship, straightway they knew him,

55. And ran through that whole region round about, and began to carry about in beds those that were sick, where they heard he was.

56. And whithersoever he entered, into villages, or cities, or country, they laid the sick in the streets, and besought him that they might touch if it were but the border of his garment : and as many as touched him were made whole.

A repetition of an old fact. Men work in many cases from the lower to the higher ; in many cases, indeed, they satisfy themselves with the lower only. The people in this instance were deeply concerned about their physical condition, but not one sign of concern about their spiritual relations did they exhibit. Jesus Christ might have made this circumstance a basis for the keenest and justest reproach. In addressing his own disciples, he constantly urged them not to think about the body, or meat, or raiment ; all these things he treated with comparative indifference or contempt ; yet in the instance of those who were not his disciples he was graciously willing to meet them on their own terms, and to do as much for their bodily welfare as if they had no souls. His great object was to lay hold upon the moral attention of the world. In some cases the proposition of Christian doctrine would have been a waste of energy and of time ; in such cases Jesus Christ began with the physical condition and necessities of those who were around him, and so sought to quicken the ear of the heart to receive the doctrines which heal and bless the soul. The lesson to the Church is clear. The Church must begin wherever an opportunity is offered ; it may be in relieving the necessitous, in giving education to the ignorant, in seeking the social improvement of the masses ; Christ's injunction to the Church is, " Begin somewhere." From his own example we are to learn that the physical is but to be introductory to the spiritual ; because to heal the body without seeking to relieve the soul is actually to aggravate the sinfulness of sin by giving the sinner a new lease of power in his evil way. The idea that the shadow of Christ passing over the sick would heal them is suggestive of the fact that there is no waste of power in the ministry of Jesus Christ. A look broke Peter's heart. A touch of the hem of his garment healed a poor woman. His shadow passing over the sick cooled the fevered and gave rest to weariness ;—truly the shadow of the Saviour is better than the lustre of all suns !

The action of the people is most suggestive : they seized the opportunity of Christ's presence to secure the blessings which they most desired. "Now is the accepted time," etc. "Seek ye the Lord while he may be found." The people were not excited about Christ's coming after he had been in the country ; they were excited at the very time of his presence, knowing that if they neglected the critical hour the opportunity might never recur. The argument is this : If men were so anxious promptly to seize a physical advantage, how intense should be their urgency in seeking the higher blessings of moral and intellectual redemption and sanctification ?

Chapter vi. 1-6.

1. And he went out from thence, and came into his own country; and his disciples follow him.

2. And when the Sabbath day was come, he began to teach in the synagogue, and many hearing him were astonished, saying, From whence hath this man these things? and what wisdom is this which is given unto him, that even such mighty works are wrought by his hands?

3. Is not this the carpenter, the son of Mary, the brother of James, and Joses, and of Juda, and Simon? and are not his sisters here with us? And they were offended at him.

4. But Jesus said unto them, A prophet is not without honour, but in his own country, and among his own kin, and in his own house.

5. And he could there do no mighty work, save that he laid his hands upon a few sick folk, and healed them.

6. And he marvelled because of their unbelief. And he went round about the villages, teaching.

CHRIST CONTEMNED.

IT was not a ministry that elicited cordial response. Sometimes the teacher has to work with a conscious reluctance which disables him. There is a sense of weariness in the whole tone of this paragraph; it is discoverable even in the attitude and action of the Son of God. This, said he, is the synagogue, and this is the Sabbath day, and this is the sacred roll, historical, prophetical, poetical; but these people do not want to hear me. I know it by their countenances; every eye blinks with suspicion, every man is waiting for my halting; here I have to encounter a tremendous resistance of soul. Sometimes the teacher could encounter open hostility, and become eloquent under the pungent attack; but what can he do with the cold heart? what can any man do in the presence of indifference? Oppose the gospel, and the gospel will find its own replies: challenge it to combat, and its sword will flash out in the light instantly, and never be put back until the victory has been determined; but what could even the Son of God do with simple suspicion, unexpressed and unavowed dislike, prejudice, and distrust? Had there been open detestation the case would have been better. You can answer detestation, you cannot reply to prejudice ; you do not know where it is, where it originates, how it develops, what colour it assumes, and what subtle courses it pursues in the whole intricacy of the human mind and heart. We have seen Jesus Christ in the presence of hostile throngs, but to see him in the presence of his own countrymen, and, so to say, townsmen and fellow-villagers, and to see him encountered by simple blank suspicion, is a new view of this Man, whose ministry comprehended every aspect and every necessity of human nature.

Yet it was difficult to repress opinion. The people said among themselves, " From whence hath this man these things ? " He has no right to them ; this wine ought not to have been in this goblet ; the water is good, but how rough the vessel : could we not have had this same water in fine porcelain ? It would have tasted better in a pure crystal ; we do not like this man's way of giving it : we cannot deny what he says ; he is wise, shrewd, penetrating ; an able man, wonderful, striking, unique : but how is it that he can do these mighty works ? He was never trained in this direction ; he lacks the guinea-stamp of the schools ; he has not been ordained by rabbi or learned man or authentic authority of any kind ; there are the miracles, but how did he come to work them ? If some high priest or scribe had worked these miracles we would have applauded them, the balance of things would have been equal ; but how can the carpenter, the son of Mary, the brother of James, and Joses, and of Juda and Simon do these things ?—They, like many others, started the argument from the wrong end. They should have said : Seeing the works are so excellent, the worker himself must be good. If we would adopt that standard of reasoning, what prejudice would be dispelled, what new charities would be opened up and exercised and come to noble fruition ! Let us say so with regard to sects, communions, denominations : why say, These people are rough, therefore they can do no beautiful thing ? Why not say, contrariwise, The thing done is beautiful, therefore, under the rough exterior there must be some hidden, latent, divinely-originated loveliness ? That would be right, that would be just ; the spirit of charity would make such a criticism noble. We are apt to think that because the instruments are rude, therefore what the instruments are seeking to express must be rude also. That is false in reasoning, and it is unjust in morality : what is the thing being taught, what is the thing being done, what is the doctrine being declared, what are the results of the pursuit and the declaration ? If men are made honest, sober, wise, honourable, if they are proved to be worthy of trust and all the honours of citizenship, the thing itself which has wrought out this issue must be credited with divinity, must be regarded as an aspiration. It must be a very difficult thing for persons who have known the carpenter, the son of Mary, the brother of James, and Joses, and of Juda and Simon, to believe anything that he says. Did Jesus resent this ? When did he resent anything ? He was the Son of man, he understood contempt, he knew the evil genius of suspicion. " They were offended at him," but he held himself ready to do mighty works on their account if by faith they would allow him to show his omnipotence. This seems to be the attitude of all good men towards suspicious and suspecting persons. Whatever others do, be sure you always act the gentleman. Poor men can do so ; men who have had no advantages of a social, academic, or other kind, can by meekness and pureness of soul, sweetness and simplicity of disposition, be real aristocrats, gentlemen, knights. Whenever persons, therefore, mock you, or indulge and use mischievously prejudice against you, always show that you vindicate your position, not by your resentment, but by your gentleness, forbearance, magnanimity. Say, in sweet Christian monologue, They would not do so if they knew better; probably they only see me from an exterior point of view; they do not understand all my purpose, they only hear part of what I say, and they listen with too much credulity to what others say about me, and especially against me ; perhaps if they knew me better they would not be resentful, prejudiced, unkind, hostile, and unamiable. That is the speech for a Christian to make ; it is hard to compose, it is all but impossible to deliver ; but even this miracle lies within the almightiness of the Holy Ghost, God the Holy Spirit. Let us ask him to make us gracious when others are ungracious, magnanimous when others are supercilious and petulant and unjust ; and let us ask God to show us that there is after all no argument equal to a character. Silence may be a miracle ; a closed mouth in the presence of evil imputation may be the best exculpation : " He was led as a lamb to the slaughter, and as a sheep before her shearers is dumb, so he openeth not his mouth " : what if that silence were the consummation and expression of his omnipotence ?

There is great comfort to be derived from the incident narrated by the evangelist. One would say, given a preacher, wise, gracious, sympathetic, lovely in personal character, and un-questionably supreme in ability, and known to be ineffably tender in disposition, and the people must recognise him, welcome him, believe what he says, and repronounce in action the doctrine of his lips. That theory is dissolved and annihilated by this incident. It was the Son of God that was contemned, dis-believed, rejected. We hear even upon platforms that where the gospel is faithfully presented the people are hungering and thirsting for it, and are prepared to respond to its appeals, and invitations, and challenges. That was not the case with Jesus Christ. He was the Gospel, yet he was called Beelzebub ; he was the Son of God, and was stoned for making the claim ; there was no guile in his soul, there was no blackness of iniquity upon his sweet sacred lips ; the people wondered at the gracious words which proceeded out of his mouth, and their wonder never rose into religion, trust, and praise. Let faithful men, therefore, be not too much discouraged. The reason of failure is not in you, necessarily ; there is room enough for self-inquest, piercing examination of the heart, trying of the reins and thoughts and motives and purposes ; you may hold continual self-assize ; but the Son of God was despised and rejected of men ; we hid, as it were, our faces from him ; we spat upon his face, and plucked the hair from his cheeks. Say not, therefore, that if you had ideal beauty and loveliness and moral charm you would fall down in an attitude of piety, and accept the revelation as the very incarnation of God. History contradicts you, consciousness ought to restrain such an ebullition of impious pretension ; we ought to know ourselves enough to know that men can go from temples to cesspools, can go from the altar where the blood of the Sacrament is drunk, and drink deeply out of the cup of devils. Human nature can do miracles of this kind. We ought by this time to be acquainted with the fact that impossibility is one of the easiest exercises we have ever to accomplish.

Jesus, like himself, generalised upon the incident; he said, " A prophet is not without honour, but in his own country, and among his own kin, and in his own house." He did not say, I am suffering from a thorn that never pierced any other man; I am the victim of an unusual and unprecedented suspicion : he simply allied himself by sympathetic union with the great lines of history and said, Nothing has happened to me that is uncommon; this is but a repetition of the beginning, the very genesis of history is in this conduct. " A prophet is not without honour, but in his own country, and among his own kin, and in his own house "—because people will not look further than locality, visible characteristic, and limited uniqueness of speciality, infirmity, or other trait of disposition and relationship. Men will not listen to the music, they will handle the instrument; we have nothing to do with the organ, we have everything to do with the music. Not where Jesus came from but what he has to say should be our supreme inquiry : not the Nazarene but the Son of man can touch every point in the circumference of human relationship and human need. Judge every man by this standard; judge every Christian communion by this standard. If sects that you dislike are doing good, acknowledge it, and say, After all, there is something better in these people than I thought there was; I was wrong; by the fruit the tree shall be judged; good fruit never grew on bad trees : this fruit is sweet, therefore the tree cannot be bad. When we reason thus, I repeat, we shall get back to simplicity, trustfulness, charity, co-operation, and that wondrous exercise of mutual honour which results in mutual provocation to love and good works.

He was ready to do mighty works, but they would not allow him. You cannot drive the engine unless you light the fire. Many men have fuel enough. You have seen a grate full of fuel; was it a fire? Why do not you put your hands down to that grate and warm them? It is a grate. Your answer is simple, direct, and sufficient. The grate is there, the fuel is there; but where is the spark, the fire? So Jesus Christ

himself was prepared to do many mighty works there, but there
was no faith-spark, no love-fire, no answering heart, no cry
that made him who heard it feel that the urgency of human need
was pleading with his all-sufficiency. It is right to fix the blame
properly. If men are not saved, it is their own blame. Never
can I believe that God has said to any man, I will not save you;
I have made up my mind that you are not to be saved. God
never said such words or thought such thoughts. He is the
God and Father of us all : God so loved the world ; Jesus Christ
came to seek and to save the lost. If any man is not lost Christ
had no mission to him ; if a man can stand before Christ and
say, I am perfectly well in body, soul, and spirit, Christ says,
Then I came not to you, for you have no need of a physician.
But first let the man be found. Jesus Christ does not retire
from this sphere, saying, I could have done mighty works there,
but I would not ; he says in effect, I wanted to do mighty works,
but the people would not allow me to do so because of their
unbelief.

"He laid his hands upon a few sick folk"; they are always
ready to take what they can get ; they are always prepared
to follow the suggestion and urgency of conscious pain and
need. Jesus Christ was always welcomed to the sick-chamber
after all other doctors had left ; Jesus was never called first ;
after all the visitors had gone downstairs, saying, There is no
hope, it is a case of dissolution, then they sent for the Son of
God : a tribute, but not intended ; a compliment, but not so
expressed. Let us lay it down as a doctrine that may sober the
mind and constrain the heart in right directions, that where men
are not conscious of mighty works on the part of God, the reason
is in their own unbelief. If we had believed more we should
have enjoyed more ; if our faith had been greater, then had our
grace been larger and richer. Lord, increase our faith.

Now Jesus goes away. "He marvelled because of their unbelief." They marvelled at his mighty works ; he marvelled at
their want of faith. Why do not these people see that life is
faith, and that faith is life, and that without faith life is a mockery,
a transient dream ? Why do they not comprehend the sublime

philosophy which says that faith creates the universe and enjoys it ? Faith builds new heavens, rolls new earths into place covered with summer and harvest, and faith enjoys as of right the creations of its splendid energy. Let us abide in the confidence of this doctrine. This will do more for us than any theory, suggestion, or possession of man. We cannot explain it ; if we could explain it, it would be but a geometrical figure. Astronomy is never satisfied ; it has its glasses, and it looks on the surface, but it says in its palpitating, discontented, resurgent heart, The worlds are beyond ; these are outposts, spirit lamps : I want to be millions upon millions of miles beyond : all that height is crowded with stars, and this mean glass, this horrible mockery of optics, could only see a speck here and a speck there : and my astronomic record, what is it but an account of a phase of the moon, a throb in a cloud that means that there is another star there, pulsing, beating, waiting to be detected, weighed, measured, watched with astronomic reverence. Yet if we say the same theologically we are fanatics, enthusiasts, poor addle-brained little creatures. That is not so. Faith says, What you see is very little ; that is the outside of the cloud ; it is beautiful, but—but—but—— And in that sublime hope we endure all things ; we purify ourselves.

Chapter vii.

THE REBUKES OF CHRIST.

[An Analysis.]

1. Then came together unto him the Pharisees, and certain of the scribes which came from Jerusalem.

2. And when they saw some of his disciples eat bread with defiled, that is to say, with unwashen, hands, they found fault.

3. For the Pharisees, and all the Jews, except they wash their hands oft, eat not, holding the tradition of the elders.

4. And when they come from the market, except they wash, they eat not. And many other things there be, which they have received to hold, as the washing of cups, and pots, brasen vessels, and of tables.

5. Then the Pharisees and scribes asked him, Why walk not thy disciples according to the tradition of the elders, but eat bread with unwashen hands?

6. He answered and said unto them, Well hath Esaias prophesied of you hypocrites, as it is written, This people honoureth me with their lips, but their heart is far from me.

7. Howbeit in vain do they worship me, teaching for doctrines the commandments of men.

8. For laying aside the commandment of God, ye hold the tradition of men, as the washing of pots and cups: and many other such like things ye do.

9. And he said unto them, Full well ye reject the commandment of God, that ye may keep your own tradition.

10. For Moses said, Honour thy father and thy mother; and whoso curseth father or mother, let him die the death:

11. But ye say, If a man shall say to his father or mother, It is Corban, that is to say, a gift, by whatsoever thou mightest be profited by me; he shall be free.

12. And ye suffer him no more to do ought for his father or his mother;

13. Making the word of God of none effect through your tradition, which ye have delivered: and many such like things do ye.

THIS paragraph shows Christ's method of rebuking. The paragraph which immediately succeeds shows Christ's method of instructing. The paragraphs may be taken together in a discourse upon the outward and inward relations of Jesus Christ: his relations to the Pharisees and the general body of the people, and his more secret and spiritual relations to his disciples.

In the case of the Pharisees, there was (1) something right; (2) something incomplete; (3) something wrong. Let this be shown :—

(1) There was something right. The Pharisees noticed that a few plain men who had no right, so far as their social standing was concerned, to lead the fashion or custom of society, had treated with neglect, perhaps with contempt, a well-established custom. Men who introduce new eras, or teach revolutionary ideas, or set aside the traditions of the elders, have no claim to exemption from rigorous questioning. Social life should be more than a mere collection of personal fancies. There should be law and discipline in social habit. There is a line up to which personal independence should be claimed : beyond that line men should consider one another, and maintain a common order. In this case, the traditional discipline had been set aside, and the question, Why? is a proper one. We should make inquiries about each other, and show a religious concern about each other's habits.

(2) There was something incomplete. Ceremonialism is always incomplete. It is impossible that ritual can be final, because the moral must exceed the formal. The discipline of "the Pharisees and all the Jews" was no easy matter after all. Do we sufficiently consider that the men whom we hold in contempt put themselves to far greater trouble in maintaining their religious duties and scruples than we do ? Beware, lest contempt be mistaken for spirituality ! This frequent washing of hands, this abstinence from meat until the hands had been washed, this washing of cups and pots, brazen vessels and tables, this tithing of mint, anise, and cummin, when put together, show that the religious habits of the Pharisees were such as required time, patience, and constancy, and not a little self-denial. We have escaped the trouble ; have we within us the spirit of consecration of which all outward habits should be the sign ? Are we satisfied with mere sentiment, or do we endure hardness as good soldiers of Jesus Christ ?

(3) There was something wrong. They rejected the commandment of God, that they might keep their own tradition ; they

taught for doctrines the commandments of men; they honoured God with their lips, but their heart was far from him. Before God, life is not a question of washed hands, but of a washed heart; it is not a question of kneeling, but of praying. Religion may be a mere civility towards God,—a courteous acknowledgment of his existence, and nothing more!

In rebuking the inquirers Jesus Christ seized upon their moral defects, and showed them that God pierced the heart. His tone was spiritual. He set up no technical argument about forms and ceremonies; he held the infinite light of divine righteousness over the secret corruption of the heart.

The point to be specially observed is, that a right spirit will make to itself right forms, and that it is no sign of heavenly-mindedness to sneer at Christian formalities. Public worship, open profession of Christ, family devotion, Christian services, may express the sanctity and love of the heart as before God.

14. And when he had called all the people unto him, he said unto them, Hearken unto me every one of you, and understand:

15. There is nothing from without a man, that entering into him can defile him: but the things which come out of him, those are they that defile the man.

16. If any man have ears to hear, let him hear.

17. And when he was entered into the house from the people, his disciples asked him concerning the parable.

18. And he saith unto them, Are ye so without understanding also? Do ye not perceive, that whatsoever thing from without entereth into the man, it cannot defile him;

19. Because it entereth not into his heart, but into the belly, and goeth out into the draught, purging all meats?

20. And he said, That which cometh out of the man, that defileth the man.

21. For from within, out of the heart of men, proceed evil thoughts, adulteries, fornications, murders,

22. Thefts, covetousness, wickedness, deceit, lasciviousness, an evil eye, blasphemy, pride, foolishness:

23. All these evil things come from within, and defile the man.

The doctrine was stated in the hearing of all the people: the explanation was given to the disciples alone. Truth is not always self-explanatory. We need the living teacher as well as the divine truth.

Amongst the lessons taught by this figure may be mentioned—
(1) That men are corrupted by such outward things only as

touch some corresponding quality in their own nature. Some
men can make money without becoming covetous. Some men
can dress handsomely without becoming vain. Some men can
enjoy amusements without becoming frivolous. Other men,
differently constituted, have to watch themselves in all these
particulars as they would watch gunpowder. Hence the folly
and injustice of judging one another!

(2) That words and actions reveal the true spiritual quality of
the speaker and actor. "That which cometh out of the man,
that defileth the man." There is a common saying that no man
can injure a man but himself. It is not wholly true, yet largely
so. Not what is said about a man, but what the man himself
says, is the true standard.—(*a*) This doctrine destroys the excuse
that circumstances are blamable for our moral defilement.—
(*b*) This doctrine determines the bounds of social judgment.
For example, you accuse a man of having attended a certain
questionable class of amusements ; now observe, the amusements
may have done the man no harm, but the censoriousness of your
spirit may have defiled you! Or, again : you suppose that
because a man is prosperous he must of necessity be worldly-
minded ; now, the prosperity may have left him unspoiled, but
the criticism may show you to be envious, ignoble, and spiteful,
though it may have been offered with a pious sigh!

The 21st and 22nd verses give a picture of the human heart
as presented by Jesus Christ.

Looking at this graphic, but most terrible and humiliating
picture, four things are clear :—

(1) That the heart is chargeable with foulest apostasy. Compare this picture with the heart as it came from God. "Let us
make man in our image," etc. "God hath made man upright,"
etc. What forces are in man ! What fury,—what malevolence!

(2) That this apostasy shows itself in many ways. Read the
black list! No one man may reveal his corruptness in the whole
of these ways. A man may never commit "adultery," yet his
mind may be full of "evil thoughts" : he may resent the charge
of having committed "thefts," yet he may be degraded by the
spirit of "covetousness" : he may shudder at the thought of
"murder," yet he may be mad with "pride." We are all
somewhere in this list of devils!

(3) That such apostasy has no power of self-recovery. "The Son of man is come to seek and to save that which was lost." In a case so desperate the help must come from the outside.

(4) That the nature and scope of the apostasy includes the whole race in one condemnation. "There is none righteous." "All we like sheep have gone astray," etc. "Where is boasting?" "Let him that thinketh he standeth," etc.

Spiritual diseases require spiritual remedies. It is not thine hand, O man, but thine heart of hearts that is wrong! "Though thou wash thee with nitre and take much soap, yet thine iniquity is marked before me, saith the Lord." The day of heart-trying is at hand. "Who may abide the day of his coming? and who shall stand when he appeareth? for he is like a refiner's fire, and like fuller's soap." "Wash me throughly from mine iniquity, and cleanse me from my sin."

24. And from thence he arose, and went into the borders of Tyre and Sidon, and entered into an house, and would have no man know it: but he could not be hid.

25. For a certain woman, whose young daughter had an unclean spirit, heard of him, and came and fell at his feet:

26. The woman was a Greek, a Syrophenician by nation; and she besought him that he would cast forth the devil out of her daughter.

27. But Jesus said unto her, Let the children first be filled: for it is not meet to take the children's bread, and to cast it unto the dogs.

28. And she answered and said unto him, Yes, Lord: yet the dogs under the table eat of the children's crumbs.

29. And he said unto her, For this saying go thy way; the devil is gone out of thy daughter.

30. And when she was come to her house, she found the devil gone out, and her daughter laid upon the bed.

(1) Some things which are evil in themselves may be the occasion of good. The unclean spirit was the occasion of this mother hearing of Jesus Christ! But for the unclean spirit her interest in the great stranger might never have been awakened. So with all bad, unfortunate, painful things, they should lead to Christ. Affliction, loss, weakness, etc. On the other hand, whoever has heard of Christ should publish him to those who have never heard of him.

(2) The mere hearing of Jesus Christ may be without profit to the hearer. This woman not only heard of Christ, "she came

and fell at his feet, and besought him that he would cast forth the devil out of her daughter." Remark upon the tremendous responsibility of forming part of a Christian congregation, and yet not going to Christ. Does hearing of water quench thirst? Does hearing of medicine heal disease? Show that men should be as sensible in religious questions as in ordinary affairs.

(3) The prayer of the heart never fails. Its particular object may often be denied, but the heart itself is comforted and quieted by divine ministries. In this incident the heart does two things: (*a*) it shows the superiority of the human over the national; (*b*) it excites intellectual energy,—how sublime the reply of the woman! The mind is strongest and brightest when under the dominion of the heart. Sorrow makes the poorest lips eloquent. Under such circumstances the pleading mother might have (*a*) pronounced herself insulted; (*b*) resented the terms in which she and her child were described; (*c*) denounced the inability of Christ to meet a case so desperate as hers. She did none of these things. She shot back Christ's own arrow from the bow of her heart.

The whole incident gives, first, a lesson to mothers,—pray for your children; second, an encouragement to intercessors,—urge upon God the desires of the inmost heart; third, a sublime view of divine sufficiency,—the crumbs of God's table are better than the luxuries of all other tables; the poorest, dimmest conceptions of Christian truth are more to be prized than the fullest revelations of truth that are merely introductory or subordinate; fourth, a hint as to the limitation of the highest services,—the child was healed apart from any action of her own: the mother plucked this fruit of the highest branch, and gave it to her little daughter. There is a time when the child's own will may set itself against God. The child becomes more than a child. Whilst children are wholly yours, beseech God much in their behalf.

31. And again, departing from the coasts of Tyre and Sidon, he came unto the sea of Galilee, through the midst of the coasts of Decapolis.

32. And they bring unto him one that was deaf, and had an impediment in his speech; and they beseech him to put his hand upon him.

33. And he took him aside from the multitude, and put his fingers into his ears, and he spit, and touched his tongue;

34. And looking up to heaven, he sighed, and saith unto him, Ephphatha, that is, Be opened.

35. And straightway his ears were opened, and the string of his tongue was loosed, and he spake plain.

36. And he charged them that they should tell no man : but the more he charged them, so much the more a great deal they published it ;

37. And were beyond measure astonished, saying, He hath done all things well : he maketh both the deaf to hear, and the dumb to speak.

(1) Christ sighed,—his view of human nature touched his heart. (*a*) His natural sensibilities were touched by human suffering, and therefore he was a man of like passions with ourselves ; (*b*) his sympathies ever responded to the necessities of human life, and therefore he had all the human qualifications needful for a Saviour of men.

(2) Christ looked up to heaven. He connected the divine with the human : he showed the unity of the great system of which what we see is but a part : he made even his physical work a spiritual exercise.

(3) Christ said, Be opened. He spoke authoritatively ; the weakness of the sigh became changed into the strength of royalty.

See how these exercises follow each other in something more than a merely logical order. What an appeal to the minister of Christ ! (1) Canst thou do any great work in the world without sighing ? without tender sympathy ? without having thy very heart pierced with sorrow for human sin and pain ? (2) Canst thou work without looking heavenward ? Is the battle there ? Dost thou not need to bring down God to thy side ? O man, self-trusting, thou hast failed in thy ministry, because in the midst of work no time was found for an upward glance,—for the look which is prayer. (3) Hast thou spoken feebly, hesitatingly, apologetically ? Dost thou speak the word as if begging pardon for an intrusion ? Or, with clearness, power and authority ? How ?

The 37th verse shows what the whole world will say when Christ's mediation is completed.

Chapter viii.

FEEDING THE FOUR THOUSAND.

[An Analysis.]

1. In those days the multitude being very great, and having nothing to eat, Jesus called his disciples unto him, and saith unto them,

2. I have compassion on the multitude, because they have now been with me three days, and have nothing to eat:

3. And if I send them away fasting to their own houses, they will faint by the way : for divers of them came from far.

4. And his disciples answered him, From whence can a man satisfy these men with bread here in the wilderness ?

5. And he asked them, How many loaves have ye ? And they said, Seven.

6. And he commanded the people to sit down on the ground : and he took the seven loaves, and gave thanks, and brake, and gave to his disciples to set before them ; and they did set them before the people.

7. And they had a few small fishes : and he blessed, and commanded to set them also before them.

8. So they did eat, and were filled : and they took up of the broken meat that was left seven baskets.

9. And they that had eaten were about four thousand : and he sent them away.

HERE we have a special exemplification of the philanthropic spirit of Christ. In Christ, philanthropy was not a sentiment but a controlling power, not a dream but a fact. Some of the more striking suggestions of this paragraph are these: (1) Two different methods of dealing with social problems,— "send the multitude away;" that is one method,—"give ye them to eat;" that is another. We often have the remedy at hand while we fruitlessly seek it afar off. No man knows the range of his resources. This applies to mind, money, influence,— to all the aspects of life. A man's resources, looked at from the outside, may be as a grain of mustard seed ; but planted, used, put into right conditions, etc. The disciples took an insufficient view of their resources,—taking the account from the various evangelists, they said, " We have five loaves, we have but five loaves, we have but five barley loaves ; we have but two fishes, we have but two small fishes." Lower and lower they sink in their representation of their resources,—a picture of men who have no faith. The life that is in a man multiplies the resources that are outside. (2) The entire fulness of Christ in relation to all human need. He said, " Bring them hither to me." Christ cared for the bodies of men ; and his religion can never be un-mindful of social, secular, commercial, and physical questions. The whole man came originally from God, and to the end of time the whole man must be profoundly interesting to God. All our resources must be taken to Christ if we would make them truly availing to the necessities of men. We hardly yet understand Christ's relation to material questions. " Let the people praise thee. . . . Then shall the earth yield her increase." Man loses no bread by praying over it. The principle may be extended— no life spent in true devotion is wasted. If Christ " looked up to heaven " while using the things of earth, shall we use the things of earth as though there were no heaven ? (3) The com-patibility of carefulness with the greatest bounty,—" They took up of the broken meat that remained seven baskets full." God will not suffer loss. He makes use of every sunbeam now that fell upon the first morning of time, and the dew which glittered in Eden sparkles in the rainbow of to-day. God is the most exacting of economists.

Among the miscellaneous remarks suggested by this paragraph may be named :—(1) Christ's power in all the wildernesses of time. (2) The impossibility of loneliness or want in fellowship with Christ. (3) The union of religious exercises with daily engagements. (4) The Giver of earthly bread is also the Giver of heavenly bread. (5) The man who is prepared to give himself is prepared to give all lower property.

There need not be any difficulty in receiving this statement. If a man will closely examine himself he will find that in his own life there have been interpositions and deliverances, unex-pected and thrilling manifestations of bounty which verify this narrative, and show that in every life the miraculous element is most positive and influential.

Look at the incident (1) As showing that trials may arise through following Christ. The multitude had nothing to eat! Whatever the motive of the outsiders for following Christ, they did follow him, and in following him they were exposed to inconvenience and trial. There is no trial now in following the Saviour. Show the pitifulness and absurdity of modern whining in this matter of suffering. Following Christ is now the most successful habit of society, outside following, not vital, spiritual, self-sacrificial following.

Look at the incident (2) As showing how the impossible may become the possible. From the standpoint of the disciples, etc. From the standpoint of Christ, etc. We should always have a view of our own, but should not always act upon it. Our own view should show us the vastness and solemnity of life; should show us also our personal incompetence to meet its great necessities. Looking at these two things we shall be humbled,— humbled even to the point of despair. On the other hand, we should act on the view of Christ. We must connect ourselves with the supernatural, if we would really have dominion over all the wants and tumults of human life. God's views are to be carried out in God's strength. Now and again God sets us to do some great thing which startles us : it is so much out of proportion to our resources : we think God must have made a mistake! We often find ourselves uttering the tone of surprise in looking at unexpected demands upon our strength. This really does us good. It is well for a man to be startled out of himself, to be taken to the very limit of the possible, and to be told by God to throw himself over into the impossible. It was so, practically, in this case. Hear the startling word,—Feed four thousand people with seven loaves and a few small fishes ! This kind of demand in life does us good because it leads us to cast ourselves entirely upon the Infinite. Sometimes it is said by men in the kingdom of Christ, who have to deal with great and difficult questions,— "We are bound to look at these things as business men : " in a very superficial sense this may be true, but as a rule of Christian enterprise it is a profound and most mischievous fallacy. The disciples looked at this question as business men ! What was it that the disciples forgot ? God ! So with ourselves : we persist in ignoring the divine element.

Look at the incident (3) As showing how much superior is the man of ideas to the man of loaves. The man of loaves said, "It cannot be done;" the man of ideas said, "It must be done!" See how a man may be dwarfed by the material! The soul perishes in the absence of spiritual aspiration and communion. Don't live in your business, live beyond it, and descend upon it from the highest spiritual elevation. Loaves are for one world; ideas are for the universe. Of necessity the material must limit the power and hope of its believers : on the other hand, the spiritual ever lures the mind to enterprises higher and higher. This holds good of purely intellectual energy, how much more of energy that is religious as well as intellectual!

Look at the incident (4) As showing that the spiritual vindicates itself from the charge of wastefulness. With such power to multiply loaves, why be so careful about fragments? The one is the counterpart of the other. The spiritual is not the waste, but the accumulation of power. The crumbs of one meal should be the germs of another. The most liberal was also the most economical. In the universe there is nothing wasted, though the bounty be so liberal, and the feast so long-continued.

10. And straightway he entered into a ship with his disciples, and came into the parts of Dalmanutha.

11. And the Pharisees came forth, and began to question with him seeking of him a sign from heaven, tempting him.

12. And he sighed deeply in his spirit, and saith, Why doth this generation seek after a sign? verily I say unto you, There shall no sign be given unto this generation.

13. And he left them, and entering into the ship again departed to the other side.

The multitude did not ask for a sign, yet one was given : the Pharisees specially desired a sign, and no sign was granted. Mere curiosity should never be gratified by the Christian interpreter. There is no real necessity in human life which will be left unsupplied by the Saviour,—when an apparent want is not supplied by him, we may be assured that the want was apparent only, and by no means real. The text may be taken as the basis of a discourse upon the refusals of Christ. We often speak of what he gave : we might speak also of what he withheld. The words of the Old Testament are applicable to Jesus Christ. "No good thing will he withhold from them that walk uprightly."

The refusals of Jesus Christ were governed by three considerations : (1) Religious curiosity is not to be mistaken for religious necessity ; (2) Religious confidence is not to be won by irreligious ostentation ; (3) Religious appeals are not to be addressed to the eye, but to the heart. In applying, these points show what Christ gave in comparison with what Christ refused. He gave bread, sight, hearing, speech, health ; he gave his life, yet he refused a sign !

Understand that in some cases not to give a sign is in reality to give the most solemn and dreadful of all signs !

14. Now the disciples had forgotten to take bread, neither had they in the ship with them more than one loaf.

15. And he charged them, saying, Take heed, beware of the leaven of the Pharisees, and of the leaven of Herod.

16. And they reasoned among themselves, saying, It is because we have no bread.

17. And when Jesus knew it, he saith unto them, Why reason ye, because ye have no bread ? perceive ye not yet, neither understand ? have ye your heart yet hardened ?

18. Having eyes, see ye not ? and having ears, hear ye not ? and do ye not remember ?

19. When I brake the five loaves among five thousand, how many baskets full of fragments took ye up ? They say unto him, Twelve.

20. And when the seven among four thousand, how many baskets full of fragments took ye up ? And they said, Seven.

21. And he said unto them, How is it that ye do not understand ?

Christ gave the practical application of the refusal. This " beware " must be taken as the utterance aloud of the result of an unspoken process of reasoning. The address suggests three things : (1) That Christian thinking is to be conducted cautiously. Do not receive every suggestion that is offered. There is an enemy,—beware of him ! (2) That Christian thinking is not to be perverted by great names. The Pharisees and Herod ! Socially, these were amongst the greatest names of the day. There are many great names now, such as priests, editors, leaders, etc. Look at the speech, not merely at the speaker. Doctrine, before men. (3) That Christian thinking is not to be degraded by liberalism and materialism. " It is because we have no bread." This was paltry. Some men's thinking is always downwards. They cannot understand figures of speech. Preachers should be careful, in condescension to general ignorance and occasional imbecility, to explain that when they say leaven they do not mean bread. It is most humiliating to give such explanations, but the Master gave them!

The 21st verse supplies a basis for a discourse upon the reproofs of Jesus Christ. There are reproofs which proceed (1) upon our forgetfulness of providences,—verses 19, 20; (2) upon our bondage to the mere letter,—leaven being mistaken for bread; (3) upon our abuse or non-use of faculties,—"having eyes, see ye not? having ears, hear ye not?" There should be some difference between the eye of a beast and the eye of a man.

22. And he cometh to Bethsaida; and they bring a blind man unto him, and besought him to touch him.

23. And he took the blind man by the hand, and led him out of the town; and when he had spit on his eyes, and put his hands upon him, he asked him if he saw ought.

24. And ho looked up, and said, I see men as trees, walking.

25. After that he put his hands again upon his eyes, and made him look up: and he was restored, and saw every man clearly.

26. And he sent him away to his house, saying, Neither go into the town, nor tell it to any in the town.

This paragraph may be regarded as showing three views of Christ's work. (1) Christ's work as a salvation. The restoring of sight was a point on the brilliant line, the end of which was the salvation of mankind; so was every miracle of healing. (2) Christ's work as a process: the good work was not accomplished in this case, as in others, by a word,—it was done gradually. It is so in spiritual enlightenment. All good men do not see God with equal quickness or equal clearness. (3) Christ's work as a consummation: "He was restored, and saw every man clearly." He will not leave his work until it be finished; if so be men beseech him to go on to be gracious.

It has been to some readers an occasion of surprise that Jesus Christ should not instantaneously have cured the blind man. We should, indeed, rejoice in the variety of Christ's methods of working. His every method, to say nothing of his purpose, is full of mercy. His method is adapted to the cases which it treats. Some men could not bear instantaneousness. How many men have been ruined by sudden prosperity? Think, too, how obvious and manifold are the advantages of processes: how man is taught: how possibilities are revealed: how sympathy is excited: how dependence is encouraged: how patience is sanctified. It should, further, be understood that as a matter of fact instantaneousness is the exception, and not the rule of divine procedure: if, therefore, there is to be any surprise, it should be at the suddenness, and not at the slowness of Christ's physical ministry.

27. And Jesus went out, and his disciples, into the towns of Cæsarea Philippi: and by the way he asked his disciples, saying unto them, Whom do men say that I am?

28. And they answered, John the Baptist: but some say, Elias; and others, One of the prophets.

29. And he saith unto them, But whom say ye that I am? And Peter answereth and saith unto him, Thou art the Christ.

30. And he charged them that they should tell no man of him.

Another instance of a process as in opposition to a sudden result. The method of the inquiry, too, is a process: first, what do men say, and secondly, what do you say? The conversation may be taken in three points of view:—

(1) Jesus Christ, the subject of universal inquiry. All men talk about him: he appears to all by the variety of his works and by the vitality of his teaching: as the Son of man he appeals to all men.

(2) Jesus Christ demanding a special testimony from his own followers. "But whom say ye that I am?" We are called to knowledge: we are called to profession: we are called to individuality of testimony. We are not to be content with taking part in common talk, and sheltering ourselves behind general opinion; having special privileges, we must have special judgments regarding Christ and his doctrine.

(3) Jesus Christ, revealed by his works rather than by verbal professions. See how the case might be paraphrased: " I have been with my disciples for a considerable period; they have known my spirit, and seen my manner of work: they have not been told in so many words who I am: my appeal has been conveyed through service and through doctrine: it is now time that they should have grown far enough in spiritual strength and spiritual discernment to know the mystery of my personality,—I shall ask them therefore to declare my name and status."

Regard this as the true method of disclosing every individuality.

A teacher may say, "I am a very great man, therefore believe
me:" it is beginning at the wrong end : let the doctrine produce
its own effect : let the works be such as shall compel observers
to inquire, What manner of man is this ?

In the light of this suggestion, see the value of the charge that
the disciples should tell no man of him.   Men must be conquered
by great deeds, not by great names : men must be trained to
strength by thought, inference, comparison, and moral discrimination ; not by sudden and startling displays of personal glory.
God himself has adopted this method.   His glory has ever been
shown through his goodness,—his name has been approached
through the beauty and splendour of his works.

31. And he began to teach them, that the Son of man must suffer many
things, and be rejected of the elders, and of the chief priests, and scribes, and
be killed, and after three days rise again.

The disciples needed to be specially prepared for this disclosure.   See the infinite and gracious wisdom of the course: as
soon as they are strengthened by a distinct acknowledgment of
his divine personality, they are called to bear the revelation of
his sacrificial character !   No sooner does he fully acknowledge
his glory than he stoops to the depth of his sacrificial humiliation !
To have told of the rejection and killing first would have overpowered the disciples : therefore (and herein are the subtle signs
of his Godhead) he prepared them for the shock by the splendour
of the supreme revelation,—I am the Christ !   The personality
gave value to the sacrifice, and at the same time gave an assurance that for once death would be made a servant rather than a
master.

Regard this verse as showing (1) Christ's foresight ; (2) Christ's
preparedness for his work ; (3) Christ's dominion over events,—
" After three days rise again."

32. And he spake that saying openly. And Peter took him, and began
to rebuke him.

33. But when he had turned about, and looked on his disciples, he rebuked
Peter, saying, Get thee behind me, Satan : for thou savourest not the things
that be of God, but the things that be of men.

Peter rebuked Christ, and Christ rebuked Peter,—an alterca-
tion of more than mere words.   It is charged with practical

truths : (1) Man's shortsightedness ; (2) man's sentiment ex-aggerated ; (3) man's audacity,—to think he can help or save Christ !

On Christ's side: (1) He rebukes the oldest; (2) he rebukes the wisest,—it was Peter who said, " Thou art the Christ ; " (3) he shows that men are only worthy of him in proportion as they enter into his spirit.

34. And when he had called the people unto him with his disciples also, he said unto them, Whosoever will come after me, let him deny himself, and take up his cross, and follow me.

35. For whosoever will save his life shall lose it ; but whosoever shall lose his life for my sake and the gospel's, the same shall save it.

36. For what shall it profit a man, if he shall gain the whole world, and lose his own soul ?

37. Or what shall a man give in exchange for his soul ?

38. Whosoever therefore shall be ashamed of me and of my words in this adulterous and sinful generation ; of him shall also the Son of man be ashamed, when he cometh in the glory of his Father, with the holy angels.

These words seem to mark an epoch in the Saviour's teaching. The announcement has all the formality and solemnity of a new beginning. The principle had been the same from the first, but it had not been plainly stated in so many words. Henceforth there is to be no mistake. The " follower " is not the man in the crowd who can hardly give any account of himself; who is there because other people are there ; he is the man who carries a cross, who rules over himself in Christ's spirit, and takes the law of his life from Christ. At first, Christ said, " Follow me." Now he says, " If you will follow me, take up your cross." It is an enlargement in words, but there is no change of spirit. Still, it is beautiful to mark how the cross is introduced into the ministry of Jesus Christ. First of all he takes it himself, and then he says, You must do the same. This is following ! Doing what Christ does, and doing it because of his example and com-mand. Sometimes we find it extremely difficult to say the key-word of our meaning. Other words we can say easily enough, but how to get out the master-word that says everything at once ! In Christ's case that word was—" Cross." It has been a burden on his heart for many a day, and now he has spoken it out loudly. There are some words which if we do not say loudly, in high and hallowed excitement, we shall never say at all. The minister says words in public which he could never say in private; he speaks from the whirlwind what he could never say in a whisper.

The words in this paragraph, 34—38, are spoken with great energy, as if spoken in haste which never allowed the speaker to take breath. He had so much to say, and he said it every whit in one brief paragraph! See how much he spoke in that flashing moment :—

(1) I am the leader of men,—" whosoever will come after me."

(2) My leadership is based upon the principle of self-sacrifice.

(3) This principle is of universal application,—" Whosoever."

(4) Though the principle is universal, the cross may be personal,—" his cross :" what is a cross to one man may be no cross to another. Every man has his own cross: he may break it or carry it : he must carry it if he would follow me.

(5) The world says, " Save your life ; " I say, " Lose it,"—but mark the conditions, " for my sake and the gospel's ; " not suicide, but martyrdom ; not recklessness, but courage.

(6) To lose the soul is to lose the world. To lose your eyes is to lose summer and beauty. To lose your hearing is to lose music and eloquence. To lose your soul is to lose all.

(7) There is a law of inversion operating in human affairs : one day I shall be ashamed of all who are now ashamed of me. I shall come in my glory, and in the glory of the Father. Strange conjunction of words,—" Cross," " Glory."

In view of these words three things are clear : (1) That the application of Christianity to daily life is not easy ; (2) that such application can only be made in the strength of him who demands it ; (3) that whosoever makes such application will share the glory of the Son of man.

"Having eyes, see ye not?"

SEEING DIFFERENCES.

OUR Saviour would have us use all our faculties. Christianity never forbids a man looking and listening and considering and concluding for himself. The great complaint which Jesus Christ made when he was upon the earth was that men would not look, would not hear, would not consider, would not sit down and think out for themselves great questions. They were traditionalists, they were believers in legends, and tales, and glosses, and ceremonies; but they would not use their faculties. Jesus Christ says, " Having ears, hear ye not?"—you must hear something: what is it you hear? noise, tumult, uproar? but you ought to hear more, you ought to hear music, whispering voices, minor tones, winds that come down as if by stealth from heaven, fragrance-laden, and attuned to the very symphonies of the sky. Having eyes, what do you see? surfaces, appearances? What do you see in the city? a network of thoroughfares, a panorama of street-life, a great confusion of traffic? That is not the city. The city is within all that; it is in the home life, in the beneficence, in the purpose, in the education, in the discipline of the citizens; the citizens are the city. "Having eyes, see ye not?" You see broad differences; but a beast could almost tell the difference between night and day. Things are not classified into right hand and left hand, and are not thus roughly distributed; there are fine distinctions, gradual shadings, colours that run into one another and run out of one another again, making strange alternations of expression and suggestion and symbol: why do ye not see the fine lines, the microscopic lines? it is there that the difference is to be really found. When difference comes to be a mere vulgarity, then anybody can be trusted with it; but as to critical difference, the soul needs to be trained, taught, inspired. The natural man receiveth not the things that are of God, for they are spiritually discerned. The naked eye is assisted by the lenses of inspired reason and inspired faith. So our Saviour would have us use every faculty we have :—be up and stirring, ask questions, knock at doors, insist upon answers, show yourselves to be enthusiastic students, and God will give you some reply. He never answers indifference ; he pays no heed to patronage ; he is deaf to mere eulogium : but how he listens to the sighing of the broken heart, and to the prayer of him that is ill at ease! We are face to face, therefore, with a teacher who means to prosecute his inquiries to the end. Men do injustice to Jesus Christ if they suppose that he never wants them to ask any questions or raise any difficulties or state any doubts : he says, Empty your heart, be your own very self; if you are blaspheming, out with it ; if you are doubt- ing, speak your doubt ; if you are wondering, tell like a little child what your wonder is. Thus he would deal frankly with men and lovingly ; he would handle them like a creator, he would bless them like a saviour. Yet what a false impression exists regarding him ! To go to church is now considered by some people to be a species of weakness. To read the New Testament is considered to be a kind of attention to ancient literature that no man of ample and complete scholarship would like to neglect. It should be otherwise,—never man spake like this Man. We should hasten to where he teaches as hungering men would rush to bread, and thirsting men would speed and almost fly to water, to fountains, and wells in the desert. Let us commune with him awhile ; if he will touch us we shall feel the glow in our hearts.

We are called to sight, to discernment, to careful critical readings of all things ; so the Saviour would challenge us, and say to men who are hastening along the road, See ye not that there is an end as well as a beginning to things ? Men do not see the end ; they see the beginning, the frothing glass, the glittering gold, the immediate pleasure. Who sits down and counts costs and reckons up and says, The sum total of this is——

and then states the whole in plain figures? It would seem to be part of our policy to shut our eyes, and to butt at things with a deadly fatalism. Why do not men hold up their heads, and look, and perceive, and penetrate, and detain things until they have been analysed and examined and cross-examined, and made to bear frank and complete testimony? If your religion has come into your souls without cross-examination and practical test and severest handling, let me say plainly that you have no true religion; you are simply giving house-room to a mocking and burdensome superstition. Look at the end; mysteries will then be solved, perplexities will then be disentangled, embarrassments will be smoothed down, and all things that have troubled even the conscience will be made to stand up in simplicity and be invested with self-vindication. To a little fellow-traveller I once said, " We may save a great deal of this journey by taking this cross-lane,"—a little path which lay like a diagonal across the field,—" shall we go? " He was a little philosopher; said he, "I always find "—it was a short " always," but it was the only always he had—" that there is something at the other end, a wall to climb over, or a ditch to leap over, or something very hard to do at the other end; " so he preferred taking the longer way round. I wish we could lay that more to heart. There are easy roads, tempting paths, and we say, Why not thus, and so, and be home almost at once? And, lo, at the other end we find we are in a blind alley, or there is a pit, or a ditch, or a high hedge, over which to leap or through which to force our perilous way. If men would look at the end as well as at the beginning they would be saved from a good deal of rash adventure.

See ye not that in the structure and economy of nature one thing bears upon another, that there is nothing alone, isolated, by itself, but that everything is part of something else; and that therefore we stand within a system of Providence? We do not always see how things are to connect themselves one with the other. Occasionally we have said, This is a solitary instance, and must be regarded as such, and must be wholly neglected with regard to all possible issues. Yet in seven years' time that very solitary thing has come up and said, You will need me now: I have been waiting all this time; this is your opportunity;

if I were not here you could not complete the case ; you neglected
me once, but to-day I am a necessity. We cannot escape the
idea that there is a Providence. We may write it with a little p
or a large P; we may call it Force, or Fate, or Necessity, or
Mystery : but there it is,—an invisible Hand that puts things
together, that stretches itself out beyond common lines to bring
back things that have been ejected. There is a shaping hand.
Each man may see it in his own life. Do not throw your
experience away. It would be like murdering your best friend ;
nay, it would be a species of suicide. What is a man but his
experience ? What is to-day but the gathered past, the culmination of the centuries that are gone ? Who made you, directed
you, nursed you? Who was kinder than mother, gentler than
nearest friend ? Who opened the gate when you had lost the
key ? Who saved you in the peril, the danger, the household
extremity, when there was no light and when no voice could be
heard but your own, and that voice was lifted up not in thanksgiving but in agony and distress ? Some of us could not go back
from this testimony. If we did we should write upon our hearts
—Liar, Coward, Ingrate, unfit for the society of the beasts that
perish. We have had strange lives; they have been wondrously
handled and directed ; and we are here to say that many things
that we thought were hard and cruel, and at the time intolerable,
were amongst the richest of our treasures, the most sacred of our
possessions and memories. But Providence means two things;
it does not stand by itself; if it may be represented as having
two hands it lays one hand upon Creation and the other hand
upon Redemption. Only a Creator could be a true Father in all
this ministry of Providence. The one necessitates the other.
Only he who created the world can guide it. We may have to
take it back to him again and again that he may pay attention to
it, because we have spoiled part of its mechanism. He alone
knows all its intricacy, all its economy, and he alone can guide it
and bring it to its proper issues. If God care for one blade of
grass, he must redeem the world. This is the sublimity of his
love; it does not end upon little things; it begins upon them to
show that it means still greater sacrifice. If God built one
rosebud he built the heavens ; and if he made man he meant to
save him : and it will go hard if Omnipotence be worsted. I

know not what will happen; no man may make conjecture into
a dogma, and set up his own speculations as authoritative conclusions; but it will go hard if God do not win at the last.   No
man can tell when the last is.   God never gives up, until he
finds the case utterly hopeless.   Yet has he given to man the
power of electing at last to be lost.   What controversies God and
man will have we cannot tell, but man has the dread power of
telling God to his face that he has elected to be damned.

   See ye not that there is a great difference in the functions, the
gifts, and powers of men?   Who made all this difference?   It
cannot be self-arranged.   Self-arrangement of this kind would
be scouted in all things material : why should it be admitted in
things that are immaterial, intellectual, spiritual, and that lie close
upon the metaphysic line that is not far from the existence of God
himself?   Let us say that every building in the town elected its
own shape.   Not a child that can go to school but would smile at
the foolish idea.   Let us propose to the child that the pillar said it
would be a pillar, and the window a window, and the lamp a lamp,
and the beam a beam, and that thus it was all settled,—see how the
little one chuckles his unbelief, and looks upon you as a species
of intellectual fool.   Am I then to look upon society and say—
Painter, poet, farmer, merchant, preacher, you arranged all this
among yourselves?   Nothing of the kind.   If men are going
along the right line of development they are carrying out a divine
economy.   The poet never could be anything but a poet.   The
adventurer never could be anything but an adventurer.   You
cannot keep an explorer at home ; you may attire him in the
clothes of civilisation, and set him down by your fireside with the
very nicest book that has lately been issued from the press, and
you may whisper to one another that you think he is now likely
to remain at home.   He will never remain at home.   The spirit
of travel is in him.   He would crush his destiny if he remained
at home longer than to please us for a moment or two.   He must
be off,—child of the wind, child of the sea, he is at home in the
wilderness, in the black continent, in the far-away places of the
earth ; otherwise he is not at home.   All this difference makes
society possible.   If we were all alike we could not have society
It is because we differ that we can cohere ; it is because we are

not alike that we can hold companionship one with the other. This makes society tolerable. Without it society would be intolerable, because it would be monotonous, flat, blank; no man would have any idea different from any other man, and all speech would be useless. And this makes society progressive. We live by friction, we live by attrition; it is because we have conflict, controversy, contention, that we advance in our highest education and complete our spiritual manhood under the inspiration and guidance of divine providence. If men do not see these things, these things will become to them mysteries, elaborate confusions, stunning and stupefying bewilderments. Keep your eye open and watch, and see how cunningly he works who builds the stars and paints the flowers. He doeth all things well; give him time; pray to him with your patience; praise him with your forbearance; show your confidence in him by your long-suffering, by the end he elects to be judged.

See ye not that all this wondrous economy of nature and life is marked by a very marvellous system of compensation? so that the little may be great, and the great may be little; he that hath much may have nothing over, and he that hath little may have nothing under, and the very frailest life known to us has its own palace, and its own crown, and its own sceptre, and its own unique ability. What a study is here! Along this line men may meet with revelations every day. The microscope writes its own bible; the telescope unfolds its own revelation. There are some poor weak animals that in the daytime have an almost contemptible appearance, but they can see in the dark— and you cannot; you must judge by the night as well as by the day. You cannot tell how very contemptible you look in the night-time when you are stumbling about and do not know where you are; and the creatures you laughed at in the hours of the daylight are looking at you and wondering how you dare venture out at all. There are creatures that have enormous strength, and there are other creatures that have no strength at all, but they have all but infinite cunning, and they do not fear your mightiness; they will make no noise or demonstration, and yet they will overturn you, and bring you to ruin. There is a power of cunning as well as a power of muscle. The whole

scheme of nature is written over with the word Compensation.
One bird wants to be an eagle, but the Lord says, You have got
something the eagle would like to have.   Some poor things look
very feeble on land, but they become poetical symbols of grace
when they move into the water.   Is there a more ungainly
figure than that of a swan trying to walk?   It attracts universal
attention; it is smiled at as a very grotesque thing: but the
moment that same swan presses the waves poets come to write
about it, and painters come to paint it, and people say, How
exceedingly graceful!   There are compensations all through and
through nature.   You, for example, are very poor: but look how
cheerful you are!   Your cheerfulness is worth—who shall say
what it is worth?   What hope you have!   How you sing in the
night-time!   How in the coldest winter day you come upon men
like a cheerful fire!   Is no consideration to be paid to that?
You have no social standing; but look what health you have!
what a digestion! what a monstrous digestion!   Is that to be
set down in cyphers?   Is no account to be made of that?
Reckon up your mercies.   You are not tall; but how alert you
are!   You have no vigour in muscular fight; but what sagacity
you have in counsel!   Draw the balance well, be just to God.
What bird shall fight the eagle?   None.   Yet there is a bird
that shall drive the eagle mad; and the eagle cannot get at it.
Which is the smallest bird?   The humming-bird, and the
humming-bird can kill the eagle.   The eagle would strike a
lion, but the humming-bird is so small that the eagle cannot get
at it.   Naturalists have told us that the humming-bird, dear little
ruby throat, settles on the head of the eagle, and pecks out the
feathers one by one; and the eagle flies away, mad with agony,
screaming through the infinite arch; it is only a little humming-
bird that is just taking the feathers out, and pecking away at the
head all the time.   "Fly away," says the humming-bird, "I like
this very mnch."   If the eagle could get at that humming-bird
we know what would happen.   Alas! that parable has more
interpretations than one.   It is your little trouble that bites you.
You could fight a whole court of lawyers, but some little care
lays hold of your head and takes such interest in you that sleep
is an impossibility; and a man dies for want of sleep.   The
conies are a feeble folk, but they make their houses in the rock.

Spiders have been found, saith the proverb, in kings' houses. Other animals that are very weak in themselves go forth in bands, all together, then how mighty they become ! There is a locust that has defied an army of soldiers, a beetle that has beaten a standing army, that has gone forth night and day and eaten up all the crops ; and soldiers have had swords and sabres and spears and guns, and none can tell how many other weapons of war, and the beetle has still gone on eating. It is a curious system in which we live. It never made itself. Is there anything more melancholy than that a man should go through the world blind ? " Having eyes, see ye not ? "—that a man should go through a whole day's history and have nothing to write about at night ?—that a man should walk through the city, and have seen nothing of poverty, necessity, sorrow, pain ? This is to lose the world ; this is to lose all that is best in life.

One great question may sum up the whole : See ye not a difference, large and vital, between Christ and every other teacher ? Compare them. Jesus Christ is always willing to be compared, to have a true opinion formed, to have himself tested by the spirit which he inculcates, and the conduct which he inspires. What has done for the world what Christianity has done ? Let us be just. We have seen what was done for Terra del Fuego by Thomas Bridges ; we have seen how a place which British ships of war were forbidden to touch has become a civilised and Christian garden through the ministry of Christ. Have you seen a remarkable book called " Metlakahtla," edited by Henry S. Welcome ? No man can read that book without becoming a Christian. Everything may be risked upon that one testimony. The Metlakahtlans are described in that book as amongst the most ferocious and murderous tribes on the North Pacific coast—men of intellectual capacity though in barbarism ; men civilised enough to be able to make very cunning workmanship in bracelets and jewellery ; men philosophical enough to find that fire may be produced by friction ; men civilised enough to get mad by drinking rum. One man, William Duncan, had it laid upon his heart that he would like to teach the people Christianity. His thought was laughed at and scorned. The people who were approaching the frontier had to build strong fortifications, and to watch them night and day lest these ferocious and murderous people should break through and work havoc and ruin in so-called civilised life. William Duncan still had his dream of evangelisation. He enlisted the services of one who could initiate him into the mysteries of the language of Metlakahtla. He found it a picturesque language, full of metaphorical colour and image and force; he studied it, made a phonetic representation of it—for there was no written language—and acquainted himself so far with it as to be able to tell a little plain simple tale. He told the people he wished to tell them about the white man's God, if they would allow him. He went a step at a time, cautiously, little by little; and without professing now to give the detail of the wonderful volume, the end was a garden of the Lord, every man subdued; within thirty years the whole place transformed, transfigured. And if certain metaphysical Christians had not gone there the simplicity of the Metlakahtlans would have remained uncorrupted. It is when your unbalanced theologian or mere metaphysician wants to vex the human mind with distinctions that are not vital that great Christian labour is brought to an unhappy end. But there stands the fact. The Metlakahtlans were found in this condition ; a man goes amongst them with nothing but a warm heart and a clear conception of Christ's work, and the end is civilisation, education, an interest in spiritual things, a falling down before the Cross of Christ, and an acceptance of Christ as the God and King and Saviour of men. Who did it ? What was his name ? Buddha ? No. Mahomet? No. What was his name ? " Jesus Christ the Son of God." He never loses his power. To-day he will make the wilderness to blossom as the rose. Why not tell the world this, and turn its wildernesses into smiling fruit-fields ?

Chapter ix.

THE TRANSFIGURATION.

[An Analysis.]

1. And he said unto them, Verily I say unto you, That there be some of them that stand here, which shall not taste of death, till they have seen the kingdom of God come with power.

THIS verse would seem to belong to the preceding chapter. It may be taken alone for homiletic purposes, and treated under the form of an inquiry, viz.,—When does the kingdom of God come with power?

(1) When it so comes as to show the comparative paltriness and worthlessness of other kingdoms.

(2) When it brings the human heart into a state of joyful obedience to its spirit and precepts.

(3) When it throws upon the mystery and solemnity of the future a light which destroys the terror of death.

If the verse be regarded as an introduction to the scene which immediately follows, it will be seen how tenderly, as well as how wisely, Jesus Christ prepared his followers for the most startling events in his life. He was about to be transfigured : what if unpreparedness on the part of the disciples should overthrow their self-control, and disable them for further service? The light may come too suddenly, then what can happen but blindness?

2. And after six days Jesus taketh with him Peter, and James, and John, and leadeth them up into an high mountain apart by themselves : and he was transfigured before them.

3. And his raiment became shining, exceeding white as snow ; so as no fuller on earth can white them.

4. And there appeared unto them Elias with Moses : and they were talking with Jesus.

5. And Peter answered and said to Jesus, Master, it is good for us to be here : and let us make three tabernacles ; one for thee, and one for Moses, and one for Elias.

6. For he wist not what to say ; for they were sore afraid.

7. And there was a cloud that overshadowed them : and a voice came out of the cloud, saying, This is my beloved Son : hear him.

8. And suddenly, when they had looked round about, they saw no man any more, save Jesus only with themselves.

The whole incident may also be treated by way of inquiry, viz., What purposes would be answered by such an event as the transfiguration ? The event is so unique and so sensational, that we may, without irreverence, ask what purposes useful to mankind could be answered by it. Clearly, the transfiguration would, amongst others, answer four purposes :—

(1) It would confirm the newly revealed personality of the Saviour, "Thou art the Christ." Great revelations do need confirmation. They startle and unsettle the mind. Has not God generally accompanied his greatest prophecies by some outward and visible sign ? The prophecy of the Messiah, by sacrifice and various ritual ? Prophecies of destruction, by uses of the rod, and weapons of war ? Prophecies of restoration, by figures and symbols which satisfy all the longing and all the imagination of hope ?

(2) It would show that the death which he had foretold was not the result of weakness on the part of Jesus Christ. It was not a fate which he would have resisted had his physical resources been greater. The disciples, on hearing the prediction of his death, might have reasoned—" He is overborne by superior force; no man goes voluntarily to death. He is hemmed in by hostile powers ; he yields because he cannot successfully resist." The Transfiguration showed the contrary. See the heavenly light ! Behold the heavenly visitants ! Hear the heavenly voice !

(3) It would show the relation of the Christian kingdom to prior dispensations. Moses and Elias were present. The law and the prophets led up to the gospel. The hour of fulfilment was at hand. God's kingdom, though revealed in sections and phases, is but one. The blade and the golden ear are one. Sinai and Zion are (spiritually) different sides of the same holy hill. " Moses wrote of me." We miss the instructiveness and solemnity of history when we break it up into unrelated chapters.

History is one. Its sovereign purpose is the unfolding of the divine kingdom.

(4) It supplemented an individual testimony by a general and authoritative revelation. Peter had said, "Thou art the Christ." Now the Eternal One says, "This is my beloved Son." When Peter spoke, he spoke not of himself. Flesh and blood had not revealed, etc. All true sayings come down from heaven. The testimony was now established by three witnesses. There was henceforth no occasion to refer to Peter's word. Peter's word was introductory. Peter was, in a sense, the last of the prophets. The world needed a higher testimony than had yet been given : here it is—"This is my beloved Son ;" there is no height beyond this !

Observe the command which comes after the revelation,—Hear him ! Christ is the interpreter of himself. The command may be paraphrased thus : This is my beloved Son ; if you would have the proof of his sonship, listen to him, hear his speech, attend to his tone ; let him be heard for himself. If Christ were more listened to, he would be more profoundly loved and honoured. How many people, even in Christian congregations, have gone regularly and seriously through the word of Christ for themselves ? The question is not, How many people have heard sermons ? but, How many have studied the whole life of the Saviour for themselves ? We never knew an infidel who quoted the words of Christ accurately and completely.

"Hear him" may be regarded not only as an indication of authority, but as a challenge to human intelligence and consciousness. Hear him, and say if he speak not to your hearts; hear him, and say whether any voice be so full of music, of sympathy, of love ; hear him, and say if he speak not in the language of heaven the things which have been dumbly struggling within you, and set in cloudless light the hopes which you could never get beyond the region of misty and self-contradictory speculation.

Peter, James, and John alone accompanied the Saviour. The world's profoundest secrets and sunniest hopes have ever been in the keeping of two or three men. Lonely men, scattered here and there, have told the world when a great event was to be expected : they have predicted comets, and set men watching for new stars, and started men on expeditions full of peril and proportionate riches. We cannot all be treasurers; we cannot all be librarians. Thank God for mountaineers, for the strong climbers who first see the coming on of the new day !

9. And as they came down from the mountain, he charged them that they should tell no man what things they had seen, till the Son of man were risen from the dead.

10. And they kept that saying with themselves, questioning one with another what the rising from the dead should mean.

We have been dwelling upon the scene which disclosed itself on the top of the mountain : we now enter upon the scene which took place on the way down,—a scene which shows Christ giving a charge, and the disciples displaying intense interest in the revelation conveyed in that charge. We are amazed that silence should be enjoined upon the disciples : why should they not be allowed to tell this thing to all men ? Surely such a statement must have a good effect upon the public mind. Instead of enjoining secrecy, why does not Jesus Christ summon thousands of witnesses to behold a repetition of the transfiguring glory ? We are impatient to secure results. We would, in our imperfectness, try to do by a stroke what he takes many days to accomplish. Was it not a waste of power on the part of Christ to be transfigured in comparative secrecy ? Would not the transfiguration have done more for his interests than the sermon on the mount ? Yet the sermon was heard by a multitude, and the transfiguration was seen by three uninfluential men ! This is one of the divine processes which we should have reversed. So foolish are we, and ignorant !

(1) All physical phenomena are but temporary.

(2) Wonderful deeds are only permanently valuable as expositions of spiritual truths.

(3) Every miracle or wonder in Christ's life was incomplete until the resurrection had been accomplished. Half-truths or unfinished statements often do more harm than good. When the resurrection had been accomplished, all the other miracles would fall into their proper proportions,—the resurrection itself would be the one miracle of universal and eternal importance. It is the epitome of all the rest.

(4) What the disciples have already seen is to be eclipsed by what they have yet to see. They have seen the transfiguration,

they shall yet see the resurrection ! Is not this the law of divine discipline and progress ? Can we ever see the richest jewel in God's treasures ?

(5) The speculation of one age is the dogma of another. The disciples questioned one with another what the rising from the dead should mean. They had the resurrection before them ; we have it behind us. Wonderful in its width of meaning was this rising from the dead ! What did it mean ? It meant Redemption completed, Death overthrown, Heaven opened ! "If Christ be not risen from the dead," etc.

11. And they asked him, saying, Why say the scribes that Elias must first come?

12. And he answered and told them, Elias verily cometh first, and restoreth all things; and how it is written of the Son of man, that he must suffer many things, and be set at nought.

13. But I say unto you, That Elias is indeed come, and they have done unto him whatsoever they listed, as it is written of him.

The disciples now begin the deepest questions which they had to propose. They showed themselves students as well as observers. Men misread prophecy. They do not see the principles which are represented by names. John the Baptist was the pre-Christian Elias. Men do not always fully understand their representativeness; even the poorest of men are more than they seem to be : even a little child may typify the kingdom of God.

14. And when he came to his disciples, he saw a great multitude about them, and the scribes questioning with them.

15. And straightway all the people, when they beheld him, were greatly amazed, and running to him saluted him.

16. And he asked the scribes, What question ye with them ?

17. And one of the multitude answered and said, Master, I have brought unto thee my son, which hath a dumb spirit ;

18. And wheresoever he taketh him, he teareth him : and he foameth, and gnasheth with his teeth, and pineth away : and I spake to thy disciples that they should cast him out ; and they could not.

19. He answereth him, and saith, O faithless generation, how long shall I be with you ? how long shall I suffer you ? bring him unto me.

20. And they brought him unto him : and when he saw him, straightway the spirit tare him ; and he fell on the ground, and wallowed foaming.

21. And he asked his father, How long is it ago since this came unto him ? And he said, Of a child.

22. And ofttimes it hath cast him into the fire, and into the waters, to

destroy him : but if thou canst do any thing, have compassion on us, and help us.

23. Jesus said unto him, If thou canst believe, all things are possible to him that believeth.

24. And straightway the father of the child cried out, and said with tears, Lord, I believe ; help thou mine unbelief.

25. When Jesus saw that the people came running together, he rebuked the foul spirit, saying unto him, Thou dumb and deaf spirit, I charge thee, come out of him, and enter no more into him.

26. And the spirit cried, and rent him sore, and came out of him : and he was as one dead ; insomuch that many said, He is dead.

27. But Jesus took him by the hand, and lifted him up ; and he arose.

28. And when he was come into the house, his disciples asked him privately, Why could not we cast him out ?

29. And he said unto them, This kind can come forth by nothing, but by prayer and fasting.

Different diseases require different treatment,—" this kind goeth not out but by prayer and fasting." Illustration may be found in common life ; among diseases of the soul may be set down— Pride, Lust, Covetousness, Self-confidence, etc., the cure of which may require variations of treatment. However many and subtle the variations, Christ's power is available for all.

On the expression, " This kind goeth not out," etc., LANGE remarks : " It were a mistake to regard this demoniacal posses- sion as different from others in kind, and not merely in degree, and hence as constituting a peculiar kind, for which specific prayer and fasting were required. The Lord rather conveyed to his disciples that they had not preserved or cultivated the state of mind and heart necessary for the occasion, that they were not sufficiently prepared and collected to cast out so malignant a demon. . . . The demons of such complete melancholy could only be overcome by most earnest prayer and entire renunciation of the world." STIER says : " Our Lord says two things in the *But :* first, that he had meant the casting out of devils by the similitude of removing mountains ; and, secondly, that to control spirits, to break the evil will, the wicked power in the kingdom of sin, and of rebellion against the Almighty, who tolerates it according to the law of freedom, and even only thus removes it, is, indeed, another and greater thing than the simple working of miracles on helpless nature."

In this incident, note : (1) A household in misery because of one of its members. Trouble may be intensive as well as extensive. One prodigal may destroy the peace of a whole family. (2) A household troubled by an uncontrollable circumstance. The sufferer in this case was not blamable. Some troubles we bring upon ourselves; others are put into our lot by a power beyond us. (3) A household united in deep concern for one of its members. The father spoke not for himself only, but also for others : " Have compassion on us, and help us." The beauty of individual and social sympathy. An unfeeling heart a greater calamity in a family than the most painful affliction.

The incident may be viewed not only from the point of the household, but from the point occupied by the Church. Thus : (1) The Church expected to have restoring energy ; (2) the Church overborne by the evil which confronts it ; (3) the Church publicly rebuked for its incapacity ; (4) the Church shown to be powerless in the absence of Christ.

Look at the incident as showing Christ's position : (1) Christ calm in the midst of social tumult ; (2) Christ exposing himself to severe reprisals in the event of failure,—he spoke rebukingly before he performed the miracle ; (3) Christ asserting his independence,—" Bring him unto me." Jesus needed no help : "Without me ye can do nothing,"—but without us he can do everything. (4) Christ over-ruling and destroying evil : he never put evil into any man,—always he sought to cast it out ! Christ's antagonism to evil was implacable and eternal.

Learn something from the incident respecting the restoration of men : (1) The worst of cases are not hopeless ; (2) devils do not come easily out of men ; (3) Jesus Christ not only expels the devil, he gives his own personal help to the recovered man. "Jesus took him by the hand, and lifted him up." We need Jesus even until we are set in heaven. It is not enough that the devil be expelled ; we must have the direct, daily, gracious help of the Saviour. The devil throws down ; Jesus lifts up.

30. And they departed thence, and passed through Galilee ; and he would not that any man should know it.

31. For he taught his disciples, and said unto them, The Son of man is delivered into the hands of men, and they shall kill him ; and after that he is killed, he shall rise the third day.

32. But they understood not that saying, and were afraid to ask him.

Antecedently, there is nothing more improbable than that a

man who has worked so beneficently should be "killed." The very miracle which he has just performed should itself bring around Jesus Christ a whole army of protectors. Men should say: "The man who has done this good deed shall never be injured: we take him under our care, and not a hair of his head shall perish." We must, then, go deeper than mere circumstances to find the meaning of this mortal antipathy. What is its meaning? The meaning is that evil and good are in eternal antagonism, and they must come to a final contest. Jesus has cast out a devil; now the devil will try to cast him out.

The 32nd verse shows how mystery is the occasion of fear. The fear in this instance was most pathetic. Even Peter was silent. There are circumstances which make the most flippant and talkative of men solemn. There is no mystery in a straight line; when the curve begins, mystery begins. Jesus Christ was going out of sight for a time,—a specified time, and therefore under the dominion of the very power which seems to be worsted in the fight.

"He shall rise,"—the word of hope spoken in the day of gloom.

"The third day:" (1) A full separation; (2) a brief separation, —"For a small moment I have forsaken thee," etc.

About this announcement there are two remarkable things :—

(1) Jesus Christ gave his disciples the advantage of preparation : so in all our life, could we but see the meaning of things, we are always being prepared for further disclosure of God's purpose and method.

(2) Jesus Christ followed the surprise of grief with the surprise of hope,—"He shall rise the third day." The surprises are equal. That such a man should be killed is impossible. He can work miracles, why, then, should he not save himself? That a man who was weak enough to be killed, should also be strong enough to rise again, was a counterbalancing surprise! Why not use this very strength to prevent suffering and death? If he could overcome death itself, why not overcome those who sought to kill him? He who can do the greater can of course do the less. Herein is the mystery of sacrifice,—the problem of atonement.

Jesus "gave himself;" he laid down his life : socially there was murder,—spiritually there was sacrifice.

33. And he came to Capernaum; and being in the house, he asked them, What was it that ye disputed among yourselves by the way?

34. But they held their peace: for by the way they had disputed among themselves, who should be the greatest.

35. And he sat down, and called the twelve, and saith unto them, If any man desire to be first, the same shall be last of all, and servant of all.

36. And he took a child, and set him in the midst of them: and when he had taken him in his arms, he said unto them,

37. Whosoever shall receive one of such children in my name, receiveth me : and whosoever shall receive me, receiveth not me, but him that sent me.

(1) This dispute about greatness can only be prevented by a deep attachment to Jesus as head of the Church.

(2) All selfish discussions degrade Christian dignity, and impair Christian usefulness.

(3) This dispute is proceeding to-day more vigorously than ever. Who is to be high priest? Who is to be leader? Who is to go first in the procession? Who is to sit on the right hand? The Church is still fighting the battle of etiquette and status. Poor Church!

In Jesus Christ's statement of the case two things are clear :—

(1) That selfishness defeats its own object.—"He that exalteth himself shall be abased." "He that saveth his life shall lose it."

(2) That greatness is a spiritual condition, not a social distinction.—The child-spirit is true greatness. "Whoso abaseth himself shall be exalted." "Let this mind be in you which was also in Christ Jesus." "Pigmies are pigmies still, though perched on Alps, and pyramids are pyramids in vales." A man may be great in grace. By the very necessity of the case all outward distinctions must become less and less, but spiritual attributes endure as long as the being of the soul.

Notice the beautiful picture set forth in the 36th verse. Jesus with a child in his arms !

(1) Childhood teaches simplicity, dependence, trustfulness.

(2) Childhood represents freedom from care, anxiety, and fear of the future. The apostle put away childish things, not child-like things.

(3) Jesus values life, not mere age. We baptise human life, not human birthdays.

Jesus Christ has set a child in the midst of the whole world to teach the highest lessons. The child's dependence; the child's ignorance; the child's affliction; the child's death,—these things teach us evermore.

38. And John answered him, saying, Master, we saw one casting out devils in thy name, and he followeth not us: and we forbad him, because he followeth not us.

39. But Jesus said, Forbid him not: for there is no man which shall do a miracle in my name, that can lightly speak evil of me.

40. For he that is not against us is on our part.

41. For whosoever shall give you a cup of water to drink in my name, because ye belong to Christ, verily I say unto you, he shall not lose his reward.

42. And whosoever shall offend one of these little ones that believe in me, it is better for him that a millstone were hanged about his neck, and he were cast into the sea.

A sign of great self-importance was this on the part of John! The veto would sound well as the voice of the Church. The right use of authority has always been a subject of special delicacy; and the danger of narrowness has always threatened to impair the primary design of the gospel.

The incident may be homiletically treated as showing five things :—

(1) Whoever attempts to cast out devils has the sympathy of Jesus Christ.—Instead of the word ·devils, use evils, and the meaning will be clear. Intemperance, ignorance, idleness, etc. The whole reformatory system which society has set up, etc. The outworks are Christ's, as well as the citadel.

(2) All who work in a right spirit are in reality one body.— "No man which shall do a miracle in my name." There are two classes excluded—(1) Miracles wrought to satisfy vanity; (2) miracles wrought to promote selfish ends. A beautiful picture is that arising out of the unconscious unity of all good workers.

(3) The solitary and unclassified worker is not ignored by Jesus Christ.—"We saw one casting out devils in thy name." Here is individuality of effort. Each man has his own way of working. Some men cannot work in companies. The solitary

worker should not be cynical towards companies. Companies should not be harsh to solitary workers (ver. 42).

(4) There are more good people in the world than are gathered around conventional standards.—" Because he followeth not us." We are all prone to make ourselves the standard of measurement. This may be more than weak, it may be sinful. Sects seldom know much of each other. Their mutual animosity is in proportion to their mutual ignorance. Sectarianism is hateful ; denominationalism may be convenient and even useful.

(5) Long before men reach the point of miracles, they may reach the point of acceptance with Jesus Christ.—The man in the text had been working a miracle ; but Jesus says that the gift of a cup of water shall be treated as a miracle of love. See the variety of work : one man casts out a devil, another gives a cup of water ! They are both servants in the same household.

As an interlocution between Christ and the Church, see the infinite superiority of the Master ! He speaks the noble word of charity. He draws within his love the strange worker. It is better to fall into the hands of God than into the hands of man ! Thanks be to God, the Church is not to pronounce the decisive word !

The 42nd verse must be guarded from selfish and paltry interpretation. It is easy to offend some people. We may offend a man's vanity, and it is right to do so : we may offend his ignorance, and have the Master's approval,—we are not to offend the Christ that is in any man ; we are not to discourage him in doing good ; we are not to grieve the Holy Ghost that is in him.

43. And if thy hand offend thee, cut it off: it is better for thee to enter into life maimed, than having two hands to go into hell, into the fire that never shall be quenched :
44. Where their worm dieth not, and the fire is not quenched.
45. And if thy foot offend thee, cut it off: it is better for thee to enter halt into life, than having two feet to be cast into hell, into the fire that never shall be quenched :
46. Where their worm dieth not, and the fire is not quenched.
47. And if thine eye offend thee, pluck it out : it is better for thee to enter into the kingdom of God with one eye, than having two eyes to be cast into hell fire :
48. Where their worm dieth not, and the fire is not quenched.

49. For every one shall be salted with fire, and every sacrifice shall be salted with salt.

50. Salt is good : but if the salt have lost his saltness, wherewith will ye season it ? Have salt in yourselves, and have peace one with another.

A perusal of distinguished commentaries has not made the whole meaning of some of these expressions plain to us. We question whether "the kingdom of God" (ver. 47) and "hell fire" (ver. 47) refer to the future and invisible state. The whole expression is figurative. A man does not enter into heaven because he has one eye, nor is he cast into hell because he has two eyes. The hand, foot, and eye, are not to be taken literally, but symbolically ; otherwise what a spectacle would the Church present ! The meaning may be this : It is better for thee to mortify every passion in the name and for the sake of Jesus Christ, so as to enter into true life, than to gratify every lust so as to create within thee corruption full of worms, and a heat terrible as hell. The heart of a depraved man is a Gehenna. There the worm dieth not, and the fire is never quenched. The salt of Christ's presence and discipline can alone save the heart from loathsome corruption.

Homiletic use may be made of the symbolism :—

(1) The hand,—strife, defiance, theft, oppression, etc.

(2) The foot—trespass, wandering instability, supposed solidity of position, etc.

(3) The eye,—covetousness, lust, the fallacy of appearances, the temptation of the visible as against the invisible, etc.

The 49th verse has been variously commented upon, thus :—

"By salt understand the spirit of wisdom and grace, seasoning the effect, and by fire tribulation, whereby the patience of the faithful is exercised, that they may have a perfect worker." (Beda.) "Salt is just reproof, which is to be tempered with love, and wherewith our love is to be seasoned." (Jerome.) "It is an exhortation to the vigour of faith, by which others are preserved also, when we use our gift to season them ; and lest the acrimony of salt should be too acting, he adds the other member of love." (Calvin.) "The interpretation of the sacrifice of the condemned—and the fire and salt as eternal fire—except in the case of the salt having lost its savour, is contrary to the whole

symbolism of Scripture, and to the exhortation with which this
verse ends : 'Have this grace of God—this Spirit of adoption—
this pledge of the covenant, in yourselves ;—and,' with reference
to the strife out of which the discourse sprung,—'have peace
with one another.'" (Alford.)

General Note on the Ninth Chapter.

The transfiguration may be compared to the full noontide light.
The scene is one blaze of such glory as the disciples had never
beheld. The conversation in passing through Galilee is full of
the shadows which point towards eventide. The miracle which
intervenes shows Christ at work, though the shadows were
lengthening ; the conversation which follows shows Christ teaching the very doctrines which would be best illustrated by the
humiliation which he had predicted. In this chapter we have
brilliant light, solemn shadows, noble service, pathetic instruction.
Learn how to meet death, viz., in the midst of holy labour, and
in the strength of holy principle.

Chapter x.

AMBITION REBUKED.

[An Analysis.]

1. And he arose from thence, and cometh into the coasts of Judæa by the farther side of Jordan: and the people resort unto him again; and, as he was wont, he taught them again.

2. And the Pharisees came to him, and asked him, Is it lawful for a man to put away his wife? tempting him.

3. And he answered and said unto them, What did Moses command you?

4. And they said, Moses suffered to write a bill of divorcement, and to put her away.

5. And Jesus answered and said unto them, For the hardness of your heart he wrote you this precept.

6. But from the beginning of the creation God made them male and female.

7. For this cause shall a man leave his father and mother, and cleave to his wife;

8. And they twain shall be one flesh: so then they are no more twain, but one flesh.

9. What therefore God hath joined together, let not man put asunder.

10. And in the house his disciples asked him again of the same matter.

11. And he saith unto them, Whosoever shall put away his wife, and marry another, committeth adultery against her.

12. And if a woman shall put away her husband, and be married to another, she committeth adultery.

THIS passage, which will hardly ever be required for public use, suggests some points which ought not to be neglected by the preacher.

(1) Jesus Christ taught. The word is very significant. Ignorance was never approved by the Saviour. He saved through light, never through darkness. He conducted specific intellectual processes, as well as processes distinctively moral. It was his delight to simplify truth.

(2) Jesus Christ taught the people. Not a particular class,

but the people as a whole. His appeal was to humanity. His teaching was as impartial as the sunshine. This is the glory of Christian truth. It challenges all hearts, in all ages, and in all lands. It is a heavenly rain, not a local fountain.

(3) Jesus Christ honoured the holy teachers who had gone before him : " What did Moses command you ? " Truth is one. We are not to go to new teachers for new truths. We find new phases, new applications, and the like, but Truth is one, because God is one. This is our security amid all changes of ministers and teachers. In so far as the men have been true to God, each can say, What did my predecessor tell you ?

(4) Jesus Christ honoured the tenderest relations of the present life (vers. 7–9). He did not ignore the present because of the future. He treated no vow with levity. There is a spurious spirituality which overrides social bonds and human compacts, but Jesus Christ never gave his sanction to such blasphemy. Without a home himself, he yet guarded the home-life of the world ; able to live alone, he yet upheld the sacredness of social institutions. He taught the whole law—the law of home, the law of society, the law of the Church : " There is one lawgiver."

This profound exposition was given in reply to men who tempted him. Even the enemy may occasion some truths to be more fully revealed. The lawyer tempted Christ, and behold the picture of the Good Samaritan was painted ! We are indebted to the darkness for the stars.

13. And they brought young children to him, that he should touch them : and his disciples rebuked those that brought them.

14. But when Jesus saw it, he was much displeased, and said unto them, Suffer the little children to come unto me, and forbid them not: for of such is the kingdom of God.

15. Verily I say unto you, Whosoever shall not receive the kingdom of God as a little child, he shall not enter therein.

16. And he took them up in his arms, put his hands upon them, and blessed them.

Even the disciples did not know their Lord. The persons who are nearest to us may actually know nothing of our character. The disciples had mistaken ideas of greatness : to them the greatness was not in life, but in circumstances. Jesus reversed this idea : the tree is in the seed : he cared for children, and so he profoundly cared for men. Jesus " was much displeased ; " this displeasure enhanced the value of the benediction. The blessing was thus shown to be no cold compliment, nor a merely social courtesy; it was an act of the heart. The displeasure would be as memorable as the blessing. The disciples measured themselves by their manliness; Jesus taught them to measure themselves by their childlikeness. Notice three remarkable things:—

(1) The power of parental instinct. The mothers knew, without having received any formal intimation, that a man like Jesus Christ must love little children. They did not wonder whether he did or not, they knew that he must. The heart soon finds out the quality and purpose of Christ. Let thy heart speak, O man, and it will tell thee that the Saviour is thy friend, and that he will hail thee as a suppliant.

(2) Parents may be interested in the Christian welfare of their children without being much concerned for their own. This is a startling possibility. There are men who seldom open their Bibles who rejoice in the Biblical knowledge of their children: so with Sabbath-keeping, church-attendance, and the choice of companions. They have more than a merely outward respect for religion, yet its redeeming mystery has no place in their hearts! They admire, but they do not repent.

(3) Jesus gives more than even parental love expected. The parents wished that Jesus would touch their children. They would have been pleased had he taken the children's hands into his own. What did Jesus do? "He took them up in his arms, put his hands upon them, and blessed them." See what he was asked to do, and see what he did! "He is able to do exceeding abundantly above all that we ask or think." The children were almost in heaven! A practical question may be asked here: Are our lives worthy of the advantages we enjoy in childhood? Some of us were brought to Christ, and were given to him in many a fervent prayer: have we gone upwards or downwards since?

17. And when he was gone forth into the way, there came one running, and kneeled to him, and asked him, Good Master, what shall I do that I may inherit eternal life?

18. And Jesus said unto him, Why callest thou me good? there is none good but one, that is, God.

19. Thou knowest the commandments, Do not commit adultery, Do not kill, Do not steal, Do not bear false witness, Defraud not, Honour thy father and mother.

20. And he answered and said unto him, Master, all these have I observed from my youth.

21. Then Jesus beholding him loved him, and said unto him, One thing thou lackest: go thy way, sell whatsoever thou hast, and give to the poor, and thou shalt have treasure in heaven: and come, take up the cross, and follow me.

22. And he was sad at that saying, and went away grieved: for he had great possessions.

The young man was farther from Christ than was the young child. The child was brought: the young man came, but he was farther away. His earnestness was good, for he "came running," as one in great urgency; his attitude was good, for he "kneeled" to the Saviour, as one who is humble-minded; his inquiry was good, for he asked, "What shall I do to inherit eternal life?" Men are not saved by good points, but by a good spirit. Men who ask great questions should expect great answers. Was the demand excessive? Manifestly not; it cannot be excessive to give up time for eternity, to forfeit a troubled hour for a happy immortality, to give up a speck of dust for an infinite inheritance. In his treatment of this young man, Jesus Christ showed—(1) That he was not anxious to add to the mere number or respectability of his followers. What an opportunity of doing so was here! A man with a carriage! A man who could make money questions quite easy! Some of us would have smoothed the way for his entrance into the Church —we should have talked about culture, refinement, speciality of sensibility, and the like. Jesus Christ showed (2) that outward amiability is not to be mistaken for spiritual character. "Jesus beholding him loved him." There was charm of countenance: there were remnants of a beautiful child-life; there was a struggle with the spirit of worldliness. Every man is more or less beautiful as he knocks at the gate of the kingdom: he stands between two worlds: the far-off light flushes his face with peculiar glory. (3) That the wisest and the best, as well as the dullest and the worst, must bear the same cross. "Take up the cross and follow me." What, the cross in youth? Yes. What, the cross where there is so much morality? Yes. Will it not be enough to lighten the crosses of other people? No! A requirement like this, made under such circumstances, ought to secure for Jesus Christ, viewed as a merely human teacher, the confidence and veneration of mankind.

23. And Jesus looked round about, and saith unto his disciples, How hardly shall they that have riches enter into the kingdom of God !
24. And the disciples were astonished at his words. But Jesus answereth again, and saith unto them, Children, how hard is it for them that trust in riches to enter into the kingdom of God !
25. It is easier for a camel to go through the eye of a needle, than for a rich man to enter into the kingdom of God.
26. And they were astonished out of measure, saying among themselves Who then can be saved ?
27. And Jesus looking upon them saith, With men it is impossible, but not with God : for with God all things are possible.

How hard it is to give up one world for another! Wherein lies the difficulty? (1) This world is seen, the higher world is invisible ; (2) this world gives immediate pleasure, the expectation of the higher world is often associated with sacrifice, self-mortification, and pain ; (3) it seems so easy to work for both worlds, as the division between them is so marked. What has business to do with theology? How can money interfere with prayer? Can stocks, funds, investments, speculations, become as a cloud between a man and his Maker? See how Jesus Christ puts the matter: "How hard is it for them that trust in riches to enter into the kingdom of God !" The emphasis is upon the word "trust." There are rich men who are poor in spirit. We should rejoice when the riches of the world fall into the hands of good men, because it is better for all great forces to be under Christian than under unchristian control. There is no merit in poverty. There is no wickedness in wealth. The one question relates to the spirit, not to the circumstances. The 25th verse must be read in the light of the 24th: "It is easier for a camel to go through the eye of a needle, than for a rich man who trusts in his riches to enter into the kingdom of God !" The confidence that is put in riches is so much confidence subtracted from the honour of the Father.

28. Then Peter began to say unto him, Lo, we have left all, and have followed thee.
29. And Jesus answered and said, Verily I say unto you, There is no man

that hath left house, or brethren, or sisters, or father, or mother, or wife, or children, or lands, for my sake, and the gospel's,

30. But he shall receive an hundred-fold now in this time, houses, and brethren, and sisters, and mothers, and children, and lands, with persecutions; and in the world to come eternal life.

31. But many that are first shall be last; and the last first.

Peter's all! What a tone of self-compliment there is in Peter's statement! "We are the right men: we have done the right thing: we are comfortably off; let the rich young man do what he may." Is there anything more deadly in its effect upon the spirit than religious self-satisfaction? The piety that gathers its skirts up, and avoids the mud of common life, is the most diseased and intolerable of all respectability. How pathetic was the reply of Jesus! No man serves him for nought! He who loses his life for Christ's sake, finds it,—finds it immortalised and glorified. "Seek ye first the kingdom of God," etc.

32. And they were in the way going up to Jerusalem; and Jesus went before them: and they were amazed; and as they followed, they were afraid. And he took again the twelve, and began to tell them what things should happen unto him,

33. Saying, Behold, we go up to Jerusalem; and the Son of man shall be delivered unto the chief priests, and unto the scribes; and they shall condemn him to death, and shall deliver him to the Gentiles:

34. And they shall mock him, and shall scourge him, and shall spit upon him, and shall kill him: and the third day he shall rise again.

Jesus went before: went alone: separated himself from the people and from his disciples. There was something in the action which filled the observers with painful amazement. His own thoughts were society enough for him meanwhile. He had seen the end. He had come to a turn on the life-road from which he could point out the Cross to others; as for himself, he had always seen it—seen it from unbeginning time, but now he had to point out to others that grim, dread object. No wonder he wished to be alone for a time. It is not easy to find the beginning of a sentence which is to convey tidings so startling and so terrible,—so Jesus goes alone to prepare himself to tell of the sacrifice. Observe (1) Jesus knew all that was coming upon him, so he was not surprised into suffering and death; (2) Jesus himself told the disciples, so he showed his perfect knowledge of the future; (3) Jesus said he would rise again, so his death was a sacrifice, not a martyrdom. He who had power to rise again, had power to prevent the taking of his life. The resurrection showed that the crucifixion was not a necessity arising out of Christ's weakness.

35. And James and John, the sons of Zebedee, come unto him, saying, Master, we would that thou shouldest do for us whatsoever we shall desire.

36. And he said unto them, What would ye that I should do for you?

37. They said unto him, Grant unto us that we may sit, one on thy right hand, and the other on thy left hand, in thy glory.

(1) The natural result of extreme ambition is selfishness. What did the sons of Zebedee care for other people? (2) Ambition may not be the less criminal for being associated with religious position and influence. The feeling shown by these men should always be discouraged. There is an earnestness that is fanaticism. The ambition that is unholy is always also unreasonable.

" That the sons of Zebedee wished for ecclesiastical, rather than secular honours, may be thought probable from the allusion that is made here to the supreme dignities in the great Sanhedrin. The prince of the Sanhedrin (HA-NASI) sat in the midst of two rows of senators or elders; on his right hand sat the person termed AB (the father of the Sanhedrin); and on the left the CHACHAM or sage. These persons transacted all business in the absence of the president."—(*Adam Clarke.*)

The sons of Zebedee asked for honour in the kingdom, they did not ask for fellowship in the preliminary suffering. Bengel well remarks : " Very different were those whom our Lord was first to have on his right hand and on his left."

38. But Jesus said unto them, Ye know not what ye ask : can ye drink of the cup that I drink of? and be baptized with the baptism that I am baptized with?

39. And they said unto him, We can. And Jesus said unto them, Ye shall indeed drink of the cup that I drink of; and with the baptism that I am baptized withal shall ye be baptized:

40. But to sit on my right hand and on my left hand is not mine to give; but it shall be given to them for whom it is prepared.

Lange says : " Different views are entertained of this reply." De Wette explains it : " Your request arises from an incorrect view of the character of my kingdom, which is spiritual." Meyer paraphrases : " Ye know not that the highest posts in my kingdom cannot be obtained without sufferings such as I have to endure." Luther says : " The flesh ever seeks to be glorified before it is crucified, exalted before it is abased." Referring to the latter part of verse 40, Adam Clarke says : " The true construction of the words is this : To sit on my right hand and on my left, is not mine to give, except to them for whom it is prepared of my Father." Dr. Clarke argues that the words " it shall be given to them," " are interpolated by our translators." Bishop Horsley says the meaning is, " I cannot arbitrarily give happiness, but must bestow it on those alone for whom, in reward of holiness and obedience, it is prepared, according to God's just decrees."

The practical ideas of the passage might be homiletically expressed thus :—(1) Human ignorance should restrain human ambition,—" ye know not what ye ask ; " (2) human weakness should modify the expression of human confidence,—" are ye able ? they say, we are able ; " (3) human history should be left to the development which God has purposed for it,—" ye shall drink ; ye shall be baptised ; but—— ; " (4) human position will be determined by human character.

41. And when the ten heard it, they began to be much displeased with James and John.

The primary conditions of brotherhood had been violated by the two brethren and their mother, and the ten had a right to be angry. All men who wish to outreach their brethren deserve indignation. Religion does not annihilate anger, it regulates its expressions and penalties. The incident may be homiletically used, as—(1) A warning against an unbrotherly disposition ; and (2) an example of Christ's method of treating unbrotherly men. Jesus Christ does not expel them ; he declares their ignorance, he points out their weakness, he shows that suffering is the portion of those who follow him, and that such suffering is to be endured, apart from promised official position in his kingdom.

42. But Jesus called them to him, and saith unto them, Ye know that they which are accounted to rule over the Gentiles exercise lordship over them ; and their great ones exercise authority upon them.

43. But so shall it not be among you : but whosoever will be great among you, shall be your minister :

44. And whosoever of you will be the chiefest, shall be servant of all.

45. For even the Son of man came not to be ministered unto, but to minister, and to give his life a ransom for many.

This exhortation shows that the spirit of self-abasement is to distinguish the entire course of the Christian life. The Church is not to look to secular governments for precedents or patterns, but to the Son of man alone. The ἄρχοντες were proud, domineering, fond of power, and self-sufficient; nothing could be more foreign to the spirit of Christianity, and this was emphatically the time to say so. Jesus Christ adapted his teaching to the varying phases of human nature; at this time the phase of ambition was uppermost, and the exhortation took its course and tone accordingly. Adaptation is the secret of successful teaching. The teacher who speaks to the line of actual experience will never want a theme, and if his teaching be wise he will never speak without profit to his hearers. (1) Christian influence is not official; (2) Christian influence is spiritual; (3) Christian influence can be legitimately attained only by the Christian spirit,—" whosoever will be great among you let him be your minister (διάκονος), and whosoever will be chief among you let him be your servant (δοῦλος)." It has often been explained that διάκονος means a servant of a superior order, always near his master's person and admitted to a certain degree of his confidence, whereas δοῦλος means a slave, one who may be employed in the most menial service. The distinction, however, is not always maintained in the Christian writings. For example, in Matthew xviii. and 23rd verse, we have a king " which would take an account of his servants (δούλων);" all the officers of Oriental courts were regarded as slaves, but the servants here referred to are the provincial officers employed to collect the revenue for government; in the Persian court they were called *satraps*. In Matthew xxv. 21, the word is used, " Well done, good and faithful servant (δοῦλε)." Without insisting upon any fanciful or even real distinctions between these words, the spirit of the exhortation is perfectly intelligible; abasement is the condition of true and permanent eminence. The simplicity of the condition is not without its dangers, for is it not possible to simulate humility? Is there not a stooping to conquer, which is merely an attitude of the body, not a gesture of the soul? There is an amiability which covers a hard and relentless heart ; there is an outward austerity which may conceal the tenderest geniality of spirit.

The expression, " to give his life a ransom for many," is not to be taken as limiting Jesus Christ's atonement. The atonement is not the subject of discourse ; Jesus Christ is speaking of himself simply as an example of service,—a service so profound and so pure as to include even the surrender of life itself.

The whole address bears upon Christian position, the spirit by which it is to be attained, and in which it is to be held. Jesus Christ is not speaking against secular authority, civil magistracy, and the like ; his remarks are exclusively confined to the affairs of his own kingdom. There must be rulership in civil society, and in religious society as well. Rulership is by no means arbitrary ; it is founded upon the instincts and necessities of human nature. In civil society sovereignty may descend from generation to generation without regard to the fitness of the sovereign ; in Christian society true rulership is a question of character and capacity. The modest, cultivated, intellectual Christian will, in time, attain his proper position. Zealous and foolish mothers may secure for their children an external position of authority, but the real authority will always be held by men who have drunk most deeply into the spirit of Jesus Christ. Such men care nothing for authority for its own sake ; they are not the slaves of officialism ; yet even in the absence of nominal status they wield the profoundest and most durable influence over the thought and sentiment of the Church.

46. And they came to Jericho : and as he went out of Jericho with his disciples and a great number of people, blind Bartimæus, the son of Timæus, sat by the highway side begging.

47. And when he heard that it was Jesus of Nazareth, he began to cry out, and say, Jesus, thou Son of David, have mercy on me.

48. And many charged him that he should hold his peace : but he cried the more a great deal, Thou Son of David, have mercy on me.

49. And Jesus stood still, and commanded him to be called. And they call the blind man, saying unto him, Be of good comfort, rise : he calleth thee.

50. And he, casting away his garment, rose, and came to Jesus.

51. And Jesus answered and said unto him, What wilt thou that I should

do unto thee ? The blind man said unto him, Lord, that I might receive my sight.

52. And Jesus said unto him, Go thy way; thy faith hath made thee whole. And immediately he received his sight, and followed Jesus in the way.

(1) A man representing the side of human life which is marked by deprivation,—no sight, no bread. (2) A man seizing a great opportunity,—" when he heard that it was Jesus of Nazareth." (3) A man resisting the most obstinate difficulties,—" many charged him that he should hold his peace." (4) A man repeating his prayer until the answer came,—" Jesus commanded him to be called." (5) A man stating his own case in his own words, —"Lord, that I might receive my sight." (6) A man turning to a right use the gifts of God,—" he received his sight, and followed Jesus in the way." Application—(1) You are needy; (2) you have heard that Jesus passeth by ; (3) you have sight; how are you using it ?

Chapter x. 23-30.

23. And Jesus looked round about, and saith unto his disciples, How hardly shall they that have riches enter into the kingdom of God!

24. And the disciples were astonished at his words. But Jesus answereth again, and saith unto them, Children, how hard is it for them that trust in riches to enter into the kingdom of God!

25. It is easier for a camel to go through the eye of a needle, than for a rich man to enter into the kingdom of God.

26. And they were astonished out of measure, saying among themselves, Who then can be saved?

27. And Jesus looking upon them saith, With men it is impossible, but not with God: for with God all things are possible.

28. Then Peter began to say unto him, Lo, we have left all, and have followed thee.

29. And Jesus answered and said, Verily I say unto you, There is no man that hath left house, or brethren, or sisters, or father, or mother, or wife, or children, or lands, for my sake, and the gospel's,

30. But he shall receive an hundredfold now in this time, houses, and brethren, and sisters, and mothers, and children, and lands, with persecutions; and in the world to come eternal life.

THE DISCIPLES ASTONISHED.

JESUS CHRIST is here moralising; that is to say, turning an incident to moral and spiritual account and use. He is musing aloud. The little transient anecdote has passed, but Jesus Christ's doctrine respecting the event abides for ever, an eternal voice in the Church. Mark is the only writer who takes notice of the look and gesture of our Lord on this memorable occasion. We have noted often that Mark is the one who takes most notice of the Lord's looks,* as if the devoted disciple never turned his eyes away from the Lord's expressive face; as if indeed the tongue could not say all that Christ wanted to say; as if he who would know the Lord's meaning wholly must keep his eyes steadfastly on the Lord's countenance. Although Jesus Christ is moralising, he is not conceding anything. He does not call the young, rich man back, and say, You can take this kingdom upon your own terms. Jesus Christ does not build up his party

---

* See "The Silent Looks of Christ," *post*, p. 176.

or Church or society by compromise.   The Lord's Church is a
Church of the Cross, a society of crucified hearts.   No man is in
the Church who has not been crucified.   He may be inquiring
about the Church; he may even entertain admiration for the
framework and general policy of the Church; but he is not
inside until he has entered by the door of the Cross.   There
is no other door.   We are crucified with Christ, or we are
not in his society.   Who, then, is in the Church?   We must lay
emphasis upon this word " hardly," so as to get out of it the
meaning—with what infinite difficulty shall they that have riches
enter into the kingdom of God.   They will barely get in ; they
will hardly be in at all ; if they do enter in it will be by an
agony not to be expressed in words.   It is much to have a Lord
that recognises difficulties.   This Lord of ours is not one who, by
a wave of the hand, passes men into the Church ; he says, It is
hard work getting into the kingdom of God ; it is difficult to give
up one world for another.   Here is the one world ; it is visible,
tangible, what we call real (though therein we are false), what
we call certain (though therein we repeat our falsehood).   Where
is the kingdom of God ?   When you have found God you will
find his kingdom.   The kingdom of God is not in meat or in
drink; the kingdom of God cometh not with observation ; the
kingdom of God is not a visible framework which men can estimate and walk around and form opinions about ; the kingdom of
God is a new consciousness, a new selfhood, a new creatureship,
a new life, the beginning and pledge of eternity.   If the kingdom
of God were a set of doctrines which we could buy or appropriate
or understand, we might as well have that kingdom as not have
it ; for it amounts to nothing more than assenting to a number of
things which other men have written at the dictation of other
men ages past, and if there is anything in it we may as well have
it.   That is not the kingdom of God ; that is a make-up of man's
own ; the kingdom of God is spiritual, penetrative, vital ; changing
the spirit, changing the soul.   If any man be in Christ Jesus, he
is a new creature; the old self is not only dead, but buried,
forgotten ; every thought, every impulse, every desire is new.
If the Lord did not recognise difficulties some of us could not live.
It is hard for some men to pray ; it is good for you to whom it
is hard if you can get as far in prayer as " Our Father."   If you

put a full-stop there it will be taken as if other men had spoken all the prayer, clear away down to the resonant and grateful Amen. That is all you could do. You did that with difficulty; you are of the earth earthy; you love the world, you hug the dust, you are the victims of the senses: yet there is just one feeble ray of the upper light struggling with the darkness of your materialism, and you have got as by miracle and agony to " Our Father." It is easy for other men to pray ; prayer becomes their native tongue: silence to them would be penalty ; they must speak devotional language, fall into devotional attitudes, and their very sighing is attuned to a religious emphasis. But it is hard for such men in some cases to give. That is their curse ; they will pray with you all day, but they will not give you anything. It is easy for some men to give time, advice, sympathy; but it is impossible for them to give money. It is easy to others to give money, but they cannot or will not give time ; they are busy, busy—doing nothing ; busy wasting their lives ; busy pursuing nothing, and overtaking it. One man's difficulty is another man's pleasure. For want of this discrimination we have talked in cruel generalities, so that they to whom another feather's weight would become a burden intolerable, have been distressed for want of that fine discrimination which separates character from character, not in vulgar lumpishness, but in fine gradation, in exquisite weight and balance.

" How hardly shall they that have riches enter into the kingdom of God." Then is it easy for poverty to enter that kingdom ? It is as difficult for poverty to get in as for wealth to get in. There is no virtue in poverty ; there is no vice in wealth. The more the good man has the better. I pray that every good man may become just as rich as he can bear to be, and yet retain his piety, because the more he has the more the poor have ; he is only treasurer, steward, custodian for Christ. How hardly, with what difficulty, shall they that have any kind of riches enter into the kingdom of God ! Do not limit the word " riches " to the word " money." There are many kinds of riches, and all kinds of riches constitute difficulties in the way of spiritualisation. The poorest, commonest kind of wealth is money. Some are wealthy in morality. They can never see the kingdom of God. No " good " man can enter the kingdom of God : his goodness will be the ruin of him. Here is a young man who has kept all the commandments ; not a day or a week, but all his life ; handled them with consummate ease, made familiars of them, pets, idols ; done them over and over again, could not help doing them, liked to do them. Was he in the kingdom of God ? He was not within millions of leagues of that dominion of light and love and liberty, growth and progress and beauty, sweetness and security, benevolence divine. The difficulty is that some persons cannot distinguish between morality and Christianity. Morality is a question of manner. Etymologically, " morals " is a word which means manners ; it means indeed manners that might be limited by attitudes, relations of an external and mechanical kind. Does piety of the true sort, then, exclude morality ? Nay, verily, it includes it and glorifies it ; puts it in its right place ; divests it of all propitiatory value, and looks upon it as a necessity, arising spontaneously out of vital relations with God. It is not to be exhumed, it is to be emitted as flowers emit their fragrance. Persons who are rich in their respectability are not in the Church ; persons who can sneer at the ill-behaviour of others are not in the Church ; people who can point a finger of scorn at an erring life are not in the Church of Christ ; people who are so noble as never to forgive have nothing to do with Christ, and ought never to mention his name by way of profession. There are men who are theologically exact enough to preside over a theological perdition, but who are not Christians ; they can hold grudges in their hearts against other men. The man who can hold a grudge cannot pray ; no prayer can get through a throat stuffed with that wool. We know nothing about this kingdom of God as revealed in Christ until we are prepared to be crucified in every finger, in every hair of the head, and to have spear-thrusts all over the life. Who, then, is in the kingdom of God ? O thou cruel question, ring on ! we cannot answer thee. Some are rich in ancestry. They are the most difficult persons in the world to deal with ; they are nothing in themselves, but, oh, how grand they are in their predecessors, who in their turn were nothing, but grand in their progenitors. The most curious part of the psychology of such a case is that such people are often as humble as humility itself in ninety-nine points, but on the hundredth point the sky is not blue enough to shine upon them, and the sun acquires his dignity through lighting them to their occupation. All this must be cut off, or there will be no kingdom of God. Little mechanical morals, musty antiquated respecta- bility, and even intellectual genius, and money, must all be cut off, one after the other, or all together : such tumours overswell the man, so that he cannot crush himself into God's narrow door. This is Christianity.

Look at the poor disciples! "They were astonished at his words;" and again (ver. 26), "And they were astonished out of measure." What a difference between the Lord and his followers! Jesus Christ spoke from an altitude that made the whole universe on a level; but those who were dwelling a thousand worlds lower down in the great house of space were amazed and bewildered, embarrassed and overwhelmed, by everything the great Lord said. This is not wholly to be deprecated. Even astonishment has a part to play in our spiritual education. When we have reached the *nil admirari* stage of development, at which we wonder at nothing, we might as well have the extinguisher placed upon us, for the universe is played out, and creation is underfoot, a thing without value, fascination, or utility. Blessed is he who keeps his astonishment young, fresh, expressive; happy in perpetual estival is he who still loves the wayside flowers, and who when he sees the first violet exclaims as if he had seen a new planet. Do not let little things lose their charm; do not allow spring to come back with her lapful of simple beautiful field-flowers and you take no notice of the largess; welcome the vernal queen. What she brings is from heaven: all flowers grow there; here they are exotics: let them take you back, by progress, beauty, suggestion, unspoken sympathy, to their native clime : flowers are the thoughts of God. At the same time our piety must pass beyond the stage of astonishment, and find its rest in the point of service. Christianity must renew its youth by giving itself away for the benefit of others.

How impossible it is to crush all self-consciousness out of men! No sooner had Peter heard this discourse, so tender in its eloquence, than he began to say unto the Lord, "Lo, we have left all." Think of Peter's "all"! How long would it take to write an inventory of that fisherman's "all"? Yet he pronounced. the word "all" with such elongated emphasis that anybody would have thought he had really made some sacrifice for Christ. How nobly did the Saviour reply; how he blotted out Peter's contribution; how he made the senior apostle ashamed of himself, as he "answered and said, Verily I say unto you, There is no man that hath left house, or brethren, or sisters, or father, or mother, or wife, or children, or lands, for my sake, and the gospel's, but he shall receive an hundredfold now in this time, houses, and brethren, and sisters, and mothers, and children, and lands, with persecutions; and in the world to come eternal life." Every man is overpaid. Here we see the right use of religious hyperbole or exaggeration. Think of a man having a hundred mothers! Jesus Christ often uses self-correcting phrases. The Lord often puts our lessons at the point of impossibility, that we may next drop to the point of reality. "An hundredfold now in this time, houses, and brethren, and sisters, and mothers, and children, and lands." Every Christian has these; the realisation is already accomplished. All houses belong to the Christian heart; all children belong to the regenerated, Christ-expressing soul; the last born into the family of God owns creation: other ownership is legal, nominal, mechanical. The poet holds the landscape, and no other man ever did hold it; the Christian holds all wheatfields and vineyards, the cattle upon a thousand hills are his; nay, saith Paul, when we are counting up our little riches, all things are yours, angels, and principalities, and powers, and things present, and things to come, and height and depth, and life and death, are yours. We do not realise our possessions; we turn whiningly away from infinite riches, and groan because the body has certain wants which cannot be instantaneously appeased or satisfied. We must live in divine exultancy; we must find our riches in God. Herein is it true that no good soul can ever be poor; herein is the twenty-third psalm the psalm of life—"The Lord is my shepherd; I shall not want."

Chapter xi. 1-19.

CHRIST'S ROYALTY.

[An Analysis.]

1. And when they came nigh to Jerusalem, unto Bethphage and Bethany, at the mount of Olives, he sendeth forth two of his disciples.

2. And saith unto them, Go your way into the village over against you: and as soon as ye be entered into it, ye shall find a colt tied, whereon never man sat; loose him, and bring him.

3. And if any man say unto you, Why do ye this? say ye that the Lord hath need of him; and straightway he will send him hither.

4. And they went their way, and found the colt tied by the door without in a place where two ways met; and they loose him.

5. And certain of them that stood there said unto them, What do ye, loosing the colt?

6. And they said unto them even as Jesus had commanded: and they let them go.

7. And they brought the colt to Jesus, and cast their garments on him; and he sat upon him.

8. And many spread their garments in the way: and others cut down branches off the trees, and strawed them in the way.

9. And they that went before, and they that followed, cried, saying, Hosanna; Blessed is he that cometh in the name of the Lord:

10. Blessed be the kingdom of our father David, that cometh in the name of the Lord: Hosanna in the highest.

11. And Jesus entered into Jerusalem, and into the temple: and when he had looked round about upon all things, and now the eventide was come, he went out unto Bethany with the twelve.

FOR homiletic purposes the narrative may be used to show the features which will characterise the day of Christ's recognised royalty. When Christ's royalty is fully recognised—

(1) All possessions will be consecrated to his service. Jesus Christ gave his disciples a word whose power was to overcome all hesitation on the part of the owners of the colt; that word was—"The Lord hath need of them." The expression itself is peculiar. Why should the Lord have need? Strange combina-

tion of ideas—lordship and necessity ! Yet, on the other hand, what necessity can he have who has but to express it in order to have it satisfied ? By a legitimate exercise of fancy, we may amplify the idea and include all orders of men, all degrees of talent, all capacities of endurance and activity. Say to the poet, the painter, the musician, the orator, the rich man, the man of influence, "the Lord hath need of thee," and there will be instantaneous and grateful response !

When Christ's royalty is fully recognised—

(2) All the services of Christ will become the subjects of ardent and universal praise. According to Luke, "the whole multitude began to rejoice and praise God with a loud voice for all the mighty works that they had seen." (1) The true worker will eventually be recognised ; (2) works will be the basis of just and permanent elevation ; (3) God will be praised as the fontal source of all true benefaction,—the multitude praised God.

When Christ's royalty is fully recognised—

(3) His essential greatness will overcome his momentary humiliation. "Blessed be the King that cometh." (Trace Jesus Christ's life, and show how much there was in it to depress and crush ; yet, through all, there is a shining of his divine lustre.) In addition to doing this a contrast may be drawn between what is transient and what is permanent in the Messianic life : poverty, sorrow, humiliation, all kinds of social and temporal disadvantage, on the one hand ; on the other, riches, rapture, exaltation above every created height, and all the honour and homage of the universe.

When Christ's royalty is fully recognised—

(4) Religious enthusiasm will overwhelm or absorb all Pharisaic formality. According to Luke, "Some of the Pharisees from among the multitude said unto him, Master, rebuke thy disciples ; and he answered and said unto them, I tell you that, if these should hold their peace, the stones would immediately cry out." Enthusiasm is natural ; stoicism is unnatural. When the soul is inspired, the lips must speak. About enthusiasm three things should be remarked : (1) That it is essential to success in all pursuits ; (2) that it reaches its highest intensity in the development of the religious life ; (3) that its suppression would excite the reproaches of nature.

The whole scene shows the effect of a true view of Jesus Christ upon the heart of man. Such a view transports the soul with the holiest delight, and draws the worshipper, even while in the poverty and feebleness of the body, nearly into the ecstasy of the heavenly worshippers. The scene gives a hint of the joy which shall one day fill the hearts of all men.

12. And on the morrow, when they were come from Bethany, he was hungry:

13. And seeing a fig tree afar off having leaves, he came, if haply he might find any thing thereon: and when he came to it, he found nothing but leaves; for the time of figs was not yet.

14. And Jesus answered and said unto it, No man eat fruit of thee hereafter for ever. And his disciples heard it.

This incident may be homiletically used to show: (1) The doom of those things which do not meet the wants of the time; (2) the terrific prospect of meeting a disappointed Christ; (3) the perfect dominion of the spiritual over the material; (4) the vast possibilities of undoubting prayer.

Olshausen has some striking observations as to the cursing of the fig-tree: "The difficulty is diminished here, if we understand by it that kind of figs which remain hanging on the branches all winter, and are gathered in early spring. In that case, the sense of the words would be this—while the common kind of figs were not yet ripe, and the time for gathering them in had not come, Jesus yet perceived that this tree on which he sought for figs belonged to that other kind, which bore at that time ripe and refreshing fruit, and thus he could rightly expect figs on the tree."

15. And they come to Jerusalem: and Jesus went into the temple, and began to cast out them that sold and bought in the temple, and overthrew the tables of the moneychangers, and the seats of them that sold doves;

16. And would not suffer that any man should carry any vessel through the temple.

17. And he taught, saying unto them, Is it not written, My house shall be called of all nations the house of prayer? but ye have made it a den of thieves.

18. And the scribes and chief priests heard it, and sought how they might destroy him: for they feared him, because all the people was astonished at his doctrine.

19. And when even was come, he went out of the city.

These verses, taken in combination, present a vivid view of

Christ's twofold method of conducting his ministry : that method
was first destructive, then constructive.   About the cleansing of
the temple four things are noticeable : (1) Jesus Christ did not
connive at abuses for the sake of securing popular favour; (2)
Jesus Christ did not allow abuses to be continued on the ground
that the circumstances were temporary,—he knew that the
temple was soon to be destroyed ; (3) Jesus Christ showed that
man's convenience was to be subordinated to God's right,—" my
house is the house of prayer " (Luke xix. 46); (4) Jesus Christ
showed in this, as in all other cases, that the right one is morally
stronger than the wicked many.   The healing " the blind and the
lame " (Matt. xxi. 14) occurs most impressively in this connection ;
after anger came peace ; after an assault upon strength came a
gentle ministry upon weakness.   The incident may be separately
treated, as showing: (1) That the temple is spiritual not in
an exclusive but in an inclusive sense,—the wants of the spirit
include the necessities of the body; praying included healing,
but money-changing did not include praying ; and (2) that society
should be taught to connect the temple with the most benevolent,
practical, and spiritual ideas.   It is a great error in any com-
munity to shut up the house of God six days out of seven.   When
society is penetrated with true Christianity, the house of God
will be a library, a hospital, a school, and a prayer-house, all in
one.

Chapter xi. 11.

"And Jesus entered into Jerusalem, and into the temple; and when he had looked round about upon all things, he went out."

THE SILENT LOOKS OF CHRIST.

THIS is one of the passages of Scripture that the reader may easily pass without allowing his attention to be sufficiently arrested. The *singularity* of this act will not escape your notice now that the verse is read as a text. Jesus Christ entered into the city, and into the temple; merely looked round about upon all things, and went out. The *comprehensiveness* of this act will make you feel as if you were girt about with eyes. Jesus Christ entered into the city and into the temple, and looked round about upon *all* things. The great things, and things minute and obscure and comparatively worthless. If he thought it worth while to create the daisy, will it be beneath him to stop and look at the little beauty which he painted? We do not look upon *all* things. We look upon faces, surfaces, transient aspects of things; but Jesus looks into spirit, purpose, motive, heart, impulse, will, and all the secrets of that supreme mystery amongst us called human life.

The *silence* of this act will almost affright you. Jesus came into the city, looked round about upon all things, and did not say one word. That is terrible! When men speak to me, I can in some measure understand what they are aiming at. But there are some looks, even amongst ourselves, that are mysteries; there are some glances shot from human eyes that trouble the beholder! Can guilt bear the lingering enquiring gaze of innocence? Does not the corrupt man fear the eye of the just man more than he would fear the lightning at midnight? May not that look *mean* so much, even if it be a look of unsuspicion and of entire ignorance, so far as the immediate circumstances are concerned? Yet it *may* mean so much; and that potential mood is the hell of the bad man.

176

You see, then, that our text leads us to look, not at the miracles and words of Jesus Christ, but to study his *looks*, as indications of his character. And it may be profitable, after we have spent some time in examining the eyes of the Saviour, to enquire how we should *return* the looks that are so full of meaning. The subject is, *The Silent Looks of the Son of God!*

In reading the Evangelists, have you ever noticed that Mark above all the other writers, takes note of the looks of the Saviour? Different men see different phases of the same object. Luke began his Gospel by saying that he was going to tell Theophilus *everything*. Who can tell everything about the Son of God? I speak not only for myself, but for every minister in this house, and, I believe, for the whole Church of God, in saying that, after we have written our sermons and our books, the thing that strikes us most is their *emptiness*. We seem to have missed the very point we intended to indicate, and when we have ceased our talk and our effort, there comes upon us a sense of having ill done what we aimed to do, and we feel as if we had not yet begun the story that is as a centre without a circumference.

"And Jesus looked round about" (Mark x. 23). It would appear that Jesus Christ's look was, then, a *circular look*. Instead of fixing his eye upon one point, he fixed his vision upon all points, and, as it were, at the same moment of time. "And Jesus looked round about." This is an action specifically by itself. "And having looked round he saith unto his disciples, How hardly shall they that have riches enter into the kingdom of heaven!" The look of the preacher should mean something. Earnest men should have a look peculiarly their own. What, my friend, if thy sermon has failed to take effect because thy face gave the lie to thy voice? There are looks *and* looks. When will men discriminate between things that differ? when will they cease to regard all things as alike? and when will the time come when men can see *meanings* even in unlikely things? I have seen on the plainest faces looks that had soul in them. I have seen poor people look at me, in telling the story of their trouble, in a way that has gone to my very heart, and melted it in tender sympathy with their sufferings. I have seen persons to whom intelligence of a startling nature has been brought—intelligence of broken fortune, of expired friends—who could not say one word, and yet I had rather seen a tiger than the look of disappointment and shame and fear and pity that I have seen upon some human faces. Go and tell a man who is laughing—innocently laughing—that his only child has been found dead on the roadside. The man does not *talk* to you, except with his eyes and his face. There is no storm so terrible as the darkening and the raining of grief! Jesus Christ accompanied his words with a look, and sometimes left his look unaccompanied by a word.

"But when he had turned about and looked on his disciples, he rebuked Peter." He looked them all into attention, and then gave them the lesson. Is he not looking here to-day? Should there be any turned heads amongst us, any indifferent eyes, any careless hearts? I thank God I believe that so many people as I see before me would not come together at twelve o'clock without earnestness in their hearts regarding this ministration of the gospel. Observe the peculiarity of the occasion. "When he had turned about, and looked on his disciples, he rebuked Peter." The look was a general caution; the rebuke was an individual application. The look was as a common judgment; the rebuke was a personal law. Jesus looks when he does not rebuke, but he never rebukes without looking. My friend, thou wouldst see more of the eye of God if thou wouldst drop the scales from thine own. But my subject is the *silent* looks of the Saviour. Luke, in his twenty-second chapter, indicates a remarkable instance of such looks—viz., "*The Lord turned and looked upon Peter.*" Did he speak? No. Did he cry out, "Shame!" No. What did he do? He turned and *looked* upon Peter, and broke the man's heart. May he break our hearts in the same way ere he cut us in pieces with the sword of his anger, and utterly slay us with the breath of his judgment! He had told Peter that before the cock crowed he would deny his Master three times. Peter had just given the third denial; immediately the cock crowed. The Lord turned and looked upon Peter, and Peter's heart of rock melted into a river of tears. What was there in the look? Does the eye of Jesus look memories at us? broken vows, oaths, pledges? Is the eye of the Saviour like a mirror, in which a man may see himself ?   Is the eye of Jesus Christ terrible as a sword of judgment, that it can cut to the dividing asunder of the joints and marrow of a man ?

Mark gives us another silent look in his third chapter and fifth verse. " And when Jesus had looked round about on them with anger, being grieved for the hardness of their hearts, he saith unto the man, Stretch forth thine hand." He said nothing to the individuals themselves ; he only looked round about on them with anger.   I have heard of the sword that flamed in Eden, that moved from the east to the west, and back again, night and day. But oh, I could have run through that sword, methinks, compared with this circle of fiery anger which now surrounded the Son of God ! anger of the most terrible kind, —anger arising out of *grief.* The anger of malice who cares for ?   The anger of mortified pride, vanity, ambition—who heeds it ?   The anger of mere selfishness,—what is the meaning of that ?   But when *grief* turns to anger ; when *love* itself becomes wrath,—who can abide the day of its coming?   Is there anything so terrible as " the wrath of the Lamb "—that greatest contradiction in words, apparently, yet that consummation of purest anger in reality ?   " The Lord looketh on the heart."   The Lord is *always* looking.   He looketh from heaven, and beholdeth the children of men.   The Lord looked to see if there were any that feared him, and that honoured his name.   There is no *protection* from his eye.   This is a terrible statement to be delivered to the bad man !   You are never alone ! When you think you are alone, your solitude is but relative.   You can take the thinnest veil and hide yourself from men, but who can hide himself behind impenetrable curtains and screenings from the eye of fire ?   All things are naked and open unto the eyes of him with whom we have to do !   " Whither shall I flee from thy presence ? "   The question is unanswered and unanswerable.   God fills the universe, overflows infinitude, and thou canst not escape his eye !   I think I have heard something before of this silent look.   You may recall it.   When I read in the Apocalypse, as I have just read our morning lesson, about John seeing, on the Isle of Patmos, eyes like a flame of fire, I felt that I had read something like that before.   Where ?   Can you tell me ? Young friends, who are supposed to have just read the Bible, you who have the youngest, tenderest, freshest memories, can you

tell me? Where? You read something like it in the Book of
Exodus. The eye of the Lord never dims. If you have once
read of it, you never can forget it ; if you have once seen it, it is
an eternal presence !

When the Egyptians pursued Israel, and there was a halt made,
a cloud came between the Israelites and the Egyptians ; the one
side was brightness—that is on the side towards the Israelites—
and the other side was darkness ; *and the Lord looked out of the
cloud and troubled the Egyptians !* Have I your attention? Do
you follow me? The Lord *looked* out of the cloud and troubled
the Egyptians, and his glory struck off the iron from the wheels of
their chariots, and they were dismayed ! Not a word was spoken ;
there was no thunder in the air. What was it then that troubled
haughty Egypt, proud of her resources, fat with the marrow of her
accursed victories over a bound people,—what was it that troubled
the haughty queen? It was a look, *a silent* look ! An argument
could have been answered mayhap : if not answered, it could
have been replied to. But a *look !* who could return it? When
the lightning strikes a man, who can look at it? Ay, when the
summer sun goes behind a cloud, as it were, and suddenly strikes
down upon the lookers up, who can bear the sting of his fire. So,
then, you will find that the eyes of the Lord are often spoken of
in the holy Book. Are these eyes *terrible* then? May any one
look at them? Herein is the mercy of the Lord seen. What is
terrible is also gentle. "Our God is a consuming fire !" "God
is love !" "He numbereth the stars !" "He bindeth up the
broken in heart !" He walketh upon the wings of the wind, and
the clouds are as the dust of his feet, and his utterance shakes the
kingdoms and dominions of the universe ! Yet not a sparrow
falleth to the ground without your Father's notice ! If the looks
are terrible they can also be benign. Hear the proof of this : " I
will guide thee with mine eye." Lord, what is the history of thine
eye? the eye that troubled Egypt, and struck off the iron from
the chariot-wheels of the host of Pharaoh? the eye that divided the
waters, and made them stand back, that the Lord might pass in
the person of his chosen one? "I will guide thee with mine eye."
The eye that makes day, and summer, and beauty, and the eternal
light ! Behold the goodness and severity of God ! "I have
heard," said the Psalmist, "that power belongeth unto God !"

And he trembled, and he took up his pen again, and wrote, " To thee also, O Lord, belongeth mercy ! " Omnipotence in the hand of mercy is the idea of righteous government. So the eyes of the Lord are very terrible. Flames of fire are the only symbols by which they can be likened amongst us ; but they are also gentle, melting with dewy tenderness, yearning with unutterable pity ; looking out for us ; watching our home coming, looking over the hills and along the curving valleys, if haply they may see somewhat of the shadow of the returning child !

Will it not be profitable for us now to enquire : If such be the looks of God the Father and the Son, how should we *return* looks that are so full of significance and purpose ? Are we not able to use our eyes to advantage ? Hear the Word of the Lord. " *Look* unto me, and be ye saved, all ye ends of the earth." How ? Look not with the eyes of the body, nor with curiosity ; but with reverence, with eagerness of heart, with determination of love, with all the urgency and importunity of conscious need. He asks us to look ; to look at himself ; to look at himself, not on the Throne of Judgment, but in his capacity as Redeemer and Saviour of the world. Have you looked ? Pause ! There is no need to be in haste. Have you *looked?* Observe our earliest lesson this morning—viz., there is looking *and* looking. I have seen a dog look towards the sun, but he saw it not ! The beast always seems to be looking upon the flowers of the meadow, but it is not seeing them ! Have you *looked* with your *heart*, with your hunger, with your urgent need ? Have you looked with that expectant, piercing look that means, " I *will* see " ? " Yes," says one of my hearers, " I have looked, and I have a comfortable sense of having seen the Lord ; but I get so weary, and jaded, and worn out by the difficulties, frets, temptations, and chafings of this earthly life, that sometimes I do not know what to do." Then let me tell you what to do. If, for a moment, I have the advantage of you, I will use my advantage to teach and comfort you, if I can. You are weary, worn, dispirited, tempted, discouraged, and do not know how to go on. Go on thus—*looking unto Jesus !* You will see how the various texts belong to one another, and constitute one piece of solid religious teaching. *Looking* unto Jesus. Returning the look of the Saviour. Not a hasty glance, but a steady, importunate, eager, penetrating " looking for." And he is only behind a veil.   If you did but know it, there is hardly a cloud between !   He will come from behind, and say to the heart that has waited for him, " For a small moment I have forsaken thee, but with everlasting mercies will I gather thee."   It was better to have that small moment.   There may be a monotony of kindness, a monotony of light.   Better to have a momentary sense of orphanage, and then to be embraced with a still fonder clasp by the infinite love of the eternal heart !

Look unto Jesus even through your tears.   Tears are telescopes. I have seen further through my tears than ever I saw through my smiles.   Laughter hath done but little for me; but sorrow and a riven heart have expounded many passages in the inspired volume that before were hard, enigmatical reading.   Blessed be God, we can see Jesus through our tears.   He knows what tears are.   Jesus wept!   The eyes that John saw as a flame of fire the Jews at the grave of Lazarus saw as fountains of water.   "And coming near unto the city, when he beheld it, he wept over it."   No man can fathom the depth of that river, or tell the bitterness of that sorrow. You have tears.   Every man amongst us has his tearful times. But we use our tears wrongfully if we do not lift up our eyes and look through them unto Jesus in the heavens!   So much for the comfortable side of this.   Dare I turn to the other side?   Surely, for I am a steward only.   May I say another word that shall not be so tender?   Surely, for I am an echo, not a voice.   Am I here to make a Bible for the comforting and soothing of men, and not to expound a Bible that looks all ways, and pierces all things?   If I now speak with apparent harshness, believe me that it is a cry of pain, that I may bring some men to consideration and decision in a right direction.   My subject is the silent looks of the Saviour—the silent looks of God—and the method in which men are to return the glances of the divine eyes.   Let me say that those who will not look now *shall* look !   The great sight shall not perish from the horizon without their beholding it.   Hear these words—"They shall look upon me whom they have pierced ! They would not look upon me, but they *shall* do so !"   The great cross shall not be taken up and set away in the heavens as a centre of holy fellowship without those who despised it having one look at it !   What will be the consequence of their looking ?   They shall look upon him whom they have pierced, and mourn !   The look was too late; the look was not in time. You have put your fingers in your ears while the sweet music of the Gospel has been appealing for the attention of your heart; you have shut your eyes when the king has come in to show you his beauty. But he says he will not break up this scheme of things without every eye beholding! Every eye shall see him, and they also that pierced him shall look upon him. Shall I add another word that no human tongue is fit to speak? How shall I utter it? If I could let my heart say it, I would. But it must be spoken with all the incompetence and brokenness of the voice. There shall be a cry in the latter time, and the cry shall be this—" Hide us from the face of him that sitteth on the throne!" Hide us! What from? " The sword?" No. " The terrible phenomena?" No. But from the *face*—that anguished face, that smitten face, that insulted face! Oh! I see the marks the thorns made! I see the red streaks upon it that I made when I smote him in the face and said, "Prophesy!" Oh, hide us from the face of him that sitteth on the throne! Shall it come to this? Is he not the fairest among ten thousand and altogether lovely? Is there any one whose beauty is to be compared with his? You say, " Our God is love." Yes, " Our God is a consuming fire!" You say, " The eyes of the Lord are a comfort to his people." So they are. But the eye of the Lord struck off the iron from the wheels of the Egyptians on the night I have just spoken about.

We shall have to look: the only question is, how? Are we prepared for his coming? How are we prepared for his face? By going to his Cross. He proposes that we should meet him in his weakness. He appoints the place. He says, " Meet me where I am weakest; when my right hand is maimed, and my left, when my feet are pierced with iron, and my side is gashed with steel, and my temples are crushed with cruel thorns,—meet me there!" Then having met him there, when the Son of man shall come in his glory, and all his holy angels with him, he will be the same Saviour, as gentle and as pitiful as ever. And now, the Lord's hands are his again, he will use them for the opening of the door of his kingdom, and the lifting up of all who put their trust in him!

Chapter xii.

JESUS CHRIST'S METHODS OF TEACHING.

1. And he began to speak unto them by parables. A certain man planted a vineyard, and set an hedge about it, and digged a place for the winefat, and built a tower, and let it out to husbandmen, and went into a far country.

2. And at the season he sent to the husbandmen a servant, that he might receive from the husbandmen of the fruit of the vineyard.

3. And they caught him, and beat him, and sent him away empty.

4. And again he sent unto them another servant; and at him they cast stones, and wounded him in the head, and sent him away shamefully handled.

5. And again he sent another; and him they killed, and many others; beating some, and killing some.

6. Having yet therefore one son, his wellbeloved, he sent him also last unto them, saying, They will reverence my son.

7. But those husbandmen said among themselves, This is the heir; come, let us kill him, and the inheritance shall be ours.

8. And they took him, and killed him, and cast him out of the vineyard.

9. What shall therefore the lord of the vineyard do? he will come and destroy the husbandmen, and will give the vineyard unto others.

10. And have ye not read this Scripture; The stone which the builders rejected is become the head of the corner:

11. This was the Lord's doing, and it is marvellous in our eyes?

12. And they sought to lay hold on him, but feared the people: for they knew that he had spoken the parable against them: and they left him, and went their way.

INSTEAD of telling men their faults in so many words, Jesus Christ often set forth a parable which avoided personality, and yet vividly represented the features which he wished to correct or condemn ; not only so, he drew men into a condemnation of themselves by showing their own conduct at such a distance as brought a new light upon it. The parable before us is a case in point. The people having heard the parable, " knew that he had spoken it against them." There is a moral interpreter in every man's heart.

In this parable we have—

(1) A striking way of teaching the highest truths. For the moment Jesus Christ turns aside from what is distinctively religious, and assumes a case which might occur in ordinary life. Here are men in certain business relations : they act in such and such a manner : what do you think of their conduct under such circumstances ? Jesus thus begins on common ground. There is not a word of what is ordinarily known as religion in his statement, and yet his inferences are directed to the highest spiritual ends. This is a striking way of teaching truth. Begin with men on their own ground ; force them to apply their own conclusions ; show them that they must either accept Christianity or give the lie to their own reason. Thus : Men complain that without faith it is impossible to please God ; but why should they so complain when, as a matter of fact, it is just as impossible to please themselves without faith ? Or again : Men say, why does not God give us all we need without our having to pray ? when they act daily on this very principle of prayer in relation to their own children ! So throughout the whole scheme : if men would but narrowly look into their own way of doing things, they would find in the human a germ of the divine. Christianity completes and glorifies human reason, and never impairs or dishonours it. This striking way of teaching the highest truths is open to all Christian teachers. They must study human nature, and show men the full meaning of the partial moralities which are too often mistaken for perfect righteousness.

(2) A vindication of the simple justice of God's claim upon mankind. Look at the reasonableness of the case as shown in the figure of the vineyard. The vineyard belonged to the man ; he did all that was necessary for its protection and cultivation ; and at the season he sent for the fruit. On these simple lines God finds foundation enough for his claim upon the homage and love of the world. (1) Here is proprietorship : " All souls are mine." (2) Here is culture : " What more could I have done for my vineyard that I have not done ? " " He maketh his sun to rise," etc. (3) Here is reasonable expectation : " At the season he sent to the husbandmen a servant, that he might receive from the husbandmen of the fruit of the vineyard." This is God's case in relation to ourselves. We cannot get out of it.

We are imprisoned by our own reason, and the measure of our sanity is the standard of our obligation.

(3) A gracious view of malignant behaviour. The owner of the vineyard did not take vengeance at first. He gave the husbandmen the benefit of every doubt. The servant might have acted unwisely, so he sent another; the second might have brought himself under just condemnation, so he sent a third; and so on until the bitter end. God is slow to anger. Judgment is his strange work. Is he quick to mark our iniquities, and eager to bring down upon us his terrible sword? But see how bad behaviour encourages and strengthens itself in wickedness! The husbandmen beat the first, they wounded the second, they killed the third! Vice emboldens itself quickly. The youth who laughs at an oath to-day will himself blaspheme openly to-morrow. There is a lesson here to those who neglect sermons, or undervalue opportunities, or treat slightingly all good advice. See the culmination! The men who began by beating a servant ended by killing the Son! This is not exceptional. It is the natural and necessary course of sin.

(4) An assurance of just vengeance upon all bad men. The Lord of the vineyard will come and destroy the husbandmen, and will give the vineyard unto others. According to the account given by Matthew, the men who heard the parable pronounced the judgment themselves. When Christ asked what the Lord of the vineyard would do, the people answered, "He will miserably destroy those wicked men, and will let out his vineyard unto other husbandmen, which shall render him their fruits in their seasons." This is a solemn fact, viz., that men will judge themselves, and pronounce the heavenly vengeance just. The wicked will say Amen to their own condemnation! In the long run the sense of justice that is in every man will assert itself, and acknowledge the righteousness of God.

13. And they send unto him certain of the Pharisees and of the Herodians, to catch him in his words.

14. And when they were come, they say unto him, Master, we know that thou art true, and carest for no man: for thou regardest not the person of men, but teachest the way of God in truth: Is it lawful to give tribute to Cæsar, or not?

15. Shall we give, or shall we not give? But he, knowing their hypocrisy, said unto them, Why tempt ye me? bring me a penny, that I may see it.

16. And they brought it. And he saith unto them, Whose is this image and superscription? And they said unto him, Cæsar's.

17. And Jesus answering said unto them, Render to Cæsar the things that are Cæsar's, and to God the things that are God's. And they marvelled at him.

(1) Flattery missing its aim. Sin of all kinds always misses its aim; its apparent successes are all momentary and unsatisfactory. Sincerity can see through flattery. When a man is right in his own heart the words of other men cannot do him any harm. Flattery is poison to the weak, but it has no effect upon the strong. (2) Patriotism directed by righteousness. "Render to Cæsar the things that are Cæsar's." Be honest. Whenever there is a claim honestly made it must be honestly met. (3) The twofold duty of man pointed out : to Cæsar,—to God. He who fulfils his obligations to God fulfils them also of necessity to man. The greater includes the less. Religion does not hold political obligations in contempt. Prayer and taxation must go together so long as we are citizens and subjects as well as saints. (4) Insincerity turned into reality. "And they marvelled at him." There was no pretence about this wonder. The answer stunned the flatterers, and brought to their cheeks every drop of real blood that was in them. Who can stun like the Almighty!

18. Then come unto him the Sadducees, which say there is no resurrection; and they asked him, saying,

19. Master, Moses wrote unto us, If a man's brother die, and leave his wife behind him, and leave no children, that his brother should take his wife, and raise up seed unto his brother.

20. Now there were seven brethren : and the first took a wife, and dying left no seed.

21. And the second took her, and died, neither left he any seed : and the third likewise.

22. And the seven had her, and left no seed : last of all the woman died also.

23. In the resurrection therefore, when they shall rise, whose wife shall she be of them? for the seven had her to wife.

24. And Jesus answering said unto them, Do ye not therefore err, because ye know not the Scriptures, neither the power of God?

25. For when they shall rise from the dead, they neither marry, nor are given in marriage; but are as the angels which are in heaven.

26. And as touching the dead, that they rise : have ye not read in the book of Moses, how in the bush God spake unto him, saying, I am the God of Abraham, and the God of Isaac, and the God of Jacob?

27. He is not the God of the dead, but the God of the living : ye therefore do greatly err.

This is the case of men who spend their time in getting up little neat arguments. They think their cases complete. They feel quite sure that such instances must carry conviction to every mind. Such men, too, are fond of the *reductio ad absurdum,* their logical recreations. It amuses them. They chuckle hilariously over the feats of their nimble wit. Look what a case the Sadducees had ! A woman had seven husbands on earth, which of them will she choose as her one husband in the next world ; and are the remaining six men to have no wives hereafter ? " Ha ! ha !" said they, " how ridiculous he must look when we put such a case to him ! Come, we have caught him now, and the public shall see how we pluck his stolen feathers." Away they went. On the road they stopped a moment here and there that they might laugh just once more by way of anticipation. The man who had undertaken to state the case declared that he could not keep his gravity, the thing was so infinitely amusing, and so dazzlingly self-evident as an argument. One woman : seven husbands : resurrection : all the seven putting in a claim : the woman bewildered and unable to make a choice : ha ! ha ! The man who reported the case was regarded as having found a pearl beyond price. Lucky dog ! it had fallen to his lot to puncture the Christian balloon. So away they went, merry enough, and sure enough of an easy and brilliant victory. They stated the case. The Saviour was not agitated. As soon as they ceased he said to them, in effect, " You fools, in the resurrection there is no marriage : unities are established on a new basis : you are wrong in your fundamental position : go home and learn common-sense before you put any more riddles to a Christian teacher." Jesus Christ will show that all objectors are fundamentally wrong. They have no ground to stand upon. Their cases are all bubble-like. The wittiest objector will find that his blade has no handle. Every objector forgets the one thing which makes all the difference between genius and insanity.

The reference which Jesus Christ made to Abraham, Isaac, and Jacob, is very suggestive. He showed the Sadducees that if they gave up belief in the spiritual state, they must also give up belief in God himself; forasmuch as God called himself the God of

Abraham, who had long been absent from earth, so God was the God of the living. It is even so. We cannot surrender one part of Christ's teaching without surrendering the whole. If we break one commandment we break all. If we subtract we destroy. Tender is the life of Truth ! And yet how gentle its corrections,—"ye do greatly err." Solemn, even to sadness, are some of the rebukes of the Saviour.

28. And one of the scribes came, and having heard them reasoning together, and perceiving that he had answered them well, asked him, Which is the first commandment of all ?

29. And Jesus answered him, The first of all the commandments is, Hear, O Israel ; The Lord our God is one Lord :

30. And thou shalt love the Lord thy God with all thy heart, and with all thy soul, and with all thy mind, and with all thy strength : this is the first commandment.

31. And the second is like, namely this, Thou shalt love thy neighbour as thyself. There is none other commandment greater than these.

32. And the scribe said unto him, Well, Master, thou hast said the truth : for there is one God ; and there is none other but he :

33. And to love him with all the heart, and with all the understanding, and with all the soul, and with all the strength, and to love his neighbour as himself, is more than all whole burnt offerings and sacrifices.

34. And when Jesus saw that he answered discreetly, he said unto him, Thou art not far from the kingdom of God. And no man after that durst ask him any question.

This incident shows that indirect influence may be exerted by Christian teaching. Even if the scribe had not proposed this inquiry he would have received advantage from the answer which Jesus Christ returned to the Sadducees. He was evidently impressed with the wisdom, self-control, and high spiritual claims of Jesus Christ. Ministers should take a lesson from this. Besides the persons who are immediately interested in our ministry, there are others who are quietly and almost under concealment looking on, and forming their opinion of our temper and competence. We know not where the influence of a sermon may penetrate. Our preaching should always be such as to encourage serious listeners to ask such questions as may be secretly engaging their thoughts. The scribe was evidently clearer-minded and more earnest than either the Herodians or the Sadducees. The Herodians put a political question, the Sadducees proposed a speculative question ; but the scribe made a profound and spiritual inquiry, "Which is the first commandment of all ? " This is the kind of question which is worthy of the most anxious consideration. Life should not be spent in paltry disputes about tribute money, or in studying questions of barren speculation, but in finding out the principles which are at the very centre of things and shall abide for ever.

Jesus Christ answered the scribe in the scribe's own spirit—a spirit of the deepest solemnity and veneration. The words of the commandments as pronounced by Jesus Christ are simply majestic. Without exposition, paraphrase, or enlargement, Jesus Christ repeated the words of eternal life. There is a scriptural answer to every great spiritual question. He who returns answers in the words of Scripture will most satisfy the desire of every earnest heart. Jesus attempted no philosophical exposition of law, obligation, judgment, or any related subject ; he pronounced the commandments with the authority of the Lawgiver. Man needs two commandments because his life has two aspects. The one aspect is upwards towards God, the other aspect is lateral towards society. Both commandments have a common root, viz., love. True love is a compound feeling. It is more than mere admiration, fancy, prejudice, or esteem based upon superficial qualities and attractions. It comprises the assent of the judgment, the approbation of the conscience, and the fervent sanction of the best feelings. We may reverence God without loving him. For our neighbour we may have admiration without affection. We are to try ourselves by the severity and comprehensiveness of the divine requirement.

The answer which the scribe returned to Jesus Christ shows that in the heart of man there is a voice which confirms the claim of God. " Well, Master, thou hast said the truth." We should speak so as to compel those who hear us to acknowledge that our word is true. We can do this by our tone as well as by our reasoning. The tone of the ministry is quite as important as its argument. A hard, dry, dogmatic method of stating the truth will repel : a solemn, sympathetic, tender tone will constrain and persuade. We lose half our power as ministers of Christ if we neglect to appeal to the spirit of man as itself the best witness of God. " There is a spirit in man, and the inspiration of the Almighty giveth him understanding." It is the highest prerogative of man to be able to distinguish the false from the true, and to discover in the moral chaos of society the line of rectitude and order. Let ministers appeal to that prerogative, and they will put many to silence who are too obstinate to be convinced.

Jesus Christ recognises every particle of good that is in a man. He told the scribe that he was not far from the kingdom of God. Jesus Christ recognised good directions and tendencies, as well as successful results. We should tell men when they are setting themselves upon a right course, even though they may have gone but a few steps upon it. Encouragement is as food to the soul. Do not let us be afraid of telling any man that we see some good in him. Point it out rather, and urge him to persevere in the holy way, walking by the same rule, and minding the same thing. Men may be so told of their excellences as to abash and humble them, as well as so told as to encourage self-exaggeration. The scribe was a type of men who require a word of encouragement. They have great questions to ask, and already in their own hearts there is an answer to such questions, but they wish that answer to be pronounced by some outward authority that may come back upon themselves as a revelation and an appeal. There is much in our own hearts which we would be glad to hear other people say, for we could then rest upon it with a redoubled sense of security.

35. And Jesus answered, and said, while he taught in the temple, How say the scribes that Christ is the Son of David ?

36. For David himself said by the Holy Ghost, The Lord said to my Lord, Sit thou on my right hand, till I make thine enemies thy footstool.

37. David therefore himself calleth him Lord ; and whence is he then his son ? And the common people heard him gladly.

This gives us some insight into one of Jesus Christ's methods of teaching. He raised great questions for discussion. He did not always stop to explain the difficulties which he suggested, but rather left them to create a healthful excitement in the minds of his hearers. Ministers are often urged to be simple in their preaching, and there is undoubted wisdom in the exhortation ; at the same time we ought to take license from the example of Jesus Christ to propound inquiries, and suggest courses of thinking, which seem to lie somewhat afield from the line of simple gospel preaching. Every mind is the better for having some great theological question constantly before it. A sense of awe comes over the traveller when he enters the primeval forest, stands within the shadow of inaccessible heights, or feels his loneliness in the midst of the great sea : there is something analogous to this in some departments of theological inquiry,— we are perplexed, awed, overwhelmed ; and in many a scene we are constrained to exclaim, " How dreadful is this place ! " Jesus Christ raised great scriptural questions. He went back to Moses, the prophets, the Psalms, and found in the whole range of inspired statement bases on which to ground inquiries relating to his own person and mediation. He found himself everywhere. How is it that some of us see so little of him in the great sanctuary of his own revelation ?

Notwithstanding these great problems, " the common people heard him gladly." The common people know a great deal by sympathy, which they do not receive through the medium of their understanding. It is unwise to suppose that every word has to be broken up into simple meanings for the sake of the common people. They can read the countenance, they can understand the tone, they can interpret all the feeling which pervades Christian discourse; and whilst three parts of the statement may be perfectly simple in an intellectual point of view, they can enter with deep appreciation into those portions which are far-reaching and sublime.

38. And he said unto them in his doctrine, Beware of the scribes, which love to go in long clothing, and love salutations in the marketplaces,

39. And the chief seats in the synagogues, and the uppermost rooms at feasts :

40. Which devour widows' houses, and for a pretence make long prayers : these shall receive greater damnation.

The Saviour here returns to the great practical line of his ministry. He who had just proposed a solemn theological inquiry, utters a word of caution regarding some of the men who were immediately around him. Every honest minister is called upon to point out the false men and the false influences which are in society. This is a part of our ministry in which many of us fail. Who is courageous enough to lay his hand upon the vices which are immediately before him, presented in some of the members of his own congregation, and to condemn them specifically and vehemently? No word is hard which is true.

To call a man a hypocrite because he has in some way disappointed or offended us is mere spite; but to call him a hypocrite
when we know that such a term is deserved by his conduct is
not to speak severely. We find in the Scriptures such words
as vipers, hypocrites, whited walls, liars; and these words have
no harshness in them : employed in passion or in ill-nature they
would recoil upon the speaker, and constitute a charge against
his judgment and honour; but employed righteously they justify
themselves, and do their proper work in human speech. No
man used hard words, commonly so-called, so specifically and
tellingly as Jesus Christ; the danger is, that with less wisdom
and less authority some of his followers may abuse the holiness
of his example. Jesus Christ condemned persons as well as
actions. There is a shallow policy which says, Condemn the
sin, but let the sinner alone : this was not Jesus Christ's method;
he pointed out the sinner, and openly set upon him the mark
of his righteous disapprobation. Long clothing, salutations in the
marketplaces, chief seats in the synagogues, uppermost rooms
at feasts, did not hide from Jesus Christ the fact that men bearing
sacred names were devouring widows' houses, and for a pretence
making long prayers. So terrible in penetration and judgment
is the word and gospel of God !

41. And Jesus sat over against the treasury, and beheld how the people
cast money into the treasury: and many that were rich cast in much.

42. And there came a certain poor widow, and she threw in two mites,
which make a farthing.

43. And he called unto him his disciples, and saith unto them, Verily I
say unto you, That this poor widow hath cast more in than all they which
have cast into the treasury:

44. For all they did cast in of their abundance; but she of her want did
cast in all that she had, even all her living.

A story without an equal in the whole history of human beneficence. It abounds in practical points. Take a few of them :—

(1) There is a treasury in the Church. Treasury may stand
for all means of doing good : supporting the ministry; spreading
the gospel; teaching the ignorant; visiting the sick, etc. Into
this treasury some may cast money, some time, some influence,
others may cast the whole of these. The treasury, taken in this
large sense, is one severe test of the piety and consecration of
the Church. The treasury is not spoken of here as if it were

an exceptional institution, or brought into occasional use. It was a permanent fact. It was part of temple-worship. So it must ever be. When the Church ceases to give it will cease to live.

(2) Jesus Christ himself presides over the treasury. He did so, virtually, in this case. This fact redeems the treasury from all sordid and vulgar associations. What we give we give not to this man or to that, but to Jesus Christ himself. This consideration turns the act of giving into a holy service. When a shilling is given to a poor man it is given to Jesus Christ; when money is given to any Christian object it is handed to the Saviour himself. Work from any lower action, and giving will become a vexation; work from this high level, and it will become a sacrifice of joy. Jesus Christ is the Treasurer of the Church. Every farthing, every cup of cold water, every gentle service, he puts down in his book. All human officers are but sub-treasurers and sub-secretaries: the Saviour holds everything in his own hand.

(3) To this treasury men are to give as God has prospered them. Uniform rates of gift are unnatural, unreasonable, and unjust. It is scandalous that the great merchant and his clerk should be asked to give the same amount to Christian service. Pew-rents, as defining the final line of giving, ought not to be known in the church. They may be tolerated as bearing upon certain fixed expenses, but as a channel of love and gratitude they are infinitely worse than ridiculous. Love is the only sufficient law of giving. What has God done for us? What have we benefited from his word, his providences, his manifold ministries? These questions will settle the measure of our gifts to the consecrated treasury.

(4) Jesus Christ pronounces judgment upon the gifts of men. He knew what the rich had given; he knew what the widow gave; he knew how much was left behind in the hands of the rich, and he knew that the widow had parted with her whole living. Our judgment, then, is with God. Mutual criticism loses all sting when we bring ourselves immediately to the divine bar. Nothing that we have ever done shall be forgotten! "God is not unrighteous to forget our work of faith and labour of love." The poor will not be lost sight of in the judgment. What if they who gave most in quantity gave least in quality?

Chapter xvi. 15.

A DIVINE COMMAND.

SO said Jesus Christ, according to the report given in the
Gospel according to Mark. "And he said unto them, Go ye
into all the world, and preach the gospel to every creature."
Can we make these words more universal? Can we add
another province to the sphere? Let us see :—"Go ye into all
the world." Can you add one island to that geography—a little
island? Can you? "And preach the gospel to every creature."
Is there one left out—a little one, a black one? Say what
omissions mark this census. Not one. Is this like Jesus?
Was he always so big in thought, in love, in care? Was he
never little, mean, economic, sparse, critical? Did he always
keep house for the whole universe? What is the characteristic
of Christ along this line ot thinking? Is it not universality,
inclusiveness, godliness? How many men did God make, and
who made the rest? Where is there a man that shaped himself,
called himself into existence, maintains an independent individuality and relation to things, comes and goes as he pleases?
Where is that man? As at the first God's hand was upon all,
so through and through all the story God's love is upon all, and
Christ's dear Cross overshadows all, and Christ's infinite heart
welcomes all. If there be anything contrary to this, then we are
mocked ; false words have been spoken to us, promises have been
spoken to the ear and broken to the heart. Is this the God we
can worship? Is he a trifler? Is he a verbal necromancer,
saying one thing and meaning another, indulging in the *double
entendre* ; ambiguous, uncertain? or is he positive, definite, clear,
plain, meaning just what we expect him to mean when we are
told that he is Love?

"Preach the gospel to every creature." Then every creature needs it? What is Man? I have never seen him; you have never seen him. You have seen a man, you have not seen Man. Only God can see Man. Until we get thorough hold of that simple thought we shall make no progress in our Christian studies. We cannot know human nature, we cannot know Man, we have never seen Humanity. Humanity is the sum-total of innumerable details; it is the total form of infinite variations and combinations. We have seen a man and many men, but Man is a singular-plural, a contradiction in grammar, a glorious unity in thought. You have never seen vegetation. What is vegetation? You have seen your own little garden and the field adjoining, and you may have gone even further, and you may know a little about English vegetation; some may go still further, and know a little about American vegetation. These are nothing. Who has seen all the vine-lands, corn-lands, spice-lands, all the lands watched by the zodiacs, the angels, the stars? We are very curious about this. We have near London built a large glass house at great public expense, and we watch it scientifically, and write reports about it, and treasure it as a national blessing. We call the place Kew. Let us enter this great glass house. What are these wondrous leaves, plants, trees? They are all named classically, and labelled and registered and cared for; but in the tropics they are all weeds. They grow out of doors; there are far too many of them; they are a nuisance. What do you know about Man? You have built him a glass house in some cases, and said, This is Man. Nothing of the kind: this is a man; but he who is an aristocrat here is a plebeian over yonder. Ah, that over yonder, that new place, that unknown territory, that unsuspected province! At Kew we are treasuring all kinds of weeds: we know nothing about sum-totals, we have no wisdom; we have little facts and small entries and minute memoranda about parishes, provinces, districts, and what we call empires. Only God can see the globe at one glance. We must therefore go to revelation if we would know what Man is.

Hear this and blush—You have to be revealed to yourself. Until you know that you cannot make much out of Christ Jesus. He will not only be a mystery to you, but a mystery of darkness;

not only will he be a mystery, he will be a perplexity. **I have
to be told what I am.** I think I know myself, yet myself I have
never seen. I do not know which is myself. My name is Legion,
for there are many of us, and all within is riot, tumult, shouting,
noise, war, bitterness, strife, prayer, blasphemy, seeing of angels
and devils. What is this? Who is it? Father-Maker, come
and tell me all about myself; I do not know what I am : reveal
me to myself. What impudence it is therefore, what sheer
impertinence and perversion of cleverness for any man to arise
and pretend to tell us what Man is ! Human nature is matter
of revelation. If there is a book which reveals God, that book
will reveal Man. As Christians we accept the Bible in this
regard. We have come to look upon it as a divine revelation,
below the letter, above the letter, glorifying the letter, and
otherwise making the letter an inconvenient convenience, but
still independent of it, as we shall come to know when our
education is further advanced. The Bible tells us a poor story
about Man,—a most incredible story to man, because man does
not want to believe it. It is very difficult to satisfy any man
with his own biography. If you were to write your dearest
friend's biography, he would wish, without saying so, that you
had been a little more emphatic here, and a little more compli-
mentary there, and without indulging at all in flattery you might
have brought out three or four other points more vividly, so as to
have thrown a softer glory upon his beautiful personality. This
he would not say for the world. Man has great power of self-
concealment, and still greater power of social concealment.
It is therefore extremely difficult to satisfy any man with his
biography. It is well, therefore, that he should be dead before
his biography is written ; the severest of all critics would be
himself. So when man comes to read the Bible story or
himself, he says, This cannot be true ; this is evidently fanatical,
suppositional, allegorical; this is a Jew's account, this is a perverted
statement. Man,—why, I know what man is, quoth the critic. So
impudent can man be, so bare-faced and shameless. Until we
know every creature that ever lived, and every creature under
every climate and under every civic, geographical, and celestial
condition, we do not know Man, and we must accept a statement
of man from a revelation.

We as Christians have accepted the Bible as God's revelation of himself and of humanity, and, accepting the Bible so, man stands before his Maker lost—lost. How dare you take the responsibility of denying this? Who are you? and what will you do for us if you are wrong? If we believe all your nonsense what will you do for us in the crisis-hour? Where will you be? What will be your address then? How many of us may call upon you? If you do not make a revelation you suggest one; if you do not issue a new revelation of the universe you take upon you a still greater responsibility in contradicting one which has been believed by the piety, the benevolence, the purity, and the heroism of ages. What is the Bible account of man? The heart is deceitful above all things : God made man upright, but he hath sought out many inventions. There is none righteous, no, not one. All we like sheep have gone astray, we have turned every one to his own way : there is none that doeth good, no, not one. This is the Biblical account of humanity, and the Bible is a large book; it takes large views, suggests infinite conceptions, grapples with the mysteries and problems of the universe, it lets nothing alone; it is a heroic book. It is not content with walking round little questions, and making little remarks upon them; it deals with God, man, sin, sacrifice, atonement, reconciliation, spiritual ministry, conquered death, and entered heaven. This book reveals man as lost. Hear this sweet voice, "The Son of man is come to seek and to save that which was lost,"—not some of it, not a little of it, not much of it, not most of it, but "that which was lost." If these words do not mean what they say, then we are—let me repeat, solemnly and reverently—mocked by an abuse of language. What is it that is to be preached to every creature? A new theory, a very intricate and most ingenious hypothesis about nothing? No. What then is "the gospel"? What does "gospel" mean? Good news, glad tidings, blessed intelligence, the most astounding and musical revelation of love ever addressed to the ear or the heart,—musical music; and what is it in words? No words can express it all, as no instrument can exhaust a musician's soul. But some of the words are these, As Moses lifted up the serpent in the wilderness, even so must the Son of man be lifted up, that whosoever believeth in him might be saved. God

so loved the world, that he gave his only-begotten Son, that whosoever believeth on him should not perish, but have everlasting
life. While we were yet sinners Christ died for us : he died the
Just for the unjust, that he might bring us to God : he bare
our sins in his own body on the tree : he shed his blood for the
remission of sin : and he cries, Come unto me, all ye that labour
and are heavy laden, and I will give you rest. Why, this is
what we wanted ; somebody has dreamed or invented the very
thing man most needs. If this is not a dream, an invention, it
is what it professes to be, a revelation of the infinite Heart, a
declaration of the ineffable, inexhaustible Love.

How do we stand in relation to it, then ? We have either
believed it, or we have not believed it. We cannot take up a
neutral position, and say we have nothing to do with it. That
is impossible. No man can so treat the sunlight. If a man shall
be charged with doing something that is contrary to the laws of
life, society will not allow him to say, There may be a sun, but
I really maintain a totally neutral position in relation to it ; I
do not regard it, I do not look to it at all. Society would call
him fool, and put him down ; and if he had done anything wrong
society would lock him up and punish him. Society will not
allow a man to be so indifferent to the light as to commit a crime
when he might have left it undone. You cannot maintain a
neutral or negative position in relation to the Cross. Christ, as
a matter of history, has died, has sent forth his ministers, has
declared his gospel, has opened his heart-door, has breathed
upon every one the welcomes of his love; so you cannot say
you will take no heed of it, but will receive destiny as it comes.
You do not act so in other matters : why do you lay down and
abandon your common sense when you come to face the deepest
and most solemn questions of life ? I believe every man may
be saved. I have not a gospel given to me which reads, Give
every creature a hearty welcome ; but I will take care that there
is only room for a few. Go into all the world, and tell everybody
he may come ; but when he is half a mile off I will take care
that he falls into a pit and cannot come. My gospel does not
preach so ; my gospel is a gospel of love, entreaty, of universality.
It says to the very worst man, You may come. It says to the

thief upon the cross, already half in hell, There is still time for saving prayer. " Fly abroad, thou mighty gospel ! " This is what we need. We may not feel our need of it at some particular moment, but there are other moments in our life when we must have it all, and when we say to our friends, " Tell me the old, old story of Jesus and his love ! " Then we become little children again, broken-hearted men. And God never loves us so much as when we are of a broken and a contrite spirit.

NOTE.

The following list of references to the Old Testament is nearly or quite complete :—

Mark i.	2.	Mal. iii. 1.		Mark xii.	10.	Ps. cxviii. 22.
„	3.	Is. xl. 3.		„	19.	Deut. xxv. 5.
„	44	Lev. xiv. 2.		„	26.	Ex. iii. 6.
ii.	25.	1 Sam. xxi. 6.		„	29.	Deut. vi. 4.
iv.	12.	Is. v. 10.		„	31.	Lev. xix. 18.
vii.	6.	Is. xxix. 13.		„	36.	Ps. cx. 1.
„	10.	Ex. xx. 12 ; xxi. 17.		xiii.	14.	Dan. ix. 27.
ix.	44.	Is. lxvi. 24.			24.	Is. xiii. 10.
x.	4.	Deut. xxiv. 1.		xiv.	27.	Zech. xiii. 7.
„	7.	Gen. ii. 24.		„	62.	Dan. vii. 13.
„	19.	Ex. xx. 12-17.		xv.	28(?)	Is. liii. 12.
xi.	17.	Is. lvi. 7 ; Jer. vii. 11.		„	34.	Ps. xxii. 1.

" Though this Gospel has little historical matter which is not shared with some other, it would be a great error to suppose that the voice of Mark could have been silenced without injury to the divine harmony. The minute painting of the scenes in which the Lord took part, the fresh and lively mode of the narration, the very absence of the precious discourses of Jesus, which, interposed between his deeds, would have delayed the action, all give to this Gospel a character of its own. It is the history of the war of Jesus against sin and evil in the world during the time that he dwelt as a Man among men. Its motto might well be, as Lange observes, those words of Peter : 'How God anointed Jesus of Nazareth with the Holy Ghost and with power; who went about doing good, and healing all that were oppressed of the devil ; for God was with him ' (Acts x. 38). It developes a series of acts of this conflict, broken by times of rest and refreshing, in the wilderness or on the mountain. It records the exploits of the Son of God in the war against Satan, and the retirement in which after each he returned to commune with his Father, and bring back fresh strength for new encounters."—SMITH's *Dictionary of the Bible.*

THE GOSPEL ACCORDING TO LUKE.

Chapter ii. 11.

" Unto you is born this day . . . a Saviour."

THE WORLD'S NEED.

THIS is just what the world wanted. This is just what the
world always wants. The world wants this not the less
that it is in some instances not aware of the necessity. What
does a drowning man want? A lecture on natation? That would
be exceedingly profitable to a man who was drowning! Tell
him how to use his right arm, and his left, and his lower limbs;
remark on the gracefulness of his action. All this would be
exceedingly gratifying to a man who is struggling for life. You
would not mock a drowning man; you are not cruel enough for
that. What does the drowning man want? A strong grip: no
reasoning; let him be reasoned with by-and-by; let him work
his way into the metaphysics of the occasion when he has leisure.
First of all get him out, and bring him into safety. Everything
depends upon our circumstances as to what religion we want. If
we are members of Parliament, with an abundance of leisure on
our hands, and with some little capital that will enable us to
publish agnostic pamphlets, and to give them away, we shall not
want a religion of agony. There need be no Cross in that relation ;
a little scented water, a few difficult sentences written on gilt-edged
paper would be very admirable, and would have about them some
hint of the higher æstheticism; but men and women such as
we meet any day in coming to church,—the peeps we have had

into slums and alleys and back places, into which civilisation dare hardly go; poor, poor women trying to snatch a moment's sleep in some little off-hand alley, with the inevitable black shawl around their unkempt heads,—what do they want? By-and-by they may become metaphysicians and philosophers, and even agnostics; I cannot tell what they may become in two millenniums: but now, this moment, they want a "Saviour." If Christ the Lord will not do, get up some other man; but do get a Saviour. We do not want you to be finding fault with one Saviour if you can get another. Why hold a controversy on the shore when one of you should plunge into the sea and save the drowning man? Jesus Christ is willing to stand aside if you can supersede him by one more excellent, by one mightier, by one of larger heart. When did he ever usurp the first place arbitrarily? Even his enemies said that the works which he did gave him a right to the primacy. He wants to hold the primacy on no other terms. If any man can save the soul more completely and beneficently, Jesus Christ would be willing to let that man go forward and perform this sublimest miracle. They take a mean course— selfish, dishonourable, inhuman—who simply say Christ is not the Lord. He is willing to be displaced if you can bring forward any man who will do a deeper, truer, larger, nobler work.

"Unto you is born this day . . . a Saviour." The world did not want an adviser. The world had advised itself almost into hell. The world did not ask for a speculator. Everything that man could do had been done, and men sat in the darkness of their own wisdom. The world did not want a reformer, a man who could change his outward and transient relations, an engineer that would continually devote his time (for appropriate remuneration) to the readjustment of the wheels and the pulleys and the various mechanical forces of society. The world wanted a Saviour. "Saviour" is a pathetic name. It is not an official title; it is not an image you could robe in scarlet, and bow down before on account of its majesty and haughtiness; "Saviour" is an angel with tears in his eyes; arms mighty as the lightnings of God, but a heart all tenderness. "Saviour" is a complex word. It has in it all human nature, all divine nature, all the past of history, all the possibility of prophecy, all the mystery of apocalypse; the tenderness outvying the love of women, the majesty humbling the haughtiness of kings.

Suppose we take the world apart altogether from religious definition and description; suppose for the time being we set aside the term "sin," and look at the world concretely, exactly, as it then presented itself to the eyes of an earnest observer, what kind of world was it? Men were hostile to one another. That is an undeniable fact. A spirit of enmity was the spirit of such civilisation as there was, rude or elaborate:—Who could be uppermost, who could rule, who could plunder and overwhelm and destroy? That was the aspect presented by one large section of the world. If there was another section apparently refined and cultivated, it was a section that had refined itself into weariness, and cultivated itself to surfeit. On the other hand, it was a world given over to daily and unaccountable suffering. Account for it as we may, there is the suffering world before our eyes day by day. Every heart knows its own bitterness. Life cannot throw off its load. When we laugh we are sad; if for a moment we make holiday, and endeavour by legitimate friction to excite one another into merriment, we hear a whispering full of trouble; there is a noise in the heart that will not be stilled. Where there can be no distinct trace of suffering to actual or positive disobedience or infraction of divine law, still there it is; the child is dying, the heart is breaking, the home is violated by invisible but mighty enemies; there is a canker even in the purse, there is rust on the gold, so that men take it out and look at it, and wonder if they may accept it, or whether they shall arrest us as dealers in base coin; heaven at its bluest has streaks in it that may at any time come together and constitute a storm. This is the world; what will you do with it? What does that kind of world want? It wants a "Saviour." If any man has dreamed himself to be the Saviour of the world, he should be welcomed; by so much as he has dreamed of possible salvation he will do good, he will be gentle, he will be sacrificial; in the degree in which he earnestly says, "I want to save the world," he may be trusted, be he Greek, or Roman, or Jew. Jesus Christ came and proposed to save the world. Whatever we may say for Christianity or against it, there is the fact that Christianity sought to put down hostility by the creation of brotherhood; and, on the other hand, Christianity sought to mitigate human suffering, even when it could not be wholly removed, by sanctifying it, by turning it to the highest practical uses. Christianity addresses itself not to sections of the world, little classes and coteries of philosophers and speculators, but to the heart of the world—the heart that is broken, the soul that is in agony, the life that has given up the last hope of self-salvation. It is a bold religion; it is a noble, glorious proposal.

I have just read a pamphlet entitled "A Friendly Correspondence with Mr. Gladstone about Creeds," by Samuel Laing. Mr. Gladstone wrote to Mr. Laing—an eminent controversialist, and a thorough-going student, and a gentleman in controversy—asking Mr. Laing to state the negative points in series, that he might have some conception of the new position to which the later religious thought would call the world. Mr. Laing replies, and in the course of his first letter he says, "But we are not an aggressive or proselytising race. . . . In fact, we prefer to wait." Christianity does not. Christianity will not wait a moment. Christianity says, The people are dying. Wait? By what authority? Verily here is a popish assumption. Here are men who are proposing to wait! Christianity separates itself from such men by instantaneous, urgent, passionate, tremendous earnestness. It may be wrong, but it is sincere. "We are not an aggressive or proselytising race." But Christianity is. Christianity is nothing if not aggressive. Meet Christianity where you like, and its arms are out for battle or for salvation, and its voice is lifted up saying, "Come now, let us reason together." Behold, here is a new leisure that baptises itself, and names itself "non-aggressive." Let us lie down now a little on the other side, and let the world go its own gate: we are not aggressive or proselytising. If you like to have that religion you can have it. But, Mr. Gladstone says, let us have your propositions as it were in the form of an indictment; state them in consecutive order and enumeration. Mr. Laing begins the first article. You will have a difficulty in making out thirty-nine articles—he begins with one:—" That the subjects which positive creeds profess to define are, for the most part, unknowable,—*i.e.*, beyond the scope of human reason or

conception. Whose human reason ?   Whose human conception ?
Verily, here is authority with a vengeance !   Here is one man
who stands up to speak in the name of human reason and human
conception !   These are the men who dislike authority in the
Church, and dislike dogmatism in the pulpit, and who are so
extremely modest that they would only speak each for himself,
except when under extraordinary and uncontrollable pressure
one of them ventures to speak in the name of human reason.
Archbishops and bishops, pastors, ministers, and professors of
every name, close your books !   Here is a man who speaks in
the name of human reason.

Suppose we treated social questions in this way, what would
be said about us ?   Let us talk thus :—Human sorrow, human
suffering, human poverty, is so vast, and the whole question is
so complicated, that it is simply impossible for human reason to
grasp it, or human conception to evolve a new scheme of social
philosophy—call me to-morrow as late as you can.   Christianity
says, If we cannot do everything we must do something; we
must begin to-day ; to-morrow the people may be dead.

Having perused this pamphlet, I am struck with several
things about it.   There are here propositions in italics.   It
does not require any great genius to be a proposition-maker.
This pamphlet might have announced itself as indicating a
" Proposition-formulating manufactory : propositions formulated
here on the shortest notice, and on moderate terms."   The
formulation of propositions makes no difference in this great
agony of human life, this tremendous struggle of human progress.
Suppose we should describe household economy as some of these
able writers describe the Christian idea.   Would you be satisfied
to have household life described by things that are external ?
Suppose I were called upon for a definition of household life, and
I should give it in a series of propositions or descriptions—thus :
First, rent ; secondly, rates and taxes; thirdly, weekly bills;
fourthly, fifthly, and sixthly, highway arrangements, police
arrangements, general relations to the people round about ;—that
is household life.   Is it ?   No, no.   The household life is inside
—in the birth, the death, the suffering, the joy, the mutual trust,

the common honour; household life is in the mingling of tears
and laughter, in the exchange of hearts, in copartnery of sorrow;
these are not things that will submit to be set in propositions
and printed in italics; they must be lived, they must be experienced to be known. So when men talk about the Christian
religion, indicating its creeds, its metaphysics, its ecclesiastical
organisations, and all the rest of such environment or accompani-
ment, we say, That is not all: the Christian religion is within,
is to be found at a place called Calvary; it is in Bethlehem, it
is in Gethsemane, it is in Golgotha, it is on Olivet, it is on the
eternal throne. You have not settled the claims of Christianity
when you have disputed with the highest scholarly authorities
that are arrayed on the side of Christian defence. He only
understands Christianity who has felt it. No other man has a
right to speak about it. Christianity is not a proposition to be
discussed, it is a gospel to be received.

Reading this pamphlet through, I find it wholly destitute of
moral enthusiasm. There is no passion here; there is not a
tear in the whole argument. There is nothing in that paper
that says, I want to help the race. There is, however, some
degree of consolation even in this manifesto. That consolation
you will find in Article 8—"Polarity is the great underlying law
of all knowable phenomena." What does a man want more than
that? It seems to be a respectable word, and to convey nothing
by way of mischievous implication; at the same time it does not
speak to me in my sorrow; it plants no flower on the grave;
it does not turn my crust of bread into sacramental flesh as I eat
it through lips that have burned with prayer. This may be the
way to progress and liberty, purity and nobleness, but I cannot
think it is. Sirs, I would see Jesus! He knows me better than
any one else. His words drop as the small rain, and as the gentle
dew and the healing balm: I want him; he is my Saviour.

A great injustice may be inflicted upon Christianity by attempting unduly to intellectualise it. Christianity has suffered from
the human intellect. Men would be clever where cleverness was
a sin. Men have no business to write creeds. That is where
the Church has been disloyal to the Cross. The Cross cannot be

formulated in propositions and articles and items, to be received, accepted, signed, and held for ever in certain cast-iron human forms. You have no right to a creed that is of the nature of finality. If you choose to regard it as marking a stage in holy progress, so be it; if you submit some statement of faith as indicating how far Christian thought has advanced, that may be done with great utility; but if you set up a creed and say, This is final, this is the only way to heaven, this is orthodoxy; if you do not accept this you cannot have fellowship with God through Christ,—then you are telling lies in the sanctuary. Suppose we are going to the North, and we have arrived as far as Barnet, and I say, I must just put down two or three things as to our position :—Barnet : nice-looking country; nothing romantic, still a place that a man might live in if he had the means of doing so ; moderate climate ; partially wooded ; some nice views here, no doubt, at certain periods of the year : that is where we are ; that is our creed. So it is. The great express rolls on for two hours, and we say, Where are we ? Where are we ! We settled that long ago ; I told you where we are—Barnet. Why do you raise these questions now ? I raise them because the train has been going on ; that is all. And so the great progress of the age advances. We are not always at Barnet; we are not always at the old outworn creed. The faith that is in the creed may be just the same, but it requires new expression, new incarnation, new adaptation to new circumstances. It is the creed we have abandoned ; we still, blessed be God, grasp and love the faith. In Christian inquiry always suspect the intellect ; not in any bad sense, but in the sense of vigilant caution. Men are victimised by their own sagacity ; men are led into extremes by their own vanity and their own cleverness. A clever religion is a bad religion.

I speak to some whose life-duty it is to represent Christian thought in its latest forms and in its best aspects. Using that function in the spirit of Christ, they may confer inestimable advantage upon the Church and upon the world ; but if they say, This is all, this is the beginning and the end ; my form is the only possible form, I speak in the name of human reason and human conception : this is the whole mystery of God,—believe them not; they are hirelings and not shepherds. That is the worst kind of popery; it is the popery that is not surrounded by the dignity of a historic sentiment, it is the popery of personal vanity and ignorance. What then is to be trusted in this great religious pursuit? The heart. What do you mean by the heart? I mean three things—I mean purity of motive, I mean tenderness of feeling, I mean self-crucifixion. In the Scriptures the heart is often used as a convertible term with mind and intellect; that we perfectly well know; but there is also a sense in which the heart separates itself, and becomes motive, emotion, sacrifice; a Christ-like passion and agency, dominating, subli-mating, glorifying the whole life. We shall never have unity of opinion. We have no unity of opinion in business, we have no unity of opinion in architecture, we have no unity of opinion even in politics, we have no unity of opinion in art; but does this divergence of opinion split up society and endanger the altar, and bring the throne into peril? Men may be patriots, to whatever political party they belong. Patriotism is not the birthright or the heritage of any one party in the State; it touches a common sentiment, and there are moments when men throw down their party flags, and lift up the national banner, and are proud of their country's name. So with this great Christian thought and action. Blessed be God, there come moments when we forget whether we are Episcopalians, Congregationalists, Baptists, or Presby-terians, or Wesleyan Methodists; for the moment we forget all that is little, partial, and individual, and a common impulse drives us forward in the arms of trust, brotherhood, and generous comradeship, that we may proclaim a common salvation, and declare to all men everywhere—" Unto you this day is born . . . a Saviour." Ministers, that is your gospel. God give you and me grace to preach it. Believers, that is your gospel. Do not you be making your little mechanical creeds and orthodox con-trivances and small ecclesiastical gateways. Let all men feel that the Church is not a debating club, is not even an academy formed for the higher disputes of metaphysics and philosophy. Let not the world get the impression that only scholars can find their way to the Cross. Oh, outcast, ignorant, blind, there is one traveller that can find his way to the Cross. What is his name? The Broken Heart.

PRAYER.

COME to us, Lord, in thine own way, and according to thine own measure; only delay not, but come quickly ! We live when God is with us; without God we cannot live. We pray thee, therefore, at the Cross of our Saviour, to come; Father, Son, and Holy Ghost, dwell with us, break bread to us, reveal thyself to us, and give us a perpetual blessing. We rejoice when we see God ; it is like seeing the morning light, the summer glory, the noonday in all its cloudlessness. Say to our souls that have been mourning thine absence, The winter is over and gone, and the time of the singing of birds is come. May the birds of heaven make their nests in our hearts, and sing to us songs of the summerland. We bless thee if our hunger has led us to thy table, then the hunger was sent from God ; we rejoice if our thirst has brought us to the right fountain, then was our thirst no accident, but part of God's leading and education of the soul. We rejoice that in our Father's house there is bread enough and to spare ; and as for the river of God, it is full of water. Blessed are they that do hunger and thirst after righteousness, after love and beauty and purity, and divinest fulness of thought and life, for they shall be filled. Giving doth not impoverish God ; withholding doth not enrich the Lord. Thou hast been giving unto us with both hands since we were born ; thy right hand has been opened in power, and thy left hand in succour and tenderness. We have nothing that we have not received ; it is of the Lord's mercies that we are not consumed ; we are the children of compassion, we are spared by the tears of God. We rejoice that all this highest thought of our souls takes us to Calvary. The Cross is the river of God, the fountain of joy, the beginning of immortality ; yea, in it we see all figures and emblems signifying purity through pardon and peace, through righteousness, and bringing us into closer alliance with the living God. We would live on Calvary ; we would build our house near the Cross. We can only live in mercy, for we are inclined to sin every moment ; our prayer is but occasional, our sin is permanent. Yet we have hope in God through Christ ; the Cross was not set up in vain, the Lord cannot be foiled in battle. Thou dost mean to save this little world, every man, woman, and young child in it; thou wilt lose no lamb from the flock. We leave it all with thee, only give us the answering heart when thou dost send to us the appeals of thy grace. Make us great in goodness ; may we be strong and valiant in modest courage ; may we derive all our strength from God; then shall our weakness be strength, and our extremity shall be God's opportunity. Help us to be better men, in innermost thought, in nobleness of aspiration ; make us eloquent in secret wordless prayer; may we commune with God all day, all night, then the morning shall give us a baptism of dew, and the day shall be succeeded by no gloom or darkness of night. Holy Spirit, dwell with us;

come down out of heaven upon us, and abide upon our shattered lives, a new hope, a new defence, an inextinguishable glory. Rebuke us, but in mercy; let not thy rod smite us in all its scourging power, for which of the sons of flesh hath strength enough to stand against the scourge of God? We own our sins; we do not get rid of them by confessing them, but if we confess, thou art faithful and just to forgive, and thus by the divine act we have release from the guilt and the torment of sin. Behold how we have wasted our prosperity; we have written our own name upon it, and we have swollen ourselves with pride in the presence of the poverty that has fallen at our feet, and we have said to ourselves, Behold, we are not as other men. We have not been kind to the point of nobleness; we have given nothing, we have kept all we could, and therefore nothing has been given. If anything has been parted with, it has been forced out of us by shame, by social pressure; we would have kept it, every crumb and farthing, if we could. So we are before God as criminals: give us to know that we are pardoned by feeling that we can do the wrong no more. Wherein any have been just and generous and good, beneficent and useful, they desire to trace all to the action of the Holy Ghost. Not unto us, not unto us, say they, but unto God's name be all the glory. We think of our loved ones at home, and far away, specially those who are weakened by pain, who have not been able to do their day's work, and therefore have lost their day's bread. We think of the weary, and the sad, and of those who are saying, Is this never to end? is the darkness always to deepen, and is the wind always to be filled with the sound of nearing wolves? Oh, the heartache! Oh, the world's great misery! Saviour of the world, is it our impatience that prays or our faith, when we say, Lord Jesus, come quickly! Amen.

Chapter iii. 22.

"And the Holy Ghost descended in a bodily shape like a dove upon him."

THE DESCENT OF THE HOLY GHOST.

IT is that " bodily shape " that creates all the difficulty in some lumbering and wooden minds. How to connect spirit and body is the profound and insoluble problem. Some persons can believe in matter; they think they see it. Others have a dim notion of the possibility of there being a force in creation that might be called Mind or Spirit. But how to connect the two, how to get the Holy Ghost into a bodily shape,—that is the puzzle, the problem, the impossibility. Yet that connection is plainly declared in this text if words have any meaning. The terms are very explicit and vivid: "And the Holy Ghost descended in a bodily shape like a dove." In that event the problem would seem to be solved; solved by illustration, it not by exposition.

The whole Trinity is here. Let us count the persons indicated in this twenty-second verse : "And the Holy Ghost"—that is one—" descended upon him "—that is another—" and a voice came from heaven, which said, Thou art my beloved Son "—that is a third. Here is the threefold action of a threefold Personality : the descending Holy Ghost, the baptised Christ, the approving Father. We cannot get away from the Trinity unless we get away from the Bible. It is not necessary that we should explain it, or understand it, or have even the dimmest conception of its possibility. Some things we are bound to accept without handling. A man might handle the earth, but he cannot lay his fingers on the sky. All things do not come into possession through pen and ink, or through a process of handling and counting. All the greatest blessings we enjoy come without explanation of a human kind ; yet their coming is indisputable ; yea, their coming marks the vital point of the day and the vital point of all destiny. We only know God when he puts himself into relation. He must be in the dove, or in the man, or in some shape, before we can know fully and impressively that he is, and that he is near. We have no mental room for the Infinite ; we lack space for that accommodation : but when God puts himself into visible shape, when he comes to us in the person of his Son, we see him through that living medium. We shall miss the true point of the Incarnation if we stop only at the bodily or physical appearance and presence of Christ. All things physical are emblematical. All stars are but an index. They are not the text, they are not the body of the poem ; they mark its lines : the poem is spiritual, metaphysical, wordless, and it comes to us through any medium that we can best appreciate or comprehend. God must become man before we can know him with any sense that warms the heart, enlarges the understanding, and brightens the outlook of the mind.

We shall have to face one difficulty, and that is the difficulty that some persons can only think of one bodily shape. But all bodily shapes are available to God. "Body" becomes quite a large term when God interprets it and utilises it. In the text it was the bodily shape of a bird. It seems to us sometimes as if some birds required but a touch from heaven to turn them into angels; they have such beauty, such voices, and they are altogether marked by such qualities that it would be easy to some minds to conceive that a mere breath from the mouth of God might transform them into celestial visitants. They are more than birds. Not to the bird-fancier, the bird-dealer, but to the man who listens to the gospel poured out of their throats. In the text the bodily shape was that of a dove, so soft, so beautiful, so gentle, so emblematic of peace and serenity. God chooses his mediums and his instruments, and whatsoever they may be when he takes them up for his use, they all become beautiful by his habitation of them.

Are we willing that this descent of the Holy Ghost in the form of a dove should be simply a point in ancient history? Are we still reluctant to give modern enlargements and interpretations to the spiritual ministry of God in his own creation? The truth is, that the Holy Ghost is coming down always in bodily shape; only we deprive ourselves of celestial visions by talking about the New Testament as a book a thousand years old and more; whereas we should accept it as an indicator, as a book pointing to events that are now taking place, to descents which are the true creators and sanctifiers of human history. The Holy Ghost sometimes descends upon us in the form of a little child. All the little children are heavenward-bound. No one ever went to hell out of a cradle. "Suffer the little children to come unto me," said he who was man, woman, and child in one; "for of such is the kingdom of heaven." When the disciples would inquire as to ecclesiastical status, and especially with regard to ecclesiastical primacy, saying, "Who is greatest in the kingdom of heaven?" Jesus took a little child, and said, "He is." There is nothing greater in heaven than the child-heart. All the rest is decoration; all the rest is of the nature of embroidery, fringe, accident, detail. Heaven is childness. Yet we are prone to think of the child as another element in statistical inquiry. We call him part of the population, and allow the little wave to fall into the great sea without special reckoning and individuality and care and love, speaking for the bulk of mankind. Yet that child is the Holy Ghost in bodily shape. You could see it if you looked well into the eyes; you could hear it if you listened to the mighty throb of that weakness. Why let things pass by you without catching their apocalyptic meaning, their highest references? Why live in dry, dull, bare commonplace, when you might be living in a continually opening heaven?

Sometimes the Holy Ghost descends upon us in bodily shape in the form of a man, a great teacher, a great prophet. Who is the great prophet? Not the fortune-teller; the after-teller is the real prophet. Any mind of an audacious turn can make a bold dash at the future; but he is the real prophet who post-tells, who reads you the writing of moss and lichen on the old wall, who takes you down to the rocks, and reads you all the stony eloquence millions of ages old. Sometimes the man is not only a prophet, but he is a reformer. He says, This is out of square, this is not plumb; here geometry has been violated; there the foundations are out of course. He has an uneasy time of it. No man likes to be told where he is wrong. It is in human nature, whilst protesting modesty, to be drinking in whole rivers of flattery. We are liars. Why not see God in man? Why not know fully and graciously that humanity is God's dwelling-house, and that the poorest, meanest cripple that halts from one step to another is part of the mystic building? Why keep your theology in a book two thousand, five thousand, years old, when you might have it newly written for you according to the old pattern every morning in every life? Until we realise these great conceptions of childhood and manhood we shall not begin the right work of education, reform, or progress. So long as the metaphysic is wrong the concrete must be false. Wrap nothing up; let us have no veneer and covering and bandaging. We are wrong until the heart is right.

Sometimes the Holy Ghost descends in the bodily shape of events, and how have events been treated by modern men? As wholly secular. If the pulpit so much as referred to them, it would lose its dignity. We have made a special department in life of the treatment of events, and we have taken care that the Church shall have nothing to do with them, the pulpit shall ignore them; whereas these events are divine incarnations, writings of human history, the things that ought to constitute the

texts of the pulpit. But the pulpit will not have it so, and therefore the pulpit is becoming effete. We leave events to the
newspaper; we leave events to the fireside; we leave events
to constitute the investments of liars and persons who act from
sinister motives, as well as to persons who do their very honest
best to interpret them in their largest and truest sense. But who
can instruct the Church? Who can make the Church other than
the most grievous, blind, halt, maimed old grandmother? Who
can waken up any preacher to read the events of the day? Yet
there is God in every one of them ; here rebuking, there approving,
yonder shaping, and over the whole adjusting, balancing, weighing, and working them out to holy and blessed issues.

Here, then, we come face to face with the perpetual Incarnation,
the daily, unceasing descent of the Holy Ghost. Yet we cannot
get men to believe these things. They will believe whatever
was written two thousand years ago. Man loves antiquity; he
loves superstition; he loves the anonymous. That man rightly
interprets God who sees him in the precious inspired Scriptures,
the beginnings of things, the outline and the symbol of ever-
evolutionising history. We might have had a stronger faith if
we had been more wise and pious in our treatment of the things
that are happening round about us every day.

Descent—descending from heaven. The earth needs the
heavens. The old earth wants something which it has not got.
Its very weeds want to be paradises. Its beginnings are full of
pain, and the cry of the earth is, When will it come—the light, the
morning, the joy? I cannot thus be left alone, I was not meant
to be solitary; I am part of something else : where is that something? what is it? when will it come? Oh, nameless Force,
descend upon me! Let the heavens withdraw from the earth,
and what is it? An ice-heap. Let the heavens come to the
earth, and what is it? A garden. Children run out to play in
the sunshine, not knowing in words, but feeling in soul, that
heaven is come down to make holiday for them. The sun
governs all things. As we have often had occasion to say, the
sun is your tailor, the sun is your house-builder, the sun spreads
your table. You did not know it, but then you did not know

God. The earth needs the descending heavens, in warmth, in growth, in comfort. Man needs the descending heavens in sympathy, in special inspirations, in particular and immediate qualification for the discharge of solemn trusts. Sometimes a man may not awaken until the finger of God touches his eyelids. Sometimes, having awakened out of the physical sleep, he shrinks from the age he lives in; it is so crooked, so tortuous, so perverse, so loath to listen to anything of the nature of purity, righteousness, and noble exhortation; and he cannot go out to his duty until the Holy Ghost descends upon him; then he is a thousand legions, then he will never strike his battle-flag until the victory be won.

Some men are more spirit-gifted than others. Some men have hardly begun their manhood. They are dealers of a low type. The true business man is a truly inspired man, just as much so as any prophet, according to the level he lives upon. But some men are mere hucksters; it is give and take. I do not call them business men. I hold that the title " business men " means education, sagacity, statesmanship, power of arrangement and adjustment and government. There are some men who have not begun to be. They have never prayed; they cannot sing. All beauty is wasted upon them; the gilt is gilt, not gold; the colour is a violation of whiteness, a staring challenge to dull eyes; not symbolism, not poetry, blushing before their very sight. They are animals. Never take the clue of your life from them. They will always tell you how not to do a thing; they will chill you like icebergs. Other men have hardly any body; they are all soul, all spirit, all sensitiveness. They feel that a thing is coming; they know it is in the air; they see it in flashes of the face, in kindlings of the eyes; they know it by the tips of the fingers of those who touch them. Man is not one and the same; he requires definition, according to personality and environment. Some men have fire, genius, sight; it is a great gift of God; it is the pledge and seal that the Holy Ghost has descended out of heaven upon them, and that they are approved by the Father, ruling all the household of mankind. We should hail such men; we may not understand what they are talking about, but we feel that they have brought with them fragrance from an upper garden. They may often bewilder us, but we feel that the very bewilderment is part of a higher education ; it lifts us up, it never drags us down. Christ was full of the Holy Ghost. In him dwelt all the fulness of the Godhead bodily. It was in his cloak. Said one, " If I may but touch the hem of his garment I shall be made whole." It was in Christ's hands. Oh those wondrous hands ! We shall one day come to believe more in manual healing. One day the true healing will be in the true touch. There is healing in some hands ; they are mother's hands, they bring us nearer to the heart, they talk masonically. Christ's hands have healing in them. " He laid his hands upon him " ; and as for the children, he laid his hands upon them and blessed them. It was in his voice. Some men who went to arrest him said, We could not touch that man : never man spake like this man. On another occasion, all the people wondered at the gracious words which proceeded out of his lips. They were old words, but never so spoken ; the words had been written upon the scroll until the ink had become yellow with age ; but uttered by Jesus they were new words, syllables of fire, glints of light. We might have more light. Jesus came to give us life, and to give it to us more abundantly, like wave on wave, so that we not only breathe, but fly, and burn, and go upward to meet our kindred in the skies.

Christ's spirit, or genius, or divinity, was in his Beatitudes. He blessed whom none had blessed before. Other men had been blessing riches and honours, crowns and thrones, and glories of many kinds and degrees ; but Jesus blesses the poor in spirit, and the meek, and the merciful, and raises them all to heaven. The Deity of Christ was in his welcomes. Were ever such welcomes breathed ? Broad as the firmament, generous as the all-inspiring air. Read his welcomes if you would take the measure of his soul. Yet at last he was forsaken. Said he, " My God, my God ! why hast thou forsaken me ? " That only the body might be killed ; that only the flesh might be dishonoured in the final blasphemy. Was he forsaken ? Say, is the sun forsaken when for a moment he is eclipsed. Not a beam of him has been shorn. His centre has not been changed. He is still the sun. The eclipse will pass. The sun will abide.

PRAYER.

ALMIGHTY GOD, help us to hear all thy truth. Give us the hearing ear, the understanding heart, lest we reject any portion of the counsel of heaven. Speak, Lord, for thy servant heareth. We want to hear every tone of thy voice. Not one word of thine would we allow to fall to the ground. We want to hear thy commandments. The thunder and the lightning and the great earthquake shall not keep us back from the commandments of God. We want to hear thy beatitude, thou lovely One, fairest among ten thousand, whose voice is music, whose eyes are morning. We would hear the commandments and the beatitude, the great law and the tender benedictions. We would keep company with the prophets and with the minstrels, and with the apostles and with the evangelists. We would hear all their utterances, and treasure them in our hearts as revelations from heaven. Forgive us wherein we have neglected one portion of thy Word, or cultivated one at the expense of another. We have lost the proportion of faith; we have heeded not the balance of thought; we have not known all the way and all the counsel of God. Dost thou not speak in great thunder, and hast thou not also a still small voice? Are not thine the torrents and the cataracts, and are not thine also the rills and the streams that make glad the city of God? The Lord give us fearlessness of soul that we may pursue our quest after truth amid all dangers, difficulties and perils, and when the voice is harsh and terrible may we still listen to it, for in the judgments of God there is no want of music. Find a way for thyself into our hearts; abide in our judgment and in our conscience; accept the sovereignty of our will. These prayers will be prevalent because we baptise them with the blood of atonement. We offer them all at the altar of the Cross, we make them mighty in the name that is above every name, in which name the universe evermore bows its knee before God. Amen.

Chapter iv. 28, 29.

"When they heard these things, they were filled with wrath, and rose up, and thrust him out of the city, and led him unto the brow of the hill whereon their city was built, that they might cast him down headlong."

EXCITING SERMONS.

ARE there any such perorations in connection with the pulpit eloquence of this day? The preacher retires amid thunders of applause, or amid tepid compliments, or without recognition, or with more or less of well-calculated or ill-calculated criticism.

But when does a congregation ever rise up, and, filled with wrath, seize the minister, lead him to the brow of the hill, and threaten to cast him headlong from the eminences of the city? Never! We have fallen upon other times. Hear the trumpery criticism of this day :—The sermon was so quiet, so delightfully quiet; the preacher was so pleasant, so tranquil, so composed; he never betrayed the faintest excitement. Or, hear it again in another form :—The sermon was so comforting, soothing, healing; there was balm in it; the preacher was a son of consolation : how richly he dwelt upon the divine promises! how aptly and happily he applied them to human necessity! There is room for all that kind of preaching. It is not a kind of preaching in either case to be despised or held in light esteem. Sometimes we need quietness, oftentimes we need healing. The broken-hearted are the majority in every congregation, if they knew themselves. We need the balm that is in Gilead, and we need no other physician but the One that is there. All that is true ; create space for such ministry, for we need it all.

But where is the other kind of eloquence? It must be the right kind in some instances, at least, because it is associated in this text with the name of Jesus Christ. This was not some wandering speaker who had gone forth without licence or authority, or without adequate cause, and had aroused popular passions, or excited religious hatred. The speaker was the Son of God, he who spake as never man spake : and yet when he had uttered a few words, to us apparently so simple and so inoffensive, the whole congregation rose up in a mass, being filled with wrath, and led him forth to the brow of the hill on which their city was built, that they might cast him down headlong.

There should be room for that ministry as well as the other. We do not like it. Therefore, perhaps, we need it the more. We would rather not be disturbed. We have disturbance enough in business and in politics. When we go to the sanctuary we want to hear something to soothe us, and lull us, and comfort us. That is bad reasoning. When we go to the sanctuary we should go for truth. Sometimes truth will be like a child-angel, so sweet, so tender, so familiar, so domestic, so necessary to the completeness of the household ; sometimes it will be as the voice of the lute, just what we need ; and sometimes it will rage and storm and judge the world and thunder against its iniquities and corruptions : we need it all.   Christ's was the perfect ministry, and in Christ we find all this kind of preaching.   And only that ministry is right, four-square to the edge, that can be both tender and judicial, comforting and critical, sympathetic and damnatory.

Nor must the preacher be afraid of the people or of his own income.   That is the great curse of every age of the pulpit, that a man should think whether he is diminishing his own resources when he declares this or that part of the counsel of God.   Those who do not like it must go, and take their gold with them.   It will buy them nothing.   For such metal there is no exchange with God. It will be a mistake to upbraid the ministry of the time for self-consideration to that degree.   The preaching of this day is as fearless as it has been in any other day.   Not, perhaps, so fearless in every church ; but wherever there is fearless preaching there is a congregation rising to thrust the preacher out of existence. The fearless, all-truth-speaking preacher is hated everywhere. He is not and cannot be a popular man.   He can have no sympathy with the majority of his race.   He must be prepared for consequences.

What a wondrous ministry was Christ's !   In verse twenty-two we read, in the same chapter, " And all bare him witness, and wondered at the gracious words which proceeded out of his mouth."   A few verses after, the whole of the people in the synagogue " rose up," " being filled with wrath."   What a change he wrought !   What a wizard he was !   Now look at the people. How beaming, how radiant, how benignant ! they say.   Did charmer ever charm like this ?   Hear that music, and say, was the like ever heard in Israel ?   In five minutes more, by historical allusions which the people alone could understand, the same people rose up, being filled with wrath, and would have killed the very charmer whose entrancing power they had just acknowledged.

Was there ever any exciting preaching in the Church ?   Read : " And as they spake unto the people, the priests, and the captain of the temple, and the Sadducees, came upon them, being grieved that they taught the people, and they laid hands on them, and put them in hold." They do the same to-day. If you were to preach apostolically you would be put in prison. The magistrate before whom you would be tried would not understand the case. What case is there that a magistrate really and thoroughly understands all round and round where the gospel is concerned, where high moral impulses are involved, and where the real good of the people is the question of the hour? The magistrates have never been on the side of apostolical preachers. The magistrates have always suggested prison as the best treatment for men who preach the gospel. It looks energetic; if a magistrate were to sympathise with the preacher it would look sentimental. A magistrate seems to be doing something for his dignity when he puts somebody in prison. Read the life of George Fox; read the Life and Journals ot John Wesley; study the biography of George Whitefield; read the present-day records of the Salvation Army, and say when were apostolical preachers otherwise treated than Christ himself was treated in the very instance before us.

Understand that we are not saying a word against this same popular quiet preaching, in which a man speaks for an hour, and says nothing that can at all offend or exasperate his audience. We are not undervaluing healing preaching. God forbid. For we all need it; if not to-day, yesterday; it not yesterday, to-morrow we shall need it. But we want to point out that the counsel of God is full-orbed, now soft as when Zephyrus on Flora breathes, and now a wind that silences Euroclydon.

But the times have changed! Have they? Who changed them? Is the devil changed? Has that miracle at last been wrought? Has evil washed its hands and come out of the process pure and stainless? What has changed? Is the thief honest? Why, that is a paradox, a contradiction in terms. Are there no thieves to-day? Is the miser generous? When did he convert himself? If he is generous he is not a miser; if he is a miser he is not generous. The times have changed! When? Services may have changed, transient relations may have been transformed and modified, but the times have not changed in the sense of making sin less sinful, dishonesty less thievish, miserliness less avaricious. We find these great radical principles and policies abiding now in the deepest sense. What if we should be the real thieves ? That is a harrowing suggestion. But what if the magistrate should be the real thief, and the little boy who took the pocket-handkerchief should be honest in his soul and only thievish in his fingers, because of some impulsion or compulsion not easily understood by those who are outside the circle and atmosphere within which he lives ? What if the man with the fine clothing and the gold ring and the high position be the real thief ?—not a vulgar, common, street thief, that is the very poorest kind of felon ; but a calculating, long-headed, nimble-fingered gentleman, who writes well and reads much, and talks fluently, and has his turns of piety—what if he in the soul of him and in the whole trick of his policy be the real thief ?

Have the times changed ? In that direction they may have changed. Refined sin may have displaced rough criminality, but the devil is inconvertible, and will be the same when the hour of doom has struck. Do not misunderstand things, and do not be such wonderful optimists and poets as to see improvements where there really are none at all. If there are improvements prove them, recognise them, be thankful for them; but understand that the devil cannot change. If he is dead the times may have changed. If we have any reason to believe that he is still hidden in some corner of God's universe, he is as fruitful of poison and iniquity as he ever was. What if we be the misers ? That is an exasperating suggestion. The man who makes it ought to be led out, and cast down from the top of the highest hill that is accessible. What if we be the misers ? Ay, that ! You who gave a hundred pounds all at once may be the miser. Why did you give it ? In what atmosphere did you act ? What was your regnant motive ? Go into your soul, and ask your soul torturing questions until you get at the truth. If you gave it honestly, lovingly, gratefully, you will be blessed ; you shall have it tenfold back again. The question is, Did you, or did you not ? and that question I must force back upon myself until I bleed. Is not every man more or less miserly ? Who gives what he ought to give ? Who gives to the point of dividing his last crust with Christ? Does he give anything who withholds anything? Does he answer God's appeal who has his meals regularly and fully, and who sleeps through all the night of the world's darkness and sorrow? These are questions which I must put to myself and hold a long inquest with my own life. And it may turn out that I am the thief, the miser, the felon, the self-indulgent, the wrong-doer. If judgment thus begins at the house of God, what wonder that everybody in the synagogue should rise up inflamed with wrath, mad with resentment? Yet so curiously are we constituted, so wondrously made, that we have a positive delight in hearing the sins of other people denounced. Thus we eke out our own virtue. We do like the man in the next pew to have the truth told plainly to him. We love to hear drunkenness denounced, whereas we may be the real drunkards. The man who drinks his potass may be the real winebibber. That is no paradox; it is a plain, literal possibility in life. Men are what they are in the soul of them. Less the habit, more the spirit, must be taken as the judge and estimate of the man's spiritual quality.

Speaking thus, how different an aspect is put upon everything. The first shall be last, and the last shall be first; and many shall come from the east and from the west, from the north and from the south, and shall sit down in God's kingdom of light, and we ourselves, pretentious, ostentatious, pharisaic professors, shall be cast out because we nodded our heads at certain dogmas, but gave no heed to the commandments. We sought to suck the honey of the beatitudes, but never attempted to obey the law.

Great mistakes may thus be made about any ministry. You hear a man once, and judge him altogether. How foolish and unreasonable, how wholly unjust as well as unwise is this course! If you had heard Jesus Christ in the twenty-second verse, so to say, you would have gone away with this report: "So gracious in his speech, so musical, tuneful, tender, comforting." If you had gone away at the twenty-eighth verse you would have said, "Exasperating, maddening his congregation. Instead of taking that people into his hand, and playing upon them as a skilful man would play upon an instrument, he roused them to madness; yea, so vehement and terrible was he in style that all the people rose up and seized him, and led him out, and would have killed him on the spot." Neither report would have given a fair idea of the ministry of Christ.

Yet this is just how ministries are treated to-day. A man who never heard a minister before falls upon some occasion when the minister is very tender and sympathetic, and thinks he is always so; or falls upon another occasion when the minister is denunciatory, and goes away and reports him in terms that are full of all evil suggestion. You never know any ministry that has anything in it until you have heard it seven years long, in all its moods, tenses, variations, aspects, colours, in the whole gamut of its strength. What is true of a ministry is true of God's Book. We must read it all if we would judge it fairly. It is true of the gospel; we must hear it all if we would pronounce upon it with wisdom and ripeness of judgment.

So with Christ our Lord. Hear him : Blessed are the pure in heart, blessed are the merciful, blessed are the meek, blessed are the peacemakers. Oh, how the beatitudes flow from his sacred lips! Hear him : Woe unto you, scribes and Pharisees, hypocrites; woe unto you, ye lawyers; woe unto thee, Chorazin; woe unto thee, Bethsaida. Where are your beatitudes now? It is the same man, in the same brief three years' ministry. Behold, you must take in the evening and the morning to make the day. God's great sky has in it four directions, and every one must be estimated and set in its proper relation to the other if you would understand the geometry of God's canopy. Blessed be God, the severity is always against the sin. It is sin that is predestinated to go to hell. It is sin that is foreordained to be damned. Some persons do not like these words, "hell" and "damned"; yet how wondrously men change in their estimate even of such terms and of the doctrine and preaching with which they are associated. I know a remarkable artist who came to a church with which I am very familiar, and heard a sermon on the damnation of wickedness, and fled away in horror because she did not believe in hell and in damnation. Years have come and years have gone, and she is now in the Roman Catholic

Church, where there is a real hell, where there is no want of
literal fire. So curiously are we made, and so mysterious is the
reaction which is the possibility of our lives.

We must have the whole counsel of God. We must hear
of the night as well as of the day, and we must not as ministers
and churches allow ourselves to be cozened out of half the truth
because there are people who will come in thousands to hear
our musical utterances about Christ, who would be exasperated
and offended if we held up the law in its terror. We must lose
them; we must bear our lot as bravely as we can. Better the
pews be empty to the point of desolation; better that the minister
should starve than that we should never hear that God is Judge
as well as Saviour. All the gentleness is for the sinner. God
never turns against the prodigal; he is always against the self-
righteous. The self-righteous is, of course, the greatest sinner,
but God has no pity upon him, because he cannot have pity
where there is no pity for himself, that is to say, for the sinner,
the man himself. The man is self-righteous, self-satisfied; he
has enough, he wants no more; he is a perfect man and an
upright, yea, he is the temple of the living God, and other men
are the filth and the off-scouring of the race. God can have no
pity for that man. He can only encounter him with sternness
and judgment, and visit him with the final penalty. But where
there is a broken heart, where there is a contrite spirit, where
there is a desire to come home again, all the angels are sent
down to make the way easy, and great welcomes await the
returning prodigal. God is gentle and good towards any soul
that can weep over its own guilt and its own sorrow. Let us,
therefore, take heart and come before him with tears. He will
dwell with the contrite in spirit.

This is my conclusion: It ought to be the greatest blessing
of society to have within it a pulpit that can be both gentle and
terrible. When you lose that pulpit you lose a saving element
from your social constitution. It ought to be the supremest
educational force in morals to have a pulpit that is afraid of
no face of clay; to have a pulpit that will speak all the counsel
of God, come weal, come woe. Do not let us misunderstand this.

He is the great preacher who preaches to himself. Yea, he is the man to be trusted who first takes up the law and smites himself with it, and tells you across the ruins of a broken law that he is criminal as well as preacher. I would listen to that man. It is an infinite impertinence on the part of any man to preach the law as if he kept it. It is an infinite help to us to hear any man preach the law who says he has broken it all through and through, yet by the mercy of God, as shown in the Cross of Christ, he has crawled home again, and has begun to taste the sweets of divine forgiveness.

NOTES.

[From the *Speaker's Commentary.*]

Ver. 28. *Filled with wrath.*—They were indignant at his rejection of his countrymen which he points by citing the examples of the two great prophets. They may also have understood him to hint that he had a mission even to the heathen.

Ver. 29. *Thrust him out.*—Drove him out with violence.

The brow.—Or *a brow*, according to a great preponderance of authority. Two natural features, in the neighbourhood of Nazareth, may still be identified. . . . " The second is indicated in the Gospel history by one of those slight touches which serve as a testimony to the truth of the description, by nearly approaching, but yet not crossing, the verge of inaccuracy. 'They rose,' it is said of the infuriated inhabitants, and cast him out of the city, and brought him to a brow of the mountain. . . . on which the city was built, so as to cast him down the cliff.' . . . Most readers probably from these words imagine a town built on the summit of a mountain, from which summit the intended precipitation was to take place. This, as I have said, is not the situation of Nazareth. Yet its position is still in accordance with the narrative. It is built ' upon,' that is, on the side of, 'a mountain,' but the ' brow' is not beneath, but over the town, and such a cliff . . . as is here implied is to be found, as all modern travellers describe, in the abrupt face of the limestone rock, about thirty or forty feet high, overhanging the Maronite convent at the south-west corner of the town, and another at a little further distance." (Stanley, "Sinai and Palestine," ch. x.) One such cliff, about two miles from Nazareth, is shown as the " Mount of Precipitation."

That they might cast, etc.—Read, *so as to cast.*

PRAYER.

BLESSED JESUS, thou knowest all things; thou readest every heart; thou needest not that any should testify of man, for thou knowest what is in man. Truly we bear the image and likeness of God, and thou, being in the bosom of the Father, knowest all things that are in our nature. We can hide nothing from thee; but, blessed be thy name, thine eyes are not eyes of justice only, they are eyes of love, compassion, tenderness; they see us as we are, they see us as we might be, they see us in the purpose of God. Behold, we come to thee; to thee all men must come; thou canst find the piece we have lost; thou canst bring back our whole being, our highest quality, our truest character; thou canst restore us to our standing in the household of God. Blessed One, we love thee; we do not only revere thee and admire thee, and offer the homage due to great power; but we love thee, we yearn towards thee, we struggle after thee, we struggle after thee in the crowd, knowing that if we can but touch the hem of thy garment we shall lose all our disease. O thou Great Speaker, Great Healer, Friend of the broken heart, and Helper of the helpless, come to us day by day, bringing the daily bread we need for the body, and the bread of life we need for the soul. We have read thy life—we have sat down with thee, we have looked at thee; we have been with thee when we thought no eye could see us, when hardly thine own vision could detect us, so deep was the darkness and so complete our concealment; and after all we have heard and seen and known and felt of thee we love thee all the more. Lord, abide with us, for it is towards evening, and the day is far spent with many: break bread to us with thine own dear hands, and when we begin to touch what thou hast blessed we shall see thee, a vanishing glory, but a light to come again. Amen.

Chapter vii.

A CONSPECTUS OF CHRIST'S MIRACLES.

MY purpose is to show the congruity of Christ's miracles; to point out with what beauty and precision they accommodate themselves to one another; to indicate the family likeness of the miracles; how much soever they may seem to differ from one another, yet there is a central and all-uniting line bringing them into perfect congruity, and showing how possible it is in the midst of great diversity to have real spiritual unity.

Observe what is in the chapter. Here is a servant cured who was ready to die; a dead man raised to life whilst he was being carried out to be buried; an hour crowded with wonders, such an hour as probably never occurred before even in the history of Jesus Christ; and, lastly, a sinner forgiven, in connection with which a human heart was revealed to itself. Let us suppose all these miracles occurring just as they are found in this chapter: our immediate purpose is not to find precise dates, or to rectify chronologies if needful, but to look at the chapter as it is written for us in our English Bibles; and looking at it so to find out the congruousness, the moral unity, the benevolent and beneficent solidarity of the whole work of Jesus Christ. Note how we come into this gallery of miracles: by what door did we enter? If we knew it, we should find that the door itself is greater than any miracle it opens upon. The door is indicated in the first verse of the chapter—" Now when he had ended all his sayings." The speech was the great miracle; how it welled up out of the heart; how it brought a taste of eternity with it; how it sounded unlike all other music, and put all mere philosophy, speculation, and intellectual adventure to shame ! How simple the sayings, but how profound ! A child thinks he can carry them all; yet an angel cannot see the depth of their wisdom, or measure all the scope of their meaning. When we come to judge by right standards, we shall find that words are the greatest miracles when they are employed to reveal infinite wisdom, when they are set up as sanctuaries in which God himself is enshrined, when they are used sacrificially for religious purposes; for all words must be slain by the very deity they would convey, if they attempt to represent God. Truly we drag our eloquence to the altar to slay it and burn it by the message which we would convey through its tones. We do not, however, judge spiritually; we are still victims of our senses: to see the brilliant sight, to hear the startling sound, to observe the new phenomenon,—to these base uses do we drag ourselves. The time will come when we shall rather say, Blessed is he who is revealed in these words which constitute our mother tongue; wonderful is the might of God, that in words so familiar to us he can show us all the surprises of his love,

Notice the motive or line of reason which runs through the
whole of this narrative. Jesus marvelled at the faith of the
centurion, saying, "I have not found so great faith, no, not in
Israel." It was more than amazement, it was gratitude; there
were tears in his voice as he expressed this astonishment. He
loves faith; he will do anything for faith. Believest thou that
I am able to do this? Yea, Lord. Then take it all! said he.
Christ withholds nothing from faith. That is the miracle he
looks for. We cannot surprise him by genius, by brilliance, by
boldness of intellectual conjecture and speculation, but we can
surprise him by trust, faith, confidence. He looks for spiritual
miracles. We can amaze him by our love. If we kiss his feet,
he thrills with an infinite sensation of delight. When he praises,
what does he commend? If we read the history of Christ
aright, we shall be struck with the fewness of the instances
in which he uttered commendation; but when we bring them
together we shall see that they are all of the same quality. He
praised a prayer: what was it? The Pharisee's pompous self-
defence? No. The publican's self-abasement—"God be merciful
to me a sinner." That prayer pleased the Son of God: it
sounded like prayer; it was all prayer; it startled him into the
utterance of eulogium. He praised a donation: what was it?
The widow's two mites: he saw so much in them, a whole
fortune, an absolute devotion, a miracle of wealth. He praised
a servant: in what terms did he commend him? In moral
terms—"Good and faithful." Christ's commendations are all
on the same line, all directed to the same point, all rich with the
same quality; and his commendation runs upon a line on which
all men may stand. This is not a tribute to gigantic stature,
to phenomenal genius, to occasional brilliance, to eccentric gift;
it is a benediction pronounced upon actions which children can
commit, which the common people can execute. When he saw
the widow following her dead, "he had compassion on her."
He is easily touched with the feeling of our infirmities; he could
have looked upon all the Pharisees in the universe, and passed
by them with an infinite disdain; but when we need him most,
and cannot see him for our tears, he will move all heaven
to help us. He was condescending to the weakness of his
forerunner. When John sent a doubt to him he sent back a

gospel ; he said, I will perform a thousand miracles to heal this heart of doubt. In that hour—such was the lustrous focal point of the omnipotence of Christ—" In that same hour he cured many of their infirmities and plagues, and of evil spirits ; and unto many that were blind he gave sight." What a day of festival ! What an amnesty was proclaimed that day ! Not only that the men may be healed who were ailing in body, but that a man might be healed who was sick at heart, saying, in his imprison-ment and darkness, After all, I wonder if this is the Son of God ?

Then, finally, came his response to love. When did he say no to true affection ? He gave the woman all she wanted—a new girlhood, a new morning, a new heart, a new conception of God. Observe that all these feelings are of the same quality—wonder, compassion, condescension, and recognition of love. Jesus never worked a miracle for the sake of working it. They were but miracles to the observers ; they were no miracles to him. If " miracle " means surprise, alteration, unexpectedness, incalcul-ableness, it would be impossible for Christ to work a miracle to himself ; all the ministry of Christ is but miraculous on its human side, on the aspects which it bears to observers. Christ was no specialist. Observe what he did :—" Go your way, and tell John what things ye have seen and heard ; how that the blind see, the lame walk, the lepers are cleansed, the deaf hear, the dead are raised." The whole circuit of miracles is swept. There are men who are strong at points ; they are men who rejoice in the name of " specialists,"—that is to say, they have made particular studies of particular diseases, and in the treatment of those diseases they have earned a very just reputation ; but Jesus Christ was not a specialist, so we have infinite variety in his miracles—" blind," " lame," " lepers," " deaf," " dead." Jesus Christ did not treat symptoms, nor did he ever merely lessen human suffering, saying, Now the burden is not quite so heavy as it was; you are considerably relieved after this mitigatory treatment to which I have subjected you ; you will be able to return home with more ease than you came from it. Jesus Christ never performed half a miracle ; all his wonders are associated with the most perfect ease of action. He commanded, and it was done ; his word was the miracle. He said, Let there be ! and there was, so quick the change of tense and reality, of time and space and fact of every kind. Why? Because he penetrated to the heart of things. He said, The disease is at the centre; other men are looking at symptomatic changes, and are inferring from those changes what they can of the nature of the disease : the deadly disease is here, in the very heart, at the very core. So he touched that, and in the cheek there flamed red health, and in the voice there sang new energy and consciousness of power.

We ourselves can supply the conditions of the miracle. What were those conditions in this chapter?—need, faith, sorrow, love. Observe, there is a line of co-operation in all this action. So in nature we do something. Why rip up the ground? why sow the seed? why close the furrows? what are you expecting? We have buried this seed, say you, in sure and certain hope of a glorious resurrection. That we can also do in the Church. We can be working as if we expected a miracle. Jesus will never disappoint that expectation. He will say to us, What do ye here, building an altar, filling the trench with water, laying the wood, supplying the offering—what mean ye by all these things? And the answer is, We are expecting the descent of God : we know we shall realise it; nothing shall be wanting on our part; if this fail, the blame be God's. When the Church speaks so, the Church will not be disappointed—when we leave the onus with God, when we can truly stand up and say, Nothing has been wanting on our part; we have prepared for a miracle, we have prayed for a miracle, we have been expecting a miracle, we have pledged God to a miracle, and all the jibing crowd is come to see whether God will answer prayer. Could we conduct the process in that spirit, in that high tone of reverence, with that sublimity of expectation, God would not be wanting on his part.

There is another line running through the narrative which in the blaze of glory may be entirely concealed; so to say, there is a deity higher than we have yet seen in these gathering wonders. What if the compassion was greater than the healing? What if the moral was grander than the miracles? We are surprised at miracles, as we have said, and Christ is surprised at faith. Is it nothing that the first miracle was done at a distance? Jesus

never saw the first man who was to be healed ; Jesus Christ did
not go near the man, did not observe him with the eyes of his
body ; and yet the man was healed.   Distance is nothing to
Christ ; with God there is no distance.   We ourselves are beginning to talk of annihilating distance, annihilating time and space :
thus we grow in the knowledge of the Lord Jesus Christ ; thus
science brings us to the altar ; thus we are trained to know the
meaning of words which once were but symbolic, algebraic,
charged with spiritual possibilities which we could not compass,
—slowly, gradually, we are being brought round by all manner
of lower education to be able to grasp in some degree great
spiritual significations.   Is it nothing that the second miracle
was not asked for ?   Did the widow pray Jesus to help her ?
Poor sufferer, she could not : her heart was full, her throat was
choked, her eyes were dim with the waters of sorrow ; she never
spake a word to Christ about the matter, and yet the miracle was
done.   There is mute prayer—an awful, silent, looking supplication.   Sometimes we get beyond the region of words, and Jesus
Christ looks at our attitude, listens to our breathing, numbers our
tears, and says, Poor soul ! he would ask me to-day for seven
miracles if he could, but not a word will come to his dry lips ; I
will go to him, for he cannot come to me.   The greatest miracle
of all was not asked for.   We get greater things for not asking
than we ever get by supplication.   The Son of God came to earth,
not in answer to prayer, but in realisation of divine purpose and
divine love.

The coming of the Saviour is the supreme miracle of the
universe, and that was brought about by no man's prayer.   How
much we get that we do not ask for !   Who asks for sunrise, who
asks for summer, in the broadest significations of these terms ?
Who asks for all the great benisons that are sent down from
heaven for the warmth and comfort and culture of this little cold
earth ?   Is it nothing that by the healing of others we are healed
ourselves ?   To heal John's doubt, Christ cured other men's
bodies.   He sent John a whole galaxy of miracles, a gathering-
up, a summation of phases of almightiness ; not one miracle only,
for that might have been misconstrued, but miracles at every
point of the circle—blind, deaf, dumb, lame, widowed, palsied,

dead ; they could not forget that message ; they might have confused one incident, but when a whole encyclopædia of miracle was wrought it would be impossible wholly to miss the point and accent of that great gospel. The same evidence is open to us. When we ourselves doubt, in some prison of darkness, go abroad into the world, and see the miracles Christ is working every day, and let the miracles done for others be miracles of healing in our own heart—of fear, or hopelessness, or doubt. Thus the miracle is twice wrought : first, wrought upon those who need bodily release ; and, secondly, wrought upon those who need spiritual light and comfort. Is it nothing that Christ notices the neglects of our life and worship—the simple omissions with which we are chargeable ? Hear how Jesus speaks to Simon :—" Thou gavest me no water. . . . Thou gavest me no kiss. . . . My head with oil thou didst not anoint." He went to be the guest of the Pharisee : did he notice what the Pharisee did for him ? Everything ; he knew everything that was on the table ; he recognised it if he did not eat it. He does not like to be treated as if he were no one of particular dignity or consequence. He does not consume the feast, but he notices every little device of love. Thus he noticed what the woman did : " She hath washed my feet with tears, and wiped them with the hairs of her head. . . . This woman . . . hath not ceased to kiss my feet. . . . This woman hath anointed my feet with ointment." Jesus knows all we do. When we go out on errands for him in the snowy night, in the cold winter, in calculated secrecy so that nobody may know what we are about,—when we open our hand to give as if we were not opening it, but looking at something beyond, he puts it all down in his register ; and specially does he notice neglect on the part of those whose neglect is not due to poverty. We may not insult Christ ; alas, we may neglect him. It is not enough not to have blasphemed : our silence may be blasphemy ; we may have omitted to sing, to praise God with a loud voice, to laud and magnify him with fearlessness of worship. Christ thus notices the negative aspects of our character ; and herein he works a miracle as great as any of the wonders which startled us in the earlier parts of the chapter. He read the Pharisee's heart ; the Pharisee thought he was reading Christ's spirit, and detecting in him inability to penetrate the character of another, when in a moment he turned upon him all the lightnings of creation, and Simon was revealed to himself. Notice the tender delicacies of love, the little attentions. The Pharisee gave Christ meat, but he omitted the water, the kiss, the ointment—the little things that finish with grace what was begun with large hospitality. It is in the detail that we discover our characters. The cabinet maker cannot furnish a house ; he may put down all his mahogany and walnut, and the house is quite cold and bare ; we must have little touches of colour, artistic devices, not necessarily representing wealth and great affluence of resources, but the woman's touch, the gentle, simple thing, the new turning which only a skilled hand can give to a common object or article ;—all these things that give fascination to home are done not with great broad rough hands, but with genuinely delicate fingers—delicate because the heart is charged with the courtesy of love. It is not enough that now and then the son has done some great thing for his mother— plunged his hand into his pocket and produced a handful of gold, and said with some roughness, Take that, and never charge me again with being unkind to you. The son was never unkinder than when he made that speech. The mother wants a thousand other things beside, or perhaps instead of, that glaring gold : a little sympathy, a little attention, a little consideration ; a hundred things done for her without her attention being called to them, so that when she comes she finds that some one has been there to anticipate the wish, to be before her, to have all things ready for her. O thou generous Giver of all good, dost thou not set thy sun in the heavens before we awake ? and is not thy glory standing there when we open our eyes ? Thou preventest me. Thou goest before me with thy goodness.

Here, then, we have healed suffering, healed heart-ache, healed sin, and the healed sin is the greatest miracle of all. My friend, is thy sin healed ? If the answer is, " Yes, by the grace of God," then be not ashamed of him who forgave it, but publish that sweet gospel everywhere : through the miracle wrought in thee another miracle may be wrought in some listening observer. Thus all the miracles of Christ fall into beauteous rhythmic congruity. In reality there was but one miracle, and that one miracle was himself.

PRAYER.

As the hart panteth after the waterbrooks, so panteth our soul after thee, O God—living, good, and wise evermore, gentler than all motherhood, and more majestic than all kingliness. Verily thou hast all things in thyself; thou commandest, and it is done; thou utterest the word, and behold what thou callest for is there, present in all its reality, to do thy bidding. Thou dost turn water into wine, thou dost turn common bread into sacramental food, and thou dost make all things new, yea, even new heavens and a new earth. But there is one renewal above all others we long to know, and that is a renewal of our own spirit. If any man be in Christ Jesus he is a new creature: old things have passed away; all things have become new. This is the newness we want to experience; then we shall see it with our eyes that are within, and feel it in all the outgoing and purpose of life. Thus thou dost deliver us from the power of monotony; thou art making new heavens and a new earth every day, did we but see the mighty creation as we ought to see it; and thou art renewing the inward man day by day by subtle ministries of spiritual assistance, did we but yield ourselves to the working of thy compassion. Thou dost work in many ways: the chariots of God are twenty thousand in number—yea, thousands of thousands; and thou comest into the heart as thou wilt, by many a door we know not of; thou hast access to our life in ten thousand ways: come by any one of them, only come; even so, Lord Jesus, come quickly! through our imagination, or our judgment, or our pain, or our contrition, or our expectation,—choose thine own way, only hear the sighing of the heart as it says, Lord Jesus, come! When thou comest the heart-house will be made beautiful by thy presence, and there shall be great hospitality, for thou wilt spread the table as with thy blood, and minister unto us of the wine of thy grace. Lord Jesus, come; come by healing our diseases, by satisfying our mouth with good things, by renewing our youth as the eagle's, by giving unto us assurance of pardon whilst we tarry at the Cross; in thine own way do thou hasten to us, only hear us when we say, Lord Jesus, come! Amen.

Chapter viii.

CHRIST'S SUSTENANCE ACCOUNTED FOR.

WE have wondered how Jesus Christ subsisted. The explanation would seem to be given here. There are with him not only the twelve, but also "certain women," some of whose names are given, "which ministered unto him of their substance." We are not wholly unfamiliar with that species of action; we have read in the ancient books of a woman who "said unto her husband, Behold now, I perceive that this is an holy man of God, which passeth by us continually. Let us make a little chamber, I pray thee, in the wall; and let us set for him there a bed, and a table, and a stool, and a candlestick; and it shall be, when he cometh to us, that he shall turn in thither." It was not unusual in Bible times, and even down to New Testament days, for the richer women to keep a Rabbi or a prophet out of their income, sustaining the good man in his educational and evangelistic works. Here we find the Son of God subsisting by similar means. "There were with him many others, which ministered unto him of their substance." Yet the Son of man came not to be ministered unto, but to minister. And yet both statements are open to the most perfect reconciliation. Thus we work in different ways—the divine Minister who does everything, the Christ of God; and the lesser ministers who do their work on a small scale, but whatever is done is taken, and is magnified and glorified by the living God. Some of the names are given. We ought always to be thankful for what is written, not only because it shows itself within its own boundaries so vividly, but because it enables us to draw inferences regarding many things which are not explained. "And certain women, which had been healed." What a key is there! Jesus Christ does not want any others to follow him than those to whom he himself has first ministered. It is possible so to read the passage as to omit the fact that Jesus Christ's ministry was first. The mind comes suddenly upon the statement that certain women ministered unto him of their substance, and the mind is apt to dwell upon that circumstance with magnifying emphasis; whereas we ought to read the narrative so carefully as to get out of it all its music, and so reading it we shall find that Jesus was first, for the women who followed him "had been healed of evil spirits and infirmities," and, as we shall presently see, their attachment to him was grounded upon a still wider basis.

"Mary called Magdalene, out of whom went seven devils." Some have said, seven evil spirits or dispositions; unwilling to recognise what is termed demoniacal possession, they have regarded these as seven evil tempers, bad dispositions, wicked desires. Practically, it comes to the same thing: whatever they were, devils or dispositions, they were cast out by the Son of God ; there is the working of the divine power; there is the miracle of wisdom and grace, of human compassion and divine ability. "And Joanna"—do we know anything of her ? She was "the wife of Chuza, Herod's steward." Some have traced her by critical processes to be the mother of the nobleman's son who, when at the point of death, was healed by the Son of God. Out of her there was cast no evil spirit, and she was not cured of any personal infirmity : why, then, did she follow this Nazarene ? Ask her. Try to detach her from his following, and she will tell you, with tears of gratitude and joy, that Jesus Christ was the resurrection and the life in her house ; say of him what others may, she knows that he cured her son, and from that point she cannot be dislodged by any evil suggestion or by any sophism. Hers was a personal gratitude for personal favours. Jesus Christ thus is followed by people who have understood him at some point. It is not necessary that all who follow Jesus Christ should understand every phase of his personality, and be able to explain every section of his ministry, and to answer all the questions which may be put concerning him ; the people who followed Jesus Christ knew him at some point, and that became emphatically their point, and one of them gave expression to the sentiment of the whole when he said, "One thing I know, that, whereas I was blind, now I see."

How much has Christianity itself suffered from the delusion that those who profess it must be able to answer the questions ; that every Christian must be a theologian, a man of science, a profound philosopher, an accurate logician, and an eloquent speaker. Nothing of the kind. It is for every Christian to have his own view of Christ, his own particular song of praise concerning what the Son of God has done ; and so long as men keep to that personal testimony their utterance will be unbroken as to emphasis, and direct and unanswerable as to practical appeal. "And Joanna"—do we ever hear of her again? The time came when Jesus Christ was in the tomb, and certain women went to see where the Lord lay. "It was Mary Magdalene, and Joanna, and Mary the mother of James, and other women that were with them." Here is constancy. The names do not appear upon great occasions of triumph ; the women were not ornamental pillars who came out on state occasions ; they were not sun-flowers that could live only in all their freshness at midday : they were with the Son of God, ministering unto him, and when he was dead they still thought they could do something for him. Who can allow the dead to go without some last touch, or kiss, or flower reverently laid on the door of the black prison ? There is always some other little thing that can be done. This is how Jesus Christ subsisted then—taking nothing from any one to whom he had not himself first ministered.

This is the only way of sustaining Christianity. It lives by the enthusiasm of its followers. It is not to be mechanically buttressed and supported and patronised. Jesus Christ, so long as the earth exists and his Church abides, must be ministered unto by those out of whom he has cast devils, whose children he has blessed, whose houses he has lighted up from the very·fountain of the sun. Christianity lives upon enthusiasm, or it does not live at all. Christ has a right to look to those who bear his name, because if they bear it honestly they bear it on account of what he himself has done for them. Men do not come and take up Christianity for the purpose of doing it some favour, saying, We have looked at you from a distance, and the more we have looked the better we have been pleased with your banners, and now we are about to show you some regard for your general respectability, and therefore we will speak of you wherever we have suitable opportunities. Christianity disdains the paltry patronage. Christianity must be spoken about because it is in a man, and will not allow him to be dumb ; it is a new spirit, the eloquent spirit, the burning spirit, and it must declare its presence in the soul by touching the tongue with eloquence, and leading the hand forth into constant and generous service. When we are asked why we minister to Christ, we reply, Because he first ministered unto us : we love him because he first loved us.

That is one view of Jesus Christ which this chapter supplies.

Now we have another aspect of the Son of God in relation to his teaching. He taught positively, and he taught negatively. How did he teach positively ? By fact and by parable, and by giving the larger meanings of things. He found a man sowing, and he said, That is my text. He found a woman putting leaven into three measures of meal, and he said, That is my subject. He found men selling all that they had for the purpose of buying one particular gem, and said, That is what you have to do in your spiritual education, if you are wise. Sometimes all things must go for the sake of one thing. To the eye of Jesus Christ all men were revealing the kingdom of heaven in some aspect, although they were doing it unconsciously : the sower did not know that he was supplying the Son of God with the basis of a parable. We limit ourselves too severely by excluding the poetry and the apocalyptic view and issue of things, supposing that when we lift a hand we do nothing more ; when we utter a word we have simply uttered a vocable, and there is an end of the exercise : whereas, if we were wise, we should find that our outgoing, our incoming, our downsitting, our uprising—yea, every breath of our respiratory system,—all things—are parabolic and suggestive, the beginnings and the germs of great spiritual thoughts and possibilities. So Jesus came to give the great meanings of things. In explanation he said, " The parable is this : The seed is the word of God." What a key is here, as in the former instance ! Jesus Christ seems always to deliver up the key to men when they are in a right mood of mind and heart. Once Peter gave such a great answer to a question put to him by the Son of God, that Jesus Christ took the keys and gave them to him at once. Thus he rewards faith, the genius of love, the passion of enthusiasm. We should have more keys if we had more qualification for sustaining them and using them aright. Not only was this a key to a particular instance, it is a key which opens a thousand locks. The seed is the word of God ; the leaven is the spirit of truth ; the pearl of great price is truth itself ; the returning prodigal is the returning soul ; the music and dancing in the father's house is heaven's rapture when heaven's number is increased. Oh that we had eyes to see and hearts to understand ! then all the world would come with its spring lessons and summer and autumn and winter lessons, and the snow would be as eloquent as the blossoms, and the hard ice would have its gospel as well as all the rains of summer.   He that hath ears to hear, let him hear !

Not only did he teach thus positively, but he exhorted ; he said, " Take heed therefore how ye hear" (ver. 18).   In Jesus Christ's sermons there is always a line of exhortation.   We ought to notice more and more that without exhortation a sermon is not complete, and is little worth.   The preacher must come down upon the hearer with all the power he can command of appeal, persuasion, entreaty ; he should beseech men to be reconciled to God.   Here, again, is a key.   " Never man spake like this man ! "   He begins by pronouncing a number of beatitudes, and we listen with delight to his mellifluous voice ; his lips were formed for eloquence, his eye was set in his head for illumination, for it assists the tongue to make his meaning plain : but presently we are awakened out of this intellectual reverie, and are withdrawn from this spiritual luxury, by an exhortation sharp as a crack of thunder, and we are called to be, to do, to stand, to go, to die !   How many of us leave Christ at the point of exhortation !   In exposition we like to hear him, because then we can partly contradict him, and contend our own opinion after he is exhausted as to speech ; in poetry we love to listen to him, for the words know one another, and recognise their mutual kinship, and the whole speech flows like a deep and all but silent river ; but when he comes to bid us follow him, take up our cross, deny ourselves, take heed, we begin to feel that he is imposing upon us discipline, and discipline is never acceptable to a nature that loves indulgence.   But Christianity is discipline.   Christianity is a commandment as well as a theology.   Some can obey who cannot fully understand, and, alas, many have great understanding who never attempt to obey.

Not only did Jesus Christ teach positively, but he taught negatively.   There was an occasion upon which he went into a ship with his disciples ; and " he said unto them, Let us go over unto the other side of the lake.   And they launched forth. But as they sailed he fell asleep."   Can he teach in sleep ?   He

always teaches. Every look is a lesson; every word a condensed volume. How will Jesus Christ teach by falling asleep?
He will teach by showing the disciples what they can do without
him. This is the only way, if we may so put it, that Jesus
Christ can awaken us to true self-consciousness. So long as we
have the sun in the heavens we expect him to return; we treat
him as in some sense a hired servant : he is looked for, and
if he does not do his duty we complain of his neglect : but we
cannot restore him to his place ; we have no power over the
clouds, and we must wait until the sun reappears. It is so with
the Sun of Righteousness ; Jesus Christ must withdraw from
us to teach us of what value he has been. We do not know
sometimes that a prophet has been amongst us until the prophet
is dead. Then we feel a strange vacancy ; we miss a personality,
an influence, a presence, an effect, a blessing; then we ask
questions, and then we discover that the King has passed by, and
we failed to recognise his crown and sceptre. Jesus Christ might
have lived with his disciples so long that they imagined they
could do very well with him or without him ; they had seen his
method, they knew the lines which he traversed, and they could
supply what was lacking if he himself was not present. Such
was their infatuation upon some occasions that they attempted to
work miracles when Jesus was not there, and they said to devils,
Depart, and the devils mocked them with bitter laughter, and
tore their subjects with still greater strength, and inflamed and
excited them by still more appalling paroxysms. Then Jesus
himself drew nigh and said, What is it? And the man most in
question as a sympathiser said, I brought my son to thy disciples
that they might heal him, and they cannot. Thus Jesus Christ
teaches by withdrawment, by falling asleep, by simply standing
aside, by becoming an onlooker, instead of an active worker.
Thus he teaches. The withdrawment is not an arbitrary act, the
sleep is not merely a natural necessity ; out of these things must
come lessons, showing how true it is that without Christ we can
do nothing. Evil spirits utter their scorn at our incantations, and
the waters pour their billows upon our little craft, heedless of our
impotent cry. Do not let us have any Christianity without
Christ, any mechanism that is not wrought from within by a
dynamic agency, a spiritual inspiration ; then every wheel will

roll smoothly, and the whole machinery (which we are obliged to have for the execution of religious purposes) will move on, each part answering the other part as with intelligent obedience and co-operation. We may retain the altar without Christ, but there can be no sacrifice upon it; we may retain the Church, but it will be but a set of gilded walls, not a centre of power and a fountain of refreshment, if Jesus Christ himself be not In it.

Then see not only how he subsisted and how he taught, but how he healed. A man representing the uttermost distress had come under his attention, and Jesus had renewed the man, and the issue is thus stated—" Then they went out to see what was done; and came to Jesus, and found the man, out of whom the devils were departed, sitting at the feet of Jesus, clothed, and in his right mind." These are the tests, and we cannot alter them; we cannot lower the standard; these alone, and standards equal to them, are the tests by which Christ's work in society must be judged. Let us judge ourselves by them. What was the man doing? He was "sitting at the feet of Jesus." Then he was subdued, chastened, refined, docile. Has the same miracle been wrought in us? sitting as a learner; not as an equal, not as a dictator, not as a critic, but sitting at the feet of Jesus to hear what the Master had to say, and to embody it in beautiful and generous life. " Sitting at the feet of Jesus." If I may but touch the hem of his garment I shall be healed ; if I may sit at his feet it will be heaven enough for me; if I might but just feel his shadow passing over me I shall ask for no other benediction. Thus we begin. To what heights we may ascend none can tell ; but Jesus Christ himself says that if we overcome, being faithful unto death, we shall sit with him on his throne. Meanwhile, it is enough to be led into the city like the blind Saul ; in after years he will be blind again, but it will be in the third heaven. " Clothed," that is a common expression to us, but in this instance it was a most uncommon circumstance. The man who had been healed had not been clothed a long time—"A certain man, which had devils long time, and ware no clothes, neither abode in any house, but in the tombs," is the description we read of him in the 27th verse. Now he is renewed in habit, civilised, part of a commonalty; no longer a rude solitary man, but tesselated socially, related civically, and now part of organised society.

Sometimes little things show what has been wrought in a man,—sitting in a new place, sitting in a new attitude, sitting in the house of God reverently; not looking at other people and wondering what they are doing, but looking to the centre with an eye that cannot be diverted. For some men to sit still is a miracle; for some poor light heads to listen betokens that God has been at work with them; such their natural frivolity that they cannot maintain an attitude of reverence and dignity in the house of God, and when you see them in such attitude then know that Omnipotence has not failed. " And in his right mind " : the clouds all gone, the trance broken, the madness subsided, ruled like an angry sea that has been tranquillised by a divine fiat; now looking squarely at men, the eye no longer unsteady, fiery, wandering, but fixed and calm as a planet. These are the standards by which we must judge. Are we sitting at Christ's feet? Have all our habits been changed, and are we in our right mind— humble, modest, self-distrustful, dependent upon God every moment, saying to him, " Hold thou me up, and I shall be safe : do not leave me for a single instant to myself, or I shall commit suicide, and go to hell " ? These are the tests; not our little power of criticising one another, and distinguishing between Christian sects and denominations, and playing the artificial theologian, and talking unintelligible metaphysics; but these practical standards—seated as scholars at the great Teacher's feet, part of the great society and brotherhood of man, with a steady, calm, aspiring mind that has realised its dignity, and is endeavouring to discharge its obligations.

How many ways there are all leading to Christ! Here are the women who have been healed doing something for him according to their resources and their opportunities; here are others coming in through the gate of parable, having had the kingdom of heaven revealed to them by signs and by things which are being done in common life, and by spiritual interpretations of the commonplaces of the day; and here are others being taught by feeling how nothing and less than nothing they are when Jesus Christ is not actively present—how they bungle over their work, how they begin at the wrong end, sow in the wrong field, reap nothing but darkness in the harvest-time, and at winter are left in desolation and poverty ; and here are others who are healed from great extremities—drunkards, who had been given up as losses, turned into sober citizens; madmen, who never spoke but irrationally, subdued and chastened into a docile spirit; wanderers on the face of the earth set in their right places in society.   Let us go to Christ in some way.   It is not for any man to say, This is the only way by which you can come.   The chariots of God are twenty thousand, yea, thousands of thousands, and men may go to God in twenty thousand different ways ; and provided they wish to go to God with their whole love, they will realise their desire.   "While he was yet a great way off, his father saw him, and ran."   That is how God does towards us.   Whilst we are yet a great way off, wrong in our thinking, mistaken in our intellectual conceptions, hesitating as to certain moral positions, poor and ignorant and weak, he sees us, and has compassion upon us, and runs toward us, lest another step should turn us backward, lest the foe should prevail were he himself to tarry too long.   The question which each man has to ask himself is this, Can I get to the Son of God in any way ?   I cannot understand the preachers, the theologians, the churches, the literature religious, and therefore I feel that I am kept outside ; but here is an opportunity given to me, because a preacher says, Come to Christ in some way—your own way—only insist upon seeing Christ.   Then perhaps some poor heart may say, I will go in this way—broken-hearted, contrite, desolate, ashamed ; I will go at night, when everybody is asleep, and I will utter my first prayer when the house is quiet as a cemetery : I think I dare go in that way.   Then—Go !

Chapter ix.

TYPICAL MEN.

THIS chapter shows us how very different men may be from one another. It also shows us the point of union by which all men are kept together, notwithstanding their contrariety to make and fire and purpose. There is no monotony in human nature; yet human nature is one. It will be interesting to give speciality of position in the eye of our imagination to some of the typical men who are so graphically described in this chapter.

First of all, here is the perplexed man:

"Now Herod the tetrarch [see note, p. 252] heard of all that was done by him: and he was perplexed " (ver. 7).

This is a singular word. When we have a pictorial dictionary we shall see a very graphic illustration of the meaning of this term. We use another set of words which are very homely but quite memorable; words which are often quoted, and which are not always fully understood in their etymological references. This word διηπόρει (dieporei) imports that the man who was in this condition was perplexed, really stuck in the mud. That is the literal import of the word. He could not move easily, and in all his movement he was trying to escape,—now he was moving to the right, then he was moving to the left; now forward, now backward, now sideward; he was making all kinds of motion with a view to self-extrication, and he could not deliver himself from this mood of hesitancy and incertitude. Herod was perplexed about Christ, and curiously perplexed; for his instinct put down his dogma, his conscience blew away as with a scornful wind his theological view of life and destiny.

Why was Herod perplexed?—

"Because that it was said of some, that John was risen from the dead; and

244

of some, that Elias had appeared; and of others, that one of the old prophets was risen again " (vers. 7, 8).

Why did Herod trouble himself about these dead men ?   As a Sadducee he did not believe in spirit or in resurrection.   If he had been quite faithful and steadfast to his creed, he would have said in answer to all these rumours, Whoever this man may be, he has nothing whatever to do with another world, for other world there is none: as to resurrection, dismiss the superstition and forget it.   But Herod had never been in this situation before. Circumstances play havoc with some creeds.   They are admirable creeds whilst the wind is in the south-west, and the way lies up a green slope, and birds are singing around us, and all heaven seems inclined to reveal its glories in one blaze ; then we can have our theories and inventions and conjectures, and can play the little tricky controversialist with many words : but when the wolf bites us, how is it then ?   When all the money is lost ; when the little child lies at the last gasp ; when the doctor himself has gone away, saying it will be needless for him to return,—how then ?   Men should have a creed that will abide with them every day in the week without consulting thermometer or barometer ; a creed that will sing the most sweetly when the heart most needs heaven's music ; a great faith, an intelligent, noble, free-minded faith, that says to the heart in its moods of dejection, All will come well: hold on, never despair, never give up ; one more prayer, one more day, in a little while.   A faith of this kind saves men from perplexity ; it gives the life of man solidity, centralisa- tion, outlook, hope.   It is an awkward thing to have a creed that will not bear this stress.   Herod's Sadduceeism went down when a tap came to the door by invisible fingers.   We can do what we will with matter ; if the fingers are of bone and flesh, they can be smitten and broken : but who can touch invisible fingers !   Then what have we to take down by way of comfort ?   We have declared that we know nothing, and have taken quite lofty pride in our boundless ignorance ; but here is a hand at the door, and the door must be answered, and you must answer it.   Herod was perplexed, hesitant, now on this side, now on that side ; he could not tell what to do.   So are men perplexed about Christ to-day who do not believe in him.   It is one of two things in regard to this Son of man : cordial, loving, positive trust, the whole heart-love poured out like wine into a living flagon ; or it is now belief, now unbelief, now uncertainty, now a prayer breathed to the very devil that he would come and take possession of the mind so as to drive out all perplexity and bewilderment. The latter course ends in deepening confusion and darkness. The only thing that will bear the stress of every weight, the collision of every conflict, is Faith—simple, loving, grateful faith. Lord, increase our faith.

Here is the helpless and despairing man :—

" Then the whole multitude of the country of the Gadarenes round about besought him to depart from them ; for they were taken with great fear : and he went up into the ship, and returned back again. Now the man out of whom the devils were departed besought him that he might be with him : but Jesus sent him away, saying, Return to thine own house, and show how great things God hath done unto thee. And he went his way, and published throughout the whole city how great things Jesus hath done unto him. And it came to pass, that, when Jesus was returned, the people gladly received him : for they were all waiting for him. And, behold, there came a man named Jairus, and he was a ruler of the synagogue : and he fell down at Jesus' feet, and besought him that he would come into his house : for he had one only daughter, about twelve years of age, and she lay a dying. But as he went the people thronged him " (viii. 37-42).

Why did not the man help himself ? Why did not his friends help him ? Why did not the disciples come to his assistance ? Luke takes note of many particular incidents. His narrative is distinguished by points of observation which we do not find in the other evangelists ; he alone says "for he had one only daughter." So with regard to the widow of Nain ; speaking of her son, he says, " the only son of his mother, and she was a widow." There are men who see little pathetic points in history. They sprinkle their history with the dew of tears. Other men see nothing but hurrying events, a rush and a tumult. Blessed are they who see heartbreak, and signs of sorrow on the cheek, and channels wrought in the flesh by flowing grief. Why did not this man heal his child ? The clamour of twelve children was not in his ears ; he had but one daughter : why did he not make her immortal ? Alas, we are limited ; we soon come to the last bottle of medicine, the last prescription ; even the pharmacopœia may be emptied. Does this man represent those who only come to Christ in extremity ? Whilst there is another recipe in the house they will not pray; whilst there is another draught that may be taken they will not lift up their eyes appealingly to kind heaven. We cannot tell. There are men who do just so. They come to prayer at last,—they end where they ought to have begun. There is no medicine that prayer will not sweeten; there is no application that prayer will not assist the working of. It has a magical influence upon the life. If it does not take away the burden, it increases the strength; if it does not enlarge the print, it increases the light by which we read it. This is the testimony of men—strong men, wise, shrewd, penetrating men, who know the value of words; and they are prepared to stand up and say that but for the power of prayer the night would have been too dark for them, and the wind would have blown them over the brink.

The disciples could do nothing in the case. It is right that there should be limitation on that side. It would never do for the Church to be omnipotent. It would never do for us to reach an ideal faith, because then confusion would follow : If ye had faith as a grain of mustard-seed ye should say to this mountain, Depart, be removed into the sea, and instantly it would plunge into the deep like a stone thrown by the hand. That is ideal, that touches another region, and falls into the action of another gravitation; but it is along that line that men must climb. See what confusion would arise if every man could say to a mountain, Depart! Because, therefore, it is literally impossible, it is spiritually educative and inspiring. But we must not reason from that circumstance that therefore little faith would do, a crippled Christianity would be enough : Jesus Christ rebuked the disciples, and traced their failure not to their modesty, but to their perversity and faithlessness. We might do more miracles than we accomplish. Where is there a man who might not sit up five minutes later at night to finish the appeal, to complete the letter, to add a last touch to the tender entreaty? Where is there a giver who might not have added something to his donation? Where is the preacher who might not have reached a higher level of inspired eloquence, exposition, and appeal? Where is any life that is not conscious of shortcoming? We might do more. And it would be helpful to us if, having given our last loaf away, we were obliged by a common hunger all to go to Christ together. Our appearance would be a prayer, and his look would be an answer. Take heart, poor suffering one; at the core of things there is Love. It does not always appear; sometimes, indeed, the appearance is quite to the contrary; sometimes we feel as if we were under discipline that is penal and almost excessive; then we cry out, and no answer comes from the wind that bears our cry away into oblivion: but at other times we get revelations, we see light, and we ought to put down such occurrences and read them as we read the Bible. The Bible does not end upon any given age; it continues itself into the experience of mankind; so much so that a man should come back and say, Isaiah, thou art my companion to-day, I understand thee now. Ezekiel, I have got some hint of thy wheels and colours, thy flashing light, thy mysterious imagery. Job, I will cry with thee to-day; let us lean upon one another and pour out our love in a common psalm. Psalmist, Asaph, David, I can sing to your harps; oh, accompany me whilst I sing the goodness of God. So every life ought to be a comment upon the Scripture. We cannot all comment upon the same book. Some do not understand the book of Genesis, or the book of Revelation; others can make nothing of the historical books, because they are filled with long names, and apparently have no home music in all their polysyllables; but other men can touch even the deepest parts of the Bible, the most mysterious instances of revelation, and all can gather around the Cross.

Here is the ambitious man :—

"Then there arose a reasoning among them, which of them should be greatest" (ver. 46).

How shall the hierarchy be formed? Who shall be first? Which of us shall stand bracketed as equals? Who shall speak the determining word, who shall give the casting vote? Who shall be crowned? When men are left to themselves we see the kind of questions they ask. These are the inquiries men put when they lose hold of the spiritual, the immaterial, the immortal. What conflict then arises, what petty controversy, what contention battling against contention! We need eternity to keep us

up to the true level. That is the great use of religious thinking
and religious worship. We cannot always explain the mystery,
but we can feel its elevating influence. Whatever enlarges our
veneration, quiets our spirit, turns our wonder into a telescope
that can search the heavens,—does the soul real good : it is not
fanaticism, it is instruction ; it is not sentiment, it is the beginning of conduct. When Jesus Christ enters into any conversation,
the conversation instantly rises to another level. We know his
voice; there is none like it. We all speak much in the same
tone, but when Jesus joins the conversation he makes us ashamed
of all we have said, and teaches us the beauty, the utility, and
the dignity of silence. Whoever multiplies the ceremonial officers
of the Church, departs from the spirit of Christ. All high-
sounding titles, all ambitious distinctions, all differences in status
and in function that imply inferiority on the part of others,
were never learned at the Cross of Christ. Whoever makes
the ministry a profession, and speaks of a minister as if he were
separate from the people, having access to sealed secrets, having
a key that can open the arcana of God, does not understand
the spirit of Christ. "One is your Master"; all ye are brethren.
What distinguishes one brother from another will soon be evident
to the brethren themselves, and men have that instinct of recognition and justice which will soon settle all classifications; but
purple, and velvet, and crimson, and gold, and gem, and staff of
office are unknown to the Cross of Christ.

Quickly following is the sectarian man.

"And John answered and said, Master, we saw one casting out devils
in thy name; and we forbad him, because he followeth not with us"
(ver. 49).

He thought he had a great message to deliver, and that the
Lord would be exceedingly pleased with the news which he
brought that day. John did not understand anything about the
kingdom of heaven at that time, or he never would have done
what he did. Yet still it enables a man to increase his stature
by standing upon his toes when he can forbid some other man.
Where is there a man who does not enjoy his food all the more
since he has the consciousness that he has exercised a little
brief authority? There is a pleasure in snubbing other people.

There is a subtle comfort in telling another man to sit down. That is what the sects are doing to one another all the week long. I am not now speaking of denominations, for we must have them to the end of the chapter, as we must have families, households, separate communes; I am speaking now of the sectarian spirit which says, Because you do not worship under my roof, therefore you are not of Christ; because you do not accept my credenda, therefore you are without faith; because you do not call yourself by my name, therefore you cannot be going to the kingdom above. That is the spirit of hate, the spirit of illiberality; let us renounce it with detestation. It is beautiful to see what different views men can entertain. These differences of opinion ought to occasion us delight, when they are held with reverence, and when they are defended with reason. The idea that a man can see differently from me ought to enlarge me, in my thinking, my faith, my hope. When two men pursue the same text and each comes with a conclusion of his own, we should not think of the petty differences between the two men, but of the greatness of the text. It is because Christianity, as we have often said, is so large that men have so many different opinions about it. There are more differences of opinion about a firmament than about a gasometer. It is wonderful how sectarian some people can be. They never travel, and that is an infinite disadvantage. Always to live in the same street, mingling with the same people, going out at the same hour, returning at the same time, speaking always the same language, reading only one class of literature,— why, but what angel could endure it? It is destruction. Men should travel; they should go into countries where they cannot speak a word of the language, to learn how ignorant they are; into countries that are established upon novel lines, and yet are as solid as rocks, to see that things can be done in other lands that are not done at home. Men should often turn themselves as to all their thinking upside down, so as to get hold of a larger view. The artist will tell you that in order to lay hold of the real image and colour of a landscape he puts his head down and looks at the landscape as from below. Any person coming behind him, not understanding art, would of course remark upon the eccentricity of the individual—for some people cannot be eccentric. To the artist it is needful to see the landscape just from that angle; he sees what cannot be seen from any other angle, and he gets colour and lights that are otherwise impossible of recognition. To think that a man boasts of never having been absent from his own church for forty years! What a ridiculous little man he must be! How exceedingly uncomfortable to live with! I believe in all churches, in all forms of life, in all variations of music. We may pride ourselves on that which ought to be our humiliation; we may belittle the Christianity which we have undertaken to patronise.

Following the sectarian man comes in due sequence the religiously vindictive man :—

"And it came to pass, when the time was come that he should be received up, he steadfastly set his face to go to Jerusalem, and sent messengers before his face : and they went, and entered into a village of the Samaritans, to make ready for him. And they did not receive him, because his face was as though he would go to Jerusalem. And when his disciples James and John saw this, they said, Lord, wilt thou that we command fire to come down from heaven, and consume them, even as Elias did ? " (vers. 51-54.)

You cannot make Eliases. You may do just the very thing that Elias did, and so make the greater fools of yourselves. Elias is sent when the world needs him,—son of thunder, son of consolation, each will be sent from heaven at the right time, and be furnished with the right credentials. But how delightful it is to set fire to somebody else! The dynamitard is a character in ancient history. Would it not be convenient for the Church always to have in its pocket just one little torpedo that it could throw in the way of somebody who differed in opinion from somebody else? The Lord Jesus will not have this; he said, "Ye know not what manner of spirit ye are of." The spirit of Christianity is a spirit of love, a spirit of sympathy, a spirit of felicity, a spirit that can weep over cities that have rejected the Son of man.

Then said he, or said the historian—the words might be his, for they are part of his very soul—

"For the Son of man is not come to destroy men's lives, but to save them " (ver. 56).

Tell this everywhere. Go ye into all the world and say to every creature, "The Son of man is not come to destroy men's lives, but to save them." The strongest man amongst us might devote his life to that sweet, high task. The brightest genius that ever revelled in poem or picture might devote all its energies to the revelation of that sacred truth. There are destroyers enough. Nature itself is often a vehement and unsparing destroyer. We are our own destroyers. There needs to be somewhere a saviour, a loving heart, a redeeming spirit, a yearning soul, a mother-father that will not let us die.

NOTE.

"Tetrarch (τετράρχης). Properly the sovereign or governor of the fourth part of a country. In the later period of the republic and under the empire, the Romans seem to have used the title (as also those of *ethnarch* and *phylarch*) to designate those tributary princes who were not of sufficient importance to be called kings. In the New Testament we meet with the designation, either actually or in the form of its derivative τετραρχεῖν, applied to three persons:—

"(1) Herod Antipas (Matt. xiv. 1; Luke iii. 1, 19, ix. 7; Acts xiii. 1), who is commonly distinguished as 'Herod the tetrarch,' although the title of 'king' is also assigned to him both by St. Matthew (xiv. 9) and by St. Mark (vi. 14, 22 *sqq.*). St. Luke, as might be expected, invariably adheres to the formal title, which would be recognised by Gentile readers. Herod is described by the last-named Evangelist (ch. iii. 1) as 'Tetrarch of Galilee'; but his dominions, which were bequeathed to him by his father Herod the Great, embraced the district of Peræa beyond the Jordan (Joseph. *Ant.* xvii. 8, §1): this bequest was confirmed by Augustus (Joseph. *B. J.* ii. 6, § 3). After the disgrace and banishment of Antipas, his tetrarchy was added by Caligula to the kingdom of Herod Agrippa I. (*Ant.* xviii. 7, § 2).

"(2) Herod Philip (the son of Herod the Great and Cleopatra, *not* the husband of Herodias), who is said by St. Luke (iii. 1) to have been 'tetrarch of Ituræa, and of the region of Trachonitis.'

"(3) Lysanias, who is said (Luke iii. 1) to have been 'tetrarch of Abilene,' a small district surrounding the town of Abila, in the fertile valley of the Barada or Chrysorrhoas, between Damascus and the mountain-range of Antilibanus."—SMITH's *Dictionary of the Bible.*

PRAYER.

ALMIGHTY GOD, thou hearest the prayer of men when spoken in the Name that is above every name, which Name alone do we now breathe in approaching the throne of the heavenly grace. We come by the new and living way, henceforward the only way, and we humbly beseech thee to grant unto us such blessings as our hearts require. We pray for the forgiveness of our sins. God be merciful unto us sinners! We come to the Cross of Jesus Christ our infinitely sufficient Saviour, and there confess our sins, and humbly seek the pardon of God. If we confess our sins, thou wilt surely forgive us. We now make confession of our iniquity, we now speak of our transgressions, that they may be taken away by the blood of the one Sacrifice. Create within us a clean heart, renew within us a right spirit, and give us to know the meaning of holiness as thou dost know it. Purify us by the blood of Jesus, and there shall be no stain upon our hearts or upon our life. Put within us thy Holy Spirit, so as to enlighten the understanding, to regenerate the heart, and sanctify the whole nature; then shall we grow in grace, and shall become beautiful with the purity of God. Let the Holy Ghost descend upon us! Now may we know that he is here by the warmth of our affections, by the loftiness and purity of our desires, and by a holy resolution to give ourselves, body, soul and spirit, to the service of the living Lord. Prepare us to hear the messages of the gospel. May we receive them as good seed cast into good ground. May no word of all the message of thy love escape us. May every tone of the music of the gospel enter into the ear of our hearts and charm our life. May we know thy truth more perfectly, and love it more truly, that men, noting our behaviour, may wonder concerning the sources of our power. We would live in God, we would live according to the law of Jesus Christ. Daily would we carry, with unmurmuring patience and cheerful hope, the Cross of our Lord and Saviour. Direct all the way of our life. Suffer none of our steps to slide; when the wicked, even our enemies and our foes, would come upon us to devour and to destroy, save us in the time of peril. Set our feet upon a rock and hide within our hearts thy word, that we may not sin against thee. We now await thine answer, O living One! We have spoken our prayer at the Cross; we now abide the answer of God. Let it be an answer of peace and love and tender mercy, and our hearts shall burn within us: Now unto him that is able to keep us from falling, and to present us faultless before the presence of his glory with exceeding joy, to the only wise God our Saviour, be glory and majesty, dominion and power, both now and ever. Amen.

253

Chapter x. 25.

"And behold, a certain lawyer stood up and tempted him, saying, **Master,** what shall I do to inherit eternal life ?"

INHERITING ETERNAL LIFE.

YOU will observe that the man who asked this question was a lawyer, a man of education and of good standing; a man, therefore, from whom good behaviour and reverence of spirit might reasonably have been expected. You would think that when such a man spoke, he would speak soberly, he would mean, under such circumstances, exactly what he said. You find, however, that the inquiry,—the very greatest that can possibly engage human attention,—was put in a spirit of temptation. The lawyer was not an earnest man. He asked a right question, but he asked it in a wrong spirit. See, then, the possibility of asking religious questions irreligiously. You would suppose, when a man puts a grave religious inquiry, that his spirit is concerned in the meaning of the question which he propounds. Here you see a direct contradiction of that reasonable supposition. A man may be learned and intelligent, may have good social position, and may in many respects deserve the regard and confidence of society, so far as appearances go ; and yet he may put the gravest questions in the most flippant and irreverent spirit. Then is it possible for a man to open the Bible without really desiring to know what it contains that can minister to the ignorance of his mind and the hunger of his soul ? Truly, alas, it is so possible. Many men attend the house of God, and sit amongst those who profess themselves to be saints, and yet care nothing for the place and nothing for the service, beyond a little momentary excitement or entertainment of some kind or other. Verily so. If men are to be judged religious because they put religious questions, then snall religion become the cheapest exercise of life. Learn the possibility of asking great questions in a merely controversial spirit, without any profoundly anxious desire to know the answer that God will return to such inquiries. We, being present at a religious service, may be supposed to be in a grave mood, to be listening with all, intentness for some word that shall touch the hunger and the necessity of our life. Yet it possible, and in some respects even likely, that we may be in a reverent attitude without a reverent spirit, and asking a religious question without a religious intention.   If so, let no man think that he will receive anything of the Lord.   God understands the irony of our attitude. The Living One knows whether we are hungering and thirsting for him; he can see through our hypocrisies and concealments, and only into the broken heart and the contrite spirit will he come with redemption and life and helpfulness and grace.   We know the conditions upon which alone we receive the revelations of God : That we be quiet, self-renouncing, reverent, sober, anxious about the business ; and wherever these conditions are forthcoming, some light will be flashed upon the life, and some healing word will be dropped into the sorrow of the heart.

We look up to certain men for examples.   We say we cannot surely be wrong if we follow the type which such men set before us.   Probably one would have looked up to the lawyer referred to in the text as a man who could give us an example ; and yet here are the so-called pillars of society rotting away ; the men who ought to be the trustees of decency proving traitors to their stewardship ; men of education and intelligence and standing exerting a pestilent influence upon young and untrained but susceptible life.

"And Jesus said unto him, What is written in the law ? how readest thou ? " (ver. 26.)

Jesus himself answered one question by asking another ; and so he not unfrequently disappointed men who had undertaken to ensnare him in his speech.   They thought that if they did but put a case to him he would commit himself, and they would entrap him.   Here is a man accustomed to put questions, and to put questions again upon the answers that are given, and so to cross-examine those with whom he came in contact.   Jesus undertakes to deal with him according to the spirit which he presents ; and before he lets him go he will show what the man's meaning is and his nature, and he will expose him as he never was exposed before.   Thus quietly he begins, "What is written in the law ? Thou art a lawyer, a man of reading, a man of many letters, and of much understanding probably,—how readest thou ? "   God has never left the greatest questions of the human heart unanswered. The great answer to this question about eternal life was not given first of all by Jesus Christ as he appeared in the flesh. Jesus himself referred to the oldest record ; inferentially he said,—That question has been answered from the beginning ; go back to the very first revelation and testimony of God, and you will find the answer there. Yet the question is put very significantly, "How readest thou ?" There are two ways of reading. There is a way of reading the letter which never gets at the meaning of the spirit. There is a way of reading which merely looks at the letter for a partial purpose, or that a prejudice may be sustained or defended. And there is a way of reading which means,—I want to know the truth; I want to see really how this case stands ; I am determined to see it. He who reads so will find no end to his lesson, for truth expands and brightens as we study her revelations and her purposes. He who comes merely to the letter, will get but a superficial answer in all probability. It was, therefore, of the highest importance that the lawyer should tell how he had been reading the law.

But before passing from this point let us observe that Jesus Christ never treated the Old Testament lightly. I am afraid that some of us imagine that we have got beyond the Old Testament, and therefore hardly ever turn to its ancient pages. Believe me, the testaments are one : as the day is one—the twilight and the noon-tide, as the year is one—the vernal promise and the autumnal largess—so are the Testaments of God one. And no man can profoundly interpret the New Testament who is not profoundly conversant with the Old. A man will come upon the New Testament from a wrong point altogether, except he come upon it along the line of Moses and the minstrels of Israel and the prophets of Zion. He who comes so will find it to be a New Testament in the best sense ; the Old re-pronounced ; the Old set forth in a new light, and brought to bear with wider and more vital applications. Have we read the law ? Are we really conversant with all the old statements about sin and duty ? Do we know the history of human kind as it is written in the Old Testament ? If not, we are unprepared for the deepest and truest consideration of the new covenant. Let me, therefore, in passing, urge young men in particular to read the Old Testament through carefully, seriously, minutely, and they will see how marvellously

the way was prepared for the final covenant, which we know by
the name of the New Testament.

"And he answering said, Thou shalt love the Lord thy God with all thy
heart, and with all thy soul, and with all thy strength, and with all thy
mind; and thy neighbour as thyself. And he said unto him, Thou hast
answered right: this do, and thou shalt live" (vers. 27, 28).

The lawyer, remember, knew the answer at the time when
he asked the question. He said, "What shall I do to inherit
eternal life?" and all the time the answer was in his own
recollection had he but known it. Alas! we do not always turn
our knowledge into wisdom. We know the fact, and we hardly
ever sublimate the fact into truth. We know the law, and we fail
to see that under the law there is the beauty and there is the
grace of the gospel. Is there any man to be found amongst us
who does not know what to do to inherit eternal life? Is there
one who dare say, "If I knew what to do I would do it"?
Does not every man's heart say to him, "You know perfectly well
what to do and how to do it"? If you ask a question, with a
view of misleading your teacher, understand that you must suffer
the pain of that sin. Jesus said, "Thou hast answered right."
Men can give right answers to great questions, if so be they set
themselves really to do so. If the lawyer had returned a blundering
or imperfect answer, Jesus would—had the man's spirit been right
—have sat down for days together to talk the matter over with
him, simply and tenderly as he alone could talk. But the lawyer
knew the answer, at the very moment he put the question; and
he intended to put the question so adroitly as to escape the
application of the answer to his own case. What if at the last
this be our condition; if in the winding up of things we venture
to say, If we had known the right path we should certainly have
taken it! God will show, out of our own mouth, that at the
very time we were doing the wrong we perfectly knew the right.
I charge every man who hears me, who is not in Christ, with
knowing perfectly well what to do; though he may cheat himself,
and wrong himself by putting questions, with a view of escaping
the application of the answers, or postponing a decision upon the
great question.

"This do," said Jesus, "and thou shalt live." What had the

lawyer to do ?   To love the Lord his God with all his heart, and
with all his soul, and with all his strength, and with all his mind.
Love is life.   Only he who loves lives.   Only love can get out of
a man the deepest secrets of his being, and develop the latent
energies of his nature, and call him up to the highest possibilities of
his manhood.   Criticism never can do it ; theology never can do
it ; power of controversy never can do it.   We are ourselves, in
all the volume of our capacity, and in all the relations of our
original creation, only when life becomes love and our whole
nature burns with affection towards the God and Father of our
Lord Jesus Christ.   Hast thou knowledge ?   It will not save thee.
Art thou well versed in ancient reading upon the deepest
theological questions ?   It will not save thee.   Dost thou know
the truth when it is spoken ?   It will not save thee.   What then
will save a man ?   The turning of all his knowledge and all
his power into love.   And upon what object is that love to be
concentrated ?   Upon the Lord God.   Then is a man a loving
creature in che true and proper sense of the term.   The measure
of our love is the measure of our life.   In proportion as we
love God do we live.   In the degree of our affections towards
purity and truth and holy service are we the heirs of a blessed
immortality !   Then the question becomes a very practical one.
How is it with ourselves ?   Let us look less at our knowledge and our intellectual capability and our training and our
circumstances, and more at the degree of our religious love.   The
end of the commandment is charity ; the summing up of all true
law is love.   Do we, then, know this mystery of religious love ?
or is ours a religion that hangs itself upon the outward letter and
the ceremonial form ?

Then observe that the law goes still further than love to God ; it
includes love to one's neighbour.   Mark the exact expression ot
the text, "And thy neighbour as thyself."   Love of God means
love of man.   Religion is the divine side of philanthropy ; philanthropy is the practical side of religion.   We must first be right
with God, or we never can be right with man.   If we begin by
endeavouring to get right with our neighbour, we shall fail.   But
if we begin by establishing right relations with God, according to
the conditions which he himself has laid down, we shall find that

being right with God our whole life is elevated and all social relationships are redeemed from error, and our neighbour is loved with a lofty and pure charity. Was the lawyer satisfied ? Read :—

"But he, willing to justify himself, said unto Jesus, And who is my neighbour ?" (ver. 29.) *

It was the question of a sharp man, but not the inquiry of an honest one. Such a question as this does not need to be answered in words. Every man knows in his own heart who his neighbour is ; and only he who wishes to play a trick in words, to show how clever he is in verbal legerdemain, will stoop to ask such a question as this. Why did he ask the question ? Because he was willing to justify himself. It is precisely there that every man has a great battle to fight, namely—at the point of self-justification. So long as there is any disposition in us to justify ourselves, are we unprepared to receive the gospel. One of the first conditions required of us at the Cross is self-renunciation. If any man shall say, " I think I can defend my behaviour ; I am sure I can excuse myself before Almighty God ; I know that if opportunity be given to me I can put another face upon things in my life which are regarded as transgressions and shortcomings,"—let a man talk in that tone, and the gospel has nothing to say to him ; he has shut the door of his heart upon it. But let him, on the other hand, know that all power of self-redemption is gone out of him ; let him know that he can do nothing towards his own recovery in the sight of God; let him be driven to this prayer—all prayers in one—"God be merciful to me a sinner !" and then Calvary is heaven, the Cross is the ladder the head of which rests against the sky !

My reader, why art thou not saved ? Because of a desire to justify thyself ; because of thy power of self-excuse ; because thou hast it yet in thine heart to say that the conduct which is charged with blame may be defended by some species of eloquence, or by some effort of immoral, because degraded, wit. Not until we come to the point of self-renunciation, do we come to the point at which Jesus meets us with all the preciousness and infinite sufficiency of his own atonement !

* See also *post* p. 272.

Jesus was willing to answer the lawyer even here; but he answered him by putting another question. So he proceeded to relate the parable which has come to be known amongst us as the "Parable of the Good Samaritan." Let us take notice of one or two points in that parable. A certain man was wounded upon his way from Jerusalem to Jericho; he was left on the road half dead. There came down the road a certain priest; the priest saw the wounded man, and when he saw him he passed by on the other side. See how possible it is for a man to have a great office and a contemptible nature. See how a great name may mean nothing in the way of great service. See even how the holy name, the name of priest, may be associated with an unholy spirit. He passed by on the other side. There are two sides in this human life of ours. There is a side upon which the wounded man lies, and there is a side that is crowded with men who are hurrying upon their various errands—some good, some bad. There is a side in life on which you may find weakness, helplessness, poverty, starvation, and death. You have it in your power to step to the other side and go about your business, on a path more or less clear of everything that can offend your senses,—and the priest chose that other path. The man with the holy name, that ought to have allowed temple or tabernacle or holy service to stand still, till he had redeemed a man who was lying on the verge of the grave,—passed by on the other side; and the Levite followed his example, looked upon the wounded man, and passed on to the opposite road. Then comes this beautiful expression: "But a certain Samaritan." Sometimes we quarrel with the word but. When we hear it we say, Yes, there is a but in every life; there is an if in every statement. Everything seems to be full of sunshine and beauty until we suddenly come to but, and then we expect to turn round the corner and see nothing but gloom and difficulty. Here is a case upon the other side. The light in this instance comes with a but. We turn from the gloom and the ugliness of the scene to look upon an unexpected light, and be charmed by beauty from an unexpected quarter. Mark the boldness of Christ in saying it was a Samaritan who did this. This is an instance of the Saviour's courage. It required a bold, true, brave man to say even this simple word under the conditions which surrounded the speaker. He was addressing the

Jews; he himself was a Jew; the Jews had no dealings with the Samaritans. The Samaritans were on the gloomy side, and more or less proscribed. Yet Jesus, Son of God, talking to a Jewish lawyer, said, It was a Samaritan who did the noble deed! We cannot over-pass these incidental touches without remarking upon them. We must pause here, to see how even casually there comes in the divinity which was ever present, and showed itself occasionally in great breadths of lustre, and almost constantly in those little flashes and touches which make up so much of our common daily life. Jesus was the Son of man, and therefore he spoke well of what-ever good was done by any child of Adam. He was a Jew, but a Jew for a moment only. He was the Son of man and the Son of God, and therefore, whether in favoured or proscribed circles he saw aught of nobleness or moral beauty, he commended it with a generosity which came of the perfectness of his own nature.

When the lawyer had heard the parable, a question was put to him, and he answered again rightly. So that all the time the lawyer knew the answers to the very questions he was putting. You observe he got nothing out of Jesus Christ that he himself did not before know. The Saviour simply put the case to him, and got him to answer upon it. You might have expected, when the question was put, "What shall I do to inherit eternal life?" an elaborate exposition of the moral condition of humanity, a profound and intricate statement concerning the revelation of God in the flesh, a magnificent dissertation upon redemption by sacrifice, and the necessity of the shedding of blood for the remission of sin. Instead of these expectations being satisfied, Jesus Christ asked the man certain questions which he answered rightly, and those answers were returned to him as a response to his own inquiries. This ought to have a very serious application to ourselves; because we are to be no longer self-deluded by the impression, that if more was said to us we should do more; if we had a better minister we should soon have higher knowledge of truth and keener perception of moral beauty; if revelation had been more minute and specific, we should have had the advan-tage of that minuteness and should have been better men. To talk so is to talk lies,—infamous and unpardonable lies! Jesus

Christ showed in this case, that all the while there was in the man's heart the very answer which he professed himself eager to ascertain. So it is with ourselves. We know the right; yet oftentimes, alas! the wrong pursue. We know the truth, and we hoodwink ourselves to a degree which enables us to say, lyingly, that if we knew its meaning better we should carry out its purpose more fully. O man, the answer is in thine heart; the law of God has been before thine eyes, and thou hast known it to be true, to be simple, to be right; now say that though you know the truth you will not follow it, or say, "Knowing the truth I yield myself to its persuasion, I put myself under its discipline." Decide at once. Decide ere it be too late! Begin to live whilst you may! If you have not this life in your heart you are not living. You are alive without life; you have existence without being; a pulse without immortality! Where in all this is the evangelical element? It is possible for men, who do not distinguish between words and things, to be surprised at the answer which Jesus returned to the lawyer, because they do not see in that answer the full statement of what is known amongst us as evangelical truth. The lawyer came for eternal life, and he was referred to the law. The lawyer asked who his neighbour was, and he was told to do as the Samaritan had done and he would certainly live. Read the Sermon on the Mount, and say, Where is the evangelical truth? It is precisely here that a profound mistake is often made by men. Let any man try to carry out literally and morally the Sermon on the Mount, and he will soon find where the evangelical element is. Let a man set himself when he is smitten on the one cheek to turn the other also, patiently and nobly, and he will soon begin to inquire for the Cross of Christ! When a man is compelled to go one mile, and is able to answer he will go two—he will find that he derives his ability so to reply from his being one with Christ, in all the sympathies of his nature and all the desires of his heart. Let a man try to love his neighbour as himself, and he will soon find that all his attempts will end in ignominious failure if he have not drunk into the spirit of Jesus Christ, who made himself of no reputation, who took upon him the form of a servant, and became obedient unto death. The evangelical element is not a matter of mere statement. It goes beyond all expression; it never can be set fully forth in any words that man can employ. Yet in all our endeavours to carry out a truly noble and heavenly life, we feel that we cannot take one step in the process without knowing Christ alike in the fellowship of his sufferings and the power of his resurrection. Am I to suppose that any man is asking, What shall I do to inherit eternal life? Do not misunderstand that word "do." It may be so employed as to convey a wrong sense. The obtaining of eternal life does not come through any action or merit of our own. There is not a certain journey that is to be taken, a labour which is to be performed, a specific duty that is to be discharged. What, then, is there to be? Consciousness of sin, conviction of guilt in the sight of God, self-despair, self-torment, such a knowledge of the nature and reality of sin as will pain the heart to agony; and then a turning of the eyes of faith to the bleeding Lamb of God, the one Sacrifice, the complete Atonement; a casting of the heart, the life, the hope, upon the broken body of Jesus, Son of God! Dost thou so believe? Thou hast eternal life! This eternal life is not a possession into which we come by-and-by. We have hold of it now; for to love the Son of God is to begin eternity, is to enter upon immortality!

How is this life to be exhibited? In other words, how is it to prove its own existence and defend its own claim? By love. "But I can talk theology so well." So you may, and yet be an alien to the commonwealth of Israel. "But I can give critical distinctions between one statement and another." So you may, and be a fool. How then am I to show that I am living the eternal life? By love. God is love. And if we be in God we shall be filled with love. Say a man is narrow, censorious, unkind, cruel; and whatsoever may be his attainments, without charity, he is as a beast in the sanctuary of God! But see a man who knows but little, and yet whose heart burns with love towards God, and with a desire to know him more perfectly, and serve him more devotedly, and you see eternal life.

Let us then henceforward know that there is in our hearts and minds information enough upon these great questions, if so be we are minded to turn that information to account. Let no man say, he will begin a better life when he knows more. Begin with the amount of your present knowledge. Let no man delude himself by saying that, if he had a good opportunity of showing charity to a stranger, he would show it. Show charity, show piety at home. Let no man say that if he was going down a thief-haunted road, and saw a poor man bleeding and dying there, he would certainly bind up his wounds. Do the thing that is next thee ; bear the cross that is lying at thy feet ; start even upon the very smallest scale to love, and thou shalt grow in grace. We do not expect men in Christ to be men in one day, fully grown, finally completed. We expect growth, process : first the blade, then the ear, then the full corn in the ear. First, a rude attempt, it may be poorly and clumsily carried out, but done with the best spirit, with the highest desire to be right. Given such a condition of affairs as that, and God will see to it that the bruised reed be not broken ; that the smoking flax be not quenched ; that a little strength be cultured and reared and defended until it become a gigantic power. And as for those of us who are in Christ, and who know this sweet mystery of eternal life, let us prove it by the depth, the ardour, the purity of our love.

Chapter x. 26.

"How readest thou?"

HOW TO READ THE BIBLE.

NOTHING would seem simpler than to open the Bible and read the verses as they came. Few people read the Bible. Many people make a charm of it; others approach it along false lines. Some treat the Bible superstitiously; it is not a divine revelation to them, but something about which they have to be mystified, and they suppose that the less they understand it the better. "How readest thou?" What is the method of reading? Have you any general principles, any guiding maxims, any philosophy of reading? Do you merely pass through chapter and verse as they come, accepting everything, testing nothing, proving nothing, but simply reading so many words, and extending towards these words so much of unintelligent respect as you may care to bestow upon them? How read you your own children's letters? Are they only a jingle of words, or is there some central meaning even in the child's communication? What is the vital point? what does the writer want to be at? what is the one thing to which he addresses himself? Except we consider these questions, and reverently obey the direction in which they point, we shall read the Bible mistakenly, we shall constantly be in fear of every assault that is made upon it; we shall suppose, with criminal ignorance, that it is in the power of some man mighty in dialectics and rich in information to take the Bible from us. There is a certain kind of Bible we ought never to have had. No man can take any revelation of God from us, if our spirit be in sympathy with the revelation, and if our life be moulded and inspired by its highest meaning. Men can rearrange chapters and verses, and dispute authorships, and point out discrepancies; and when they have done all that, they have not touched the Bible. When the Churches learn this there will be greater calmness in the midst of all uproar and tumult, and a noble voice will say, We will be calm in God, for he is our refuge and strength, though the mountains be removed and be carried into the midst of the sea.

"How readest thou?" Take the first chapters in Genesis, and how many people have been hindered and injured and upset and mystery-beclouded and befogged by those chapters, when they need not have been so troubled for a moment. The people who thus suffer begin at the wrong point; they look for the wrong thing; they would not read a friend's letter as they read what they suppose to be God's Bible. All this comes from want of asking, What is the vital point? It is thus we must read a parable, and with this illustration I will begin at the difficulty I have referred to. How do you read the parable of the Prodigal Son? There is only one line in it. So many people begin with the decoration, the colouring, the poetry; they do not see that the whole thing is in one sentence—Come back! Suppose men were to say, On what day in the week is it probable that that young man went away? There are seven days in the week, and every day would have its friend in that controversy, and so we should have seven different schools of thought based on distinct and dogmatic conviction—that he went away upon every one of them. Suppose they should say, On what day is it probable the young man came back again? Would they be discussing the parable? would they be reading God's Book? would they be students of Christ's religious philosophy? They would lose everything by beginning at the wrong point, and looking for the wrong thing: the one cry of the parable is: Return! thy father waits for thee. So in the creation of the world, what troubles we have: one school setting up the idea of specific creation; another setting up the theory of evolution, development, the whole apocalypse of the universe coming out of some tuft of fire-mist by persistent force. I do not care which it was; that is not the thing the Bible wants me to believe or cares about for one moment. What is it the Bible says? "God created." That's all. I do not give up the first chapters of Genesis any more than I give up the parable of the Prodigal Son, because I do not care what day the young man went away, or on what day the young man returned home; nor do I care how the feast was spread and who served it; I know he came home, and I want to follow him as he hastens to his father's refuge. All the Bible wants me to believe is, that " God created the heavens and the earth." As for the rest, all that will come in due time; we shall have space enough for the consideration of these questions when we get higher, where the light burns more steadily, where the day is master of the night. Yet there are some people who will knock at doors that are marked *Private.* You cannot get rid of intruders, trespassers, and vulgar people; they rush in where angels fear to tread. He who believes that " God created the heavens and the earth " is ready for any theory that can vindicate itself by reason, fact, history, and other stable proof. How troubled some have been about the tragedy of Eden ! " How readest thou ? " You may have been attacking the wrong points; puzzling yourselves to dizziness over things you have nothing to do with. The serpent betrayed the woman, and she did eat. How did the serpent betray her ? You have nothing to do with that. How readest thou, then ? I read only one thing in all that Eden transaction, namely, that the human heart was tempted. All history confirms that reading, our own consciousness bears us witness there ; let all the rest stand for scrutiny in other days and other places; far away there stands the one grand awful fact that the human heart disobeyed God, ate, and has since evermore been eating things that are bad for it. If men would confine themselves to the vital point, and not trouble themselves about things that are collateral, subsidiary, and merely meant for minor purposes, they would love the Bible. It speaks the right word, it alone has the truth, and " in the process of the suns" every theory will come to offer gold and frankincense and myrrh to the right thought in Genesis.

" How readest thou ? " Let us go to Sinai. Shall we consider about the thunders and the lightnings, the personality of the legislator, and shall we ask how Moses wrote the law, or whether God wrote it with his own finger, and in what language he wrote, and how the symbols looked to the uninitiated eye ? These are not questions fit for us ; we are earnest men. What is the question ? The question is, Has there been any distinction made between right and wrong ?   The answer is in the law.   Whoever wrote it, there it is.   It is written on stones, and stars ; on flowers, on hearts ; this truth lies at the basis of secured society ; without this we could not live.   Shall we discuss about the number of the commandments, the order in which they were given ?   Shall we begin to wonder how it is there were not more or there were not less ?   Then were we frivolous, then would we give up all that is worth holding ; but who will give up this great fact, that there has been made a distribution of moralities, there has been a classification of things right, things wrong ?   You cannot get rid of that Sinai ; it is in your houses, it is in your nurseries, it is in your schools, it is in your houses of business ; it is the very life of civilisation ; it is the guarantee of property, it is the sanction under whose protection human life is sacred.   " How readest thou ? "   Thou hast been pottering about a thousand things that do not belong to the subject.   Any human author, distinctively so-called and known, treated as the Bible is treated, could not stand for a moment, if there were aught in him of poetry, high thinking, far-reaching suggestion : the mechanic might live—the artist would be killed.

" How readest thou ? "   How many have been troubled about the wars and the destruction of the Canaanites and the Perizzites and the Hivites and the Amorites and Jebusites, and how they wondered how all this could take place as it did !   That is not the point.   You miss the author's meaning.   " How readest thou ? "   We should so read all these mysteries as to see that there is a meaning in the ages, a shaping, directing power,—call it Fire-mist if you like, if you prefer that to Deity ; have your idol ; call it Chance, if in that syllable there be more poetry than in the syllable God ; keep your little pet, and gorge him till he die : we call history Providence, the shaping out of God's kingdom the onward line that aims at and will terminate in righteousness ; and Hivite, Perizzite, Canaanite, and all other opposing forces must go down. Nor is this an outworking of divine purpose, as if that were something arbitrary, far away, metaphysical, and impossible of human conception.   God has no interests inconsistent with human welfare. That is the key of the whole position.   If yours be an ivory god, I do not know what he may do, I will not be responsible for him ;

my God is Father, royal Father, everlasting Father; his name is Wonderful, Counsellor, The Mighty God, The Everlasting Father, The Prince of Peace : and there poetry may take licence, and write the firmament with the choicest epithets descriptive of majesty, patience, tenderness, and love. *That* God has no interests inconsistent with the salvation of the child that was born an hour ago. *That* God is working out nothing that does not contemplate the good of the meanest vagrant that disgraces our civilisation. So there are those who are hard of mouth because hard of heart, who talk about God as if he were working out something far away in the clouds that man has nothing to do with, and man must be crushed and ground to powder that that mighty Invisible may have his way. It is a lie; God is love; God is thinking about every man, woman, and child when he is working his mighty way; yea, when he whets his glittering sword and his hand takes hold of judgment, even then God is love. We cannot tell all the mystery of the action of love ; it has a side that is marked by chastening, discipline, trial, loss. Our God is a consuming fire, but at the last it will be found that he has consumed nothing that even he could save.

" How readest thou ? " At the Cross, how readest thou ? How many theories of the atonement we have ! How many theological hairsplittings and metaphysics we have seen around the Cross by blasphemers who thought they were praying ! There is but one meaning in that Calvary transaction : what is that meaning, all-inclusive, all-explaining ? It is that the world is redeemed. If you add one line to that your addition is subtraction ; if you begin to theorise and speculate and dogmatise you are lost. We only dogmatise when we are fat and prosperous and self-conceited ; when we are self-convicted, penitent, contrite, broken-hearted, blind with tears, we seize great meanings, and when language fails we express ourselves in mighty cries of love. Have nothing to do with theorists and theological mechanicians, and people who have plans and schemes of God. God is love; the meaning of the Cross is, The world is redeemed, not with corruptible things as silver and gold, but with the precious blood of Jesus Christ, as of a Lamb slain from the foundation of the world. Pilate writes in Greek and Latin and Hebrew, but above all the superscription there is written the true meaning—God so loved the world that he did this—he died for it. Do not be as a beast in the sanctuary, trampling upon things that ought to be taken up and reverently treasured in the heart. Do not seek for meanings in words ; words are deceptions, words are mockeries, words are either infirmities or falsehoods. It is the heart that knows. There is no word-ladder that can reach even unto heaven, but there is a heart-power that wings its way unerringly through all the clouds, and finds the father-mother God.

How readest thou, finally, in the fifteenth chapter of the first Epistle to the Corinthians respecting the resurrection ? We have actually had volumes written on the resurrection ! The whole doctrine is in one line, like every other doctrine of the Bible— the doctrine is, we shall not die. There is a power mightier than death ; the sting of death is for a moment, and the victory of the grave is for the twinkling of an eye ; the grave will not be able to felicitate itself upon its victory until it is crushed by the resurrection. But some man will say, Just so. Paul anticipated the whole of the fussy-mindedness of the theological genius, whether it be a genius of affirmation or of denial. But some man will say, How ? You cannot get rid of that " some man " with his little questions and foolish peddling inquiries. As if God could always come into a " how," and live there ; as if there were room enough in a human " how " or a human " why " to tabernacle the Infinite. Thus we believe in the Resurrection ; we believe in Creation, we believe in Law, we believe in Providence, we believe in Redemption, we believe in Resurrection. If we could get hold of the central thought, the living, vital principle, how few infidels there would be ! Infidels are made by details. Infidels are all born on some sort of theologico-colonial line away out yonder. If there are scoffers, mockers, profane persons, we have nothing to say in their defence ; but if there are persons who have been puzzling themselve with externals and collaterals and subsidiaries, my purpose in this exposition is to ask such to find rest in central thought and in vital conception. Never think that words can express God. Theology, falsely so called, has done itself mortal injury by picking out a few words or many, and calling them final. There

are no final words. All words are alphabetic or symbolic. Do
not suppose that the ripest student in God's sanctuary is able to
comprehend God or tell all about God. It is his joy that he cannot
find out the Almighty unto perfection. But there is room in history
for prayer ; there is scope in reverent distance to see many aspects
of the divine movement that derive not a little of their beauty and
their fascination from the very perspective into which they are
thrown. Here, then, amid all tumult and controversy and
conflict, is a man who holds to the Bible ; and he holds to it
because of its vital points, and he beats off the rude hands that
would seek to take to pieces the mere decoration of the work.
Your child is not its clothes, the clothes are not the child ; within
it, and within it still, further, further, is the real child. So the
depredator comes and takes away in the night-time much that I
used to think essential ; but I find that it is not essential, because
I can live without it, pray without it, do good without it, suffer
heroically without it, and be like God without it. What has the
thief taken ? What he is welcome to. He cannot take away from
me the doctrine that God created the heavens and the earth,
though I know not how ; the doctrine that man is tempted and
disobedient, I cannot tell by what mystery of evil ; nor can there
be taken from me the distinction between right and wrong, thou
shalt and thou shalt not ; nor can there be taken from me the
conviction that life is ruled, shaped, directed, inspired, and not
the sport of chance. No man can take away from me the doctrine
that the world is redeemed ; and as for death I mock it, taunt it,
call it grim, lean, ghastly, hungry, and ask it, O death, where is
thy sting ? because of a conviction regarding rising again, ultimate
triumph, the final conquest of life over death. Think on these
things. Comfort one another with these words.

PRAYER.

ALMIGHTY GOD, we approach thee in the name of Jesus Christ, thy Son our Saviour, who was wounded for our transgressions and bruised for our iniquities. We see not the Infinite, but we see Jesus. We see not thy glory, but we see thy goodness; and so far as thou hast enabled us to behold Jesus Christ in all the wondrousness of his beauty and holiness, we are constrained to exclaim, each for himself, "My Lord and my God!" We rest in Jesus Christ,—he is our peace; he has answered the demand of law; he has broken down the middle wall of partition which separated us from God, and he hath made God and man one in holiness and in love. We have come to consider his gospel. To every one of us may it be good news from heaven. May we recognise the utterance of it as the only music that should charm the heart and appeal to the love of man. Enable us to know the sinfulness of sin, that we may the more clearly understand thy love in the gift of thy Son. Help us in this hour to be sincere worshippers. May our hearts be bowed down before the Holy One, and may our souls know their hunger and be able to express it in earnest urgent prayer. Let thy Spirit be given unto each hearer, as a spirit of life, of interpretation, of comfort, of stimulus; that this hour spent in this place may enable us to go in the strength of its memories many days. Dry the tears of our sorrow; uphold us in the day of sore distress; find bread for us in the time of famine; and when we are in the desert make pools for us. Thou art able to do exceeding abundantly above all that we ask or think. We leave, therefore, in the Name that is above every name, this poor prayer at thy footstool, for surely thy grace will turn it into a great answer. Amen.

Chapter x. 29.

"But he, willing to justify himself, said——"

SELF-JUSTIFICATION.

MY intention is to examine some of the excuses which men make in this matter of the religious life; to ascertain some of the causes or reasons which keep men back from entireness of consecration and completeness of Christian love. If the excuses are good, verily I shall embrace them myself, and repeat them with you, and help to heighten the thunder in which you speak them, when you are called upon to avow the reason of your indifference or of your opposition. If they be bad excuses, and

272

if they will not stand fire, I shall ask you to renounce them, to disclaim them, to be ashamed of them, and, as far as possible, to do double work in the future, to make up, in some degree, for the negligence or wastefulness of the past.

"The lawyer said——" Then comes his own particular plea or excuse, to which I intend to pay little or no attention now, it was so completely and triumphantly answered by Jesus Christ. Read his parable in reply. Next to the parable of the Prodigal Son, it is the sweetest word ever spoken even by the lips of Jesus Christ. I intend each man to fill up the sentence for himself, only having from the lawyer the preface : " He, willing to justify himself, said——" What words do you insert after the word "said"? How is it with your self-justifying and self-excusing heart? Do I hear correctly when I say you are now reasoning thus: " If I am sincere in my spirit and convictions, no matter whether I believe what is in the Bible or not, all will be well with me here and hereafter"? Is that a correct statement of what you are now thinking? It sounds well. I admit, with all candour, that it seems to sound conclusive and to admit of no refutation. Yet it surely will admit of a question or two being put, in order that we may fully understand the position. You speak of sincerity. I ask, What are you sincere in? Does anything turn upon the object of your sincerity? If you are sincerely giving to a customer over your counter what you believe to be the thing he has asked for, will you be fully justified in the day that you find you have poisoned the man? You sincerely believed that you were giving him precisely the very ingredient that he asked for, and that he had paid for, but you did not give him that ingredient, but something else, and ere the sun go down the man will be dead. What does sincerity go for there? If you indicate to a traveller, sincerely, to the best of your knowledge, the road along which he ought to go to reach a certain destination ; if it be the wrong road, and if in some sudden darkness the man should fall over a precipice, will your sincerity obliterate everything like self-reproach ? Were you sure it was the road? " No, but I was sincere in thinking it was." Did you explain to the man that you were speaking upon an assumption ? " No, I thought there was no occasion to do so, I felt so sure." But you see that the mere element of sincerity goes a very short way in cases of that kind. We love sincerity. Without sincerity life is but a mockery, the worst of irony! But what are we sincere in? Have we ascertained that the object of our sincerity is real, true, and deserving of our confidence? We are responsible not only for the light we have, but for the light we may have. It sounds very well, I have no doubt, to some young men, when a man says, "I intend to walk according to the light I have, and to take the consequences." Believe me, the man who so speaks talks in mock heroics. There is nothing in his statement that ought to deter you from investigation, or from anxious and devout pursuit of truth. I repeat, we are responsible not only for the light we have, but for the light that is offered to us. If you go into some dark chamber, and say you can find your way about well enough, and I offer you a light before you enter the apartment and you refuse it, and trust to your own power to grope your way in the dark; if you should fall into some mischief or be tripped up or thrown down, so as to injure yourself, who will be to blame? You walked according to the light you had, but the light that was in you was darkness! Your injury will be associated with a memory of neglect on your part, which, when the injury itself is healed, will yet be a sting in your recollection and your heart. Am I speaking, then, one word against sincerity? Certainly not. God is a Spirit, and they that worship him must worship him in spirit and in truth. I am speaking about that degree of sincerity which might be increased, and that quality of sincerity which might be enriched, by knowing more perfectly the object upon which it is terminating. Who are you, that you should be a revelation to yourself? Look at the mistakes of your lifetime and shut your self-written Bible. He ought to be a very wise man who can, gracefully and with aught of authoritativeness, close the Book of God and say, "I can do without it." He may be speaking sincerely, but he is speaking ignorantly. There is a sincerity of fanaticism, as well as a sincerity of philosophy. There is a sincerity of ignorance, as well as a sincerity of knowledge. Merely, therefore, to say, "I am sincere," is to say nothing. We must inquire, What is the object on which your sincerity fixes itself? What is the degree of its intelligence, and what is the degree of its conscience? When any man has returned clear earnest answers to these inquiries, my belief is, that he will find himself short of something, and that that something which is absent will be found to be the truth as it is in Jesus,—the Cross, the one Cross, out of which every other cross that is true and useful must be made!

But he, willing to justify himself, said—"I have been looking round, and it strikes me that I am every whit as good as other people that are about me." Would it be rude to contradict you? Will it be polite to admit the truthfulness, generally, of what you say? Either on the one hand or the other it does not touch the point at all. If the question lay between you and me, it would be right for each to compare himself with the other, and to exalt his superiority at the expense of his brother's infirmities. The case is not as between one man and another. We err in circumscribing the question so. The question is between the soul and God; between the heart and the absolutely right; between man and Jesus Christ; between right and wrong. How does the case stand when viewed thus? We injure ourselves by comparing ourselves one with another; setting shoulder to shoulder, and saying, "My stature is as high as yours;" laying hand beside hand, and saying, "My fingers are as clean as the fingers of other men." We are to come to the law and to the testimony; we are to proceed to the Cross of Jesus Christ; we are to go to the standards and balances of the sanctuary; we are to shut ourselves up with God, alone! He who can then boast, must be a madman or a devil! There is a disposition, I know, amongst us all, and exercised more or less, to compare ourselves with one another. One flippant and cruel man will say, looking upon a number of professing Christians, who may not exactly have been pleasing him, "Well, if this is your Christianity, I don't think I shall have much to do with it." All the while he knows, perfectly well, that the men who have been doing anything wrong have been so doing, not because of their Christianity, but because of their want of it, or in spite of it. A man looks over a lot of copper and sees one bad penny in it, and says, "Well, if this is your currency, I do not think I shall have anything to do with it." What do you think of that man? Would you introduce him to your family? Would you make him the tutor of your boys?

Would you in any way express esteem for him? A man goes into your orchard and picks up a rotten apple and says, "Well, if these are your apples, I don't think I shall have much to do with them." What do you think of him? Do you say, "He is an admirable man; a sagacious creature; a counsellor to be consulted"? You turn aside, and you say, "The man must be a fool." Not that I am going to say so about you on these solemn questions. But shall I say to you this?—When you compare yourself with another man, especially to your own advantage, you are not in the spirit which is likely to elicit the truth and lead you to sound and useful conclusions. Your disposition is wrong; your temper is wrong. You must cease such a method of comparing advantages and honours, and must go to the absolute and final standard of righteousness.

But he, willing to justify himself, said—"Though I do not believe and act as they do who call themselves Christians, yet I trust to the mercy of God." The man who makes this plea talks in some such fashion as this: "I do not care for doctrines; I do not care for churches; theologies trouble me very little indeed; if I live as wisely as I can, and do what is tolerably fair between one man and another, I shall trust to the mercy of God, and I believe all will be right at last." Do you know what you are talking about in talking so? Do you understand the value and the force of your own words? Are you aware that the word mercy is one of the words in our language which it is very difficult to understand? What is mercy? In your estimation, perhaps, it is mere physical sensibility, simple emotion—a gush of feeling. Is that mercy? No. What is mercy? The highest point of justice,—justice returning and completing itself by the return. Mercy is justice in tears. Mercy is righteousness with a sword just transforming itself into a sceptre. Is mercy a mere freak of sentimentality? Do you think God will say at last, "Well, well, come in, come in, and say nothing more about it"? I would not go into his heaven if the conditions were such. It would be no heaven. Where there is not righteousness at the centre, there is no security at the circumference. Where the throne is not founded upon justice, mercy is but a momentary impulse, to be followed by a terrible recoil,

"The mercy of God," you say, "where do I find the mercy of the Living One?" I find it in Bethlehem, in Gethsemane, on Calvary. Where is the mercy of God? It is in that dying Son of his, who was delivered for our offences, and raised again for our justification. Your notion of mercy is superficial. You use the great word in one of its aspects only; you do not seem to understand that the word mercy is a composite word, that has within itself many elements. As peace is not death, mercy is not sentiment. You propose to trust to the mercy of God. So do I, but in a different sense. Is it right to trifle with his law, to despise his word, to crucify his Son afresh, and then to say, "I will trust to his mercy at last"? Is that decent, fair, honourable, sensible? We are all living, in so far as we are living truly, in the mercy and grace of God. We trust to his mercy now. The question is not one of ultimate conditions, but of present experiences. Every morning we hallow the day with this prayer, "God be merciful to me a sinner!' and every night we recover the mistakes, the infirmities, and the sins of the daytime with this cry, "God be merciful to me a sinner!" What do you mean, then, when you talk about trusting to his mercy at last? Trust to his mercy at first. Where is his mercy? It is in the life, the ministry, the death, the resurrection, and the whole mediation of Jesus Christ.

But he, willing to justify himself, said,—"There is so much mystery about religion that I cannot really attempt to understand it." I answer, There is mystery about religion, but there is ten thousand times more mystery without it. There is mystery with the Bible, but there is nothing but mystery without it. There is a mystery of grace; yes, and there is a mystery of sin. Life is a mystery. All that is great touches the mysterious. In proportion as a thing rises from vulgarity and commonplace, it rises into wondrousness,—and wondrousness is but the first round in the ladder whose head rests upon the infinite mysteries. Understand it! Who asked you to understand it? You make a mistake if you suppose that religion is to be understood in the sense that you apparently attach to the word understand. It is to be understood by the heart, to be felt as the answer to the sorrow of the soul, to be understood through the medium of love

and sympathy, and not through the medium of dry intellect.
Do I understand the method of salvation? No. Can I explain
it intellectually, so as to chase away every lingering shadow of
mystery? No. What then? I feel it to be right. My heart
says, "Though you have often brought me bread I could not eat;
you have now brought me this bread,—and it is life!" I cannot
give the lie to my own heart. Would I part with the mystery?
Nay, verily. Are not the clouds God's as well as the blue sky?
Are not the mists around the mountain tops his, as well as the
bases of the mountains and the foundations of the earth? Is not
he, himself, the living God, the culmination of all mysteries, the
sum of all wonder—the Alpha and the Omega—not to be understood, but loved and served? There is a point in my religious
inquiries where I must close my eyes, look no more, but rest
myself in the grand transaction which is known as faith in the
Son of God.

But he, willing to justify himself, came at last to this : "There
are so many denominations of Christians that it is impossible
to tell which is right and which is wrong." Think of a man
going off on that line! Think of a man saying, that he has been
looking round and sees that there are so many denominations,
that really he has made up his mind to give up the whole thing!
Does he know what he is talking about? Is he really serious
when he speaks so? Shall I follow his example? If I do it
will be to show how great is his folly. "I have been looking
round, and see so many different regiments in the country that
really it is impossible to tell which is right and which is wrong,
and I do not think I shall have anything to do with the country."
Yes, there are many regiments, but one army; many denominations, but one church; many creeds, but one faith; many aspects,
but one life; many ways up the hill, but one Cross on the top
of it. Do not lose yourself among the diversities, when you might
save yourself by looking at the unities. "There are so many
mountains about, that I really do not know that there can be
any truth in geography." Many mountains—one globe! There
are a great many denominations, and I do not regret it. I believe
that denominationalism, wisely managed, may be used for mutual
provocation to love and to good works. It may be better that

we should be broken up externally, that each may do his own work in his own way, than that we should be bound together by merely nominal uniformity.   When an enemy arises to make an attack upon the Christian citadel, when he writes a book against Christ, or against the Bible, or against any aspect of Christian truth—who answers him?   Not one denomination in particular.   No.   When a hand is lifted up against the Cross, who seizes it?   Not one section of Christendom.   No.   When an assault is made upon Calvary, the whole Church, in all colours, all attitudes, rushes to protect—what indeed requires no defence except as a sign of love—the Cross of Christ, which sets itself above the storms and outlives the puny assaults of puny men!

I have looked into all the excuses that I could find, and verily I now pronounce them, so far as my intelligence will enable me to judge—rubbish!   Is that word understood?   It is my business, as well as the business of every man, to understand really what excuses are made of; what the value of self-justification is. Because I am as anxious to be right, I trust, as most other men; and having examined all these grounds of self-justification, I say I would not risk so much as a day's health upon them, not to speak of an immortal condition.   There is not one of them will hold good in the market-place if it were commercialised.   Shall any one of them stand good as between us and God?   If, then, there is not to be self-justification, what is there to be?   Self-renunciation.   A man must empty himself of himself before he is in the right condition to understand lovingly and gratefully the offer which Jesus Christ makes men.   So long as there is, in the remotest chambers of his mind, anything like the shade of a shadow of a supposed reason to imagine himself in any degree right, he is not in a position to consider the offers of mercy. Who receives the Eternal One as guest and friend?   Name him. Hast thou heard his name?   Tell it.   His name is a broken-hearted man!   God guests with the contrite and companies with the self-renouncing soul.   I will go to my Father, then, and will say unto him, not, " Father, I was tempted; somebody lured me away; I did not intend to leave thee, but I was beguiled;" but I will say unto him, " Father, I have sinned!"

This, then, is the ground of coming to God; the ground of self-denial, self-renunciation, self-distrust, self-hatred on account of sin. "O Israel, thou hast destroyed thyself, but in me is thy help." "Come unto me, all ye that labour and are heavy laden, and I will give you rest." "Jesus cried and said, If any man thirst, let him come unto me and drink." "I am come that they might have life, and that they might have it more abundantly." Who accepts the invitation? Some have accepted it. Pray that this word may not be in vain. Some require just one more appeal, and they will decide. Take this, then, as the appeal you want. Now is the accepted time; now is the day of salvation. I want to see men decide for Christ. I want to know that men who have been thinking so long, have at last been enabled by the Spirit of God to say, "I will cast myself on Jesus, the one Saviour of a sinful race." Our fathers used to plead for decisions. The men who made the pulpit of England the grandest of its powers—pleaded with sinners that they would decide. If aught of their mantle has fallen upon me, even but for the occasion, I would speak with all their voices, now dead; I would stand upon their dead bones and turn their graves into a pulpit, and cry, "Ho! every one that thirsteth, come ye to the waters; and he that hath no money, come ye, buy wine and milk without money and without price." "How long halt ye between two opinions?" I am not the one speaker; all the holy dead speak in my voice; the general assembly and church of the first-born written in heaven; your dead pastors, your sainted fathers and mothers, all the companions of your life who have passed away into the other world, all prophets and apostles, make me their mouthpiece when I say, Now is the accepted time; now is the day of salvation!

Chapter xi. 42.

"Ye tithe mint and rue and all manner of herbs, and pass over judgment and the love of God."

PIOUS AT THE WRONG PLACES.

IN other words, you are pious at the wrong places. That is the point. It applies to us all. We think we make up for lack of the right, and complete piety by fussing about a thousand things that are secondary, subordinate, and hardly of any consequence. Thus man writes his poor programme of service. He has his little fads and likings and prejudices, and if you will allow him to cobble away at these he thinks he is about as good as anybody else. When men work according to their prejudice they are not working at all in the sight and love and acceptance of God. They are working on their own account, for their own purposes, with their own wishes in view; they are fools, and blind, and it requires the Son of God to tell them this in the right tone. What they are doing has its own importance if set in the right perspective,—"these ought ye to have done, and not to leave the other undone." If you carefully examine men's Christian life and Christian profession you will find they are doing the little things they like to do. They have not attained the dignity of sacrifice. They like to go to church, they like to hear good music, they like the general society of the Christian congregation. That is the fatal word—they "like." When we are doing the things we like, we are doing nothing. That has to be broken down; that bad root has to be gotten right out of us; every fang and fibre of it has to come out, and to be thrown into the fire. So long as people only do the things they like to do, they are in danger of supporting their little prejudices by a loud invocation addressed to their own consciences. There are points at which there should be a general conscience; that general conscience will only occupy its right sphere and exert its right

influence in proportion as the individual conscience is watched
and cultivated and sanctified.   There should, however, be times
when men give up their little likings, their small, drivelling
prejudices, and unite with the infinite stream of devotional and
noble sentiment.

We may do the little without doing the great.   That is the
mischief; and we may so do the little as to imagine that we are
doing the great, which is the still deeper and more fatal mischief.
Men like to keep their piety well under their hand, so that they
can take it up and set it down and manipulate it with perfect
ease; then it is no real piety, for true piety is discipline, aspiration, discontent with present achievement, and determination to
conquer some loftier, sunnier altitude.   "I count not myself to
have apprehended," said the chiefest of us, the mightiest runner
in the race, the stoutest champion in the war.   We cannot do
the great without doing the little.   That is the beautiful relation
and issue of things in Christian life and experience.   We cannot
pay attention to "judgment and the love of God," and allow the
little taxations to escape notice.   This is how Christ would work;
this is the programme of Christianity.   It says, Get the people to
do the great things, and then they will surely do the little things
in due time and turn.   Christianity addresses itself to vitalities,
not to accidents and externalities.   Christianity is the spiritual
religion; the book it carries is the sword of God, quick and
powerful, mightier than any two-edged sword ever forged by
human hands.   It makes its way into the innermost parts of life,
and by war brings peace into the soul.   Does Christianity trouble
itself about washing hands, and tithing mint and rue and all
manner of herbs?   Not at all.   Is Christianity a little reformer
going up and down in the world, seeing where it can patch up
broken walls and repair broken glass?   Nothing of the sort.
Has Christianity any little detailed platform of reformation?
None, none.   Then how can Christianity get at the habits of the
people?   By getting at their hearts.   Christianity is not a little
outside day-labourer, who comes for an eight-hours' spell at the
dilapidation of human life; Christianity is the spirit of love,
which is the spirit of God, and it does not begin its work until it
gets into the heart; its watchword is, Behold I stand at the

door and knock ; I cannot begin outside, the ruin is not external, I must start from the innermost core and root of things, and work my way to circumferences and outlying relations and engagements. How does Christianity address itself to the health of the people ? Through the heart. Of course the little fussy reformer goes in at once for an immediately new and absolutely sparkling and dazzling programme of sanitation. Christianity says, Why so hot, my little sir ? Health is the expression of the heart. When the heart is right there will not be lacking the colour of health upon the cheek. You are painting skin. I am touching life at its font and central spring. Christianity does not build a new house for a man ; it creates for him a new atmosphere. Atmosphere is always the largest quantity. It is larger even than light ; it abides when the light has gone away. Atmosphere stays with us all night. Atmosphere makes life ; we take from it our health, our vitality, our temperature, we take from it our colour. What Christianity wants to create, therefore, is a Pentecostal air, —fire-filled, angel-thronged, pure and health-giving, as that which flows over the hills of heaven.

Christianity, therefore, does not begin with your little reformer, fussy, urgent, tumultuous, self-exploding. Christianity begins with "judgment and the love of God." Hence its slowness. That is the explanation of the tardiness of the kingdom of God, because when it does come it will never go away. Our little reforms have their day, they have their day and cease to be ; but when the kingdom of God comes—it has taken uncounted centuries to come—it will abide, and God shall be all in all ; the last enemy that shall be destroyed is death. The greatness of Christianity is the explanation of its tardiness. It is being out-run at present by many competitors, and so impatient are those competitors that they jeer Christianity, and they jeer the Church, and they jeer the pulpit, and they say that the ministers of the Church are always the last to come along ; then arises the loud vulgar laugh of ignorance. Those who take but superficial views of life and duty want us to be getting on. I have been watching two buildings in my own neighbourhood : the one was being put up by a speculative builder, and he put it up almost before I had time to turn round ; the other dwelling was being put up for the owner, and directly by the owner, and every stone seemed to bear the impression of individual appreciation. The house was a long time in being built, and it will be a long time in being blown down : already I have seen the ladder five times against the chimney of the speculative builder. We cannot build the kingdom of heaven according to this spirit. God will not have it so. He is content to be mocked for slowness that he may work his way into everlastingness.

Here the Christian ministry is blamed. I have letters from Cornwall, and from Scotland, and from Ireland, from physicians, and working men, and men of business, and young men, who, if all gathered together, would constitute the largest cave of Adullam that ever existed upon the face of the earth, and they are all telling us ministers and preachers and Christian teachers to get on. They are fools, and blind. A little plan can be pushed on very much indeed. You can have a ladder made by contract, but not a tree. That is the difference. You can pledge that this day week at three o'clock in the afternoon that ladder shall be ready under a penalty of two pounds, but you cannot pledge that about an oak-tree. It will be ready when it likes, so to say ; it will be ready when it co-operates with the sun, and the soil, and the air, in other words, with God ; but when the oak does come it will make your ladder look both useful and vulgar.

The question is, What is the work we have to do ? Is it to " tithe mint and rue and all manner of herbs " ? or is it to establish " judgment, and the love of God " ? The work may be in process of being done when there seems to be nothing but a spirit of indolence over the whole Church. Reason takes a long time, because it means to abide for ever when it works out its holy purpose. The pulpit has absolutely nothing to do with the little questions that may be ranked with " mint and rue and all manner of herbs." If any man stood up in a pulpit and delivered his opinion about strikes, he would prostitute his vocation, he would dishonour the altar. He would be beginning at the wrong end : pious in the wrong place. We have nothing to do in the pulpit with competing politics ; we have nothing to do with civic administration in the pulpit : and yet we have to do with them

all, but in another and loftier and grander sense. You cannot
have "judgment and the love of God" operating in human understanding and conscience and life, without mint and rue and all
manner of herbs having due attention paid to them. This is the
glory of the pulpit. This is the glory of the pulpit because it is
the glory of Christianity. Yet there are persons all round about
us who tell us how we ought to preach; especially is a man
delighted when he can come in and say, "That is the very thing
I have been saying, sir, the last five-and-twenty years." Man loves
to hear himself loudly preached. But what about the other man
who has been saying the exact contrary these five-and-twenty
years? Of course it is easy to relegate him to old-fogeydom;
easy to say that he is out of the running, out of the swim, out
of the spirit of the times; that is a rough-and-ready method with
your opponents: but is it just, is it reasonable, is it right in the
sight of eternity?

My contention is that the pulpit has nothing to do with the
details of controverted or contentious questions, and yet the
pulpit can exert upon them the profoundest and most beneficent
influence. When I go into the church I must hear honesty so
expounded and so enforced—sweet, wholesome honesty, frank-
faced, open-eyed honesty—that I dare not go out and do the
little mean dishonesty which I had intended to do. Has the
pulpit been talking metaphysics when it has been so talking and
so affecting my life? It is absurd and unjust to maintain any
such contention. My preacher did not say a word about little
detailed acts of theft, of felony, but he so exalted honesty, snow-
white honesty, that I burned with shame when I thought of the
mean thing I was going to do to-morrow morning. When I go
into the church I must hear justice so expounded and so vindicated
as to make it impossible for me to be unjust, whether I am man
or master. Is the minister therefore doing nothing? Is Christianity dumb amid all your strikes and elections and contentions?
The Sermon on the Mount would settle everything; yet the
Sermon on the Mount is a great moral revelation and a sublime
moral appeal. The Golden Rule would reconcile capital and
labour, all political contention and uproar, all selfishness and
greed. Yet we are waiting for some man to write a large book

that will philosophically adjust and determine everything. We have been waiting for him so long that I have long ago given up any expectation of seeing him. I find the Man has come and the book has been written—the name of the Man is Jesus Christ, the name of the Book is the Golden Rule, and all contentions and controversies should be settled by that rule alone. Herein is he Prince of Peace, Reconciler of the nations. When I go to hear my minister I must hear Charity—sweet, tuneful, beauteous, mother-like, sister-like Charity—so expounded and applied that I cannot and will not write my bad criticism to-morrow. I thought of running that man down, but I cannot now. If what I have heard is true about charity,—great, noble, all-hoping, divinest love—if that is true, I should be ashamed of myself if I wrote that bad-blooded criticism upon my fellow-worker; I will burn it. Is the pulpit, thus interpreted and thus applied, doing nothing? It would seem to be doing more if it placarded the church walls with —"Discourse next Sunday morning on the Great Strike." I should be ashamed of any sanctuary that was blistered with such a brand. Yet the pulpit, I may repeat again and again almost to tediousness, does take up every quarrel, contention, difficulty, threatening of war, and would settle them all upon the altar of Christ.

Here, then, let us refresh our memory by saying here is the reason of the slowness of many Christian means. It is not the business of the pulpit to discuss politics, but it is the business of the pulpit to rouse and educate conscience. Many of my correspondents call for practical preaching—that is to say, they mean by "practical preaching" a very sound whipping of the man who sits next to them. They insist that the pulpit is not practical; but when the pulpit inflicts upon them a just laceration, then they say the pulpit is transgressing its province, is becoming personal and intolerable. God be thanked! I would it were intolerable by some wretches! I would that justice and the love of God could be so expounded and enforced that every man who is going to cease work to-morrow morning before the clock strikes twelve should be ashamed of himself, and say to himself, "I am a bad thief," and keep his hand going till the clock strikes right up. I would have justice so expounded that if any employer were thinking of withdrawing, curtailing, pinching, and unjustly treating the humblest boy in his charge, he should say, Instead of stinting him I will increase his income. I will encourage him by all manner of kindly recognition. If great principles, divine religion and maxim, do not work out these issues, nothing can work them out. They may appear for a time to be doing well; but all your plans, policies, programmes, schemes, arrangements will come to nothing, they will wither away because there is no deepness of earth; and the thing that will abide is the regenerated life, the soul born from above. If any man be in Christ Jesus, he is a new creature; old things have passed away, and all things have become new. If we are not born again, we may do very much in speculative building and in new programme drawing, we may make great excitement as if we were going to readjust the relations of individual, social, and imperial life; but it will come to nothing, it will be as an idiot's tale—sound, fury, signifying nothing. Have faith in "judgment and the love of God"; in other words, have faith in truths that are fundamental, vital, that spring from Christ and return to Christ; in other and better words still, have faith in the Cross. That, and that alone, will bring the nations to brotherhood, will unite earth with heaven.

PRAYER.

ALMIGHTY GOD, our lives are precious unto thee, for thou dost create them, and thou hast redeemed them with a price beyond all reckoning. We are redeemed not with corruptible things, as silver and gold, but with the precious blood of Jesus Christ. And inasmuch as thou hast freely delivered him up for us all, with him also thou wilt surely give us all things. Help us to trust in the Lord, and to wait patiently for all the way that he himself is taking, knowing that at the end thereof we shall see some new and beautiful vision of thy love. We oftentimes hasten thee, because we are weak,—our prayers show our weakness ; every hour we urge thee where thou dost need no importunity. We wonder at thy slowness, and at much of thy method of governing man, because we ourselves can see but a little way, and what we do see is beheld very indistinctly. Thy will be done. We put ourselves into thy hands ; we are to thee children and sons and redeemed ones, and surely thou wilt magnify thy grace and thy power in our life. We know not what a day may bring forth. We are of yesterday, and know nothing. We cannot tell what is passing around us, and as for the secret of the next hour, behold it is too deep for us. What, then, shall we do ? We will rest in the Lord, and wait patiently for him. We will put our case into the hands of God, and we will say, Judge thou ; direct the way of our feet ; uphold our lives in righteousness, and by-and-by, when it seemeth good in thy sight, bring forth our judgment as the light, and our righteousness as the noonday. We will trust thee in Jesus Christ. It is through Jesus Christ alone that we know the meaning of true faith. May the faith which he called for be found in us ! Lord, increase our faith. May we by faith lay hold of thy words of love, and fully realise them ; enter into their meaning and live upon them, as a child lives upon his inheritance. What is it that hinders us from the full realisation of thy presence and thy care ? Surely it is our unbelief. Help us, now that we are gathered around the Cross of Jesus Christ, to renounce our unbelief and to begin our life again. May it henceforward be a life of faith on the Son of God, who loved us and gave himself for us. We humbly beseech thee to pardon our sins. God be merciful unto us sinners ! The blood of Jesus Christ, thy Son, cleanseth from all sin. May we know its purifying power. May we know the joy of pardoned men, and the blessedness of those whose iniquity is covered. Enable us now to worship thee with simplicity and sincerity and love, and whilst we tarry before thee, may a great light fill our hearts ; may a new joy take possession of us ; may each hearer listen to the gospel as he never listened to it before, and answer the appeal of thy love by the entire surrender of his heart. Break down the stubborn will, dispel the prejudices of an evil mind; destroy the power of temptation, and the whole system of our spiritual enemy ; do thou upset and utterly put him away, and give us again to feel that we are children of God ; that we have stewardship imposed upon us ; that we ourselves are not our own, and that what is in our hand belongs unto the Giver of every good gift. Lord, hear us and be merciful unto us, and read the secret of our heart, and come to us as a God of truth where we need instruction, as a God of comfort where sorrow is swallowing us up, as a God of light where we are groping and stumbling in darkness; and above all and including all, come unto us as the God and Father of our Lord Jesus Christ. Show thyself to us as we need to see thee. We hope in God ; we pray for the gift of God the Holy Ghost. We would be solemn, quiet, thoughtful. We would be inspired whilst we abide in the sanctuary. We would be filled with the Holy Ghost ! Let the Lord hear us ; let our cry prevail with our Father, and our hearts shall be filled with blessing ! Amen.

Chapter xii. 16-20.

" And he spake a parable unto them, saying, The ground of a certain rich man brought forth plentifully : and he thought within himself, saying, What shall I do, because I have no room where to bestow my fruits ? And he said, This will I do : I will pull down my barns, and build greater; and there will I bestow all my fruits and my goods. And I will say to my soul, Soul, thou hast much goods laid up for many years; take thine ease, eat, drink, and be merry. But God said unto him, Thou fool, this night thy soul shall be required of thee : then whose shall those things be, which thou hast provided ? "

THE RICH FOOL.

LET us find out where this man, called a " fool," got wrong. There seem to be some points of common-sense in the man. One is, therefore, curious to know where he breaks away from good thinking into foolish planning, and where he proves himself to be an atheist.

" The ground of a certain rich man brought forth plentifully " (ver. 16).

There is nothing wrong in that. There is no harm in having good crops, fields beautiful with the produce of nature. You cannot stand beside a man's farm, and say, " This must be a very bad person, because his fields bring forth so plentifully." In Old Testament times abundance of harvest was considered a sign of the divine favour, and men regarded the increase of the ground as a token of God's approbation. It is a practical fallacy to suppose that a man must be wrong because he has plenty. A man may be a very child of God, a saint, and a crowned one in the spiritual kingdom, and yet have an abundance on every hand. He may also be a very bad man, and yet be poor and destitute and homeless and friendless ; and contrariwise, forasmuch as nothing depends upon the circumstances, but everything upon the spirit. The rich man before us derived his property from the ground ; and agriculture is of all professions the most honest, the most natural, and the most beautiful. Some of us would like to follow that pursuit above all others. What can be more simple and beautiful than to till the ground, and to get out of the kindly earth sustenance for our daily life ? So far, therefore, we find nothing amiss. The man was rich, and his ground brought forth plentifully. Herein, there is no indictment against him. Let us, then, proceed :—

"And he thought within himself, saying, What shall I do?" (ver. 17.)

There is nothing wrong there. A man must reflect. A man must put questions to himself regarding the disposing of the property which has come honestly into his hands ; he must put a value upon his possessions, and know how to act with prudence. There are times when we must stand still, call our lives up, and ask ourselves some plain, practical, business questions. So far, therefore, the man appears to be a man of sense, —he is reflective, he is thoughtful, he sees what he has, and wishes to dispose of it. Let us, then, proceed one step further :—

"Because I have no room" (ver. 17).

There he is wrong ! He had plenty of room, if he had known it. Not barn-room ; but soul-room—life-room ! He measured his room by measuring his barn. What, hast thou no room for all thy goods when so many thousands of people are starving upon the face of the earth ? No room for thy surplus property, when many men have not where to lay their heads ? The man begins to get wrong at this point—in thinking about his barns only, and in taking too limited a view of the scope of his life. Perhaps we shall find something wrong a word or two farther on. So we do :—

"All my fruits, and my goods" (ver. 18).

There he is wrong again. My fruits, and my goods, and my soul, and my barns. That is all wrong. He has narrowed down things to a point. He has made himself the centre of reckoning ; he has constituted his own individuality into the standard of life.

But surely a man may say "my soul"? No. Only in a
secondary sense, at least, may he say that. "For all souls are
mine," saith the Lord. The fundamental error in life is that a
man should call himself his own. And until that deadly, fatal
reasoning is driven out of him, he will never take hold of life by
the right end. The discussion is not, "Is what I have in my
hand my property or not?" Your hand itself is not your own.
Why, then, be wasting your life in some little peddling debate
about what you hold in your hand? No man can live wisely,
deeply, truly, until he has got rid of the notion that he is his own
property. Herein is the great mystery of the Christian faith:
Ye are not your own; ye are bought, ye belong to another.
Glorify God in your body and your spirit, which are God's. I do
not, therefore, follow a man into any debate when he says, "My
barns, my fruits, my goods." I let him chatter on; but when he
says, "My soul," I arrest him! He may fight all day long about
his barns and his fruit and his goods, and no useful result would
testify to our wordy debate. But if I can convince a man that his
soul is not his own, except in a secondary sense: that it is God's;
that it is a bought soul; and that it must take its law and its way
from the utterances of God,—I shall have brought the man to the
right point from which to start all the courses and all the discipline of his life. Is not selfishness at the root of all evil? Is
not a man little in proportion as he debates everything in the
light of his own personality? This man committed that great
error. He spoke of nobody but himself; he seemed to imagine
that creation was absorbed in his own little life; he was his own
lawgiver, and he undertook to decide his own way. Let us read
further, because we shall perhaps find that the man's character
more fully develops itself:—

"And I will say to my soul, Soul, thou hast much goods laid up for many
years; take thine ease, eat, drink, and be merry" (ver. 19).

What had he laid up? Much goods. Truly! But had he the
years laid up? Barn enough—goods enough. But where are
the stored years? Can a man lock up even one day, and say,
"Thou art mine; I will come for thee"? He seemed to think
that all things came within the range of his individual ownership;
and yet there was a point when his poor little "my" dropped
down dead, and had no longer any hold upon his property. My

fruits, my barns, my goods, my soul; but not my years. No!
God must, now and then, just put in a little claim of proprietorship, must he not?   He says, "Hitherto shalt thou come, but no
farther; and thou shalt even go to this line only in a secondary
sense.   But when thou dost take into thy keeping the years, and
make a covenant with time and mortgage the future, I must say,
No; boast not thyself of to-morrow, for thou knowest not what a
day may bring forth." Ye must not say, We will go in to such and
such a city, and tarry there a year, and buy and sell, and get gain.
But ye ought to say, If the Lord will.   There are unseen forces
we have to consult; stubborn as we may be and self-resolved, there
are great walls set round about us, that we cannot break through
—invisible walls, but there they are—and he only is wise who,
knowing the limit of his little power, and holding it as secondary,
says, "Not my will, but thine, be done."   We can lay up the
goods, but we cannot lay up the years.   We can, in some sense,
call the fruits ours, but no man can call to-morrow his.   There
are limits to proprietorship, there are boundaries to property, and
ever and anon God comes down to us in some way, to say, "The
earth is mine, and the fulness thereof."   No nation can live long
in sweltering prosperity; sometimes, therefore, God comes down
about harvest time, and scatters a blight upon the wheatfield, and
people wonder.   Why?   "The earth is the Lord's, and the
fulness thereof."   May he not do what he will with his own?
Sometimes he says to the wind, "Blow," and the poor little
structures of human skill are toppled over.   Sometimes he says
to the flood, "You may go over the line to-night—rush on!" and
then men run away from the invading waters.   Is it not right
that now and then he should put in some kind of claim upon
his own property?   We hold it only as stewards; at best we
have it but secondarily; it is his, and if it please him to shake
the roots of the earth—"The earth is the Lord's, and the fulness
thereof."   And what shall we, even the mightiest, require?
Just a handful of it at last, under which to hide our dead bones.

Let us read again.   We may discover that the iniquity deepens:

"I will say to my soul, Soul, take thine ease, eat, drink, and be merry"
(ver. 19).

The man was all animal.   There was not one little bit of blue sky in all his universe. His universe was a great dinner-table, or a great wine-cellar. He told his soul to eat, drink, and be merry; not knowing what a soul lives upon, or what its proper food and drink are. So he told his soul that it would find heaven in the barn. I thought as much. The moment he said soul and barn in the same sentence, I was confident his intention was to feed his soul with chaff and with wind. Some men are doing this to-day. They are starving their minds and begrudging proper sustenance for their souls. The literature they read is the literature that poisons their best life. The conversation they hold, being destitute of the truly spiritual element, tends to the impairing of their manhood and the destruction of every holy energy of their nature. A man, as in this case, may make promises to his soul that are the worst threatenings. A man says that he is going to treat his soul well, not knowing that his "well" is the deadliest threat that could ever be uttered to the life that was within him. Let us not be altogether animalised. Let us know that we cannot live by bread alone, but by every word that proceedeth out of the mouth of God. For there is a way of feeding the soul which means destroying it. He who learns this in time may yet save something out of the wreck of his nature: having spoiled the most of a lifetime, he may yet gather up some of the fragments, that he be not wholly lost!

So much for the man's own speech. Now we turn to another side:—

"But God said unto him, Thou fool, this night thy soul shall be required of thee : then whose shall those things be, which thou hast provided?" (ver. 20.)

What had he forgotten from his calculations? Only God. He had his slate and his pencil, and bent over and wrote his memorandum, and it looked well; and when he had added up what he had set down, he said, "That is the sum total." What had he omitted from his slate? God! The one thing that most of us are omitting from all our calculations. You cannot build a house without God; because the winds are his, and the rains, the lightnings, and all natural forces, and no man can take a lease of them, or have any right of property in them. You must believe either in that way, and by a kind of natural theology take note of God; or in the better way of homage and spiritual trust. But there you are—he has you in his grip! It is one of two things. It is either to be held by him, or to say, "Hold me." If I take the wings of the morning, and flee unto the uttermost parts of the earth, he is there, waiting for me. If I say, I will linger in mid-sea, behold, every wave that breaks against my vessel says, "God is here!" If I make my bed in hell, even there a shadow passes over me, and I know it to be God! And as for heaven, it is made by his presence. You see life does not divide itself sharply, thus: One man can live without God, away from his administration and control and sovereignty; and another man can live under God, working out his laws, and living in harmony and peace with all his dispensations. The earth is full of his presence, and whatever I touch has his autograph upon it. The rich unthinking man had omitted God from his calculations. God allows us sometimes to go so far along the road, and all things look very pleasant, and we seem to feel as if-we had left all care behind us, and had only to open another gate or two and then—liberty without bounds, and enjoyment without end! Yes,—only another gate or two! Go up to the first gate; try your key. No use? Shake the gate, perhaps it only requires a little strength, because some of the hinges are rough. No! Look well at the wards and appoint-ments to see where the difficulty is. Cannot! Try it again. And a great mist falls upon it,—you step away from it but one inch, and you can never find it any more; darkness has settled upon it, and you are groping about like a homeless, blind man! God allows us to proceed in our monologue, sentence after sentence, and we seem to have things all our own way; and then, when we have set up our little plan, he puts a question to us which makes us drunk, but not with wine; he puts one view of life before us, and we turn dizzy as we look. We have come to the last step, and we are just going to take it, and then, as we imagine, all will be well with us. We take it,—and we are never heard of more. Who can dig a pit so deeply as God? Who can scoop out abysses so terrible as those which are made by the hand of the Almighty?

"But God said unto him, Thou fool, this night thy soul shall be required of thee" (ver. 20).

"Thou fool." Why use this expression ? The man was very wise, on one side of his nature. So many of us are clever in little points. So many people are prudent and sagacious and wise in one aspect of their nature, and are utter and irredeemable fools in others. If the light that is in us be darkness, how great is that darkness ! Few men are foolish altogether. The man in the parable talked wisely up to a given moment, and from that time he went down into the utterest and worst imbecility. What does God say ? "This night." God sometimes gives but short notice to his tenants. Oftentimes the Most High cometh suddenly upon us. May he rightfully do so ? Yes. Why ? Because "the earth is the Lord's and the fulness thereof." All souls are his. All lives are but throbs of his own heart. No man hath right or title of proprietorship in himself, nor can have evermore.

Does not Jesus Christ in this parable disclose the method of the divine government ? God comes suddenly to men, so that not a man amongst us can surely say he will be living upon the earth to-morrow morning ! Oh, that men were wise; that they understood these things ; that they would consider their latter end ! "Lord, so teach us to number our days, that we may apply our hearts unto wisdom." "He that, being often reproved, hardeneth his neck, shall suddenly be destroyed, and that without remedy." Is there a man amongst us who knows of a certainty that he will reach his home again ? Can the wisest of us say, with sureness, that he will live five minutes longer? This is the reality of affairs ; this is the kind of thing we ought to look at and estimate in making up the scheme of our life. We are walking upon a very thin line. On the right hand there is an abyss, on the left hand there is a precipice. There is barely foothold between the two. "Hold thou me up, and I shall be safe." As a mere matter of fact, we hold our life without a moment's guarantee that we shall have it to-morrow. What becometh us, then, but diligence and watchfulness and prayerfulness ; a spirit that makes the best of the passing hour ; a disposition that cries to be taught what is best to be done within the brief space allotted to human life ?

"This night." The man had forgotten the nights! He talked about years in whole numbers; about the bright spaces called day, but did not think of those black lines called night. Between to-day and to-morrow there rolls the black night-river, and we may fall into it, and never step on the shore of the morning. "Whatsoever thy hand findeth to do, do it with thy might."

"Then whose shall those things be, which thou hast provided?" (ver. 20.)

Can the man not take them with him? Not one of them. But they are fruits of the earth? Yes,—but not required in the other world. What, then, is it impossible for a man, after having been anxious and thoughtful, after having worried himself to death in the amassing of a little property, is it impossible for him to take it out into the next world? Yes,—impossible! "We brought nothing into this world, and it is certain we can carry nothing out." "Lay not up for yourselves treasures upon earth, where moth and rust doth corrupt, and where thieves break through and steal: but lay up for yourselves treasures in heaven, where neither moth nor rust doth corrupt, and where thieves do not break through nor steal. For where your treasure is there will your heart be also." Make your ground bring forth plentifully; be the best farmers in the neighbourhood; be successful in every kind of business or profession; and, if you possibly can, rise to the very top of the line along which you are working. But all the while hold all these things loosely; hold them in a spirit of stewardship. Then you will hold them rightly, and when God says, "Let go!" it will be but a step into heaven. The only things we can carry out of this world are our thoughts, our feelings, our impulses, our desires,—all the elements which make us spiritual men, and invest us with moral character. We take out of this world our moral and spiritual condition,—and as the tree falleth, so must it lie! What, then, do I find wanting in the speech of the foolish man? I find no grateful heart in it all. The man never blessed his banquet in the name of God. Not a word do I hear to this effect : "God hath dealt bountifully with me: praise God from whom all blessings flow. He hath put all these things into my care; he hath entrusted me with all this large estate, that I may administer it in his name. Lord, teach me how to use it, so that not one crumb be wasted, but that the whole be so ordered and dispensed as to bring honour to thy name, and satisfaction and gladness to thy children that are round about me." He doubles his enjoyment of worldly things who uses them gratefully; he drinks the best wine who drinks out of the goblet of thankfulness; he has most who gives most; and he grows most truly who, for Christ's sake, expends himself for the good of others most fully.

How, then, are we to live wisely in the world? How, then, are we to be wise in the dispensing of the produce of the earth and the results of honest trading? We meet the whole thing only in one way. We come back at a bound to the old, old gospel. Only he who lives in Christ Jesus, and has Christ Jesus living in his heart, can use wisely and well the things of the present world. A great deal has to be learned by sheer force of thought, by mental diligence, by comparing notes one with another, by meeting in associations for the purpose of discussion; but under all, and over all, and including all, there must be a profoundly religious spirit that sees God in everything, that feels his presence, and that acknowledges his sovereignty and his right. Because, after we have made our ground do its best, and we have pulled down our barns and built on a larger scale; after we have stored up our goods, he may say to us suddenly, "To-night I shall want you!" And we cannot say him, No. You may say No to your best friend; you can refuse the invitation of your most importunate associate; but when God says, "I shall want you to-night," you cannot write a note of excuse! When God says, "Thy soul shall be required of thee to-night," you cannot say, "Lord, let it stand over for a week." See, then, our weakness, as well as our strength; and know this, O man, as a matter of dead certainty, whatever our religious faith may be, though we are the vilest, vulgarest, and most stubborn atheists, that we cannot escape the final day—the great deed—the deed of death!

How, then, am I to become prepared for the last great scene? for I think it worth preparing for. As a wise man, I think I shall be doing right in turning this over in my mind, and making some reflections upon it; and thus have I resolved, by the strength and grace of God, to do: I will put my confidence in God—in God as revealed in the person and ministry of Jesus Christ; in God as known to me through the Cross, as the one Saviour; God the Son, who loved me and gave himself for me. I will walk in the way of God's commandments, and I will diligently study his precepts; I will make his Book the man of my counsel and the light of my way. All that I can do I shall do according to the strength he gives me, and I will praise him for the power with which he may invest my life. This I will do; and I think it is the right thing. I ask you who are hovering between two opinions to decide so; and I ask those of you who are already on the right side to pray without ceasing; and let him that thinketh he standeth take heed lest he fall. " Watch and pray, lest ye enter into temptation." The strongest of us is not stronger than his weakest point; and the very subtlest of temptation may even elude us, if our eyes be not anointed with the eye-salve that God himself alone can give.

Seeing, then, that there is to be a day of departure from this world, when I must leave my fields and my barns and my goods and my fruits and my present relationships,—what shall I do? This. Live for eternity. Look not at the things that are seen, but at the things that are unseen; for the things that are seen are temporal, but the things that are not seen are eternal.

PRAYER.

ALMIGHTY GOD, we bless thee that thou hast made us understand thy will in some degree. We glorify thee that we have heard of thy will through Jesus Christ thy Son, who was able to explain it and make it clear to our dull understanding. Now thou hast laid upon us a great responsibility: to him that knoweth to do good and doeth it not, to him it is sin. Verily thou hast done much for us: what can we do in return? Thou dost daily load us with benefits; we would that thy goodness might lead us to repentance, and not unto presumption and boastfulness; may the goodness of the Lord humble our souls, and open our eyes, and constrain us to walk in the paths of obedience; may thy mercies not be wasted upon us as rain is wasted upon the barren sand. Having received much at the hand of the Lord, may we be proportionately diligent, growing in grace, adding to virtues all the graces which thou hast named, bringing forth all the fruits of the Spirit, and justifying our communion with God by our kindness and love and service towards man. Thou knowest our life, its frailty, yet its immortality; thou knowest how abject is man, yet how almost divine. Thou dost lead us by strange ways, thou dost interpret thyself unto us by the events of life: take thine own course with us, O loving Father, gentle Saviour, and lead us at last to the open heavens, where the morning is, where the summer lingers, where the light continues; where there is nor death, nor pain, nor parting; the homeland, the place of gathering, made sacred and secure by the eternal presence of him who died that we might live. Amen.

Chapter xii. 42.

"And the Lord said, Who then is that faithful and wise steward, whom his lord shall make ruler over his household, to give them their portion of meat in due season?"

SOMETHING FOR EVERYBODY.

OUR Lord commends the faithful and wise steward who gives a portion of meat in due season to the household placed in his charge. A portion of meat to each; not necessarily the same meat, not necessarily the same quantity of food; but the faithful and wise steward looks at the whole situation, sees what is best to be done, and does it conscientiously and to the best of his ability. So far the faithful and wise steward may be taken as a type of the faithful and wise pastor, or minister of a congregation, or teacher of a household or school, whose business it is to study variety of character, and to adapt his communications of doctrine, or truth, or suggestion of any kind to the capacity and the training and the circumstances of those with whom he has to deal.   The man who continues steadfastly upon one line may appear to be doing more good than the man who studies a large variety of human character, and zealously tries to adapt himself not to one class of hearer or people, but to all classes.   His work is often too much diffused to be estimated and measured as would be the work of a man who toils only at one kind of labour.   Our Lord, however, commends in various instances that steward who studies his peculiar circumstances; who recognises and develops his individual responsibility, and who thus endeavours to serve his day and generation.   Consider the variety of a human assembly : no two men are precisely alike; what one man believes another heartily discredits and zealously repudiates; what is sacred to one conscience is looked upon by another as a fanaticism or a superstition, a piece of pedantry hardly to be excused—a narrow, dwarfing, humiliating morality that ought to have been forgotten years ago.   Yet the teacher must consider all these varieties, and see that by no lack of his shall any man leave his table over which he has been set by the lord of the house without having a portion of meat in due season.   There should be mutual sympathy in the congregation; all exasperating and narrow individuality or personalism should be lost in a sacred and ennobling fusion of feeling, thought, desire, purpose, so that individualism shall be magnified into largeness and representativeness of humanity and aspiration.

Consider, for example, that in all assemblies you will find the slow-thinking, slow-minded hearer, untaught, unskilled, wanting much nursing and care and patience ; he cannot be hastened; he has always moved at a certain pace, and his pace cannot be quickened.   If you attempt to stimulate him you plunge him into confusion; if you urge him to the next sentence he completely forgets the one that has just been spoken.   Yet side by side with him is a man who sees the end of a discourse in the very first word—that too-quick, too-sharp man, who anticipates every speaker, and who knows the course of every argument before it has even been dimly outlined.   What is to be done in such cases ?

Nothing can meet such exigencies but mutual sympathy; the quicker, keener, more penetrating the mind, the greater should be the patience, the more complete and noble the indulgence. Some credit, too, should be given to the speaker for knowing what he is about; when he is slow or diffuse, when he repeats himself in some degree, what if in his pastoral heart he be considering the untaught and slow-minded that needs his instruction a line at a time, sometimes a syllable, and a halt before the next syllable is uttered? If a man were really clever, quite a genius at hearing, able to swallow up a thousand preachers before they had opened their mouths, he ought to be as great in patience as he is brilliant in self-conceit. We cannot all travel at the same rate. Be patient with the slow one. You would not leave any behind; you will have a poor account to give at the end if you have only brought the strong, and the agile, and the audacious along with you, and have left all the little children, all the slow-footed, all the infirm—how shall you tell the lord of the house that you have only brought those who were able to gallop your pace? It will be a poor account to render; it will bring to the Lord's sweet face a flash of righteous anger.

Here is the strong, prosperous man, who wants everything done quickly; he reduces life to one philosophic motto—namely, Get it over. He does not want any particulars, distinctions, analyses, fine traceries in colour, and new combinations of geometric outlines; he wants to take his gospel in large boluses and let them work their mystery within him as they like. Near to him is one who is weary and ill at ease; all life is entangled in knots and perplexities, and no sooner is one hand filled than the other is emptied, and no sooner is one step taken in advance than half a step is fallen backwards. The light is always be-clouded, grey; June cannot bring full day to such eyes, summer must linger long to prove that it has ever come at all. What is to be done? The fat, prosperous, dominating man takes no heed of those who are weary and ill at ease, and by so much he does not deserve his prosperity. The great law of Nature will get hold of that man some day; he can only be taught through his flesh, you can only get any hint of theology into him through his purse: impoverish him, and he may begin to pray; strip him, and in his nakedness he may cry out for the gods. Honour him who is of faint heart and sad wounded spirit; be angry with the brother who is so strong and bold and urgent: let each have his portion of meat in due season. The mature Christian must have his doctrine, and the hardened sinner must be brought under the hammer of God's love; before some must flame the law, a living, avenging Sinai, a mountain of fire—paled by a crown of lightning. To another must be spoken poems, idyls, dreams, hints of things large and bright and ever-abiding. Yet one mind has to do all this. One mind can do it under the blessing of God if the congregation itself be intelligent, responsive, sympathetic.

No one hearer should expect the whole discourse to himself. He must be a wonderful man who needs a whole discourse; what can he do with it? No man wants the whole bill of fare. There are men who would swallow the menu, and think they had dined: why do they not swallow it? There is all the difference in the world between crumpling up the bill of fare and drinking it, and really enjoying some two or three of the viands indicated on the hospitable paper. Some men will find their refreshment in a sentence; that is enough for them. Take your sentence, eat it, live upon it, and pray that others may be able to seize some little word, some flashing simile, some coloured parable, some hint of larger things and larger actions. Thus let there be established in a congregation the principle of mutual sympathy, so that the strong shall say, The pastor is now after the weak: God bless him; he has a great tender woman's heart, and he will not stir one inch until he picks up the very frailest of those who want to follow him in his holy wandering. Sometimes the weak will have to say, The pastor is now struggling with the strong: he is a valiant soul, he has never been thrown yet, and in this contest by the power of Christ he will be conqueror again. God bless him! see how he tugs with the broad Hercules. Thus a discourse shall be a thousand sermons; every sentence a gospel; every appeal a new chance; every exposition a vision of the brightness and grandeur of life. Do not take your one sentence and run away. That would be selfishness. If any one would study selfishness let him be often at church. There are hearers that take just what they want, and then leave the preacher and his hearers to do what they can for themselves. Where is unity? Where is masonry? Where is the household spirit? Where the family genius? Oh! where that divine shepherdliness that carries the lambs in its bosom? Thus a congregation should be the co-pastor of the preacher. Some will pray whilst he wrestles with the hardened ; some will thank God as he drops the honey of sacred promise upon those who are hungering for heavenly solace, and throughout the whole assembly there shall breathe a spirit of unity, and the discourse in its wholeness shall belong to everybody, because parts of it in their adaption belong to somebody. You may have had your portion in the prayer ; when the portion of Scripture is read you may say, That is enough ; I can go in the strength of that sweet word full forty days and more. So be it ; now wait for the others. You are not other than part of humanity ; subdue your selfishness ; a little trial of patience may sometimes chasten you, and refine and enlarge your best education.

To whom shall we go for examples of all this doctrine but to Christ himself? He was the universal Preacher ; he had no style of preaching—he had all styles. Have you studied Christ as a minister, pastor, preacher, teacher? How infinite the variety! How humiliating to the miracles when they are set beside Christ's teachings! In his doctrine he was greater than in his miracles. He spoke the beatitudes, whole philosophies in little sentences, life condensed to a point, a point that flashed, and that gleams in ever-brightening beauty as the ages come and go. Will he always speak beatitudes? Shall we always hear this Man in this key? Is he one line of music? Has he founded a school of style? No. When we hear him again he will pronounce no beatitudes, but there shall roll from his lips a torrent of overwhelming Woes! And yet if our ear be quick enough to hear inner music, minor tones, undertones, we shall hear in the malediction a voice of pity, a tone that says, I would it were otherwise ; and if our eyes be quick to see all life's mystery as pictured in the face, we shall see tears coming that would have prevented the Woes if they could. Does this Teacher exhaust himself in beatitude and malediction? No ; the next time we hear him he will be speaking pictures ; he will be uttering those wondrous parables that hold all the stories and romances that ever really took place in human consciousness and experience. Nothing ever happened in all true fiction that cannot be found in the parables of Christ. " True fiction "—is not that a contradiction in terms ? No. No fiction is worth reading that is not true —true to human nature, true to reason, true to the possibilities of life; however grand, eerie, wild it may be, the world will shake it off as a nuisance if it cannot lay hold by a thousand tentacles upon human recollection, human consciousness, human experience, the whole tragedy of human endurance and aspiration.

But besides all this Christ was a great painter of character. Perhaps we have not dwelt sufficiently upon this phase of the divine ministry. Jesus was always sketching some individual, always contributing some new picture to the gallery of human art. He did not always enjoy the advantage of being fully reported ; we have to put things together in making up the ministry of Christ; we have to enter into his spirit and method of looking at things, and then, out of the fragments that are related in the evangelists, we can shape temple and poem and altar and picture as Christ meant them to be represented to the eye of the religious imagination. See how he struck off a character in a sentence. Who can forget the man in long robes ? The description may be so read as really to have little suggestion in it ; or it may be so read as to fill the eyes with pictures of hypocrisy and skill and partially successful deceit. Who could but remember the men standing in the market-places and praying to the empty clouds, as if God could stop to listen to voices without hearts ? There they stand, mockers, actors, liars ; and there they will stand until the end of the world's tragedy. Then see how quickly he turns his eyes upon men who are seeking out the chief seats. Is it a synagogue ? He watches the man who is urging his way to the uppermost place. Is it a feast ? He says, Look at this fool who is urging himself to the top, only to be ordered down to the bottom again ; watch him, see how the little comedy will end. Then he turns and paints, with wondrous ineffable skill, a heart, young, passionate, riotous, that lost its filial instinct and wandered away into far places, the habitations of dragons and the abodes of desolation and hunger. One man he described as simply well clothed, and faring sumptuously every day, and dropping into hell.

So we have justification for the various treatment of men in the example and in the authority of our blessed Lord and Master Jesus Christ. There should be great variety in Christian teaching. Society should provide texts for the preacher. The Bible is a book of seeds, germs, alphabetic hints ; the newspaper should be as a bible to the reverent and eager reader; he should study the journal of the morning to know what God is doing amongst mankind. The journal will be what you make it : regard it as so much gossip, news, to be scanned and bandied about in frivolous conversation, and it will amount to nothing; regard it as indicating a providential action, a ministry of rulership, a ministry that seemingly delights in contradiction, controversy, conflict, paradox, and yet over all exercises a sovereignty which shapes things out to their best uses ; then every incident will be as a pillar of cloud by day or a pillar of fire by night, or a whispered word indicating the continued presidency and the continued beneficence of God. He preaches Christ who denounces hypocrisy. The hypocrite will be the first to regard such preaching as wanting in evangelical sentiment. The hypocrite is very fond of a really juicy, savoury doctrine. It does him no harm ; he can sleep through the most of the exposition ; there will be no shot-mark upon his mask. Let a preacher arise amongst us who has the gift of denunciation, the genius of objurgatory speech, a man entrusted with thunderbolts and flashes of lightning, and the hypocrite will publish his name as one who is wanting in evangelical unction. The man must bear the penalty; it is his prize, it is his commendation. He preaches Christ who protects women and children. The cruel man will object to such preaching on the ground that it is a great departure from the lines that were taken by the unread Puritan divines. Abuse some other sin, and he will applaud you; lay your hand upon his cruelty, and he will be impracticable in his anger and madness. A man who shall stand up in the Christian pulpit and plead for women and children who are helpless, friendless, or cruelly used, is preaching the gospel, is uplifting the Cross of

Christ. He, too, preaches the gospel who tells the worst that they may come back again. It would be unworthy preaching that omitted to take notice of those who have wandered far from light and truth and beauty, virtue, honour, and nobleness. We do not want stay-at-home shepherds who, being sure of the ninety-and-nine, care nothing for the one that is lost. They are not shepherds, they are hirelings; the true shepherd cannot sleep because one of the flock is missing; when he appears to lie down his mind is full of solicitude about the absent; what if he but watch for the first hint of dawn, that he may be away to seek that which is lost, only to return when he has found it? Blessed be that teacher, in church, in school, at home, who cannot be happy so long as there is one unhappy person over whom he can exercise some gracious influence. He preaches Christ who denounces censoriousness; he preaches the Sermon on the Mount over again. That is sadly wanting in evangelical sentiment; it will disappoint the man who lives either in cant or in sentiment.

What does your evangelicalism amount to if in five minutes you can blight fifty reputations? If you profess to be evangelical, and can so do, I will not be one of your number. Let me rather invite the charge of heterodoxy than sit down and pluck the flesh from the bones of better men than myself. He preaches Christ who proclaims pardon by the Cross. There is no other pardon. "This is the way; walk ye in it." We are not called upon to invent some theory of pardon; the question is not put to us how to get back our yesterdays, and to purge and cleanse them from the infinite staining they have undergone at our profane hands. Can you get back your yesterdays? Can you go back five-and-twenty years and heal the heart you then wounded? Have you the stealthy foot that can go noiselessly back, and put in again the treasure that you stole? Can you drive a nail into polished wood, and take it out without leaving a wound? Can you shatter crystal and then put it together again so that no flaw can be detected? The question is not put to us, How shall a man be pardoned? We have not to answer an inquiry, but to accept a welcome. "Let the wicked forsake his way, and the unrighteous man his thoughts: and let him return unto the Lord, and he will have mercy upon him; and to our God, for he will abundantly pardon." There is none other name under heaven given among men whereby we must be saved but the name of Jesus Christ. Yet this wonderful Son of God represents every aspect of humanity, looks in all directions. His was the fourfold ministry that had the face of a lion, the face of a cherub, the face of an eagle—but oh! had it no other face? Yea, it had the face of a man. This is the ministry the age needs. If this ministry be not exercised in its fourfoldness; if it be wanting in eagle, and lion, and cherub, and humanity, or in any one of these, it is not the ministry of Christ's ideal. It is not a reproduction of the ministry of the Son of God who was also Son of man. Each man may find a portion of meat in every service if he will seek for it; only he is disappointed who will not search. It is impossible that God's house can be opened, and God's praise sung, and God's Word read without a portion of meat being furnished, to every man as he wants it; and there is no sermon, how poor soever in intellectual conception, in vocal utterance, that has not in it somewhere, if the preacher be faithful to Christ, a touch, a hint, a gleam, that can be used in life's great warfare. In this respect, Seek and ye shall find; knock and it shall be opened unto you. Say,—Lord, which sentence was meant for me? and he will show you. Eat it, and live evermore.

Chapter xiii.

NOTES OF CHRIST'S SERMONS.

LUKE undertook to be very minute and exhaustive in his statement of Gospel facts. He was going to do better than many other writers had done. He said so with cool frankness: "Forasmuch as many have taken in hand to set forth in order a declaration of those things which are most surely believed among us, even as they delivered them unto us, which from the beginning were eye-witnesses, and ministers of the word; it seemed good to me also"—that is a curious expression. We expected him to say: Forasmuch as many have done this work there is no need for me to do it. But he makes the very fact that there were other writers a reason why there should be one more. That was good reasoning; it should prevail in all the lines and departments of Christian life and action. The contrary policy often supersedes it, and brings ministers and churches into great discomfort and enfeeblement. Men will say, You have so many helpers, you have no need of me. They are always more or less dishonest men,—not intentionally so; intentional dishonesty is perfectly vulgar and wholly detestable, and nobody lays claim to it; but when men say, "There are so many preachers I need not be one; so many deacons I need not be another; so many helpers there is no need of me," they are not conducting a Christian argument, they are, with all their graciousness, unconsciously jealous and spiteful,—but not sufficiently so to prevent them conducting family prayer in the evening as if they were as good as their neighbours. Luke reasoned in the right way; he said, Many men are taking up this subject, I will do what I can in it; I think I can beat some of them: "It seemed good to me also, having had perfect understanding of all things from the very first, to write unto thee in order." Will the book be as good as the preface? I fancy not—when the subject is Jesus

Christ. The first sentence is often the best. Why? Because
the subject grows. No man can ever prepare his imagination
for the glory of that theme. The young preacher feels this; he
buckles to with a brave heart, and says he will work honestly all
day, and pray most of the night, and produce such discourses
as will satisfy his best ambition. He empties his inkhorn, does
all he can, and then puts his young hand upon his mouth and
says, Unprofitable! I have failed! I had an ambition high as
heaven, bright as the unclouded noon; but I have failed! He
does not do justice to himself. The Lord does not pronounce
that judgment upon him; he says, Thou hast not failed: industry
never fails; conscience always succeeds; thou hast won a right
bright crown. Cheer thee! It is not the man who has failed,
it is the God who has exceeded all ever thought of in prayer,
ever dreamed of in poetry.

Still we expected more from Luke than from the others, and
we get more. He does not see some things as Mark saw them.
It is fashionable—shall we say, with due mental reservation,
pedantic?—to point out that Luke was the observing writer.
Mark observed a great many things that Luke never saw, or
at least never recorded. Matthew also had his own way of
looking at things: and as for John, what was he looking at?
Apparently at nothing, his inner eyes were fastened on the
soul of Christ. If Luke had sharp eyes, what ears John had!
he heard whisperings of the heart, throbbings and beatings
and sighings. And what a gift of expression! he turned all
that he heard into noble sweet music for the soul's comforting
in all the cloudy days of the Church. But Luke says he will
set down things "in order"; the others have been good historians, but a little wanting in the power or grouping and classify-
ing; good historians, but poor editors. Luke will break things up
into chapters, and verses, and paragraphs, and sections, and he
will attend to chronological sequence. We need mechanical men
in the Church, people that know when to begin a new paragraph,
and to codify laws, and to do a good many useful little things.
But when Luke comes to his thirteenth chapter he is obliged
to condense. He cannot overtake Christ except by condensation,
—a note, a line, a catchword, a significant phrase, and he thinks

he can find all the rest when he goes home to write it out. He
cannot. Even Luke says he must put things together in a
somewhat hurried and condensed fashion. Blessed be God ! It
would seem as if God himself must condense, because he cannot
overtake himself; so he must put here a syllable, and there a
sign, and otherwhere some hint of meaning, in burning bush,
in sacred wine, in bread blessed—so blessed that it becomes
flesh ; he will condense, he will bring things to a sharp issue ;
he will put in a memorable word, and that word shall stand for
a whole library.

This is the way with his book. As we have often said, all
other good books are in the Bible. They are variations of it ;
they are never improvements upon it ; they do nothing outside its
lines, but they wisely turn to highest advantage what is to be
found within its limits. The Bible is the condensed wisdom of
God. There are commentators who find sequence in this chapter ;
there are men bold enough to say that the parable concerning the
fig tree follows admirably after the short discourse about what
occurred to the Galilæans and those eighteen upon whom the
tower of Siloam fell. Without seeing the sequence literally we
may feel it spiritually. Let us, then, regard this chapter as a
series of notes of Christ's sermons. They were sermons that
bore reporting. Sometimes the most humiliating thing you can
do to a preacher is to try to quote something he has said. He
never recognises it ; he is perfectly sure he never said it, he has
a latent conviction that you made it up : but as you get good
from it he is content that you should assign it to his authorship,
if you please. But Jesus Christ had a sermon in every sentence,
so that if you could not quote in detail you could quote the whole
in condensation and suggestion. His were little sentences, but
the little sentences were focalised infinities of thought. Luke,
therefore, gathers a good deal even in this condensed chapter, and
gives us a many-sided view of Jesus Christ. What would we give
for a handful of notes used by the Saviour ? He never wrote
a word. He never preached what is called—with blasphemy—a
" finished sermon." We now have " finished " preachers. There
is a sense in which that is true. This man so talked that little
children opened their eyes in amazement, and women wondered at

the gracious words which proceeded out of his lips, and old age said, "Never man spake like this man." He himself was the discourse; he was in very deed the Gospel—"I am the truth"; he therefore never did anything but preach, because he preached as he breathed; it was a continual forthgiving of deity to humanity. He remarked upon the anecdotes and stories of the times most tersely and instructively. In nearly all ages men have loved startling anecdotes. There were men who told him of the Galilæans whose blood Pilate had mingled with their sacrifices, and they thought they were giving him some information. He said, Pay next to no attention to the anecdotes of the day; do not ground upon the incidents of the time generalisations which cannot be sustained. You suppose that these Galilæans were the supreme sinners because they suffered such things: you are wrong. God is not fantastic in his action. You say that if they had not done so much that was wrong they never could have suffered as they did at the hands of Pilate: nothing of the kind: by so talking you despoil history of its genius and providence of its purpose. I tell you, except ye repent ye shall all perish: attend to yourselves: do not live upon the anecdotes which relate to other people, but enter into self-judgment. The "likewise" does not refer to a literal vengeance or method of punishment, but it refers to the inevitable, unchangeable gracious law, that whatsoever a man soweth that shall he also reap. Jesus Christ was not so much interested in the anecdotes as the people were. They had heard of eighteen people being killed by a tower that had fallen down, and Jesus said, "Suppose ye that these Galilæans were sinners above all the Galilæans, because they suffered such things?"

Here we have a doctrine capable of broad application. How foolishly we judge the Almighty! We say that certain men sought their own pleasure on the Lord's Day, and they were drowned. Nothing of the sort. Do not degrade the universe. We say that certain persons having done certain things were struck down dead, and this was a sign of the divine wrath. Such is not the God, the Father, in whom we believe. Are the people therefore wrong in their inferences? They are wrong because they are too narrow. They might avail themselves of the same great truth, and do it on the right lines, and thus save themselves from contempt and their doctrine from repudiation. From eternity, it is necessary that whoso does wrong should go to perdition. He cannot go anywhere else. That is the law. It was not made by the New Testament; it is not a dogma invented by Christian thinkers: it is the necessity of the universe. Creation casts out of her motherly heart those that will plague and destroy the purpose and intent of God. The son of perdition can only go to hell. Then we are so very apt to be liberal in awarding divine judgments, under some peculiar and inexplicable semi-consciousness that by so doing we are almost equal to the divine Being himself. There is a great comfort to some hearts in judging other people; in this, as in other respects, we are fearfully and wonderfully made. Jesus Christ will have no false interpretations of events; he will have no false morals drawn from accidents and anecdotes. We are bound every man to consider his own life, his own conscience, his own duty; let him learn from history to apply history to himself. How prone we are to look upon history as a riddle which we have to guess if we can! Now why did that tower fall upon those eighteen people? Then we have a series of conjectures, and these we call exposition. One minister asks with solemnity too awful to be sincere, "Why is not the name of Job's wife given?" Then he answers himself with a wit too profound to be genuine, "Why should it have been given?" And this we call exposition! Jesus Christ sweeps away all this rubbish; he will have none of it. He says, You are despoiling the meaning of God's providence: you do not comprehend what God is doing: he means all death to teach life; all punishment to teach caution; all judgment to indicate the solemnity, the grandeur, the all but divinity of his universe. Luke takes down enough of this to make it perfectly clear that it was useless to go to Jesus Christ to tell him the last anecdote. He was an awful man to talk to if you wished to fritter away his time or to turn trifles into events of importance.

Why can we not get the Church to be serious, real, funda- mental,—to get at the philosophy of things? Ministers have no encouragement to search into these matters, because there is hardly a congregation in the world that would endure a prolonged and exhaustive study of the Scriptures. Now Jesus Christ, according to some commentators, speaks a parable upon this very subject. The anecdote of the newsmongers suggested a parable to the divine genius. Some people mistake an anecdote for a parable, and a parable for an anecdote. A parable has infinite colour, throb, suggestion, wisdom. Jesus now began to tell what happened. Did it happen literally? Perhaps not. But literal happening is nothing. What we want is the truth, the necessity of life. Truth is larger than fact. Fiction is the largest truth, when rightly managed, when properly interpreted. So Jesus Christ relates a parable :—"A certain man had a fig tree planted in his vineyard." He lays down the doctrine in this parable that he will have nothing to do with uselessness. He makes nothing of ornament; he will not listen to the plea that the fig tree looks well, is an ornament in the place which it occupies, and although there is no fruit, there is an abundance of leafage, and an artist would be very pleased to take a sketch of the tree. The meaning of the whole universe is utility. Utility is a word which has been abused by being narrowed, depleted of its force and meaning. Utility is a wide word. He is useful who grasps a hand in silence; but it is a masonic grip and a masonic sign. He is useful who gives a little child a red and blue and yellow picture —oh, so crude in colour that the trained eye could not look upon it : but the child's eyes round into bigness and delight when they see such vividness. He is useful who gives a shoot of ivy to some poor man to plant in his inch of garden that it may climb round his windows and talk spring and summer to him. He is useful who suggests ideas, excites noblest thought; he most useful who having the gift of prayer lifts men right up to heaven's gate. It is in this sense that Jesus Christ will have nothing but that which is useful, fruitful, real :—"Herein is my Father glorified, that you bear much fruit."

But is there not something higher than usefulness in this wondrous parable? Yes. When did Jesus Christ speak without telling all he knew, in suggestion? Every sentence of his contains every other sentence. We have to search for it, to grow its meaning, and for that we want summers warmer

than any that have shone upon earth and time. The first verse
of the Bible is the whole Bible. There is nothing more in the
Bible than there is in the first chapter of Genesis, and there is
nothing more in the first chapter of Genesis than is in the first
verse. How it grows! How it reveals itself! How it looks at
us, and withdraws; broadens upon us and contracts! How it
tantalises, and yet gratifies! How it fills the imagination, how
it thrills the heart! So in this very parable we have the great
doctrine of intercession. We cannot explain it; but it having
been revealed to us as a doctrine we acknowledge it. We have
been told that there is one who prays our prayers over again,
and makes them by his spirit and addition his own prayers—
"He ever liveth to make intercession for us,"—to translate our
meaning, to keep back our ignorance and selfishness, and as it
were to offer the wine of our realest love and need to God. This
is our comfort in prayer. When the prayer has fled away from
us like a liberated bird the Lord Jesus undertakes the next
office, a sacred, self-imposed duty; and when we hear of our
prayers again we hear of them through the same medium, in
answers of quietness, rich peace, contentment, ineffable restful-
ness. This is how the Lord's intercession is granted to us in
gracious answers. We cannot tell how, but we know it. We
make mistakes in our ignorance. We are mocked because we
pray for a fine day that the children may enjoy their summer
excursion. There be long-headed philosophers, too courteous to
laugh outright, but too human not to smile, who tell us that we
want to re-arrange the solar system. These unbaptised brethren
are always anxious about the solar system. It is a wonderful
thing to them, because they have never seen anything else. If
they had once seen God, they never would have mentioned the
solar system any more. But when man's great idea of space, and
weight, magnitude, force, and velocity, is all concentrated in the
solar system, it is exceedingly desirable that Sunday school
teachers should not disturb the comfort and the peacefulness of
that sublime mechanism. They may be right; but whether they
are or not, their view has nothing to do with the energy and the
success of prayer. I can pray for a fine day for the excursion,
for fine weather that the harvest may be got in; I can pray God
to send the haymakers a whole heavenful of sunshine because we

want food in for the beasts that perish; and having said my
prayer I shall have an answer. I have prayed for that dear little
wasting child, now almost skin and bone, and he will live—even
the doctors cannot kill him. He will live. But the word "live"
may have to be enlarged; I may have to pass from one lexicon to
another to get broader, deeper, truer definition; and when the
little child, in the language of earth, dies, I shall see him in every
glittering star and every blooming flower, and hear his little
chatter in every babbling brook, and he will seem to fill all nature
with his little blessed presence.

We must not narrow terms and rob them of their meaning
because every word we have does not end in itself, if it be a
vital and important and necessary word. Bread does not end at
the baker's shop. It is not in the power of any baker to limit the
meaning of the word bread. Water is not limited by channels
and torrents and pouring clouds: water there is for the soul's
drinking—cool, refreshing, pure water. "Live" does not mean
some action of the body, some attitude of the anatomy: *live*
means something, we cannot yet tell altogether what, in reference
to love, thought, development, service, pureness, worship.
Blessed are the dead that die in the Lord: for they do but
enlarge their sphere of service and get nearer to their Maker.
The intercession of the text was answered. The intercession of
Christ is answered. The answers which are received to our
prayers are greater than the prayers themselves; otherwise man
would be equal to God; man would say, I prayed for so much
and got it. But the Lord gives exceeding abundantly above all
that we ask or think.

What do you suppose the people did after all this? A parable
like this ought to have saved a man from all criticism, and given
him the very highest place in his time. Any man who spoke
that parable ought to have had, according to material measure,
the very finest house in the land, the noblest position in the whole
country. The creator of a parable like that might have created
all the stars, and the doing of it would not have been equal to the
creation of the parable. What became of him?

"And he was teaching in one of the synagogues on the Sabbath. And,
behold, there was a woman which had a spirit of infirmity eighteen years,

and was bowed together, and could in no wise lift up herself. And when Jesus saw her, he called her to him, and said unto her, Woman, thou art loosed from thine infirmity. And he laid his hands on her : and immediately she was made straight, and glorified God. And the ruler of the synagogue answered with indignation, because that Jesus had healed on the Sabbath day, and said unto the people, There are six days in which men ought to work : in them therefore come and be healed, and not on the Sabbath day " (vers. 10-14).

The Jews had their own way of doing things. It it was a case of life and death the doctor might prescribe on the Sabbath day, but the doctor was not to pay the slightest attention to chronic cases of any kind ; they were there on Saturday and they would be there on Monday, and they would be there the next week, and they would be there the next month, and therefore no particular heed was to be paid to them. Here again we find the narrowing spirit. All ailment is the same to Jesus Christ. Transient as men call transient, or chronic as men call chronic, the great fact is that the man wanted healing, and he was there to heal ; if he had done anything else he would have thwarted his own election, and stultified his own sovereignty. This was the necessity of his very make, build, constitution,—he came not to destroy men's lives, but to save them. Having spoken as he only could speak, " all his adversaries were ashamed." He made them hold down their heads that the redness of their blush might not be seen. Whoever encountered him and stood upright after an interview, when the purpose was a purpose of hostility ? We have seen how many men came up to him in fine attitude, in studied posture, thinking they had a case that would constrain his attention and secure his approbation. How often we have seen them coming up young men, going away about a hundred years old, so blanched and withered and humiliated, and so ashamed that they dare not speak to one another, or if they did speak they wanted to say, " It was you that would go—I did not want to go, but you made me—I will never go again." " And all the people "—Bless God for the people. What would the kings do without the people ? They would die of loneliness. " And all the people "—Yes, it is true oftentimes that the voice of the people is the voice of God. There may be mysterious variations of this, and yet there is a central truth in it. " And all the people rejoiced for all the glorious things that were done by him." Yes, let judgment be upon the " things," and we have no fear. We must not be word-mongers, logic-choppers; we must take our stand upon the facts, the conversions, the changes of heart and disposition and character and tone and temper, and Christ asks no other standard of judgment. See what Christianity has done for the world, and by the glorious things it has done let the whole Christian argument stand or fall. We are not all called upon to argue. Many are called upon to suffer, and suffering may be borne with such gracious heroism as to constitute itself into an argument. The great talker proceeded. He gave philosophic symbols of the invisible and infinite kingdom ; he said, The kingdom of God is like a grain of mustard seed : like leaven, which a woman took and hid in three measures of meal, till the whole was leavened ; and thus he started imagination on a wondrous course of inquiry, and to this day the poets are finding new symbols. When a man arises who can construct a new parable, true to the purpose of the kingdom of heaven, the people acknowledge him to be a true servant of Christ.

But did the matter end there ? No. There was an application to this sermon as there ought to be to every sermon. He said unto them, " Strive to enter in at the strait gate." What is the meaning of this " strive " ? Literally, wrestle ; throw your arms around the adversary, and throw him ; struggle ; say you will begin. He is a giant with whom you have to grapple, but it is God who tells you to enter into the encounter. " Strive to enter in at the strait gate : for many, I say unto you, will seek to enter in, and shall not be able." They shall only seek : but that is not the whole meaning. We must dislodge the narrow-minded theologian from this passage. Have not some good men said, Many will seek to enter in and shall not be able because of the decree of God ? Who says so tell lies. When will they seek to enter in and not be able ? The Lord gives the time :—" When once the master of the house is risen up, and hath shut to the door, and ye begin to stand without, and to knock at the door, saying, Lord, Lord, open unto us ; and he shall answer and say unto you, I know you not whence ye are " (ver. 25). The time is when the Lord himself has risen, has closed the dispensation, has terminated the economy of grace, has gone to some other department, so to say, of his universal empire. But, blessed be his name, he has not risen yet; he has not shut to the door yet. Now men may come. In this holy moment those who are outside may strive to enter in; may wrestle, struggle, determine in God's strength to enter in. If you fail to do this you fail altogether, no matter what admiration you may have of Christianity as a theological system; no matter what knowledge you may have of Christianity as a theological argument; no matter how liberal you may be in the support of Christian institutions. If you do not strive to enter in, determine to enter in, if you do not struggle and agonise; if you do not make it the supreme object of your life to get in, all else is failure. "Ho, every one that thirsteth, come ye to the waters!" Sweet word! How sweet to those whose throats are burning with thirst! "Let the wicked forsake his way, and the unrighteous man his thoughts: and let him return unto the Lord, and he will have mercy upon him; and to our God, for he will abundantly pardon." What! "abundantly"? Yes. What does that mean? Wave upon wave, billow upon billow of love; he will multiply pardons; give them a thousand thick; so give them that conscience and memory and imagination shall have no more record of sin.

Chapter xiii. 31-34.

"The same day there came certain of the Pharisees, saying unto him, Get thee out, and depart hence: for Herod will kill thee. And he said unto them, Go ye, and tell that fox, Behold, I cast out devils, and I do cures to-day and to-morrow, and the third day I shall be perfected. Nevertheless I must walk to-day, and to-morrow, and the day following: for it cannot be that a prophet perish out of Jerusalem. O Jerusalem, Jerusalem, which killest the prophets, and stonest them that are sent unto thee; how often would I have gathered thy children together, as a hen doth gather her brood under her wings, and ye would not!"

PICTURES OF JESUS CHRIST.

HERE, then, is a picture of a threatened man. Jesus Christ was continually being threatened. There seemed every day to be but a hair's-breadth between him and death. He was despised and rejected of men; there was no beauty in him that man should desire his presence. Yet there was something about him which excited the passion, the most terrible vengeance of mankind. He held his life in his hand, in a special and peculiar way. Who was there that did not lift up a hand against him? Who was there not too mean to pucker up his face into a sneer when he saw the Son of God? And who was there not too feeble to suppose that even he could do some damage to the name of the Messiah? What was there, then, to induce Jesus Christ to live upon the earth? The foxes had holes and the birds of the air had nests, but the Son of man had not where to lay his head. Why, then, should he not have made short work of it; have turned right round and said, "I leave the dust of my feet behind me as a testimony against you; I have made you an offer of truth and of life and of love, and you have rejected that offer. I leave you now to all the consequences of your obstinacy"? Yet he came to be upon the earth in this very position in which we find him. He knew the kind of hospitality that awaited him; he knew how homeless he would be; how hard would be the

319

pillow on which his weary head was to rest; how unkind the looks that would be waiting for him here and there, on the right hand and on the left. Yet, for our sakes, he became poor, that we through his poverty might be made rich. There was nothing strange in the revelation of this lot which met the Saviour—that is to say, there was nothing strange to his mind; he was not startled by the mode of reception that was accorded to him. From the height of heaven he foresaw it; before coming to the earth at all he knew all the courses through which he must of necessity pass. Still, in the face of it all, he came to seek and to save that which was lost. Behold, then, in this text, a picture of a threatened man. There is a sword against thy life; there is a king against thee! Thirty years before Herod the Great had sought the young Child to destroy him; and now, after the lapse of a generation, Herod the Tetrarch sends messages by the Pharisees, that his hand was against him. What a threatened life! What a position of discomfort, of misinterpretation, of utter friendlessness, of sore distress! I want you to look at Jesus Christ in this aspect, and to keep your eyes steadily upon him whilst such messages are being delivered; because it is under such circumstances that we may get some hint of the real quality of his character.

Why did Herod threaten Jesus? Why was the life of Christ a threatened life from the beginning to the end? Because good is always unpalatable to evil. That which is good always torments that which is bad. But had not Herod far greater influence in the world than Jesus Christ? No. But Herod could strike! True, but in doing so his arm would rot. Wherein, then, is the superiority of the influence of this threatened man? It is in its goodness. Good men have everything to hope from time; bad men have everything to fear from the lapse of days. Beauty can stand the wear and the tear of life—the inward and imperishable beauty of consummate goodness and divine truth. Goodness is a perpetual quantity, all penetrating, all searching, impartial, noble, a comfort in distress, a refuge to the weak, a tower and a defence to all men who wish to be right and to do right. Had it been a case of man against man, position against position, hand against hand, truly Herod would have made short work of this controversy; he would have thrown down his antagonist, set his foot upon him, and with a loud " Ha, ha!" would have declared his triumph. But it was a question of light on the part of Jesus Christ,—light against darkness, truth against falsehood, God against the devil. No wonder, therefore, that when the controversy was so vital and so keen Jesus Christ should have been surrounded, if I may so express myself, by an atmosphere of menace, of threatening, of ill-will, and of latent determination to shed his blood. I am anxious to know how Jesus Christ will conduct himself under such circumstances. Herod has pronounced the authoritative word. Kings ought not to be forced to the humiliation of eating up their own messages. When the Tetrarch speaks he ought to have meaning in his speech. It will tell to the disadvantage of Herod if, after all this, he come to humiliation and shame. Some men think they have only to threaten and the earth will quake at once. It would appear that some persons are under the delusion that they have but to shake their finger in the face of the sun, and it will be night presently. Herod sent word to Christ to get out of his jurisdiction, or he would kill him. I am anxious to know how Jesus Christ, without home or friend, will conduct himself under such circumstances. Let us read how he answered the message of Herod the Tetrarch :—

"And he said unto them, Go ye, and tell that fox, Behold, I cast out devils, and I do cures to-day and to-morrow, and the third day I shall be perfected " (ver. 32).

Here you have a picture of impotent rage on the part of Herod the Tetrarch. He thought that Jesus Christ would tremble under the message. He instantly treats it with disdain, with noble haughtiness of conscious superiority to the shaft that is levelled against him ; and he describes Herod according to the moral traits of his character. He does not hesitate to call Herod a fox ; a mere cunning, designing man, only courageous when there is no danger at hand; scheming and plotting in his den, but having no true bravery of heart; an evil-minded person, whose whole character is summed up in the word "fox." What —did Jesus Christ, then, call men names ? Not in the usual sense of that expression. Did he call Herod a fox out of mere defiance or spite ? He was incapable of doing anything of the kind.

When Jesus Christ spoke a severe word, the severity came out of the truth of its application. Is it not a harsh thing to call a man a liar? Not if he be false. Is it not very unsocial to describe any man as a hypocrite? Not if he be untrue. Wherein, then, is this wickedness of calling men names? In the misapplication of the epithets. It is wicked to call a man true if we know him to be untrue. There is an immoral courtesy; there is a righteous reproach. We do not use harsh words when we tell men what they really are. On the other hand, it is a matter of infinite delicacy to tell a man what he really is, because, at best, we seldom see more than one aspect of a man's character. If we could see more of the man, probably we should change our opinion of his spirit. In the case of Jesus Christ, however, he saw the inner heart, the real and true quality of the Tetrarch; and, therefore, when he described Herod as a fox, he spoke the word of righteousness and of truth. It was not an epithet; it was a character in a word; it was a man summed up in a syllable. Let us, therefore, be very careful how we follow this example, because we ought to have equal knowledge, before we take an equal position in this respect. On the other hand, let us beware of that simulation of courtesy, which is profoundly untrue, which is despicably immoral—the kind of thing which sets itself to catch the favour and the flattery of the passing moment. As men in Christ, we ought to be true with our speech; we ought to study morality of language, and never to say anything merely for the purpose of pleasing or passing through the temporary occasion with something like self-satisfaction. Then Herod's message produced no effect upon the work of the Son of God? Not the slightest in the world. But Herod was a man in authority, "brief authority"! Jesus Christ was the sovereign, and Herod was but the servant of a servant. What then did Jesus Christ profess in the jurisdiction of Herod? To cast out devils and to do cures. It was a moral work upon which he was set. Preachers of the gospel are not to be turned aside by the threatening hand of any man. If any one should, indeed, be doing aught to unsettle the minds of the people in relation to these political things which we hardly understand, he ought to be brought to law and called to order. But whoso is casting out devils and doing cures, here or there, under this form of government or that, let him not heed the king's words, but proceed in the strength of God, and in the sufficiency of divine grace, to do his beneficent work !

We thought that Jesus Christ's labour would be cut short by this message from Herod. Jesus Christ must finish what he has begun. But is it not in the power of the great and the mighty to say to Christ, " You must stop at this point"? It is in their power, truly, to say it, and when they have said it they may have relieved their own feelings ; but the great, the beneficent, the redeeming work of the Son of God proceeds as if not a word to the contrary had been said. The kings of the earth set themselves, and the rulers took counsel together against the Lord, and against his anointed ; and behold, their rage came to nothing, and their fury recoiled upon themselves ! "He that sitteth in the heavens shall laugh ; the Holy One shall have them in derision." Are we opposing Jesus Christ ? Are we in any way setting ourselves against the advancement of his kingdom? It will be an impotent rage. Go and strike the rocks with your fist,—perhaps you may batter down the granite with your poor bones. Try ! Go and tell the sea that it shall not come beyond a certain line, and perhaps the hoary billows will hear you, and run away and say that they be afraid of such mighty men. Try. You have nothing else to do, you may as well try. But as for keeping back this kingdom of God, this holy and beneficent kingdom of truth, no man can keep it back, and even the gates of hell shall not prevail against it. Men may rage ; men do rage. Other men adopt another policy; instead of rage and fury and great excitement, they set themselves against the kingdom of God, in an indirect and remote way. But both policies come to the same thing. The raging man who pulls down the wooden Cross and tramples it underfoot, and the man who offers a passive resistance to the progress of the kingdom of heaven, come to the same fate. The light shines on, noontide comes, and God gets his own way in his own universe. Behold, then, this is our glory and our strength and our hope, that none can hinder. In a secondary sense they may retard, they may put stumbling-blocks on the road, and for a moment they may be seeming to succeed ; but, in the long run, this kingdom goes on until it has covered the earth with its lustre, and set a universal throne amidst mankind !

"**Nevertheless I** must walk to-day, and to-morrow, and the day following; for it cannot be that a prophet perish out of Jerusalem " (ver. 33).

Here is a picture of perfect reliance in the divine protection. On the one hand, Herod threatens; on the other, Jesus says, " I must walk to-day, and to-morrow, and the day following." Every man is immortal until his work is done. You cannot injure a hair of a man's head until the work that he is entrusted with be so far fulfilled as to ensure its entire completion. Men should not be soured by the opposition of their enemies. Some of us are prone to be so. When our lives are threatened, when our peace is jeopardised, we are disposed to say, " Then we shall have no more to do with this thing; we shall utterly abandon it; we shall settle down into peace and tranquillity, for we have had enough of vexation and disappointment." It is feeble to say so; it shows the poverty of our nature, if we talk in that way. I know not whose example we may be copying, but I know we are not transcribing the example of the Son of God. He did not resign his functions, he did not decline to go on with his work. He said, " I work in the name of God and for the good of mankind, and I must not be stopped." If we had more of that spirit, we should do more work in the world; we should have fewer resignations of Christian positions, less slinking away from the road of difficulty, and the path of bewilderment, and the course of pain. We should have more steadiness and consistency, not arising from pride and a sense of self-sufficiency, but coming out of the consciousness of a divine call, and an assurance that divine grace is more than sufficient for every occasion. What is the cure for all this willingness to run away from difficulty ? The cure is in looking to the Master and not to the servant. We are the servants of God, and therefore the servants of one another. Tell me that I have received my ministry from man, and I shall take one view of the difficulties which may beset it. But tell me that that ministry has been imposed upon me from heaven, and that I am called and elect of God to do a certain work; and whatever may be the impediments round about me, there shall be sunshine in my heart, there shall be deep inexplicable peace in my soul; I shall regard the difficulties of the present occasion as but momentary, and the strength upon which I rest shall be nothing less than the omnipotence of God.

Whose servants are we, then? Who has called us to this
Christian work? We are called of God, we are not called of
man; and we must take our orders from heaven, and not from
earth. But Herod threatens. Herod's threatening is but
impotent breath! The king shakes his hand. His hand will
drop off in the shaking! But our work must go on because we
are called of God to do it. What rest this gives a man; what
dignity in the midst of vexation and difficulty! What an assurance
that all tumult and opposition can be but for a moment! How
it assures us that in the long run the kingdom of heaven shall
suffer nothing at the hands of mere violence! It is established
upon a rock, and it is guaranteed of God. Jesus Christ saw the
end from the beginning. In proportion as we have a wide outlook upon things, shall we have peace in our work and assurance
of the blessedness of its end. Let us look at nothing in itself
alone, or we may be discouraged by it exceedingly. But let us,
following the example of Jesus Christ, think of to-day and to-
morrow and the day following, and then we shall see how things
bear upon one another, how they modify one another, and how
what is difficult in detail becomes solved and harmonised in the
great result. The Church would be quieter if the Church could
see further. How far ought the Church to see? To this
law, namely, God is on the throne. Christ has promise of the
world, and whatsoever may be the difficulties and perplexities
in the meantime, there will be worked out this great result.
Are you threatened? Have you difficulty? Is the road very
thorny, steep, hazardous? You have nothing to do with these
things, except in a very temporary and secondary sense. God
has promised to-day and to-morrow, and he has promised that
on the third day things shall be perfected. Take him at his
word, rest in his love, and as for the resources that are required,
they are hidden in God's power!

"O Jerusalem, Jerusalem, which killest the prophets, and stonest them
that are sent unto thee; how often would I have gathered thy children together, as a hen doth gather her brood under her wings, and ye would
not!" (ver. 34.)

Here is a picture of rejected and wounded love. We have had
a picture of a threatened man; we have had a picture of impotent
rage; we have had a picture of perfect reliance on the protection

of Almighty God. And behold, we have now the most pathetic of the pictures—a picture of rejected and wounded love. " O Jerusalem, Jerusalem, how often would I have gathered thy children together, and ye would not ! " Jesus Christ's ministry, then, in this sense, was a failure. There are men amongst us who would not hesitate to say, that Jesus Christ's endeavours to save men had ended in a disastrous disappointment. This indeed is a wail, a cry of failure, an utterance of disappointment, —it is love in agony! Viewed within a certain limit of time, no ministry has been less successful than was the ministry of the Son of God. No man amongst us ever uttered a cry so heart-breaking as this over the apparent failure of his ministry. Jesus Christ went, with all his power, into some districts, and could not do many mighty works there because of the unbelief of the people. Was his ministry then a failure ? Jesus wept over Jerusalem and said, he would have gathered the children of the city together, but the children would not be gathered by his love. Was the ministry of Jesus Christ then an ignominious failure ? We must not look at things within these limitations. " Thou fool, that which thou sowest is not quickened, except it die." You have striven for the better life of your child, and no good result seems to have blessed your ministry. Do not suppose that you have failed altogether in your efforts. You have been sowing seed ; you have been laying up memories ; and the time may come when the child will get a right view of all you have done for his welfare. Despair not; hope on. No man can speak a loving word or deliver a wise message, even to a child, without in some sort having his reward either in the approbation of a good conscience, or in seeing the work of the Lord so far prospering in his hand, that his child shall be twice born to him. We speak ignorantly oftentimes when we speak of failures. We only see parts of the case. We want to see everything within the compass of one day. We cannot wait until the day following, and the third day. Oftentimes our impatience betrays us, and we mourn a failure where we ought to see but an ebb in the tide. A man's heart-waves will come again, by-and-by, with still greater force and fuller volume !

The offer of salvation had been made, and the offer of salvation

had been rejected.   This appears to me to be one of the most
astonishing facts° in human life.   Given this state of affairs:
An assembly of men, and a declaration from heaven that God is
willing to save every man in the assembly, and that most of
them should refuse to believe the message.   Is there any
anomaly so great?   Is there a state of affairs less likely to
secure our belief than that?   And yet this is the condition of
things.   No man is so little believed as is the Word of God.
Sometimes we feel wounded because our messages do not
produce proper effect.   But the heart of Almighty God is continually grieved, because of the rejection of the gospel.   Jesus
Christ here puts himself into an attitude most pathetic and
touching.   He says, "I would have gathered you.   Why are
you not gathered?   Not because of any want of opportunity;
not because of any deficiency of love on my part, but because
of the stubbornness of your own will."   After all, whatever
metaphysical mysteries there may be about this view of the case,
it satisfies the heart and the deepest love of mankind more than
any other view.   Christ entreating—men rejecting; the gospel
offered—the gospel despised; and the blame coming down in
judgment and condemnation upon those who have rejected the
truth.   I know not of any view of the case which goes so far
to satisfy one's present intelligence and sense of right, and
consciousness of religious concern for the children of men.

It is so with ourselves.   The gospel is offered to us.   Jesus
Christ comes to every man, comes to us, and says, "I would
gather up your life; I have redeemed you.   Will you believe
it?   I have bought you with a price; may I not claim you as
my own?   I have an answer to your sin, a solution of your
difficulty, a comfort for your whole being—will you believe
it?"   It is possible for us to turn round and say to him, No!
Then what is the end of all this?   The end is that God himself
is exhausted.   Mercy is the culmination of justice, and when
mercy is despised the whole government of God is exhausted, so
far as the possibility of human salvation is concerned.   What is
it that is offered to us then?   Is it some great and hard thing
that God requires at our hands?   Verily not.   It is that we,
consciously sinful, consciously needy, shall listen to the appeals

of his love, and say, We believe those appeals with our whole
heart, and we will live by them! That is the true meaning of
faith. Not a mere assent of the mind, not a mere indisposition
to controvert any statement which is made, but this,—I live by;
I believe. Reverse the word "believe," and it is live by. It is
the rendering up of the life to a certain truth, a governing of the
whole being by the spirit of a certain statement. What is that
statement? "God so loved the world, that he gave his only
begotten Son, that whosoever believeth in him should not perish,
but have everlasting life." "This is a faithful saying, and
worthy of all acceptation, that Jesus Christ came into the world
to save sinners." "The Son of man is come to seek and to save
that which was lost." When a man can, with all the love and
energy of his heart, lay hold upon this statement, he is a saved
man. He is not a learned man, he is not a skilful controversialist, he is not what is generally known as a theologian.
But he is a saved man; he has a germ in his heart that means
pardon, purity, peace, heaven, rest, service!

Then there is a possibility of saying, as Jerusalem said, "I
will not be gathered." What is the consequence of our availing
ourselves of that possibility? This:

"Behold your house is left unto you desolate" (ver. 35).

No man can explain the meaning of that word desolate, as used
by Jesus Christ. Different words have different meanings,
according to the position, the education, and the character of
speakers. When you say desolate, you may mean uncomfort-
ableness, a sense of loss and of want. When Jesus Christ says
"desolate," no wind that ever moaned could speak it as he spoke
it; no desert that ever withered could represent it as he meant
it to be seen and felt by the heart. When Jesus Christ says,
"Your house is left unto you desolate," I cannot describe what he
meant by that word. It was no longer a home; it was no longer
a place of safety, or a place of comfort, or a place of rest. When
he said "Desolate," I may not tell what he meant. God grant
that we may never know! It must be something indescribably
awful when the face that has love in it and life and heaven is
turned away! It is never turned away suddenly. It is turned
away gradually, little by little, almost imperceptibly, until the

moment does come when it is turned utterly away, and then language fails to describe the blank, or properly set forth the dire desolation of the scene.

Are we to understand, then, from these words, that there is to be a limit to the period of trial which is allotted to mankind in this matter of salvation? Is there but a day of grace? Verily. A day! Then it has an end? Yes. "The sun of grace once set, will rise no more." When is that period of trial? Now. How long will the period of trial last? No man can tell. Shall I be spared another year? No man can promise thee that. Shall I hear another offer of salvation? I dare not say thou wilt. May this be the last time the call of heaven resounds in my ears? Yes. What then? "Now is the accepted time; behold, now is the day of salvation." But I am old?

> "While the lamp holds out to burn,
> The vilest sinner may return!"

But I am young? Thou mayest never be old; for the young die, the little child withers off its parent-stem, and the youth in the very flush of his powers is sometimes cut down suddenly as with a stroke of lightning! What then? "Now is the accepted time, now is the day of salvation." "To-day, if ye will hear his voice, harden not your hearts." But I am told that the will of man must be affected in some metaphysical and difficult way by the Spirit of God. Verily, we have not time to talk about metaphysics. Do you believe in your heart that you want salvation? "Yes." Do you believe that Jesus Christ offers you salvation? "I believe,—oh that my unbelief were helped!" It is enough to begin with; by-and-by you will be able to see further into the metaphysics of the case; you will be able to know more about the doctrine of the whole subject. In the meantime the first thing to be done is to avail yourself of any spark of desire towards the Son of God. We grow in knowledge as well as in grace; and the point at which we are saved is the point of faith. "But I have not great faith." Hast thou faith as a grain of mustard seed? Can any man say no to that? "I have no passionate, enthusiastic love." Hast thou one throb of affection? Is there anything in thy nature equal to a sigh of desire for the Son of God to save thee? That is enough to begin with. As eternity discloses itself, thou shalt grow up into rapture and perfectness of love. Do not, I pray you, omit the pathos of the Saviour's words, " O Jerusalem, Jerusalem ! " It is a burst of grief, it is the cry of a wounded, pained love ! Yet all the while he is pronouncing judgment. We mistake God when we suppose that his judgments are pronounced harshly, severely. He cries as mother never cried for a rebellious child, when he is passing condemnation upon any son of man. I know how possible it is even for preachers of the gospel so to pronounce words of judgment as to give a false impression to those who hear them. When Jesus said, "Your house is left unto you desolate," his voice was not haughty ; there was no triumph or defiance in his tone. He wept tears of the heart when he spoke this word of judgment. And at last when he is on his throne and the angels are round about him, think you that he can say, " Depart, ye cursed ! " without the tears coming into his eyes again ? Will it be a stern word ? Will it be a word pronounced with hardness, with harshness, with delight, that the hour of his triumphing is come ? Oh, there will be memories enough of his love, recollections enough of his Cross, reminiscences enough of the Calvary which he bedewed with his blood, to cause his voice even then to falter !

Yet even here is mercy. Even perdition itself is an aspect of the divine mercy. Indiscrimination, as to character, would be unjust. God is merciful in the " depart," as he is merciful in the " come." We shall see it one day. May we never see it from the lower aspect, but from the higher. What then have I to offer to men ? This : A present Saviour, a sufficient Redeemer, Jesus Christ, God the Son, willing to gather men. It is a tender word, " The Son of man is not come to destroy men's lives, but to save them." " As I live, saith the Lord, I have no pleasure in the death of the wicked." No,—and we can never tell how much it costs the heart of God to say to any man, " Your house is left unto you desolate."

Chapter xiv. 7–11.

"And he put forth a parable to those which were bidden, when he marked how they chose out the chief rooms; saying unto them, When thou art bidden of any man to a wedding, sit not down in the highest room; lest a more honourable man than thou be bidden of him; and he that bade thee and him come and say to thee, Give this man place; and thou begin with shame to take the lowest room. But when thou art bidden, go and sit down in the lowest room; that when he that bade thee cometh, he may say unto thee, Friend, go up higher: then shalt thou have worship in the presence of them that sit at meat with thee. For whosoever exalteth himself shall be abased; and he that humbleth himself shall be exalted."

OUT OF PLACE.

THERE is a fitness of things. We all know it. We feel it, though we may not be able to explain it in words. There is an instinctive judgment about proportion, and social rightness, and personal action. There is a regularity in irregularity. Life is not so tumultuous as it seems. If we could see the action of all the lines of life we should see that beneath all the tumult and uproar, all the eccentricity and irregularity, there is a steady line, direct, inevitable, persistent. It is upon that line that God looks when he talks of progress and the final out-blossoming of all the things he has sown and planted in the earth. There is what is called tendency. It can hardly be measured; it is often imperceptible; it may require whole centuries in order to note the very least progress that that tendency has made. It is in the air, it is in the remoter thought of men, it is in the things which they say to themselves when nobody hears them. It is thus that God leads us on from one point to another, whilst we ourselves imagine that things are irregular and upsidedown and wanting in order and peacefulness. There are two looks: there is the outward and superficial look that sees nothing, and there is the penetrating and spiritual look to which you may trust for a true and profound criticism. There is therefore, I repeat, a fitness of things, a sense of proportion, and colour, and weight, and values. We know one another at once; in a few minutes we soon learn whether the man should be here or there, or elsewhere : there is a spirit in man, and the inspiration of the Almighty giveth him understanding. There is an order of things which every one must approve. You may talk as much democracy and vulgarity as you please, but there is an order appointed of God, and you cannot upset it. It is not an order based upon mere money. When money is mere money there is nothing so poor on all the earth: nobody wants it, nobody will change it, nobody will trust to it. Money by itself is mockery, imposition, disappointment. There is no order or classification founded upon mere golden sovereigns. It is not an order of dress. Men shine brightly through their clothes. The clothes of a poor man are always radiant, not to the eye of vulgar judgment; but there is something about the man that makes his very cloak shine and glisten as no fuller on earth can whiten it. It is a marvellous process, wholly mysterious, and out of the way of the common run of criticism; but there it is, and we feel that the man has a right to be at the top. He does not look much, but let him give a judgment, let him utter one sentence, let him put his finger down upon one point in the argument; and at once the primacy is conceded. It is the ghostly, the mental, the spiritual, that rules all things in the long-run.

This order or fitness of things is not merely hereditary. We do not despise that which is hereditary. Because it ought to bring history with it. There ought to be a good deal of grey moss on certain names, and grey moss ought to be full of wise writing, it ought to be the treasure-house of experience and character and honour and service. But the fitness of things I refer to now is not founded either upon money or dress, or heredity, or anything that is external. It is a house not made with hands. Hands spoil everything. No man can pluck a flower without killing it. Plucking means killing. You cannot put back the drop of dew on the rose-tip that you shook off just now. That dew will not be handled. How sweet a thing it is, and beautiful, to know that our hands have done so little! And whatever our hands do time wears out, nature begins to quarrel

with at once. You no sooner put the roof upon your house than
nature begins to take it off. There is an inner fitness, a spiritual
relation and kinship, and when souls that know one another meet,
how accidentally soever, they know one another instantly; an
introduction would be a dishonour: the introduction comes up
from eternity and is stamped upon the face of the occasion.
There is a spirit in man.

I could imagine all the bankers in London gathered together
with all their gold with them, pile on pile, and quite a snow-
storm of financial paper; and I could imagine it being announced
to them that Robert Burns, who hardly ever had a sovereign in
his life, was at the door, and would be glad to look in if they
would allow him. I could imagine all the bankers of London
starting to their feet to receive the ploughman. How so? He
has a right to such salutation. He has no paper, he has no
bullion, but he has written words that make life doubly precious: he has sent angels through the air singing of common
things and little things; he makes the house the pleasanter
whenever he comes by his songs into it. He would be recognised
at once as welcome, and honoured, and honourable. This is also
a marvellous thing, that the spirit that is in man bows to spirit.
For a time it may bow to the gold, but there are times when
it recognises its true kinship, and when it rises and bows itself
down again in humble and reverent homage before its own
higher kindred. I could imagine all the lords of Great Britain
and Ireland assembled under their gilded roof, and I could
imagine circumstances under which they would also rise to their
feet to welcome a stranger. Let it be announced to them that
Beethoven was at the door and would like to come in, and
there is not a lord amongst them that would not rise and say,
Welcome! Why? He was no peer, he was a poor man. He
has been set down even at great royal festivals to sit and dine
apart, but he also was so much of a man and a king that when
they set him down at the side-table he took up his hat and went
out, and left them to dine without him as well as they could ;
and on other occasions he was called to the chief seat, where he
had a right to be. It is mind that must be at the top : beauty of
soul, pureness, grandeur of imagination, massiveness of intellect,

that must rule; and every other aristocracy must pay tribute to its majesty. There must always be an aristocracy of mind. I do not like the free-and-easy way which I have seen in some countries. I do not care for that broad and vulgar doctrine which says that all men are equal, because I know that is a lie. All men are not equal. There are masters and there are servants, and there must be so to the end of time. I am not now using these words in their ordinary social sense. There are master minds, master thinkers, men who catch the light of the morning first and throw it down upon the valleys. All men are equal?—is the landscape all equal? are the stars all equal? is nature all equal? Why, we must have masters, rulers, kings, and sometimes what we call tyrants; there must be an order or level of mind that must domineer for the time being, and prove its rectitude and harmony with the higher sovereigns after long time, so that we shall salute the dead. We often reserve our encomiums for the dead. We kill them, we crucify them, and then we sing hymns to their memory. We slay the prophets, and the next generation will come and build marble tombs over them, with elaborate epitaphs. But there should be and must be inequality now: it is inevitable, we cannot alter it. There must be class after class, lower and higher; and blessed is that nation the citizens of which can recognise these great distinctions of mind, and moral force, and pay appropriate tribute to them. I have no right to be equal in the presence of a man like Longfellow; a servile mind like mine must bow down at the feet of such a man, and look up to him. We know what he has written, we know what a master of music he was; his words are now part of the air we breathe, and when we see him we do not accost him with some false bald doctrine of " All men are equal, and I will stand in your presence covered." There are not many men who have a right to keep their hats on when Longfellow comes in. And what is true of the one poet is true of poets of our own. I would have therefore an exaltation of mind, genius, character above all things. The pure-minded man should be the sovereign of the age in which he lives.

But the speaker of this parable is no Epictetus, he is no Seneca, he is no mere moralist; he did not hang up these little pictures

for the purpose of having them admired as men admire cameos
and forget them. He was the Son of God, and therefore there
must be even in this parable, simply ethical and social as it
appears to be, a gospel element, a sacrificial doctrine and
thought and purpose. What is it? Is it true that Christianity
is a religion of manners? Certainly Christianity teaches men
how to behave themselves; and when a man does not know how
to behave himself he is no Christian. But he believes in nine
hundred and fifty-nine articles and doctrines and other addenda.
So he may do, but he is no Christian if he be not courteous, if
he does not know how to behave himself and restrain himself and
exhibit excellence of conduct; I do not care if he multiply his
beliefs by ten, it is nothing. If he have not charity, love, all-
teaching, all-guiding love, he is nothing, and less than nothing.
So Christianity is a religion of manners. "Be not weary in
well-doing." We misunderstand that word oftentimes. It is
not well-doing in the sense of doing well, doing things that are
excellent, but doing things that are excellent excellently. The
emphasis is on the adverb. A man may do excellent things and
do them roughly; a man may preach the gospel in an ungospel
tone; a man may bid you welcome to heaven as if he were
threatening you with punishment. Literally, the apostle says,
Be not weary in courtesy, in good manners, in the civil treatment
of one another. A man is not candid because he is brutal.
Courtesy does not ask for bluntness to sustain its charter and
its dignity. Christianity is therefore, I repeat again and again,
a religion of manners, of behaviour, of conduct. When thou art
bidden of any man to a wedding sit not down in the highest room,
but seek out the right place. Never be out of position; and if
you have to elect the position always proceed upon the assumption that you are not the best man that is coming to the feast.
Christianity insists upon self-knowledge. How honourable are
you? How many men are there who are more honourable?
Suppose there are fifty men coming to the wedding-feast, who
is the most honourable? Blessed is he who says, Not I; I must
wait until I see all the guests before I can form a judgment; it
is my business to wait until all others are in. And depend upon
it sooner or later there comes a destiny, a gentle, genial, beautiful,
yet inexorable fate, that says, Friend, that is not your place, your

place is further up. You cannot keep men back from the places they are destined to occupy. God goes by the fitness of things which he himself has established. You need not edge and elbow and crush your way, in obedience to the vulgar exhortation, Now make your way in the world! Do nothing of the kind. Depend upon it, we are under a fatherly providence, and if you will look back upon your life you will see that you have never forced your way to any real position worth having, but have been led to it; men have heard a voice in the air, saying, This is the man. It is so in statesmanship, and in commerce, and in literature, in journalism, in preaching, in everything. There is a master of ceremonies, an angel of God, a spirit of right that says, You are wanted higher up : or, Sit where you are until you are sent for. God knows where you are, and when he wants you he will not forget you. You are in a little village, and you want to be in a great city, and you are impatient because a man of your bulk almost occupies the whole of the village. Draw yourself in, and wait just where you are, and when God needs you in the great city he will come for you certainly. If you live in this faith, you will have peace, you will have great measure of enjoyment in life. Oh, rest in the Lord, and wait patiently for him, and he will arrange the wedding-table ; and when the whole geometric figure is completed, and all the living people are at the table, they will look round and say, Why, this is a mosaic ; this is a mosaic not made with hands. How well fitted we are, how admirably thrown together! Yet there was no throwing in it, except in the sense in which the clouds throw their showers upon the thirsty ground. Believe in God, live in God, and know that he knows you better than you can know yourself. You think you could occupy the top seat, but you could not. If you could believe that we should have no fret at home, no chafing, no mortified ambitions, but just that wonderful silence which often says to itself quite inaudibly to others, What is this? I wanted to be otherwhere, and yet I am here; for a time I was impatient, but now I see I would not change my place : all has been ordered wisely ; he who is the Master of the feast hath done all things well.

A marvellous Christianity is this for continually—shall we say eternally ?—striking the self out of the man.   It will not rest until it has got out of you and me every little weight of selfishness that is lying in the most secret part of our hearts.   In this very chapter the doctrine is laid down in graphic language :—" If any man come to me, and hate not his father, and mother, and wife, and children, and brethren, and sisters, yea, and his own life also, he cannot be my disciple.   And whosoever doth not bear his cross, and come after me, cannot be my disciple."   What, may I not retain one little atom of my very self ?   And the gospel says, No.   Then what are the terms of acceptance with the higher life ?   God the Father, God the Son, and God the Holy Ghost. The words are at least four in number :—humble himself, deny himself, crucify himself, mortify himself.   Are these the terms of entrance ?   Name them again : Humble, deny, crucify, mortify. Then where am I ?   Nowhere ; killed, slain, the last shred of selfishness crushed : now you are prepared to receive the kingdom of heaven.

An awful word is the word " mortify."   What does it literally mean ?   Make dead.   Unless a man make dead himself, he cannot begin to live.   You know the term well enough in your deeds of partnership and deeds of arrangement and deeds of settle-ment—" That he the said A. B. shall be as if dead."   You have often written yourselves dead on your legal parchments : that is just what you must do in this entrance into the wedding chamber ; you must have no self, no selfishness, no self-idolatry, no self-trust ; you must hate your own life ; then God can begin to do something with you.   Ambition killed the race ; wanting the next and higher thing brought us to ruin.   That spirit will ruin the Eden of your life, and blight the Eden of your home, and bring you down to disappointment and shame and misery.   What you have to do therefore is to get rid of self.   " Unless a man deny himself he cannot be my disciple."   You say it is necessary for you to live, and God says it is not.   There is no need for you to live another moment.   A man may say, " I must do something for a living."   No ; that is atheism ; there is not one whit of gospel in that.   It is absolutely needless that you or I should live another moment.   And if we cannot live without sharp practice, and without injustice, and without taking up the room that belongs to other people we had better not live; it is not life. In some money there is no comfort. Once a man got hold of thirty pieces of silver, fifteen in each hand, and his hands were scorched, and he took it back and could hardly shake it off, and he said, " Take it again, I have betrayed innocent blood ! " Why not make the confession and keep the money ? You cannot; restoration follows confession. There is some honour in which there is no real sense of dignity; it is a thing of feathers and air and paint and gilt. True honour cometh only from God ; it belongs to righteousness and to obedience.

Here then is the great Moralist and the great Teacher, and especially the great Saviour, saying to us by parable and by doctrine, If you want to come into my kingdom one man must be killed. Who is that one man ? Yourself. " Strait is the gate, and narrow is the way, that leadeth unto life, and few there be that find it." We might all find it if we really wanted to do so.

Chapter xv.

THE PRODIGAL SON.

"And a cert.in man had two sons. And the younger of them said to his father, Father, give me the portion of goods that falleth to me. And he divided unto them his living" (vers. 11, 12).

THE man was a man of substance. It may be a fortunate or an unfortunate circumstance, as events may prove. There is nothing wrong in being a substantial man in society; yet the very fact of a man having great riches may be one of the greatest calamities that ever occurred in his life. The younger son did not say, "Father, I am tired of a lazy life, and now I am determined to do something for my own bread. I have been turning over this great problem of life in my mind, and I find that life is a responsibility, life is a discipline, and though I have been born under circumstances of conspicuous advantage, yet I think it right to go out and do something to make my own position, to establish my own title, to be called and to be treated as a man." What did the young man say? He said, "Father, I am a youth of fortune; please give to me the portion of goods that falleth to me." He had been scheming, it appears, but scheming in a wrong direction. He had been scheming in the direction of self-enjoyment; he was going out to taste the sweets of liberty; the time had come, in his consciousness, when he thought that he would enjoy a little more freedom, and the first notion that occurred to him was to get clear of his father. Many a man has had precisely the same lucky suggestion presented to his mind by the great enemy. The father has stood in the way; the father's old-world notions have been impediments in the path of supposed progress and enjoyment and liberty; and the young man's great concern has been to get rid of his own father! It looks well. "Let me open a door in my father's house, go into the wide world with the portion of goods that

falleth to me, and all will be sunshine and beauty, music and
rest." It is evident that the young man was not a man of robust
understanding; yet he was not to be blamed for having had very
little experience of the world. He thought that life would be
enjoyable if only he had liberty. I propose now to follow him
in his journeyings, to see what his experience was, to collect
it for the advantage of all who need a moral exhortation upon
this point, and to inquire at last whether there cannot be some
better way of spending the days which God has put into our
keeping as a trust.

The young man gathered all together, took his journey into
a far country, thinking that the farther from home the sweeter
and larger would be the liberty. I fear he has planned something in his heart, which he would not like to do just within the
neighbourhood of his own father's house. If not, he gave way
to the sophism which exercises a very malign influence upon
a good many of us, namely this : That we must go a long way
off in order to be blest, not knowing that the true blessing grows
just at arm's length, forgetting that the fountain of the truest
joy springs within us and not outside of us. Yet how many
there are who travel mile on mile to get joy, to secure rest;
when they are forgetful of the fact that they might have it without
going out of themselves, except in so far as they go into God
and truth and purity!

The young man has gone then, and a merry day he has of it
at first. His pockets are full, he has health on his side, many
a pleasant memory sings to him, he has not yet tasted of the
bitterness of life. It would be cruel if a man who is going to
serve the devil could not have just a few hours of introductory
enjoyment, or something that he mistakes at least for delight.
A man cannot cut off good ties all in a moment; the ligaments
require some time to get thoroughly through; and whilst the
spell of old memories and traditions is upon the man he imagines
that he is going out into a large and wealthy place, and that every
step he takes is a step in the direction of comfort and honour.
When he got into the far country what did he do ? He wasted
his substance in riotous living; stepped out of liberty into license.

At one bound he seems to have cleared the region of discipline
and entered into the sphere of licentiousness. He wasted his
substance. There is nothing so easy as waste. It does not
require any genius to waste property, to waste beauty, to waste
life. Any man can waste what he has. It is easy to do the
destructive part of life's work; the difficulty is to gather, to
accumulate, to amass, and yet to hold all that has been brought
together in the right spirit, and to administer it to the right ends.
Why did he show such bad skill? How does it come that in a
moment he was master of the art of wasting? Because he had
never mastered the art of earning his own living. Everything
had been provided for him. When he came down to breakfast
—towards ten, the family hour being seven in the morning—
he found the things still waiting for him, and at dinner he
found the table lavishly spread without his having worked for
a single morsel of food that was upon the board; when he was
sick the physician was within call; and when he felt any desire
to please himself his father and his mother were but too ready
to gratify his desires. Now the young fool goes out into the
world to find his joy in wasting, destroying, trampling under foot
all the things that he has got! And what blame? We wonder
if the rod ought not first to have been used upon his father? It
is a question (if we may modernise the instance) whether the
old man at home was quite blameless in this matter. But so it
is; men mistake enjoyment and the scope of pleasure; they
forget that in the absence of discipline there can be no true
profound enjoyment of any of the greatest gifts of God. He who
escapes discipline escapes one of the purest enjoyments; he who
mistakes license for law goes downward to the pit at a rapid
rate! Let us read:

"And when he had spent all, there arose a mighty famine in that land;
and he began to be in want" (ver. 14).

Such men help to bring about famines, —men who eat all and
produce nothing, men who are consumers and non-producers.
These are the men that make famines. A man that will eat up
a whole wheatfield and do nothing in the way of sowing, is
the man that will make a famine anywhere,—logically, necessarily. He is eating, appropriating, consuming, absorbing,—**never**

working, never doing anything in return. Why, here is cause and effect. The man is eating the things that are round about him, and when the last meal has gone, he says, "There is a famine in the land." Of course there is. A man cannot always go on consuming and not producing without soon coming to the end of his patrimony, and finding a famine staring him in the face. "And when he had spent all"—all that he possessed admitted of being spent! You see my meaning? He had nothing that could not be spent. All that he had was outside of him. A man could get through the very stars of heaven if every one of them was a golden coin; a man could spend the sands upon the sea-shore if every sparkling atom was a silver coin! He could get through it all and be a pauper at the last! Who is he, then, who cannot spend all? A man who lives spiritually, a man of character, of purpose, of high conception, of noble sympathy, a man who knows truth and loves truth never can spend his fortune. Once that fortune was attempted to be described, and the words of the description I remember well. "An inheritance incorruptible, undefiled, and that fadeth not away." May I ask any young man what he possesses in the way of property, substance, security? If he says that all he has is outside of him, then I say it is very possible for him to get through it all, and at the last be compelled to face a famine. Gold can be spent; ideas cannot be wasted by the wise man. There is that scattereth, and yet increaseth; there is that withholdeth more than is meet, and it tendeth to poverty. Be sure of this, that any man in society who has not given back a fair equivalent for what he gets in the way of bread, and dress, and physical blessing, is the man who is working mischief in society,—that man is one of the causes of destitution and famine.

"And he began to be in want" (ver. 14).

A new experience came upon him. And oh! it is pitiful when a man who has never known want just begins to feel it. Better be born at the other end of things; better be born in poverty than in riches to be spent so. You should have seen him when he felt the first pang. It was pitiful! The man had a fine face; there was a gentle expression upon it at times, all the signs and tokens of refinement had not been quite taken out of it; and when the young man began to feel the pain of want, I was sorry for him; I saw his blanched face, and saw him look round as if he might see his father somewhere, or his mother, and there was nothing but strangers, emptiness, desolation! He called out, and the mocking echo answered him. It was very sad, but it was right,—it was right! If a man can go upon a course like that, and at the end of it be prosperous and joyful, having fulness of satisfaction; why, then, life is not worth having, and destiny is cruelty. I saw him in want, friendlessness, pain, hunger ; and, though I feel that it might have been myself standing there, yet I own that it was right.

"And he went and joined himself to a citizen of that country ; and he sent him into his fields to feed swine" (ver. 15).

He was nothing to the citizen ; the citizen cared nothing for him. The citizen did not say, "Let me see your hand, and I will tell you whether you were born a gentleman." He did not say, "How have you been brought up, young man? and I will try to fall in, as far as possible, with the traditions of your youth." Nothing of the sort. No, no. It seems a little way from the man's father to the citizen,—but oh, it is a long, long way! He left his father and went to the citizen. Both men! But the one was as a shining angel, and the other as a tormentor sent of providence to bring the young man to his senses. Yes, sir, you will say good-bye to your father, and care nothing for him, but the first man you meet will be a rough one. Thank God for that! I thank God that there are rough men into whose hands young people fall, who have not known how to value a father's care and a mother's love. Young men must at some time or another come under the rod. They may delay the time of discipline, they may put off the time of judgment, but it comes upon them. Events are God's servants ; the great purposes of Heaven are working themselves out by events which we cannot number, and which we cannot control. At the end it will be seen that there is a rod in the law, that there is a God on the throne, and that no man can do wrong without having judgment brought to bear upon him !

But could he do nothing better than feed swine? No

There was the great mischief. His father (again we modernise the instance) had never taught him a trade. Shame on his father! We blame the father more than we must blame the young man, in so far as this may be true. What could the young man do? Nothing. He had no skill in his fingers; he had no power of putting things together so as to make a living out of them. All he could do was the meanest work,—he could feed swine. Do you feel it to be somewhat a hardship, young man, that you are sent to work? It is the beginning of your prosperity, if rightly accepted. Do you say that you ought to have been something finer? There is time to prove how far you are worthy of elevation and honour. Meanwhile, whatever you are, do your work with all patience, believing that he who does so will in the end have a sufficient and appropriate reward. Let us follow him in his menial employment and see how it fares with him,—with him who was once so pampered, who was the delight of the household and the hope of his father's life.

"And he would fain have filled his belly with the husks that the swine did eat : and no man gave unto him " (ver. 16).

Is that true? It is literally true. Is it true in this young man's experience? Then it is true in ours. We cannot allow any dispute upon this for a moment, so far as the book is concerned, because the same thing is done every day amongst ourselves. While the man spent his substance in riotous living he had friends, he had companions; there were many who shared his bounty and hospitality,—where are they now? They are not within his call; they do not know him now. He spent his money freely, and so long as he had any left they lived with him, and were his friends—they prostituted that sweet and holy name friend, in order that they might the better accomplish their own purposes ; and as soon as they saw him lay down the last coin, and they had helped him to devour it, they turned their backs upon him and declared they never knew him! No man gave unto him, though he had given to so many men. Bad men always disappoint their victims. Bad men always make dupes and leave them. I would to God I could teach that thoroughly, effectively. The bad man cannot be a friend! The bad man who follows you, tracks you about, waits for you at the warehouse door, and spends your substance for you, cannot be a friend. He looks like a friend, but he is an enemy in disguise. "He apparently loves my company." Not a bit of it! He loves what you have; he loves your money. "He seems to prefer my society to anybody else's." He will ruin you to suit his purpose! The bad man cannot be a friend. He can be a sneak; a vampire; he can suck your blood, but he cannot be a friend! Only he can be a friend who can suffer for you, sympathise with you, own you in darkness as well as in light, defend you in danger, as well as smile upon you in the time of prosperity. I know this to be true. It has been burnt into our history as with a red-hot iron. This is no poet's fancy; this is no touch of dramatic genius,—this is sadly, tragically, awfully true. It is not long since that a case in point occurred within the sphere of my own observation. A young man was taken up by a crafty villain, pursued by him, flattered by him,—he could call upon this man to do what he pleased for him; there was plenty of money on the one side, and a bottomless pit of perdition on the other, along with a smooth outside, with a fair tongue, with a gentle tone of expression. As long as there was any property to be squandered the villain was at hand. He would do any-thing; set the young man up houses, and find him means of so-called enjoyment; he was his right-hand man, making all his arrangements, opening all the gates for him, and indicating the road that he was to take. And when the young man had spent thousands upon this policy, it came of course to a break, it came to a crisis. Where was his friend? Did he turn round and say, "I will be your friend still"? No. He said, "I will drag that young man through the mire." This was not an accident— a single separate event standing by itself. It is a doctrine, a truth, that badness never can be sincere, that badness is always selfish, and that selfishness will always allure and destroy its dupes. And the young man's future went so. The old man at home perhaps had some difficulty in getting the property together. He used to be a workman himself, a man of good understanding and of great industry in matters of business, and it took him some twenty-five years to amass the property, and the young man spent it in a month! Be your own executor; you lay up money and you know not who will spend it. You say, "Five

—seven—ten thousand for my youngest boy. That will be a nice start in life for him; he will never know hardship as I have known it; he will never have to eat brown bread as I have eaten it; he will begin in very comfortable circumstances, and be able to take a very high position at once." Take care! He may spend it in a fortnight! See, at one toss of the dice your estate may be gone! He may be doing but a poor thing for his child who tries to turn nine thousand into ten thousand for him. Better send him to shoe-blacking, to crossing-sweeping, better make him a boy waiting in the shop, than so to train him as not to know the value of what you have amassed for his advantage. It may seem hard that he should begin where you began; but depend upon it that unless the young man be of singularly high principle and fine integrity, you are laying up for him that which will turn into a scorpion and sting him!

"And when he came to himself, he said, How many hired servants ot my father's have bread enough and to spare, and I perish with hunger!" (ver. 17.)

Mark the beauty of the expression,—When he came to himself. All sin is insanity; all wickedness is madness. A wicked man is not himself. He has lost self-control; all his best memories have been darkened or forgotten; and he is no longer to be counted a sane man in the true and proper sense of that term. Wickedness blinds the intellectual faculties, disorders a man's vision—spiritual, intellectual, moral; gives him exaggerated notions of all other persons and things. A course of wickedness has a madhouse at the end of it! How much we are mistaken upon this matter of insanity. We think only those persons insane who are imprisoned in asylums, who are restrained by a strait waistcoat, who have watchers and keepers appointed over them. We say about such, "Poor creatures, alas! they are insane!" not knowing that there is an insanity of wickedness, a moral insanity,—and of all insanity moral insanity is the worst. Responsibility begins there. If a man's reason be blighted, then responsibility goes along with it,—he cannot distinguish the right hand from the left in morals. But where the insanity is moral, where there is a love of evil, where iniquity is rolled under the tongue as a sweet morsel, then there is obligation, there is responsibility, and where there is responsibility there is the possibility of damnation! "When he came to himself." He never would have come to himself but for his poverty, his desertion, his pain. So, Almighty God has strange ministers in his sanctuary. All his ministers are not mere speakers of holy and beautiful words. He hath employed some grim teachers to instruct a certain class of mankind in the first principles of right: grief, hunger, pain, homelessness, ill-health, desertion. These are all the hired servants of the Father. He sends them out after sons that have left the old, dear home. This young man had to thank his swine-feeding, his experience of famine, his homelessness, as the beginning of his better life. Many of us probably have had to do precisely the same thing. We found no religion in luxury; no altar in the carpeted room; so long as we had everything within reach and call, our hearts never went out of us in incense of praise, in utterance of prayer. Not until we were breadless, homeless, until we exchanged fatherhood for citizenship; not until we got under influences that were keenly bitter and tormenting in their effects, did we begin to know that we had done wrong. Some of us, again, have had to thank God for poverty, for ill-health, for friendlessness, for being left out on the streets, without bread to eat or a pillow to rest upon, the rain dashing into our faces and no man knowing us. It was then we called for God, and it was then the Father met us! What did the young man say? Did he say, "Now I have taken this step, I cannot retrace it; I have said farewell to my father, I am not the man to succumb, to go back to my father's door and say, 'Please be kind enough to open this door to me again.' No, no; I will rise up from this state of poverty— I have been suffering by a heavy hand—I will yet make a man of myself; I will get back my fortune, I will renew my companions, and my latter time shall be better than my first"? If he had done so he would have shown but another phase of his insanity. He took the right course; he humbled himself; he got a right view of his way. He felt it to have been bad—bad in its purpose, bad in its conception, bad in its whole course. He said, "I will go without a defence; I will get up no argument; I will not explain how it came to be; I will just go and throw myself at his feet and say, 'Make a servant of me, only take me back again.'" He won the battle then! The moment he threw off his pride, the moment he said, "I shall not stand before him, but fall down at his feet," he was victor! So long as there is a spark of pride left in a man, as between himself and God, a great battle has to be fought. So long as a man thinks he can make out a sufficient statement, an explanation of how he came to be wrong, and to do wrong, and can defend himself, in some degree at least,—he is far from the kingdom of heaven.

What, then, is this that we have to say? This: there must be no excusings, no pleadings, no apologies, arguments, defences or palliations. Man must surrender; he must say, "There is no health in me; I yield; I have grieved thee, insulted thee, wounded thee: it seems as if I never could be a son again. Make something of me in thy house still. I will keep a door, I will follow the poorest of thy servants to be his servant,—only have me somewhere in thy care, dear, grieved, broken-hearted Father!" When a man begins to talk so he is saved—is saved! The young man went forward with his speech, a beautiful speech, not a single strain of selfishness in it; all a speech of condemnation, self-renunciation. He got so far with it, and the father interrupted him, fell on his neck, and kissed him, and said, "Make a son of him again." It is God's way with the sinner. He never lets us finish our speech of penitence. We struggle and sob on to about a comma, or at most a semicolon, and then his great love comes down and says, "That will do; begin again; begin at the Cross, my son; my child, begin at the Cross!" Were I to talk through many hours, even until sunrise, I could say no more than this, that a right state of acceptance before God is a state of self-abhorrence, self-distrust, self-renunciation. So long as we stand, God will not have anything to do with us, because he cannot. But when we fall down at his feet; when we feel our nothingness and own it—it is then that he would put all heaven into our hearts.

Chapter xv.

PERSONAL PRONOUNS.

W E have often lectured on the parable of the prodigal son without bringing out these pronouns vividly and emphatically :—" My son "; " thy brother "; " let us eat, and be merry." " My "; " thy "; " us." The prodigal has his own pronoun; he says, " I will arise, and go to my father," not my brother's father, but my own. Repeat these pronouns—" my," " thy," " us." We cannot keep great joys in the singular number. You must at one point or another pluralise. Let us follow the course of this little river pronominal.

" *My son*."—The father recognised facts. He said, " My son was dead." He was not in a school, he was not a boy of equivocal behaviour ; he was not a diamond oft colour, a little yellow but still a diamond. The father did not thus confuse his own understanding and conscience. He looked facts dead in the face. Until we do that we can make no sound progress. We shall never evangelise the world if we think the world is only in a swoon. The Son of man is come to seek and to save that which was lost. He has not come to prop up a reeling polity ; he is going to reconstruct shattered ruin. " Dead "—how dead ? There is a dead that has poetry in it; there is a dead, a death, which means that the family have taken a bulb and planted it, sure that it will flower in heaven. That is not death : but the dear friend is thus merely planted or sown. We might sing at such a planting. But for this poor little natural feeling of ours which overflows its own narrow channels, we might sing loud sweet psalms in the cemetery, praising God that another bulb was put into the earth with the assurance that it would be all flowers presently. The son was not dead in this sense, or the father never would have wished him back again ; he would have

349

---

made no feast for him if he had returned. Given the conviction, not the mere sentiment, that our departed ones are in heaven, and when we are asked to give a judgment in the court of the highest reason and reverence, we should say, Do not disturb them, let them alone in their high ecstasy; it is too cold down here for such as they are now. " Dead "—twice dead, all dead; the body alive but the soul dead; understanding, conscience, imagination, heart, all the highest powers and qualities of the soul dead. That is death. Death is not the worst evil that can befall any man or any family or any nation. There are living men who are too dead to be buried, there are living forces emitting continual and devastating pestilence. When we have them in the house the house is no longer sweet; though we open all the windows of the dwelling and let in the strongest west wind, it cannot quell that miasma. Such were some of us : " we were by nature the children of wrath, even as others." Do not let us trifle with realities, and say that the human heart is " not as good as it ought to be." Whilst we are thus talking we never can understand Christ and his gospel. We must get to the tragedy of sin before we can get to the tragedy of the Cross. They go together ; in a sense, they balance one another ; in a sense they are equivalent to one another. If you set down a unit on the one hand and say that it is equal to a fraction on the other, you are arithmetically wrong ; and if you set down sin on the one side as a mere offence against moral colour and the Cross on the other, then are you guilty of creating an infinite and shocking disproportion.

" *Alive again,*"—alive in his soul, in his conscience, in his reason, in his sense of right ; alive in his broken-heartedness. That is the point at which true life begins. True life begins at contrition, at self-renunciation, at self-hatred. When we are most deeply in tears we are nearer than we ever were before our loudest, sweetest song. "Alive," because he has come home. Life seeks the centre; life yearns for fatherhood; life turns round, as it were, and in dumb quest asks for home. The young man was alive the very moment he said, " I will arise." He was alive before the father knew it. He had been alive some considerable time, walking on it may be day after day, for he had to come

from "a far country"; yet he was alive all the time, and he
himself hardly knew it. We sometimes pray without fully
seizing all the meaning of the act. Many a man who would almost
resent the idea that he prays cannot help praying, in some form,
in some degree, in some sense. The yearning, the backward
look to the things left long ago, the question in the heart as to
how they all are at home; the unconfessed looking out for the
post if haply there may be a letter from the old place: all these
are aspects of prayer, they are expressions of desire, they are
hints at a great gnawing want in the soul. It is a good thing
for a man to have even a passing feeling of this kind. It is an
excellent thing for a man to take pen and paper and sign some
holy vow. He may break it to-morrow, but he has had four-
and-twenty hours of it. That has done him good. He may
not break it to-morrow; the four-and-twenty hours of release
which he has had may prepare him for four-and-twenty more,
and the eight-and-forty may constitute quite a defence between
him and the old temptation. It is good for a man to come to
his old church and hear one of the old hymn-tunes and try to
take part in the singing, though it be musically but a poor
part: somehow it connects him by fine filaments with things
sacred and ineffable. The whole world is changed from that
point of view; the grass is greener, and the birds never sang
with so penetrating and comforting a trill before. These are all
mysteries, but they are mysteries of education, they are all
stimulants in an upward direction, they are all part of that
marvellous and inexplicable apocalypse which we call Life.

" *My son* " *:* did not distance destroy both the noun and the
pronoun ? No. We go back to our mother tongue: and it was
part of this man's mother tongue to say concerning each of his
children, "My son." We are sometimes suddenly startled into
our real way of speaking. There is a conventional way, or there
is a way to which we have schooled ourselves, so that we say,
The next time we meet the offender we will address him swiftly.
So we might if we had a week's notice of his coming; but the
Lord oftentimes makes suddenness quite a part of his process of
human education. Before we are aware of it there stands the
man straight in front of us,—the prodigal, the lost son, the lost

daughter, and we have not time to do anything but cry. We were going to be very haughty; we were going to treat the offender off-hand. Trust the heart that was once really in love with you, that truly and deeply felt the necessity of your nearness and comfort; and though there may be for a time alienation between you, yet there shall come another time when the old language shall utter itself and familiar cries shall put down all the meaner music. John B. Gough told us of a husband who had acted so badly that he could no longer be kept in his own home. He had been taken into that home again and again, and again and again he had wrecked it. In his old age he thought he would try again. He found his way to his wife, who would not speak to him, or approach him, or have anything to do with him. She recited the story of her wrongs, and no honest man could listen to her without taking her side and rejecting the so-called husband as a plague intolerable. Mr. Gough was present at the interview. It was a fruitless communication. The old man, he said, rose to retire, and taking up his old muffler for his throat, he was trying with feeble and fumbling hands to put it on. He could not do so, and his wife gave it just one touch in the right direction : but that one touch brought her to herself; she fell on his neck and kissed him. It is the touch, the sudden impression, the unlooked-for vision, the thing we never calculated—it is that that touches us with a new and higher, brighter and diviner relation.

" *Thy brother.*"—The pronoun " thy " comes out of the pronoun " my,"—" thy " because " my." An hour before the elder brother had no brother. Even nominally he would reject and scout the idea, but the father called him " thy brother " because he first called him " my son." Until we get the larger relation right we never can get the inferior relation put right. The one depends upon the other. Thou shalt love the Lord thy God with all thy heart, soul, mind, strength, and——it is out of that " and," that copulative word, that falls all neighbourliness, all true fraternity, all sacred and noble quality. The mischief is that men will try to work the other way. Why do we attempt to overget gravitation ? Gravitation never has been overcome but temporarily. The little lark overcomes it ; the ascent of the lark is an argument against gravitation, but a very short and lame argument. The lark will soon come down again. Even larks, and singing birds of every name, and eagles, and eagles that dare the sun, soon tire of wrestling with gravitation. The action of gravitation in this sense is a movement from God to man, from the first commandment to the second ; and until we have obeyed the first commandment we cannot touch the second, or if we do touch it we shall soon drop it again as involving a tremendous and impossible task. Here therefore stands the Church in its supreme majesty as the reformer and saviour of the world. It works along the right line, it keeps step with gravitation, it moves with the action of God. Of course, the elder brother had an argument. He is a despicable fool who cannot argue about something. He would be an intolerable person who could not find fault with some other person. That *rôle* is always open to us if we care to make havoc of life's finest opportunities. Find a man with an argument, and you find a man with a grievance, and find a man with a grievance and he can never go into the feast. He feeds on hunger, he asks a blessing in the open air upon tables spread with nothing; he takes a pride in his very food. He is a home-made martyr to a home-made conscience. Never trouble about the elder brother. Why do preachers try to explain such a character ? He is not worth explaining. You join the sacred revel, find your way to the interior banqueting-room where soul is brought to soul in new wedlock, and new fatherhood, in new sonship, and let the elder brother fill himself to satisfaction with the east wind.

" *My* "—" *thy* "—" *us.* " Who is meant by that " us " ? The explanation is in the parable. The father said to his servants, Take such and such a course, " and let us eat and be merry." And they began to be merry. It is a poor joy that does not overflow the parlour and get down to the kitchen. It is a party not worth going to if the servants are not interested in it ; it is a mean, despicable kind of uninviting show ; it is not a festival. Great emotions do not know who are men or kings or peasants or servants or masters. Great emotions touch our human nature ; they are humane, civilising, fraternising, uniting, consolidating. Herein is the marvellous miracle that is wrought by Christian sympathy. Men who are under the influence of the Cross have all things in common. That rule has never been suspended and has never been put out of practice. There is a literal way of reading the story which ends in saying, All this sort of thing has passed away. Nothing of the kind. It cannot pass away. It is immortal because the love of Christ is eternal. Our love for Christ may have removed, our passionate loyalty to the Cross may have gone down in volume and quality. If we could bring back the love we could bring back the true communism. No man would say that anything he had was his own. Blessed be God that miracle is always possible. It is always possible that love to Christ may be so great, efflorescent, exuberant, that man shall simply forget his own individuality and petty concerns, and call all hunger to share his loaf. We shall certainly go down at the social end if we go down at the spiritual beginning. There is a law of cause and effect in these things. Keep up your religion if you would keep up your morality. Keep up your Christianity if you would keep up your socialism. Keep up your prayer if you would keep up your service. Knees unused to bending before God soon tire in endeavouring to run the errands of men.

Blessed be God for these eternal pronouns. You could not live on "it" and "they," although "they" is plural enough to include a great many things. You want the "my," the "thy," the "us,"—personal, warm, sympathetic, human. This is what Christ came to work out amongst us. This is Christ's own sweet parable. The Man who spoke this parable ought not to have been crucified. This parable should have saved him from murder. It is a beauteous poem. It has the music of all generations in it. He who spake it was the Son of the carpenter so-called. True: but Christ was not murdered. The speaker of that parable never could have been merely killed. He gave himself. Said he, "I lay down my life : I have power to lay it down, and I have power to take it again." That man was not a victim, he was a Priest. To his priesthood I call all the sons of men who have wandered into a far country.

Chapter xvii. 6.

"And the Lord said, If ye had faith as a grain of mustard seed, ye might say unto this sycamine tree, Be thou plucked up by the root, and be thou planted in the sea; and it should obey you."

FAITH POWER.

YOU either believe these words, or you do not. Probably there is not a man who has not neglected them. Was there ever such a declaration made by human lips? How we hasten over verses of this range and quality, and get into easy reading as soon as we can! But here stands the solemn, incredible word. Words of this kind should not be read once only, for the ear may refuse them full admission, and the memory may perform quite a miracle of forgetfulness; we should say the words themselves over and over again until they become part of our very consciousness. "And the Lord said . . . ." It requires an introduction not less august. Had it been—"And Peter said," we should have made short work of the speech. "And the Lord said, If ye had faith as a grain of mustard seed, ye might say unto this sycamine tree, Be thou plucked up by the root, and be thou planted in the sea; and it should obey you." If this is not a fanciful speech it is the most neglected doctrine in all the book. Not a Christian soul in the wide universe believes a tittle of it: so we cannot call ourselves Christian. We only become Christians at the difficult points: along the common road we belong to all denominations of thinkers; it is at hard places, at new departures, at cross-roads, at the Cross, that we become real Christians. We always seek to lessen the meaning of supernatural declarations; we call them figures of speech, we refer to them as mystic idealities; things written in clouds, and framed with stars; we are willing to give them any amount of transcendental honour, but we never accept them as direct, imposing immediate responsibilities, and offering an instantaneous heaven. What wonder that spirituality is at a discount? We hold our

355

religion with the fingers of our reason ; we take it up and set it
down as an argument, we surround it with many learned books
we have never read, and think that so surrounded it is perfectly
secure.   The one thing we have not done is the only thing we
are asked to do, and that is to live our piety.   It is for the men
of faith to recall and re-establish the doctrine of faith.   Even
believers that seem to be supreme carry with them a measuring-
rod with which to mark off the ideal, the spiritual, and the infinite
into inches.   We are never lost in God.   We exclude the supernatural, and then praise God ; we write moaningly—and
remuneratively—about the decay of supernaturalism, and then
never think of using our soul's wings, but always do we walk
with the feet of our body.   All this must be reformed and driven
away.   Nothing is clearer to me than that the Church is dying.
The Church ought to die when it loses its distinctiveness ; when
it ceases to represent faith, it is effete, it has survived its function,
it is fit only to be cast down and trodden under foot of men.
When the Church is only one of a number of kindred institutions,
decent, respectable, self-protecting, self-promoting, the Church has
ceased to have any reason for existence.   We need the voice of
the Lord—great, noble, resonant, musical ; a majestic voice—to
speak to us some doctrine the reception of which will give us
distinctiveness and therefore holy influence.

What can be more rational than the basis of the doctrine which
the Lord thus declares ?   What is it when put into other than
distinctively religious words ?   It is simply that mind is greater
than matter.   " If ye had faith "—a high mental condition, a new
spiritual consciousness, the faculty which lays hold upon God—
you could uproot mountains, and transfer forests to the midst of
the sea ; you could give eyes to the blind, you could wake the
dead from their undreaming sleep.   Thus divested of theological
colour and prejudice, we come face to face with a new philosophy,
namely, that mind in its spiritual fire, in its conscious dominance,
is greater than all things we denominate material.   Yet we have
put our necks under these things, and have accepted the yoke of
a humiliating bondage.   We who ought to have played with the
laws of nature have lassoed ourselves with them, and asked what
they were going to do next.   We have lived inverted lives, we

have given away our heritage, and have not received even a mess
of pottage in return. Is it possible that we have not faith as a
grain of mustard seed? Does that refer to quantity or to quality?
In the first instance evidently to quantity, for the apostle said in
the preceding verse, "Lord, increase our faith": give us more
faith;—and the Lord said, "If ye had faith as a grain of mustard
seed," which is the smallest among seeds, ye should work
miracles with it. Yet, in the next place, it may be a question of
quality; for, though the mustard seed is the least among seeds,
yet when it is grown it becomes an exceeding great tree, and the
birds of the air lodge in its branches. So with this Christian
faith: though quantitatively small, yet in its quality it is vital,
expansive, always ascending into largeness, fruitfulness, hospitality. We are not called upon to ask for a little faith, small as
a grain of mustard seed, but we are called upon to ask for the
mustard-seed-like faith, that being planted will not die, but will
rise and grow and strengthen, and be a church for the singing
birds. It ought to be possible to receive from our Father in
heaven direct guidance as to all the practical affairs of life.
Observe the expression "direct guidance," not some hazy,
cloudy, impalpable impression. Otherwise history is living
backwards. We have less communion with God than the old
prophets had; where they heard the word of the Lord we simply
catch an impression which we translate according to our uppermost instinct or our most recent prejudice. Let the Church lay
down this doctrine: It is possible to receive from our Father
in heaven direct guidance in all the practical affairs of life; then
the Church has a distinct position to occupy. Those who do not
belong to the Church admit an intellectual action in life; they
speak of having impressions, convictions, and refer with great
confidence to the action of instinct and the play of reason: it is
only after that we must look for the beginning of Christian faith,
and the distinctiveness of spiritual action and reliance. If we
pass through all the tragedy of Calvary merely to accept the
nostrums and the dogmas of old paganisms, or current rationalities,
we have squandered our strength, and by elaborating our circumlocution we have lost time and pith and quality.

We must, perhaps with a ruthless hand, clear the ground of

certain misconceptions. For example, this doctrine will not admit the proposition of frivolous inquiries. "Thou shalt not tempt the Lord thy God." The Lord will not listen to inquiries that are not burning with sincerity, and that do not relate to the very centre and dignity of life. Nor will this doctrine for one moment tolerate presumptuous inquiries, as to what shall happen on the morrow, or as to who shall live or die ten years hence, or what is the mystery of the universe. "The secret things belong unto the Lord our God; but those things which are revealed belong unto us and to our children for ever, that we may do all the words of this law." God will not allow violation of boundaries, trespass of limitations, which are good for us as little children, as lives trained on a cloudy day to aspire after forgiveness and immortality. Nor will the doctrine for one instant tolerate prejudiced inquiries. For example, a man might come saying, that he knows in his heart what he will do, whatever the divine answer may be supposed to be. A man so coming will be disappointed; his inquiry will be regarded as an impiety and will be disallowed. How difficult it is to get rid of prejudice in our inquiries, and even in our prayers! We pray for certain events, but we spoil our prayer by a bias; we want them, but not for the right reason; we suggest certain possibilities to the Lord, but he knows by the reading of our heart that we do not want those possibilities to transpire, but that we are really craving for another set of possibilities and facts. To no such inquiries will the Lord respond. Nor will he answer those who turn evident duties into moral perplexities and spiritual problems. When things are plainly revealed there is no need to pray about them or to inquire concerning them. No man need pray saying, Lord, send me an answer to this inquiry : shall I pay my debts? shall I forgive my penitent enemies? shall I continue in Christian worship and spiritual aspiration? shall I really love my neighbour as myself?—questions that have no real point, no sacrifice in the heart of them, no Calvary at any point of their statement. Thus we lay down limitations, and within those limitations I do not hesitate to propound the doctrine that to an honest and true heart there should be no difficulty whatever in ascertaining the right course, in business, in enterprise, or in any practical department of life. If you have the childlike, sincere, loving heart, you can have an answer to-morrow as to whether you should take up that venture or not: but if you want to take up the venture, and then make a mock of prayer for heavenly guidance, you will have no reply, or God will make a fool of you. "He taketh the wise in their own craftiness." What is your heart? Is it childlike, obedient, docile, without a thought, a prejudice, a bias? Then you can have an answer direct from heaven as to whether you ought to take up that new business, enter into that new enterprise, accept that glittering offer. When the Church lays down this doctrine, and lives it, the Church will have a distinct function in society; but at present the Church is in danger of having nothing to do but repeat its old ceremonies, its old dogmas, its old propositions, every pulse of life having gone out of them, and nothing being left but a dead form of dead words. All men cannot, it may be, attain this supremacy of faith. But the men who have attained it should be the ministers and the prophets of their age. Men should hasten to them for guidance and direction: but they should come in a spirit of docility and faith. Men who can ask God for us are the greatest ministers of the time: no honour too great for them, no tribute too costly. We pay musicians for music, and chaplains for prayers, and preachers for sermons: what should be given to the man who can guide us in the practical affairs of life?

How will the answer come? I cannot tell. What will be the process through which the divine being will communicate with the suppliant soul? I do not know. By mental impressions, by a series of events following each other in a certain order, by uncalculated and unconscious coincidences, by some definite physical action, or in some way that cannot be mistaken for a merely human sensation or event. The answer will be according to the sincerity of the inquirer. Bad faith on the part of the inquirer will receive nothing of the Lord. The Lord will even deceive the prophet himself, and will lead the foolish or selfish inquirer astray. "I will set my face against that man, and will make him a sign and a proverb, and I will cut him off from the midst of my people; and ye shall know that I am the Lord. And if the prophet be deceived when he hath spoken a thing,

---

I the Lord have deceived that prophet, and I will stretch out my hand upon him, and will destroy him from the midst of my people Israel." And the prophet himself may have his security endangered by the wickedness of the wicked applicant. I have never hesitated to act upon this doctrine in my own life, and it has never led me astray. I have risked everything upon it. To the sight of men I have in one or two instances or more played the fool that I might magnify faith in God. The answer may not always justify itself by immediate results : God takes time for the declaration of his economies and inspirations. I have sat down the day after committing myself thus to God, and cried like a disappointed child, and have said aloud, Surely in this case my faith has been misplaced, or God has trifled with me. But in another day, or month, or year, a vision has glorified the whole heaven, and all doubt has been dispersed, and they who mocked me as a foolish man have come round to offer their tribute too late, and have even then sought to magnify a man's sagacity above the inspiration of God. Do you feel that you cannot rise to this elevation of faith ? Then do not attempt it. Does some tempter say to you, "after all—" Then you are in the tempter's hands, and do not contract the guilt of venturing to speak to spiritual men on spiritual subjects. You have no right to use such language ; it is a currency unknown in your world.

Might not false prophets arise ? Certainly. What then ? If you cannot keep false prophets down, do what you may; you may lay down the doctrine. You fear there will be men who will scoff at it, or misappropriate it, or pervert it, or degrade it ? Here is a man who has given up all commercial life because he once knew an individual who attempted to pass a bad half-crown : how noble he looks, how lofty in reason ! He had his ground for retiring from the world ; nothing we may say can persuade him to return to commercial usages. Here is another man who has given up all friendship and all society because he once proved a man to be a hypocrite. Now he never speaks—now he simply waits for extinction. If he thinks, it is after this fashion, namely : Friendship may beget hypocrisy ; men may presume upon it, men may misuse it, may degrade it into selfish and mischievous perversions : therefore I have ceased to have anything to do

with the culture of friendly relations.   Here is a noble soul who
has retired to a hermitage unknown to every human being
because he found self-seekers in politics.   He could not bear it—
he has gone! We must not therefore be afraid of a doctrine
simply because false prophets would arise to trade upon it,
because the element of betting, and gambling, and speculation
might be introduced into it.   What we are in search of is sound,
true, spiritual doctrine.

If the Lord Jesus Christ has not taught some such doctrine
as we are now attempting to state, he has taught nothing.
Therefore I see no scriptural argument against faith-healing.
I have never seen any healing by faith, but to my knowledge
there is not a single verse in all the Bible which forbids that
the prayer of faith will heal the sick.   Let us admit that.   I do
not see any scriptural argument against the possibility of mind
communicating with mind, spirit holding sacred relations with
spirit : are they not all ministering spirits, sent forth to minister
for them who shall be heirs of salvation ?   The angel of the Lord
encompasseth round about them that love him.   Surely there
are more passages of Scripture that would seem to indicate
the possibility of spiritual communion than would seem to dis-
allow that possibility.   I see no scriptural argument against
personal inspiration.   God surely does not live backwardly,
going from much to less, and from less to nothing.   The other
course of revelation and providence would seem to be more in
harmony with what we know of human consciousness, and
human history, and divine revelation.   The Spirit of God was
promised to the Church, and was promised for the express
purpose of leading the Church into all truth ; men were told
not to think about what they should say when they were brought
before human tribunals for faith's sake,—as if the Lord had said,
You will not be convicted or condemned on the ground of cleverness, or on account of faculty, intellectual inventiveness or
personal eloquence.   All these things have nothing to do with
the case ; in the hour of your agony you shall have an answer
which cannot be finally gainsaid.   This is the upper life ; this
is the life of faith.   I see greater danger in the discouragement
of faith than in its stimulus and even exaggeration.   Do not

imagine that we escape all danger by disallowing the possibility
of communing with God, in the sense of receiving from above
direct answers to direct inquiries.   Do not suppose that we live
a noble life by saying to young and ardent hearts : Do not expect
answers from God of a direct and pertinent kind, but construe
events, look at the outlines of Providence as they are indicated
in the history of the current day.   There is a danger in all such
discouragement of faith, more danger than in the doctrine which
says, Increase your faith ; distrust your senses; be sure that
your reason cannot comprehend the whole economy and meaning
of things.   But may not that end in fanaticism ?   Certainly.
Still, what does that prove ?   If it prove anything it proves too
much, and by proving too much it proves nothing.   I contend that
the sound reason points to the culture of faith, and encourages that
marvellous plunge which a man takes when he says, My reason
can do no more for me, my senses cannot go one stride further :
now, my God, I leap !   Take me : leave me not, O thou great
Jehovah !   To the world that is insanity, but the world never
understood faith.

Let no man imagine that this gift is dissociated from obedience.
It is not a solitary gift, it is not an eccentricity, it is not given
to one man and withheld from another by any merely arbitrary
arrangement or purpose.   There is a distribution of functions and
gifts in the Church ; Christ gave some, apostles; and some,
prophets ; and some, evangelists ; and some, pastors and teachers.
You do not find all these specialities consummated and expressed
in one ministry.   To one man Christ gave the keys.   The man
who really holds this trust will be most modest, most faithful,
most consciously dependent upon God.   The high office to which
this doctrine points is, let us repeat, not open to gamblers,
speculators, curiosity-mongers, and fortune-tellers.   The argument that such people would abuse it, let us further repeat,
proves nothing by proving too much : for what holy office or
sacred trust have not such people abused ?   They have prostituted every natural instinct, they have broken every honourable
compact,—nay, they have sacrificed their children unto devils.
Not for fear of them, therefore, must Christians either lower
their flag or shade their light.

Chapter xviii. 24.

"How hardly shall they that have riches enter into the kingdom of God."

THE DANGER OF RICHES.

IS it easy then for poor people to enter into the kingdom of God? Jesus Christ does not say so. It is always difficult to enter into the kingdom of heaven. It is not entered by wealth, nor is it entered by poverty; for wealth and poverty are incidental and external circumstances. Let us fix our attention upon the fact that this was probably the first rich applicant at the door of the kingdom of Christ. There have been many since; familiarity may have made some processes in their external relations easy enough: but this young man was in all probability the first rich applicant. Did he think he would add something to what he already had? Was the kingdom of God, or, as he termed it, eternal life, a kind of annexe to the property which he already had? and did he suppose that he might on the whole as well have eternal life as not? it would cost nothing, it would entail no heavy responsibility; it might invest the young man himself with the dignity of novel thought and speculative enterprise, and give a kind of sparkling accent to his general situation. We cannot enter into the reasoning of the young man's mind; we should be foolish to condemn the young man: Jesus Christ loved him, was struck either by his personal beauty, or by his modesty, or by something bewitching in his geniality; he looked upon him as the young man had never been looked upon before, and loved him. If he could have saved him he would; if he could have made the gate of the kingdom a little wider he would: but the kingdom has its laws. Jesus Christ represented those laws, obeyed them, and insisted upon them, and therefore the comeliest young man of to-day would not be allowed to take in with him all his burden.

It was a critical moment for Jesus Christ himself. He had to set precedents in his own Church, he had to create examples by which all succeeding Christian ages and Christian institutions should regulate their policy. Was it no temptation to the Lord ? Was it no temptation to attach a millionaire to the cause that elicited social contempt? Might not one rich man act as a decoy and bring a thousand other rich men, and so might not a fashion be created ? There can be no fashion in crucifixion. Calvary can never be popular. The Cross can never be a custom of the day. That is the spirit of Christianity, these are the conditions upon which alone eternal life can be realised ; we do not enter by money, by wit, by genius, learning, pedigree, or aught that is incidental and external : only by way of the Cross do men pass into the kingdom. The disciples were troubled ; they thought that an opportunity had been lost ; they started the proposition that if this were to be the policy of the Master, salvation was simply impossible. How could the kingdom get on without such people as this young man ? " Who, then, can be saved ? "

But Jesus Christ explained the whole occasion by saying, " them that trust in riches." There is no harm in riches themselves, they may be instruments of the greatest possible good, in right hands they are well administered, and the world is better for a Christian administration of wealth. The Lord is not abusing riches or condemning riches ; he is pointing out that men may trust in riches, men may idolise their own wealth, their own possessions, and may be unwilling to take the step between the material and the spiritual. He did not say it was impossible, he said it was "hard." There was a touch of agony in the process ; there was a conscious wrench in making the change—Ye must be born again—and admission into the greater kingdoms, all morning and all summer as they are, must be an admission through the gate of pain. Jesus Christ often calls us to do the impossible that he may stimulate us to do the difficult. Christianity is the great impossibility of the world. In all its higher ranges it is not within our reach ; but its loftiness is an encouragement to those who otherwise would succumb to difficulty, and yield the field to the enemy. Jesus Christ calls us to climb the clouds in the air that he may tempt us a little way up the solid hill.

Christianity will never be easy ; it can never be thrown in with
something else ; it is not a supplement, it is the integral and
dominating quantity.   There are those who wear their Christianity as they wear their garments newly bought and much
valued for the moment : but Christianity is not to be worn, it is
a robe of the heart, it is the clothing of the soul.   Hence Jesus
Christ calls us to do things that mortal man cannot do, in order
that we may be stirred to nobler aspiration and purpose.   No
man, being smitten on the one cheek, can turn the other also ;
yet we could not do without that impossibility in the divine
vocation.   It makes our best endeavours look poor ; it humbles
our virtue into prayer   The spirit, not the letter, reaches the
discipline of Christ in the soul.

Nor must we think of riches as referring to mere money.
There are riches of many kinds—centres of pride, centres of
vanity, centres of self-trust and idolatry, and the whole fabric
must be shaken to its base, and torn up by its foundations before
Christ can begin to build.   There are those who are proud of
things they have no concern in.   You remember the titled lady,
whose name we have ungratefully forgotten, who called upon a
distinguished artist, and on being shown into a drawing-room was
perfectly wonderstruck.   When the painter appeared the lady
said, "I am seeking Thrift, the painter."   "Well," said the
gentleman, "that is my name."   And looking round at the beauty
of the place, she said, "Is this your house ? "   "Yes," he said.
She thought a painter lived in a garret, and had a portmanteau for
a wardrobe and a three-cornered cupboard for a larder.   A
painter with all these nick-nacks and curios and little touches of
refinement about him—what right had a painter to such environment ?—as if a painter were not a greater man than a king
that sits upon a throne he never worked for and never deserved !
People are very fond of talking about the aristocracy of the body :
they never know that there is a spiritual aristocracy, that many
a man who has no money and no title and no pedigree that can
be written down in plain ink, is related to Aristotle, and traces
his progeny beyond the Plantagenets even to the great thinkers
that have ruled the world by the energy and splendour of their
genius.   All this rubbish must be cleared out of the way

before spirit can rule, and genius be invested with its divinest influence.

Notice the deceitfulness of all kinds of riches. Riches may corrupt the very simplest of you—take care ! How many men have we seen go to the gallows and hang themselves just through the deceitfulness of riches ! How delightful it would be to trace the life of many a man and see how he died in the bank—that great mortuary. The man began simply, and was a right genial soul ; he brought with him morning light and fresh air wherever he came, and as to cases of poverty his hand knew the way to his pocket so well that he could find that pocket in the dark ; as for religious services he was there before the door was open ; he never thought the Sabbath too long, he loved the sanctuary, and was impatient to be there ; he even went to the week evening service, but then he was only a working man, and only working men should go out in the night air—what does it matter about a few working men being killed off by the east wind ! The man whose course we are tracing doubled his income and multiplied it by five, and then doubled it again, and then found that he must give up the prayer meeting. Certainly ! Then he proceeded to double his income again, and then he gave up the Sunday service—there was a draught near where he sat, or there was some person in the third pew from his, the appearance of whom he could not bear. How dainty my lord is becoming ! Oh, what a nostril he has for evil savours ! He will leave altogether presently. He will not abruptly leave : he will simply not come back again, which really amounts to the same thing. He will attend in the morning, and congratulate the poor miserable preacher on the brevity of the service. Did he mean to do this when he began to get a little wealthier ? Not he. Is he the same man he used to be ? No. Is he nearer Christ ? He is universes away from the Cross. He is killed by wealth, trusted in, misunderstood, misapplied. It is not the wealth that has ruined him, but his misconception of the possible uses of wealth ; he might have been a leader of the Church.

How is it that Jesus Christ does not attract more poor people to his Church ? Because the Church has ceased in some degree

to be Jesus Christ's at all. Jesus Christ is as fond of the weak
and the poor and the blind and the halt as he ever was ; he is
just as tender and beneficent to lepers as he ever was in his
earthly ministry ; but we have changed the whole situation : now
the masses go to the socialists, and the classes go to scientists,
and they can treat them better than we can do. The Church
has lost its Lord. They have taken away my Lord, and I know
not where they have laid him. But was not Jesus Christ crucified in the days of his flesh ? Yes, and he would be crucified
if he came back again ; the first thing we should do with the
Christ of God would be to stone him and then to slay him. It
must be so : this is the necessary treatment of the infinite by the
finite, the pure by the impure, the ineffably holy by the unspeakably corrupt. There are those who in the midst of the greatest
splendour remember the days of their poverty. Blessed be God
for such men, so sweet of soul, so unpresumptuous, so ready
to help. The more wealth they have the better am I pleased,
because the better is the world, the better is the Church provided
for. " I want," said the late Emperor of Germany, the last but
one, the great William, " I want a lamp such as so-and-so has "—
naming some distinguished member of the court. A lamp was
provided according to the very pattern, but his majesty complained on returning to his study after withdrawment that he
could not bear the savour of the room, the lamp was emitting
smoke, and it was altogether intolerable. One of the secondary
servants knew the reason, but dare not name it to his majesty ;
one of the higher servants learned the cause and brought it under
his majesty's attention—" It is because your majesty turns down
the light when you leave the study, that occasions the emission
of smoke and vapour, and if you will cease to do that, all will be
well." " Ah," said the good old patriot of his nation, " I know
how that is ; I learned that in the days of our poverty : after the
battle of Jena we were very poor, and my mother never allowed
us to leave a room at night without turning down the light, and I
continue to turn down the light in memory of my mother." A
beautiful economy ! a tender domestic story that ! Here is a man
who could have had a thousand lamps, and yet in memory of the
days of his poverty, when his mother taught him the uses of
money, he kept turning down the light, saying, " Sacred to the

memory of my mother." There are men to-day who are practically doing the same thing :—In memory of the days when we struggled, here is our gift; in memory of the time when we had nothing but hard work to do, here is a token of goodwill to those who are carrying heavy burdens up steep hills. The Lord multiply your wealth a thousandfold ; you are the trustees of God, you are the stewards of heaven.

With regard to the whole surrounding of the Church, we should lose heart altogether if we did not hold on to Christ himself. We must come back to the living Lord. If any man were to ask me, as I have recently been asked, to discuss the present position and action of Christianity, I should decline to debate because the man would silence me ; I should have no answer to his poignant eloquence. If I endeavoured as a special pleader to make a show on the other side, my own soul would blush for shame whilst I heard my own hollow words and pleas. Because Christianity is now ecclesiasticised, it is an ecclesiastical institution, and I will not defend it. Because Christianity is now a formulated creed, the separate clauses of which are all duly and arithmetically enumerated ; and the clauses run into tens and twenties, and only trained intellects and self-deceived metaphysicians can even begin to understand the unintelligible farrago. Because Christianity is now turned to the uses of selfishness I will not defend it. I have challenges from men of various grades, and I decline them one and all, because the challenges are all directed to a vindication of ecclesiasticisms, credal formularies, controversial dogmas, and I renounce them all. If any man will discuss with me the Christ of God, his personality, his claims, his propositions, his life, his priesthood, the Lord that has delivered me all my lifetime will deliver me from any assailant who would lay violent hands on the Son of God ; there I will debate and contend vehemently and zealously, because I know the Saviour Christ to be the one Saviour of the world, the one Saviour of my sinning soul—" His blood can make the foulest clean, his blood availed for me." Ecclesiasticisms, institutions based upon narrow conceptions, controversial propositions, man-made creeds, are all doomed. Blessed be God ! I will be present if I can when a great bonfire is made of the whole of them, and if anybody wants any quarter of that great pile lighted I shall be willing to lend both hands on the occasion. You can burn down everything but the Cross. That cannot be burned : it is the same yesterday, to-day, and for ever : grim, bleak, bare symbol of agony, type of suffering, consummation of woe. And yet it is breaking out like a tree in the springtime, there are little glints of green, forthputtings of power. There is every assurance that the Cross will be the tree of life, the most beautiful tree in the gardens of the universe, every leaf designed to heal the wounds of the heart.

You cannot bring your riches with you into the kingdom, if you are going to trust in them : if you are going to offer them to Christ and sanctify them to his use, bring them all. You cannot bring your intellectual pride with you : if you are going to consecrate your intellect to the study of the profoundest mysteries, if you are going to cultivate a childlike spirit, if the greater the genius the greater the modesty, bring it all. You can bring with you nothing of the nature of patronage to Christ. It is because he has so little he has so much : because he is so weak he is so strong. You cannot compliment him : he lies beyond the range of eulogy : we reach him by his own way of sacrifice, self-immolation, transformation,—a great mystery outside of words and all their crafty uses, but a blessed conscious spiritual experience. Blessed are those to whom that experience is a reality.

"He asked what it meant."

INQUIRY INTO MEANINGS.

THE speaker was a blind man. He sat by the wayside begging. Though he was a blind man, he had the use of other faculties. Let us be just to facts, and cognisant of the law of compensation. " Hearing a multitude pass by "—then he was not deaf. To be deaf is worst of all. There is nothing to compare with deafness. So the Bible says in all its analogies and teachings. The deaf heart, the deaf soul, the deaf devil,—these are given as instances of the horribleness of deafness. This man was not deaf, he heard the multitude pass by. " And he cried, saying "—then he was not dumb. If we really search into the case of men who are marked by some special disadvantage or infirmity, how many instances of alleviation shall we find ! Yet these go for nothing in the fluency of our description. We make much of this man being blind ; we say nothing of the fact that he was neither deaf nor dumb ; that he had an obstinate and determined will of his own ; and that all the multitude passing by could not stifle his prayer. We forget much.

" He asked what it meant." We can at least do this. In asking a question we begin a hopeful experience. The difficulty Christianity has to contend with is that people do not sufficiently ask what it means ; they let the procession of miracles pass on and do not say, What is the significance of all that is proceeding round about us ? We are bound to ask what these things mean. No man can be just to his own intelligence who does not interrogate the history of Christianity, and insist upon definite replies. Men can live without intelligence, they can elect to be ignoramuses, they can go a step further down and be absolute fools ; but no man can be just to his intelligence who does not ask what Christianity means ? Christians in their turn are bound to ask what Buddhism means, what Mohammedanism means, what idolatry means ; Christians ought to study the philosophy of history, and to know everything that can be known within the region of fact. Here is a marvellous thing, that one name should have become uppermost, a ruling dominant name, that the centuries cannot put down—nay, that the centuries lift to a higher elevation age after age. Here is a name, a person, an actor on the stage of history, confessedly unrivalled in his influence and power, exercising a wondrous charm : what does it mean ? However he came into the world, he is in it, and he is the most conspicuous fact in all its history. Say he came in by the historical gate—how did he get in ? Why have not others come in of equal magnitude and quality ? Why should there be only one man ? why should he be peerless ? Say he came in by the dream gate. Still, here he is; if he was dreamed, he is, if possible, more wonderful than he is in his historical relations. Here is a dream that has fascinated the ages, over-turned thrones, established dynasties, ruled policies, made thrones bow down in homage. Who dreamed this dream ? What is his name ? Did he ever dream again ? These inquiries enable us to reassert the statement that no man can be just to his own intelligence who does not seriously ask and faithfully pursue the inquiry, What does this thing mean ? Here is a name that has tamed tigers and made them gentle as lambs; here is a power that has turned the poor man's little house into a gate opening towards heaven; here is a power that has liberated slaves, sustained the cause of the poor and needy, never been silent in the face of oppression. What does it mean ? How did it get amongst the agencies that constitute human history ? Tell us about it. When men ask questions like these they begin, let us repeat, a hopeful experience. Great questions will always elicit great replies.

There is another side to this circumstance. When any man asks what it means, there should be some other man standing close to him who can answer. That may be a serious deficiency in the Church,—qualified men, persons who can speak with the authority of experience, and not with the authority of office, people who can definitely say, We will tell you what he has done for us, and what he has done for us he will do for you, he loves to do it; come nearer to us, and we will tell you all the story of wisdom and love as we ourselves have been enabled to receive and understand it. That is the function of the Church. The Church has a great teaching ministry to discharge. Do we cultivate and encourage the spirit of inquiry. Do we so deport ourselves that men feel they may venture to ask us serious questions? It is well that the Church should wear its robe of humility and speak of its ignorance. But the Church ought, on the other hand, to have some definite message to deliver, the Church ought to be able to answer certain great questions. It will be no sign of pride, but a distinct proof of faithfulness, when the Church says, Whatever I can tell you I am willing to communicate. Nor should the Church be dumb until she can be eloquent. There is a halting-place between silence and noblest utterance: there is the point of serious attempt; there is the point of being willing to say how much divine wisdom has been acquired : and so wondrous is the law of spiritual communication that when we begin to speak we begin to find somewhat to say, if so be we are inspired by the spirit of earnestness, and are deeply solicitous about the eternal welfare of the people who have asked us questions. It will be vain, and even worse than vain, it will be simple and most culpable hypocrisy, to say that we will not tell what we do know until we know more. What should we say of a man who refused to give bread to the hungry until he has multiplied his own loaves by a hundred? Give what you have; start where you can; speak the one little sentence that is addressed to you in all your presently-acquired treasures of the kingdom of heaven. We want a communicative Church as well as a communicative ministry. Inquiries are handed on to the minister. That might be right if the inquirers wanted to know something technical, recondite, pedantic, if they wanted a literary schoolmaster, a veritable pedagogue ; but they want encouragement, sympathy, and they will feel that sympathy all the more tenderly if spoken to them on an obvious level which is not unattainable by themselves. All this reference to ministers for answers to questions is superstitious, popish, and infinitely mischievous; in the Christian kingdom every man is a priest, a minister, a teacher sent from God.

Those who are able to answer should not be content to rebuke inquirers. We read in this connection, "And they which went before rebuked him, that he should hold his peace." We are not to encourage the spirit of rebuke. We cannot impoverish Christ, therefore we need not rebuke appellants and suppliants; they can appeal and supplicate and cry and desire, and the more he gives the more he will have remaining in his power. The Church has always been delighted to rebuke men. The more highly organised the church the more has it been characterised by the rebukeful spirit. A highly organised church—be it Popish, Episcopalian, or Congregational—always means authority, dictation, standard of orthodoxy, repulsion by authority. All this need not be put down by force, because all time, all progress, all spiritual ministries are on the other side. The rebukeful spirit must go down, and the spirit of sympathy must take its place, and exercise a blessed function in reference to the education and progress of mankind. The Church—by which I mean any highly organised and elaborated Church—has always stood in the way of progress, has been the mother of superstition, has been the occasion of infinite mischief. The whole history of progress has run away from the lines of the Church. When we say the lines of the Church we take liberties with imagination, for the Church has no lines. In speaking thus of the Church we are not speaking of any particular church, but of the organisation which for the time being represents the supreme spiritual authority of the day, by what name soever it may be described and defined.

There was a time when it was pronounced a heresy to declare the existence of the Antipodes. To us this is incredible, but we must not throw away the history of our own race. There was a time when a man could have been imprisoned for declaring that the earth moved. A great monk arose in Alexandria, by name Cosmas, who was charged as it were by the Church to refute the awful and soul-destroying doctrine of the Antipodes. He devoted the remainder of a long and laborious lifetime to the refutation of the heresy. The result of his thought and labour was that he declared the earth to be a parallelogram, whose length is twice its breadth, that the sky is glued round its sides, and the sun and moon and stars are the decoration of its firmament; and to say anything contrary to this was to be anti-Christian, to be in a distressing spiritual condition. If a man arose to say anything to the contrary he was rebuked, that he should hold his peace. Now men go to the Antipodes as a matter of course. Cosmas said the Bible speaks of "the face of the whole earth"; so how can it have anything on the other side of it? He was a literalist, and the letter-mongers have nearly ruined the whole cause of Christianity, and would have done so if it had not been divine. That Christianity has survived the patronage of its friends is the culminating proof of the divinity of its origin. We must therefore beware of this spirit of rebuke, inasmuch as we have history to guide us in reference to its action. When men arose to declare on the evidence of geology that death was known hundreds and thousands of ages ago, the Church rebuked them, that they should hold their peace. Now every child knows that death has been in the world from the beginning, that the cemetery is the oldest of its institutions, or may at least rank amid the most venerable of its antiquities. Poor Church, authoritative empurpled Church! holding a sceptre of its own cutting and its own gilding, which has always been shouldered out of the way by men, for whom God be praised. Hence our great object should be to shatter all great organisations of a spiritual kind; all poperies and hierarchies and man-made mechanisms, and to simplify Christian relations to the utmost, and cultivate a spirit of reverent freedom, so that every man shall tell every other man, as opportunity may arise, what he has heard in his own tongue concerning the wonderful works of God. The disciples would seem to speak with authority. Who dare contravene the dictum of a disciple? The blind man dared. If he had not been blind he would not have dared; but conscious need defies the Church. Said the blind man in effect—I am blind, and this man can give me my sight; stand back and let me speak to him for myself. This is the individuality we ought to encourage—no prayer by proxy, no choking of supplication by official authority, but each heart, conscious of its own need, coming to Christ to tell its own tale.

When men get the right answer they should offer the right petition. When the blind man was told that Jesus of Nazareth passeth by he got the right answer, and having got it, he offered the right petition: "Jesus, thou Son of David, have mercy on me." This is the point we must all begin at. This is evidently true. We could not amend the terms, we could add nothing to the dignity of the spirit, we could increase by no instalment or increment how small soever the dignity of this man's position— have mercy ! The reason we have not received answers to many prayers is that we did not begin at the beginning. Many persons begin their prayers at the wrong end; they do not take up the sequence of things. There is no logic in the progression of their sentiments and desires : we must begin by crying for mercy. The publican said, "God be merciful to me a sinner." The suppliant came to him saying, "Lord, have mercy upon my child." Whoever begins there begins at the only right point. We do not come to discuss questions of law and righteousness, of ordinance and institute, of sovereignty and destiny with God, we come to ask for mercy ; having obtained mercy, we advance, we grow, and our prayers enlarge, until they become reverently familiar communions with God, long fellowships, talks that take up all the sunlight, and that Christ himself must needs conclude by coming into the house and breaking for us our bread. Are there any who are standing outside, saying that they have many questions to ask Jesus Christ before they will ask him to heal them ? He will not answer; he has no time ; earnestness cannot dally; the king's business requireth haste. You could retain him for ages in your own house if your earnestness could last so long; he will never go so long as your simplicity and sincerity have any question to ask : but to discuss with us on equal terms, to make Christianity a kind of schoolmaster revelation, he will never consent,—it is a flash of light, it is a dawning day, it is a spirit whispering in the soul, an infinite subtlety operating upon every point of life, and working a miracle without name or limit.

Having got the right answer, men should adopt the right course. What did the blind man do? "And immediately he received his sight, and followed him." There are many who have received sight, and have gone the other road. "Were there not ten cleansed? but where are the nine? There are not found that returned to give glory to God, save this stranger." Ingratitude is easily learned; if it is a fine art we seem in many instances to be to the manner born. We have received all that men could give us, and have rewarded them with tepid applause or discriminating criticism: enthusiasm, devotion, avowal of indebtedness, who can find? Yet when found how precious are they, how they multiply life and increase influence, and establish the teacher in a kind of natural and holy authority. Who will be the last man to leave that travelling Christ? The man whose sight was restored. He will get to the front presently. He has not received his eyesight that he might not make use of it. This man intends to be on the front line presently. We have seen what force he had in blindness—his energy has not been destroyed by his restoration. Do we not make mistakes regarding Christian influence in this way? A man is converted, and henceforth we hear nothing more about him. That would not be conversion, that would be extinction. A man has been a great singer in the tavern, in the saloon, in the family circle; his voice has been praised for richness and sweetness of tone: he has been converted, and now he sits in the church, and no one ever hears his voice. That is not conversion, that is annihilation. The man who was blessed with restored sight was a man who put the church down when he wanted his eyesight, and he will put down any church that wants to keep him from his right place. What we want is not so much further instruction but simple gratitude. We do not go too far in our statement in saying that gratitude will outlast all mere information, all external training, and will be heard at the very end glorifying God. How can a man go from Christ who has received his sight? This would seem to be absolutely impossible. Other men may go who have only received external gifts, such as bread for passing hunger, water because of immediate thirst; these things may be forgotten: but restored sight! why, every star that glittered, every flower that bloomed, every bird that flew in the air would be a rebuke and a reproach if such a man turned away from Christ—yea, he could not have seen the way to go but for the very sight which he received from the Son of God. Let us take care how we turn our Christian instruction to immoral uses. Let us beware, we who learned to read in the Sunday School, lest we turn our power of reading to the service of the devil. Christianity found us when no other agency cared about our life; elicited our interest, fascinated our imagination, evoked our confidence, and made us men. The question now is, Shall we, having been thus discovered, re-created, inspired,—shall we turn our back upon our Creator and Inspirer, and spend the treasures of his benevolence at the counter of the devil?

Blessings bestowed on others should make Christians joyful and grateful. " And all the people, when they saw it, gave praise unto God." This is the spirit of festival. If we were to continue our hymn as long as we could discover any instances of divine interposition, our psalm would never cease. Yet this is precisely what we are called upon to do. The missionary comes into the church in breathless haste and says an island has been purged of its idolatry, a house of prayer has been set up there, and the people are eagerly flocking into it, and are crying mightily for light and love from heaven. Such a speech ought to fire the enthusiasm of the mother country from whose shores the missionary went forth. To-day they are but an insignificant minority who care anything as to what any missionary may declare. You can empty almost any church by putting a missionary in the pulpit to tell his tale of Christian triumph. When we hear of benevolent institutions being founded, we should sing another hymn of praise; when we hear that any one solitary heart has been made glad by news from heaven, we should join the festival and increase the gratitude. We are involved in other engagements; we care for spectacles, demonstrations, great occasions: unhappily, we seldom care for the right thing. That a king is to be executed would excite all the civilised nations of the globe: that a man has been converted would excite the suspicion of the few people who cared anything concerning it. We are living upside down. We are availing ourselves of false standards and estimates of things. When the world is in the right course the things that are now highly esteemed will be of no repute, and when a little child begins to sing its first Christian hymn with the intelligence of tears the whole church will pray with holy joy.

Blind men should avail themselves of all the light they can

secure. But of what use is light to a blind man? None. But the question does not end with the blind man. We have read of a man who was travelling on a dark night, carrying a brightly shining lantern; we have read of some one meeting him, looking him in the face, and discovering that he was blind; we have further read of him inquiring of the man who carried the lantern, " Are you not blind?" and receiving an affirmative answer. "Why, then," said the astounded inquirer, "do you carry a lantern?" Said the blind man, "To prevent other people stumbling over me." A philosopher that as well as a blind man. He was protecting himself by carrying a light. As he could not see others coming, and others might not take heed of his blindness, there might be collision and loss; so the blind man carried the lantern. So it may be in many of our moral and spiritual relations. We should show what we are even if we are blind. We might prevent other people injuring us and injuring themselves by declaring in some way our blindness. The mischief is that some men who are blind declare that they see, and having declared that they are in the possession of sight they incur responsibility. If they had not said "We see," their sin would not have remained: " but," said Christ, "now ye say, We see; therefore your sin remaineth." God judges by facts, by limitations; he takes all things into account, and his mercy endureth for ever.

Chapter xix. 1—10.

"And Jesus entered and passed through Jericho. And, behold, there was a man named Zacchæus, which was the chief among the publicans, and he was rich. And he sought to see Jesus who he was; and could not for the press, because he was little of stature. And he ran before, and climbed up into a sycomore tree to see him: for he was to pass that way. And when Jesus came to the place, he looked up, and saw him, and said unto him, Zacchæus, make haste, and come down; for to-day I must abide at thy house. And he made haste, and came down, and received him joyfully. And when they saw it, they all murmured, saying, That he was gone to be guest with a man that is a sinner. And Zacchæus stood, and said unto the Lord; Behold, Lord, the half of my goods I give to the poor; and if I have taken any thing from any man by false accusation, I restore him fourfold. And Jesus said unto him, This day is salvation come to this house, forsomuch as he also is a son of Abraham. For the Son of man is come to seek and to save that which was lost."

JESUS CHRIST AND ZACCHÆUS.

YOU may build God out of cities, or you may throw open the city gates and bid him welcome with all reverence and thankfulness. You cannot build him out with common masonry. He can crumble our rocky walls to pieces, and drive the plough-share through the foundations of our fortresses; he can touch the mountains, and they will go up before him as the smoke of incense; wherever mere power is required, God can break us down by a stroke. How then, you will say, is it possible to build God out of the city? I answer, by corrupt institutions, by depraved laws, by tricks of trade, by knavery and fraud, by selfish dispositions and oppressive usages, by forgery, by unjust balances, by defective measures, by practical lying, by false-heartedness, it is possible to build God out of a city more thoroughly than he could be excluded by the most elaborate masonry. Ancient Jericho attempted to enclose herself within solid walls, but men appointed by God threw down all her boasted defences. Can anything resist the thunder of the march which is commanded by God? When men walk according to the divine order, when they step in harmony with the rhythm of the divine movement, they overturn the rocks, and cast the mountains into the sea. Yet, alas! there is a region in which Omnipotence itself is weakness : even a child can shut the door of its heart against God, and Almightiness may be defied by an evil will! Jericho was favoured of God in exceeding measure— bountifully supplied with water, having a tropical climate, her palm trees equalling the palms of Egypt, rich with fruits, spices, and perfumes, growing in abundance the sweet-smelling camphire and the balm of Gilead ; yet, while the beasts of the field, the dragons and the owls honoured the Most High, she departed from her Maker, and praised not the goodness of her Lord. She trusted in her walls, and confided in the strength of her arm, until God smote her by the breath of his mouth! Gladly do we come to the words before us, as marking a new era in the annals of Jericho. And Jesus is passing through our own city to-day ; and, busy as we are with the claims of daily life, we may see his beauty and learn his will.

"And, behold, there was a man named Zacchæus, which **was the** chief among the publicans, and he was rich " (ver. 2).

A whole paragraph devoted to the delineation of one man's life, whilst so many great subjects are hardly touched upon in the Christian Scriptures. Yet let us not complain of what looks to us like the capriciousness and incompleteness of divine revelation, for in these portrayals of individuals, we have not only the most practical aspects of the Christian faith, but we get nearer to God than would otherwise have been possible. When we see Jesus Christ face to face with an individual sinner, we see the whole scheme of redemption as it were in miniature ; and we have the advantage of concentration ; our minds are not distracted by the bewilderment which is occasioned by a vast scale of operation ; everything is brought to a point ; and to us is given the benefit of the conciseness of individuality. Does not one man require in his own experience the whole scheme of divine redemption ? Is it not with this as with the light, the atmosphere, and the whole mechanism of the world ? Were there but one man upon the globe, he would as much require the sun, the summer, the harvest, as do the millions who now exist upon it. We shall see God's love perhaps more vividly displayed, because more intensely concentrated, in the case of one man than when applied to the necessities of the whole world. Each man should have a paragraph of Christian history specially his own. Is your life to be found in Christian history? Can you point to any record of a personal interview with the Saviour? Blessed are you whose lives are part of a great unwritten Bible, which is continually before God.

"And he sought to see Jesus who he was; and could not for the press, because he was little of stature" (ver. 3).

Let me take out of this verse three words which set forth the highest object of human life; these three words are—"To see Jesus"! Zacchæus sought to see him through natural curiosity, yet such curiosity may be turned to the highest uses; Zacchæus sought only to see the Man, but in the end he saw the Saviour; he desired to see a wonder, and in the end he was made into a wonder himself. So it is evermore,—a man is made either infinitely better or infinitely worse by coming into contact with Jesus Christ; the Gospel kills or makes alive. This man found a difficulty in attempting to realise his wish. Is it not so with some of us who are listening to this story to-day? Zacchæus was little; every man is little somewhere. The signature of defect is upon every character; we cannot write a complete biography of any man without having to use this word little, in one relation or another. Men are truly little when they are little in spiritual force, in moral sympathy and tender-heartedness, in appreciation of objects that are noble, progressive, sublime. Any other littleness is but a trivial defect; this is a mortal blemish. Hear how the descriptive words go in the case of Zacchæus—chief, rich, little! It is possible for a man to read his life in this fashion, and to complain that it has been set on a descending scale; but it is also possible to reverse the order of these epithets, and so to get a more inspiring view of life. He will then say, not chief, rich, little, but little, rich, chief! Take care how you read your life! Some lives may be read thus— little, less, nothing! If we look at those who are higher than ourselves, we may become censorious critics of the divine way; but if we make ourselves familiar with those who are in the lowest positions of life, suffering pain, hunger, loneliness, we shall abound in grateful praises to the Giver of all good. Did Zacchæus give up his object because of the difficulty of the situation? Let us read :—

"And he ran before, and climbed up into a sycomore tree to see him: for he was to pass that way" (ver. 4).

He never would have been chief among the publicans and rich if he had succumbed to difficulties. His character was brought out by opposition. I contend that, whatever a man's disadvantages may be, he can see Jesus Christ if he so determine in his heart. There are men, now-a-days, who profess that they have endeavoured to see Jesus Christ, but have been kept back by the press of sects, sceptics, speculators, critics, commentators, and controversialists; but, in the face of an incident like this, the triviality of such pretence is made evident. I allow that there is a great press of the sort described; no doubt it is, more or less, a difficulty to urge one's way through the throng surrounding Jesus Christ, yet there is a sycomore tree up which we may climb if we are truly in earnest. Zacchæus was little, but he could run; Zacchæus was short of stature, but he could climb. How very shocking—how manifestly improper of one who was chief among the publicans and rich, to be seen running along the road and climbing up a tree! Such enthusiasm in pursuit of his object is in keeping with the whole character of the man. Are you willing, if need be, to go out of the so-called regular way to see the Saviour, or are you sacrificing your destiny to the tyrannous claims of conventionality? Then I exhort you to climb up any tree, to enter any church, from which you can more clearly see the face of the Redeemer. Break up your old associations, cast off your creeds and usages, and incur the censure of established proprieties, rather than not see the Friend of sinners. Incidents like this make me impatient of all the excuses which are urged in explanation of not accepting the salvation of Jesus Christ. Can we not do as Zacchæus did? What is the value of our earnestness, if it does not enable us to overcome difficulties? No excuse should detain us, except such as we can tell Jesus Christ himself. Remember that it is written, "Strait is the gate, and narrow is the way." The Saviour himself acknowledges the difficulty, yet he never says it is insurmountable, and never promises that it shall protect men from the consequences of unbelief. Oh, ye men who are exhausting yourselves in the pursuit of riches; ye who rise early and retire late, that you may increase your worldly substance; you that are prepared to make any sacrifice of strength and time, that you may compete successfully in the strife of scholarship; you that are prepared to encounter every form of suffering and incur any danger, that you may extend your knowledge of the world and your influence among men as legislators and economists, say not that you have been driven back from seeking Jesus Christ by some petty inconvenience or contemptible barrier! Sobriety is undoubtedly the snare of some men; they must needs take their first considerations from what is called prudence; and whilst they are deliberating whether it be proper to adopt some extraordinary method of attaining their object, the Saviour passes by without being seen. Better run the risk which comes of the intoxication of enthusiasm, than be rendered powerless by a benumbing conventionality. Zacchæus would never have been the man that he was, had he been incapable of enthusiasm; he would have succumbed to propriety, where he overcame by a noble passion.

"And when Jesus came to the place, he looked up, and saw him, and said unto him, Zacchæus, make haste, and come down; for to-day I must abide at thy house" (ver. 5).

Observe the development which is traced in this verse. Jesus Christ looked, saw, and said. It is possible to look without seeing; many men can look upon the throngs of the world without emotion; human history has to them no deep significance; in their eyes men are but customers, clients, patrons; the idea of immortality never mingles with their coarse thinking. On the other hand, it is possible both to look and to see; to the highest type of mind, the sight of a crowd brings sadness of heart; every man is seen to be a mystery—to be the bearer of untold sorrow—to be the distracted subject of many ambitions—to be weak through sin, and to be bearing the black seal of death; to such types of mind life becomes one long sigh, by reason of the wickedness which enfeebles and dehumanises the race. It is possible, however, both to look and to see, yet not to say. There is a want of moral courage, even where there is a deep appreciation of the necessities of the case. Many men will tell you, that when they have been brought into contact with men of extreme depravity, they have just been on the point of preaching the Gospel, yet they have forborne to speak the Word of life. When Christians look, and see, and say, there will go forth into the world such an evangelising commission as never yet sought the recovery of men. Have you ever spoken to one human creature about his personal salvation? You tell me you have looked upon your friend, and that you have seen the deepest want of his life, yet you have not delivered the message of God to his soul. Believe me, this is not friendship, and that there is a day coming on which you will feel that in neglecting these opportunities—you have risked your own salvation. Is it not noticeable, that Jesus Christ addressed Zacchæus by name? To the reverent mind, this circumstance justly suggests the omniscience of the Son of God. Did not the Lord say unto Moses, "I know thee by name"? We, too, are known in our individuality. If we have set ourselves in any position, ordinary or peculiar, for the purpose of seeing the Saviour, the All-seeing Eye is upon us, and our personal name is associated with the act. How did Zacchæus receive the word that was addressed to him? Did he hesitate? Did he excuse himself on the ground that he had been seeking to gratify merely a natural curiosity? Many persons take up positions of observation in the sanctuary, and when they are personally invited to active service on behalf of Jesus Christ, or closer communion with the Church, they instantly plead a merely general interest, and excuse themselves from consenting to the appeal on most trivial grounds. They turn the sanctuary into a convenience; they make use of the vantage-ground without any pledge of loyalty to the claims of Christ, and treat with coldness the invitations which might call their souls in a most fruitful and glorious development. How did Zacchæus act? Let us read :

"And he made haste, and came down, and received him joyfully" (ver. 6).

This is in striking harmony with all that we have seen of Zacchæus. The man who could run and climb was just the man to make haste in coming down, and to give a joyful answer to such an appeal. Men would be better if we spoke to them more kindly. Take high ground with a man, and you instantly put him on his own defence; speak to him in a conciliating tone, and you may gain audience of his very heart. Be sure, as Christian teachers, there is something in every man to which you can address yourselves with good effect. We may clearly infer from this text, that the unlikeliest men may yield the most blessed results of our ministry. Here is a man, chief among the publicans and rich, despised and avoided by a large portion of society, who returns a joyful answer to the appeal of Christ. Has it not been so in our own experience? Some of the men on whose adhesion we had reckoned most confidently have fallen back into coldness and unbelief; and some whom we had regarded as hopeless have responded to our ministry with most unexpected and startling joy. We must be more cordial with neglected men. In all congregations there are men little counted of, or even hardly known, lying under the ban of suspicion, or misunderstood by reason of some social disfavour, who only need to be personally addressed in the language of Christian love, to yield themselves with overflowing joy to the gentle demands of the Saviour.

"And when they saw it, they all murmured, saying, That he was gone to be guest with a man that is a sinner" (ver. 7).

What a life of criticism Jesus Christ endured! Always reproached, always suspected, often despised, truly had he been less than God, he would have abandoned his ministry in disgust and returned to the world whence he proceeded. The whole of the religion of his day was hostile to his spirit and method, and no man entered into sympathy with his world-embracing schemes; his brethren distrusted him, and his friends fell away from his standard, and he was left to work in loneliness that would have been terrible, but for the divinity that was in him. Even the most despised worker amongst us can have but a faint notion of what it is to live under a fire of continual reproach; to have all one's motives misunderstood, to see our whole purpose resented with contempt, to have one's name made synonymous with that of the devil. Think of what was the condition under which Jesus Christ worked, and let us learn from it patiently to endure the contradiction of sinners.

The relation of Jesus Christ to sinners enforces a lesson which the Church has yet to learn. We shall not severely criticise the Church in the exercise of moral discipline; but we shall ask most earnestly whether the discipline of exclusion should not be followed by the discipline of recovery? It is perfectly right to depose from the honour and privilege of Church standing those who have brought the Church's name into disrepute. Justice to those who have maintained a consistent profession demands this, not to speak of the higher consideration in which Jesus Christ himself is involved; yet, when such deposition has been effected, there should be a most kindly concern on behalf of the Church to recover the excluded. Discipline is not exhausted by the mere act of excision; it is doubtful whether this is not the lowest aspect of discipline. It is easy to thrust out the offender, but not so easy to go after him and to say, that having fulfilled the law of penalty, we have come to attempt the law of restoration. It is to be feared that we have not been filled with God's love towards backsliders; we have not pursued them with our prayers; we have not stood around them in masses to put before their feet every possible impediment in the road to hell. Which of us would dare to go into the house of a publicly known sinner, such as Zacchæus was thought to be, for the purpose of drawing him towards higher life? Our own virtue has often been so feeble, that only by associating with the best men could we escape the reputation of being vicious. Only where there is superabounding spiritual life can there be a graceful descent into the haunts of evil which defies the tongue of scandal, and ignores the murmuring of outraged respectability.

This verse shows very strikingly that the path of duty often lies across the prejudices of society. It is not an easy thing for one man, poor and friendless, to set himself against the current of public opinion. A word of caution is, however, necessary here, for there are self-opinionated men enough, who boast of their singularity, and imagine themselves to be somebody, because they are foolhardy enough to throw out a challenge to the whole world. Singularity, considered strictly in itself, is no virtue. When it is the expression of self-confidence, it is neither more nor less than detestable affectation; when it is the expres-

sion of intelligent and anxious conviction, animated by a profound
humility, and dictated by a self-sacrificing desire to do good, it is
noble and praiseworthy. Men should not aim at singularity ;
but, being forced into it by their loyal constancy to Jesus Christ,
they should not fear its consequences. Some consciences seem
to describe an eccentric orbit, and, in doing so, become whimsical
and fantastical in what, from want of a better word, may be
called their moral phases. Out of this eccentricity there comes
a narrow and censorious criticism, which gives just offence to the
most honourable and generous minds. Jesus Christ was never
singular merely for the sake of singularity. It was the divinity
of his virtue which compelled the loneliness of his life—more
earthliness would have meant more popularity.

"And Zacchæus stood, and said unto the Lord, Behold, Lord, the half o
my goods I give to the poor ; and if I have taken anything from any man
by false accusation, I restore him fourfold " (ver. 8).

You have seen flowers which have been closed during the
night, opening to the morning sun ; so is it with human hearts
shut up in the cold dark night of selfishness, when the Sun of
righteousness arises upon them with healing in his wings.
Zacchæus would never have known himself if he had not first
known Jesus Christ. It is ever noteworthy that by contact with
the Saviour men become greater, and to their fuller strength is
added all the charm of generosity. In this case there is a noticeable combination of liberality and justice ; the poor and the
wronged alike feel the blessed influence of this man's renewal ;
all with whom he had to do were to be the better for his having
received Jesus Christ into his heart. This kind of evidence ought
to form the most powerful vindication of Christianity. Renewed
men explain God's revelations to the soul. Instead of saying,
Examine this or that doctrine, we ought to be able to point to the
poor man who is being comforted, and to the wronged man who
is being compensated, and to say, These are the claims which we
we set up in exposition and defence of Christian truth. Let me
beseech you to think of Jesus Christ, not only as the Saviour, but
as the revealer of men. See how all generous resolutions, all
divine aspirations, and all unselfish impulses result from contact
with him. In the presence of such evidences of new life, I am
constrained to say that no man need hesitate to decide whether

or not he is really under the influence of the Son of God. He has only to put to himself such questions as these : Am I doing my utmost to repair the wrongs of the past? Do I measure everything by a divine standard? Do I make myself the centre of the circle in which I move, or do I refer everything to Jesus Christ as the one Lawgiver and Judge? Am I the friend of the poor? Is my presence as a light of hope in the dark places of oppression and misery? These are the questions that determine the quality of our manhood. We have heard of professing Christians who were narrow in their creed, selfish in their policy, grovelling in their dispositions, and illiberal in their judgments; we have no hesitation in charging upon them the high crime of dishonouring the name that is above every name. It is the glory of Christianity that it ennobles human life. Do you know of any man who has been made less true, less generous, less compassionate, less forbearing, since he identified himself with the cross? My bold and lofty challenge on behalf of Jesus Christ is this, that he meets man dwarfed and crippled by sin, and glorifies him with the dignity, and enriches him with the blessedness, of eternal life. Let men receive the spirit of the Saviour, and every transaction of their lives will be simplified, elevated and made pure, their business will be regenerated, their houses will become sanctuaries, and their whole character a living persuasive defence of all that is wise, and true and good. We do not for one moment deny the heightening and refining effect of intellectual education ; but we have seen evidence enough in the history of the world under all conditions of civilisation, to justify the opinion that man's best estate, apart from Jesus Christ, is but as the artificial plant to the living and fruitful garden.

"And Jesus said unto him, This day is salvation come to this house, forsomuch as he also is a son of Abraham" (ver. 9).

Have you had such a visitation in your house ? Truly, there are special days in our life which seem to throw all other days into insignificance. Chiefest and brightest of them is the day on which salvation becomes the culminating fact of our history. I am afraid that this word salvation is becoming somewhat unfamiliar; nor am I sure that it is always used in its fullest meaning, even by those who are not ashamed of the Gospel of

Christ. It is possible to think of salvation as a distant blessing, but Jesus Christ speaks of it as a present reality. He gives eternal life to men now, and we fall short of the happiest realisation of our privileges, if we allow the heart to dwell upon anything less than the immortality which has been given to us by the Son of God. It may not always be possible to point out the exact day on which salvation came to us; I do not press for the identification of mere dates, but I do contend that it is impossible for Jesus Christ to have been received into any house as Redeemer and King, without his entry having made such an impression as can never be effaced from the memory or dislodged from the liberated and rejoicing heart. It ought not to be a merely senti-mental exercise to recall the hour in which we received the blessings of salvation. Men are poor when they give up the great memories of the soul. It is one of the most blessed enjoy-ments of the Christian life to fall back upon hallowed recollections, and to summon them to our aid in anticipating a future on which there may rest somewhat of the shadow of doubt or fear. Men can say, This day I was ruined in trade; this day I undertook a most important commercial engagement; this day I fell under the power of a terrible disease; this day I came into possession of great riches—blessed are they amongst whose recollections is the transcendent day on which Jesus Christ set up his kingdom in their hearts.

Whilst dwelling upon this verse, it is important to observe the view which Jesus Christ takes of Zacchæus. The multitude had called him "a man who is a sinner"; Jesus Christ openly declared him to be "a son of Abraham." * Little natures delight to take lowering views of human life; it is the delight of great souls to give high interpretation and sublime significance to the capacity and destiny of men. See the mercifulness of the

---

* "Many ancient and some modern commentators understand this to mean that Zacchæus, whether or not a heathen by birth, now became a 'son of Abraham' in a spiritual sense, by his conversion; but it probably signifies that he was a son of Abraham literally (compare ch. xiii. 16), and had claims and rights by reason of his covenant relation to God, as well as other Jews ('he also'), although a publican. Nevertheless, he was one of 'the lost sheep of the house of Israel,' whom the Son of man is sent 'to seek and to save' (compare Matt. xviii. 11)."—*The Speaker's Commentary.*

Saviour's judgments! If there is one spark of light in us, he increases it to a great flame; if he can possibly classify with the children of Abraham, he will never identify us with the sons of perdition. It is better to fall into the hands of God than into the hands of men.

After this came the last grand word, worthy of being written in letters of fine gold—

"For the Son of man is come to seek and to save that which was lost" (ver. 10).

Had men not been lost, he never would have come as a man. In what form we might have seen him it is impossible to say To our sin we owe his incarnation; what if sin shall prove to have brought us views of God which could never have been seen in the light of unfallen virtue? As we see most truly what is in man when Jesus Christ reveals him, may it not also be true, that we see most deeply into the heart of God when he is moved to the condemnation of sin and the redemption of the sinner? It is premature to say what part sin will play in the economy of the universe; we know little about it now; at best, it is but morning twilight; yet, if through the sin we have even now seen so much of the mercy, there may remain still brighter and more inspiring revelations, and hell itself may be made to contribute towards a fuller understanding of the infinite love and glory of God. Turning away from the mystery, let us take heart in presence of an incident so graphic and touching as this; let no sinner despair; let none who would see Jesus give up the noble purpose. He receiveth sinners still; he braves the reproaches of the narrow-minded still; he is mighty to save—he is unwilling to destroy.

Chapter xix. 41.

"And when he was come near, he beheld the city, and wept over it."

THE CLAIMS OF THE CITY.

THE city was Jerusalem; the beholder who looked at it through his tears was Jesus Christ. Our difficulty is that men will not come near the city. They live in it, and do not see it; they have their little accustomed macadamised roads, hardened by the feet of business, but as for what lies behind, just ten feet from their own turnpike, they know nothing. No man knows London. The people who live in it mayhap know less than those who only visit it now and then. The familiar way, the daily swing, the repeated routine : that is not London; that is not the city. It is but so much custom, so much paved road; what was done yesterday, done again to-day, and to be repeated to-morrow, and so on to the end of life's little day. London is behind all that, and below it, and immeasurably beyond it; a city of sorrow, a city of death, a city of health. London is not at church to-day; London is never at church. Respectable London is there; custom is observed, old superstitions are repeated, or ancient reverences are observed with gracious concern and gratitude; but million-headed London is not at church; does not want to go to church; finds nothing at church, but mockery, disappointment, things hung so high up in the air that hunger cannot seize them with the clutch of its eager hand, or the tooth gnaws it like a cruel beast. It was when Jesus Christ came near the city that he wept over it with a heart that could not hold all its sorrow. There are men who dare not go off their own beaten way in the great city; in the smallest number of minutes they might make themselves strangers in their own metropolis : they would not know the faces—faces out of which God has been expunged; they would not know the voices—voices that might once have been made tuneful, musical, but are now instruments of harshness, clamour, vulgar noise and tumult. Some of us are bound to know a little about the city. We would rather live in a garden; it would be quieter, sweeter, altogether more in accordance with cultivated taste. Some of us would rather live in an art gallery; it would be serener; it would be more favourable to oblivion as regards all things unpleasant. But because we belong to the Cross we belong not to the respectability of society, only to the part of it that is already half-condemned.

The Cross has nothing to do with respectability; it loathes it. If the Cross is not this day and every day going down the city's darkest roads, then the men who professedly bear that Cross have broken every oath that makes life sacred. Go to the poor and see them pay their rent. When will the counting cease? The shillings are but a little handful, and there is one, two, three, four—what for, poor woman? What for? For a floor to sleep on, for space to toil in. Climb high and find in the unfurnished room the sufferer who has no friends—silent, solitary, cursing this world and defying every other, and determined if ever he should see a God to face him as tyrants should be faced, for calling men into such existence that is all pain and no joy. The poor, irrational sufferer no doubt will be spoken about as eccentric, and wild, and lacking in self-control : but a sufferer nevertheless, in every pore of his skin, in every nerve of his curiously complicated body—a body as well made as if it had been the body of a prince, with exactly the same capacities of enjoyment, but capacities that are sealed with the black seal of death. The statistician knows nothing about the city; the politician knows nothing about it, unless he be more than a merely political student. The sick-visitor knows a little about the city; the city missionary goes where many philanthropists would prefer not to go, but would be willing to throw the missionary a guinea that he—he— might work it out, whilst the philanthropist drank his wine and said his unheard prayer. A real sight of the city would convert any man to Christianity—to Christianity as exemplified in the person and ministry of Christ himself. When we speak of Christianity it is not of Christianity as professed by preacher or hearer, but as embodied in the Son of God. When you answer Christianity, please to answer Christ. As for answering us, you could grind us to powder. We cannot stand before you if ye be righteous men, pressing the claims of morality and honour and truth and benevolence and sincerity; if you pelt us with our inconsistencies we are stoned to death. When you would plead against Christianity make your assault upon the Son of God himself.

How beautiful is this text in every aspect! Take it as a picture: Is there anything finer in art? Take it as a sentiment: is there anything deeper in human pathos? Take it as a revelation of God, and surely to the weeping God even a little child might go. God should be so pictured that little children would run to him. Call him invisible, eternal, immutable, omnipotent, and no one wants to see him: point him out crying over the city, and a child might want to go and catch some of that sacred rain. It is to this Saviour, and to none other, that we are committed. As for speculation about him, away with it; as to this man's theory about him, and that man's contradictory theory concerning him, and some other man's elaborate philosophy about the Son of God, they have injured, hindered, degraded the Cross. The only Christ to whom I have given my poor soul, my little frail, dying life, is yonder Christ, blind with his own tears. Take it as a revelation, a sentiment, a picture; and what can go so far towards inflaming with celestial life and fire the imagination of mankind?

There is some grim encouragement about the spectacle—" And when he was come near, he beheld the city, and wept over it." Then even he had his disappointments in life. The ministry was not a "success," even in the hands of Christ. How easy to blame the minister because he does not make all the city good! That miracle, being moral and spiritual, and not of a nature that comes within the limits, even of almightiness, the Son of God himself could not accomplish. The youngest child can double its fist against God. Every heart can shut the door in the face of Jesus Christ. Let us accept the circumstance as an encouragement marked by many limitations. Let us first be quite sure that we have done for the city, in our degree, what Christ did for Jerusalem before we plead that where Christ failed it is impossible for us to succeed. This is not an encouragement to indifference; this is

not a sanction to careless work ; this is not a plea that should bar
the soul against the claim and agony of sacrifice. When Jesus
Christ wept over the city he realised this fact, that even he could
do nothing more. Is omnipotence exhausted ? There is no
omnipotence in moral suasion. Omnipotence has to do only with
vulgar things. The almightiness of God is but a pagan attribute
—almighty in moulding star bubbles, almighty in keeping the
infinite machinery in action, so that there can be no collision,
friction, or tumult amid all the roll of the stars. There is no
omnipotence amongst hearts. God has, so to say, divided his
sovereignty with man in this particular. Even God can only
reason with man ; at last, indeed, his almightiness may become a
destructive agent, but even that does not relieve it from the
comment we have made upon it, as relating only to those things
which come within the sphere of creation and destruction. Men
have to be persuaded to be good. O mystery, miracle, wonder,
greater than any other surprise—a man has to be wrestled with
to keep him out of hell ! These are the difficulties of unbelief and
these the difficulties of faith. You would justly say that it would
be impossible for any man to have any other conviction than that
which is spiritual, lofty, pure, beneficent ; such reasoning would *à
priori* be pronounced correct, inevitable ; that a man with brain,
mind, mental fire, moral sensitiveness, should ever do one mean
thing is impossible. So it would seem, so it ought to be ; the
only difficulty in the way is, first, personal consciousness and
experience, and secondly, universal history. It is quite in our
power not to see the city. You can get rid of the comfortless
spectacle if you like. You can live at the financial centre, and
gamble all day ; you can live at the political centre and gamble in
another way both day and night; you can live at the literary
centre, and enjoy yourselves in sweet companionship with "the
dead but sceptred monarchs who still rule our spirits from their
urns"; you can live at the home centre, and when the wind
howls you have only to stir the fire and the answering flame will
make you warm, you have only to touch the bell and order bread
and wine and manifold luxury. You can thus live in London
and know nothing about it. For such seclusion, monasticism,
selfishness, literary luxury, there is no sanction in Christianity.
You can come home every night with a broken heart because of

misery you can hardly touch, and can never heal ; you can come home to hug your children with a tenderer embrace because of the orphans whose fathers are not dead, the widows whose husbands are still alive, the agony that defies even the approach of prayer. All that any of us can do is to undertake the little area within which he personally, socially, or ecclesiastically lives.

As a minister in the city of London I appeal to men who do not spend their sabbaths in the City. We have a claim upon you. You make your money in the City—where do you spend it ? Are you the men to talk about absenteeism as a political blemish on the history of landlordism ? Come, we are not going to talk about that until we have first cast the beam out of our own eye. You do not make your money in the suburbs, you only reside there. It is the City that feeds the world. Is it right that a man should be six days in the City and then turn his back upon it on the seventh day when moral agency, spiritual activity, is to be set in motion for the redemption of those for whom there is no country, no green field, no singing bird in the blossoming hedges ? Is this right ? Nor can I allow you to escape on the lie—the lie—that you have so much to do in the suburbs. So you have, but you never do it ! Do let us tell our lies anywhere but in the house of God. In the suburbs you say you have so much to do for the City ; in the City you have so much to do where you reside—you who could pay off that little chapel debt with one scratch of the pen, you talking about having so much to do for the little or the great suburban place. But whatever you have to do for that place you owe your prosperity to the City : you sell your goods in the City. The whole commercial pulsation of the world is, in a sense, in the cities of the world, and not in the villages and suburbs. In this connection the word " city " must apply to London, Paris, New York, and all the great centres of population, enterprise and activity. It is easy to mount the wagonette, and touch the steeds that will hardly bear touching, so fiery are they, and drive away into the green and beautiful places ; but what of those who are left behind, to curse society, because they know not what else to curse, for deprivation that gnaws like hunger, and for solitude that is aggravated by a sense of neglect ? Is it right that these

City churches on all hands should be dying out ? Is it right that great Episcopal churches should be torn down or sold because it is impossible to maintain them ? Is it right that the whole City should be left and that Sunday should be a suburban luxury ? Every family that goes into the suburbs and leaves London on a Sunday to take care of its own churches and schools is a guilty family and ought not to prosper ; some member of the family should say, We owe what we are and have to the City, and part of the day shall be given to visitation, to teaching, to exercises of Christian sympathy within the boundaries of the City.

Nor does the matter end here. Given a thoroughly spiritual, Christianised city, and the influence of it will be felt thrilling through every point of the great circumference. A converted London is a converted world. When London is religiously in earnest, all its wealth, education, and intellectual force and social eminence devoted to the good of men, the world will know it, must feel it, and will inevitably respond to it. I would have our City churches the greatest of all. In speaking thus, I do not speak of one communion, but of all communions. I want every City church to be crowded to the doors, and if this were all I would not repeat the desire ; but it is not all. It is suggestive of the further possibility, which ought to be the further assured fact, that crowded churches should mean energetic, evangelistic, devoted communities. A crowded church is nothing in itself ; if it be a sign, a symbol, a symptom, meaning that behind all this, and after all this, there is a spiritual inspiration and Christian consecration, then a crowded church is an honour, a glory, a profound and inexhaustible spiritual satisfaction.

Chapter xx.

JESUS TAUNTED.

" AND it came to pass, that on one of those days, **as he taught** the people in the temple, and preached the gospel "—not an exceptional work, but on a particular and memorable day. This was the circle within which Jesus Chrtst móved—namely, he taught the people in the temple and preached the gospel. A familiar word to us is the word "gospel," but not a familiar word in the four evangelists. Does Mark ever use it ? Does John ever use it ? Is it ever used in the Gospel according to Matthew ? —but once; and that not in a direct and positive sense. But Luke cannot do without it. So it is that we choose our particular words, and men become attached to forms and expressions and ideas and methods, and their names become involved with the outworking of these, so that sometimes a feature which to others would be regarded but as transient becomes a permanent expression of an individual genius and consecration. Luke uses the word "gospel" some ten times in his narrative. When he writes the Acts of the Apostles the word "gospel" has been counted in the record in about twenty instances. The man who uses the word "gospel" most frequently after Luke is the Apostle Paul. What wonder ? They were companions ; they talked much with one another, and took sweet counsel together ; and thus, by the action of a spiritual masonry, they came to use one another's favourite expressions. There is a plagiarism that is honest ; there is a talk that is contagious ; there is a way of uttering Christian experience that so commends itself to others that they must needs reproduce it. Jesus Christ taught in the temple, and evangelised, told the good news, related what men could then receive respecting the kingdom of God upon earth. And never was such talk heard by human listeners : they were spell-bound. They were not all believing : some were of a doubtful and

sceptical mind; yet the spell that was upon them wrought like
a divine fascination, and made immediate contradiction difficult,
if not impossible. Sometimes we think we could answer an
argument; but we are restrained from attempting to do so by
the sweetness of the music which accompanies its utterance.
The argument failed, but the music soothed. It is often so with
character, consistency, beneficence. Some put to silence the
ignorance of foolish men, by simply doing well; doing good, by
being liberal with both hands; and tender, ineffably tender,
towards all human infirmity and weakness, so that listeners say,
We could not accept his argument; but it would be impossible
to reject the man himself. In this way all may acquire most
beneficent power, most sacred and elevating influence. It is not
possible for all to be great: blessed be God, it is possible for all
to be good.

As Jesus Christ was engaged in this work, "the chief priests
and the scribes came upon him with the elders, and spake unto
him, saying, Tell us, by what authority doest thou these things?
or who is he that gave thee this authority?" So they had their
favourite word; they, too, must have their badge and pass-word,
their mechanical, unsympathetic, chilling masonry. Where is
thy name written? where are thy certificates? who accredits
thee? open thine hand, and let us see how the thunder lies in it:
we are startled and perplexed when we compare the instrument
with the effect; what we know about thee does not correspond
with what we see thee do and what we hear thee say: explain
thyself. When a man can explain himself he is done. There
are those who delight in vivisection; and in hunting for the life,
they kill it. There are those who would try to make a man out
and cannot do so, and they give him up as an enigma. The
gospel can never be made out, in the sense of getting behind it;
for it covers infinity, as it came up from eternity. The authority
is in the thing that is done. If you cannot explain the metaphysic
you can estimate the practical; if you cannot get behind so as to
see all the secrets of God, you can get in front and see what
those secrets do when they embody themselves in living character
and active exertion. Christians should be the proof of Christianity.
Let the men speak the praises of the Saviour who has redeemed

and inspired them. Christians, too, should be inexplicable as to root and core and essence, and innermost spring of life and purpose. But there should be no mystery on the disc of their conduct, nothing evasive, shuffling, ambiguous, equivocal. Whatever mystery may attach to the spirit there must be no mystery about the conduct as to its purpose, beneficence, nobleness, charity;—let the mystery lurk in all these if you will, but let there be enough of explanation, clearness, and frankness of thought and action, to constrain confidence and elicit healthful approbation.

By what authority do you preach ? By the authority of the issue. We have seen the effect of the gospel, and therefore we preach it. Others could account for preaching metaphysically; most of us can account for it practically. We have seen a man healed, we have seen a leper cleansed, we have seen a barbarian civilised, chastened, refined, ennobled ; and this has all been done by Jesus Christ of Nazareth ; therefore we preach, that others may be touched by the same power, renewed by the same divine energy, and brought to the same perfectness of spiritual quality, and the same dignity of moral intention. It is always forgotten that Christianity can ask questions as well as Unbelief. It seems to be thought by some that the mark of interrogation is the private property of infidels and sceptics and scribes and Pharisees, and that poor dumb Christians can only sing hymns and psalms, and never ask any questions. They are difficult men to meet in interrogation. All things are not plain on the side of unbelief, opposition, hostility. There are riddles in the open book of providence as well as in the metaphysics of divine rule. Jesus Christ could reason, inquire, discuss, and impale men with a gentleness which did not at all mitigate the agony of the impalement. If Christianity chooses rather to be positive in its action, distinctly beneficent and aggressive rather than verbally controversial, Christianity has its reasons for choosing that policy. Christianity says, Time is brief, the case is urgent; the remedy is here : instead of paltering with word-mongers, let us declare the positive redemption, the immediate, gracious, ever-present kingdom of God, and truth, and light. But the enemy always created an opportunity for the Saviour. We have already shown that we owe more to the enemy than to the friend in the New Testament. If there had been no enemy there could have been no New Testament as we have it now. All the great parables were spoken in reply to hostility. It is difficult to continue in a monotonous course of instruction, not because there is any failure of genius on the part of the teacher, but because the people so soon weary and tire. Thus opposition becomes useful, controversy becomes an ally of the pulpit, and question-asking is turned to high account by men who watch the signs of the times, and show to all who care to see how the kingdom of God is always the question of the day.

Having been thus taunted through the medium of interrogation, having been thus insulted by circumlocution—a favourite method with men who even in cruelty cannot give up politeness—Jesus Christ "spake a parable unto them." To their credit be it said, they could read between the lines. They were shrewd men; they knew what they heard. "They perceived that he had spoken this parable against them." They were, therefore, good men to preach to. The infinite difficulty of the preacher is when the people perceive nothing. He can preach well who knows that every man is saying to himself, The preacher means me; he is hard upon me, but he will be gentle before he closes; he has now dragged me to the seat of judgment, but presently he will speak to me gospel music, and he will show me how to escape this great dilemma. It is pointless preaching that nobody applies. Preaching of this kind could be continued for ever, and the minister would acquire a reputation for being a very harmless and a very quiet, and it may be kind, sort of a man, who is finding his way down to oblivion without giving anybody any trouble. We have lost in too large a degree the courage of our convictions. The pulpit should be an institution feared by every scribe and chief priest and Pharisee. Let some pulpits find their fame in their odiousness to wicked men. Whilst others may be acquiring renown in other directions, would God some pulpits could acquire first notoriety and then solid repute as instruments that are feared by every evil-doer, every tyrant, every statesman who is playing falsely with the destinies of his country! We may do this in various ways, sometimes through the medium of parable. A great deal can be said through the agency of an active imagination. We need not always say everything directly and frankly. There are more instruments in the world than cannon-balls. The resources of civilisation are not reduced to paving-stones. Let us now and again try a parable, an image, a mirror held up to evil nature, that it may see itself and cry out, Take away that duplicate; I will look anywhere but at a visage so indicative of evil purpose, so suggestive of evil life. So Jesus Christ was a judge through parable. He could speak in all styles. Many of the beatitudes approach the conciseness of epigram; some of his retorts might be characterised as specimens of the highest wit; then as to his parables, every one of them is a judgment or a gospel, a condemnation or a reward, or a door swinging back upon all the amplitude and glory of heaven. No one minister may be able to take this range, but each of us can find out his own department, sphere, faculty, opportunity, and all can combine in a testimony the clearness and emphasis of which it would be impossible to mistake.

"By what authority doest thou these things?" By the need of the hour. The minister finds his authority in human necessity. By what authority dost thou speak against evil? Because it is evil—that is the authority. Oh, blessed halcyon days when the pulpit can look upon all manner of evil and never recognise its existence! Who would attend such a pulpit? Who would love it and desire it? Not men of justice; not strong-minded, earnest, equitable men. Sometimes even silent men are forced to speech, and the very fact of their speech being only occasional lends to it a quaint but poignant emphasis; it is known that they would not have spoken but for the pressure of the times. Wise are they who take such note of occasion and historic development as to know when they ought to speak and in what tone they ought to deliver themselves.

This is one aspect of Jesus Christ's work; another and almost totally different aspect is given in other parts of the chapter :— "Then came to him certain of the Sadducees, which deny that there is any resurrection"; and they had a case of infinite interest to their finite minds. It was a novel case. When they

collected the particulars they gloated over the anecdote as one
that would upset the whole fabric of distinctively Christian
revelation. Where they got the case nobody knows. Who
cares to inquire into the genealogy of an anecdote? If they
made it up they were clever, and if they did not make it up they
were probably easily imposed upon. But the case was stated, and
they waited with that patient impetuosity which can hardly hold
its tongue, that wants to laugh because it is sure it has conquered.
When they had told their tale, Jesus Christ answering said unto
them: You are wrong at the foundation; ye do err, not knowing
the Scriptures: there can be no such possibility as you indicate
in reference to the resurrection; they who rise again "neither
marry, nor are given in marriage; neither can they die any
more; for they are equal unto the angels; and are the children
of God, being the children of the resurrection." They were
wrong, where all men who oppose Christ are wrong, on the base
line. The error was not only in the superstructure; the sophism
or the mistake was in the foundation. Jesus Christ withdrew
the corner-stone, and all the Sadducees went home again, sorry
that they had troubled him. It is always so with the Son of God.
His answers are fundamental, and therefore inclusive. We
tamper with details, and inquire into vexatious incidents, and
puzzle ourselves about what we call phenomena, and when we
state our case we are told that we were wrong in the first line.
He only can be really sound in all thought and Christian service
who is sound in the foundation, who has got hold of first principles
about whose quality there is no doubt. If we are wrong in the
foundation we cannot be right in the superstructure. We must
know on what we are building.

Jesus Christ having disposed of these men made a grand
popular appeal. "Then in the audience of all the people."
Christianity is an open religion: it invites the consideration, the
criticism, the judgment of the popular mind. It has its secrets,
which eternity will be required to unfold; but its sublime moral
appeals may be heard and answered by all. "Then in the
audience of all the people he said unto his disciples, Beware of
the scribes." Then he described the men, saying, "which desire
to walk in long robes, and love greetings in the markets, and the

highest seats in the synagogues, and the chief rooms at feasts; which devour widows' houses, and for a shew make long prayers: the same shall receive greater damnation." This is the man who uttered the beatitudes! Is that the tongue we heard on the mount, saying, "Blessed are the pure in heart: for they shall see God; blessed are the meek: for they shall inherit the earth"? What says he? "Beware of the scribes!" His voice changes; he becomes another man; he thunders, lightens, denounces, and already drives into darkness those who have opposed the commandment and counter-worked the purpose of God.

We must put all these aspects together if we would see Jesus Christ in anything like the totality of his character. We find him, in the first verse, teaching the people condescendingly, breaking up all the long words into little ones, that he might get down to all classes of mind. We find him preaching the gospel or evangelising, bidding men welcome to God's banquet, to God's forgiveness, to God's heaven, and doing it as if his whole life were, as it was in reality, involved in the issue. We find him raising his head, as it were, from the book, and looking at the chief priests and scribes. In the seventeenth verse we read, "And he beheld them." That word "beheld" is pregnant with meaning. It is not the ordinary English word which signifies he saw them, he cast a glance upon them; but it means that he fastened his gaze upon them, looked through their hypocrisy, burned them with his look, scorched them with his eyes. "He beheld them," and they fell back from that gaze as men flee from advancing fire. Then we see him for a moment interested in some poor creatures who had got together a number of impossible details for the purpose of puzzling him with a question, and we hear him saying in a tone which cannot be printed—a tone half of judgment and half of compassion—"Poor souls! you are wrong at the foundation; you do not understand the Scriptures; you have to begin the alphabet yet." Then we see him answering certain of the scribes; and then we hear him expounding by interrogation a glorious psalm; and then we see him rising into the dignity of moral indignation. It is the same Christ throughout. His voice is a voice of a tempest, yet it is the whisper of anxious love, the music of infinite pity.

This chapter, therefore, gives us an outline of the great work which the Christian ministry has to do in this and in every age; teaching the people and preaching the gospel—that is the basis work; answering objectors in a way which gives them to feel that they have approached the wrong man if they have desired to overthrow him by shallow questioning and moral impertinence; correcting men who have made great mistakes in fundamental lines, and then judging the age as represented by its chief personages. Who would dare to rebuke a Prime Minister? Are we not too eloquent in denouncing Agnostics, and too silent in reproving men who are misleading a nation? We should, if pursuing that policy of denunciation, create a great revolution in our churches. That is precisely what we want everywhere—a great expulsion of all seat-holders and an opportunity for the return of those who are really in earnest about the kingdom of God. We are always hindered by the presence of the one man, rich, or prejudiced or peculiar, the exceptional man: we wonder what he will think and what he will do. We ought not to count him; he ought not to be in the census at all, unless he finds some vague position in a great etcetera. What we have to do is to reveal a kingdom, to declare a gospel, to set forth a judgment. I am not saying on which side that judgment should be, except that it should always be a word for the helpless, the weak, the down-trodden, the friendless. It should always be thunder against iniquity, unrighteousness, cupidity, perverseness, and all meanness of soul. When he comes who will so talk he will have a hard time of it; he will be taken out to be crucified. This must be so. No man can commit himself to judgment and be allowed to die in his bed; he must, in some way or sense, be hanged by the neck until he be dead. Could I speak to young ministers I should not hesitate to foretell such a course, and to urge them to be faithful to conscience and to duty. It is not necessary that they should live, but it is necessary that they should be true and faithful and just

Chapter xx. 38.

"God . . . of the living."

THE GOD OF THE LIVING.

PERHAPS the text might be made more vivid in its expression by taking the words before, namely, " not a God of
the dead, but of the living." This is the very thing which
nobody believes. It is probably believed universally in words,
but when in this connection we use the word "believes" we
use it in its intensest and fullest meaning, and in that sense
probably there is not a man under heaven who believes that God
is the God of the living. They are not the worst atheists who
openly call themselves by that dreary name; such persons are
comparatively harmless : the man who is injuring God the
Father, God the Son, and God the Holy Ghost is the man who
professes to believe in that God and yet does not. It is the
Church that is killing God. If men believed that God was the
God of the living, there would be no more fear, or darkness, or
sorrow, or tears; nothing would come amiss, nothing would
inflict upon the soul humiliating surprise; we should live in
the very quietness and peace and glory of God. The kind of
atheism that is ruining life is the atheism which says in words
" I believe in God," and then goes away and lives as if there
were no God to believe in. It is merely theoretical belief that
is sowing the earth with the seed of perdition. Yet there will be
many a protest against this suggestion; many a man will say,
speaking for himself, that he believes that God is the God of the
living: but I would press upon him the inquiry, In what sense
do you believe that? Do you believe it with limitations? Do
you believe it with certain qualifications which you could hardly
put into words? Do you really, intensely, and unchangeably
believe that God is the chief factor in the present life? Does he
look in through your window every morning? Does he watch

you in your sleeping hours? Does he direct you in all your ways? And do you never put on hat or boot, or take up staff to walk with, without first asking if you may? "In all thy ways acknowledge him, and he will direct thy path." Is that only a verse in the Bible, or is it a principle that rules and and elevates and guides your whole course of conduct? We have a kind of general faith, or faith in theological generalities; we are somewhat partial to propositions that have about them the haze and the dimness of old age: but what about the immediate life, the present necessity, the temper of the moment? Do we ask God when we shall lie down and when we shall get up, or do we assume ninety-nine hundredths of our life, and leave God the odd hundredth to make of it what he pleases? Let us be earnest and searching in these matters; otherwise our so-called religion will sink into superstition, and our superstition itself will sink into ruin, and ruin will bring with it moral contagion, moral pestilence, social blight and death.

Men are so prone to worship somebody else's God. This is not the spirit-of Christ, this is not the dominant message of Christianity to the soul: every man must worship, so to say, his own personal God; he must not have indirect commerce with heaven, he must do immediate business with the skies. Do not receive anything intermediately, except as a kind of incidental help; open up a great, wide thoroughfare to God, and travel on that road night and day, and never be found on any other road; then you will believe that God is the living God of living men; not an Old Testament idea, or a New Testament idea, or a first century idea, but the one all-including, all-glorifying fact of creation and eternity. We do not want any books of references or any books of evidences. If a man's religion stand upon the foundation of argument, it stands upon no foundation at all. A man's religion must stand upon the ground of experience, of immediate, personal, loving intercourse with God, so that a man shall be able to say, I saw God this morning: I will refer this to my Father; having had an interview with heaven, I will give you my answer: God is behind me, before me, on my right hand, on my left hand, and he lays his hand upon me, and everything that I do seems to be of importance to

my Father in heaven.   When a man has to go to some book
to find out what he believes, he believes nothing.   You must be
your faith.   " The word that I speak unto him," said Christ,
" shall be in him " : he does not take it with him as an external
article, he does not hold it in his hand, as who should say, Behold
my belief is written in this paper, and if you would know what
I believe read these words in black and white.   That is not
faith.   As with faith so with preaching.   A man must not have
his sermon, for then he would be no preacher; he must be his
sermon, and then he never can be other than eloquent.   It is
just here that the Church has been making its mistakes with
painful consistency.   It has had a library to which it has gone ;
it has kept God in the library.   I want God kept in the living-
room, wherever that is; if we live in the library, so be it.   We
must not keep God in the ornamental rooms, but in the place
we live in, and so realising the nearness of the divine presence
the humblest chamber will become as the vestibule of heaven.

It is possible to dishonour the very God that we pretend to
worship.   We say God is in heaven.   Nothing of the kind : God
is not in heaven in any sense of the word which implies distance,
palatial luxury, and security and delight; God is in the field, on
the highroad; God is in thee, thou poor fool, if thou wouldst
open thine eyes and see him in the sanctuary of thine heart.
We will have God in heaven; nothing can persuade us that he
is anywhere else : we forget that wherever he is his presence
is heaven.   The Church will not have it so : it will have God
in heaven, immeasurable number of miles away, and it will have
all its arrangements formal and mechanical : immediate absorption in God would appear to the Church to be a kind of sentimental blasphemy, whereas it is the central doctrine of Christ,
it is the essential principle of the Cross.

We also dishonour the very men whose memories we celebrate.
Who honours the Apostle Paul ?   No man, except in the character
of a historical personage, somebody who lived, maybe, eighteen
centuries ago, somewhere, under certain circumstances detailed
in some book.   That is not the Paul to honour.   The Paul to
honour is the man who living to-day would repeat the Paul of

eighteen centuries ago.   Paul asks no granite stone at our hands ;
the mighty heroic prince of God does not ask for our memorial
brass ; speaking from his urn he says, If I lived amongst you
nineteenth-century men, I would tear society to pieces.   The
revolutionist, inspired by justice and chastened by reason and
ennobled by reverence, is the only man that really honours the
Apostle Paul.   Other honour is worthless flattery, encomium that
never reaches the object of the worthless eulogy.   There are
those who honour, almost worshipfully, Martin Luther.   Martin
Luther is honoured when Lutherism is propagated.   We cannot
honour Martin Luther, but we can repeat Lutherism, and
Lutherism is Martin Luther in his noblest form.   If Luther lived
to-day he would eat and drink amongst the people, he would
have his music, he would sit down at the table and discourse
eloquently upon all the affairs of earth ; he would rise, and,
shaking himself like a lion, he would condemn all evil things ;
he would flame and burn against all restrictions placed upon
individual conscience and private judgment ; he would hurl his
thunders against the little popes that are trying to snub the
rising genius of immediate progress.

   If Martin Luther were himself to come back again, we should
kill him.   If Christ were to descend to the earth again, we should
take him to a place called Calvary.   It is not Christ in any
historical sense we want, but Christianity, Christ's own deep sweet
saving truth, Christ's blessed spirit of sacrifice and obedience.
There are those who honour everything that is about a hundred
years old as against things that are of immediate conception, and
immediate purpose and use.   Only give some people a tune that
Wesley sang, and they think that they are as near heaven as
they ever will be—which is indeed probable, now I think of it.
Only give them a tune that was sung a hundred and fifty years
ago, and the very fact that it was sung a hundred and fifty
years ago is the only fact they care about ! whereas if Wesley
were here now he would be listening to the tunes on the streets.
That will do ! the fine old statesman would say, if that tune
were baptised and consecrated it would be useful in the church :
I will fit it to words.   He would take the tune home and link it
to worthy expression, and that tune would be sung in the church

next Sunday. Why do not men see that the very things they praise as belonging to a hundred years ago were a hundred years ago quite novel ? They had not at that period of time the advantage of antiquity, they were then new, they had to run the gauntlet of all kinds of opposition, and establish themselves in the confidence of the Church : and that is what we must do now. If any man can make a new tune, let him make it, and the common heart of humanity will soon pronounce upon its merits. It is possible so to use history as to debase it. There is a kind of evil disease in some men which will not allow them to believe that though Wesley is dead God lives. Theirs is a God of antiquity : ours is a God of antiquity, but also the God of the present throbbing moment. We must have no patience with persons who take the life out of God, and worship him as a mere term in ancient history. It is what God is to me at this moment that is the all-important and all-determining factor in my life. Of what avail to tell me that there was once a God called the God of Abraham ? Any God that can die is no God. The only God I can worship is a living present God, who is giving me new experience, new history, new faculties, new inspirations, new tunes, always giving me new grace and new power to reveal himself. There is a novelty that is rich with an eternal secret. By what means can we get rid of the people we do not want to keep, the whining, sentimental, superstitious worshippers of something that happened a hundred and fifty years ago ? Will any infidel build a church to hold such people ? I would transfer them all in one letter. They are the infidels. We had better call them by their right name and put them to their right uses. They who believe that God is here, now, in all the fulness of his light and love and grace, they who believe that every step they take is ordered from heaven, if they have put their life into God's keeping, they are the believers, and they never can be argued down.

We are then called upon by this train of suggestion to believe that Providence is not something that expired long ago, but that Providence is in beneficent and detailed action now. Who can draw himself up to that stature of faith ? What, God in action now ! I could believe that he may have been in action five hundred years ago, but to believe that everything is under his control now, at this very present moment, baffles my imagination, and puts my religious faith to severe tests. Yet I must accept that doctrine. Appearances are sometimes against the theory that God is in action now; we are oftentimes the victims of appearances, we do not take in field enough, within whose amplitude we can judge fairly and justly of God's purposes in life. When, in a great flood that carried with it village after village, a mother put her lost child upon some driftwood, and the child said, "Mamma, you have always told me God would take care of me: will he take care of me now?" I must say there is one way of looking at that which utterly shatters our religious faith; there is another way of looking at it which may confirm the faith which is momentarily in peril. We have formed a wrong conception of death. We first of all take our logical sword and cut the filaments which connect the worlds, and then we say, Will God take care of me now? What is care? What is taking care of a little human life? All men must die, they must go out of this world by fire or flood or disease: what is, in the largest sense of the term, taking care of human life? In that case, so pathetic and so tragical, I would say, Pity the living, not the dead; pity her who has to wait a few months or years and carry all the trouble in her soul, do not pity those who by flood or fire or pestilence or disease are urged into their destiny. We must talk of such tragedies fifty years hence; time must work out its ministry of soothing and suggestion and comfort, aye, and in many a day-dream we must see from what awful possibilities they have been saved who under circumstances of violence have been detached from our side. Let those who can testify as to God's presence in their life be no longer silent. I can bear testimony that God has been with me. I have felt him. There be those who with cold pen and ink write whether we know God by some intellectual process. I know him by my feeling, by my experience, by my spiritual elevation; I know him by the view I have been enabled to take of all past things in my life: they were painful, humiliating, tormenting; they were full of disappointment and distress; yet every one of them was right. You cannot put that down by any argumentative process. This is not an affidavit in the court of intellect, it is sworn testimony in the court of conduct, character, and human feeling.

must therefore believe, if faithful to this line of suggestion, that inspiration is now going on. Can you believe in a God who has nothing more to say to his human family? Has God quite gone from his Church? Does he never whisper to any of his sons and daughters? Does he never interpret the Scripture by some ministry of the Holy Ghost known and felt by the individual heart alone? May not God have changed the method of his inspiration without changing the fact? May not he who once inspired individual men now inspire whole communities and nations of men? May there not be a thought common to civilisation? May there not now be a tendency in movement which can only be accounted for by a sovereign action on the part of God? May he not now inspire actions, great acts of self-sacrifice and generosity; may he not now so work in the human mind that men shall keep back nothing from him, but make themselves poor every night that every morning they may go forth and reap a harvest of gold? What is your God? an antiquity, a mythologic conception, some dim nebulous impalpable thing? or is he Father, Shepherd, Friend, in you, near you, round about you? Is he the builder of your house from the basement to the roof; is he the chief guest at your table; does he keep all your account books; does he watch you with eyes of love? And has he never anything new to say to his ministers? Do they go forth Sunday after Sunday to tell something that he has not told them? Does he not now say to his servants, Arise, the time of battle has come, or seed-sowing; rise, I will go with thee, the people are waiting for us, and I will tell you in the same hour what ye shall say: put away all your own little ability and cleverness and smartness, and put away all attempts to patronise your Father in heaven; I will go with you, and fill you with the Holy Ghost, and the opening of your mouth shall be as the sounding of music, and the people will answer with a glad amen? This is the God we worship, this is the God for whose presence we pray. Unchangeableness in providential action does not mean monotony. God " spake at sundry times " and " in divers manners," We will not allow that expression " divers manners," although it is part of the very economy of heaven. God does nothing by mere repetition : he gives every man an individuality ; every atom casts its own little shadow, every soul has its own momentum from God, every voice has in it a tone that no other voice can utter. Let us therefore find God's consistency in his providence, and not in the methods of it ; let us find God's inspiration, not in some mechanical theory concerning it, but in the feeling that it is created round about us in the minds and hearts of men. When men say in great bodies, whether in families, municipalities or nations, Come, let us go unto the house of the Lord ! that is inspiration ; the wind is from heaven, rushing and mighty, and there is no dust of earth in all its sounding tempest.

We are not then to limit the Holy One of Israel. Let God work as he may. All ministers are necessary to form a ministry. No one preacher can say everything. When you say, What about the preaching of Christianity ? you can say nothing about it until you have heard every preacher under heaven ; the man you have not heard is the man who may contribute the completing touch. God looks upon his ministry as one : we unfortunately look upon the ministry as a series of individuals, one personality having little or no connection with another. To God it is a solidarity, not an association of atoms that have no relation to one another. So with Providence, the great movements of the world are one in purpose and in tendency ; and so with inspiration, there is an inspired sentiment, and who dare say that jurisprudence to-day is not in the highest Christian countries inspired ? The noble lord comes before the law, or the noble scion of a noble house, and the one who brings him before the law is some poor orphaned friendless woman : what will jurisprudence do in the highest countries ? It will do right, and the noble scion of a noble house must make compensation to the life he has wronged. When that voice of judgment is heard God is heard. When our laws are good, when our judgment is impartial, when our honour is without a stain, when we speak truth and fear no consequences, let us know that God is in the tabernacle of his people, and that he is leading the civilisation of the world. What we want, then, is living character, a living Church. When we hear discussions of an ecclesiastical kind, what are they all about ? Listening to these controversies about words and phrases, see how warm these men become. They smite the table. Why so hot, my little sirs ? What do you know about it ? Nothing—nothing. It will require eternity to settle the things you want to handle as if they were so many pennyweights of gold. What you can do is to love justice and mercy and truth ; what you can do is to be honest, helpful, noble, Christlike ; what you can do is to realise God in conduct. Yet how pitiable it is to see doxy versus doxy, and many clouds of words. There is a friend of yours, it may be, who settles everything by saying it. The Unitarians, he says—the block-heads ! Of course the Unitarians, then, are all settled. Strauss and Renan and Wellhausen—the blockheads ! That is one way of treating the case ; but it is a useless way in all instances. We cannot settle metaphysics or eternal questions within the little cage of time, but this, through Jesus Christ, our dying, risen Lord, we can do, this by the power of the Cross of Christ lies within the compass of our ability—we can do justly, we can love mercy, we can walk humbly with God.

Chapter xxi. 14-29.

"Settle it therefore in your hearts, not to meditate before what ye shall answer: for I will give you a mouth and wisdom, which all your adversaries shall not be able to gainsay nor resist. And ye shall be betrayed both by parents, and brethren, and kinsfolks, and friends; and some of you shall they cause to be put to death. And ye shall be hated of all men for my name's sake. But there shall not an hair of your head perish. In your patience possess ye your souls. And when ye shall see Jerusalem compassed with armies, then know that the desolation thereof is nigh. Then let them which are in Judæa flee to the mountains; and let them which are in the midst of it depart out; and let not them that are in the countries enter thereinto. For these be the days of vengeance, that all things which are written may be fulfilled. But woe unto them that are with child, and to them that give suck, in those days! for there shall be great distress in the land, and wrath upon this people. And they shall fall by the edge of the sword, and shall be led away captive into all nations: and Jerusalem shall be trodden down of the Gentiles, until the times of the Gentiles be fulfilled. And there shall be signs in the sun, and in the moon, and in the stars; and upon the earth distress of nations, with perplexity; the sea and the waves roaring; men's hearts failing them for fear, and for looking after those things which are coming on the earth: for the powers of heaven shall be shaken. And then shall they see the Son of man coming in a cloud with power and great glory. And when these things begin to come to pass, then look up, and lift up your heads; for your redemption draweth nigh."

HOW TO TREAT COMMOTION.

JESUS CHRIST is teaching us how to conduct ourselves in the midst of tremendous commotions. The chapter should be read from verse 5 to verse 36: within that space you hear thunder, and great winds blowing like tempests; you are made familiar with the shock of earthquake and the falling of things supposed to be immovable. There is in very deed what we have termed tremendous commotion, nation rising against nation, and kingdom against kingdom, and great earthquakes, and famines, and pestilences, and fearful sights and great signs shall there be from heaven. How are we to conduct ourselves amid all this infinite storm? Can we do anything? Nothing. There are occasions upon which we are taught that we have no strength, and that our strength is to stand still.   What man can turn away the whirlwind by a wave of his impotent hand ?   What skill can control the earthquake, or keep that perpendicular which the Lord has shaken at its root ?   But may not men have the gift of eloquence under the sting of accusation ?   If they have that gift they had better hold it in abeyance.   The accusation is also a great whirlwind, a tempest let loose.   A storm must be left to cry itself to rest.   Even cyclones cannot work always : they have their little sweep of madness, and then they pass away as if they begged to be forgiven.   What a voice of calmness is this amidst all the storm !   The voice could rise to the dignity of the occasion.   The speaker shows how energetic he can be in portrayal, description, and representation of elemental war and scenic havoc : now his voice becomes all the tenderer because of its louder tones in the other direction ; like whispered love falls the injunction—" Settle it therefore in your hearts "—not to trouble yourselves about your own defence : the case is not yours ; you are only representatives, you are only speaking a word which you have heard from heaven ; the answer must come whence the word came : God does not give half a blessing, the Lord does not give you a gospel, and then leave you to defend it—he will use you in both instances as an instrument ; therefore settle it in your hearts to let God be your strength and refuge.   He will know how much you trust him by feeling how much you lean upon him,—" Casting all your care upon him, for he careth for you."   He loves us when we do not keep back so much as one finger that it may work for us in some little skilful way, but when we give ourselves wholly up to him, saying, Lord, undertake for me ; I can see nothing, do nothing ; I am poor and blind and helpless ; I hide myself in thine almightiness,—the roof of that pavilion was never shattered by any storm.   Be instruments in the hand of God, and wait for the divine word.

" For I will give you a mouth and wisdom, which all your adversaries shall not be able to gainsay nor resist."   He will give the mouth as well as the wisdom.   He will not only give the great lesson in sacred philosophy, but he will shape the lip, and tip with fire the tongue that shall express the divine thought and purpose : it is all of God.   We have nothing that we have not received.   Do leave room in your lives for the action of your Creator.   If you have sketched out anything you are going to say, let it be but a framework within which God can operate in all the sweep of his power and all the radiance of his wisdom.   We should pray better if we did not think about it beforehand.   We should qualify ourselves to pray by first feeling the depth and agony of our want.   Feel the hunger, and the petition will come, in urgent and prevailing words.   No man who is in real hunger prepares a speech about it ; he has but to open his lips, and he becomes livingly eloquent.   All this instruction is part of the larger scheme of education.   Jesus Christ knew what was in men, he knew how apt they were to be self-reliant, self-defensive, and how much they would trust to their own craftiness, and to their own choice of words, so that they might resist the enemy.   There is only one resistance effectual in the case of the oncoming foe :— " When the enemy shall come in like a flood, the Spirit of the Lord shall lift up a standard against him."   We cannot keep these mischievous fingers from some little erection, and some small miracle of self-protection.   Why not live nakedly before God ? The sword is long and sharp, but it is blunt beside God's lightning.

Thus trusting upon God, we are to expect the very worst that can come.   Some idea of that worst is given in verses 16 to 18. Looking to the Revised Version we receive at the opening of verse 16 a point of light.   In the Authorised Version the first word is " and " ; change it into " but "—" But ye shall be betrayed both by parents, and brethren, and kinsfolks, and friends."   The emphasis can only be received fully into the mind by reading verses 15 and 16 together :—" I will give you a mouth and wisdom, which all your adversaries shall not be able to gainsay nor resist.   But" for all that you shall have trouble enough. How double-sided is the whole economy of God's ministry amongst men.   At the end of verse 15 we thought we had nothing to do and nothing to fear ; the paraphrase of the Saviour's words would be, Keep yourselves perfectly quiet, wait for the living God, plan nothing in the way of self-excuse, mitigation, palliation, defence, rest the whole thing upon your Father, and I will give you a mouth and wisdom which shall confound all your adversaries. There is a happy end. No: but, notwith-standing all this, you shall have the ground struck from under your feet by the very friends that ought to support you most constantly and lovingly; your own children shall fasten their teeth in your flesh; those that ought to make your reputation their own will pour slanderous words upon your fame. You shall have mouth and eloquence enough, but some of you shall be put to death before you have a chance to open your lips. Could not this Man that gave us mouth and wisdom have caused that we should not have been betrayed? Yes, but that would not have been for our advantage: we only understand one another in times of crisis; we do not know one another in fair weather and in prosperity, in smooth seas and in the middle of golden harvest-fields, where there is plenty for both hands, and where all the birds of heaven seem to have been gathered for our entertain-ment and delight. Betrayal tests friendship. Real religious conviction tests the household. We must put such verses as 15 and 16 together; and even 17 must come in, for it says, "Ye shall be hated of all men for my name's sake." It is easy to be Christian now. Not to be Christian is to lose some measure of social standing; not to name the name of Christ now is to incur the opprobrium of being atheistical and untrustworthy and morally pestilential. There was a time when to be a Christian was to be a martyr, when to be a Christian was to live in darkness and contempt and derision, and ostracism from every fireside that was indicative of the higher respectability.

In verse 18 the Saviour seems to take up the thread of the thought in verse 16. We could have done well without verses 16 and 17; every man could have done very well without the storm. Verse 18 reads—"But there shall not a hair of your head perish." Change this "but" into "and," then hear the weird music, listen to the paradoxical exhortation—"Ye shall be betrayed both by parents, and brethren, and kinsfolks, and friends; and some of you shall they cause to be put to death. And ye shall be hated of all men for my name's sake. And there shall not an hair of your head perish." Who can understand this talker Christ? We have been deprived of a good deal of meaning by the insertion of this English word "but" in verse 18; now that the revisers have replaced it with "and," although they involve us in a paradox yet they surround us with a new and beauteous morning light:—And ye shall be betrayed . . . And ye shall be put to death . . . And ye shall be hated . . . And there shall not an hair of your head perish. This is the paradox of truth ; this is the mysterious eloquence that takes up into its musical thunder all the emphases of human experience and Christian utterance. How can I be betrayed by parents, brethren, kinsfolks, friends, and yet not a hair of my head perish ? How can I be hated of all men for my Lord's sake, and not a hair of my head perish ? How can I be put to death, and yet not a hair of my head perish ? Here is the exaltation of the larger life over the smaller ; here is the elevation of our little roof, hand-made and hand-adorned, into God's great sky not built with hands, flaming with uncounted lamps. What say you of a man who thus talks ? Your house shall be burned down, and you shall not be left without a home. How aggravating is such speech. Every picture on the wall shall be cast into the fire, and you shall not lose one vision of beauty. But I have lost all the pictures ! So you have ; but you have not lost one hue of colour, one gleam of beauty's tenderest light. You shall lose every penny you ever possessed, and ye shall be richer than ever. This is the paradoxical talk of Christ. Paul caught the same feeling, he was the victim of the same contagion ; for he said, " I am crucified with Christ, nevertheless I live ; yet not I, but Christ liveth in me." What shall we say to the paradox that we shall fall down dead and be buried with our mother in the churchyard, and there shall not a hair of our head perish ? It is all true. We live our selves into the higher meanings. Poor grammar, willing to lend us what oil it can, and willing to trim our lamps as far as it can, falls back at certain points, and says, You must go to rest on the road alone. So there be in God's Church those who have suffered the loss of all things that they might gain all things, who have died that they might begin to live, who have ceased their individuality that they might be translated into sympathy with the almightiness of God himself. There have been those who have glorified exceedingly in tribulation also. These are the practical paradoxes that cannot be understood from the outside ; they reveal themselves in all the tenderness of their meaning and all the lustre of their wisdom to those who pray without ceasing.

"In your patience possess ye your souls." That cannot be explained as it stands. "Patience" has a meaning that must be dug for as men dig for silver. "Possess" is not the right word there. Say, rather, In your patience, or by your patience, you win your souls, you win your lives, you win yourselves. Patience always wins. "He that endureth unto the end"— one more day—"shall be saved." Many cannot endure, therefore they know not what is meant by the salvation of God: for a time they run well, but they soon give up the race, and fall down dead, where they ought to have prayed some larger and tenderer prayer. "Ye did run well; who did hinder you?" "In your patience,"—patience means keeping on, persisting; and persisting means sisting through, pushing by, insisting upon progress: it does not mean aggressiveness, it means persisting by submission; it is the mystery of resignation, it is the miracle of union with him who, when he was reviled, reviled not again; when he suffered, threatened not; but committed himself unto God wholly,—that is patience. Patience is not languor, indifference, reluctance, unwillingness to work or suffer: patience is continuance in submission. "Whosoever shall smite thee on thy right cheek"—O Man of Gethsemane, who but thyself could have said it?—"turn to him the other also." We cannot do it, but thou didst it, and art not thou the Son of man, and may we not hide our infirmity in thy majesty? What is "possession"? It does not mean the mere act of holding, it means the act of winning, acquiring by a process, seizing hold upon by right of conquest. You have seen some skilled player, some chief in the tournament, who has a silver cup, and we say to him, "That cup is yours?" and he replies, "Not yet." He has it in possession, but he has not yet won it. He says, "If I succeed in two more encounters the cup will be mine." "But you have it in possession?" "Yes, but possession is not final; there is yet a process of conflict, noble test to be passed through: if I succeed on two more occasions no man can take the cup away from me." Here you have exactly what is meant by possession and winning. The cup is in the possession of the man, but it is not yet his by right; he means to contend for it, and he will be disappointed if he succeed not. That is precisely how it stands with us. You have your souls in possession? Yes. Now win them. Seven years' more fighting. The devil will not let you have one quiet night's rest if he can help it; he can be quiet, he can be siren-like, he can be seductive, he can be defiant, aggressive, threatening; he can be as an angel of light, he can be "that old serpent," or he can be the roaring lion; but he can never be anything except your enemy. Are not our souls our own now? Partially. They are our own to fight for and to win. In your patience you shall win your life. Have I to fight for my own soul as a man would contend for a prize? That is exactly so: now you know the truth. Yourself! what a mistake you make in thinking of your completeness, and how you boast yourself in the sophistical reasoning when you say, "May I not do what I will with my own?" You have nothing your own; you are not yourself your own yet. We are men that we may fight for our manhood; we are souls that we may escape being beasts; we have a touch of immortality, now fight. This is the talk of Jesus Christ to men who were surrounded by cyclones, whirlwinds, tempests, storms, in the highest degree of violence. What a prize to fight for! We say in our songs that men will fight for hearth and home and liberty. They are chivalrous words, they cannot but touch the heroic nerve in every soul, but the sweeter hymn, the louder thunder psalm is this, Win yourselves, win your souls, take up your poor selves to Christ and say, O Captain of my salvation, I bring myself as prey won by thy sword: bind me to thy chariot wheel.

What a revelation we have in these verses of the character of Christ! He calls himself the Good Shepherd: is there anything shepherdly here? Why, every tone is the tone of a shepherd's voice. He calls himself the Bread of Life; is there any nourishment here for the soul? Every word is meant to sustain the soul in its most strenuous endeavours at self-conquest and self-perfecting. He is called the Captain of our salvation: is there aught of a captain's tone here? It is the tone of a general leading on the army to victory. Here is the power of the Church. See it in all these commotions; all evil maddened, all hypocrisy in arms, all vested interests resentful. O Church of the Crucified, thou wilt trouble the world until the devil is cast out! All these details have changed, but the governing principle remains. To the end life will grow and act within the zone of commotion. To that tumult what is to be our relation? Are we to answer wrath by wrath? Are we to hide ourselves as men who are afraid? Or are we to perform the miracle of controlling uproar and vengeance by the dignity of patience? This method is in harmony with the whole spirit of Christ. This method is not worldly; it would not commend itself to men of the world; it is not in harmony with the militarism, the pomp, and the arrogance of cardboard thrones that have nothing to trust to but scarlet and steel, powder and cannon. But to what vulgar ends do vulgar processes inevitably come! The cannon roars, but the sap rises silently in all the anatomy of the forest; the blood that soaks the soldier's steel feeds no root of corn or flower, but the noiseless dew is secretly working to feed the hungry with bread, and satisfy the tongue that burns with thirst. The army, proud army, mad with resentment or ambition, overwhelms the city in destruction and calls it triumph; but the force we know as gravitation—impalpable, imponderable, invisible—cries not, nor lifts up its voice whilst it holds in perfect sovereignty the empire of the stars. Christ was the Prince of Peace. It was left to him to show how much can be done by quietness, and to show what miracles are possible to patience.

Chapter xxi. 28.

"And when these things begin to come to pass, then look up, and lift up your heads; for your redemption draweth nigh."

COMFORT AND DISCIPLINE.

"AND when these things——" What things? Trumpets, and dances, and festivals? What things? They have been named, generally and in detail, so that there need be no difficulty in ascertaining their scope and quality. The things that were to take place were unpleasant things—"Nation shall rise against nation, and kingdom against kingdom: And great earthquakes shall be in divers places, and famines, and pestilences; and fearful sights and great signs shall there be from heaven"— as if all things had gone mad. Nor were they material phenomena only, such as could be gazed upon from quiet towers, and estimated by geometricians and men skilled in other law and science:—"But before all these, they shall lay their hands on you, and persecute you, delivering you up to the synagogues, and into prisons, being brought before kings and rulers for my name's sake." So then, all the action did not take place in sun and moon, in earthquake and famine and pestilence; the prophecy came very near to flesh and bone and spirit,—"And ye shall be betrayed"—worst cruelty of all: a blow is not to be named in quality with treachery,—"And he should be betrayed both by parents"—an impossible revulsion of feeling, and yet historically and literally true in every syllable,—"And ye shall be betrayed both by parents, and brethren, and kinsfolks, and friends; and some of you shall they cause to be put to death. And ye shall be hated of all men for my name's sake." And so the dark eloquence rolls on, until we come to the words, "Men's hearts failing them for fear, and for looking after those things which are coming on the earth: for the powers of heaven shall be shaken."

422

Now Christ adds, "And when these things" [earthquakes, famines, pestilences, darknesses sevenfold] "begin to come to pass, then——" Everything depends upon the point of time. It is no difficult thing to look up on a summer day, to see the light and the verdure, the blossom and the shaking fruit; but to look up when all the heaven is churned by reason of humanly ungovernable violence of action, and to sing as if standing on solid marble and domed by radiant heavens,—what is this but a miracle, God's supreme miracle of providence and grace? What can these words mean but—Play the man : be strongest when danger is nearest : let the heads that are lifted up be the heads that were bowed down in prayer? No man can look up aright who has not first looked down, with genuine devoutness, self-distrust, and reverent anticipation of seeing that the foot of the ladder is resting on the earth.

There can be no doubt that these words uttered by Jesus Christ refer to the destruction of Jerusalem, and there they might be left: but when can Jesus Christ's words be left at any one point as final? They serve historical purposes, and then take upon themselves new indications; they flame out into omens and signs, and suggestive indications never ripening except intermediately, always having an after harvest, a subsequent revelation and benediction. There can be no doubt that Jesus Christ spoke much about the destruction of Jerusalem. There have been books written full of critical care and learning, which go to show that Jesus Christ has already returned to the earth, has already fulfilled all his prophecies, and has in the destruction of Jerusalem completed the testimony. Some of these books are striking in their method of representing the whole case; their learning, within given bounds, is unquestioned and unquestionable; they are etymological or grammatical books; they are skilful in the analysis and application of terms; but they are false from my point of view. If the universe were a letter these books would be admirable and unanswerable, but the universe is not a letter, it is a thought, a purpose, a beginning; it is something growing. Let men beware how they thrust in the sickle. To thrust in the sickle before the harvest is ripe is to bring back an armful of nothingness. God is a Spirit: therefore never attempt to define him in catechism or standard of orthodox or literal creed. He is the fulness of all things: lay not upon him, therefore, the measuring-line of an alphabet, as if he could be caught within the few inches covered by the frail letters out of which as out of a root we get our daily speech. Unquestionably, much that Jesus Christ said referred to the fall of Jerusalem. Unquestionably, some of the apostles believed that Jesus Christ was coming back almost immediately, and therefore they said— Let them that are married be as if they were not married; do not complete the furrow ripped up by the plough; pay no heed to these things that are round about you,—he will be here presently! Parts of the New Testament can hardly be read intelligibly without coming to the conclusion that the apostles were expecting Christ—to-day, to-morrow, or in the night between. They were right too. That is the only state of mind in which a wise man can live—never knowing what is going to happen, but always believing that something great is going to occur:—Therefore! If all were accomplished at the time of the destruction of Jerusalem, then the whole Bible, Old Testament and New, is an exhausted light. But I can admit that very much did happen then, and that Christ in a certain sense came then, and yet that everything has yet to take place on a wider scale, and with fuller meanings. Jesus Christ never ends. He comes, shows himself, departs; comes again, shows himself, vanishes; he always comes, and is always coming. Without, therefore, disputing with men of letters concerning the destruction of Jerusalem, I can accept very much that they say as to criticism: I would endeavour to turn them from criticism to prophecy, to enlarge the literalist into a seer. Occupying this position, I can find in the text lessons of eternal import, suggestions that come upon our immediate life, blessing it as with light and dew, calling our life to discipline, and enriching our life with rarest, sweetest comfort.

"When these things begin to come to pass"—Then appearances are not the measure and value of life. When these things begin to come to pass, common reason would say, All is over; the battle is lost, the foe has conquered; all we have to do is to accept the destiny of despair, and die as quickly as we can. At

some points of history we need the strong man more than at
others,—some mighty, chivalrous, hardy brother who can say,
Now, be men! His voice may be an inspiration, for we thought
no one dare speak in darkness so dense, and in the face of
violence so ungovernable. Behold, this Man of Nazareth, this
teacher sent from God, is calmest when the storm is loudest.
It would seem to take a tempest to reveal his real peacefulness
of soul : if he had so much as fluttered the battle would have
been lost; but as violence came after violence, like billow upon
billow, his tranquillity became more evident, and influenced
others more like an all-inclusive benediction. Yet we seldom
learn much from these things, because we will persist in taking
the case into our own hands. We think that if we grow hot the
Lord will probably avow our side as his own, and Providence
might descend to help us. Some men cannot sit still; some
cannot be quiet : if they could but be kept under the influence
even of an opiate the universe would feel more contented; but
they will act, they will run, and stir, and move about, and
develop plans, and set up institutions, and if they cannot build
a solid house they will do something with tarpaulin. Why will
they not love ? Why will they not sweetly pray when other
speech would be impertinence ? Why do we not lie down in
the arms of Omnipotence and say, The case is too large for
us, dear Lord ; we cannot handle these awful materials ;
but we will sleep in love, and in the morning thou wilt bring
back the sun, unshorn of a beam, and we shall get back to
our ploughing and our commerce and all our household life
because we have lost our fatigue in the embrace and blessing of
God. We have nothing to do with appearances; we ought to
leave these to the journals of the day that have nothing else to
live upon. We are men of faith, men who have found a castle
in providence that never can be violated. The face of the saint
should never be writhed with a care; it should always be radiant
with a sweet, wise confidence.

" When these things begin to come to pass "—Then appearances must be under control. That is the point we have forgotten. When nation rises against nation and kingdom against
kingdom, the Former of nations and the Creator of kingdoms

must have the whole mystery in his hand. He is manipulating his own systems, and astronomies, and infinities: let him alone. All things are under control, if the Bible doctrine be right, and that it is right has been proved now for thousands of years. The Bible doctrine is, "The Lord reigneth." May he not sometimes invest himself with clouds and darkness? May he not wear the night as a robe, and go forth to the trumpeting and the drumming of the storm and the tempest, as well as to the quieter music of dawning day and westering sun flooding the whole heaven with purple? "The chariots of God are twenty thousand"; "the clouds are the dust of his feet"; "On cherub and on cherubim full royally he rides." We have not correctly interpreted the darker sides of nature. When the Lord shaped things, and sent them forth with names, he called one part Day, and another part called he Night. Did he fix an hour at which he would withdraw from the astronomy, and say, The dark time must take care of itself, for I now retire to needed rest? He never uttered such words—God never blasphemed. God never left his providence for a moment in the care of any being; he never vacates the throne. All things, therefore, must be considered as under control, management; they are working together for good : at this moment how violent, how portentous, how impossible of settlement! And yet, another revolution of the wheel, where is the noise, where the storm, where the tempest ye spake of, where the darkness that made you afraid? Gone! What queen is that which presides now—what king?— the Lord. This faith is not sentiment, is not rhetoric, is not poetry, because it comes so down into the soul as to make a man doubly strong; this faith says to a man, Dry your tears, and go forth to battle; lift up your head, and begin to sing; fear not, for the deliverer is coming in his own way, and will arrive at his own time, and will make all things work together for good. It is by this practical action that the Christian faith saves itself from the futile, sometimes malicious, charge of being but a sentiment. It inspires, it invigorates, it makes men ; it has made some men forget the weight of the burden in the growing strength of their confidence. Any religion born at Athens or born in Bethlehem that can do this is a religion that the world will never willingly let die.

We must always distinguish between historical providences and personal discipline. Some men are born in rough ages We cannot fix the time of our birth, the period within which our little life shall revolve among the visible stars. It was hard to be born when nation rose against nation and kingdom against kingdom ; to be born amid earthquakes and famines and pestilences and fearful sights and great signs : it would have been better to have been born at midnight, with a star to watch the birthplace, and angels to sing the natal song, and quiet shepherds to come and knock at the mother's door and make inquiry about the child. But we cannot fix the time of our nativity. Circumstances develop men, test their quality, shape their course, call them to their destiny. We cannot overget the fixed environment of life. We may accept it, make the best of it, pray to take hold of it and use it aright; but there it is. It is right that lions should be born in jungles ; it would be a misfit if tigers were born in the nursery where the children have their toys and their letters. The ages have been mapped out, and the earthquakes have been set down ; every famine and pestilence has been in the counsel and view of God, and all the births that were to take place under circumstances so disturbed have all been matters of the divine providence. What wonder if some men should feel that they have been born a day too late ? When they read of what happened when the sea was a battlefield and the land an Aceldama, the soldier starts up in them and says, Why was I not born then ? To-day I am dying with dotards, passing the food to toothless lions. But these misfits are not so numerous as one might imagine from those who suppose they could have done better if they had been born last century. They might have done better then ; certainly they could hardly do less and worse than now.

What is the inspiring comfort ? What is the doctrine that lifts this exhortation above rhetoric, and fixes it amongst the severest realities of history and logic ? Jesus Christ explains : he says— You are to be superior to the action of events, because they do not hinder the coming of the Son of man :—"And then shall they see the Son of man coming in a cloud with power and glory." That is the comfort. Only that which hinders him can or ought to hinder us. How is the night ? Stormy. At what rate drives

the wind ?   A hundred miles an hour or more, and blows from
the cold east with intolerable bitterness.   Are there any stars
alight ?   Not one.   Is all over ?   From a human point of view,
yes, all is over.   What is that which breaks through the cloud ?
It is an image like unto the Son of man.   How it brightens, how
it enlarges, how it descends ; how all things are afraid of it that
are hostile to it, and how all praying life leaps to greet that
image as if by an instinct of kinship !   In that doctrine Christianity
stands.   If anything can keep back the Son of man from coming
in power and great glory, then the case of the Church is lost.
But if nothing can happen to hinder Christ, nothing can happen
to hinder the Church.   When Omnipotence is foiled, then strike
your tents, and flee away with the heels of cowards ; and let the
universe watch those feet as they run, while you are asking for
some woman to house the white-livered deserters.   So we now
interpret Providence as to comfort ourselves and call ourselves to
discipline.   So, when nation rises against nation and kingdom
against kingdom, and great earthquakes are in divers places, and
famines, and pestilences, and fearful sights and great signs are all
operating, we simply open our eyes and say, Has the sun risen
this morning ?   Yes.   Then all is well ; if the sun is not hindered,
peace will not be hindered.   When there is great upset and fear
in the land, we have simply to say as Christian men, Are the
seasons still revolving ?   Do seedtime, and summer, and harvest,
and winter still appear in the land ?   Do they come in regular
order ?   Yes.   Then be quiet ; pray on ; you may even sing a
little : if the four seasons have not been hindered in their course,
have not fled away in fear and lost the path by which they have
come these thousands of years to the earth, then pray without
ceasing ; God is master, the Lord reigneth.

This was the reasoning of Christ :—Because all these things
spoken of in the text could not hinder his own advent, therefore
men were to lift up their heads, and look up, and know that their
redemption was drawing nigh.   In that hour all self-dependence
was to be renounced :—" Settle it therefore in your hearts, not to
meditate before what ye shall answer : For I will give you a
mouth and wisdom, which all your adversaries shall not be able
to gainsay nor resist."   Do not trouble your memory to reckon

up dates and facts and circumstances and phenomena that you
can shape into a reply; have no words, and thus be more eloquent
than if you had charged your memory with all the riches of
rhetoric and eloquence.   So he says to preachers : If you are
only preaching what you have learned in the study, you will
never preach : what you have to do is to read the Scriptures, get
into the spirit of them, pray night and day as strength will allow,
and then stand up and I will do the rest.   But men will " prepare "
themselves.   Self-control is to be exercised :—" In your patience
possess ye your souls."   [R.V.—" By your patience ye shall win
your lives."]   In your doing nothing you are doing everything ; in
a negative position you are achieving affirmative results ; in your
patience hold ye your souls, keep your souls quiet, and if you
have not patience no matter what genius you have.   There is a
time when virtue is everything; there is another time when
grace is larger than virtue.   Patience is a grace.   Self-culture is
to be a law :—" And take heed to yourselves, lest at any time
your hearts be overcharged with surfeiting, and drunkenness, and
cares of this life, and so that day come upon you unawares."   Do
not be beasts, do not be mere animals, do not be mere eaters
and drinkers, gluttons and winebibbers ; let the spirit be larger
than the body ; live in your soul, and for your soul, and through
your soul; then the word " unawares " can never happen in the
journal or the diary of the true heart.

Then comes a sublime injunction :—" Watch ye therefore, and
pray always, that ye may be accounted worthy to escape all these
things that shall come to pass, and to stand before the Son of
man."   That is what we are called upon to do—to watch.   He
may come from the east, from the west, from the north, from the
south.   May he come from the north—that north which never
held the sun, but only looked at the south burning with his
majesty ?   Yes, he may come from the north.   May he come
from the east, whence the cold wind blows ?   Do not speak of
the cold wind.   The dawn comes from the east ; day is born
orientally.   Speak no more of the biting wind, but think of the
summer dawn.   When may he come ?   Now.   How may he
come ?   No man can tell.   What should we do ?   Be ready—be
caught on our knees.

Chapter xxii. 3.

"Then entered Satan into Judas surnamed Iscariot, being of the number of the twelve."

SEEKING OPPORTUNITY.

HERE is a vivid instance of the craft of that old serpent the devil. He did not seek out a stranger, a prominent politician, or statesman, or leader of the general public; he entered into one of the twelve. We should recognise ability wherever we discern it. Here is a lesson for the Church. Only one of the twelve could have done this work. A singular qualification for mischief indeed, a qualification undeniable; that which ought to have been the secret of the best influence was the secret of the worst. It is always one of two things with this Christianity: it is our life, or it is our death; it is a savour of life unto life, or of death unto death, just as we may appropriate and use it. Let us give credit even to evil ingenuity. Satan entered into one of the twelve. He always wants to do that : to get hold of a nominal Christian, that is his supreme intent and desire. Nobody can hurt Christ so much as one who professes to follow him. It does not lie within the scope of so-called infidel power to hurt the Son of man in the sense in which he can be hurt by those who have touched his dear hand, and joined with him at least nominally and apparently in tenderest communion and prayer. What a lesson is this to the Church ! How the Church should be continually on its guard ! A man who would be of no account were he outside the Church becomes a rather important factor by the very incident of his being within the Church. We get influence from our environment which does not properly belong to our personality. The whole stress of the terms is upon " being of the number of the twelve." Only break up that unit, make it into an odd number, let there be schism at the heart. As for you, quoth the devil, discoursing with one another in market-places, speculating, inventing, dreaming, blaspheming, it amounts to nothing ; last

night I caught a Christian at his prayers, and sowed black seed in
his heart, to-morrow there will be a harvest.   Think of the doubt
of a Christian !   From my point of view a Christian should never
doubt.   Let me tell you why.   If Christianity were a matter of
intellectual speculation only, doubt would be timely and reasonable and inevitable; but Christianity is not wholly speculative,
Christianity is profoundly, essentially, eternally moral.   Why do
you not hold on there ?   If you have doubts about the moral
content and purpose of Christianity, then you are not of the
number of the twelve ; but if you are of the number of the twelve
whatever speculative difficulties you may have should be lost in
your moral enthusiasm, that is to say in your spiritual conviction
regarding the righteousness and beneficence of God and Christ.

People will not take hold where they can.   Is it an infirmity
of the mind or an infirmity of the body that men will allow themselves to be led about in places where there can be no immediate
certainty ?   The infinite never can be expressed in the terms of
the finite : it is not the infinite that is to blame.   You cannot put
the ocean into any vessel that man ever made : it is not the fault
of the ocean that it cannot be so included and contained.   Why
dwell upon these matters that lie away innumerable miles from
life's tedious, dreary, suffering road ?   If any man have pinions
strong enough to fly through these infinite firmaments, do not
hinder him ; the most of us, however, must hold on to commandments, beatitudes, duties, and responsibilities : and of God's
goodness I have never had the shadow of a doubt.   There I stand.
If I had read about it, or listened to some high and eloquent
defence of it, I might have forgotten what I had read and w'
had heard, but I have seen it, known it, lived it; from the very
first God has done all things well for me.   When he stripped me
naked and lacerated me to the bone, it was well, it was right, it
was good ; when he took me out into the wilderness, and left me
there at midnight, it was for my benefit ; I cried against him then,
and vehemently complained, and said, The Lord hath forgotten
to be gracious : I was wrong, wholly, absolutely wrong.   When
he dug the first grave under my very hearthstone, I said, Can
this be kindness ? can this be love ?   God does not expect you to
turn the grave into a garden the very first day; he gives you

time and space, and sets life before you in new perspectives and distances and colours, and then you go back and say, Where is that grave ? and, lo, you need not make a garden of it, for God has done that already. Why not then cling to this ? What can the most of us know about high terms in speculation, so-called philosophy, and the higher thought ? There may be men who have rights on these elevations, and we should be foolish to dispute those rights ; but no man has a right to take from me my own recollection of God's goodness to me. Every Christian should say that about his own case. Let me repeat, therefore, that if Christianity were purely intellectual, imaginative, ideal, or speculative men might have a thousand doubts, and have them naturally and justifiably; but seeing that it is moral, practical, beneficent, seeing that there is something we can lay hold of and testify about clearly and with a good conscience, we should hold fast there, and the rest shall be revealed and declared as we may be able to bear it.

Why are we of the number of the twelve ? The answer ought to be that we may help Christ, co-operate with Christ, make Christ better known, represent Christ, so much so that men coming to us may as it were come to the Lord himself. Be ye imitators of God, be ye imitators of Christ. The word "imitators" we do not like, but it is the right word. If we first of all impoverish terms of their meaning, and then deride them, it is not the terms that are to blame, but our ill-treatment of them. To imitate it now means to affect, to endeavour to produce a kind of similitude ; it means also to appear to be what we are not in reality : that is the corrupt meaning of the word imitation ; but the Revised Version has restored that word to its right place, and now we read, "Be ye imitators," of God, of Christ, of truth. The question which we shall have to decide is this, whether we shall use our influence for good or for evil. If Christians are doubting God, if Christians are speaking coldly about inspiration and spiritual enthusiasm and duty, the world cannot be expected to take up these great themes and glorify them. Why not stand a little aside for a time ? why not cease to be of the number of the twelve until certain doubts be removed, or a new position can be taken up rationally and strongly ? There need be no sense of exclusion or excommunication on the part of others. This may be a duty which a man owes to himself. I could conceive it perfectly possible for a minister to say : I want a month or a year alone ; I want to be away among the hills or on the sea, far hence, where I know no man's language round about me, that I may think it all out again, and mayhap I shall come back and ask for the old mantle and the old position, that I may declare God with new influence, new emotion, and new energy. That man is not to be banned as an infidel or a traitor ; he is rather to be regarded with admiration as one animated by the spirit of stewardship and faithfulness. Every man's life should be his own Bible. Why ask questions about other people's doubts and faith ? What of your own soul, your own life ? Have you forgotten your own yesterdays ? You do not need your faith to be supported by a buttress on the outside, you only need to remember God's goodness to your own life in the past, and you shall have lifting up and strengthening within. That is the abiding and gracious power.

What did Judas do under this bad inspiration ? He "sought opportunity." That is a simple expression, but there is a whole tragedy in it. What self-involution, what scheming, what balancing of probabilities, what shading and blending of colours, what weighing with the right hand and weighing with the left hand and deduction of inferences ! What a recall of Christ's methods—when he rises, whence he travels, what he does, what he prays ; what is his weak point : at what time can I catch him ? He "sought opportunity." Whoever does that will find it. Whoever seeks for the door of hell will find it. We read of Herod, " when a convenient day was come." Have you sufficiently lingered upon that word "convenient"? It is a suggestive word—when things come together, from east and west, from north and south ; when circumstances are made to focus—"when a convenient day was come." We make our opportunities, we make our conveniences ; we write our diary so that it may lead up to the day of red murder. What do you want to make, what do you want to create ? You can do it. Happily, this doctrine holds good not in the evil direction alone, but in the beneficent and sacredly happy direction of the soul. We can make opportunities for doing good ; we can put ourselves in the way.

We understand how certain actions move, and how certain events
develop, and we can throw ourselves by skilful accident into the
way of doing good without at all appearing to be aggressive or
obtrusive. We could create sweet incidents. If we liked we
could almost any day meet poverty and help it without poverty
ever suspecting that we have been parties to a gracious conspiracy.
There may be those who go out hooded and ulstered, saying,
Where art thou, poverty ? I want thee : stand up, grim spectre,
and let me talk to thee ! I hope poverty will have more sense
than to do so !

There is a way of seeking an opportunity, as who should say,
Behold ! good day ! and good luck to thee ! I have had sweet
fortune singing to me, and helping me, and it may be that in this
happy chance I have an opportunity of sharing something with
thee. You can make the opportunity ; you can be standing in
the road ; you can be saying, It was on this path that the awful
incident occurred, there may be some repetition of it ; I intend to
be close at hand, so that if any chance be given me of doing good
I may do it with both hands earnestly. And all this you can
say to your own soul and to God. It is not to be written large
or spoken aloud ; it is to be a soliloquy that the soul shall turn
into music. Lord, when saw we thee an hungred, and gave
thee no bread ? When saw we thee athirst, and gave thee no
drink ? When ? O lying soul ! O dead, dead conscience !
The Christ was standing beside you all the time, and you mistook him for a stranger, for the gardener, perhaps for an enemy :
why did you not seek opportunity of testing the man's necessity
without making him feel it doubly ? It might have been worth
while to risk something if haply you could have identified the
Son of God in a brother man. It is worth while to burn this
kind of excuse out of the Church, that if men had only known,
they would have done wonders. Why did they not know ? Why
did they not inquire ? " The cause which I knew not I searched
out." You might have given that minister something that would
have saved him from broken-heartedness. If you had known,
you would. No, you would not, thou wicked servant ! You
might have known. And you, minister, might have helped some
poor creature in darkness, and poverty, and misery, if you could

have withdrawn yourself from what to you was luxurious enjoyment, it may be of a literary or intellectual kind. Do not say
you would have gone if you had known; it might have been
worth while for you to have tried to know. So if you want
opportunities to do people harm, you can have them. You can
find fault with any man. I find now that it is supposed to be as
near as possible to having heaven, that "nobody was ever heard
to breathe one word against him." That was how it was with
the Apostle Paul! Nobody ever spoke a word against the Apostle
Paul, either about his bodily presence or his public speech.
Paul would not have had a heaven of that kind; he would not
have had room in it. No man ever spoke against the apostles,
not a breath—O beautiful obscurity, celestial orphanage! Yet
this is the highest encomium we can now pass upon men, that
we never heard anybody in the world take the slightest notice of
them; and there are ministers who say, "We have been forty
years together in this town, and never had a cross word."
What a miracle! How often have you met? "We have not
had many opportunities of meeting." Then why did you not
make them, create your opportunities, and test one another's
trust, and chivalry, and love? If I could address the mischief-
maker, I would speak to him words intended to scorch his
insignificance. Do not do harm in your churches, do not make
yourselves the mediums of harm-doing and mischief in your
churches in London, or in the country, or in the mission-field.
Have nothing to do with evil-minded men; seek opportunities for
helping one another, and blessing life, and when other opportunities occur, avoid them.

Here is, lastly, an instance of what may be termed indirect
mischief: he "sought opportunity to betray him unto them."
It is in the last words that we find the indirectness of the
mischief. There are plenty of people willing to do the sin if
they can escape the crime. There is a temptation to do the first,
and seeking to avoid the last. We are willing to point Christ
out, and then to run away and leave others to do the murder.
That is what you did when you told the young man, *that* was the
book that he ought to read. You never saw him again; you
knew that if he read that book he was a dead soul. All you did

was to say that the book was interesting, fascinating, and very novel and suggestive, and then you ran away. Are you guiltless of that young man's death ? Will he have nothing to say to you when you face one another at the bar ? You bought the book, named the book, lent the book, watched the effect of the book, and professed to deplore the result. What if I tell a child that the cup is there which contains a very pleasant draught, and if I run away, and hear afterwards that the child drained the cup and fell down dead, which is the criminal ? Can I retain my social status and respectability, and allow the blackness of infamy to fall upon the name which I cursed ? There is nothing so easy for Judas to do as to point out to others how murder may be done, how vulgarity may be perpetrated, whilst he himself escapes in darkness. He does not escape long ; the Lord is against him, and the Lord will bring him to judgment, the Lord will avenge his own cause.

What we have to do is to support Christ, uphold Christ, and to do this by the eloquence of example as well as by the eloquence of speech. Can we all be perfect ? Certainly not, but we can want to be perfect, aim to be perfect ; we can desire above all other wishes to be imitators of God and of Christ Jesus, and the bent, the trend, of the mind will be accepted as an actual fact. O blessed Saviour, keep us from betraying thee, from pointing out any weakness, even in thy poorest followers, over which the scorner can rejoice and the mocker can be glad with malignant joy. May we be solicitous to find or make opportunities for doing good, speaking good, and being good. May we know that we do not represent ourselves, but that we represent thee. O thou Man, wounded in the right hand, and in the left hand, and in both feet,—thou Son of man, whose temples bled under the piercing thorns, may we know that we represent thee, and may every unkind speech, or word, or thought, or evil deed, be felt by us to be a sharp sword thrust into thine own heart. Thus keep thy Church, thou who didst buy it with thy blood !

Chapter xxiii. 8-11.

"And when Herod saw Jesus, he was exceeding glad: for he was desirous to see him of a long season, because he had heard many things of him; and he hoped to have seen some miracle done by him. Then he questioned with him in many words; but he answered him nothing. And Herod with his men of war set him at nought, and mocked him, and arrayed him in a gorgeous robe, and sent him again to Pilate."

DIVINE RESERVE.

ALL subjects reveal themselves according to the mental mood in which they are examined. This is true in every ramification of life. Men's decisions are influenced by the state of mind in which they receive either evidence or sensations. With regard to the external universe, for example, if it is surveyed when the heart is agitated with sorrow, it fails to produce those impressions which majesty and beauty naturally convey. When the landscape is gazed upon by a mind free from anxiety it elicits feelings and utterances accordant with its own gaiety or grandeur; whereas, when the spirit is "wounded," or crushed with care, the landscape is to it but a cemetery, and the brightest star but a torchlight to the tomb. The same principle is illustrated in the diversified estimation of personal character: urge one man to suspect another, and in all probability the party so urged will imagine that he sees reason to justify the advice. Words will be twisted—actions will be misconstrued—and the very glance of the eye will be made to confirm the impression that the man is a decidedly suspicious character. Instruct another that the very same man is a trustworthy friend, and, in all likelihood, his words, actions, and glances will be made to concur in verifying the commendation. Such is the immense influence which mental moods exert on human reasonings and judgments. That which is looked for is found, or thought to be found. The same person or principle examined through the respective media of sympathy and antipathy, will reveal aspects the most different. It is of vital importance to remember this fact in all our investigations of creeds, or balancings of contradictory evidence, so that we may escape both the traductions of prejudice and the blindings of partiality. The non-recognition of this truth has induced the grossest misrepresentations of social life, of individual belief, and of denominational doctrine. Each man is apt to consider his own mental mood right, and to be deficient in charity towards the contrary mood of his fellow-student, or fellow-labourer. Seeing, therefore, that our mental conditions act so powerfully on all the developments of life and thought, it becomes us to watch them with a jealous eye, and to bring our minds into continual contact with the divine Purifier and Teacher. Thus much, however, is general, and simply introductory to the sublime particular truths which this remarkable passage is so eminently fitted to teach.

The divine being discriminates our mental moods. Apparently, Herod was in a pleasing state of mind. Superficial observers would have been delighted with his animated and cordial bearing. What could be more gratifying to Christ than that Herod was "exceeding glad" to see him? There was no royal hauteur—no cold rebuff—no vengeful triumph. Why then that awful silence? Why those sealed lips? Could Herod have done more to conciliate the favour of his renowned prisoner? Was it not an act of incomparable condescension for Herod to wear a smile in the presence of a reputed blasphemer and seditionist? For Christ's significant reserve there must be some peculiar but satisfactory reason. It was not fear of the judge, for he was the judge's Creator and Sovereign; it was not contempt, for he entertains a just regard for all the creatures of his hand; it was not constitutional sullenness, for none could be more open and engaging than he; it was not consciousness of guilt, for his most rancorous foes failed in their attempts at crimination. Why, then, did Christ thus treat a man who was "exceeding glad" to "see him"? The only satisfactory answer which we can suggest, is that Herod's gladness did not arise from a proper cause; or, in other words, was no true index to his mental mood. Christ looked deeper than the smile which lighted Herod's countenance, or the mere blandishment of his manner; he discriminated the mood of mind, and acted accordingly. Christ was not misled by external appearances, "The Lord seeth not as man seeth; for man looketh on the outward appearance, but the Lord looketh on the heart." "For thou, even thou only, knowest the hearts of all the children of men." "The Lord searcheth all hearts, and understandeth all the imaginations of the thoughts." Christ here displayed his divinity; his all-searching eye penetrated the recesses of the monarch's heart, and noted every passion which surged there; there was no escape from that glance to which the " darkness and the light are both alike " ! There is something in this thought calculated to awaken most earnest solicitude regarding our mental moods: the smile does not necessarily reveal the true intellectual condition; nor does " exceeding gladness" always indicate genuine sincerity, or a lofty intelligence. Consider this well: your earnest gaze—your profound attention—your sparkling eye, may not convey a correct impression of your moral or mental state! We cannot infallibly decide by exterior manifestations, however pleasing or hopeful: but know this for an eternal certainty, that the divine Being discriminates your mental moods, analyses your conduct, and understands your motives! Every thought that flashes across the intellect, every vision that enchants the fancy, every emotion that swells the heart, is most surely known in heaven! God knoweth your thought " afar off "; ere it is fully matured in your mind, it is transparent to his! Sublime, yet overpowering, is the fact that " all things are naked and open to the eyes of him with whom you have to do "! That there is a dread Being in the universe who watches all the evolutions of life, all the processes of thought, and all the executions of will, is a truth less terrible in its abstract grandeur than momentous in its moral suggestiveness. Ever to be overlooked, ever to have an eye resting on the springs and outworkings of existence, never to have a moment perfectly to one's self, is surely sufficient to prove that man is no trifle—that life is a stupendous and glorious reality —that human deeds are not mere bubbles on the wave—that human responsibility is a fact, and that retribution is an unalterable certainty !

Certain mental moods deprive men of the richest blessings of

Christianity. Of this proposition the text supplies a striking proof and illustration. Had ever man a better opportunity of hearing words of eternal life than Herod had? The divine Teacher was before him—the Man who could have opened his eyes to the grandest scenes, and poured into his ear the sublimest strains—the Man who could command the resources of infinite intelligence, and thrill the heart with the gladdest tidings : and yet that opportunity was unimproved—that memorable meeting a blank! But why so? Why that solemn silence on the part of Christ? Because of Herod's mental mood. The judge wished his curiosity gratified ; he had heard of the great wonder-worker, and longed to behold his feats of skill, or his displays of power. Christ knew the treatment proper for the oblique-minded judge, and acted accordingly :—he would not work miracles to gratify a king ; he would smile on a child, or dry the tear of misery, but he would not court the applause, or solicit the patronage, of royalty. To whom, then, will the Lord Jesus deign to reveal himself in tender speech or loving vision? Is there any intellect on whose conflicts with scepticism he will bestow his attention? Is there any heart on whose strugglings with sin he will lift up the light of his countenance? Since he was silent before Herod, will he be communicative to any of his creatures? He shall answer for himself : " To this man will I look." Suppose the divine Speaker had paused here; what inquisitiveness and suspense would have been occasioned! " To this man "; to which man, blessed Lord, wilt thou look? To the man who has slain kings, and wandered to the throne of power through the blood of the warrior and the tears of the widow? To the man who has enrolled his name among the proudest of conquerors? To the man who boasts attachment to the cold exactitudes of a heartless theology? To the man arrayed in purple, and enshrined in the splendour of a palace? Is this the man to whom thou wilt look? Nay! 'Tis a grander spectacle which attracts the divine eye :—to the man " that is poor, and of a contrite spirit, and that trembleth at my word." Here then we have two conditions of divine communion, viz., contrition and reverence : apart from these there can be no spiritual fellowship. In Herod these conditions were not found ; hence Christ was dumb. So with us : if we would truly worship God we must fulfil the conditions herein demanded. Would ye

commune with the eternal spirit of the universe ? Be contrite and
reverent ! Would ye walk in the light of the divine eye ? Be contrite and reverent ! Would ye understand the meaning of the
divine will ? Be contrite and reverent ! Would ye find in the
Bible words of hope and joy and love ? Be contrite and reverent !
" For thus saith the high and lofty One that inhabiteth eternity,
whose name is Holy ; I dwell in the high and holy place, with
him also that is of a contrite and humble spirit, to revive the
spirit of the humble, and to revive the heart of the contrite ones."

Here is presented a truth of solemn importance ; viz., we may
be self-deprived of the richest blessings of Christianity. Certain
men leave the house of worship as they enter it : they carry no
heavenly spoil to their homes : they have no expanding of
heart, no illumination of mind : and why this leanness ? It is
true they reproach the minister for want of energy or skill—they
rail against the arrangements of the sanctuary—they complain
that there is " no food for the soul," but they forget the fact
that spiritual improvement is contingent on the conditions of
reverence and contrition. I would ask such whether they are
sure, beyond all misgiving, that their spiritual dwarfishness is
attributable solely to the inefficiency of the pulpit ? I would
adjure them by the living God to pause ere they accuse any of
his ministers of the stunting or starvation of their souls. I would
charge them by the solemnities of an eternal destiny to beware
lest they seek to remove their guilt to the account of the innocent !
Is it likely that such men can be profited in sanctuary service ?
All the week long they toil for earthly possessions—their energies
are engrossed in " buying and selling, and getting gain "—on the
morning of the Lord's day they hurriedly wash the gold-dust from
their busy fingers, and, while yet the din of commercial life rings
in their ears, they hasten to the gates of Zion ! They have had
no secret preparation of heart—they have not in the calm of
solitude invoked the pardon or the guidance of the Lord—they
trust all to the excitement of the occasion—and if their animal
impulses are not aroused, they complain of the feebleness of the
ministry ! Can we wonder that God is dumb before such men ?
Can we wonder that they have no relish for simple and quiet
devotion ? Can we wonder that to them there is no music in the

supplication of saints, and no beauty in the tear of penitence? Can we wonder that the heaven is as brass to their heartless formalities of worship? Nay! God is ever silent before such men: he meets them on their own ground: he judges them by their own spirit. If men would carefully prepare their minds ere entering on the exercises of the temple, instead of panting for displays of human genius, they would feast on the devotional part of the service—God would deign to speak to their waiting hearts, and they would leave the sanctuary fertilised and refreshed by a baptism of blessing!

I may enumerate a few classes of hearers, whose mental moods deprive them of spiritual enjoyment:—

(1) Men of violent personal antipathies.—Such persons confound the minister with his message; so that if any whim has been assaulted, or any favourite dogma contravened, they forth-with resort to misinterpretation—they turn every appeal into a personality—and that which was intended as a blessing they pervert into a curse! God will not commune with them: they fulfil not the condition of fellowship—they are neither contrite nor reverent—and Christ answers them nothing! All our paltry and miserable prejudices must be renounced ere we can rise into the loftier regions of spiritual manifestation. It is beneath our dignity as immortal beings to suffer our minds to be warped or poisoned by antipathy; let us rather cultivate such a reverence for truth as shall bear our souls far beyond the polluting touch of prejudice or bigotry.

(2) Men of large speculative curiosity.—Herod belonged to this class. They wish to pry into the secrets of the Infinite: not content with the ample disclosures which the divine Being has graciously granted, they would penetrate into the deepest recesses of his nature, and scale the loftiest altitudes of his universe. They conceive a philosophic dislike for the commonplace truths of Christianity; and regard with patronising pity the minister who lingers on the melancholy hill of Calvary. Such men would understand all mystery: they would break the silence of the stars, or detain the whirlwind in converse: they would summon angels from their high abode and extort the secrets of heaven—

they would even dare to cross-examine the Deity himself on the propriety of his moral government! God will answer them nothing. He will meet them with a reserve more terrible than an utterance of thunder, and cause their souls to quake, in a silence which was never broken but by their own presumptuous voice! Were men content to approach the volume of Inspiration with a simple desire to know the truth in relation to themselves, God would shine upon the page, and make it radiant with the most glorious manifestations of his goodness and mercy; but when they open the Bible for purposes of mere speculation and debate, the music of his voice is not heard, nor the majesty of his presence revealed! Wouldst thou behold the King in his beauty? Let thine heart be contrite. Wouldst thou hear his paternal utterances? Be reverent and humble! While curiosity amuses itself with propounding questions, Faith revels in the green pastures of positive blessing; while the carnal mind seeks after the sensuous, Hope regales itself on the anticipation of future and endless felicity! Let ours be the wisdom of attending to the revealed, and waiting with patience the sublime development of infinite purpose and power.

(3) Men who accept rationalism as their highest guide.—They reject all that reason cannot comprehend. Their own intellect must see through every subject, otherwise they consider it as worthy only of repudiation. They read the New Testament as they would read a work on mathematics, or a treatise on physical science, expecting demonstration of every point. Such men leave the Bible with dissatisfaction. Christ treats them with silence: their flippant questions elicit no response: their feeble reason plunges in hopeless confusion;—Infinitude refuses to be grasped in a human span, and Eternity disdains to crowd into one little intellect its stupendous and magnificent treasures. The mere rationalist is denied fellowship with God: so long as he defies reason, God will be dumb before him: he may utter the most pretentious claims, and make the most philosophic professions of attachment to truth, but he who reads the darkest secrets of all hearts is not to be deluded by lingual protestations or exterior show. Reason has its own peculiar province which it may cultivate to the utmost; but when it would seek to trespass its

appointed boundary God awards it the terrible rebuke of divine silence!—He answers it "nothing."

(4) Men who delight in moral darkness.—Such men have no objection to theological discussion;—they may even delight in an exhibition of their controversial powers, and, at the same time, hate the moral nature and spiritual requirements of the gospel. So long as attention is confined to an analysis of abstract doctrines they listen with interest, but the moment the gospel tears away the veil from their moral condition—reveals their depravity— upbraids their ingratitude—smites their pride—and shakes their soul with the assurance of judgment and eternity, they sink back into sullenness, they take refuge in infidelity, or they curse and blaspheme! Your Herods care not for moral betterance;—they wish their fancies gratified—they desire their questions answered, but they persist in following the devices of their imagination, and imprisoning themselves in the bond-house of bestial passion.

Men so deprived resort to opposition. "And Herod with his men of war set him at nought, and mocked him, and arrayed him in a gorgeous robe, and sent him again to Pilate." This is a striking illustration of the manner in which the truth has been treated in all ages. Men have approached the Bible with fore- gone conclusions, and because those conclusions have not been verified they have revolted, and assumed an antagonistic attitude. The course of reasoning has been this:—Here is a book professing to have come from God; if it is truly divine it will contain such and such doctrines, but if it is an imposition those doctrines will not be represented. Against such reasoning we must carefully guard; the argument would stand more correctly thus;—God has presented this book to the human race; whatever it contains must be founded in wisdom and goodness, whether we compre- hend it or not. Man has no right to assume anything in reference to a divine revelation : such is our intellectual and moral constitution that it is utterly impossible for us, *à priori*, to determine what kind of revelation God should grant. It is a matter about which we can have no conception;—but now that we are in actual possession of the book we presume to dictate what it should have been! Amazing presumption! Merciful indeed is the divine Being, or he would blast with death the miserable quibblers who audaciously question his wisdom ! Shall we suggest improvements in the constitution of suns and their attendant orbs ? Shall we remould the great fabric of the universe ? Shall we impose nobler laws on the organism of nature ? Shall we accelerate the majestic march of the seasons ? Why not ? If men are wiser than God—if men know better than their Maker the kind of revelation needed—if men can criticise the moral government of the Eternal—if they challenge the Infinite to debate the spiritual economy he has developed—why should they not intermeddle with the minor arrangements of the physical creation ? It were easier to add splendour to the sun—to increase the universe—to extend infinitude—to prolong eternity, than for the unaided intellect of man to have determined the nature and limits of a divine revelation !

As Herod expected to have his curiosity gratified by the disclosures and miracles of Christ, and resorted to opposition because his expectations were disappointed, so in modern times men have formed certain notions of what a divine record should be ; and because these notions are not recognised by the Bible they complacently decide that their judgment is correct, and that the Bible is an error.   This is the secret of much of the infidelity which has prevailed in all ages—the out-growth of pride which God has mortified.   Infidels seek to destroy the Book which does not contain what they have imagined was necessary : when they open the Bible they cannot discover the cause of the Christian's gratitude and exultation ; no voice of gladness appeals to their ear ; no solution of the problems which perplex the ingenious is given ; to them the prophets and apostles are dumb, or, if they speak, it is in tones of reprehension and warning ! How so ?   Because it is written, " With the merciful thou wilt show thyself merciful, and with the upright man thou wilt show thyself upright.   With the pure thou wilt show thyself pure ; and with the froward thou wilt show thyself unsavoury."   Thus, God reveals himself according to the mental mood of the party desiring a revelation.   To the penitent thief in the agonies of crucifixion he addressed the promise of eternal life, but in the presence of the marvel-loving tetrarch, though arrayed in robes of judicial authority, he embodied a silence more appalling than the solemn stillness of the untrodden desert! What was the consequence? Opposition, mockery, torture! The disappointed and chagrined Antipas resorted to the lowest form of vengeance; he yielded to the petulance of his temper, and sought relief in the display of bitter and malignant scorn.

Ample illustration of the proposition might be adduced from the history of infidelity, bigotry, and persecution; but instead of lingering on that, we hasten to indicate the practical bearing of the thesis on the matter more immediately in hand. As men responsible in some degree for the dissemination of Christian truth, it is important to understand how we can best fulfil our mission. In prosecuting this inquiry let me remind you of two things :—

(1) That the Bible is God's appointed representative.—What Christ was to Herod, the Scriptures are to us, viz., the embodiment of divine truth and love. We have this representative in our dwelling-places—we have it in our native tongue—it is a great national fact. We can retire from the din of secular life into the calm of our secret chamber, and there commune with this divine guide. Though we have not the personal presence of Christ, we have what is only one degree less valuable—the intelligible record of his life and will. His Spirit is there embodied, and that Spirit will reveal himself according to our mood of mind : two men representing contrary states of feeling may find in the same chapter thoughts the most different:—the contrite and reverent Christian will find instruction, comfort, hope—while the wonder-seeking Herod will find, as it were, words of fire, or a blank heart-dismaying silence! Let me adjure the teachers of the young to make this record their constant study ; other books may be read as subsidiaries, but the Bible must ever remain supreme as a volume for study. Borrow light from every quarter —roam in every realm in quest of illustrations—make every incident useful as an encouragement or a warning—from history, poetry, travel, and biography, bring fact and metaphor, but I charge you in the name of Christ, and in the prospect of eternity, to regard the Volume of Inspiration as the "chief among ten thousand, and altogether lovely." Imagine not that you have

sounded all the depths or grasped all the amplitudes of this great Book—the greater your genius the more prolific of thought it will appear ; and in proportion to the vigour of your piety will it flow with the water of life ! The very fact of our having the Bible involves a tremendous responsibility. Christ is in our house : he will speak to us if we properly address him. The man who neglects the Bible, neglects Christ, and deprives himself of the countless and inestimable advantages attendant on fellowship with God !

(2) **That the Bible must be approached in a sympathetic spirit.**—Would you gather from its pages " thoughts that breathe " ? Come with an earnest mind, humbly seeking divine illumination, and your desire will become reality ! God will approve your aim, and angels may be missioned to quiet your quivering hearts and thrill you with immortal thoughts. Blessed is the reverent student of this Holy Book ;—he never opens it without being charmed with its beauty, fired with its ardour, soothed by its tenderness, and transported by its visions of glory ! In his eye the light of other literature is but the dimness of a rushlight compared with the overpowering splendour of the sun in his might ! To his ear other words are harsh and discordant contrasted with the melodious flow of supernal song. Do you complain that to your investigations the Bible yields but poor returns ? I blame your spirit. Do you allege that general literature is more enchanting to your mind ? I blame your spirit. When the spirit is out of sympathy with God and truth, no book is so difficult as the Bible to understand ; it is all mystery, dark as starless midnight—voiceless as the silent grave. But when the heart is contrite, the vision is quickened to behold a lustre dazzling as the purity of God.

" Wondrous things " may we behold in God's law if we study it in the right mental mood. In fact, all nature is vocal to the ear of the true student ;—there is a voice in the opening year, in the budding spring, in the glorious dawn, the pensive twilight, the star-lit firmament, and the spreading sea—there is a suggestive beauty and an impressive grandeur everywhere ; and could we but walk through this material temple with unclouded intellect and pure heart, we should find a lesson in every breeze, a thought in every atom! But some men find no joy in communing with nature—to them there is no poesy in a flower, and no music in a tempest; the mountain, the landscape, and the sea "answer them nothing,"—all is vacant to their unappreciative eye. So with the great Volume of Revelation, some readers feel not the force of its appeals—to them it is but a common book, which fails to captivate their genius, or entrance their imagination, or subdue their heart. In the plaintive Psalms of Israel's sweet singer no note affects their being—in the fiery majesty of Ezekiel they behold no glory; in the mystic prognostications of Daniel nothing arouses their wonder; in the genial, tender, propitiatory life of Jesus no incident breaks open the fount of their sympathy. Can such men feel any interest in the moral culture of the young? Can such men be expected to support the benevolent institutions of their age? No, is the only answer. Our leaders, ministers, teachers, and supporters must be found in the ranks of the lowly-minded, the contrite, and the reverent. The Herods of society applaud us so long as we can amuse their fancy or gratify their curiosity; but so soon as this power fails they exchange compliment for mockery, and "exceeding gladness" for determined persecution.

Let our prayer be, "Create in me a clean heart, O God, and renew a right spirit within me," that so our minds may ever be open to the reception of divine light. It is a glorious and a hallowed thing to commune with God. We know the conditions on which this privilege can be realised. Let us tremble lest we forfeit it: for Saul, after he had been deposed from the throne of Israel, and found himself weak in the presence of a mightier foe exclaimed, in an agony we cannot describe, "I am sore distressed; for the Philistines make war against me, and God is departed from me, and answereth me no more neither by prophets nor dreams." Time was when God held fellowship with the illustrious potentate; of this he was reminded by the faithful Samuel in this burning question, "When thou wast little in thine own sight wast thou not made the head of the tribes of Israel, and the Lord anointed thee king over Israel?" And what is this question but another form of the proposition that contrition and reverence are the necessary conditions of fellowship with the Infinite? Let us then be lowly, if we would be wise—let us be humble if we would be great—let us worship at the footstool if we would be raised to a throne—let us pray in filial trust if we would awake the responsive sympathy of God.   Would we be mighty teachers and preachers of the gospel?   Let us commune with Jesus. Would we break the mountains in pieces and turn our enemies to confusion?   Let us commune with Jesus.   Would we elevate the truth, and drive error from her ramparts?   Let us commune with Jesus.   Would we silence the miserable reproaches of infidelity?   Let us commune with Jesus.   Would we make life a joy, death a friend, and the tomb an avenue to glory?   Let us commune with Jesus.   'Twill make us strong in battle, swift in race, patient in suffering, and triumphant in death.   His thrilling words will awaken our courage—his genial smile will develop our powers—his gracious promises will inspire our hope.   We may be rich in grace, valiant in fight, strong in confidence, and successful in labour, if we commune with Jesus.

Chapter xxiv. 50.

"He led them out as far as . . ."

PARTED FROM THEM.

THAT is what he is always doing. In the case of the text the incident was personal and local, but it contains a principle of very wide and gracious adaptation. There is a point in life at which visible leading ceases. It may be at Bethany; it may be at eighteen years of age; it may be at nominal and legal manhood. It may vary according to individuality, but there is the principle:—Now I have brought you out so far, go on. This is education, this is providence. We are almost conscious of the moment when we felt our feet squarely upon the earth, with no one near at hand on whom we could rest for a moment. That was a crisis; that was a fine point in life-education. Some people seem never to get out of leading-strings. They have no faith, no courage, no spiritual consciousness that says, I can do it; I can do all things through Christ which strengtheneth me. Where is thy Christ? Taken up into heaven. Canst thou trust an unseen Leader? It is there, at that very point, so vital and so sensitive, that faith comes into full fruition and gracious operation, and man feels that he is no longer dependent upon visibleness and tangibleness, that he has entered upon a higher level of life, that he breathes the air of an infinite and sabbatic climate. Some are farther on than others. This is the difficulty of conducting a thousand men all at once through the same line of argument, because one man is saying, I am not so far on, why do you hasten on? And another man says, if we begin to slow down for those who are weary and weak, Why do you not make more haste in your argument? We have left that point half a century ago; we feel the budding wings, we are about to fly. What is the poor speaker or teacher to do? He must ask his contrastive hearers to throw themselves together and strike an

450

average line, that they may meet for the moment at one common point and receive the impulse and edification of one common thought.

"He led them out as far as "——— Walking. Is there a more interesting exercise than to teach a little child to walk from one chair to another ? The journey is not a very great one to the observer, but it is like going through all Africa to the little traveller. We look upon the exploration with a genial and sympathetic smile, but there is no smile on the child's face; that is about the most solemn moment that has yet taken place in its history. See how it wavers, how it walks, partly with its hands and shoulders, and how it balances itself, and overbalances, and at the last just touches the other shore ! Then we say the child can walk by itself; we turn over a leaf in the family book and write that on such a day at such an hour so-and-so began to walk by himself. We leave him there; he must now find his own legs; we cannot always be putting our arms round the little traveller. There comes a point when even the mother must say, Do the best you can as to walking; you know you can walk well enough : come, find your feet ! And only in this way can the little traveller be made really to walk ; only in this way can toddling become walking and walking become rapid and energetic, only by leaving us can even God himself sometimes make men of us.—"He led them out as far as to——— " books, school, initial instruction, alphabets, forms of things. When we have mastered all these, he says, Now go on : you do not need me to sit down with you and spell out the words : we have passed through that process; you must not always be children, you must not always read the words individually, one by one, as who should say, "And—it—came—to—pass." That is not reading. You must learn to cause the words to flow into one another quickly and musically, so as to make one word out of twenty. But much of that has to be done by yourself. Your teacher leads you out "as far as," and then says, From this point go on, because I am going to begin with a number of little children just such as you were twelve months ago, and try to bring them up to this point. So he has parted from you, and you see that kind and degree of teacher no more.—" He led them out as far as to——— " business.

Then even a father has to say, My boy, carve your own way: I have done all I can for you, I gave you a good schooling, I tried to show you a good example, I have endeavoured to create a very healthy home climate for you, and now it has really come to this that the rest must be done very largely by yourself: pluck up courage, only be of a good courage, and nothing shall stand before you; be faithful, honest, wise, magnanimous, and life will open a road for thee through all its thickets, and we shall meet again in heaven. Our teachers and leaders cannot always be with us. They lead us out as far as to some Bethany, then as to visibleness we say Good-bye! and we return to work with great joy; we are alone, yet not alone; a sweet gracious companionship still drives away all solitariness from the soul, and we live in holy presences. It is withdrawment, not abandonment; it is the ascension of the teacher, that he may become more a teacher still.

This is in common life analogical to what takes place in spiritual life. The Lord leads us out " as far as," and then he says, Now do all you can in your own strength, and, lo, I am with you alway, even unto the end of the world. He has gone that he may be nearer to us; he is higher in the heavens that he may be closer the earth,—a contradiction it may be in mere words and letters, yet they know it to be sweet music who have felt that Christ has gone away, and yet is coming to the soul in every sunbeam and in every quivering of the nightly stars. We are led out as far as—the Bible. But the Bible is not revelation; it is the beginning of the vision; it is the seedhouse, not the garden, the orchard, and the forest. We cannot move without the Bible, and yet it must continually enlarge itself. We can add nothing to the Bible, and yet it can unfold its own wealth, until we exclaim, Behold! these are unsearchable riches. This is the proof of inspiration. It is not a letter, it is a letter only to begin with; the Bible is full of algebraic signs pointing onward to infinity. We do not need any book in addition to the Bible: only those books are good which reproduce the Bible itself in ever-varying forms, and repronounce it in ever-changing but ever-mellifluous and soothing music. Many are accounted heretics who have not the slightest tinge or taint of heresy about

them.   They may only be larger thinkers ; they may only suffer
under the penalty of genius ; they may see through the letter
much of what the letter means.   Each century has its own Bible,
each man has his own revelation : and what we want to get at is
the point at which all men shall say, This is how God shows
himself to me ; how various the vision, how wondrous, how
panoramic this marvellous apocalypse ; we are not divided, in the
heart we are really one.   We shall never have geometric and
mechanical unity, God forbid : we shall have inward and spiritual
unity, God speed the day !

" He led them out as far as "——the Church.   The Church is
not one institution ; the Church could not worship under one and
the same roof.   The Church is invisible ; the Church has indeed
its outward indications, its geometrical magnitudes, it has even
its arithmetical statistics ; but all these are useless if they do not
point to something invisible, spiritual, immeasurable, ineffable
What part of the Church are you in ?   You are only in the
alphabetic-church, you are only in the vestibule ; you may be
only in the outer court of the Gentiles.   Manifold and infinite is
the Church of the Cross, and it should be our business to include
men and not to exclude them ; let excommunication be the last
act, the unavoidable, the tremendous finale.

" He led them out as far as to "——the symbol.   It has been
beautifully shown again and again that God is always leading us
out to something larger than we can express in terms.   That idea
has formed the basis of many a noble and inspiring discourse in
various sanctuaries.   Thus to Abraham the Lord said, I will give
thee a land flowing with milk and honey—come !   If the Lord
had said, I will give thee a heavenly Jerusalem, an invisible
Canaan " a land of pure delight, where saints immortal reign,"
the sheik could not have been touched, he did not know that
music, there was no home-strain in all that celestial melody ;
when, however, he heard of a land, a land flowing with milk and
honey, a land of acres that bloomed like flowers in the sun, he
rose, and then at the last he would not have the very thing he
went for.   He had grown in the meantime, he had become a
larger man, he had become dematerialised, spiritualised, elevated ;

his whole imagination had become as a lens through which he saw further distances and brighter glories, and instead of looking upon the green Canaan, growing grass and herbs, he said, I seek a country out of sight. God meant that from the very first, but if at the first he had said that, he would have overpowered the man and left him in bewilderment and dismay. Thus we are led on from point to point, and God has so arranged the economy of life that sometimes we seem to be left to ourselves; as if the Lord would set us a task or lesson in his own Bible, saying, as sometimes a pastor says to an inquirer, Read the third chapter of the Gospel by John, and see me in a week. Thus I have been able to help many inquirers myself, and other pastors have done the same. Instead of sitting down and reading the chapter with the inquirer, we have said, Take it home, read it every word, get it into your heart, talk with the passage and get the passage to talk to you, and then let us meet this day week and compare our investigations, and seek the blessing of God upon our individual and mutual inquiry. So the Lord leaves us to ourselves for long periods or for periods which seem long. Whenever he is absent a moment we think he has gone for ever. There are moments that are eternities: we measure time by the hunger of our love.

Having once had great companionships and noble leaderships, we can never lose them. They are taken away from us as to visibleness, but they are with us as to influence and sympathy. Thus, if we have really lived with any other soul, man, woman, child, friend, teacher, we know what that other soul would say and do under all the changing circumstances of life. What voices we hear, what counsel we receive without words! We say to ourselves, We know what he would say under these circumstances, we know what he would do, or she, under such conditions; he would say, Rise, and shake yourself from this slavery: she would say, Cheer thee: it is nightmare that is now brooding over thy soul and making thee afraid. Oh, poor heart, I have gone from thee as to visibleness, but cry thou mightily unto God, and if in some other world I can help thy prayer I will be with thee evermore. We know what the ascended husband would say; we know what the sainted wife would do: we lived so long together that there is no longer any mystery as to the counsel that would be given.   And if we will only open the ears of our hearts we shall hear music from heaven itself.   Thus our friends have withdrawn from us, and yet they come back to us in larger identity ; no longer may we shake hands, but evermore we may unite in heart.

We have not been led "as far as" in order that we might change the road, but that we might continue and complete the journey.   When men are led "as far as" and then turn their backs upon the road, they have lost their leadership in more senses than one.   Go on unto perfection : persevere along this road ;—that is the voice of Providence, that is the monition of the higher education.   We do not change the doctrine, though we may change its modes of representation.   Here again many a man is really speaking larger truth than he himself is quite aware of ; here again many a man is supposed to have left the faith when he has done nothing of the kind.   He only sees the old truths from a new point, or views them under uncalculated or unforeseen conditions : presently he will see that it is the same mountain, facing north, facing south, having a side that drinks in all the morning light, and another side that drinks in all the evening glory.   Let us have larger faith in one another, in our love of truth, in our love of Christ.

"He led them out as far as to Bethany."   He would have taken them farther if it had been for their good.   At Bethany he " blessed them."   Some places seem to double the blessing. The places themselves are memories, pictures, centres of spiritual interest.   He led them back to their birthplace, and blessed them ; he led them out as far as to the wedding altar, and blessed them ; he led them out as far as to their earliest recollection of heavenly visions, and blessed them.   He must choose the point of parting.   " And it came to pass, while he blessed them, he was parted from them, and carried up into heaven."   The sentence was left incomplete ; the benediction was broken off as it were at a semicolon.   " While he blessed them,"—it is as the song of an ascending bird, now so clear, so sharp, so sweet, and now less so, and now—and now—and now—gone !—away into the light, away to the nativity of the morning, away into heaven! We should bless God for broken benedictions, for incomplete farewells. The way of the going seems to intimate the certainty of the coming: as if Christ had said, You have heard half the sentence now, the other half you shall hear in the morning. Oh, sweet, bright summer morning, we hunger for thee! We are tired of the wild, windy, cold, stormy night!

NOTE.

The Speaker's Commentary says:—"St. Mark does not tell us where the Ascension occurred. Luke tells us afterwards (Acts i. 12) that it took place on Mount 'Olivet, which is from Jerusalem a Sabbath day's journey.' There is no contradiction between the earlier and the later statement of the evangelists. Bethany lay on the eastern slope of the Mount of Olives, and the way from the village to Jerusalem lay across the mountain. A portion of the mountain may have appertained to Bethany, and may have been called by its name. And St. Luke speaks here with a certain degree of vagueness; he does not actually assert that the apostles were led to Bethany, but 'as far as' (meaning near) 'to Bethany': and his words are therefore satisfied by supposing the Ascension to have taken place somewhere in the neighbourhood of the village. Bethany and the Mount of Olives are similarly associated in Mark xi. 1, as well as in Mark xi. 11, compared with chap. xxi. 37. The traditional scene of the Ascension is one of the four summits of the Mount of Olives, overhanging, and in full view of, the city of Jerusalem, and now covered by the village and mosque and church of the Jebel-et-Tur. The site, however, is too far from Bethany and too near to Jerusalem to satisfy the conditions of the narrative. 'On the wild uplands which immediately overhang the village, he finally withdrew from the eyes of his disciples, in a seclusion which, perhaps, could nowhere else be found so near the stir of a mighty city; the long ridge of Olivet screening those hills, and those hills the village beneath them, from all sound or sight of the city behind; the view opening only on the wide waste of desert-rocks and ever-descending valleys, into the depths of the distant Jordan and its mysterious lake. At this point, the last interview took place. "He led them out as far as Bethany;" and they "returned," probably by the direct road over the summit of Mount Olivet. The appropriateness of the real scene presents a singular contrast to the inappropriateness of that fixed by a later fancy, "seeking for a sign," on the broad top of the mountain, out of sight of Bethany, and in full sight of Jerusalem, and thus in equal contradiction to the letter and the spirit of the gospel narrative.'"—(STANLEY, *Sinai and Palestine.*)

INDEX.

457

Preaching Through the Bible

BY

JOSEPH PARKER

VOL. 22

JOHN

Originally printed
under the title,
The People's Bible

CONTENTS.

THE GOSPEL ACCORDING TO JOHN—

THE

GOSPEL ACCORDING TO JOHN.

[NOTE.—"John, the younger brother of James, who with him was called
to the apostleship, was the son of Zebedee and of Salome. His father was
a fisherman, living at Bethsaida in Galilee, on the borders of the lake of
Gennesareth. The family appear to have been in easy circumstances; at
least, we find that Zebedee employed hired servants (Mark i. 20); and that
Salome was among the women who contributed to the maintenance of
Jesus (Matt. xxvii. 56).

"Having been brought up in the knowledge and the love of the true
God by a pious mother, he appears to have early become a disciple of our
Lord's forerunner, and to have been directed by him to Jesus, whom he
followed; it being generally considered that he was one of the two disciples
mentioned in chap. i. 37–41. He was soon admitted, with his brother
James, and Peter, to particular intimacy with the Saviour, who selected
them as witnesses of the most important and solemn events of his life
(Mark v. 37; Matt. xvii. 1, xxvi. 37).

"It appears, that of all the apostles John was especially favoured with
our Lord's regard and confidence, so as to be called 'the disciple whom
Jesus loved.' He was devotedly attached to his Master; and though he
fled, like the other apostles, when Jesus was apprehended, he recovered his
firmness, was present during the trial and crucifixion of our Saviour, and
was intrusted by him with the care of his mother (xix. 26, 27).

"John is said to have remained at Jerusalem till the death of Mary, about
the year A.D. 48. After Paul had left Asia Minor John went to labour
there, residing chiefly at Ephesus, and founding several churches in that
country. Shortly afterwards, during the persecution under Domitian (or,
according to others, towards the end of the reign of Nero), he was banished
to Patmos, an island in the Ægean Sea, where he received the visions of
the Apocalypse. On the accession of Nerva he was liberated, and returned
to Ephesus, where he continued to labour during the rest of his life. He
died in the hundredth year of his age, about A.D. 100."—ANGUS's *Bible
Handbook*.]

Chapter i. 6–13.

"There was a man sent from God, whose name was John. The same
came for a witness, to bear witness of the Light, that all men through him
might believe. He was not that Light, but was sent to bear witness of that

Light. That was the true Light, which lighteth every man that cometh into the world. He was in the world, and the world was made by him, and the world knew him not. He came unto his own, and his own received him not. But as many as received him, to them gave he power to become the sons of God, even to them that believe on his name : which were born, not of blood, nor of the will of the flesh, nor of the will of man, but of God."

PRIMARY AND SECONDARY LIGHT.

THE John spoken of in the first verse of the text is John the Baptist. The evangelist says that John was sent from God. Ordinary biography begins at another point. In this case, parentage, birth, training, are omitted altogether, and the very beauty of God lights up the face of the man. Men have different ways of looking at themselves. In some cases they look downward towards "the mire and the clay," that they may keep in memory "the hole of the pit out of which they were digged"; in others, they view human life religiously, and claim the dignity and privilege of the sons of God. The influence of this view upon the uses of strength and upon surrounding life must be intense and salutary. We degrade life when we omit God from its plan. On the other hand, we descend upon our work with fulness of power when we realise that it is God that worketh in us to will and to do of his good pleasure. What is our view of life ? Have we but a physical existence, or are we the messengers of the most High ? When Moses went to his work he was enabled to say—"I AM hath sent me unto you." So when John undertook his mission he boldly claimed to be the appointed servant of God. Our greatest power is on the religious side of our nature: physically, we are crushed before the moth; religiously, we have omnipotence as the source of our strength.

"The same came for a witness,"—God reveals himself to us little by little as we may be able to bear the light. He has set forth a long and wonderful procession of witnesses, from Moses even until John, who was the last of the illustrious line. It is well when a man distinctly knows the limit of his vocation. We are strong within our own bounds. John, as a professed Saviour, would have been weak and contemptible; but as a witness he was a burning and a shining light. John the Baptist

was as the morning star. Or (changing the figure) he was a
man standing on the highest mountain, who, catching a glimpse
of the first solar ray, exclaims, "Behold, the day cometh!" And
is not such an exclamation the only originality of which we are
capable? There is no originality, except that which is relative,
in any ministry or in any church.

"He was not that Light,"—he was but a temporary ray:
the brightest light which the hand of man can enkindle is
instantly paled when the sun shineth in his strength,—beautiful
indeed is that secondary light when shining alone, and not
beautiful only, but precious exceedingly to men who, without it,
would be in darkness; yet could it speak, it would say,—"I am
but a spark of another fire; your admiration of my splendour
will cease when you see the sun." Such is the speech of the
most luminous men. Our light is lunar, not solar; or solar
only because Christ is in us, and according to the measure of our
capacity he sheds his glory through our life.

"That was the true Light, which lighteth every man that cometh
into the world." As the sun shines for every man, so Jesus
Christ lives for every man. The lamp in the house belongs to
the householder: the lamp in the street is a local convenience:
but the sun pours its morning and its noontide into every valley,
and into the humblest home; that is the true light: the freehold
of every man,—the private property of none! And every man
knows that the sun is the true light,—feels it to be such,—and
without hesitation affirms it to be supreme. There is no debate
as to whether the sun or the moon is the light of the world.
Imagine a dark night, and an observer who has never seen the
sun: a star suddenly shows itself, and the observer hails it with
delight; presently the moon shines with all her gentle strength,
and the observer says,—"This is the fulfilment of the promise;
can ought be lovelier, can the sky possibly be brighter?" In
due course the sun comes up; every cloud is filled with light;
every mountain is crowned with a strange glory; every leaf in
the forest is silvered; the sea becomes as burnished glass, and
secrecy is chased from the face of the earth: under such a vision,
the observer knows that this is the true light,—the sovereign

all-dominating flame. It is so in the revelation of Jesus Christ. When the eyes of men are opened to see him in all his grace and wisdom and sympathy,—in all the sufficiency of his sacrifice, and the comfort of his Spirit,—the heart is satisfied, and every rival light is lost in the infinite splendour of God the Son.

" He came unto his own, and his own received him not."—He came unto his own things (ἴδια), and his own people (ἴδιοι) received him not. There was no room for his mother in the inn. He himself had not where to lay his head. He was as a householder coming to his own house, and being kept out by his own servants. What is the earth but one apartment in the great house of God! Its furniture,—(its hills and valleys and rivers, fruits and flowers and harvest fields),—is Jesus Christ's, for apart from him was not anything made that was made ; yet when he came to his own house his ownership was denied by the servants who had been put into temporary possession by his own power and grace! " Hear, O heavens, and give ear, O earth : for the Lord hath spoken, I have nourished and brought up children, and they have rebelled against me."

" But as many as received him, to them gave he power to become the sons of God."—Having believed on his name they entered upon a new relation to their Father in heaven. They had been living a life of mere creature-hood ; the sense and the joy of sonship had been lost, and had become irrecoverable except by faith, which is the gift of God. Regeneration is as much the work of God as was creation. A man may unmake himself, but the power of restoration is not in his own hand. Nor is there either mystery or injustice in this. The same law holds good in the physical as in the spiritual world : a man can kill himself, but can he take back his life again? Or he can crush a flower, but can he heal it, and make it as perfect and beautiful as before ? Or he may destroy his sight, but can he recover his vision? We can only destroy ; we cannot create. " O Israel, thou hast destroyed thyself; but in me is thine help." Let us give personality to two flowers, and from their talk let us learn something on this matter : " I stand in this window from month to month, and I declare that every possible attention is paid to me ;

as regularly as the morning comes my roots are watered, and not a day passes without the window being opened that I may be revived by the fresh living air : so if ever flower had reason for contentment and joy I am that flower." So far, so good. Now, the second flower, luxuriant and beautiful exceedingly, says, "Look at the difference between us! I am of the same stock as yourself; we are called by the same name ; we live on the same elements ; yet I am strong and blooming, and you are weak and colourless." How is this, then ? The one flower has been standing in a sunless window, the other has been living in the sun! Preach the gospel of light to that flower, and if your gospel be received with faith, the light will give it " power " to become as strong and beautiful as any member of the same family. It is even so with mankind. We are trying to live without the light,—the true Light which lighteth every man that cometh into the world,—and our trial gives us over more and more to the power of death. Without light no soul can live!

" Which were born, not of blood, nor of the will of the flesh, nor of the will of man, but of God."—This, again, is most emphatically in the style of John. Never can he lose sight of the perfect spirituality of Jesus Christ's work. John shows the very religiousness of religion. Christianity is to him more than a history, more than an argument, more than a theology,—it is a spiritual revelation to the spiritual nature of man. On the part of man it is to be not an attitude, but a life,—the very mystery of his spirit, too subtle for analysis, too strong for repression, too divine to be tolerant of corruption.

Chapter i. 19, 20.

"And this is the record of John, when the Jews sent priests and Levites from Jerusalem to ask him, Who art thou ? And he confessed, and denied not ; but confessed, I am not the Christ."

THE RECORD OF JOHN.

THE John spoken of in the text is John the Baptist. John who writes the text is John the Evangelist. It is a peculiarity of John's Gospel that throughout he deals almost exclusively, though there are special exceptions, with the spiritual ministry of Jesus Christ the Son of God. The other evangelists treat very prominently of the miracles and the more public ministry of the Saviour. But the evangelist John seems to know the heart of Jesus Christ. John was the spiritual evangelist ; he had keen, spiritual eyes. True, indeed, he saw all the miracles of an outward and public kind that Jesus Christ did, but he seemed to make a special note of those spiritual miracles which deal more directly with the heart and the conscience, the inner life, and the secret motives of men. You will find somewhat of my meaning from the structure of the preface to his Gospel, which we have in this opening chapter. Matthew and Luke proceed to trace out the history of Jesus Christ from the human side ; they show how he came into the world, through what genealogical line he found his way amongst the sons of men. But John takes another course altogether. Instead of writing a genealogical table, showing us the whole human ancestry of the Son of God, he says, with the abruptness of sublimity, "In the beginning was the Word, and the Word was with God, and the Word was God." The other evangelists seemed to bring Jesus Christ up from the earth ; John opens heaven, and reveals his glory from on high. This is the key of the whole gospel ; it is pre-eminently a spiritual revelation ; it deals with the inner life

6

of things. He who is the master of the Gospel by John is a
refined and learned scholar in the school of Christ. There is very
little outwardness in the statements of John ; he does refer again
and again to miracles, but more frequently he speaks from the
interior life of the Saviour, and shows us the meaning of the
truth and the grace that are in Christ Jesus. This we shall see
more clearly as we pursue our way from the text which is now
under consideration.

John the Baptist was preaching. A deputation was sent from
Jerusalem to wait upon him, to put to him this question, " Who
art thou ? " He had been creating a great sensation ; all the
people for miles round about had been crowding to his ministry ;
he had excited very great interest and expectation, and people
were looking out for some startling and marvellous event. John
received the deputation, heard their inquiry, and when he listened
to it he passed through the hour of his temptation. Is it a little
thing to have a deputation waiting upon you from the capital in
whose heart there is evidently a very special expectation ? Is it
a little thing to hear the members of the deputation say, " Who
art thou ? " in a tone which seems to imply, " We shall not be
surprised if thou dost reveal thyself as the very light we have
been expecting ! " A temptation was brought thus to bear upon
John. The people would have returned to those who sent them,
and would have said, " Yes, this is the man ; this is the realisation of all the ancient prophecies ; he has come at last ; his name
is Messias, Son of God, King of the Jews." How did John meet
the temptation ? " He confessed, and denied not ; but confessed, I
am not the Christ." The wonder of those who waited upon him
was increased. Who was he, then ? That he was some great
man could not be doubted, so they proceeded to say, " What,
then, art thou Elias ? " and he said, " I am not." " Art thou that
prophet ? " and he answered, " No." He did not at once reveal
who he was, but allowed these people to pursue their inquiries for
a time. He baffled them, and kept them at arm's length. It is in
the same way we ourselves are treated in some such manner,
now and again, even in our highest inquiries. We receive
negatives, and not affirmatives, as answers. Instead of having a
revelation made clear, distinct, and final, we are tempted to go

further, and to repeat our inquiries in various forms. Thus God puts us under a process of training by not answering at once the inquiries with which we besiege him. Blessed is the man who will pursue his inquiry until he reaches the truth, who finds in all the answers of God licenses to ask again, to put up some other prayer, to shape his heart's wish into some other form. For truly, God is thus training the man to have a wise and understanding heart.

John knew who he was. That is one of the main points every man ought to understand about himself. He ought to be able to say who he is, what he has been called to do, what he is qualified to perform. Because a man who may have great power within a given compass may have only to step beyond the line of his limit to be utterly weak and useless. Do we know ourselves? Do we know the measure of our strength? Do we work within the compass that God has assigned us; or are we wasting our strength in those foolish ambitions which tempt us away from proper limitations and mock us, throwing us back and back again into the dust, so that at the end of the day a man who might have done some solid and substantial work in life has done nothing but follow the vagaries of a useless and mortifying ambition, and will leave the world without having done it any good? The Church ought to know what it is; the Church ought to understand its limitations. Every minister ought to know who he is, and what he is called to do. The moment a man usurps anything that does not belong to him he loses power, and the moment the Church lays claim to anything that does not fairly come within its possession as determined by Christ, that Church goes down in its best influence. " Who art thou ? " If he had said, " I am the Christ," he would have won a moment's victory, but he would have opened up to himself a most ignominious and humiliating destiny. Who art thou, O man? what canst thou do? what is the purpose of God as revealed in thy life? Art thou great? art thou little? art thou intended for public life? art thou meant for private ministry? What is thy place? what is thy calling in life? Let a man understand this clearly, and work according to a devout conviction, and his life cannot be spent in vain. But let this temptation once seize a man, " I could be as great as Elias has been ; I think I have within me the spirit of that prophet referred to so often in the Old Testament " ;—let a man extend himself ambitiously beyond his proper function and calling in life, and the result will be self-mortification, ignominy, and shame ; and he who might have done something really good and useful, will go out of the world having misspent his little day.

What is true of individual men is true of the whole Church. When a man says, " I am Christ," he lies. When a man says, " I claim infallibility," he touches the highest point of blasphemy. When a man at Rome, or in London, or elsewhere, says, " I am as God upon the earth," he knows not himself ; he has committed the most grievous sin, though there be upon his lips the holiest of names. I wish to be emphatic upon this ; I wish every man amongst us to know himself, to understand what he is, and then, though he cannot say in reply to the inquiry, " Art thou some great one ? " " Yes ; " yet, if he can say that he is sent of God to do the humblest work in the world, he is great in his degree, and shall have promotion and rulership in the world that is to come. Look at John ; see how the great men crowd around him ; hear what temptation they suggest to him. It had never occurred to John himself, in all probability, that he was Elias, that he was " that prophet," that he was some great one. So the suggestion comes to him with all the force of a subtle temptation. What does he answer ? He says, " I am the voice of one crying in the wilderness, Make straight the way of the Lord." That was his answer. What did he say of himself ? " I am a voice." What did he say of his ministry ? " I am sent to prepare the way of the Lord in the attention and the affections of the world." Thus, he who had offered to him by a very subtle temptation a brilliant crown and a high throne said, " No ; I am but a voice ; I am not the expected One ; clearly understand my ministry and function in life ; I am the herald, not the King : I blow the blast of the trumpet, and he himself will be here presently." That is just what every Christian has to do ; to go before, to proclaim the Lord, to call men to preparedness, to awaken their attention, to tell them to be ready : for the Bridegroom cometh, and then to stand out of the way, as those who have indeed done a humble,

yet a most useful work, in the world. But I repeat, he who
knows his strength as John knew it will be strong, as no man
can be who imagines himself to have a power with which God
never invested him. A stern, solemn, grand man was John.
He would receive no compliments; he would take nothing that
did not belong to him of right. He was asked why he performed
the office of baptism if he was not the Christ, nor Elias, neither
that prophet. John answered and said, "I baptise with water;
but mine is a merely introductory ceremony, I am only giving
you types, and showing you hints of things; the real work has
yet to be done, the inward spiritual change has yet to be wrought
in the hearts of men. This poor water, this shallow river, I use
as indicative of the great fact that man needs an inward change.
As for this baptism, it does nothing towards the removal of your
sins, but it offers an opportunity of saying, 'We are sinners;
we would be saved; we would repent; we would be born
again.'"

After this there came in his speech a beautiful sentence:
"There standeth one among you, whom ye know not; he it is,
who coming after me is preferred before me, whose shoe's latchet
I am not worthy to unloose." Where was the expected one?
Standing amongst the people. They were looking far away for
the blessing promised to the world, and behold, that blessing
was standing in their very midst. It is in this way that we miss
many of the great revelations and wonderful presences that God
sends down to cheer us and soothe us by gentle ministries. We
are looking beyond; we are looking afar off; we think that our
great blessings should come from some great distance. God
says, "My child, they are under thy very hand; they are close
beside thy footprints; the best blessings I can give thee may be
had at once. Seek, and thou shalt find; knock, and it shall be
opened unto thee; ask and have." So throughout the whole of
the revelations of God we are told that things precious to our
best life are much nearer us than we imagine; that God is not
a God afar off, but a God nigh at hand; that after all there is not
some stupendous thing to be done on our behalf. We have but
to open our eyes and we shall see the light; but to breathe our
prayer, and all that is good for us will be done in our hearts.

We have no long pilgrimages to make ; no great penalties to
undergo ; no long-suffering and self-infliction and self-reproach
and self-crucifixion to perform, in any outward sense of those
terms.   Christ has done the work for us ; he is within reach of
the prayer of our love ; he is amongst us ; he is nigh at hand.
" Believe on the Lord Jesus Christ and thou shalt be saved."

I believe that in talking thus I am speaking to a difficulty that
does keep many persons back from the realisation of the very
highest blessings of God.   " There standeth one among you."
Blessings are nearer than you expect.   There standeth one
among you ; but the angel is veiled.   There standeth one
among you ; stretch not your necks as if looking beyond the
hills ; open your eyes as if expecting to see God at your very
side, and the light of his countenance shall make day in your
hearts.   Have not some of us been doing some great thing, and
looking to some great distance for the incoming of God into the
human race and into our own hearts ?   There is nothing in the
creation that is round about us that does not testify to the near
presence of God.

Art thou looking for God coming far away from the east
yonder, when the morning light shines ?   Be assured that he is
in that bread, if it be but a crust that is on thy morning table.
Do you expect God to come in thunder and lightning, and whirlwind, and stormy tempest, making the clouds the dust of his
feet, and coming with the trumpet of the thunder and the shouting of angels ?   Behold, he is in that little spring of water at thy
backdoor, he is round about thy bed ; he is numbering the hairs
of thy head ; he is putting his hand upon the head of thy little
child ; he is doing home work ; he is on thy table ; round about
thy couch ; making steadfast thy feet in all thy paths, watching
all thy going, observing thy down-sitting and thy uprising, thy
going out and thy coming in.   He hath beset thee behind and
before, and he lays his hand upon thee.   And yet thou art
looking as though thou didst require some great telescope to see
the distance of God, and even then thou dost expect but to see
his hinder skirts.   There standeth one among you whom ye
know not ; God is within whisper reach : he can hear every throb

of the heart, he sees every tear that drops from the eye of penitence, and there is nothing that is hidden from the fire of his look. Believe this, and a great awe will descend upon thy life; believe this, and every mountain will be an altar, every star a door into heaven, every flower an autograph of God, and the whole scene of thy life shall be chastened and hallowed by a religious sense, and an assurance and consciousness that God is close at hand.

"The next day John seeth Jesus coming unto him, and saith, Behold the Lamb of God, which taketh away the sin of the world." This expression on the part of John the Baptist proves what I have said about the spirituality of the writings of John the evangelist. John the evangelist alone marks down this exclamation,—he heard the spiritual words of the preacher. John the Baptist called the attention of the world to the great coming One. John the evangelist saw spiritual realities, whilst men of inferior mould were dealing with so-called facts and with the outwardness of things. It was John's fine sense of hearing that caught this expression: "Behold the Lamb of God, which taketh away the sin of the world." If you will at your leisure compare the reports which are given of John the Baptist by the other evangelists, you will know what I mean by saying that John the evangelist caught the spiritual aspect of things, saw the inward, moral, spiritual intent of men who wrote and spoke, and who came as the special servants and ministers of God to the world. It will be easy for you to put together the conversations which would very likely take place regarding the preaching of John the Baptist. We have a record in Matthew, Mark, Luke, and John. There will be no difficulty in piecing these reports, so as to get a tolerably correct idea of the conversations that preceded regarding this remarkable personage. To him none could show hospitality. His meat was locusts and wild honey; he had a leathern girdle about his loins; his home was the wilderness. He wanted none of your wine and your luxury; he did not accept invitations to the banqueting boards of men; he realised what is meant by the independence of poverty. As long as there was a locust he had a meal; as long as he could put his finger out to the wild honey he had enough. The blandishments and all the refinements and luxuries of the state that was near to him had no effect upon his ambition or upon his heart. He lived independently; you could take nothing from him, and he would not have anything added to him. Oh, it was a stern, solemn, terrible-looking life that; and his preaching was very like it, was it not? If we had only had the accounts of Matthew and Mark and Luke, we should have thought that the preaching was such as eminently befitted the preacher. Look at him there. Look at his long locks, at his leathern girdle, at his monastic face, at his rugged bearing, at his simple fare. He is standing there silently; when he speaks I wonder what such lips will say? Oh, they are terrible looking lips! When he shuts his mouth he seems to have made a resolution; when he closes those lips of his it seems as if he never would open them again but to curse the world! Listen! Have you heard this preacher named John—this grim, weird man that rejects our approaches, and keeps us so much at arm's length? Have you heard him? "Yes." Can you quote anything he says? "Yes; I never heard so terrible a speaker as he is; he seems to cleave the air when he speaks. I heard him say, 'His fan is in his hand, and he will throughly purge his floor!'" Have you heard him preach? "Yes; and never heard such a speaker before." Can you quote anything he says? "Yes; he says, 'The wheat he will gather into his garner; but the chaff he will burn up with unquenchable fire!'" Have you heard him preach? "Yes." Can you quote anything that this wonderful man has said in his preaching? "Yes, I can." What did he say? "He said, 'The axe is laid to the root of the tree!'" And their report ends. Matthew, Mark, and Luke have each spoken to us, and there is an end of it. Was that preaching? Do such terrible sentences as these constitute preaching? "His fan is in his hand!" That is a threatening. "The axe is laid to the root of the tree!" That is a threatening. "The chaff he will burn up with unquenchable fire!" That is a threatening. An awful preacher! I expected as much; I thought he never could speak a gentle word; his voice could never subside into a minor tone. I turn over a page, and the page brings to me the report of John the evangelist. I inquire, "John the evangelist, have you heard your namesake the Baptist?" "Yes." Can you quote anything from any one of his sermons? "Yes." What? "Behold the Lamb of God, which taketh away the sin of the world."

Such are the different reports we may hear about a man's preaching! Some people never hear the finer tones; some persons never hear the tenderer expostulations and messages of the speaker. They remember what he said about the fan and the axe, and the unquenchable fire; but the gentle gospel, the sweet, persuasive tone, the indicated Lamb of God, they think nothing of,—they remember not; it seems to escape them altogether. This rugged preacher, with the voice of the whirl-wind and a countenance grim to terribleness, was he who preached the most intensely evangelical, the most vital gospel sermon ever delivered by the lips of man or angel. "Behold the Lamb of God, which taketh away the sin of the world." Re-member, John said that; remember, that is the upgathering of the revelation of God; remember, that to recollect everything else and to forget this, is to remember the shell and to forget the kernel, to remember the body and to forget the heart, to know the outside of things, and nothing of that inner spiritual reality which is the very joy of life. How beautifully it is put: "The Lamb of God, which taketh away the sin of the world." How it might have read! What a different expression it might have been! This would seem to have been more in harmony with the aspect of the speaker, and with all that was known about his way of livelihood. When he came out of the wilderness, having eaten the locusts and the wild honey, and girt his leathern girdle about him, and come forth amongst the people, I should have expected him to say this: "Behold the lions of the tribe of Judah that devoureth the sinners of the world!" I should have said, "Yes, that is a natural climax; that kind of expression seems to befit your mouth." Instead of that he says, "Behold the Lamb of God, which taketh away the sin of the world." Not the sinners but the sin; not the offender but the offence. That is redemption. The other course would have been destruction. It is easy to destroy; it requires God to redeem. It is easy to strike: it requires infinite grace to heal. By one stroke of his lightning he could have taken away the sinners, but it required the blood of his heart to take away the sin. We are redeemed not with corruptible things as silver and gold, but with the precious blood of Jesus Christ, the Lamb of God !

Christ came to take away sin ; we cannot take it away ourselves. If it required the divine intervention to take away sin, why should we be going to Abana and Pharpar, rivers of Damascus, when there is a fountain opened in the house of David for sin and for uncleanness ?   Why be wasting strength and mocking the heart when Jesus comes before us with the express purpose of taking away our sin ?   "Through this man is preached unto you the forgiveness of sins."   Here is the atonement, here is the sacrifice of the Son of God—complete, sufficient, final.   The priest himself becomes the victim.   Great is the mystery of godliness !   To have seen everything in life but the Lamb of God, is to have seen everything in life but the one thing worth seeing.   To have beheld all sights of greatness and glory and beauty, and not to have seen the Lamb of God, is to have seen the light from the outside of the window, and not to have gone in and found rest and welcome and home !

"Philip findeth Nathanael, and saith unto him, We have found him, of
whom Moses in the law, and the prophets, did write, Jesus of Nazareth, the
son of Joseph."

THE PRIVATE MINISTRY OF THE GOSPEL.

DO you know how difficult it is to preach to one hearer?
Some young people, who have a wish to be public speakers,
wonder how a man can stand before a thousand of his fellow-
creatures and speak to them boldly, with perfect self-possession
and confidence. Believe me, there is a higher courage than that;
namely, to speak to one man about Jesus, to direct your remarks
to one heart, and to press your urgent appeal upon the individual
conscience. Philip spoke to Nathanael, and in this fact I find an
illustration of what may be called the Private Ministry of the
Gospel—a ministry between one man and another—a ministry
between friend and friend. To this higher courage we are all
called—to this private and direct ministry we are impelled by
our own thankfulness for a revelation of the Son of God; let
us, therefore, endeavour to discover the basis and the method
of this lofty and most blessed vocation.

The Christian minister has a distinct message to deliver to the
world. Philip delivered such a message to Nathanael: "We
have found him of whom Moses in the law, and the prophets, did
write, Jesus of Nazareth, the son of Joseph." The Christian
ministry takes its stand upon facts. We are not sent to conceive
a theory to account for circumstances that are around us; we
have not to strain our minds to work out a speculation or to
elaborate an argument; we have nothing to do with dreaming
or supposition; fancy is not our business; first of all, midst of
all, and last of all, we have to deal with facts. The Christian

teacher takes his stand upon a historic rock, and only as he does
so is he safe. Clearing the ground of everything, we point the
inquirer in the first instance to facts : Jesus Christ was born,
Jesus Christ lived, taught, died, rose again,—that is our historic
outline, and we risk everything upon it ; then we proceed to
show that this historic outline has come out of a grand system
of preparation, of prophecy, of holy service as ordained of God.
Nothing else so completely, so graciously, and so gloriously meets
all the points and designs of that initial system ; so we do not
hesitate to identify all the divine elements of human history with
the person and work of Jesus Christ, and to claim for him the
title of Saviour and the throne of the One true King.

Not only so. To have the facts is one thing, but something
more is required. Philip did not say, Jesus Christ has been found ;
he said, We have found him. He himself sustained a personal
relation to those facts, and this relation was the secret of his
power. In a mighty ministry we find not only high intellectual,
but also high emotional power ; the heart gives fire to the
thought. No man can preach with the truest success if he only
knows the facts ; he must feel them as well as know them, and
then his tongue will not fail for words that find the hearts of
others. Every preacher, private or public, must, so to speak,
individualise the gospel ; must himself represent the truths which
he seeks to teach, and by so much his ministry will address
itself to the deepest life of those who hear him. Know the
gospel if you would formally teach it ; but love the gospel if
you would teach it with triumphant and blessed effect. Truly,
no man knows the gospel, except as he loves it. To know about
it is one thing ; to have it reigning in the heart is another. It
may be replied that it is not everything to know the mere facts
of the gospel, and so it is undoubtedly, if you use the term
" know " in its most insufficient acceptation ; but as intended to
be applied by me at this moment, the term includes, not only the
assent of the mind, but the loving and undivided homage of the
heart. We may know that a certain man has arrived in London,
and the knowledge may fail to excite a single sensation in our
nature ; but to those who have been expecting and longing for
him with most loving desire, his arrival is a blessing which fills

them with thankfulness and joy. So with Christ. We have been seeking him, waiting for him, crying to God for the coming of his blessed presence, and to-day the fact that we have found him causes us joy inexpressible and full of glory.

If the Church would be strong in her doctrines, she must be strong in her facts. When she gets away from facts, she gets into dangerous waters. I have no fear of speculation or of controversy so long as there is a clear and grateful recognition of facts. We may be trusted to speculate so long as we are sure of the foundations; but if we trifle with the rock, we shall be the sport of the wildest dreaming, intoxicated with our supposed independence, whilst the fetters of a cruel slavery are being bound upon our feet.

In delivering his message the Christian minister will encounter opposition. Nathanael said to Philip, Can any good thing come out of Nazareth? This is opposition. We shall encounter opposition of various kinds. The worldly-minded hearer will say, "I have enough to do in getting my daily bread. I have no time for spiritual concerns—away with your preaching and dreaming, and let me make the best of the present life." The speculative hearer will invite to controversy; he will urge objection after objection; it is not in his ethereal and sublime nature to trifle away his time in reading history and considering facts; he lives on wings, he soars through the courses of the light, and inquires in the upper circles of fancy. He says, "Away with your historic realities and your personal appearances! Answer the wonders of my imagination, and satisfy the demands of my curiosity. I care not for your dry and barren facts." All ministers have met with such opposition, and it has often been a hindrance to their ministry; but there is a deadlier opposition than this! It is possible to drag the worldly-minded man from the altar of his dust-god, and to persuade him to think of higher concerns; possible to break the awful dominion of Mammon, and to liberate a slave now and then at least; it is possible, also, to teach the speculator to be sober in his claims, to descend from his aërial car, and to look at events with the eye of temperate reason. But who can destroy the power of prejudice? Can you define prejudice? You can give me a derivation, but can you give me a definition? What is prejudice, where does it begin, how does it work, where does it end? You may have felt it, but can you describe it—define it? Take a prejudice against a man, and he can never more do right in your eyes; you will see a colour upon his purest deed, you will see a twist in his straightest course, you will see a taint in his holiest motives. Take a prejudice against a minister, and though he gives his days to study and his nights to prayer; though every word be tried as men try fine gold, yet you will shudder at his presence, you will hear blasphemy in his prayers, you will see hypocrisy in his appeals. Prejudice! What is prejudice? A devil without figure, without address, without anything to lay hold upon,—ever active, never visible; always at hand, yet always in secret,—a damnable and cruel force, yet hidden under a guise of respectability. Give a prejudiced man an anonymous book, he may read it with delight, he may exclaim by reason of joyous appreciation—hear him. " What exquisite diction! What splendid painting! What gorgeous fancy! What ruthless logic, —a grand and precious book!" Ask him, " Do you know who wrote it?" He answers, No. Tell him that it was written by the man against whom he is so prejudiced, and see the change. "Oh!" says he, "I spoke under excitement,—I had no time to form a deliberate opinion,—I spoke off-handedly; now that I look at the thing quietly, there is really nothing in it; it is exaggerated, turbid, artificial; it is shallow in conception, and poor in execution." Yes, he will say all that. Yes, he is willing to be called a fool rather than give credit to the man whom he dislikes. Such is prejudice,—yet what is prejudice? See it in the blinking of a wicked eye,—see it in the curl of a bitter sneer,—hear it in a subtly varied tone,—yet what is it? Define it, describe it, set it before us, that we may see its hideousness, and hate it with all our heart!

Let us beware of prejudice! Dislike a man, dislike his looks, dislike his works, dislike the very ground on which he walks— but do not give way to prejudice against Jesus Christ. Nathanael spoke of Nazareth, and could not believe that any good could come out of it. Prejudice may work in us also. Christianity

awakens all kinds of prejudice,—prejudice of birth, of position, of
education, of earthly taste : the manger, the homelessness, the
cross, all awaken prejudice; and prejudice may lead to our
damnation. Plain words,—yes, plain, because ruin should never
be decorated ; hell should never be decked with tempting flowers.

The Christian minister has a most practical answer to all
objections. The answer of Philip was, Come and see. When
men are thoroughly in earnest they return these short, cutting
replies to unexpected questions. Had Philip retired to consider
the best possible answer to the objections urged by Nathanael,
probably he might have written something that would have had
the appearance of argument and conclusiveness ; instead of that,
he spoke out of the holy excitement of his heart, and returned
the best answer which could possibly be given to a suggestion
such as Nathanael's. We do occasionally almost reach the point
of inspiration when we are engaged in the blessed service of the
Son of God ; questions that would puzzle us in our cooler
moments seem to be easy of settlement when we are full of the
spirit of our work. It is given unto us in the same hour what we
shall say unto men, and oftentimes we ourselves are as much
surprised at the answer as are those to whom it is directed. I
wish to point out in this connection that Philip returned, not a
speculative, but a practical answer, to the objection of Nathanael.
" Come and see " is a better reply than " Let us reason upon the
subject." Philip might have invited Nathanael to a long contention about the unreasonableness of prejudice, and might have
shown him by many instances that prejudice has often prevented
men from reaching sound and satisfactory conclusions on many
questions in common life. Instead of taking this roundabout
course, he appealed to his interlocutor to come and see the
Saviour for himself. Yes, let that be observed ; it was to the
Saviour that Philip sought to draw Nathanael. Let us be careful
how we employ this expression, " Come and see "; it is not
come and see the Church. Alas ! it is possible for men to look at
the Church, and to feel a sense of something like disgust in
relation to the doctrines which that Church professedly embodies ;
in the Church there are wars and dissensions, there are evil
controversies which vex the heart and show themselves in

perverseness of life. In the Church one teacher contradicts another ; one sect brandishes its chosen weapon in the face of another ; and there is much that looks like contradiction in the outworking of ecclesiastical principles and relationships. A man must be a very good man indeed before he can quite understand the working of Church organisations. It is only after he has held long and sweet intercourse with Christ that he is enabled to look upon discrepancies, and to regard clamours in their true light.

Observe, too, that we are not at liberty to urge men to come and see our literature : if a man should be a very good man indeed before he can be trusted to look upon the Church as an institution, he ought to be almost an angel before he be invited to form an opinion about much of our literature. We who are already engaged in the production and circulation of that litera- ture, may know how to estimate its excellences ; we can make allowance because of our knowledge of the general character of those who are concerned in that literature ; but for a young inquiring Christian to look upon it, the probability would be that by the brawling, the misinterpretation, the censoriousness of which he might discover traces, his heart might be turned away from those great principles in which alone he could find salva- tion. Nor are we at liberty to say to the Nathanaels of our own age, Come and see the preacher. No one preacher can preach the gospel in all its fulness and with all its sweetness. The true preacher of Jesus Christ is not one man, but the whole ministry of the gospel. Individual men excel in special departments— one is mighty in controversy, another is tender in appeal, a third is impressive in worship, a fourth is exact in criticism ; but if we would know what the gospel is in its entireness (if that be possible on earth), we must hear all the servants of Jesus Christ, and regard their teaching as one grand exhibition of divine truth. We are not at liberty to set one preacher against another as the man who alone represents Jesus Christ and his truth. We must go beyond the servant, and show the inquirer the Lord himself. Philip invited Nathanael to see Jesus Christ—not to look at the disciples, but to look at the Master. This is, above all things, what we desire. Once get men thoroughly to study Jesus Christ himself, and there can be little or no doubt of the result. We invite you to put aside everything that you may have heard about Christ. We encourage you in the meantime to set aside all early association and all preconceived opinion, and to go to the gospels in which the story of Jesus Christ is detailed, and to read solemnly and continuously what is said about him by the inspired writers. Nay, if possible, get beyond the reading into the spirit. And what will the consequence be ? I say it with gratitude and joy, that never did I know a single case in which an inquirer deeply studied the life of Jesus Christ, without rising from its perusal with admiration, thankfulness and delight. But to know what Jesus Christ really is, we must go to him when we need him most. We may go to him in our speculative moods, and he may be to us silent; we may go to him merely for the sake of making of his principles a momentary convenience, and we may be driven to pronounce them insufficient; but when we go to him in sin and in penitence for our transgressions, and with an earnest loving heart beseech him to show himself unto us, we are never left in doubt of his omnipotence and graciousness. I would charge it upon myself, as upon you who preach the gospel, either privately or publicly, that we are bound to urge men to come and see the Saviour himself. This is our blessed ministry. We have a short message to the world. We have a decisive answer to objections—we have to hide ourselves in the glory of our Master.

When the practical answer of the Christian minister is received, the most blessed results are realised. We have just heard Nathanael say, Can any good thing come out of Nazareth ? He has accepted the invitation of Philip to see the Saviour for himself, and now what does he say ? Hear his wonderful exclamation : "Rabbi, thou art the Son of God; thou art the King of Israel." Look at the extreme points of this experience of Nathanael. At the beginning he puts the question of prejudice ; he shows himself to be narrow-minded, exclusive, and childish— at the end he expands into a noble and magnanimous character. It is even so with all men who stand afar off from Jesus Christ, and trouble themselves about questions of absolutely no importance. So long as they look at places and at merely incidental circumstances, they quibble and contend in unworthy strife of words; but as soon as they go to the Saviour and see him as he really is, they forget, in their glowing delight, the prejudices of earlier inquiry. And how did Nathanael come to this decision concerning the Person of Jesus Christ? Whilst Nathanael was approaching, Jesus Christ said to those who were round about, " Behold an Israelite indeed, in whom is no guile !" He gave Nathanael at once to feel that he was fully abreast of his history, that he knew him altogether, and that he could instantly commence conversation on the profoundest themes. That is the great power which Jesus Christ has over all men. He asks us no questions concerning our antecedents. He is not dependent upon our answers for his knowledge of the state of our minds ; before we speak to him he reads our heart in its deepest experiences ; there is not a phase of our being on which he has not looked ; and I take you to witness that you have never gone to the New Testament without finding in it a spirit of judgment that instantly called up your whole life, and commented correctly upon its moral value. How intense must have been the joy of Philip as he stood aside and watched the progress of this interview !

We who are ministers of the Cross have had similar joy in the course of our ministry; we have seen man after man give up his prejudices in exchange for loving homage and life-long consecration. We have felt the blessedness of being enabled to turn men away from ourselves, and to fix their attention upon Jesus Christ. If it had been required of us to answer all their questions, to remove all their prejudices, and to satisfy all their curiosity, we should undoubtedly have failed in our means; but we have felt ourselves to be but called upon to point to the Lamb of God ; the question was not to rest with ourselves. We said to those who came to us with prejudices and with difficulties, All things are possible with God—take all these to him, lay them before him just as they affect your own heart, and see whether the light of his countenance cannot dispel the clouds which intervene between yourselves and the infinite beauty. I would press it upon all ministers of the gospel, upon all missionaries of the Cross, upon all who teach the truth as it is in Jesus Christ,

that in the long run we shall have a joy such as Philip had when
he saw the prejudiced man become the enraptured worshipper.
We have our difficulties, our discouragements now; often we feel
as if the work were perishing in our hands; again and again it
seems as if the prejudices of the world were too strong for us; yet
there are times when we see those prejudices so manifestly dis-
sipated, and objections so clearly confounded, as to leave no doubt
upon our minds that Jesus Christ is the same yesterday, to-day, and
for ever, and that he can do for all men what he did so graciously
in the case of Nathanael. I am only afraid that in some of our
cases we take too much upon ourselves in the way of answering
objection.   It is quite possible for controversy to become a
temptation to the Christian teacher. He may imagine that by
careful and urgent argument he may be able to counteract
prejudice, and to put men in a right state of thinking. I am
more and more convinced that our safety and our success in this
work, to which our lives have been committed, depends entirely
upon our distrust of all that is merely human. Insist upon men
going to Jesus Christ and obtaining a personal interview with
him.   Risk the results of your ministry upon a thorough scrutiny
of the life of Jesus Christ as presented in the four gospels. Protest
against any man raising questions outside that life until he has
at least made himself master of all its details as given in the New
Testament. We are bound to see that no trespass is made. As
soon as the inquirer has really exhausted the gospel narrative,
and made himself acquainted with the spirit and scope of Jesus
Christ's ministry, he may be permitted to go into abstract questions
in theology; but first of all, and until he has completely succeeded,
he must be shut up within the limits of Jesus Christ's personal
life and ministry upon the earth. I do not know why I should
hesitate to say that Jesus Christ's life becomes to me a new life
every day.   According to my increasing capacity does the
revelation of his truth and beauty increase upon me. To the
little child Jesus himself is still a babe, and to the most mature
thinker Jesus Christ stands in the relation of an all-sufficient
Teacher. Herein is the surpassing wonderfulness of this unique
life. We can never exhaust it; it grows with our growth; the
light increases with our power of vision, and we never find the
end of the perfection of the Son of God. I think that these

personal testimonies ought to be considered as of some value. I
do not ask you now to follow me in any course of abstract
argument in proof of these things ; I choose rather in the spirit
of the text to put my own personal experience and conclusions
before you, and to testify these things in my own name.

Does any man say that he feels himself in the position of
Nathanael, simply waiting to be called to see Jesus Christ ? From
this moment your plea is gone ! Never repeat that excuse. I
call upon you to come and see for yourselves him of whom Moses
in the law and the prophets did write. Let there be no misunderstanding upon this matter, because I intend to break up your
self-excusing, and to leave you without ground of delay. To-day
you hear the invitation : it is for you to reply ; but whether you
reply or not, the plea that you are simply waiting to be called is
now and for ever removed. Perhaps, however, you are saying
that you do not wait to be addressed simply as a member of a
large congregation, but you wish to be privately spoken to, so
that you may put before the speaker your personal difficulties,
whatever they be. Let me remind you of a fact in connection
with this story of Nathanael which ought to save you from the
consequences of such pleading : " Before that Philip called thee
when thou wast under the fig-tree, I saw thee." You need not
wait for the servant when the eye of the Master is already upon
you. The very fact that he is looking at you should constitute the
most potent appeal that can be addressed to your spiritual nature.
It is our joy to preach that Jesus Christ is still with his disciples ;
that they never work alone ; that he goes with them confirming
their words, and in many ways displaying the effect of his
presence. If any man who is in secret making inquiries regarding
the Christian life, or who is feeling the pressure of any special
temptation to turn away from religious pursuits, I would urge
upon him the truth that Jesus Christ himself is looking into the
very depths of his nature, and is waiting to meet all the hunger
of his heart with all the sufficiency of grace. Remember that
Jesus Christ is the minister of his own gospel, and that even
though no servant of his may ever speak to us directly in his
name, he himself is causing to operate upon us influences without
number, which we may often mistake for the agencies of ordinary

life. The fact that Jesus Christ sees us as he saw Nathanael in
solitude, and that he knows our heart-aching and deep desire,
should draw us towards himself in reverent inquiry and tender
love.

The reply which Jesus Christ made to Nathanael gives us a hint
of the ever-expanding sufficiency and glory of Christian truth ;—
with a tone that had in it somewhat of surprise, Jesus Christ said
to Nathanael, Because I said unto thee, I saw thee under the fig-tree,
believest thou ?   And then he added, " Thou shalt see greater
things than these."   Jesus Christ seems ever to have acted upon
a principle of increasing his revelations, and not of diminishing
them.   Because thou hast seen creation, believest thou—thou
shalt see greater things than these, thou shalt see the Creator
himself.   The sun and the stars, the forest and the sea, the
great mountain and the fertile vale, are but alphabetic, and he
who looks upon them with a right design shall be called to
higher revelations still—Because thou hast seen events thou
hast believed ; thou hast seen a power in society giving shape
and tendency to events that appeared to be confused and without
meaning ; thou hast put things together, and out of their union
hast come to a conclusion that there is a providence that shapes
our ends ; thou hast found in the busy streets that men were
moving in order, that they only appeared to be struggling in
confusion, and that the affairs of men, after all, were moving
round a centre that was keeping them in their places, and working
out in them some great design ; thou hast seen these things,
and thou, in so far, hast been a believer in God ; thou shalt see
greater things than these : it shall be thy joy to believe that not
a sparrow falleth to the ground without thy Father, that the
very hairs of thy head are all numbered, and that there is not
one grain of dust in the universe which bears not the impress of
God's ownership.   Because thou hast seen the Bible, the written
record,—the mere letter,—thou hast believed ; true, indeed, thou
hast been baffled by much that appeared discrepant and insufficient ; many a time thou hast been puzzled and perplexed
by things in the record which appeared to be beyond reconciliation, and of which no man can give thee a meaning that
satisfieth thy heart.   Thou shalt see greater things than these :

from the letter thou shalt pass to the spirit ; the book itself shall be forgotten in a still higher gift ; thou shalt lose inspiration in the Inspirer himself. This is the stimulating language in which Jesus Christ addresses all true inquirers. You never can find the end of divine revelation. The New Testament has no final page. We come to what we consider to be the end, and, lo ! the end is more suggestive than the beginning ; and where we expected to pause we find that it is only to pause on our feet that we may stretch the wings of a higher being, and soar in the loftier regions of divine manifestation and government. Jesus Christ said to Nathanael, Hereafter thou shalt see ;—yes, Christianity has not only a great past, it has a great future. Hereafter thou shalt see ! I venture to say that no man who is deeply learned in the Christian life is of opinion that he has reached the final line of divine revelation. He is evermore given to feel that God is able to do exceeding abundantly above all that has yet been realised.

This is our encouragement as Christian students ; yet this brings us into a deep humility of spirit, because we are given to feel that, however vast may be our attainments, we are still but little children in the great school of the universe. To increase, therefore, in the knowledge of God is to increase in lowliness of mind ; yet whilst our humility deepens we are not driven into despair, for the glory of God is not the terror, but the inspiration, of humble souls. It is not uncommon for men who criticise Christianity adversely to talk of the Christian revelation as if it were complete, as if nothing more were to be shown to the Christian mind ; we venture to say that the Christian revelation itself is yet in its beginning, and that it hath not entered into the heart of man to conceive how much light and truth there is yet to break out of God's holy Word, and how extensive and profound is the ministry of the Holy Ghost in the heart of man. I cannot preach the doctrine of finality in connection with the Cross. I believe we have yet but seen the dim outline of Jesus Christ's truth—that we are standing in the grey twilight, and that the time of the full shining of the sun has not as yet arrived. "What thou knowest not now, thou shalt know hereafter," is a doctrine which the most advanced student may rely upon as a stimulus to further study. We know in part, and in part only; towards that which is perfect we are called upon to move with patience and with sure hope. Sinful man! Thou too hast a here-after. Art thou prepared for the to-morrow that is before thee ? Thou hast further revelation of the divine throne to receive; what if it come to thee in thunder and lightning, and great tempests of judgment ? I would speak to thee tenderly about this hereafter; for it can be no joy to Christian hearts to foretell the ruin of human souls; but believe me, that whilst Christian inquirers are joyfully anticipating the bright hereafter which Jesus Christ has promised to them, those who are not in Christ ought solemnly to consider how far they are prepared for the hereafter which will surely transpire. I do not seek to frighten any man into virtue; he who is frightened into a new life may be frightened out of it again. My hope is in love; but you have understanding enough of ordinary life to apprehend me when I say that love itself is bound to disclose all the realities of the case. Among the realities of your case, so far as I read the New Testament and interpret the mind of Christ, is a fearful looking for of judgment and fiery indignation if you have not fled to the Cross and laid hold upon it as the answer to your sin. This is plain speaking, because the case is plain; this is direct appeal, because in such cases ambiguity would bring upon the speaker the just charge of exposing human souls to death.

Chapter iii.

NICODEMUS.

LET us consider how possible it is to be much, and yet to be nothing. In other words, let us consider how possible it is to be near, and yet to be at an infinite distance. If we could make this idea perfectly clear to ourselves we should begin to ask great questions; we should indeed inaugurate in our own souls the only temper in which it is possible to study the greatest theme with advantage and success. What did Nicodemus want? He impresses us favourably at every point. He went amongst men as an elder, a superior, a councillor: what more did he need? What is our idea of completeness? Now we have an opportunity of coming into close quarters with human character, and of studying human character under the inspiration and guidance of the man Christ Jesus. Probably he never talked so grandly as upon this occasion; he kept to one point in the hearing of one man, and made that one night the most memorable period in the man's recollection. Nothing could stir him; again and again he came upon his theme with renewed and tenderer emphasis. Nicodemus had not a thousand messages to take home; Jesus Christ saw the kind of man with whom he had to deal, and, like a wise master-builder, he dealt with it according to its quality and scope. He fixed that large and open mind upon one point.

It is possible to occupy a very high nominal position in the Church, and to know nothing about the purpose of Christ. That is a terrible business; let us face it soberly but resolutely. Nicodemus was a man of the Pharisees, a ruler of the Jews, a master in Israel, and he knew nothing. Literalists do not know anything. There is nothing in the letter when taken by itself, out of its context and atmosphere: "the letter killeth." If the discussion had turned upon the number of the folio and the number of the line on which a certain quotation was to be found, Nicodemus perhaps would have led the conversation; but here he stands in the presence of a Man who talks as he never heard mortal tongue talk before; he finds that his books and references and evidence are of no use to him: here is a Man who talked above them high as the heaven is above the earth. Nominal position ought to go for something. A man may be Archbishop Canterbury, and never have seen the Saviour; a man may attain a conspicuous position in the pulpit, and never have seen the Cross. That is the infinite mischief. Men may make a profession of the ministry in any communion; not one can escape saying, I am not as other men. The ministry of Christ is not a profession: ministers are not professional gentlemen; ministers of the right kind are called from eternity, and they cannot help uttering what is in them, and they are not always aware of the reach of their own meaning. They pass through periods of madness, wondering what, and what manner of time the Spirit of God within them doth signify when it tells of coming blue skies, and summers that shall encircle the globe, and songs that shall make the welkin ring with infinite joy. Do not bind the poor solitary man down as if he had invented the message, and must grammatically interpret it and bind it within parsing bounds, nor judge him by his after-conduct; he is an instrument; through him God sends sounds mysterious, messages beneficent, gospels that are saving. He is not a professional gentleman. If any young men are coming into the ministry as a profession, God hinder them; build up a great granite wall in the very face of them, and starve them until they begin to repent and pray. We are either in the kingdom of God or we are not in it; if we are not in it we cannot climb into it by ways of our own making and processes of our own invention; and if we are in it men will know by a subtle, mysterious, magnetic music and power that we have something to say not to be found on the decaying and fading pages of earthly wisdom. Here is a man, then, who occupies a high nominal position in the then Church, and who knows nothing about the kingdom of God. Probably for the first time in his life he heard the expression "kingdom of God"

as it had never been uttered before. The emphasis was a
commentary.

In the next place, we see that it is possible to be deeply
interested in comparative religion, and yet to know nothing about
the kingdom of God ruling in the heart. Comparative religion
takes up all the religions known to men, and expounds them, and
contrasts them, and compares them one with another: as thus,
—Buddhism says so; Christianity says thus. The study is
interesting; the study may be instructive and advantageous. I
do not see any advantage to be derived from ignoring the religions
of distant and unknown nations; I think that God may have
revealed himself in all lands, in idolatry as well as in rational
and spiritual worship. It is perfectly right, therefore, to trace
the operations and disclosures of Providence everywhere; that
is not the point in contention or in illustration: the point is, that
men may be deeply interested and deeply learned in comparative
religions, and may know nothing about the truth as it is in
Jesus. You say, for example, that a theological professor must
of necessity be a Christian. In Germany they say nothing of the
kind. The German professor does not necessarily profess to be
a Christian at all; he may teach Christian history and Christian
evidences and Christian apologetics, and he says, I teach these
things as I would teach Buddhism or Mohammedanism; I am
not teaching them because I believe them, I am expounding these
things to young and opening minds, giving the evidence on the
one side and the argument on the other, and asking them to draw
their own inferences and conclusions. That is a poor account for
a man in such a position to give of himself. It means that Christianity is one of the sciences, or a branch of literature, or an
aspect of philosophy; it ignores what we believe to be the
fundamental feature and characteristic and nature, namely, that
Christianity is a revelation, a sheet let down from heaven, yet
held in heaven by the four corners thereof, within which man
may find every food he needs for the sustenance and maintenance
of his strength. If a man can profess Christian theology without
experiencing Christian emotion and Christian piety, why not
preach it? It is impossible for a bad man really to preach. He
may be eloquent in words, but dumbness is more eloquent than

his rhetoric. He is not eloquent; all his sentences are a mere plash of syllables. The true eloquence is conviction, enthusiasm, reality. He is eloquent who tells you that your house is in flames; the sentence may be short, but it glows with truest eloquence. Men can only preach in proportion as they believe. The reciter is not a preacher; he is only unloading his mind of som:thing which ought never to have been in it. His heart takes no part in the delivery; his eye is not interested in this great sight; his soul is miles away. Yet the mischief is that people will run after the reciter; they like the giddy climax, they call fluency—impious fluency—eloquence. These are the people who debase the pulpit and turn the altar to unholy uses. Give me one sentence of reality, one burst of sincere solicitude and enthusiasm; I shall know it when I hear it; however blundering the construction of the sentence, however ungrammatical, yet through it there will burn the very warmth of divinest love.

Here, then, we have a pitiful state of affairs : a man may have a high nominal position in the Church and not know what the kingdom of God is; a man may be deeply interested in com- parative religion, and know nothing about the one religion that we believe is to save the world. We may come even closer, and astound ourselves with a greater amazement; for it is possible to conduct a reverent inquiry into Christian evidences, and to know nothing about their true force and compulsion. Here is a man in earnest, but he must not be taken as a master in Israel ; that is not the point at which Christ will accept us; we must throw off our master's robe and go in nakedly. We must begin at the point of ignorance. Except ye be converted and become as little children—not masters in Israel—ye shall not see the kingdom of God. You must not come in with your supposed intelligence, and your great research, and your love of exquisite diction, and your conception of the Church ; you must come in bare-footed, bare-headed, broken-hearted, and say, " I am no more worthy to be called thy son." Then you may move God into speech ; otherwise he will only blind you with dazzling glory ; otherwise he will only plunge you into what you call metaphysics. He will say, to the infinite startling of your soul, " Ye must be born again," and you will turn away and say, This is metaphysical.

So it is to any master in Israel; but when a little child hears that, it seizes the meaning by a kind of sanctified instinct, or budding reason; a singular miraculous operation by God the Holy Ghost in the soul, and, without being able to explain the meaning, it feels it and answers it.

We may come into still closer definition, and clear the ground absolutely of all sophisms. It is possible to go direct to Christ himself on the wrong business :—" Rabbi, we know that thou art a teacher come from God : for no man can do these miracles that thou doest, except God be with him." Jesus Christ does not want to talk about miracles. The miracles are but the dust of his feet. He wants to talk upon a greater subject. He will not discuss with any man the miracles. Herein we have put things into false perspective and altogether untrue relation. We have begun by thinking that if we could understand the miracles we could under-stand the Cross ; and therefore we have made a professional study of the miracles, and we have read the great argument of Hume, in which there is not the faintest fibre or shadow of reasoning ; and there we are, and there we may remain. Christ has nothing to say to such men. He says, If you will begin at the beginning, I will remain with you until you are a scholar in my school ; if you will come and ask me about inward, spiritual and vital subjects, I will tarry with you till the rising of the sun. Blessed Saviour ! sweeter than woman in love, tenderer than mother in compassion, wiser than all sages in understanding human nature ! It you want, saith he, to know how the soul may be reborn, sanctified, liberated, and finally glorified, we will take no heed of time. To earnestness there is no time.

We may therefore come to Christ himself, but on the wrong lines and for the wrong purpose ; and therefore we may get nothing from him but that which dazzles and bewilders us, so that the mind is lost in a new and infinite perplexity. Thus we see how possible it is to be near and yet far ; how possible it is to be much and to be nothing. What then can we want ? Here was lack of spiritual insight. Literal learning there was in abundance. Books are the ruin of some men. The distinction between infor-mation and genius lies there. The well-informed man says,

What does the book say about this ? He reads, and operates accordingly. Genius takes no heed of the book, but sees through the case in a moment, and prescribes accordingly. Genius knows the case before it is stated ; genius reads sign and symptom whilst the man is approaching him for the purpose of consultation. There was no spiritual insight in Nicodemus—he was a professional gentleman. Probably there was not a stain upon his professional robe ; probably he was esteemed above many in the society to which he belonged. But he was blind : many gentlemen are— especially professional gentlemen. It is the heart that sees ; it is love that pierces the cloud. Who was it that saw the Figure on the shore and said, " It is the Lord " ? Was it rough Peter ? Peter never saw anything until it was straight before him. It was John, it was the disciple of love, who said, " It is the Lord." Love sees clearest, furthest, best. If we have not love we do not know God, or Christ, or the Cross, or anything Christian. If we have not been killed we have not been made alive. " Thou fool, that which thou sowest is not quickened, except it die." What is wanted therefore to understand Christ is spiritual insight.

Many men also suffer from looking for the wrong thing. They are looking for argument, demonstration, long and elaborate statement of *pros* and *cons*. They will be disappointed with Christ. He will have nothing but pureness of soul, love of heart, a desire after the very spirit and genius of childhood ; where he sees these things there he abides, and he makes the heart burn with new love, and gives the eyes the delight of continually changing and brightening vision. Lord, make us little children ; enable us to look for the right things, namely, the revelation of thy heart, thy love, thy purpose of redemption ; deliver us from this satanic temptation of wanting to understand miracles, signs, and wonders, and impossibilities ; lead us up the green gentle slopes of loving prayer and desire ; and then when we get near the top we shall be able to look down and see the miracles as very little things ; help us, Lord, and give us vision of soul. Spiritual insight can only come with spiritual life ; in other words, if you have not the life, you cannot have the insight. Unless we live and move and have our being in God we cannot read the Bible aright. We must be in the Spirit.

This is the day of the Holy Ghost, this the Pentecostal era. Yet men are fooling away their time in asking wrong questions about wrong subjects; they are busy at the wrong door; they will agitate themselves about things that need not come within purview just now. When we can pray mightily we can treat the miracles aright. Meanwhile, if we have not the spirit, the temper, and the disposition of heart, everything will be difficult to us, and we shall be asking little questions about little things, as who should say, Who wrote this epistle ? Was it a Deutero-Isaiah? When was the first portion written ? What relation had the prophecies to the captivity ? Why trouble yourselves just now about these things? Do you see the kingdom ? Are you inside that kingdom ? Have you been killed with Christ? Has every drop of blood in your very soul gone out of you in sacrifice ? If so, you will be able to put all other questions into their right position and relation, and in due time, if there is anything in those questions that you need for the completion of your education, God shall reveal even this unto you. Meanwhile, here is the Book ; whoever wrote it, it is here. We can read it through our reason, through our conscience, through our need and pain and sorrow and woe ; we can read it best through our tears ; and as to who wrote it, better say, who has read it with wise eyes and an understanding heart ; and, maybe, when the grey day of time is gone we may alight upon some soul in the heavens that will say, I wrote the gospel you inquired about : I am the other Isaiah that puzzled you so much down there : why did you spend so much time about my personality ? I wrote the book of Genesis and the whole Pentateuch. The day is not done when we pass from earth. We only begin the alphabet here. The reading, the music begins where the day is cloudless, where the school is heaven.

Chapter iii. 4.

"How can a man be born when he is old?"

ON HUMAN REGENERATION.

NICODEMUS did not deny the doctrine of the Second Birth, he merely started a difficulty. Though a master in Israel, he was apparently destitute of that spiritual insight which sees the possibility of the very stones being raised up as children unto Abraham—that sensitive and hopeful ideality which sees everywhere the throbbings of an inner life, and believes instantly in every word which even remotely hints at immortality. Nicodemus was a literalist; his ideas were cramped by the fixed meanings of words; he never could have written the Apocalypse; seal and trumpet and vial were not for such men as Nicodemus. He was startled by the word "born"; probably he doubted its exactness; it was, in his estimation, too specific in its common meaning to be literally applied to anything else; consequently he took his stand upon nature, and judged as if there were but one way by which life could come into the world. He who had been convinced by the miracle was astounded by the metaphor. What if there were no metaphors? What if pillars never became arches? What if dogma never coloured and brightened into parable? The answer of Jesus Christ was strikingly consistent with his whole method of teaching; the strangeness of his language excited attention, provoked thought, sometimes awakened controversy, and so, through a process of troubled inquiry and anxious strife, men often entered into the mystery of Christ's rest. It is a hard way; but the men who travel it come into great strength. Simon Peter asked no questions at first, but Simon Peter denied his Master at last. Paul began with enmity, and ended with most passionate and rapturous love; Nicodemus expressed a wonder, almost dark enough to be a doubt, but in the

36

long run he took his stand by the dead body of "the Teacher come from God." It seems as if every man must at some time in his religious life have doubts and even anguish of heart respecting Jesus Christ and his kingdom ; and as if some men particularly, of whom Simon Peter may be taken as a notable example, must be utterly dashed to pieces before God can begin his constructive work upon them. Nicodemus had been an attentive observer of the public life of Jesus Christ. He was one of those persons who always ground their course upon facts ; they never throw themselves completely upon great principles, or risk themselves upon the supposed strength of an argument ; they only believe history, they never make it. The facts which Nicodemus had observed led to reasoning, and the reason was expressed in this conclusion : "Rabbi, we know that thou art a teacher come from God : for no man can do these miracles that thou doest, except God be with him." The admission is one of the utmost spiritual importance, because if the works are from God, what of the words ? Can the same fountain send forth sweet waters and bitter ? Can the worker have found his way to the Omnipotent except through the Omniscient ? Yet, important as the admission was, Jesus Christ returned an answer, which apparently had no bearing upon the subject of miracles—"Jesus answered, and said unto him, Verily, verily I say unto thee, Except a man be born again, he cannot see the kingdom of God." The subject which Nicodemus introduced was miracles ; the subject which Jesus Christ introduced was regeneration. Did Jesus Christ, then, evade the question of miracles ? No ; he incidentally showed the true position and value of the mighty works as elements in his ministry ; they were hardly to be mentioned ; they lay somewhat remote from his great scheme ; they were symbolic, and illustrative of one great miracle ; they all pointed towards the final triumph of his power, namely, the second birth of creatures who had dishonoured their first estate.

When men are not sure of their ground they make sudden deflections, and raise side issues, so as to escape a perilous topic. Read superficially, Jesus Christ's remark about the new birth looks like the stratagem of a skilful controversialist ; but looked at more carefully, we may find it to be strictly in the line of the

original subject. Earnest men often avail themselves of ellipsis.
They are impatient of mere detail. They are straitened until
their work be accomplished. Jesus did not evade the subject of
miracles ; he merely passed the intermediate points, and went at
once to the spiritual results which the great works of his hands
were meant to prefigure and elucidate. Not only so ; he taught
that unless every man himself became the subject of a miracle—
the miracle of regeneration—his belief in other miracles would not
admit him into the kingdom of heaven , other miracles were to
be looked at, this was to be felt ; other miracles were public,
this was intensely personal ; other miracles were material, this
was moral ; other miracles give new views, this gives new life.
This miracle of regeneration is the only explanation of all other
miracles ; and until a man has undergone its power, the other
miracles may possibly be stumbling-blocks to his reason—except
a man be born again, he cannot see ; cannot see anything as it
really is ; specially cannot see the kingdom of God.

    This call from outward circumstances to the deepest experiences
which the soul can undergo, not unnaturally suggested the question,
"How can these things be ? " And the answer does not attempt
to clear itself of the original mystery—" The wind bloweth where
it listeth, and thou hearest the sound thereof, but canst not tell
whence it cometh, and whither it goeth : so is every one that is
born of the Spirit." The meaning of the answer would seem to
be that we are not to deny results simply because we cannot
understand processes : we may see a renewed life, but cannot see
the renewing Spirit ; we may gather the fruits of autumn, though
we may not know by what cunning the leaf was woven, nor can
we follow the skill that set the blossom in its place. Jesus
Christ thus gives Nature an illustrative function ; all its beauty,
its splendour, its force, is to teach something beyond itself ; there
is a voice in the wind other than strikes the hearing of the ear ;
beyond the common fragrance of the flowers there is an odour
which reaches the soul ; the glitter of starlight comes from a fire
veiled from all eyes. Jesus Christ thus found a common law in
Nature and in grace ; the Spirit is the same, whether it direct the
course of the wind or renew the springs of the heart,—the earth
to the spiritual mind is but a lower heaven. This method of

reasoning from the physical to the spiritual gives great interest to life and nature; it is not meant that we should force meanings from the things which are round about us, but we are certainly taught that there is congruity between the works of God, and that the limitation of our earthly knowledge should teach us modesty respecting the things which are heavenly. Look at the words, "Thou hearest . . . . but canst not tell." Man occupies an outside position; even in common things God fixes a tabernacle of his own; he will not tell man the whole of his secret; he brings man to his appointed stature, and then says that man cannot, even by taking thought, add one cubit to it; he counts the hairs upon the heads of his saints, and tells them that they cannot make one hair white or black; he says to the master of Israel, "Thou hearest the wind, but canst not tell whence it cometh, and whither it goeth." As a mere matter of fact, then, apart from theological inquiries, there are limitations to human knowledge. Man does not even understand himself: on every side he touches immediately the boundary of his information and his power; the atom baffles him; the insect is only half comprehended; the sea sounds like a great mockery; the dwelling-place of the light is yet undiscovered, and as for darkness, no man knoweth its habitation; the wise man knows only his folly; he cannot tell by what way the light is parted which scattereth the east wind upon the earth; he knows not whether the rain had a father, or who hath begotten the drops of dew; he cannot tell out of whose womb came the ice, or who gendered the hoarfrost of heaven; Mazzaroth, Arcturus, Pleiades, and Orion pay no heed to his voice; he heareth the sound of the wind, but cannot tell whence it cometh, and whither it goeth !

These considerations show the spirit in which the subject of the New Birth should be approached. It is to be a spirit of self-restraint, of conscious limitation of ability, and by so much a spirit of preparedness to receive, not a mere confirmation of speculative opinion, but a divine revelation of doctrine. The expression of wonder is not forbidden; there is a wonder which belongs to the region of doubt; there is also a wonder which accompanies glimpses of new phases of truth. This wonder is one of the joys of the soul; it often forces the cry of delight, the shout of men who have come suddenly on much spoil. A great shock of surprise seems to come upon every one respecting this new life. The shock comes differently, indeed, but always comes. Sometimes, for example, it comes on the intellectual side, as in the case of Nicodemus, throwing into confusion the arguments and theories of a lifetime ; sometimes the shock comes upon the selfish instincts, as in the case of the rich young man who cannot give all his possessions to the poor ; sometimes the shock comes on the natural sensibilities, as in the case of Bunyan, extorting groans and lamentations the most piteous and distressing. Such men represent the most dissimilar experiences. The young man who had large property might know nothing of the struggles of the master in Israel ; and John Bunyan, who had no riches at all, knew nothing of the desperate hold which property may get upon the heart. Hence the folly of setting up a common standard of judgment, or of any man measuring all other persons by himself. The intellectual man has troubles peculiarly his own. Is it an easy thing to pronounce oneself a fool before God—to give up intelligence and conviction, and begin just where little children begin ? The man finds it is hard work to give up one by one the elements which he imagined were necessary to his manhood, and to start again empty-handed, as it were, or, at least, with nothing that bears the mark of his own wit and independence—to know as much about the great changes of his heart as he knows about the course of the wind. He would part with money rather than with theories ; he would endure the laceration of his natural sensibilities, rather than surrender his logical position. What then ? He can only know the agony of birth by giving up what he prizes most. He might give all his goods to feed the poor, and yet remain out of God's kingdom ; he might give his body to be burned and yet keep the bad heart. God will not give his kingdom other than as a revelation, and a revelation always implies the ignorance and helplessness of the man to whom it is given.

Though the mystery of regeneration may for ever remain unexplained, yet it is important to have an idea of the truths with which it is inseparably identified. It would appear that Jesus Christ delivered the most complete and formal gospel

discourse to Nicodemus that he ever uttered. That discourse
occupies twenty-one verses of the chapter in which the text is
found, and touches upon such subjects as—the work of the Holy
Ghost; the Lifting up of the Son of man; Faith ; **Divine Love** ;
Salvation; Eternal Life.   All this Jesus Christ spoke to the man
who came by night to talk about miracles.   Could he have said
more if he had called the universe to audience ?   It is as if all
the stars had come out together to light a trembling traveller
along a lonely road.

What Jesus Christ himself has left as a mystery it would be
presumptuous in any man to attempt to explain.   We hear the
sound of the wind ; we cannot follow it in all its way, yet we
know the analogy of intellectual life.   Can we explain the origin
and succession of ideas ?   How did they begin to expand,
mature ?   Do we know where the child was displaced by the
man ?   " The wind bloweth where it listeth, and thou hearest
the sound thereof, but canst not tell whence it cometh, and
whither it goeth : so is every one that is born of the Spirit."
So, too, are many of the processes of the mind.   As with
thoughts, so with affections.   Can we make plain all the secret
processes of the heart, and trace the transition through which
the soul passes from distrust to confidence, or from indifference
to admiration and love ?   The wind bloweth where it listeth,
and thou hearest the sound thereof, but canst not tell whence
it cometh, and whither it goeth : so, too, are the troubles and
changes of the heart.   All birth is mysterious.   " Thou knowest
not how the bones do grow in the womb of her that is with
child."   Can we say why one grain brings forth thirty, and
another sixty, and another a hundred fold ?   If we cannot
understand these earthly things, how can we understand things
that are heavenly ?   Yet, as the sound of the wind is heard, so
are there results which prove the fact of our regeneration.
Jesus Christ says that, if any man is in him, that man bringeth
forth much fruit, as a branch that abideth in the vine.   The
Apostle Paul says that, if any man be in Christ, that man is a new
creature, living in a new world, all old things gone.   The Apostle
John says, that men know that they dwell in Christ because
Christ has given them of his Spirit.   This is the practical side

of the doctrine of regeneration. Thou hearest the sound thereof
—"secret things belong to the Lord our God." The regenerated
man is known by the spirit which animates his life, for it is
the motive which gives quality to character ; the regenerated
man lives by rule, but it is the unwritten and unchanging rule
of love; the regenerated man advances in orderliness, but it is
the orderliness, not of mechanical stipulation, but of vigorous
and affluent life ; the regenerated man is constantly strengthened
and ennobled by an inextinguishable ambition to be filled with
all the fulness of Christ—his new life springs up for ever as a
well of water that cannot be exhausted.

It is important to dwell upon the signs of regeneration, lest
the doctrine be classed with merely speculative or metaphysical
theology, a study of deeply intellectual interest, but powerless
in the life. It is quite conceivable that an unregenerate man
may do many outwardly decent or even beautiful things, just as
it is conceivable that a watch may be altered by the hands, and
not by the regulator, or as it is conceivable that the ruddiness
of the cheek may be artificial, and not natural. If an unregenerate
nature can produce the same quality of moral life as a nature
that has been born again by the power of the Holy Ghost, the
testimony of the inspired writers is simply untrue, because that
testimony declares that " the carnal mind is enmity against God,
for it is not subject to the law of God, neither indeed can be ;
so, then, they that are in the flesh cannot please God." " The
natural man receiveth not the things of the Spirit of God, for
they are foolishness unto him, neither can he know them, because
they are spiritually discerned." Thus, on the explicit authority
of Jesus Christ and his apostles, the broadest possible distinction is made between the First Birth and the Second Birth.
That which is born of the flesh is flesh ; that which is born
of the Spirit is spirit ; marvel not that ye must be born again.

In making this great claim on behalf of regeneration, it is easy
to see the ground upon which a condemnatory charge may be
urged against those who bear the name of Jesus Christ. How
is it that new-born men often walk as the children of this world ?
The answer is, that a man has not only a soul, but a body ; that

while the soul is renewed the body remains in its own condition; consequently, though the Christian delights in the law of God with the inward mind, yet he sees another law in his members warring against the law of his mind, and bringing him into the captivity of the law of sin, which is in his members. " The flesh lusteth against the spirit, and the spirit against the flesh ; and these are contrary the one to the other, so that ye cannot do the things that ye would." It is undoubtedly true that the spirit may attain great mastery over the flesh, so much so as to explain the apostle's words—" Ye are not in the flesh, but in the spirit, if so be that the Spirit of God dwelleth in you." Still, as a matter of fact, the body is dying ; an inexorable law condemns and hastens it to the grave ; what if, in going down, it should trouble and vex the spirit ? The Christian man is an anomaly ; in a sense which unregenerate men can never understand, his body and his soul are at constant war. What, then, is the complement of regeneration ? The complement of regeneration is resurrection, and not until resurrection has done for the body what regeneration has done for the soul, can men be perfect in the stature and quality of Jesus Christ.

Is there anything suggestive in the inquiry, How can a man be born when he is old ? What does the old man care for new sights, new eras, new services ? Does the old tree ever ask to be transplanted into new gardens ? Still the old should not be left without a word of hope. We have known the spring work a wonderful transformation even upon old trees, making them strangely beautiful with green leaf and blushing blossom. I remember standing in a large forest, on an early spring day ; the sky was bright, and there was a keen vigour in the air ; the great trees were stretching their branches, as if appealing to the heavens ; they seemed to be saying, " O Spring, come quickly, and clothe us with thy verdant beauty ! We have shivered through the long cold winter, and now would be clothed upon with our house which is from heaven. O Spring, thy kingdom come ! " And what can I, a poor leafless human tree, do but carry forward that prayer to a higher significance ? " O fairer Spring, O richer Summer, O purer Light, make me beautiful as a child of God—Saviour, Father, thy kingdom come ! "

Is there anything suggestive in the circumstance that Nicodemus came to Jesus Christ by night? Oh, the night!—how many troubled doubters and inquirers are weary of its darkness! Yet they are thankful for it, because it protects them in part from the sneer of a faithless faith, and gives them an opportunity of hiding the tears which daylight should never see. It is better that the night of the soul should not write its history. Let Christian men be mindful how they throw their weapons into the night. Some honest man may be struck; some anxious heart may be wounded; some who are coming to Jesus may be hindered. Those who come by night should be encouraged. God himself made the night, as well as the day; the moon is his, as well as the sun. We know little more of Nicodemus, but what we do know is sufficient. Where do we last find him? We find him at the Cross and in the light! He has found his way through the night to the morning, from the miracles to the Cross; and there shall all true inquirers be found at last—at the Cross and in the Light!

Let it be understood, then, that in speaking of the New Birth we do not attempt to explain the mystery; on the contrary, we allow it not only as a fact, but as a necessity. We cannot have religion of any kind without mystery. We cannot construct the clumsiest mythology without having mystery; we cannot be Pagans without mystery; we cannot carve a slab to the unknown God without sinking into the darkness of mystery. But through the Christian mystery there comes a Christian fact, and it is by that fact that Christianity must be judged. We know the new man by his new life; we know the new worker by his new works; we know the heart by the hand. A Christian is the best defence of Christianity. A living man is the most convincing argument on behalf of the Christian religion. We are called not to reformation, but to regeneration—not to morality (popularly so-called), but to theology as Jesus Christ interpreted it. If we accept the heavenly call, we shall at last be found—at the Cross and in the Light. It is finished. Christ and Christians are for ever one.

PRAYER.

WE come to thee, thou loving One, because in thee are all our springs. There is nothing in ourselves; our expectation is from on high, in God we live and move and have our being. Thou openest thine hand, and satisfiest the desire of every living thing. The morning is thine, its light, its dew, its spirit of hope, its promise of opportunity; these are the gifts of God: enable us to receive them as such, and to walk worthy of the blessings with which thou hast entrusted us. Thou hast given unto us rest in sleep, thou hast called us again to duty, to worship, to endurance, to all the responsibility, the gladness, and the grief of life: may we answer thy call fearlessly, lovingly, reverently, and hopefully. The Lord will not forsake the work of his own hands; when father and mother forsake us, then the Lord will take us up, and his rod and his staff shall comfort us, though we walk through the valley of the shadow of death. Great joy have they that love the Lord; deep is the peace of those hearts that rest upon the Cross of Christ; none shall disturb them, or overwhelm them, or bring them into sudden and fatal fear; the Lord's arms are round about all who have believed in him, and no man can violate their sanctuary. How abundant are the providential mercies of God! Who shall count his compassions? who shall number the tears of his pity? who shall show where his loving-kindness begins or ends? Thou dost beset us behind and before, and lay thine hand upon us; there is nothing in our life for which thou hast not provided; thy circle round about us is without break or weakness. We praise the Lord with a common voice, we lift up our psalm of adoration, for great is the Lord, and wonderful is his way. We breathe our confessions because we have done the things we ought not to have done; we make mention of the name of our Saviour, for he alone is our Light and our Salvation, our Defence and our Comfort, our Rock and our Hope. Thy tender mercies give us assurance that thou wilt not cast us off for ever; thy withdrawment is but for a small moment, thy coming again is an everlasting summer. We rejoice in all thy promises, we are rich in all the pledges of thy love: we have in Christ Jesus an inheritance incorruptible, undefiled, and that fadeth not away. Pity our littlenesses, our vanities, our transient conceits; lay them not against us as iniquities, regard them as the expression of infirmities: then come into the deeper parts of our life, its innermost recesses, its depths and abysses, which none can plumb but thyself, and there work the miracle of pardon through the blood of the everlasting covenant. Forgive the sinner, revive his hope in the midst of his contrition, and into his broken heart come with all the presence and beauty and tenderness of thy love The day is before us: may it provide us opportunity for showing that we

45

have been with Jesus, and have learned of him; may we handle its duties
strongly, wisely, and in the fear of God ; may we accept its endurances and
trials and difficulties in the spirit of sonship, and at eventide may we know
that once more through the circuit of the sun God hath been round about us
and within us, an infinite light.   Let thy word be precious to us; let thy
word bring to us our chief delights; let thy promises be our inspiration, and
let all the duties of the life that now is contribute to the enjoyment of the
life that is to be.   Help the old and the young, the joyous and the sad, those
who are heavily afflicted, and those who live in the open sunshine: upon all
men let thy blessing come, thou Giver of the Christ that saved us.   Our
prayers we pray at his Cross : at that altar we breathe our praise, our confession, our supplication, and there we await the answer of joy and love and
peace. Amen.

Chapter iii. 10.

" Art thou a master of Israel, and knowest not these things ? "

SURPRISING PEOPLE.

NICODEMUS was a master of Israel, and "these things" he
did not know.   The question put to him by Jesus Christ
was not necessarily a condemnation; we may import a tone of
rebuke into the inquiry, but it does not follow that Jesus Christ
intended to rebuke his visitor.   A man cannot be much beyond
his age; some great men are simply abreast with it.   The child
is not greatly ahead of his toys, nor is he to blame for his nursery
enjoyments and nursery satisfactions : they suit the child, they
are the measure of his age, they represent his present capacity.
Jesus Christ was anxious to impress upon the mind of Nicodemus
that there were things which even he, though a master of Israel,
did not know.   Our knowledge is helped by our ignorance : we
are chastened by wisely recognised imperfections.   If we could
apply the rule which inspires this inquiry we should have no
uncharitableness, we should feel that some brothers are older
than others, that some students are a page farther on than other
students are ; nor is the one class of students to be praised, and
the other to be vehemently and unsparingly condemned.   Blessed
is that faithful reader who has read up to the place where he
now is, without skipping any, slurring any, but who has patiently,
thankfully, and sympathetically received the message word by
word.   Do not overchide him lest he be cast down with sorrow
overmuch ; recognise his progress, and tell him there are still
things beyond.   It is important to bring into view the things

that have not yet been fully realised, because they may change all that has gone before, not in solidity, not in substance, not in the best spiritual uses; but they may set all things in a new relation, and invest all things with a new colour, and bring the mind to feel that even in its farthest studies it has but begun its divine schooling.

Or we may take it from the point of rebuke :—" Art thou a master of Israel, and knowest not these things?" then what is the good of thy mastery?   Thine is a nominal mastership, thine is an office without an inspiration; thine is only the action of mechanism, it does not belong to the great astronomic forces and ministries of the universe. Away with thy mastership of Israel! It is a name, a label, a designation, but within there is nothing equal to the name which thou dost bear.   It is a pity that a man remains nominally a master of Israel when he has lost his real mastership.   It is one of the last lessons which a man is willing to learn, to know when it is time for him to retire.   The man thinks he has still something more to say, some other work to do, some higher height to climb; it is hard for him to see the coming man and to say, " He must increase, but I must decrease" : it is enough for a man to live in his own generation, and bless the souls that are nearest to him.   This seems to be an easy thing to say, but it is almost impossible to utter it from the heart.   Yet masterships are good, though they are temporary. A man who has taught us the alphabet has done us a service, though he may not be able to read as he ought to read the language in which he was born : yet he has introduced us to it. Let us be thankful for all past masterships, for all vanished schools of honest thinking and honest working ; they were up to date, they told all they knew, but they never said it was all that was to be told.   So let masterships be ruled by the spirit of progress, coming into full bloom, flourishing awhile, fading out, and yet not allowed to leave the world without recognition and gratitude and honour.   It is difficult to combine the old and the new: the old is looked upon with superstition, the new is regarded as turbulent; or the old looks upon the new with suspicion, and the new looks back upon the old with vexation and with a spirit of resentment.   Yet how many souls have to live as between the two, holding with the tenacity of love all things that are true and therefore old, yet willing to look forward to new developments, new aspects, new views, and to give them a welcome and assurance of hospitality. This is hard work, only a few men can do it : the great lesson to be learned by those who cannot do it is that they are not to find fault, to be impatient, to be fruitful of condemnation and eloquent in deprecation ; they should rather say, These men are our leaders, teachers, fore-runners ; we cannot keep up with them, but little by little we shall conquer the ground they have traversed. How hard it is for men to know that truth passes through phases, that every phase has its own particular time of revelation ; and how difficult to learn that no man is expected to know more than what God himself has graciously revealed for the time being. Abandon the idea that there is any finality in thought. The utmost that the most vigorous thinker can accomplish is to begin. It is not in man to end. God hath yet more to show us, teach us, and reveal unto us, and put us in trust of ; let us patiently await all further disclosures, and not await them in a spirit of contempla-tion and dreaminess, but in a spirit of industry and faithfulness The servant who works most shall know most.

All these principles have definite applications. We may admit the principles, yet it may cost us much to apply them. The application of those principles would cut down a great deal of our present action and thought. It is hard work for any minister even to indicate those applications. He may be misunderstood ; men can only go at a certain rate, and if you hurry them beyond their natural pace they complain, grow weak, and fretfully resent the scourge that is meant to accelerate their progress. What say we to a man who is found in the midst of June, with all its wealth of light and blossom and colour and promised fruitfulness, with his head prone to the earth, and voice choked with groan-ing, and who, on being asked why he moans, replies, When I think of the severity of last winter, its snows and frosts and bitter winds, I cannot be happy to-day ; I remember the winter that is gone, my thoughts live amid the cold snow, the dark nights, the tempestuous winds ? Would that man talk ration-ally ? What would be the view taken of him by ordinary observers ?　They would say, The winter is over and gone, this is summer ; we are not called to the recollection of the past winter, but to the enjoyment of a present gift of light and beauty : the rain is over and gone, and the voice of the turtle is heard in the land : stand up and praise the Lord.　That would seem to be the voice of reason and the voice of nature.　There could be no difficulty in a general acceptance of this principle ; the difficulty resides in the all but impossibility of its theological and Christian application.　There are men now who are thinking about the agonies of Christ, Calvary, its crucifixion, its pain, its cruel wounds : all these are historical verities, all these are tragedies that ought to make the heart ache, but they are over. Christ is risen, Christ is enthroned, Christ is in heaven : why seek ye the living among the dead ?　Christians are called to summer joys, and summer songs, and summer liberties and hopes.　Are ye masters in Israel, and know not these things ? Paul says, " Yea, though we have known Christ after the flesh, yet now henceforth know we him no more : " he is the enthroned Lord, he is seated upon his Father's throne, and we have to deaʹ with the present aspect of Christian history and Christian pro phecy.　Do we then forget the winter that is gone ?　We say, Probably owing to its severity we enjoy the gentleness and graciousness of the summer.　So when we think of Gethsemane and Calvary and the Cross, and the pierced hands and pierced feet and wounded side and thorn-crushed temples, we say, The summer of our joy came out of the winter of that endurance. We are not to live backwards ; our faces are towards the light, and no man can hold up his face towards the noonday of Christian truth and love and hope without being provoked by a gentle provocation to song and joy and sacred delight.　This is the precious gift of God to every believing soul.　Rejoice always, be glad in a risen Lord ; even when you sit down to break the memorial bread and drink the memorial cup, remember that the words are, " Ye do these things till the Lord come."　It is a prospective interview that makes the retrospective review sacred and fruitful of solemn joy.

Art thou a master of Israel, and readest thou the letter of the Bible ?　So many men go to the wrong Bible, therefore they are afraid the Bible may be taken from them.   No man can take love from the heart, devotion from the soul, trust from the spirit. You may steal a document, but you cannot steal a revelation.   If we have only a theologian's Bible, it may be taken from us any day.   If we have God revealed to the heart through the medium of the Bible we are independent of all criticism, all hostility ; we have a sanctuary into which we can retire and within whose walls we can be for ever safe.   The last enemy that shall be destroyed is superstition.   Even many Christians have hold of the wrong Bible ; that is to say, they have hold of the Bible by the wrong end.   So they are always living in an age of unbelief ; they are always saying, The age is oscillating between rationalism and superstition.   The men who have hold of the wrong Bible live a troubled life ; there is not a window in their houses that faces the south ; they live in gloom and sadness and apprehension ; every new volume of short essays published in criticism upon the Bible is thought to be another ebullition of the devil. Art thou a master of Israel, and troubled by any assault that is made upon the sanctuary of revelation ?   First be sure that you do not misunderstand the assailants ; they may be making no such assault, they may only be aiming to clear away clouds and demolish fictions, and cleanse the air of superstitions, and liberate the mind from iniquitous bondage ; it is due to them that we should clearly understand what they are talking about and aiming at.   There are those who go to the Bible for the wrong things, and they are disappointed.   What say you to a man who, wanting health, fixes upon the South of France for his winter's abode ; but in journeying thither he is told that he may not have sufficiently considered certain peculiarities attaching to that portion of the earth ?—Are you aware, quoth the one, that there are two distinct theories of the geological formation of the South of France ?   Are you aware that botanists differ about the fauna and the flora of the South of France ?   Are you aware that there are many contentions about the right political division of Continental countries ?   Saith the man, Why this bother ? why this rude, strange, irrelevant talk ?   I am going to the South of France not because of geological formations or botanical curiosities, or political and imperial divisions and sovereignties : there the fresh air blows, there the sun is warm, there all nature is a kind nurse, a loving mother, and back from the South of France I shall bring health, spring, hope.　That is a wise speech.　The man went to the South of France for the right thing, and he secured it, and he has returned in full enjoyment of the blessing he went in quest of.　There are those who go to the Bible timorously, and saith one, Do you know there are two theories about the first chapters of Genesis?　Are you aware that some persons have doubts whether the serpent really did speak to Eve?　Are you aware that some parts of the Pentateuch are post-exilian in their composition?　Saith the man, What is this craze? what are these long words? what can be the meaning of this muddle of polysyllables?　I go to the Bible to see if the fresh air blows there, if there be aught spoken to the soul, if there be any touch that makes me live again: as to Genesis, whether it be first or last or midst, pre-exilian or post-exilian, Mosaic or written by John the Baptist, these are not the questions I am asking.　I am saying, what is the living line of the book? what is the inner, eternal, redeeming spirit of the book? That man's Bible can never be taken from him; he has laid up riches where moth and dust do not consume, and where thieves do not break through nor steal.　That Bible is hidden in the heart; that revelation is an eternal treasure; the Spirit itself beareth witness with our spirit that this is the very revelation of God. In this sense the Bible asks only to be read—to be read patiently, thoroughly, sympathetically, to see if it cover not the whole breadth of life, answering all its deepest inquiries, and breathing gospels upon its broken-hearted penitence.　Art thou a master of Israel, and hast been seeking to bolster up some book simply because thou hast been afraid that if its mechanical structure be altered its spirit will evaporate?　That is not mastership; that is bondage.　How is it that the Bible outlives all assailants, and breathes its benediction upon awakening and enlightening souls? It is because the spirit of the book is the Spirit of God; because the message of the book is a message of righteousness, atonement, reconciliation, spiritual purification, and the ultimate triumph of grace over sin.

There is a theologian's Bible as there is a physiologist's body. An interview with a physician would frighten you.　Were he to tell you all his polysyllables you would no longer believe you are alive; were he to ask you about the curious nomenclature of the body, you would declare that you had no such things in you, you would protest vehemently that you never heard of them. And yet he would be perfectly right—he is a physiologist, and no physiologist could ever be content without an enormous quantity of Latin; he thinks that physiology depends upon the Latin language for its real construction and the proper application of all its principles. There is an analyst's water. If you were to spend a day with an analyst you would never take a glass of water more as long as you live; he could frighten you out of water-drinking, and he could frighten you out of bread-eating; if he lay before you the exact constituents of the last meal you consumed you would regret that you ever rose from your bed. But there is another body, the body that was rocked by your mother, and sustained by your friends; there is another water, there is another bread, there are great ministries in nature of the motherliest sort, meant to sustain and cheer and enrich and consolidate our life. So there is a theologian's Bible; let the theologians keep it: it has never done them any good, and it will never do anybody any good. The Bible we all want is our mother's Bible, the heart Bible, the Bible that stoops down to the life to kiss it and bless it and lift it up, and breathe into it daily inspiration of divine sustenance and assurance of immortality. That Bible is open to the poorest woman, the tiniest child, the wisest man; it is the world's wide-open book, printed in infinite letters, so that the blind may see it.

Art thou a master of Israel, and knowest not the meaning of Christ in the constitution of his visible body the Church? Yet what gateways we have put up round the Church. We have made it a theologian's church; we have admitted into the Church persons who have very clear views. Be perfectly sure that if any man has very clear views he never saw the Church. So-called clear views have torn the Cross of Christ into splinters. The only view I can have of my Saviour is that he loved me, and gave himself for me, and has by his Spirit told me to say this in all my prayers, and by saying it with my heart I shall lay hold upon eternal life. This would involve a great many persons being in the Church who are at present frightened away from it. Jesus Christ never frightened any man away from himself who really wanted simply and sincerely to see him and know his message and purpose. The disciples would have had a very extraordinary Church; there would have been no children in it, there would have been no women in it who were so earnest as to cry after the Master for pity and for the exercise of his power; there would have been nobody in it but themselves. It is a sophism of the human heart that only a man's self is really the prime favourite of heaven. The Church is hindered when one man asks another to agree with him in opinion. What is your opinion? how long have you had that opinion? who gave you the right to impose that opinion upon any other living creature? Let us develop individual responsibility; let every man be fully persuaded in his own mind: every one of us shall give account of himself to Christ. Let each soul have its own view, its own Saviour, its own rapture, its own assured heaven, and let us find our agreement in our spiritual division, and not in our intellectual monotony.

Art thou a master of Israel, and art thou fearing death? Now there is no death: death is abolished: the body drops away, but the body never truly lived; it was enlivened, but it never lived: to live is to live for ever. If masters of Israel are afraid of death, and afraid because there is panic in the heart, and afraid of loss, and afraid of affliction, and afraid because of tumult, where is their Christianity? Mastery in everything means repose; mastery means peace; mastery means rest: he only is a master of Israel who says, Let the mountains be carried into the midst of the sea, still God is our refuge and strength; let all the seas thunder themselves into everlasting destruction, no tempest can touch the river which makes glad the city of God.

PRAYER.

ALMIGHTY GOD, our cry is for thy love. Thou hast made known thy love in Jesus Christ our Lord. Without thy love we cannot live; thy love gives us light and life and hope and joy. God is love. May we be like God; may we live in God through Jesus Christ our Saviour. Help us to know that we live and have our being in God; take out of us all unworthy self-trust, and may we live by faith and not by sight : Lord, increase our faith. The just shall live by faith. We would live that higher life, we would behold that furthest outlook, we would see descending heaven : then shall our life be glad with great joy, nor shall our gladness be content with itself, it shall go out unto others, until all men who know us feel the sunshine of our joy. Enable us to know ourselves, our proper measure before God and before one another. May we never cease to do that which is right in the sight of God, come what may; may our purpose be one of righteousness and charity, and may our course be straight on, knowing that righteousness and charity can only end in heaven. Thou knowest the burdens we have to bear, thou knowest all the tears we shed in secret; thou knowest our hearts and lives altogether : minister unto us according to our need, keep us by thy love, sustain us by thy tender grace, and give us confidence that when this present day shall cease our sun of life shall arise upon the clime of heaven. Help every one of us to be better; help the best to be better still : speak a word of hope to the soul that has no hope in itself; and call men who are wandering far away back to the home they have left. Let grace, mercy, and peace be shed abroad abundantly upon us; may our hearts be warm with the love of God. Hear thou in heaven thy dwelling-place, and when thou hearest, Lord, forgive. Amen.

Chapter iv. 46-54.

" So Jesus came again into Cana of Galilee, where he made the water wine. And there was a certain nobleman, whose son was sick at Capernaum. When he heard that Jesus was come out of Judæa into Galilee, he went unto him, and besought him that he would come down, and heal his son : for he was at the point of death. Then said Jesus unto him, Except ye see signs and wonders, ye will not believe. The nobleman saith unto him, Sir, come down ere my child die. Jesus saith unto him, Go thy way; thy son liveth. And the man believed the word that Jesus had spoken unto him, and he went his way. And as he was now going down, his servants met him, and told him, saying, Thy son liveth. Then inquired he of them the hour when he began to amend. And they said unto him, Yesterday at the seventh hour the fever left him. So the father knew that it was at the

same hour, in the which Jesus said unto him, Thy son liveth : and himself
believed, and his whole house. This is again the second miracle that
Jesus did, when he was come out of Judæa into Galilee."

THE MIRACLE AT CANA.

A N incident which had occurred within a comparatively small
circle had made itself felt in a wider area.   This principle
of self-extension is most noticeable throughout the whole
ministry of Jesus Christ.   Philip found Nathanael ; the woman
of Samaria ran into the city to tell that Messias had come,
and his miracles were reported by many who had been
healed by his power.   It is interesting, too, to observe how
wonderfully a sense of the completeness of Christ's power had
seized the people.   That he had turned water into wine was
proof enough to the nobleman that he could also turn disease into
health.   Yet what parallel is there between the two ?   There is
not a shadow of resemblance obvious to the eye of mere reason,
whether trained to poetry or criticism ; but to the eye of religious
faith there is indivisible unity in divine power as essentially as
in divine goodness.   Men are skilful in this branch or in that,
and utterly unskilful in branches which are but a little distance
off; as, for example, a man who has made a study of the eye,
may have little knowledge of the ear, and an acute physician
may be but a clumsy anatomist; so much for the necessary
imperfectness of human power ; but in the case of Jesus Christ,
his ability was equal at every point of the circumference,—and
the circumference was the universe !

A nobleman whose son was sick.—Then disease finds its way
into every rank.   We need to remind ourselves of this lest we
slip into scepticism by doubting the equality of divine rule.
There are no magical lines beyond which death cannot come.
The great sea of trouble roars and foams over every line of
latitude, and the bleak wind strikes the traveller in every land.
Does the poor man suppose that pain cannot find a chink in the
strong walls of the palace or the castle ?   Does he suppose
that great advantages have made a wall of defence around the
man of wealth and learning ?   Then he knows nothing of human
history, nor can he be expected to know that the very advantages
which he covets are themselves the sources of the great man's

fiercest temptations. The poor man thinks that the high spire is a long way from the flood ; so it is, but how much nearer the lightning !

Besought Jesus that he would come down and heal his son. —Thus where there is faith in the power, there may be something of dictation as to the method. A very pardonable dictation surely ! There is always some blemish on our prayers, is there not ? Think of a prayer without a flaw ! Not that the flaw always shows itself, for it may be deeply hidden in the heart. More than that, it may be a flaw beyond the consciousness of the man who is praying ! The nobleman did not see that the power which could heal was independent of time and space. He needed to be taught this, and the lesson was given him under circumstances which would save it from oblivion. Where is your child ? On another shore ? The Healer is there ! Is the child sick ? The Healer is at his side ! Wouldst thou make all the universe a home ? Then have faith in God.

For he was at the point of death.—So, Jesus Christ may not be sent for until the very last. In this case, probably the delay was unavoidable. But what of other cases ? There comes a time in human life when men want more help than is to be found in their own arm,—a time when a strange giddiness seizes them, and spectral presences fill the air with cold and unfriendly shadows. Then man puts out his arm and cannot draw it to him again,—he shouts, and his cry is turned into laughter ! In every history this point comes, viz., the point of death ! No man can so curve his way as to avoid it. It is a point at which none but fools can be flippant. The gospel tells us that Jesus Christ can turn the point of death into the point of immortality ! He hath abolished death,—it is but the shadow of the gate of life.

Jesus saith unto him, Go thy way; thy son liveth.—Thus every promise of God challenges the contradiction of gainsayers. Mark the boldness and unreservedness of Christ's word. It was in no sense provisional. There was no parenthesis cunningly arranged for escape. It was, too, a word whose truthfulness could be soon tested. Words of this kind abound in the speeches of Jesus Christ. He set very brief trial times, and risked many opinions which every hearer could test for himself. He told Nathanael's character to men who could have confounded him with disproof in a moment; he told the woman of Samaria all that ever she did : he told Simon where to find money for the tax : he told the disciples where to find the ass and the colt : and he took but three days to vindicate his promise of self-resurrection. All these patent and testable things were the first rounds of the ladder whose head reached beyond the stars.

Then inquired the nobleman of his servants when his son began to amend, and he knew that it was at the same hour in the which Jesus said unto him, Thy son liveth.—So, things that are understood should give the mind calmness and reverence in the presence of things yet unrevealed. Some parts of the divine way are known : study them ; and if Socrates could say about human character—" What I know is excellent, therefore, what I do not know is likely to be excellent too," we can have no difficulty in carrying the criticism to its highest spiritual applications.

Hast thou a trouble in thy house ? Have all helpers told thee that there is no more skill or strength in their hands ? Is thy hope at the point of death ? I congratulate thee ! Out of weakness thou mayest be made strong. Jesus Christ, the Son of God, God the Son, has the key of the grave itself, and as for Death, it cannot bear the light of his eye. If thou wilt but sigh for him he will come, and when he comes he brings all heaven as his gift.

Have some of you been healed ? You know not how much you may be indebted for your health to the prayers of others. You cannot tell who prayed for you in the extremity of your weakness. Your father paid a special visit to Jesus Christ on your behalf: unknown even to your father, your mother crept away in silence unexplained to seek the Saviour : and one from whom you expected no such service sent, from a troubled heart, a prayer which took the kingdom of heaven by force. Think of this, and spend thy health as a talent lent thee by the King.

Chapter v. 2-8.

BETHESDA.

"Now there is at Jerusalem by the sheep market a pool, which is called in the Hebrew tongue Bethesda, having five porches. In these lay a great multitude of impotent folk, of blind, halt, withered, waiting for the moving of the water" (vers. 2, 3).

THE porches spoken of in the text were once places of luxurious indulgence; rich, self-indulgent people were in the habit of using them for purposes of self-enjoyment. They lingered there, luxuriating in ease and quiet and pleasure. In process of time the porches became hospitals, and in these hospitals lay a great multitude of people who had lost their power—power of sight, power of limb, power of brain, power of hearing—some kind of power; and there they waited for the moving of the water. There are gathering places of human pain, and want, and sorrow. Say that all the pain in the world is scattered over the greatest possible surface, it is still there, and still a fact—for the man who has mind enough to take in the fact —that this pain, though widely diffused as to area, still exists. But there are gathering places, focuses of suffering. We do not see them in walking down the public highroads; we see nothing of them, but they are just off at one side a little. If you would turn down a back street and open some door, there you would see numbers, almost multitudes, of suffering, sorrowing, dying creatures. It does us good, now and then, just to look into one of those places; it makes us sober, it makes us thankful, it sometimes makes us sad. But think of sorrow focalised, of pain, suffering, distress brought to a head—a throng of sufferers. Surely the place would be a place of weeping! Such a place is described in the text. The people were a great multitude. Sorrow has always been in the majority. There is hardly one healthy man on the face of the earth. I think I may go further, and declare that there is not a man in perfect health in existence. Pain has always been in the majority. It is a world of pain! Sometimes when we are inclined to be a little verbally poetic we say, "Surely no; it is not a vale of tears; it is a vale of light, of beauty, of song!" Thou didst speak in thy haste, my friend. It is, now that I have seen more of it, a vale of tears, and man is born unto trouble as the sparks fly upward!

A great multitude of folk represented a great multitude of diseases. Understand that the people referred to in this census of sorrow were not afflicted with one affliction. They were blind, halt, withered, and had "all the ills that flesh is heir to." Some painstaking student has counted some thousands of diseases to which the human frame is subject. I cannot undertake now, quoting from memory, to say how many thousands; but I give it you on good authority that diseases have been counted by the thousand. But let us say one thousand. Think of there being a thousand ways of taking a man to pieces; a thousand ways of whipping him to the grave. Think of God having a thousand scourges by which he can lay his hand of punishment and trial upon the sinner! It is a fearful thing to fall into the hands of the living God! Viewed in the light of this fact, health is a mystery, not disease. Think of a ship having to go over waters, where there are so many sunken rocks, or sandbanks, or whirlpools, or other impediments, difficulties, and dangers; the mystery is that it makes headway at all. Have you fire? I can run away from it. Water? I can escape inland. But who can wholly deliver himself from the hand of the Almighty? He can smite the head and the foot, the strong limb, the hearing ear, the seeing eye, the thinking brain; he can cover the skin with blotch and plague and death! Oh, who can escape the living One? My friend, hast thou health? It is a mystery; it is the beginning and the basis of true enjoyment. Without it life is a burden, and only by the highest ministries of divine grace can pain itself be said to be a discipline and a hope.

The world is an hospital, the whole earth is an asylum. Understand, that the man who is, popularly speaking, in the robustest health to-day may be smitten before the setting of the sun with a fatal disease. In the midst of life we are in death; our breath at best is in our nostrils. Man respires and cannot get his breath again, and he is gone—we call him dead. Life is a perpetual crisis. We are always walking on the cobweb string; it is snapped at any moment. "Whatsoever thy hand findeth to do, do it with thy might." Blessed is that servant who shall be found when his Lord cometh, waiting and watching and working. Great God, we are all waiting, doing nothing! There they were waiting, groaning, sighing. That was a prayer meeting, if you please. A sigh was a prayer, a groan was an entreaty, a cry of distress was a supplication. All the people in the porches were waiting. Are we not all doing the same thing? The thing we want most seems not to have come yet— it never does come. We shall have it to-morrow, and in the inspiration of this hope we are comparatively strong and joyful to-day. To-morrow comes, and the cry is repeated, "It will come to-morrow." Thus God trains us by hope and by expectation. "Man never is, but always to be blessed." We are waiting for help, waiting till we get a little round, waiting till the ship comes in, waiting for sympathy, waiting for a friend without whose presence there seems to be nobody on the face of the earth, waiting for light, waiting for relief. There are two methods of waiting: The method which means patience, hope, content, assurance that God will in his own due course and time redeem his promises and make the heart strong; the other method of waiting is a method of fretfulness, and vexation, and impatience, and distrust, and complaining,—and that kind of thing wears the soul out.

"Waiting for the moving of the waters." Every life has some opportunity given to it. "There is a tide in the affairs of men." Every one of us has had a door opened, has seen the index-finger lifted, has beheld an angel beckoning. Hast thou not? Look, then, the finger is here now, the angel present to-day! We are always living in expectation. Expectation will save us from vulgarity and lift us from the dust; will mean heaven in promise, in reversion. We do not know who are suffering. There are people suffering who are not in the porches, not in public places; and there are people suffering who have a way

of keeping in their breath, and saying nothing about it to anybody. It is a suffering world. Some suffer in fatness and plenty ;
others suffer in leanness and want. A minister came to me the
other day and said, "I am laid aside ; the physician says there
is a poison being manufactured within me which is taking away
my life." Another minister wrote to me, "The physicians have
ordered me to Germany to drink waters which are efficacious
for my disease." Physicians sometimes order a man into
Germany who has not a penny in his pocket, who has several
little children that call him father, and who, when he ceases to
preach, must cease to eat! I have sometimes been grimly
amused at doctors who order a man who has perhaps eighteen
shillings a week to drink port wine thrice a day, and to take
nourishing things, and in other ways to take care of himself. It
is a sad world. There are not five porches in it. It is one porch,
and there is nothing in it but death till the angel comes or the
Son of God!

"For an angel went down at a certain season into the pool and troubled
the water : whosoever then first after the troubling of the water stepped in
was made whole of whatsoever disease he had " (ver. 4).

So troubled waters are sometimes healing waters. Not the little
puddles you make with your own foot, but the troubles that
God makes by his angels and by a thousand ministries, by which
he interposes in the affairs of men. I thank God for some
troubles in my life ; they were the beginning of health and hope
and joy. O aged one, when you look back you see now, do you
not, that the trouble began it—began your better life, made you
mellow, chastened you, ripened you, took the rough tone out of
your voice, and infused a new music into your expression ?
Listen ! The favoured ones who were upon the mount of light,
called Transfiguration Hill, feared as they entered into the cloud ;
and a voice came out of the cloud saying, "This is my beloved
Son, hear ye him." What if thou hast heard a voice in the
cloud ? What if thou hast met God in the troubled deep or in
the storm ? Thou hast had interviews with God which could
not have been held if everything had been in a state of hush and
quietness, and the people miles away could have heard the tones
of your respective voices. What if God has created collateral
noises that he may the more quietly speak to thee ; finding in

publicity secrecy, in the very tumult of the tempest a little space of quietness and stillness, in which to talk his deepest things to thee ? I do not deprecate trouble ; I have known it. You may take hold of trouble by the wrong end ; you may abuse trouble, or you may make a place of weeping a place of thought, religious review, Christian vow, and anticipation. So all have trouble ? "No." It is indeed a very young person who says, "I have no troubles." Well, poor little child, we know that, but you may have them by-and-by ; and we are now talking not about this little day only, but about all the days, for all the days are sometimes spoken of by wise men as thy day—The day. As if life were only a flash, having one rising of the sun and one setting of the same.

"And a certain man was there which had an infirmity thirty and eight years " (ver. 5).

In all classes of people there is a special man. I am groaning over something I have had ten years; and there is a man behind me that has had something for twenty-five years and never made half the noise about it. I have only one loaf in the house. Another man says he has not tasted bread for three days. There is always somebody worse off than you are. This is the beauty of pastoral visitation. If I were now addressing a consistory of preachers I should say : This is one of the blessings of pastoral visitation ; when you are a little inclined towards grumbling and dissatisfaction and hypercriticism—about domesticities say—you go out for an afternoon into back slums, into dark, poor places, into hospitals, or infirmaries, or other asylums, and visit the poor in their houses,—see what a tea you make when you come back ! Oh, it has been medicine to me many a time! I have just got a little dissatisfied with things ; this was not smooth enough, and that was not fine enough, and there was a little black upon the toast at one corner, and life was becoming such a pain to me. I have gone out for an hour, and come back without seeing the little black upon the toast. Ah, if you could have seen this man of eight-and-thirty years' experience in suffering, you would have felt that God teaches us by contrast, and shows that even extremes may have great social influences for good connected with themselves. Richard Baxter exclaimed, who had been an invalid more than half a century, "Thank God for fifty years' discipline!" Some of us are so coddled we cannot spell the word discipline, we have to ask somebody what it means : thirty-and-eight years, and he had not got used to it ; he was still there, still wanting relief. We cannot get used to pain. The mystery is that we cannot get used to its cause. We cannot get so accustomed to pain as to care nothing for its presence, but we get accustomed to the sin that makes it. Without sin there is no pain. Sin opened the door, and death rushed in, and death will never go out again. He will be abolished, but he will never go out. So we shall have no controversy about the matter ; because I should instantly step into the witness-box and settle the case, so far as one fact is concerned. Do we not all talk more about the effect than about the cause ? We talk much of pain ; do we ever talk of sin ?

"When Jesus saw him lie, and knew that he had been now a long time in that case, he saith unto him, Wilt thou be made whole?" (ver. 6.)

When did Jesus ever say to a man, "Wilt thou be made sick?" The physician is not sent to those that be whole, but to those that are sick. "The Son of man came not to destroy men's lives, but to save them." Wherever Jesus went he sought the piece that was lost; he lighted a candle and searched the house diligently, and said, "I am seeking the lost piece," that he might put it in its place again. He is going up and down the earth to-day looking at us, his poor, broken-hearted, wounded, dying sinners, and saying to each of us, "Wilt thou be made whole?" and the very asking of the question has healing in it. Some people ask about our sicknesses and make us worse, and we are very sorry they ever came near us to make any inquiry. Other people ask how we are, and we seem to be almost better by the kind, gentle tone in which their inquiry is addressed to us. "Wilt thou be made whole?" is the inquiry of Jesus Christ to every one of us. Lord, heal me.

Let the man now speak for himself,—

"Sir, I have no man, when the water is troubled, to put me into the pool: but while I am coming, another steppeth down before me" (ver. 7).*

See the selfishness of pain! When was pain magnanimous?

---

* See this verse further treated in the following discourse.

When was suffering self-forgetful ? It is here we come again upon the subtle working of sin. Sin works pain ; pain is in our frame as sin. Does anybody say to this man who has been lying in pain thirty years, " Now you are worse than I am, I shall give you a turn this time " ? Does any man say, " You have been ill thirty years, and I have been ill only seven years ; you shall have my turn. The moment I see a ripple upon the pool I shall put you in, and wait till the next movement of the waters " ? No. Is there not an ingratitude sometimes, an ingratitude even on the side of health ? The man had been lying there a long time ; he had suffered from his disease eight-and-thirty years. Great numbers of people had been healed ; did any man of them say, " I will stand by you now that I am healed myself, and you shall have a turn " ? See how blessing, unsanctified, may but increase our selfishness. One of them might have remained ; but who can be grateful when health has been restored, when strength comes back again ? Is there not a tendency to do the old deeds, and to be as atheistic as ever ? See to it that our privileges do not deepen our atheism !

"Jesus said unto him, Rise, take up thy bed and walk " (ver. 8).

He has all power ; his instruments are not secondary, but primary ; he speaks, and it stands fast ; he commands, and it disappears ; he breathes, and the sun is dim ; he breathes again, and the sun increases in lustre ; he says, " Let there be," and there is. Jesus is Sovereign, Jesus is King.

Let us apply this whole thing to the matter of salvation. It was an angel that troubled the water. It is the Son of God that provides the fountain opened in the house of David for sin and for uncleanness. The water was moved at a certain time only. This atonement of the Son of God is open to our approaches night and day. Whosoever first stepped in was the case at Bethesda ; but here the world may go in all at once. " God so loved the world, that he gave his only begotten Son, that whosoever believeth in him should not perish, but have everlasting life." He is the propitiation for our sins, and not for ours only, but for the sins of the whole world. Let us go to the fountain, and one thing we shall never find there,—we shall never find at the fountain of God's grace one dead man !

PRAYER

ALMIGHTY GOD, thou art our Father, though Abraham know us not. We know that thou art near us because of the glow of love that is in our hearts. We live in the presence and under the blessing of our Lord and Saviour. He has gone away from our sight, but we are still within the range of his gracious vision; he beholds us from on high, he lives with us; he says, Lo, I am with you alway, even unto the end of the world. We cannot see thee, thou ascended Christ, but we remember thy word, Blessed are they that have not seen and yet have believed. Lord, we believe; help thou our unbelief! May we never look for thee in wrong directions; may our eyes be unto the heavens and unto the hills whence cometh our help; and may we know that the kingdom of God cometh in God's own way and not in ours. Save us from ignorance, from impatience, from all vain conceits and imaginings, and give us the peaceful life, the life of holy rest, the sabbath of heaven whilst yet we are upon the earth. Lead us according to thine own way; leave us but for a small moment only, that we may be gathered with everlasting kindness and mercies. When we are left alone teach us the purpose of thy withdrawment, and leave with us thy blessing which shall make us rich. Thou, O holy, wounded, triumphant Christ, wast taken up ere thy blessing was fully uttered. Thou hast left us with a half-benediction; it is bread enough and to spare, we shall hear the rest to-morrow. Look upon us now, gathered as we are in the name of holy charity. Bless all these dear boys and girls: they are all thine; may they know it, and answer the grand appeal with simplicity of heart, and with growing love towards the Cross. We bless thee for the home in which they dwell, for the love which attends to their life, and we commend unto thee all who are interested in their education and in their prosperity. For all such exhibition of love we bless the Lord: this is the proof of the Cross, this is the evidence of the ascension of the Master: may we accept it as such, and live in peace and quietness for God. Open the way in life before all these little ones; may they find the key of every gate and open the lock, and pass on under the leadership of Christ; may the least be the most cared for, and may the blind be led every step until the threshold of heaven itself is touched. Now let thy blessing come upon our hearts, rest upon us, and give us peace. Teach us thy truth, help us to see its meaning, and to feel its force. Help us in all things to follow Jesus Christ through evil report and through good report, until we sit down with him on the throne which he has promised to the saints. And unto the Father, and the Son, and the Holy Ghost, whom we adore as one God, be the kingdom, and the power, and the glory, world without end. Amen.

Chapter v. 7.

"I have no man, when the water is troubled, to put me into the pool but while I am coming another steppeth down before me."

LONELINESS.

A HUMAN being reduced to a state of helplessness ! Take a man at his full estate, when his system is healthy, when his word is law to those who are about him, when a call will bring servants and friends, and one would regard it as impossible that such a man would be reduced to the state of helplessness described in the text. Yet look at the impoverishing and withering process. First of all, there is a blight upon his business, and his thousands are reduced to hundreds ; then the great house is given up, and the proud head stoops under the humble roof. Presently, affliction strikes down wife and child, and the air becomes too cold even for the oldest friend. The next blow is at the man's own health; paralysis withers the limbs once so strong, and the hand which was once the sign of authority droops in pitiful weakness; the voice has now no meaning in it to anybody, its law and force are forgotten. There lies the man in pain, in weakness, quite alone, uncared for, lover and friend gone, and no counsellor at hand. There are hundreds of such men to be found in England to-day ; or if there be any difference in the literal circumstances, there may be other considerations which still more deeply embitter the lot of wretchedness. A man without a man ! A man left quite to himself. Such is the man in the text; he is alone in the crowd ; the eye sees him, but has no pity for him ; his unavailing struggles only add torture to his pain.

There is really a good deal of this kind of thing in society— a good deal of loneliness, helplessness, unsuccessfule ffort, and blighted hope. Oh those unsuccessful efforts, how they tear the heart right open, or heap upon it burdens which are too heavy ! The bravest will is battered down by them. A resolute and good-hearted girl, reading what some great women have done with their pens, sets secretly to work upon poem or song, the price of which is to give her a measure of independence, or is to relieve the pressure upon other members of the family ; she writes till her ill-afforded candle expires, and writes again in the greyest light of the cold morning; the lines please her, her fancy sees many a beauty in them, and the aching of her heart pauses under the exhilaration of a proud and thankful hope. Then comes the day of trembling expectation; the manuscript is in the hands of a publisher, and all depends upon his criticism. The mornings come very slowly; she can hardly sleep, and, when she does sleep, her dreams are of her book. At last the answer comes; she hastens to some secret place to read it, and the scalding tears blind her when she reads that her manuscript is "declined with thanks"; while she was coming, another stepped down before her. At that moment the sun cannot give her light; she feels a strange darkness settling over her whole life. In various ways we have had similar experiences. There are young men known to me who have traversed our city streets, "Begging a brother of the earth To give them leave to toil," until they have fainted with weariness and hunger; mile on mile they have wandered, till they thought all men had conspired to slay them; at last they feel ashamed of being seen. They have feared to meet any one who would ask them of their success, for they had nothing but the old chilling answer. A poor creature came to me lately with a tale of bitterness. She had come to London to seek employment, but nothing came of all her labour. She seemed always to be too soon or too late; at all events, no door opened to admit her even to a chance of getting her daily bread. She said, "I have walked the streets for two nights, and where to go to I really don't know." There was no professional tone in her voice; she was not a trained beggar— she was an honest, but poor and suffering creature, who gave a straightforward and veritable account of herself, which I had every means of testing. Lonely—oh, so lonely!—yet within sight of the healing pools! Most of us know what this means, for some form or other of the unhappy experience has befallen us in the working out of our life. We sometimes make merry with recollections of this sort now that we are strong, yet the gash upon the young heart is not quite overgrown; we can still find it, and happy are we when our very failures have disclosed to us the purposes of love which God was working out. Those failures strained us much at the time; they went far towards souring our temper for ever, but we were saved from that ill fate.

We have come to see how long waiting at the edge of the pool has wrought in us a lingering and hopeful patience towards other sufferers, and we have learned to be more clement in our judgment of those whose eager haste for self-recovery made them apparently cruel to feebler men. Many a time, just when we were upon the point of success, a rival has overmatched us, and left us to suffer and pine by the pool-side.

This reminds us, that according to the text there is not only much helplessness, but much selfishness in the world. Every man has a case of his own, which is right enough; the point of selfishness is, that many men having been cured, have forgotten that their cure binds them in God's law of love to see that other sufferers are aided in their attempts at recovery. Of all who had been cured at the pool not one remained to give this man the benefit of his strength. What a world this would be without social beneficence—that is, without one man finding joy in helping another! Selfishness makes the world a very little place; a very cold, fruitless, gloomy corner. It may appear to be a very grand thing to write one's own name everywhere as owner and lord, but if the name be not written on recovered and thankful human hearts it will soon be rubbed out and forgotten. Love is the only ink which does not fade; love is the only memory which strengthens with time; love is the bond which never corrodes. We have only so much as we have given; by so much as we have helped other people we have laid up reserves of strength which will give us mastery and honour in time to come. I am thankful to be associated with benevolent people, and I gladly bear record how many poor sufferers some of you have helped to the healing pool; their names are all written, and so are yours, and there is coming a day of very glad memory. You have had part of the compensation already, and you know how sweet it is. When you have taken a child off the streets, and given it food and clothing, and shelter from the harsh wind, you did not want gold and silver as a reward. God put it into your hearts instantly, as if in haste to show his approval—such a warmth of holy gladness as lifted you quite out of common worldly influences, and you wished you could be always giving.   It will be a joy to my heart for ever that, as a boy, I was seldom allowed to sit down to my own Sunday dinner until I carried a portion to some sick man or poor woman ; and that walk upon mercy's errand gave us all greater enjoyment of what was left, doubled it, made it sweeter to the taste, for it seemed as if Jesus himself broke the bread. No doubt it is a selfish world; yet, on the other hand, there is a good deal of genuine kindness among men, and it is well to think of this.   There is very much benevolence among the rich, and there is also very much benevolence among the poor ; to the poor many cups of cold water are given, and many a mite is secretly put into the empty hand.   As a general rule the complaining man is not the most deserving man, nor is destitution always to be measured by outward signs of distress; there are some who cover their sorrow with laughter, and talk so hopefully that they are never suspected of want.   And, on the other hand, there is a way of doing a kindness which looks as if no kindness had been done ; a gentle and delicate way which adds preciousness to the gift.   I have known some men do a kindness as if they were receiving it rather than giving it, so that the poor were not made to feel their poverty.   This was Jesus Christ's method, and it will be ours as we approach his likeness.   We need not look long for opportunities of helping suffering men into the pool of healing ; every day is rich with such opportunities to the man whose eyes combine with the penetration of shrewdness the benignity of compassion.

This reminds us that Jesus Christ ever, as in the text, went about doing good ; not waiting for the lost, but seeking them ; not standing still, but going after them till they were found.   Sometimes Jesus Christ's help was besought, sometimes it was offered ; but whether this way or that, Jesus Christ spent no idle hours. The stream of his most merciful help poured from an inexhaustible fountain, and no poor, broken-hearted suppliant was ever excluded from the healing waters.   This case illustrates his compassionate method.   To whom does he address himself?   To the loneliest and most helpless of men !   Truly might that man say, "When there was no eye to pity, and when there was no arm to save,

thine own eye pitied, and thine own arm brought salvation."
The same field of philanthropic service lies before us all; what
if we should all resolve that every day we should make a point
of assisting one man towards the pool of healing? A boy said
some time since, as he was writing in a diary which the fancy
of a moment had led him to buy, "Keeping a diary might change
a man's life;" and when we asked him how it could do so,
he replied, "Because at night, when he came to write in it, he
would say to himself, What have I done to-day? And if he
had not done anything, he might go out and do something." It
was a child's notion, but there is a man's wisdom in it. We may
not keep diaries, but a diary is kept for each of us, and day by
day entry is made according to our industry or idleness. How
many blanks are there in the diary! Are there many entries of
healing or few? The Christian method of service compels men
to go out and seek opportunities of doing good; and to every
man Jesus Christ says, "When thou art converted strengthen
thy brethren;" being healed thyself, help others to the place of
recovery. It is an infallible sign that a man has not undergone
Christian healing if he has no care about healing others; it is
only an external cure, some poor patchwork of morality which
fear of the law may have wrought upon him, not the divinely
vitalised energy which warms and stirs the heart with all the
impulses of far-reaching charity. The philanthropy of morality
goes at the bidding of conscience; but the philanthropy of the
Cross goes at the bidding of love. You know the difference of
the two biddings? Conscience never yet developed a grand
nature; it has striven with much urgent importunity and many
a pricking smart to keep men erect and honest, but it has never
wrought in them any overflow of good nature, and fruitfulness
of generous service. Christianity never lulls the conscience, yet
never seems to expect much from it; its chief hope is in
Christianised human love. Conscience has but a limited sway;
love has empire over the whole man. Conscience will use its
plumb and square, and with sharp-pointed compasses will describe
the range of duty; but love will wreathe every straight line with
flowers, and to the majesty of rectitude will add all the graces
and delights of beauty. Conscience is as the watchman who
travels round his beat at night time; enough for him that gates

and doors are closed, and that bolts and bars are all in their places; but love is as the friend who watches by the sleepless pillow of sickness, and with many a kind touch smooths the hard way of the sufferer. Through all Christian service the same principle holds good; conscience may tell a man what to do, but by an almost omnipotent constraint love makes him do it. You will find love at the pool-side, offering to help the poorest sufferer step into the healing water; and long after conscience is satisfied love will add something to a day's work, which has far exceeded the twelve hours of the hireling. Oh those wretched calculating hirelings, who pinch their work up to the point of dishonesty! The men who make nothing but technical rules cannot be honest out-and-out, and they will never make life very successful. People who are so clever at making rules for saving themselves, generally, and most deservedly, make fools of themselves by their very cleverness. No; throughout life, in religion, business, government, and everything else, we cannot shut up human service within rules and bye-laws; there must be grace above law, else alas for the poor lone man who has no one to help him to the pool!

This brings me to say that the lost man's hope is in Jesus Christ. He who saves the sufferer at Bethesda must save all other dying men. It is the glory of Jesus Christ that he saves when others give up in despair. He seeks the lost. When a man feels that the last human hope has gone out, and left his sky without streak or glimmer of light, Jesus Christ will come through all the darkness, and make it glow with the brightness of morning. But not till then. So long as man puts his hope in men, Jesus Christ stands off; but as soon as the dying eye turns towards him all his heart opens in one great offering of life. This is the gospel which we have to preach; can you wonder that now and again we are carried away in a perfect ecstasy of joy? We have felt the sad loneliness and helplessness of sin, and none can tell what gladness was wrought in our hearts when Jesus Christ first spoke to us. There was a tone in his voice which was wanting in all others, a persuasive kindness which quite won us back to hope. Men could not help us; but this Man said he could find for us the piece that was lost, and could add all heaven to it. We remember how glad his word made us, how we rose, and walked, and leaped, and entered into the temple, praising him with a loud voice; and as the memory comes back, we can hardly keep down the song of love and blessing. It is this memory that will give us thorough congregational singing. When the heart is cold, when the old loving memories have died out of it, and we come up to the house of God merely in the performance of a decent ceremony, no wonder that we drone and mumble lest persons in the next pew should hear us. Such singing is horribly unnatural; it amounts to insult when regarded as an offering to God. But when the heart is alive, when we recollect what Jesus has done for us, when love tunes our lips, then we could drown the storms of the sea with our rapturous yet chastened and harmonious praise. There is no praise like that which is given to Jesus Christ; it comes from the innermost chords of the heart, and is lifted up by grateful, immortal love. Think what joy will fill that crushed and suffering heart of his when all whom he saved shall be gathered into one vast company! Innumerable throng! Every man of the infinite host having his own special reason for heightening the sublime ecstatic melody. Surely in that hour all the horrors of Gethsemane and all the anguish of Calvary will be forgotten in the splendour and security of a perfected redemption.

So the text has two sides—one dark, the other bright. On the one side we see what sin would bring us to, what loneliness, helplessness, and extremity of suffering; on the other we see whence comes the light of hope and the hand of unfailing power. As the poor man at Bethesda was anxious for salvation, as Jesus spoke to that poor man, so he speaks to every one of us; and now is the solemn hour in which we may return answer to Christ's entreating love. Now are we without excuse. Jesus himself will testify against us if we complain of helplessness. His arm is our arm; his resources are ours; his divinity is our sun and shield. Do not throw from you this word of hope; hide it in your troubled hearts; listen to it when the world is gloomy and silent, and even though cast down you shall be saved by the One Saviour of helpless men. I charge you to hope in Christ!

Chapter v. 14.

"Sin no more, lest a worse thing come unto thee."

A SOLEMN WORD.

[AN OUTLINE.]

JESUS went about doing good,—that is to say, he did not ever stand in one place waiting for people to come to him, but he found out cases of need, and proposed to undertake their relief and cure. He did so in this case. The impotent man did not go to Jesus; Jesus went to the impotent man. Thus Jesus worked in both ways: he stood still that people might come to him, and he went about that he might find the weary and the lost. The great act of salvation is an act of approach on the part of God. "When there was no eye to pity," etc. ; "God so loved the world," etc. ; "The Son of man is come to seek and to save that which was lost."

Sin no more. It is clear, then, that there is a connection between moral life and physical life. Jesus did not seek to change the mere habits of the sufferer. He did not give the man a scale of diet. Nothing is said as to sleep, exercise, ablution, or any other physical discipline. The exhortation is profoundly religious—Sin no more! Where the spiritual is wrong, the physical cannot be right,—even when it is outwardly prosperous it is so but for a moment : its prosperity is threatened by a sword already poised. On the other hand physical discipline has a religious side. Cleanliness is a religious duty. Moderation is a command of God. Early rising may be necessary to the completion of the whole idea of worship. In a word, all our life is to be religious : "Whether ye eat or drink, or whatsoever ye do, do all to the glory of God."

Sin no more. It is possible, then, to leave the past, and to

73

be good for the future. A solemn yet inspiring word is this! We may turn over a new leaf. We may bury our dead selves. In the face of this declaration made by the Son of God, what becomes of our excuses and pleas, such as "we cannot help it"; "circumstances are against us"; "the flesh is weak"? The first step to be taken is the formation of an earnest resolution. "Choose ye this day!" Then will come all the helps of study, companionship, healthful service in the cause of goodness, all conducted in a spirit of believing and hopeful prayer. But suppose we cannot reach the sinless state in this life? Let that be granted, still we may be moving in the right direction. "I count not myself to have apprehended: but this one thing I do, I press toward the mark for the prize of the high calling in Christ Jesus." As it is possible to sin with the will, is it not also possible to sin against the will? God will judge the motive, and his mercy will triumph wherever triumph is possible.

Sin no more. Then it is possible to forget the greatest deliverances and blessings of life, and to go back to sin. The man had been healed. A mighty hand had lifted him out of the pit of despair and set him in the sweet light of hope; his youth had been renewed; his heart had gotten back all its best hopes; yet it was possible that all might be forgotten! The shipwrecked mariner may forget the agonies of the sea when his voice of prayer pierced the very storm, and forced itself into heaven. We say we shall never forget a mercy so great as this; yet behold in our prosperity we forget God! There is no spiritual eminence from which we cannot retire. There is a way back to hell even from the very threshold of heaven!

Lest a worse thing come unto thee. Then it is right to appeal to fear in speaking religiously to men. This is distinctly an appeal to fear. Some men are inaccessible except through the medium of terror, and they must be approached accordingly. "It is a fearful thing to fall into the hands of the living God." To those who have rejected the gospel there is a fearful looking for of judgment and fiery indignation, which shall devour the adversaries.

Lest a worse thing come unto thee. Then how many must be the punishments which God can inflict! Looking at this case one would have thought that even the wrath of heaven had been exhausted. Recall the facts: (1) Long-continued suffering,— "thirty and eight years": (2) friendlessness,—"I have no man", (3) continuous disappointment,—"another steppeth down before me"; yet in view of all this, Jesus speaks of the possibility of a " worse thing." Who can number the arrows of the Almighty? Who can tell the temperature of his indignation? Who hath sounded the pit of darkness so that he can surely tell the depth thereof? Cannot God go beyond our imagination in the infliction of penalty? After he has touched our skin with a loathsome disease, and made our bones tremble; after he has sent a chill to our marrow, and made our pulses stagger in their beat; after he has struck us blind so that we cannot see the sun, and stopped our ears so that the storm cannot be heard; after he has loosened our ankle joints, and taken the cunning from the hand of our power; after he has withdrawn the light from our eyes, and caused our brain to wither: is there more that he can do? Yea! No man can number all his weapons, or tell where the confines of hell are set.

Application :—If we would sin no more, we must pray for a daily baptism of the Holy Ghost.

"He was a burning and a shining light: and ye were willing for a season to rejoice in his light. But I have greater witness than that of John: for the works which the Father hath given me to finish, the same works that I do, bear witness of me, that the Father hath sent me. And the Father himself, which hath sent me, hath borne witness of me. Ye have neither heard his voice at any time, nor seen his shape. And ye have not his word abiding in you: for whom he hath sent, him ye believe not. Search the scriptures; for in them ye think ye have eternal life: and they are they which testify of me. And ye will not come to me, that ye might have life."

AN EXHORTATION AND AN ARGUMENT.

"HE was a burning and a shining light : and ye were willing for a season to rejoice in his light." Jesus Christ is not paying any compliment to John. The text is always regarded as if Jesus Christ were wonderfully struck by the magnificence of his forerunner. Jesus Christ is now speaking not eulogistically but contrastively. John was a burning and a shining lamp—the best light you could have at the time. When do you put out the lamp? When there is a better light to see by ; as soon as the sun comes the lamp is put out. The lamp says, " He must increase, I must decrease." John was a burning and a shining lamp only until the dawn made the eastern sky white with young splendour, and promised the noonday. He was only burning and shining because the darkness was so dense round about him—a lamp before the dawn, a little light to be going on with until the impartial sun filled all heaven with his glory. Thus Jesus Christ is not praising John, but indicating the utility of John the Baptist until the true Light came which lighteth every man that cometh into the world. You can light a house with a lamp, but not a city. The lamp is of necessity local and limited, but very useful ; so every man that came before Jesus Christ, how great soever in prophetic genius and noble in prophetic function, was a lamp that was only waiting until the sun shone ; then the lamp, as if

76

conscious, would turn upon itself and withdraw, because its little usefulness was ended.

What, then, does Jesus Christ say of himself? He says, "I am the Light of the world." How arrogant, how intolerable, if he were but a man! The very contrast which he establishes is but an exhibition of infinite impertinence, if it be the contrast of man against man. The deity of Jesus Christ is not to be established by little grammatical discussions. So long as you have grammar as your demigod you will have wondrous controversies very skilful, word-fencing most agile and keen and wonder-striking. The deity of Christ runs through his whole spiritual action; every touch was the touch of God; every word had about it some glint of a light higher than the brightness of the sun. The deity of Jesus Christ may be established by this very instance. All other men are lamps, shining only until the dawn renders them useless; the moment Jesus Christ comes into the world all lamps disappear, and the glory is that of noontide, infinite and cloudless. We could not allow any man the use of such poetry; it is not poetry, it is blasphemy. He puts himself in a wrong relation to God, and sets himself in a wrong relation to us, if he be but talking blank verse. Do not find the deity of the Saviour in a Greek preposition, or the sudden turn of some verb in its mazy conjugation. Christ is God by his deeds, by his claims. Yet he does not hesitate to correct men's notions of God by declaring that he is only the Agent of the Father; at the same time, if you read his answer to the charge that he made himself equal with God, you will find the answer more mysterious than the original difficulty. He was correcting erroneous metaphysics, and erroneous theology, and in the very act of humbling himself he was leading men to worship him. This is the mystery of godliness.

The one witness which Jesus Christ had was the Father, and the Father displays his witness in two departments: first, the works; secondly, the word. And the works and the word were one, for God is one; the word is his work, his work is his gospel: he is evermore the same, unchanging, and yet never the same in any sense of monotony that tends to weariness. How

is it then that the Jews did not see that this man Jesus Christ
was the Messiah of the Old Testament and the very Son of God
come into the world to save and deliver it? Hear what Jesus
himself says : "Ye search the Scriptures." Change the grammar
from the imperative to the indicative : instead of saying, "Search
the Scriptures," as if it were an exhortation, read "Ye search
the Scriptures," as if it were an act already engaged in. Now
mark the argument. "Ye search the Scriptures, because ye
think that in the Scriptures ye have, or shall find, eternal life :
and yet ye will not come to me"—lay the emphasis upon the
"me," as filling up the whole meaning of everything that is in
the Scriptures. Let us understand the position of these Jews.
They had the right book. Observe that particularly. If they
had mistaken the document, excuses would have been found for
them, but they had absolutely the right book in their hands.
Secondly, they took infinite pains with it, from their own point
of view, and within the limits of their own purpose. They knew
all about the structure of the book, the scribes lived to master
the particulars of the book; thus they got their living, their
eminence, their fame, their influence. And yet they missed the
point. They could tell you how many books were in the
Scripture; they could tell you how many words were in each
division of the Scripture; they could point out the exact number
of consonants and vowels in the literary composition of the
Scripture; they knew all the details about the Scripture : and
yet they had no revelation. That was the charge that Jesus
Christ brought against them. Painstaking—where could you find
the equal of such painstaking as that of the scribes in the perusal
of the Scriptures? What music will you get out of a wooden
alphabet, perfectly correct in every letter and in the number of
the whole, and turning them promiscuously upside down—when
will the music come? Yet it is the right alphabet, not a letter
is wanting, and every letter is touched with a species of reverence,
and all the letters are handled as if they contained eternal life;
and yet they are so thrown about as to reveal no literature, no
wisdom, no poetry, no hope. Precisely so did the scribes use
the Bible, and precisely so are the scribes using it to-day. It is
torn to pieces by grammarians, it is wrenched until it bleeds by
all kinds of rough handling; yet there is no Christ in it. It is

the right book, and it holds the right doctrine, but it is a murdered book.

How was it that the Jews did not find in it the Christ? Jesus gives the answer: "Ye have not his word abiding in you." A man must himself be a Bible before he can understand God's Bible. There was nothing in themselves to which the Bible could speak. They handled it manually, mechanically, daintily, with more or less indeed of superstitious reverence; but there being nothing in themselves to which the Bible could speak, there was no masonry between the thing written and the heart reading. So it must be all the world over through all time. You will get out of the Bible what you bring to it. If you want to find God's word in the Bible, you will find it. If the word be already in you in some dim, unconscious, but surely felt way, the book will talk to you, and you will talk to the book, and you will seem to have met one another in some other world, the mystery of kinship will arise between you, and the forthputting of your respective action will be sacramental and blessed evermore. No mere critic can understand the Bible; no word-chopper can preach the Bible; no murderous grammarian that thinks by taking off letter by letter he can get at the meaning will ever reach the genius of any revelation given from the heavens. Suppose a man were appointed by us to report the oratorio called the Messiah. We ask him to tell us what the oratorio is. He says, I have taken infinite pains with my analysis, and I can therefore tell you exactly what the oratorio is: it consists of two thousand words; musically, it consists of fifty breves, two hundred semibreves, and nearly eight hundred quavers; it has solos—soprano, bass, tenor; its choruses require thousands of voices. This is the oratorio. That is a woodman's report; that is the oratorio by statistics. What could be more painstaking? Yet there are men who read the Bible just so, and boast that they read the whole book twice a year. What a man that must be who can get through the Bible twice in a year! I cannot myself get through it—every verse an angel, every discourse a revelation, every history a tragedy; and yet there be some canterers that can gallop through the whole of it twice a year. That is not reading the Bible. What do you think of the oratorio from this business-like report? Could any man more industriously collect the facts? We are ruined by facts. He who can talk about oratorio and facts in the same breath does not understand either of the subjects on which he discourses. What would the oratorio be to such a statistician? Nothing. You might send him next into the woodhouse to tell you exactly how many bundles of firewood you have there: he would take the same notebook and the same pencil, and with the same hand that has not a soul in it would write down notes on bundles in one farrago. It is precisely the same through all time. We may have committed the whole Bible to memory, and yet know nothing about God's revelation. There are men who boast that they can give you chapter and verse for almost everything. That is a poor feat; it is not worth doing. A man says he got within ten feet of the top of the hill, and he wants you to praise him, and you would have praised him if you had not happened to see at the same time that there was a goat at the very top: the goat was higher than the man, the goat would not praise him. And so there be those who perform little mechanical feats with the Scriptures; they know how many chapters in each book, how many verses in each chapter, how many capital letters in each division of the book, how many verses in the hundred and nineteenth Psalm, and how many different representations of the Hebrew alphabet occur in the whole of the Psalter. All this may mean nothing. Ye search the Scriptures . . . and ye will not come. This is God's charge against us.

If we were Bible readers we would be Christ believers. In the whole course of this PEOPLE'S BIBLE we have insisted, with many a rebuking protest, that Jesus Christ is never read into the Old Testament, but is there, from "In the beginning God created the heaven and the earth." There are men who are ruining the ministry to-day by preventing their students doing anything but that which is literally grammatical. Read Christ into anything? The impertinence, the blasphemy of such a suggestion, that there is any place where Christ is not already before us! "By him all things consist." That is the reading that suits my soul better. Tell me that I may find him in every daisy in the meadow, in every little bird turned to song in the cloud, in every glint of light,—that touches and evokes the music of my soul better than binding me down to mechanical alphabets. "In the beginning God created the heaven and the earth." What for ? Who wanted them ? Why this trouble ? why this ruffling of the infinite tranquillity of the Eternal Essence ? Why ? Search the Scriptures, and you will know why. Heaven was arched that man might live under it and be saved, and pass through all the tragedy of this partial life into all the peace of immortality. The earth was made solid that it might bear Christ's Cross. For that Cross is needful to populate the realms of the blessed. Beware of those who suppose that you are introducing Christ into something ; better follow the spiritualist who finds typology everywhere than follow the literalist who finds God but in small places set up for partial uses. "Ye will not come." Oh, sweet, sweet word "Come" ! It means the toddle of a little child ; it means the running of an eager servant ; it means the hastening of one who is thirsty because he hears somewhere the plash of fountains. There is no dragging, no lashing ; it is all " coming." " Come unto me, all ye that labour and are heavy laden, and I will give you rest." "If any man thirst, let him come unto me." "The Spirit and the bride say, Come." " Let him that is athirst come." Whosoever will, let him come." Wonder of wonders it must have been to the great heart of Christ that men should be reading about him and not recognise him. It is the curse of modern reading that we do not see the thing we are reading about, feel the genius about whom we have been perusing eloquent testimonies. "There standeth one among you, whom ye know not; he it is " that shall save your souls. We do not all come at the same point. Some come to Christ because they see his miracles— " No man can do these miracles that thou doest, except God be with him. Rabbi, thou art come from God."

Let children come ; make way for all men following Nicodemus. Some came because he took little children in his arms and blessed them : the moment he did that all the mothers came in ; they said, This is he of whom Moses and the prophets did write. He had a way of handling children that showed he was the Father of them all. Some came to him because he went to be a guest with a man that was a sinner. They said, " He can touch pitch, and not be defiled ; this is the sunbeam that disinfects, but never contracts the contagion that is fatal." Some came to him because of his hatred of wrong; they love his righteous spirit; they say, He never patronised iniquity or looked with favour upon unfairness or unrighteousness or corruption ; he never would allow the poor to be trampled upon without protest and indignation. He would never allow any man to force his way by violence to supremacies which belonged to righteousness. So there are a thousand ways to Christ. Come your own way—but come. Infinite mockery to have the Bible but not the revelation ; infinite mockery to have the shell but not the kernel ; infinite mockery to have the garments of the body but not the passion of the soul. O ye Christians, falsely so-called, baptised by an evil genius into an evil faith, beware ! you can do Christ more harm than any atheist can ever do. Drop your baptismal name, curse the God whom you profess to love, and you may do some good in the world ; but to be standing there with a Bible without a revelation, with an altar but without a God, you are the fathers of infidels, you are the creators of unbelief. Infinite mockery to be near the organ and never to hear its music, as if the organ were the wooden part, the timber or the metal, and not that mysterious almost spirit that makes them quiver and thrill under the dominion of some magic spirit. Infinite mockery to be in the garden and not to see the flowers. Oh poor, poor, account to give, to say at last, Lord, we had thy book, but in it we never saw thy shape or heard thy voice ; we had the Bible, we called it family Bible, but we never saw thyself in it. It was laid down with other books, it was not distinguished from them in any way, except that we worshipped it as a fetish ; it was in the house, and we never said, Lo, God is here. Ye search the Scriptures, and ye have no Christ, simply because there is nothing Christly in you to evoke, to develop.

PRAYER.

ALMIGHTY GOD, help thy servants to do the work which will bear witness of thee; help them to work while it is called day, so that at eventide they may have peaceful and grateful recollections. May we be jealous about our purity; may our life be a sacrifice; may our speech be a call to heaven. We mourn our inconstancy, our feebleness, our ignorance; but how great is thy mercy—greater than the sea, greater than the firmament; truly it is past finding out! May our Christian name be a Christian reality, and our hope in thee a light that shall make our whole life glorious! How rich in heavenly graces might our life have been had we walked with God! We might have been princes in thy house, whereas we are but as slaves, whose eyes are ever towards the dust. Pardon us, blessed Father. Bind us to the Cross—give us hope in thy dear Son. Amen.

Chapter v. 36.

"I have greater witness than that of John: for the works which the Father hath given me to finish, the same works that I do, bear witness of me, that the Father hath sent me."

GREATER WITNESS THAN JOHN'S.

MEN are often called upon to maintain their ground in society. Specially, if a man do anything very extraordinary, and so draw attention to the sphere of his operations, society will persistently raise the personal question; the man must give some account of himself—who is he? what are his claims? on what foundation does he stand? It is not an insignificant circumstance that men take deep interest in unusual manifestations of life; it is rather a sign of their high origin and great capacity. Is there any man who would not gladly increase his power, extend the volume of his being, and carry to a higher intensity his influence for good? This is the meaning of all study, and the end of all prayer. All truly directed life is an effort after God. Men may not always have the fact present to their minds; yet, on reflection, they will acknowledge that in proportion as they make sound progress in life they work according to divine impulse and divine law. And, in proportion as they do so, they will occasion excitement and inquiry ; perhaps, also, ungenerous criticism, and even malign action.

Strange as it may appear, this is even so. Men are not always satisfied with the instruments and methods which God adopts. They limit the Holy One of Israel ; they appoint the chariots in which he shall make the circuit of the universe ; and if, rejecting these human vehicles, he shall walk upon the wings of the wind, and make the clouds the dust of his feet—if he pass by kings, and exalt mean men to his ministry ; if he refuse the silver trumpet, and elect the ram's horn—there will be wonder and disappointment among those who are the victims of their own blind and boastful conceit.

This method of criticism reached, of course, its highest application in the case of Jesus Christ. It is very instructive, as well as very humiliating, to study the discussions which prevailed about his personality, his authority, the seals and certificates of his ministry. The Jews were the very impersonation of the official mind. The first thing to be settled was descent or authority. Apart from this, all else was without value. Their intellectual operations, however exact in moving from cause to effect, seemed to be altogether unable to move from effect to cause. They saw a lame man leaping with new-gotten strength, yet they did not care to found an argument on the fact ; they saw diseased men bloom with recovered health ; yet, when they turned to the great Worker, their eyes were dimmed by a puzzled and even angry prejudice. That worker was only Mary's Son ; he had a connection with Nazareth which vitiated his prophetic lineage ; or there was some other flaw in his great claim to be heard and followed.

Is not the same kind of criticism active in our own day ? Are we not all, more or less, tempted to try men by some merely technical standard ? Do we not care more for the paper than the life, and believe a man to be good because the paper says so ; or believe him to be bad, because he has no paper to show ? If the life of Jesus Christ should have wrought one result above another

upon merely literary readers, it should have exposed the insanity
of denying a divine origin to divine works. Let those who
please demand the credentials of the sun ; but be it our wisdom
to believe that no testimony can be so convincing as his own
splendid and impartial light. This is a matter which I would
urge as of great importance. If men be looking for technicality
where they should be looking for life, they resemble thirsty
travellers who will not drink of a well until they have read the
faded inscription which tells how it come to be a well at all.
What say you to such travellers? For many a day they have
wandered along the dusty road ; their lips are parched with
thirst ; yet, when they come to a well of water, they ask who
dug it? Who enclosed it? What families have drunk of it?
Through what districts the water flows, or through what strata it
rises? The questions may not be altogether without importance, but life is more important to all, and dying nature ignores
every one of them, until its burning thirst has been quenched.
Now, Jesus Christ was as a well of living water, and the men
who were around him were thirsty ; yet those men put their
small questions, and started their small objections, it being of
more importance that their notions should be satisfied than that
their lives should be saved ; and, blame them as we may, they
were not the only people who have sacrificed the living present
on the altar of a dead routine, or rejected a spiritual Saviour
because he was not also a temporal king.

Every man, then, it would appear, is asked for his testimonials.
It was the custom of the world, and Jesus Christ must feel its
influence. Large testimonials were supposed to be valuable, but
in the progress of opinion it has been found that a man must be
his own testimonial if he is to establish himself as a fact in the
world. By this is meant that a man must not only say, but do ;
the earnest heart must express itself in the noble action, and the
final appeal must be—"Believe me for the very works' sake."

Jesus Christ said, "I have greater witness than that of John."
Let us understand this point. Jesus Christ does not despise the
testimony of good men, nor does he teach his servants to do so.
"There is another that beareth witness of me ; and I know that

the witness which he witnesseth of me is true. . . . . He was a burning and a shining light." No man is at liberty to despise the opinion of good men. That opinion should be prized on every ground, but specially as a stimulant to a still higher life. The good man's word of encouragement helps us many a time to recover heart when going up the hills of hard duty, and is often to us as a word immediately from God. At the same time testimonials are also often as the preface to a book ; the preface may be good, but the book must stand upon its own merits. When the preface written by a friendly patron is too highflown, the disadvantage accrues not to himself, but to the young author in whose interest it was mistakenly written. There are men in England to-day who would be rich for ever, if they could live upon testimonials. Their testimonials are their greatest hindrances. Modest men shrink from the very idea of assisting persons whose pedestal is so immense and imposing ; consequently the great testimonial is but a millstone round the neck of its unfortunate possessor. Jesus Christ said, "I receive not testimony from man." Paul said, "It is a very small thing that I should be judged of you, or of man's judgment." John said, "If we receive the witness of men, the witness of God is greater." We should want to know what a man is, and not what is said about him ; to see his work, and not to read his testimonial.

We are warranted in saying so by the words of the text, "The works which the Father hath given me to finish, the same works that I do, bear witness of me that the Father hath sent me." This was not the only time that the same doctrine was laid down by Jesus Christ. "When John had heard in the prison the works of Christ, he sent two of his disciples, and said unto him, Art thou he that should come, or do we look for another ? Jesus answered and said unto them, Go and show John again those things which ye do hear and see : the blind receive their sight, and the lame walk, the lepers are cleansed, and the deaf hear, the dead are raised up, and the poor have the gospel preached to them." My object in calling attention to this text is to enforce the doctrine that, both in personal and ecclesiastical life, the grand and final appeal as to authority is to works. The moral quality of the worker will be shown in his whole conduct and service among men. There may, in some instances, be crafty, and even successful simulation ; the holy word may be spoken by the unclean tongue ; the good deed may be attempted by the double-working hand ; but all this rather confirms the doctrine than opposes it, for no man would make base coin but for the value of the true metal.

It is, perhaps, hardly necessary to insist for a moment that I am not maintaining the doctrine of salvation by works ; there is no such salvation that I am aware of, any more than there is navigation in sand, or pedestrianism on the sea. I refuse to regard salvation by works other than as a contradiction in terms, and I put it in this strong way, that in a sentence I may have done with the suggestion once for all. A man's testimony, as a professed servant of God, is to be found in his works. Let a man prove his salvation by his holiness. If a man should say that God sent him, let him prove his mission by his life— having heard his word, we await his works.

Take the case of a church. You protess to be divinely called, but what is the proof ? Do not refer me to a long line of illustrious ministers, to a large and splendid sanctuary, or even to a dazzling subscription list. Are you felt in the neighbourhood to be a power for good ? Do you visit the widow and the fatherless in their affliction ? Are you eyes to the blind and feet to the lame ? Do the poor bless you, and those who are ready to perish hold you in grateful reverence ? I do not ask if the trust-deed be orthodox, if the music be scientific, if the seats be well let, if the congregation be genteel ; I ask if Jesus Christ crucified be the inspiration of your labour, and Jesus Christ risen the source of your power ?

If a man said he was eloquent, how would you judge him ? By the number of books he had read, or by the number of schools he had attended ? Certainly not. If he never moved you to tears, or compelled your consent to his reasoning, or excited you to enthusiasm, his pretension would be nothing but a barren name. On the other hand, there may be a man who has not read a book on eloquence, who could not give you a single canon in rhetoric; yet when he opens his mouth your attention is caught as by a spell; his strong, earnest, pathetic speech, though perhaps broken and inexact, carries everything before it.   Do you hesitate to pronounce him an eloquent man ?   You judge by the "works," —you believe him for the very works' sake, and you are unquestionably right.   It would fail to convince you that he was an eloquent man if he merely repeated the rules of Quintilian and of Isocrates, or repeated from end to end the orations of Demosthenes and Cicero.   You must hear the man speak.   It is not enough that he pronounce keen criticisms on other speakers, showing what canons have been violated, and what vices have been set up; after all this, the man must show his power to convince the judgment and captivate the heart and the fancy before you can yield him homage as a master of speech. Specially is this the case with the Christian minister.   He may be unlearned, yet the might of God may be in him ; he may blunder and stumble, yet a mysterious dignity may invest his whole service.   On the other hand, with spotless character, with innumerable testimonials, with a status conspicuous and influential, he may be brought to the lowest dust of humiliation, and to the distress of the most ignominious failure.   Oh, ministers of Jesus Christ—servants of the One Crown—what manner of qualification should be ours !   We must have seals of our apostleship, and these we cannot have but as we labour in our blessed Master's spirit.   Applause we may win ; a name we may make ; but wood, hay, and stubble shall perish—only the true gold will be of use to us at the last !

So there may be persons who question your standing as a Church; according to their notions, you are not a Church at all ; your foundation is a swamp, your pedigree a broken chain. What do you answer ?   Prove your call by your works.   Show that the love of Christ is the all-compelling power of your lives, and by holiness, patience, and charity set up a claim too strong to be overthrown, too lofty to be defied.   In the days that are coming we shall have much controversy on Church questions. Rival ecclesiastical theories will be zealously and ably maintained. In view of this conflict, let me say that works will be the only satisfactory standard of appeal.   Ecclesiastical mummeries must be crumbled and scattered to the winds. Artificialism must perish. Philanthropy alone will stand. The day will come when upholders of every church system will have to defend themselves by the argument of facts. What have our principles compelled us to do ? Where are the proofs of our love ? Where are the results of our voluntaryism ? What light have we shed on the world ? What sanctuaries have we built ? Away with the theory that believes much and does nothing. Blessed are the men who are drawn towards self-sacrifice ; the service that comes of love.

The appeal which Jesus Christ made on his own behalf is also the appeal which should be made on behalf of Christianity. There are two lights in which Christianity may be regarded : it may be looked at as classified in sectarian dogmas, and as upheld by any particular course of argument ; in general terms, it may become a subject of criticism. Treated in this manner, it has been alike the object of ridicule and reverence. On the other hand, Christianity may be tested by its results as a practical religion. Its history is before the world. What has Christianity done ? It has greater testimony than the commendation of its deep scholars and eloquent preachers. It has opened prison doors, broken down bad governments, aided all good causes, lifted up trampled honour and virtue ; it has saved men's souls, given men's lives higher elevation, changed death into a beneficent liberator, and turned the grave into the last step towards heaven ; it has made selfish men benevolent, harsh men gentle, timid men heroic, and sad men happy ; it has blessed the cause of freedom, succoured the efforts of charity, upheld the claims of peace ; it demands to be judged by its fruits, and its demand is reasonable and ought to be irresistible. We are called to maintain a practical testimony, to give the emphatic and convincing answer of noble living. We have had enough of literary testimonial ; we have done enough in the matter of the evidences ; we are thankful to every author who has spoken one good word for the truth ; now let the truth speak for itself, let the Christian be the best defence of Christianity, let the life of the servant commend the doctrine of the Lord. "Not every one that saith unto me, Lord, Lord, shall enter into the kingdom of heaven ; but he that doeth the will of my Father which is in heaven." "Be ye doers of the word, and not hearers only, deceiving your own selves." "The fire shall try every man's work, of what sort it is." What if our testimonials, our diplomas, our certificates, be all burnt up, and we have nothing to show but the smouldering ashes of an artificial life?

The argument which applies to Christianity applies also, of course, with equal effect, to the Bible. If the Bible is to be judged by its works, there is, happily, an end of controversy. What is the best reply to attacks upon the Bible? Circulation. When men say the Bible is not inspired—circulate it; when they charge upon it inability to address the spirit of the times—circulate it; when they say it has outlived the circumstances which called for it—circulate it! Circulation is the best argument. Let the Bible speak for itself; there is no eloquence like its own; let it reveal itself in its own pure glory, not in the artificial flare of our commendation. The Bible must be its own vindicator. Not because our fathers believed in it; not because it has a romantic history; not because of priestly exhortation; but because of its own proved power to enlighten the mind, to bless the heart, to elevate life, and destroy the power of death, must the Bible be held first in our love and highest in our veneration. "A good tree cannot bring forth evil fruit, neither can a corrupt tree bring forth good fruit." "A good man out of the good treasure of his heart bringeth forth that which is good; and an evil man out of the evil treasure of his heart bringeth forth that which is evil." What does the Bible bring forth? What of manhood? What of purity? What of hope? It must not be judged in detail; it must not have meanings forced upon it: it must be taken in its entirety; it must have free scope; it must be received into the heart—then we abide by the verdict!

PRAYER.

ALMIGHTY GOD, we have tasted and seen how good is the grace of the Lord who died for us. It was a wondrous grace. The Lord Christ spared not himself from the death that we might never die. May we understand somewhat of our own sin, then shall we understand somewhat of Christ's wondrous death. Enable us to look within with careful eyes; may we not spare ourselves in the scrutiny of our heart; may we try our own reins, and search our own motives, and penetrate to the recesses of our own spirits; then shall we be better able to approach with thoughtfulness, intelligence, and acceptance all the mercy and all the mystery of the Cross. Thou hast led us by a way that we knew not, and by paths that we had not known; thou hast led us well; thou hast brought us always from darkness to light, from bondage to liberty, from littleness towards greatness. Thou dost never call men downward; thine appeal to mankind is an appeal to rise, to advance, to grow: herein we know the truthfulness of thy word and the divinity of thy command, and herein we separate it from all human words; they do not address our inmost soul, they leave us without bread which bringeth everlasting life; but because thy Word calls us upward and onward, in ever-expanding liberty, we know it to be thine; may we accept it, live and glorify it. We pray that human life may be sanctified, divinely taught, comforted from on high by such assurances as the soul can grasp and realise and appropriate. Thou knowest how wondrous is this human life; what a tragedy, what agony, what heartache make up the history of every day; thou knowest that our tears are often hotter and more in number than aught we can set beside them to counteract their influence. Thou knowest what clouds gather in our skies, how suddenly the light goes out, and how soon we are driven downwards towards dejection. Come to us according to the necessity and quality of our life, and command thy blessing from the Cross of Christ to rest upon it. Yet thou hast given us many joys, and we would be ungrateful not to remember them: life itself is joy, life is divine, life has in it the beginning of heaven; this is thy gift, thy mystery of love, thy mystery of purpose: may we enter into it gladly, until even life itself is a root out of which shall come heaven and immortality, through Jesus Christ the Head of the universe, the Saviour of the world. Set a light in dark places; make the poor rich in hope, in love of truth, and in aspiration after things divine; then shall they know nought of the poverty of time and earth and sense, but shall be glad in the Lord. Stop the bad man on his way; take from him the instrument with which he intends to do mischief, shut his eyes with blindness that he may utterly lose himself, until he begin to think and repent and pray. If any man is laying a plot for another man, spoil his net, or ensnare him in that which he meant for the feet of others ; and if any are shedding tears that no human hand can touch, O Saviour of the world, thou who didst die for men, come, and with thine own grace turn the bitterness of grief into the beginning of the best joy. Amen.

Chapter vi. 2.

"A great multitude followed him, because——"

COMING TO CHRIST.

THAT word "because" opens the door to a thousand reasons. Every man who does follow Christ follows him for some reason of his own. Woe to the soul that has no Christ, but one that is outward, appointed by some skilled hand, preached by some eloquent tongue, imposed by some lofty authority. That is not Christ at all. Any so-called Christ will wither, will peel off the frescoed wall, will topple on the throne made for him by some cabinet-maker. Every man must lay hold of Christ with his own hand, for his own reason, and see Christ with his own eyes, and have a part or aspect of Christ which belongs to himself in an almost exclusive sense. Herein is the folly of trying to set up standards by which a million men shall be judged and tried; herein is the affront to the genius of the kingdom of heaven that would make all heaven's soldiers of one height : there is no standard of stature, there is no shibboleth of orthodoxy ; let the heart say how it sees Christ, lays hold of Christ, for what reason it in particular clings to Christ : that is enough. You cannot shake a man out of what he is really persuaded of in his own heart : if you have put him in trust of certain writings, he may lose them ; if you have in some heedless or sentimentally reverent mood persuaded the man to nod his head to certain intellectual propositions, he will straightway forget what the propositions were : but if Christ be born in a man he remains there the hope of glory—his own Christ, not some other man's Christ. When men begin to compare the Christs, then they begin to excommunicate one another. Saith one, You do not believe in my Christ, therefore you are wrong. Nay, saith the despised and banished soul, I have seen one flash of his glory, one view of his beauty, I have heard one tone of his music, and to that, what I myself have seen and known, I cling, and thou canst not excommunicate me : I am in God's own eternal keeping. Nicodemus said, Rabbi, we know that thou art a teacher come from God, for no man can do these miracles that thou doest. The romantic acts have always had an effect upon certain minds; not romantic in the sense of never having actually occurred, but in the sense of being infinitely above all commonplace, all natural conception of reasoning; something apart from the imagination, something that opens new doors into infinity. Nicodemus laid particular stress upon the quality of the miracles—"these miracles that thou doest": this particular kind of miracle—not the juggler's trick, not the necromancer's art, not the manipulation of skilled fingers, but " these miracles " —particular, distinctive, unique miracles. No man can do these miracles except God be with him; in such handling is the movement of Omnipotence. Then let Nicodemus come in, let him take his seat in the household : he has his particular con- viction regarding the power of Christ. Let him alone when he would seek to explain. Jesus Christ hindered him ; when practising his traditional casuistry and seeking to make himself master of an intellectual argument, the Lord referred him to the wind: " The wind bloweth where it listeth, and thou hearest the sound thereof, but canst not tell whence it cometh, and whither it goeth : so —— " That is the right answer to all intellectual jobbers and tricksters and cunning thimble-riggers in the Church; men who want to be able to explain what was never meant for explanation. But some men will say, How ? Said Paul, Thou fool !

Another class of men believed in Jesus when they saw the miracle of the loaves and fishes :—" Then "—every man has a birthday ; " Then "—every man has hours that are agonistic, and that result in birth and progress and illumination and consciousness of liberty ; " Then those men, when they had seen the miracle that Jesus did, said, This is of a truth the prophet that should come into the world." Nothing else would have convinced them : they had no ear for music, all voices were alike to them ; but they had an eye for curiosity, for wonder, for startling incident, and when they had seen the miracle they said This is the true prophet. Let them come in ; it is a

vulgar beginning, but it is a beginning,—and that is the fact we
ought always to rejoice in. Every man must begin where he
can. There are men who need all kinds of wonders to be done
before their eyes, and through the gate of amazement they will
get into some position in the upper and inner kingdoms of
the world. Let them come; they are the lowest kind of men,
they are the poorest quality of soul, but if nothing will get hold
of them, do not despise initial effort, opening and hopeful
endeavour. If a toy will please an infantile mind do not withhold the toy; after the toy may come the alphabet; after the
alphabet—what is after the alphabet? All knowledge, all
eloquence, all poetry. Begin when you can ; begin with Nicodemus in astonishment at the quality of the miracle; begin with
the vulgar mob in amazement that many people should have
been fed out of little food.

Others, again, are convinced by argument :—" Many of the
Samaritans of that city believed on him for the saying of the
woman, which testified, He told me all that ever I did. And
many more believed because of his own word." They are the
highest class of men; they said, " Now we believe, not because
of thy saying : for we have heard him ourselves, and know, by
the music of that voice, that it was born in heaven ; this is no
earthly wind ; this is no tumult of the dust ; this is the rhythm
of the universe, this is the tone of God." Let them come ; they
are men of doctrine, men of philosophy, men who can argue
well ; they are thoroughly equipped in controversy, and they
have that gift of mental penetration which sees realities beyond
figures, tropes, and symbols. Let them come ! How will they
company with those who believe because of the miracle of the
loaves ? They will never company with them, yet they may all
be in one Church—not the formal, limited, sectarian, little church,
but the invisible, blood-redeemed, sanctified, eternal Ecclesia ;
the assembly that shall never be broken up. It is not necessary
that men should company with one another in the Church. The
Church can exist without such fellowship. The true fellowship
is the association that is founded on sympathy, or the association
that is founded upon the giving and receiving of inspired assistance. When the loftier minds hold company with the vulgarer

minds—the word vulgarer in that sentence simply meaning commoner—it is by an act of gracious and unconscious condescension on the part of those who have walked the higher levels of sacred thinking and sacred service. One man has come in by the door of argument—let him come, and for a long time let him hold his tongue ; one man has come in by the door of wonder because he has seen a miracle—let him come ; his wide-open eyes will do us no harm ; if he be modest he may one day be great.

Others believed in Christ because of known cases of spiritual conversion. They have seen what Christianity has done in the mission-field abroad, in the mission-field at home, in the city in which they dwell ; they have known the lion turned into a lamb, and they have traced the transformation to belief in the Son of God, and they have said with honest logic and healthful thankfulness, If Jesus Christ be not the Son of God, faith in his name cannot result in such blessed and glorious issues. This matter of spiritual conversion has its outer aspect and counterpart in concrete instances which even the enemy cannot deny. Once the Sanhedrim was going to be very dignified. Peter and John were called in and rebuked—you cannot wholly destroy the impudence of the world ; its extinction is a gradual process—and whilst the Sanhedrim was about to bring down thunder and lightning upon the heads of Peter and John, there was one thing that broke up the thunder and took the glory out of the lightning : that one consideration was the man which had been healed,—" And beholding the man which was healed standing with them," they said in their souls, Confound him ! if he were out of the way we could deal with Peter and John, but there is the man, and you cannot choke him, he will speak, he will sing presently ; he has been walking and leaping and praising God, and look at his face now, eloquent with testimony, burning with gratitude. That is the way to convict and convert certain enemies of the Church. Let the Church produce the results of her working ; let the Church be able to say, We found this neighbourhood a desert, and now it is a garden of the Lord ; we found this district peopled as if by wild beasts, now the old men and little children play together as if they had consented to accept a new youth. Facts are arguments ;

the mission-field at home and abroad must be denied and extir-
pated before the enemy can get at the heart of Christ with any
fatal thrust.

Others trust to their own consciousness of change. They look
within for argument; each man says, What was I to begin with?
What am I now? What were once my hopes, my fears, my
pleasures, my apprehensions? See now how new I am: old
things have passed away, all things have become new. Once I
was as a madman living among the tombs, naked, homeless, fierce,
casting terror around me wherever I went; now I am sitting
at the feet of Jesus, clothed and in my right mind, and Jesus
did it all. I saw his look, I heard his voice, I was enabled to
catch sight of his Cross, and to know somewhat of the meaning
of that shed blood, and now I am in heaven. Blessed is the man
who can turn in upon himself when he is short of arguments;
grateful should he be who is able to say to the enemy, Although
I may not be able to answer your words in words of equal force,
I know whom I have believed, and since I received Christ into my
heart by faith, I have been a new man, a new soul, a new creature;
yea, all things are new, the earth and the heavens are new, death
is abolished, and the grave is a dry road through the waters into
the land of summer. The priests, the Pharisees were going once
to be very severe. They gathered themselves together; they
said to a man who was in their presence, Give God the glory:
as for this man, we know not whence he is; this man is a sinner;
give God the praise; be religious, not idolatrous. Said the man,
Whether he be a sinner or no, I know not; that is metaphysical,
theological; that belongs to a line of inquiry in which I have no
scholarship. One thing I know: once I was blind, now I see,
and you grey-bearded priests cannot persuade me to the contrary; you never gave me sight, this man did; you never offered
to give me my sight again, this man found me, anointed mine
eyes, sent me to the pool to wash, and I went and washed, and I
came seeing: as for your metaphysical, speculative, psychological
questions, I cannot enter into these, but so long as these eyes are
open I will mention the Physician's name. These facts are at
hand every day. Such miracles were not worked once for all,
they are being accomplished morning by morning, night by night;

the one thing men are now recovering is their eyesight.   We shall miss the genius of the whole thought if we limit the word eye-sight to some bodily function or exercise.   Sight means larger vision, keener perception, an awakening of all the faculties of the mind to a state of keen, exact, complete penetration.   Lord, that I may receive my sight!   Open thou mine eyes, that I may behold wondrous things out of thy law.   The commandment of the Lord is pure, enlightening the eyes.   Saviour of the world, Eternal One, save me from looking at surfaces, outsides, transient shapes and symbols, and give me that peculiar penetrating vision that sees without staring, and that knows afar off what lights are coming up on the horizon.

The opponents of Christianity have then a large body of evidence to overthrow.   They are not called upon to deal with any one class of evidence, their difficulty is not with one individual or two; all kinds of men are in the Church, and all kinds of men have come along all kinds of lines of approach; therefore, we have in the Church unity with diversity; one man hath an argument, another a miracle, another a personal consciousness, another a grand missionary fact, another a tongue, a prophecy, a psalm, a rapture.   Do not seek to bring all these ministries and operations into one dead monotony; the enemy will not have to break down one bastion only, he will have miles upon miles of fortification to violate and overthrow.   A single personal experience sometimes contains or combines a whole series of proofs.   All men are not of one capacity; there are men who are themselves miracles.   Sometimes a man may represent a dozen men: take him in argument, and he is strong; draw his attention to miracles, and he has seen them until they have become commonplaces; point out instances of spiritual transformation, and he will add to your knowledge instances which have come under his own observation; quote your personal religious experience, and his heart will burn within him as kindred recollections are awakened and expressed.   But taking men as a whole, we must not expect that each man shall represent the whole body of Christian evidence.   Let every man be strong upon his own one point.   There are subtle assailants who would attack a man at his weakest point, and the fear is that the man, not knowing that he has but a certain capacity, has only a certain quantity of force at his disposal, should imagine that because he has been overthrown at that point nobody else could have resisted the attack. Let each man live on his own ground, let every one speak his mother tongue ; it is possible for a man to know much about another language, and yet to be tripped up by some native of the land whose speech he speaks, on some recondite point of grammar. Every one should keep to the words his mother taught him ; the words in which his first wishes were expressed, his earliest prayers, his purest desires. Never venture upon foreign tongues in the expression of your deepest spiritual experience. If you have seen God you will be able to tell about it in English. It is wonderful how many beautiful things can be said even in the English tongue. There are those who know a little—oh, a very little—French, and a little—oh, so little— German ; but what poor English they speak ! There are many persons who know a little about theology, but they have no spiritual acquaintance with Christ, inborn, the miracle of the Holy Ghost in the heart ; and then when they come to speak about the deepest spiritual realities how they halt, hesitate, blunder, whereas they ought to have spoken with the fluency of thankfulness, with the precision of long-acquired and deeply-tested experience and familiarity. The witness of the Spirit is a great and often-neglected doctrine. "The Spirit itself beareth witness with our spirit, that we are the children of God." If this is a conference of spirit, the Holy Ghost communes with the holy man ; they exchange as it were confidences : now the Holy Spirit is a comforter, now a teacher, now the minister of Christ, taking the deepest things of the kingdom of the Son of God, and showing them to the wondering and glowing heart. When spirits meet in conference there can be no literal report of the interview : what passed must be known only to the heart itself ; but it is so known to the heart as to constitute a fortress, a sanctuary, an impregnable argument.

Have we this witness of God the Holy Ghost ? Does he speak comfortably to us ? What do we mean by comfort ? In the great majority of instances the word comfort in the New Testament means stirring up, not soothing down ; encouraging, warming, stimulating, not allowing to slumber and making life one dreary Sabbath afternoon. Let us not debase etymology : when the apostle prayed that the saints might be comforted he prayed that they might be stirred up, roused. Truly the apostles were ardent men. Great mischief will come if we begin to set one kind of experience against another in this matter of Christian life and Christian fellowship. We ought not to antagonise but to comfort one another. The man sitting next me may know nothing about miracles, but he may have a deep spiritual experience ; let us commune together/ so far as we may be able, and help one another. The next man may be mighty in argument ; let him not say to his weaker brother, If you cannot argue you cannot be saved. As well might one artist say to another, Because you cannot do my kind of work you are incapable. One man can bring into measurable canvas a whole universe of action, life, colour, suggestion ; another man can through the organ express what language can never represent, a whole apocalypse of dreamy thought. Shall the one man say to the other, Because you cannot paint, or, Because you cannot play, therefore you have no right in the sanctuary, and no right to recognition amongst men who are approved scholars and refined citizens ? Yet this is precisely what is being done in the Church. If any man's experience does not accord with mine, that man is an alien ; it would seem as if some persons ran all their thought into that unholy and despicable mould. Some men are Christians who do not know it ; there are men who have to be told what they are. When a man is troubled to ecclesiastically distribute himself or assign his precise right, if he could with a clumsy hand and too much ink and too broad a pen write down, " I love the Son of God," that would be better than anything he could indite. That is what we want more and more of all through and through the Church.

Do you suppose the world, the great million-headed world, labour-crushed, darkness-bound, is going to stop until we ecclesiastics and theologians have arranged all our little manœuvres ? The world is dying,—save it ! Testify out of your own experience, out of your own observation, out of your own knowledge ; then your testimony shall be eloquent and effective through the power of the Holy Ghost. It should be a joy to us that there are so many ways of representing Christ. One star differeth from another star in glory. It should be the delight of the pastor to know that no two men in his church can agree with one another with a view to lifting up a standard that everybody else shall accept. Listen, saith he, being a man of capacious mind, and still more capacious heart, listen to all these speeches : there is a line of unity in them though the speakers do not recog nise it. Hear : one hath a miracle, one a psalm, one a tongue, one a vision, one a dream, one a thought, one a broken heart. Listen : this is not conflict, this is not the *odium theologicum,* one man pelting another with hard words because he does not believe as he believes. Listen. What are the wild waves saying ? They say that they are moving in harmony with the great astronomic force, pulsing, throbbing, thundering on the shore, and yet they all belong to the same great sea. Let us cultivate difference ; let us accept difference as an argument and an illustration and as opening broader possibilities, and away, away with the monotony which has burdened, distressed, and hindered the Church of Christ !

PRAYER.

ALMIGHTY GOD, we come to thy house to complete our own home. The house is no home until we connect it with thy sanctuary; then the fire burns well, then is the bed the sanctuary of sleep and sweet rest; the bread then is sacramental, and the whole office of love a beauteous ministry. The tabernacle of God is with men upon the earth, sanctifying all their dwellings, and making their houses homes. Lord Jesus, abide with us; never go away: sit down with us at the table; break our bread for us, and feed our hearts with love. Be our housekeeper,—except the Lord keep the city the watchmen shall be blind. Keep our houses, our lives, all our interests. Number the hairs of our heads; watch us as if we were of importance to thee. Are we not important to thee, thou Son of God? Thou wast wounded for our transgressions, thou wast bruised for our iniquities; for us thou didst carry the Cross: we are therefore of consequence to thy love Find in us the image of God, and restore it in all its beauty and grandeur; lead us away from all that is deathly and mean and dishonourable, and lift us up to the gate of heaven, the entrance of the dwelling of God. Pity us in our littleness, vanity, and infirmity; urge not against us thy great power: for who can stand against the thunder of God? May thy gentleness make us great. Surround us with love, indulge us with mercy, feed us with grace. The Lord hear us in these things, and surprise us by great replies. Amen.

Chapter vi. 12.

"Gather up the fragments that remain, that nothing be lost."

FRAGMENTS AND PORTIONS.

YOU can easily recall the many discourses which you have heard upon these simple and useful words. The picture is vivid: the thousands have partaken of the bounty of Christ, and when the feast is finished Jesus says, "Gather up the fragments that remain, that nothing be lost": sweep up all the crumbs, pick up all the fallen pieces, leave nothing behind for beast or bird. Our fathers and our mothers have preached to us upon these beautiful words, and many admirable sentiments they have inferred from the incident which children can understand and admire. What lectures we have heard upon gathering up the fragments! Economists have said, Gather up all the odd moments of time; never have any spare moments that you do not know how to use : when there is a little break in the continuity of your labour commit to memory some portion of Scripture, or some verse of poetry, or some words of a foreign language which you are anxious to learn and to speak. Never be idle; if you add up all your spare moments you will find in the course of the year that probably they will amount to days; be very economical of time, be very miserly of periods of five minutes and half-hours : gather up the fragments that nothing be lost. And we have said, Well done, economist; what thou hast said, thou hast well said. Then the motherly economist has come in upon us and said, "Waste not, want not," and she has chosen for her trencher one that bears that motto carven on its hospitable edges. "Waste not, want not" : throw nothing away; if you have cut too much bread and cannot eat what you have cut, be careful to treasure the remainder, you will want it in an hour or two, and pick up all the crumbs, and throw no one to hungry dog or waiting bird; take care of the littles, and things that are great will take care of themselves; take care of the pence, and the pounds will manage on their own account. And we have heard the sweet old mother say all this, and have felt in our hearts that (excepting the dog and the bird) she was speaking words of truth and wisdom. Then she has said to her little seamstresses, Take care of all the little pieces, pick up all the thread ends, store away all the little cuttings; you can make something of them by-and-by —pincushions and dolls' frocks; there is no telling what you may do with these little pieces : gather up the fragments, that nothing be lost.

Have we a word to say against all this economy ? Only this, that when it is proposed to base it upon this text it is nonsense. It is very good in itself; we all need to learn something of that economy, but we must not base it upon this particular Scripture. Hence the difficulty of using single texts; hence the mischief that is wrought by many poor teachers that would build a denomination upon a semicolon. If we turn to the Revised Version we shall find a change which has been pointed out by the Very Rev. the Dean of Llandaff, himself one of the revisers, as important, showing the meaning of the text to be infinitely larger than the trifling economy which has prided itself on its own ignorance. "Gather up the broken portions that remain, that nothing be lost." "Fragments" is displaced by the word "portions," and to the word portions is attached the word "broken." "Gather up the broken portions that remain, that nothing be lost." Look at the word "broken": we have seen in Mark that Jesus took the bread, the loaves, and brake them; we have seen in Luke that the word "brake" is also used as denoting the action of Christ: now we read, "Pick up all the broken portions that remain, that nothing be lost." See the picture: observe the breaking hands of Christ: the loaves grow under his touch; he breaks until he is surrounded by heaps and piles and hills of bread; and still he breaks, and still the multitudes continue to eat, and when the feast is over he says, Pick up the broken portions that remain, that nothing be lost. Not, Gather up your leavings, but, Gather up my treasures; not, Sweep up your crumbs, but, Take care of the unsearchable riches of your Lord. All that we have heard of the little economy was neat and thrifty and domestic, but it is not authorised by this text; this verse shows the larger truth. There is no need to waste our crumbs or our leavings, but what Christ is teaching is that he has laid up treasures for ever, and we have to carry them with us wherever we go. What a different view is this! We started with economy, we end with faith; we began by keeping thrift-boxes (the thief heard of them, and took them all away one night), we end by keeping our treasures where moth and rust doth not corrupt, where thieves do not break through nor steal. I shall have enough, not because I have swept up the crumbs, but because God has broken bread enough to keep his universe through all the ages of eternity: only the universe must take care of the broken portions; that is where thrift comes in, the great thrift, the noble economy. We have had occasion to point out and denounce the miserable prudence of some people, the little nibbling mouse-like activity and industry and thrift and prudence of some small natures that always end by some act of glaring imprudence. You watch a man who is too prudent, neatly prudent, prudent on a small scale, and that man will die an open palpable fool; at the last, when nearing fourscore, he will do some deed that will topple him over, and the world will laugh at his mouse-like prudence. There is another prudence, the larger, grander philosophy, the faith that lives in God, and that says, I will dwell in the house of the Lord for ever, because the Lord is my Shepherd. That prudence will grow, that wisdom will be justified of her children; and many who trembled because of momentary eccentricity will live to see the day that he who trusted most in God had broken portions to eat that the world knew not of, the world did not give, and the world cannot take away.

Observe how characteristic this action is of the whole method of providence. God never gives just enough. If he does, tell me where. The calculator who is wise says, To-morrow month fifty guests will come to my table: for their satisfaction what shall I provide? The fare is detailed, totalised, pronounced sufficient, a little is thrown in for foam—what is the tankard unless it foam up high above its own level? That is supposed to be hospitality. With certain obvious qualifications it is what it claims to be. When does God give just enough, so that there is nothing to spare? I refer you to all you know of nature: is there just sunlight enough to last the little day and to creep to bed by? Does the one side of the earth say, I could have done with a million more beams, but they were not to be had, because the other side of the globe needed them? Why, God rains whole oceans of light upon the globe that the globe cannot retain; the little globe-vessel cannot hold the wine of the sunlight: down it comes in river and torrent, and Atlantic and Pacific—on and on—and running away over the sides of this too-little vessel to fill other globe-goblets with its largess of glory. When are there just enough leaves to cover the bare shoulders of winter, so that the Lord says, If I had more leaves I would clothe that little bare corner, that small bleak crag, but my ivy ran out, my grass was insufficient; I might have spared one flower, but that would have been all I could have done? Why, he wastes more blossoms than arithmetic can count. As for the leaves, have you numbered them? Have you had daylight enough to count the leaves upon one great oak? and what are these snowflakes under the tree? Shed blossoms! He could have clothed another globe with them as large as the globe we live upon. When does God "brake" in nature just enough? Whenever he has broken in personal providence just enough it was not an indication of his want, but a proof that he was educating and chastening our lives. He has not always entrusted us with the broken portions; he has seen that now and again we could not be trusted with them, and therefore he has had to be his own treasurer. God has had to take care of his own promises; the Lord hath not allowed all the angel promises to come and sing to us at once, but he has sent them one after another, each with his little song, enough to last out all the darkness of our fear.

It was like Jesus Christ to give ten thousand times more than the people really needed. At the wedding feast they said there was no wine, and he gave them firkin after firkin of wine, a whole Niagara of the wine of the kingdom of heaven, that never made the judgment dark, or the knees tremble in weakness, or the mind play the tricks of the fool. He began well—"This beginning of miracles did Jesus in Cana of Galilee." There never was so much wine in the little town before. When does Jesus do just enough to save the sinner? He saves the sinner with an eternal salvation, with an everlasting redemption; his Cross is not able simply and only to lift the world a little, it can lift the world to heaven. What a different meaning is this! We began by seeing the disciples sweeping up the crumbs, gathering up the little pieces that had been left over, and putting them into baskets; whereas Jesus Christ did not call them to this kind of work, he said, "Gather up the broken portions," he took the bread and brake it, and there was ten thousand times more than the universe could eat: and he said, Take care of the broken portions, my finger prints are upon them; these may be unto you some day as my broken body. Whatever Christ did he did sacramentally; he never uttered a word in any language without sanctifying that word, making it the gem of speech, the diamond of eloquence.

What about your little economy now, your small texts and neat quotations, and your religious labels? Why, all things are yours, if you will gather them up, and take care of them. God will not follow the spendthrift and put money into his pockets, but the Lord says, All things are yours, if you live in faith, if you live in love, if you serve faithfully: call upon me, and I will answer. We should have more—of everything—if we had more faith in God. "Ye cannot serve God and Mammon." That is what you are trying to do. You fail, and the universe is glad of your defeat. What, can you steal something without God seeing you? It will rot in your tents. The Lord knew that the Israelites were a gang of thieves, and he gave them just enough; and here and there some of them thought he was not looking, and they took some away with them, and when they went to laugh over it next day it was pestilent, poisonous, it had become as death in the house. You cannot outwit God. You do not want the promises every day; there are whole weeks and months when you need no promise at all, and you have nothing to do but toil and toil: but keep the promises near at hand, the day on which you will need them may come at any moment; then you will remember the words of the Lord Jesus, how he said, "Gather up the broken portions, that nothing be lost."

The Christian need not live from hand to mouth. How much of history have you gathered up? History should be prophecy. History is nothing if it end in itself; it only becomes representative of its divinely-intended meaning when it lifts up a great light over the darkness of the future. Have you stored your history? Have you turned it into prophecy, poetry, idealism, faith? Or has God governed the world in vain for you? For you have heeded not the ever-moving and all-ruling hand. How much of your own experience have you treasured? What broken portion have you ready for use? Let David teach us again as he has often taught us; looking forward to the fray with Goliath of Gath he said, "The Lord that delivered me out of the paw of the lion, and out of the paw of the bear, will deliver me out of the hand of this Philistine." That was gathering up the broken portions that remained, that nothing was lost. Some one had not to come to David and say, Have you ever had any serious encounters with any difficulties in your life? Woe to the soul that needs to be reminded of its own birthdays, its own conquests, its own days of coronation. Treasure God's goodness as seen in the past, and use it as an assurance of God's goodness in the future. He is able to do exceeding abundantly above all that we ask or think ; when he has done it, gather up the broken portions that nothing be lost. You need to be converted every day, and to be taken back to the infant school every day ; you soon fall from what little faith you have into the silliest idiocy, so that you have to be taught again the first principles and the alphabetic elements of things, instead of being rich with unsearchable riches. Lord, increase our faith. Oh that we had gathered up the broken portions ! then to-day we had been revelling in our heritage, we had been rich with unsearchable riches.

When you say to your children or your friends, "You may call upon me in the day of trouble : all I have shall be at your disposal, my experience shall be the bible out of which you shall read all day long ; when you need me most call upon me earliest, and whatever I do for you shall be eagerly and cordially done ; " then gather up the broken portions, that nothing be lost. You do not want them to-day, an easy " Thank you " covers the occasion ; but there are times when lions and wolves are after you, when the sky is one great frown, when the cross-winds howl from every point of the compass, and you cannot tell the right hand from the left ; then remember the broken portions laid up in store, you gathered what God broke : ye are fellow labourers with God.

So we are not called to save trifles, but to draw upon the treasured fulness of God. We are not called to a small economy, but to a tranquil and victorious faith.

PRAYER.

ALMIGHTY GOD, thou hast indeed set a King in Zion, and his name is Christ: the name that is above every name, around which the universe shall gather in homage. We humbly desire that we may know the meaning of that name more and more deeply every day; that its charm may become mightier over our spirits; that we may be led forth by it as by an inspiration and a challenge to many a holy fight, to much high daring, and that it may work in us all the mystery of patience and long-suffering, that in the end we may be saved as with triumph. We bless thee that we have heard of the King whose name is Christ; we love him, because he first loved us, so that now we can say, The love of Christ constraineth us. He takes the throne of our heart and sits upon it, and is the monarch of our whole life. For such a King we bless thee; we would have this man reign over us, we would be subject to no other king. Reign over us, thou whose right it is to reign; cause us to submit our will to thine, to bow before thee in continual and loving and delighted homage, and may our whole life be marked by a loyalty to divine law, to divine light, to divine love. Thus may our lives become a daily sacrifice, not living for themselves or unto themselves, but going up evermore towards the one throne where our life is hidden in Christ with God. May this account for the unchangeableness of our devotion, for the constancy of our faithfulness, for the pureness of our loyalty; may no enemy have power against us to trouble us, to torment our peace, to disturb our expectations, but in quietness and solemnity and in the perfect assurance of indestructible and unquestioning love, may we rest in God, and hope continually in the Most High. We bless thee that thou hast made us to be reigned over. Thou hast put within us the element of subjection; help us to use that element aright, to bow down before the true King, to be faithful to the one throne, never to forsake the standard of the truth. We thank thee for these aspirations; we would that they might come to fruition in our lives. Yet for them, as inspirations only, we bless thee. Their utterance does the soul good; whilst we speak them in thy hearing our life is lifted up. Enable us constantly to see the unattained ideal, to fix our minds upon the mark we have not yet reached; enable us by the ministry of the Holy Ghost constantly to urge onward towards that high mark—forgetting the things that are behind, enable us to make advancement in things divine. We would not be to-day as we were yesterday, but to-day we would have some new knowledge, some quickened expectation, some widened and brightened hope we never had before. Thus may our life continually expand and elevate until it becomes perfect with the measure of Christ's own life.

Thy Book is the man of our counsel; but how can we understand what we read except thou dost explain it to our understanding and our heart? Holy Spirit, dwell with us, revealing the hidden riches of Christ, showing us the yet undisclosed depths of his infinite truth, and constraining us to follow him with increasing diligence and devotion of heart, that we may not be left behind, but be found ready when our Lord cometh to enter into all the fulness of his joy. We have come up to thy house from divers occupations; we have brought with us memories of the world; we are pursued by anxieties, difficulties, tormenting memories, as were the emancipated Israelites pursued by the Egyptians. Enable us now fully to flee away from these things and to enter into rest, the rest that remaineth ever for the people of God. Into this sanctuary may no worldly care come; into this hidden place may nothing that is tormenting penetrate. Give us quietness for an hour, time to bethink ourselves, to collect our strength, and enable us to draw from the riches of thy grace a plenitude of thy truth and thy mercy, so as to qualify ourselves for the renewal of the conflict in the opening week. May all our battles be conducted in thy strength; may all our difficulties be approached in the consciousness that God is with them that wish to be right and to do right. Enable us, in this sure faith, in the steadfastness of this revealed truth, serenely to walk forward into whatsoever direction thy Spirit may point, knowing this, that thou wilt cause all things to work together for good if our love to thee be a pure and constant flame. Regard us as representing many human experiences, many personal difficulties, and various human estates; regard us every one with an eye of favour. Let not the fear of thy judgment be amongst us to destroy, but only to search out and to renew. May thy gospel come to every one as a new truth—old as eternity, yet new and beautiful as the summer morning shining round about us. Revive our best recollections; brighten the hopes that are momentarily beclouded; cause us to recollect the goodness that has ever passed before us, and may all our yesterdays be gathered up into an emphatic and sublime prophecy, foretelling the victories that are yet to come. Bless the stranger within our gates; may this be to him his Father's house, a place of rest, a gate opening upon the Infinite Land, where there are no strangers, where the home feeling is supreme, where the whole family gather together into one, and are indissoluble evermore. Look upon those who are in special trials and peculiar difficulties. Forget not the house that has been darkened by bereavement; remember the life suddenly desolated and impoverished; look upon the tree from which thou hast stripped the bud and the blossom and left it very bare—send summer down upon its roots, may the dew of the morning visit its branches, and may it yet bring forth abundantly, and rejoice in all the summer joy of thy glory. Be with us as individuals, families, households; remain with us as a Church and people naming the name of Christ, baptised with the Holy Ghost. Let thy ministry be luminous, mighty, powerful in tenderness, and may many people hear the Word of the Lord here, and receive it and bless his name, and give up their lives to his service. Hear this our morning prayer. Let not our psalm of praise be unheard-in heaven. Send us down answers of peace. Thou wilt surely do so, for we are gathered at the Cross of Christ, we look up to his open wounds, we remember the meaning of the sacrificial blood which flowed from his veins, and because thou hast given thy Son to die for us, thou wilt with him also freely give us all things. This thy will be done. Amen.

Chapter vi. 15.

"When Jesus therefore perceived that they would come and take him by force, to make him a king, he departed again into a mountain himself alone."

CHRIST NOT A KING BY FORCE.

THESE words enable us to come to some just understanding of the place of force in the gospel of Jesus Christ. It is a common saying amongst ourselves that some men have greatness thrust upon them. From all such men Jesus Christ separates himself, knowing that what is done by force or compulsion may by force or compulsion be undone. So he would not have a kingdom that was forced upon him, nor would he be forced upon a kingdom. Wonderful words are written upon the blood-red banner of this king. Read some of them: "Put up thy sword into the sheath." "My kingdom is not of this world." "He took upon him the form of a servant." "Behold, I stand at the door and knock." Are these kingly words? Is it the place of a king to stand outside and to knock? Jesus would not be a man-made king; in some other way he would come to the throne. The creature of a populace must live by popular favour; this man must rule by a deeper and nobler law. So he passes away from the impulsive crowd that supposes it could make a king, saying, "It is better to be alone than to be a creature of such creatures."

What then has Jesus Christ done up to this time? He has actually declined twice to be made a king. It is not every man who has two such chances in one lifetime—Jesus had them and despised them. Once he was shown all the kingdoms of the world and the glory of them, and was told that they might be his if he would bend his knee to the offerer, and he said No. Then the people who had seen him work the miracle of the loaves and fishes proposed themselves to work a still greater miracle by forcing him to be king, and he said No. Everything depends upon how you get hold of your kingdom. If you have offered false worship for your kingdom it will rot in your grip, and if you have been forced upon a reluctant heart, that heart will cast you off in the spring-tide of its returning power. We must, therefore, understand what true power is; we must go a little into the elements which constitute true might—there is influence and influence. The mystery about Jesus Christ's declining two kingdoms is this; that he actually came to be a king, yea, King of kings, Lord of lords, and he must reign till he hath put all enemies under his feet. And yet, when he was offered a kingdom for one act of homage he declined; when the people were all going to get behind him to urge him to ascend the throne, he fled, for solitude was better than such mock-royalty.

I shall claim something for Christ out of all this. A man who can act so shall not be snubbed in my hearing without protest. He shall not be reviled without indignant remonstrance. Oh, he works by a very long line, this man. When a step would take him out of the common thoroughfare into the highway of royalty, and he declines to take that step, I say there is something in this man more than in any other man. And are we, his loyal ones, going to allow our faith in him to be mitigated or impaired or snuffed out by somebody who imagines he has found some fault in him which escaped the microscopic and penetrating eyes of Pilate? For my part, I intend to stand by him a little longer. There is a breadth in his way of doing things; there is an outgo of soul in this man that I have found nowhere else. May I have strength to go with him to prison and to death! The more I study his character, the more I find that I am independent of all that series of proofs described by the theologians as evidences. I value them as introductory; they are a needful part of my alphabetical education in the things of the kingdom of Christ; but the grand claim of Christ to the supremacy of the universe is not resting upon merely temporary considerations and formal arguments, it goes right up to the very centre and necessity of things, and it will be our business to try and elucidate that proposition in a few words.

It appears, then, that nothing has to be done in the kingdom of heaven by violence—by mere force. Did not Jesus Christ come to be a king? Yes. Well, then, what did it matter by what way he was proclaimed king? Everything. A man must prove his title to his seat, or he may be unseated—dispossessed of the glory which temporarily encircled him. It is not right to do right in a wrong way. It was right that Jesus Christ should be king; it was wrong to seek to make him king by force. Let us say that it is right that men should pray. It would be wrong to attempt to force men to pray. It is right that you should come to church—it would be wrong to force any one of you to come to the sanctuary. Even a right end, therefore, is not to be attained by the wrong road; the end does not sanctify the means.

See how utterly powerless is force in all high matters, in all great concerns of the soul, the concerns that look outward towards education and matureness and destiny. For example, what can force do in this matter of prayer? You can force a man to kneel: true. You can force a man to speak, whilst he is upon his knees, religious language: true. You can force him to repeat all the devotional words of the Bible while you stand over him sword in hand: true. Can you make him pray? Never. There he defies you. A superficial observer would say, "We compelled him to pray," but he has done nothing of the kind. There is a line beyond which the tyrant cannot go, beyond which force is weakness: that is the line of perfect spiritual independence on the part of the individual judgment and conscience.

Take the matter of honesty. What can you do by mere force? You can by force compel a man to pay his debts—is that compelling him to be honest? Nothing of the kind. You can force him to pay the uttermost farthing of his pecuniary obligations, and you may be able to give him, on his so doing, a complete remittance and release from all such bond—have you made him an honest man? Perhaps you have only made him a greater thief! What is honesty? Something that force cannot create. What is dishonesty? Something that force cannot punish. You have a certain length of line, and that length of line must be used for social convenience and the purposes of social justice, but beyond that the man may pay you every penny he owes you, and be a thief in every drop of blood in his felonious heart.

They could compel a man to ascend the throne : they could not compel him to rule, nor could they compel him to be a king. Garment upon his shoulder, coronal upon his head, nimbus burning and glowing around his uplifted countenance—he is only a mean man still, a king in name, a creature of the dust in reality. What is true of the individual is true of the nation. You can compel a nation to build a church, but you cannot compel a nation to be religious. If you could do so, it would not be right—it would be out of keeping with the spirit of loyal worship ; the very bloom and fragrance of all that is heavenly in religion would be destroyed. Think of this as deeply true to human nature—the very attempt to force a man to be religious destroys the temper which alone makes religion possible. Religion, truly understood, is the joyous sacrifice of the individual will to the will of the Supreme—it is the exaltation of God over every thought and purpose of the mind. Being all this, it is infinitely beyond the control of all force and penal compulsion.

Whilst all this is true on the human side, the real point to be considered is that Jesus Christ himself would never consent to reign over the soul by mere force. Observe that this is a two-sided question ; if you could force men to Christ, you could not force Christ to men. If you succeeded in moving the finite, you could never succeed in also moving the Infinite. It is the Infinite that declines, it is God that says, No—I will not reign thus. Jesus Christ reigns by distinct consent of the human mind. Listen to these words ; they should convert us all, they should make us love him : " If any man will open the door, I will come in." That is the king's word. " If ye seek me, ye shall find me." " Come unto me, all ye that labour and are heavy laden, and I will give you rest." " He that believeth shall be saved." If there is yet left in you, O man outside the kingdom of Christ, one element that mother or wife or sister could appeal to, I level my whole argument and expostulation in the direction of that element, and ask you to consider these infinitely tender words of him who came to be king—" Behold, I stand at the door, and knock ; if any man will open the door, I will come in." Only a soul lost beyond redemption could fail to see the gospel that is in these words.

If he will not be king by force, by what means will he become king? Force would seem to hasten progress—the sword is famous for cutting a short road to remote ends. But Jesus Christ declines to be made a king by force. How then does he expect to become king over all the earth? What is his own notion? Hear it: tell me if ever in common brain there sprang a notion so divine. What is his method? Preach me, is one of his injunctions—declare me, unfold me, show my doctrine, my purpose, my spirit—go into all the world and preach the gospel to every creature. That is a roundabout way, is it not? It is, but the swing of the divine astronomy is in it, the throb that stirs the planets. It is not the thought of a common man; whilst I look at him speaking these words, arrayed in his carpenter's garments he may be, but there glows through them a light that supersedes the sun, and I claim it as a tribute of mere decency, of elementary courtesy, that when a man has a high thought, he himself should be regarded with a feeling appropriate to the loftiness of such thinking, be he carpenter, be he king.

Is it enough to preach him? He adds another word—Live me—" Let your light so shine before men that they may see your good works, and glorify your Father which is in heaven."—I have given you an example, that as I have done to you, so do ye one to the other.—Follow me, show that you have been with Christ—prove what I do for you in the mitigation of your care, in the sanctification of your affliction; tell people what it is that makes you pluck the sting from death, and spoil the victory of the grave.

It is in this way that he is coming to the kingdom. I believe he will keep it. Now that I see his plans, I hear his words with the ear of my soul, and their true meaning comes with their music—" the gates of hell shall not prevail against it, against my church, against my kingdom." What more does he say to us?—Lift me up—" I, if I be lifted up, will draw all men unto me." How lifted up? Not lifted up upon a cross—murderers gave him that elevation—but lifted up on the cross in the sense of sacrifice; in the sense of embodying the infinitely gracious purposes of God; in the sense of making reconciliation for sin ; in the sense of being offered, the just for the unjust. There you have not a wooden cross, but the cross of the heart. Yet there is another sense in which we may lift up Christ—we lift him up when we love his law ; we lift him up when we submit to his bidding ; we lift him up when we reproduce his temper ; we lift him up when we receive with unquestioning heart all the gospel of his love. He who bears affliction patiently for Christ's sake, lifts Christ up. He who says to a looking and wondering friend in the time of agony and physical dissolution, " Christ makes me more than conqueror "—lifts Christ up—" and I, if I be lifted up, will draw all men unto me." A slow process ? Yes, but unchangeable in its results. A kingdom built on these foundations is an everlasting kingdom. We are to do our utmost to create in the heart of man a deep interest for Christ ; if we do so, we shall lift the Saviour up.

Now for the truly philosophical explanation of all this. We find it in the words, " We love him, because he first loved us." If it were a question of test, mere test, momentary probation, we might change. But this man lays hold of our entire love, leaves no element of it unclaimed, dominates the whole sphere of our purified and ennobled affection. " Unto him that loved us, and washed us from our sins in his own blood, and hath made us kings and priests unto God and his father ; to him be glory and dominion for ever."

There is still the element of endurance here—there is the divine compulsion moving through the heart, working along the line of the affections, getting hold of the confidence and the love— that means an everlasting reign. When I put these things together I cannot tell how my heart glows with love to this wondrous Nazarene. His words are like no other words ; his method is self-vindicating. It looks so unhuman at the first, it proves itself so divine in its effects. The man who can proceed to capture human nature as this man proceeded, is presumably a true king. I repeat that no adventurer, no empiric, would have acted as Jesus Christ behaved. Here is the kingdom—he said " No " to the devil. If he found out his mistake he would never have repeated it a second time. He refused the kingdom from the devil, he refused the kingdom from violent men—he said he would be king, but not in either of these ways. The man who comes to take me captive by my judgment, by my conscience, by my will, by my love, by all that separates me from beast-hood, is likely to be a true king. Come and reign over us, Ancient of Days !

Let little children think of this : Jesus would not have you forced to be good—Jesus would not have you whipped to church —Jesus would not have you punished for not learning the Bible —Jesus would not have you injured because you do not care for him. He says, " I will speak to the little one ; I will say, I stand at the door and knock ; if any child will open the door, I will come in." That is how Jesus Christ would treat you, little one. He would not smite you on the head because you do not love him ; he would not crush you down by his great power, and try to make you love him ; but he says, "I am standing still outside, and knocking still ; I have been knocking all day and all night, and my hair is wet with dew : if any child will open the door, I will come in."

He makes no proposition about going out. His proposition is to get in, but to get in by your consent, on the invitation of your necessity, on the compulsion of your love. I repeat, therefore, and make an argument of it, that any man,—Galilean peasant, never in Rabbinical school, never having learned letters, trained under no settled ministry of metaphysics or philosophy,—any man who had the notion that to reign for ever you must reign by love, is presumably a true king, the king, King of kings.

The Church should be like the Master : it should not rule by force. I would never compel even a child to go to church ; much less would I attempt to compel any one who was momentarily in my power. I would not bribe a man to go to church—certainly I would in no way inflict upon him loss or humiliation for not going. I would try to make the church itself the attraction. No child should be punished for not learning its Bible. Punish a child if you please for not learning the spelling-book or the geography, but do not associate penal suffering with biblical learning.

The Church should be like the Master : it should seek to rule by love. Not one penny would I take from any man by the law to support any form of religion, either my own or yours. Whatever is done must be done of a willing mind, and everything that is given must have this written upon it—" The love of Christ constraineth us." And in proportion as Jesus Christ will not force you, ought you to love him. If it were a contest of force, then you might rejoice in the apparent victory which you win for a moment; but when he says to you, " It is not a contest of hand against hand or sword against sword, but of your obstinacy against my love ; " when he says, " I could by mere omnipotence crush you between my fingers, but that would only be a triumph of physical power. No ; I will teach you, preach to you, love you, die for you, show you my hands and my feet," the very stripping of himself of his physical almightiness should constitute his supreme power as One who wants to captivate your love, and sit down on the throne of your confidence for ever.

PRAYER.

O **THAT** this day we might see the Lord and have our whole mind filled with his light and joy! Lord, dost thou ask us what we would have at thine hands? Our answer is, Lord, that we might receive our sight! When men cry unto the Lord in their trouble, thou dost deliver them out of their distresses ; in this hope we come now before the Lord, and even whilst we speak our hearts feel the burden rising. Sweet is the day of the Lord, quiet and tender in its sacred peacefulness, opening into the very heavens, and showing us the New Jerusalem as the city in which we shall no more be threatened by fear and humbled by weariness. For every blessing we offer thee our praise. Thou didst lead us through the solitary way, and thou hast spared us from the shadow of death. Our souls are thine; our bodies are thy habitation. Thou art mindful of us with great care, and thy banner over us is love. Oh that we knew how to praise thee aright, that our hearts might not suffer pain because of the weariness of our worship! Thy judgments are very terrible, but thy mercies are greater still. Our life is full of the mercy of the Lord, and our days are made bright by his goodness. Lord, let not our feet stray from the path of thy will. Lord, comfort us, encourage our souls in the day of fear, and let our weakness hide itself in thy great power. We lay down our own wisdom as ignorance, and run away from our towers as from defences that will crush the life that built them. We come to Jesus. We stand beside the Saviour. We know the power of his blood. Lord, help us. Lord, send upon us the blessing of thine infinite pardon. Lord, show us the light of thy face. We daily see how great a gift is life; we know it not, we have not seen the divine secret, we feel the pulse beat, but we see not the power by which it is moved. We are our own mysteries. Life itself is a religion. Life is a continual prayer. How weak we are, yet how strong! We cannot just now bear the full day-light, yet we shall pass the sun on our upward way to the glory to come, and his great lustre shall be as a spark vanishing in the ever-enlarging vastness of thy universe. When we think thus of thy kingdom our light affliction is but for a moment. Thy kingdom, Lord, how great, how bright, how strong! May we one and all have a place in that everlasting house. Thy mercy is greater than our prayer, and therefore do we hope even where we cannot reason. Send the gospel to our lost ones, and bring our wanderers home. Visit our sick chambers, and whisper to our sick ones the messages of consolation, so that their very weakness may itself become a privilege, and their loneliness become the sanctuary within which thou wilt meet them. We put our own life into thy keeping. We lay aside our own poor help as a temptation, and we accept thy strength as our perfect

118

ability. O thou God and Father of our Lord Jesus Christ, when shall we
be wholly swallowed up in thy great love? When will the devil leave us,
and none but holy angels be at hand ? How long the tempter tarries ! He
wears out our strength ; he lures our fancy; he vexes our prayers ; he
tortures our very communion with thyself. Jesus of the wilderness, Jesus
of Calvary, help us or the enemy will prevail. He is so strong, so swift, so
wise ; yet we can do all things through Christ which strengtheneth us,
therefore do we pray—Jesus, save us, or we perish ! Amen.

Chapter vi. 35.

"I am the bread."   "The water that I shall give " (iv. **14**).

BREAD AND WATER.

THE subject is clearly, Bread and Water. You call these
common things, and my object will be to show that their
commonness is not a defect, but an excellence ; that their very
excellence has occasioned their commonness ; and that their
commonness corresponds to a common want in the constitution
of mankind. I will take the simple idea of bread and water, and
apply it socially in the first place, and trace it upward to its
highest and divinest meaning.

Let us look in upon the greatest feast ever spread for the
refreshment and delight of kings. All delicacies shall be there
that can be found in wood and air and sea ; the richest wines
shall sparkle and foam and glow upon the sumptuous board ;
and the fragrances arising from this luxurious feast shall excite
and regale the appetite of hungry men. Now what have we
there ? What is the fundamental idea ? What is the nucleus
of the abounding and tempting feast ? Surprising as it may
seem, the whole thing is but an adaptation of bread and water !
It is bread and water decorated ; bread and water more or less
adulterated ; bread and water supposed to be at their best as to
refinement, and richness, and power of gastronomic temptation
and satisfaction. And if you could follow the sated guests into
their privacy you would hear them say, in effect, " All this fine
living is well enough now and then, but only now and then, after
all ; let us have something plain and substantial ; " in a word, let
them have bread and water. What is this prodigious art of the
high cook ? He is bound, like other popular slaves, to produce

something fresh ; without novelty he sinks into a common baker ; a new relish may mean a new fortune ; a new gravy may give him a country house and a footman ; a new adaptation of an omelette may enable him to start a shooting box,—but it is bread and water that he works upon ; bread and water are the basis of his fortune. He lives by mystifying the public, and mightily laughs at the trick by which he has made men think that bread crumbs have some connection with far-off spice groves and Ceylon breezes. Offer your guests plain bread and water, and they will not often call your way ; but dress up the bread and water, torture them, colour them, spice them, and they will praise the delicacy and excellence of the viands. But bread and water survive ! These are the things that cannot be shaken. Empires of soups and entrées, wines and liqueurs, rise and fall, but the steady old friends bread and water remain as the unadorned and ever wholesome gifts of God. Ay, poor cook, clever trickster, half a creator, under all thy enchantments and wizardries there are the plain bread and water ; disguise them, bribe them, paint them, and wreathe around them all manner of cunning ornamentation, they are but bread and water. The image and the superscription are the cook's, but the bread and water themselves are God's ! Name the dishes that delighted Babylonian gluttons, and rehearse the menu which made the Egyptian gourmands smack their sensual lips. You cannot ; these are forgotten delights, paste-boards that perished in the fire ; but bread and water come steadily along the ages, over the graves of empires and the ashes of royalty, having escaped the tortures of the cruelest cooks, and shown themselves to be the primary and necessary gifts of God.

Well, the application of this is obvious in higher spheres of life, such, for example, as the culture and satisfaction of the intellect. Reading and writing are the bread and water of the mind. Give a child the power of reading and writing, and let him do the rest for himself ; it is worth doing (at least some of it), and let him find it out and he will value it the more. Your duty is done in giving the reading and the writing, the intellectual bread and water. But fine cookery is imitated in fine intelligence and with like results in some cases, namely, mental indigestion and ill-health. Hence, we have imperfect French, caricatured German, and murdered music, and the native tongue and the native history are passed by as quite secondary, if not beneath contempt. It is better to chatter French in a way which nobody can understand than to speak good plain exact English, is it not? We must be fine at all costs. We must have a few knick-knacks on the mantelpiece, even if we have not a bed to sleep upon. We must be able to say, Parlez-vous Français, even if we cannot pay our debts. When will people learn to prize bread and water? When will they see that it is better to know a little well, than to know next to nothing about a great deal? Oh, when? This is not a little matter; it is a matter of great importance, from the fact that it is an index of character. We do not laugh at a man whose learning ends at the multiplication table; but we may laugh with grim amusement at a man who speaks hotel French and then spells October with a "*h*." Give your children intellectual bread and water without grudging, that is to say, give them a thorough grounding in the beginnings and elements of knowledge, and let them do the rest for themselves.

These illustrations prepare the way for the highest truth of all, namely, that Jesus Christ is the bread and water without which we cannot live. He never says he is a high delicacy, a rare luxury, a feast which the rich alone can afford; he says that he is bread and water, he likens himself not to the luxuries, but to the necessaries of life, and in so doing he shows a wisdom, a reach of mind, a grasp of human nature, which should save him from the attacks of malignant men. An adventurer would not have seen in metaphors so humble a philosophy so profound. Adventurers like big words and glaring figures; they speak great swelling words of vanity; they search heaven and earth for effective figures; they disdain the sling and the stone. Not so with Jesus Christ; he is Bread, he is Water, he is Light, he is the Door, he is the Shepherd, and these words, so simple, stretch their meaning around the whole circle of human life, and by their choice alone is the supreme wisdom of Jesus Christ abundantly attested.

Let us go further into this matter by a little detailed inquiry and illustration.

(1) Man needs Jesus Christ as a necessity and not as a luxury. You may be pleased to have flowers, but you must have bread. Christ presents himself as exactly fulfilling this analogy. Our whole life is based on one or two simple but necessary lines; we must have food, we must have shelter, we must have security. But into how many glorifications have all these simple necessaries passed! We have just spoken about food. Now look at shelter. How styles of architecture have grown out of that idea! We talk of Doric, and Grecian, and Gothic; of Norman arches and Corinthian capitals; and indeed we have a long and perplexing nomenclature, all coming out of the fact that man must have a place to go into when the weather is rough and when sleep is needed. Out of the need of shelter the science or art of architecture has come! Is this wrong? Most certainly not. It is a trait of civilisation. It is a sign of refinement and progress. But let an architect of high fancy be called in to build you a house, he gives you a fine elevation, a noble porch, a splendid dome; but in the fever of his fancy he has forgotten the foundations, overlooked the drainage, omitted the joists, and made no provision for the escape of the smoke. How then? Of what avail is it that there is much elaboration of cunning masonry on the front of the house? You could have done without the stone faces above the mullions, but you cannot do without the chimneys and the joists. It is exactly after the bearing of this analogy that Jesus Christ has often been presented in preaching and in books. He has been offered as an ornament merely. He has been preached as the most curious and entertaining of all riddles. He has been treated as the successor of Plato, or Solon, or Seneca. In this way, generally indeed intended to be respectful, the whole purpose of his coming into the world has been overlooked. He has not been presented as bread and water, or the very first and most indispensable necessity of life; he has been treated as a phenomenon; cabineted as a rarity in human history; labelled as a remarkable specimen; and in this way even some of his admirers have ignorantly betrayed and dishonoured the Lord. Jesus is not a phenomenon, he is bread; Christ is not a curiosity, he is water. As surely as we cannot live without bread we cannot live truly without Christ; if we know not Christ we are not living, our movement is a mechanical flutter, our pulse is but

the stirring of an animal life. It is in this way, then, that Jesus Christ is to be preached. It is even so I would ever preach him. I would call him the water of life ; I would speak of him as the true bread sent down from heaven ; I would tell men that it is impossible to live without him ; I would say, with heightening passion, with glowing and ineffable love, that he only, even the holy Christ of God, can satisfy the hunger and the thirst of the soul of man. In this way I claim a distinct vocation as a preacher. I am not one amongst many who try to do the world good ; as a Christian preacher, or a preacher of Christ, I offer the only thing that can vitally and sufficiently touch the world's condition, and thus the position of the Christian preacher is absolutely without similitude or parallel, in that the choice he offers is life or death, salvation or ruin, heaven or hell.

(2) What has been the effect ot omitting to declare Christ simply as bread and water ? Leaving the simplicity of Christ, we have elaborated theological sciences, established and promulgated with solemn sanctions the most intricate creeds ; we have worked out a very high and cunning symbolism ; we have filled the church with incense, with garments of many colours and many signifi- cances, ceremony after ceremony we have contrived ; we have called councils, synods, and congresses ; we have constituted splendid hierarchies, with mitres and crooks, and clothing precious with gold and glaring with ardent colour. All this have we done, O Son of God, though thou didst call thyself bread and water ! We have gathered around thee liturgies and suffrages, and gowns and bands, and surplices and chants, and censers and albs, and stoles and chasubles, though thou didst call thyself bread and water ! We have drawn a long and often mutinous procession of reverends and most reverends and right reverends and very reverends, and doctors and deans and eminences and holinesses, and suffragans and novices and licentiates, though thou didst call thyself bread and water ! Horrible, indeed, and quite infinite is the contemptibleness of all this, and shall I not even say the sin ? Suppose some inquiring stranger looking on and asking, What does all this mean ? I should answer, not without sharpness and indignation, It means that man is a fool, and that he prefers vanity to truth. This is not the Saviour. This is not the way to

God. This is not the door of heaven. This is incubus and
rubbish and abomination.   Christ is bread ; Christ is water ;
Christ is the one answer to thy difficulties, the one Healer of thy
wounds, the one Saviour of thy soul.   Oh, but the curse of this
mischief is terrible to contemplate !   Poor souls are left to believe
that they can only get to Christ by seeing ministers and priests
and bishops, by learning catechisms, by swallowing dogmas
they neither understand nor appreciate, and by listening to the
mumbling and muttering of certain ecclesiastical men in livery.
Oh, the horribleness !   Oh, the blasphemy !   Is not the devil
laughing the while and filling his cruel hand with additional
prey ?   To those eager to know the truth, I say, Christ is bread ;
Christ is water ; he is nigh thee ; take the pure Bible and read it
for thyself, read it in solitude, read it with earnest desire to know
its living claim upon thyself, and thou shalt see the Lord, and
feel the Cross, and eat the heavenly bread.

(3) History furnishes a most graphic confirmation of these
views.   John Stuart Mill says, " Let rational criticism take from
us what it may, it still leaves us the Christ."   Exactly so ; it still
leaves us the bread and water !   It still leaves us all we want.   It
takes away all human conceits and decorations, and it leaves the
living bread.   It mortifies the theological cook and confectioner,
it humbles the decorator of tables, but it leaves the living water !
Theological revolutions have come and theological revolutions
have gone ; timid souls have trembled as if the sanctuary had
been destroyed, but when the noise has passed and the cloud has
rolled off, behold the bread and water remain, and " Welcome,"
is written on the tables of the Lord !   Men cannot get rid of
Christ simply because they cannot get rid of themselves.   Marvellous is it to watch how the Lord allows the chaff to blow away,
but saves every grain of the precious wheat ; and quite marvellous,
too, is it to see how some nervous people think that the wheat
is lost because the chaff has been scattered by the wind.   The
Lord will lose nothing.   Society revolutionises itself, but society
still lives.   Theologies, Eastern and Western, wear themselves
out, but the bread and water are still there, incorruptible and
unlimited.   Do we fear the dissolution of the earth because an
owl's nest has fallen ?   Will the sun not rise to-morrow because

a candle has been blown out? Bethink thee, faithless soul, they are but accidents that change, the essentials abide,

> " Unhurt amid the war of elements,
> The wreck of matter and the crash of worlds."

I fancy we should change our standpoint in viewing all the revolutions and disasters that occurred within the limits of Christendom. Hitherto we have thought of them as the results of intellectual pride or spiritual insubordination. We have mourned over men as fallen creatures because they have risen against the systems in which they were reared. But possibly we are wrong. It may be Christ himself who is at work. He is the great Revolutionist. This may be Christ's own way of clearing off the rubbish which has been piled upon his holy name. Christ pulls down papacies and hierarchies and rituals, that he may show that these are not needful, that all human contrivances are departures from his divine simplicity, and that he wishes to be known through all ages and amongst all men as the Bread and Water of human souls. He knows that our temptation is to make more of externals than of realities; hence he turns his providence against us, hurls down our cathedrals and temples and ministers, and says he will be known only as Bread and Water, not as a compound of coloured and poisonous confection. Oh the deceitfulness of the human heart in this matter of serving Christ! We tell lies to ourselves about it. We talk about enriching our services, ennobling our architecture, educating our ministers, creating universities, founding endowments, originating retreats of elegant leisure for the production of technical literature. Rubbish, all of it! Christ asks nothing of the kind at our hands. He prefers his own Spirit to our culture. It is "not by might, nor by power, but by my Spirit," saith the Lord. "Bring no more vain oblations; incense is an abomination unto me; the new moons and sabbaths, the calling of assemblies, I cannot away with; it is iniquity even the solemn meeting." What, then, are we to do? "Wash you, make you clean, put away the evil of your doings from before mine eyes; cease to do evil, learn to do well; seek judgment, relieve the oppressed, judge the fatherless, plead for the widow." Thus we are driven back to simplicity; our "culture" is thrown down and dashed to pieces as a potter's vessel, and nothing stands but the bread and the water, the first verities, the essential graces, of the Lord's Christ.

I care not how rich our music, how noble our architecture, how imposing our method of worship, if all this be kept strictly in its proper place. I love beauty; I am moved to passion and heroism by inspiring music; I would make the Lord's house glad with every expression of love; but this done, I would write on the doorposts, on the roof, and on every panel, the words of Jesus : " In this place is One greater than the temple." I prefer knowledge to ignorance, but I prefer holiness to either. Culture, when not a chattering and fussy prig, may be right noble and even majestic; but nothing is so cold as culture, and nothing so mean, when not inflamed and impassioned by the spirit of Christ. To-day the pulpit is in danger of being killed by miscalled culture. Men think that because they have been to college five years they ought to be preachers ; which is as logical as to say that a man who has driven an omnibus five years ought to be able to take a ship across the Atlantic. The Lord continually dashes these culture-pots to pieces like a potter's vessel, by making preachers of his own, and clothing them with mysterious but most beneficent power.

We must go back to bread and water. Our dainties must be given up. Our habits are too luxurious ; we are killing our souls with sweet poisons ; we are, by our fabrications and masonries and fine fancies, exalting ourselves above the Lord ; so I would call myself back to the simplicity of Christ, and find all I want in his grace and truth.

"Lord, to whom shall we go?"

THE DIFFICULTIES OF DISBELIEF.

YOU know too well that we are all tempted—sometimes tempted severely—to give up religious faith and Christian hope. The hand which grasps religious treasures is not always equally strong. In dealing with the state of things which usually attends this painful experience, I intend to raise this most practical question: Suppose we give up the Christian faith, what shall we have instead? Wise men are bound to look at consequences. They do not trust themselves to the so-called chapter of accidents. They move with critical caution, putting things into comparison and contrast, and judging the value of results. If any man were to ask you to give up your house, would you not inquire what you should do in such an event? Even if the house was not all that you could wish it to be, you would still desire to know what you were to have in exchange. Are we to be less careful about a faith than about a dwelling-place? Are we to concern ourselves about a house for the body, and leave the soul without a shelter or without a home? Be as sensible in the higher region as you are in the lower. Discern the signs of the times as clearly as you discern the signs of the sky, and the result will be acceptable to God.

Let me remind you that it is infinitely easier to ask questions than to answer them, and to pull down than to build up. This must be one of the earliest lessons which the earnest student must learn. Never forget it. The rule applies to every department of life, but bears with especial force upon the highest questions which engage the mind. Is it not easier, for example, to waste money than to earn it? Is it not easier to spoil a picture than to paint one? You can pluck a flower from its

127

stem, but can you put it on again ? With the rudest hammer
you can injure the sculptured marble ; but can you shape any
stone into beauty ?   These inquiries, made in the lower region
of life and affairs, point towards the doctrine, that it is easier to
tempt a man than to save him ; easier to ruin life than to train
it for heaven ! There are men of vigorous but most ill-trained
and incomplete ability, who give themselves to the work of
unsettling the human mind upon every subject.   They have a
genius for destruction ; they would be unhappy if there was
nothing to break ; they would kill themselves if there was no
other life to be assailed ! You who are earnest students of
these great religious questions must know these men, and value
them properly.   If you listen to their utterances you will find
that they quarrel with everything ; they lay no foundations ;
they teach no distinct and positive truth ; they give the lie to
all faith, and throw distrust upon all experience.   Mark how
easy their task is, compared with the duty of the Christian
teacher.   A malicious man can do more mischief in one hour
than a man of genius can repair in a lifetime ! Let a ruffian
have his way for one night upon any minster or abbey which
was slowly reared through generations and centuries, and in the
morning you may find it a smouldering heap ! So with your
infidels in their limited world ; wherever they go they leave the
mark of the beast, and their course may be tracked by the
desolation which they leave behind.   To all such men you must
put the practical question found in the text, viz., If we go away
from Christ, to whom shall we go ? That is the question I would
urge.   Give up religion, and what then ?   Give up the first idea
of God, and what then ?   We are bound to look at alternatives.
Sometimes a course may appear to be ready-made to our
hands, and to be simple, and to be self-justifying.   Yet when we
ask about the results or alternatives we may get a new and
correct view of the whole case.

The tempter asks you to give up the idea of God, which
we have so frequently endeavoured to explain ; and every
other idea of God which you have derived from the Scriptures
and from your spiritual teachers.   Well, what then ? Remember, you refuse to give up the humblest cottage, until you

know where you are to go; you will not throw away the poorest covering in winter until you know what you are to have in return; you will not, on a dark road, put out the dimmest lantern until you are sure of having a better light in its place. Will you, then, recklessly give up the idea of God at the bidding of any man—the idea of the living, loving, personal God, ruling over all —without asking, "To whom shall I go?" You can put away the mystery of God, and you get in return the greater mystery of godlessness. Your account of creation is then neither more nor less than a fool's account. A chair could not have made itself; but the sun is self-created. Your coat had a maker, but your soul had none. The wax flower on your table was made, but the roses in your garden grew there by chance. The brass instrument was fashioned by a skilled hand, but the voice of man, the grandest of all organs, was self-created. The figure-head on the ship was carved; but the face of the carver became a face by chance, without design and without law! We cannot believe such infinite absurdities. They not only destroy religion; they insult and dishonour reason itself. Were we to accept them and lay them down as the foundations of life, we should lose all self-respect; and feel that faith had been displaced, not only by intellectual madness (which may be a man's infirmity), but by moral licentiousness and insanity! I claim for the reverent and earnest believer in God the highest common sense. His is the only rational creed. You may ask him some hard questions, but he can put harder questions to you in return. Without doubt, as a religious man, he is surrounded by a great mystery, and he glories in it! The great must always be a mystery to the little; the arch must always be a mystery to the column; God must always be a mystery to his creatures. If we could understand all, we should be all. Only the whole can comprehend the whole; only God can understand God!

We teach that religion is the highest expression of reason. We can never consent to say that reason and religion are altogether different. Without reason there could be no religion; and without religion, reason would perish within the prison of the visible and the temporary. Religion is Reason on her knees; faith is Reason on her wings; Christianity is Reason on the

Cross, on her way to the crown! You tell me to give up the idea of God. Then, to whom shall I go? Answer that, if you can. Shall I go to you who have tempted me? Are you prepared to take the consequences of your advice? If a storm should come, will you shelter me? If a sword should be lifted, have you room for me behind your shield? When the day darkens around my soul, can you guarantee me light? You must show me some of your works, that I may have an idea of your strength. I will go round with you and see what you have done, and infer what you can do; and if you can make out a clear case, then I may give up the idea of God. What is your answer to the assaults of great natural forces? Let us begin there. You tell me that you have built great fortresses—high, broad, strong —of the best stone that can be quarried. I ask you, Is it not possible for a bolt of lightning to shiver them to their foundations in a moment? You point to the noble bridges you have made, and you say, "That is my way over rivers." I point you to the floods which tumble their proud arches into confusion, and turn your harvest fields into a swamp. Where then are your sheltering places, and where are the signs of your strength? You have told me to give up the idea of God, and I only ask you this plain common-sense question in return: If I accept your advice and give up the idea of God—to whom shall I go? Remember, it is easy work to tell a man to give up this doctrine and that faith, and to surrender the chief hopes of his life. But he has a right to ask you to take the responsibility of your advice; and especially has he the right of reason, and the right of stewardship of his own life, to ask, If I accept your counsel, to whom shall I go?

The tempter tells you to give up the idea of the future as it is viewed from a Christian standpoint. Well, what then? We are not unwilling to listen to you; but you must make your case good before we can commit ourselves to it. What do you advise? You advise us to give up our idea of the future as it is viewed from a Christian standpoint. We must put this common-sense question in return, What then? If a man asked you to throw away a telescope, would you not inquire what you were to have in its place? Here is a father, whose only son has gone to sea, and the poor old man is watching the receding vessel through a badly constructed glass. A passer-by mockingly says, "Throw away that paltry thing." Will the loving watcher throw it into the water because the mocker ridiculed the instrument? Even though the glass was known to be poor, yet in so far as it helped the naked eye, it was sure to be kept until a better glass was offered in its place. Will you act so with a telescope, and yet fling away the faith-glass through which you read the solemn and wondrous future? Look at the case. Christian revelation tells you that death is not the end of your life; it tells you that death is dispossessed of its power; that, as a believer in Jesus Christ, God the Son, you will pass from this poor weary scene into sanctuaries where there is no sin, and into activities which never tire the servant. It speaks of deeper studies, of holy mysteries, of higher engagements, of divine delights! It speaks with hallowed rapture of reunions, of immortal fellowship, of battles blest with complete and imperishable victories, of hope perfected in ecstatic and cloudless vision! If you believe in this revelation you draw water from the deep, cool well of its promises; your suffering becomes a joy through the support of its rich and inspiring grace. Under these circumstances the tempter says to you, "Give up this idea of the future." Will you give it up at his bidding without at least putting the question and waiting for an answer: If I give it up, what have you to offer me in return? I think this is a sound principle. The inquiry seems to be the very first question of common-sense.

I will suppose myself to be so tempted, and I will tell you how I should meet the tempter. I should say to him: You ask me to give up my Christian convictions about the future. I ask you, in return, Who you are that you should make a proposition so bold? Who are you? Give an account of yourself. Show me that you deserve the confidence which you ask me to repose in your judgment. You are bound to do this, and I insist upon its being done. Let me examine you. You have told me to give up my idea of the future as viewed from a Christian standpoint. You ought to be an able man; you ought to be prepared to answer some searching questions, if the counsel which you give me is to be viewed otherwise than the expression of the highest insanity.

Can you tell me, then, with certainty, what will take place in this city within one short hour ? Can you tell me without a doubt who is, at this moment, in your own house as a stranger awaiting your return ? Can you tell me the contents of a letter without opening the envelope ? Can you tell me what I shall be thinking about in five minutes from this instant ? You ought to be able to do all this lower kind of thing, or something equivalent to it. You ought to be able to make out a very strong case on your own side before you have any status which will warrant you in asking me to surrender my Christian idea of the future. You ought to have made your mark somewhere as a spiritual thinker, and see-ing that you have challenged my attention, I demand to know where that mark is, that I may examine it. Why, suppose I were to surrender my faith at the bidding of every man who came to me, without asking questions and making such inquiries as these, what a life I should have ! A believer to-day, an infidel to-morrow ! I must know who these men are, who ask me to surrender the convictions which are the inspiration and the comfort of my life. But I am not now to be easily misled. I have listened and watched ; and I must see much more and hear much more, before I give such men as I have referred to my con-fidence. If I believe you, the tempter, will you leave me in the long-run in the lurch ? Will you suffer my trial ? Will you snatch me back when I am slipping over the precipice into the desolate caverns of death ? If, as the shadows of life gather around, I begin to feel that I have been misled by you, will you show me how to repair a wasted lifetime, and how to draw the sting of mortal self-reproach ? You must not in the long-run leave the man whom you have misled ; you must not add the cruelty of man-slayer to the flippancy of the unbeliever. Tell me, if I give up this Christian view, to whom shall I go, and what shall I have ? It is easy for you to plunder me ; but I must know how you intend to replace the faith you would take from me.

The tempter tells you to shut your Bible and to believe no longer in Revelation. Well, what then ? We must still ask, To whom shall we go ? We are invited by the tempter to believe that, even assuming the existence of God, it is impossible to find any record of his will; he has never spoken to mankind; he has set forth no outline of human duty; he has written no word for human comfort; he has shed no light on the darkest questions of life; he made us, but he takes no notice of us; he fashioned us as we are, upright, above the beasts of the field in dominion as in skill, but never opens the gate of the city wherein he dwells to bid us welcome to the hospitality of his love; he never bends down to see how his children are going on; and never, never— though he sends down the light and rain, and breathes across the universe the healthful winds which bring life upon their wings—does he send any message to any creature of his hands. The man who can believe that, has a truly capacious and terrible faith; he must be a very monster of a believer! He must. His soul, if he has one, must be a bottomless pit of credulity! Before I yield my hold of the book at his bidding, I must know to whom I shall go. The Bible says to me, "The Lord is my Shepherd, I shall not want." And the tempter says, "Shut up the Bible and be your own shepherd." "But I am bruised, and wounded, and heart dead." He mocks with such advice. The Bible says, " Ho, every one that thirsteth, come ye to the waters, and he that hath no money; come!" The tempter says, "You have no thirst that you cannot slake in the muddy pools that lie at your feet." The Bible says, "God is our refuge and strength, a very present help in trouble." The tempter says, "When you are in trouble dry your own tears, and get out of your own difficulties, and snap your fingers in the face of the universe." The Bible says, "Come unto me, all ye that labour and are heavy laden, and I will give you rest." The tempter says, "Lie down on the thorns; pillow your head on the stones; rest in the wilderness; take a moment's sleep in the desert." The Bible says, "Through this man is preached unto you the forgiveness of sins." The tempter says, "You have never sinned; what forgiveness do you want? Go and wash your hands in the river and you will be clean." Jesus in the Holy Book says, "In my Father's house are many mansions." The tempter says, "Your mansion is the dark cold grave; get into it and rot away!"

After hearing the two voices I say that, considering what

human nature is, looking at its capacities, its powers, its desires, its wondrous thoughts, its marvellous accomplishments, the voice of the tempter is the voice of a liar! In all such cases I believe special importance should be attached to individual testimony, and in giving my own I believe that I am pronouncing that of a countless host of other Christian believers. When we have found God's book to be to us the book of God when we have most needed it—there have indeed been times in our history when the book was nothing to us but a piece of literature; there have been other crises in our life when the book has been to us all good books in one, with the addition of God's life and God's love—and we are asked to give it up, we only put this common-sense question in return, viz., It is very easy for us to shut up the book, but when we have closed it, to whom can we go? It is very true that we can get some satisfaction out of the earth, and out of things that are earthly. We are zealous in our pursuit of learning; we give our hearty support to every man who increases our knowledge of the universe. If a man shall come to me and say, "I have found such delight in scientific inquiry, such pure enjoyment in looking into the construction of nature and finding out the secret of the world!" I say to him, frankly, "I hail you as a friend; tell me all you can; I will consider the results under your tuition, and I will study the great stone-book of the earth, and the great fire-book of the universe; you may be able to turn over the pages and interpret the wondrous writing. I bid you good luck in your work; I say you have a right to find out still more secrets, disentangle still more difficulties, explain still more mysteries, and I shall be grateful to you for all you have done." But after the man has done all this I tell him, "Sir, I have a heart that you have not touched; I have an emotional nature that you have not yet approached. You have addressed my intellect, and I thank you for your eloquence; but you have not touched the springs of my life, you have not come near the place where my sorrow sheds her tears, where my soul thinks about the future, and where I wrestle with the deepest problems that can engage the human mind. You are on the outside, doing a wonderful work, and I give you honour for your service, and wish you God-speed in your researches; but my inner life, with its joy and sorrow, its hope, its distress and pain, you have not, with all your science, touched. Is there not a voice that can come unto my soul, and breathe a sweeter music than yours?"

In view of this, then, I have to teach that if you leave the divine life and aspect of things, there is, so far as I can see, no alternative but outer darkness! Further, I have to teach, that he only who looks at things in a divine light can see creation itself as it is. The scientific man who has no God and no Saviour has seen a great deal; but if he knew God and loved him, he would have some more keys taken from the divine girdle and put into his hands, with which he could unlock still further and deeper mystery. Hear the astronomer speak to us, and he will elevate us because of the sublimity of his pursuits. As you look up to what you call especially our own firmament—the firmament whose great dim glory lies more or less within the vision of the naked eye—the astronomer says, "In that great arch how many suns do you find?" "One." "Look again." "How many," we inquire in return, "have you found?" " What say you to a thousand?" "You have not found so many?" "Multiply it by ten, and multiply that by ten more, and multiply that again. We have found in your firmament eighteen million suns!" "And is there no other firmament?" "Yes. This telescope has searched the heavens, and found another firmament above yours, and another higher, and another again, gallery upon gallery,—four thousand such firmaments arching over one another in ever-widening expanses!" Look at them, and cease your infidel babble! Measure them, and learn how poor a speck is the dust of man! Go to Christ, and hear what he says about them. The infidel, looking up there, says, " They came there by chance; they mean nothing; you see them all now that you look at them from the outside; it is a glittering nothing, and that's all." Jesus looks upon the blazing pomp, and turning to his poor one, he says, "In my Father's house are many mansions; if it were not so I would have told you." I prefer to believe the Saviour. The other theory insults my reason, makes a fool of me. Jesus Christ comes to me with poetry, which instantly becomes faith, and which is the truest reality of hope.

Look at that great cloud of fire. Do you see it ? " Yes." Tell me what it is. Let the scientific man tell you. It is a comet. You speak about your great globe, what say you to that immensity ? What is your great globe in diameter ? " Why, about eight thousand miles, we have always been given to understand." Why, the diameter of the head of the comet, science says—not theology, not a fanatical zealot—science says, is nine hundred and forty-seven thousand miles in diameter,—a hundred thousand of your little globes, and twenty thousand more thrown in ! Look at its wondrous train ! How long is that train ? " Two thousand miles—five hundred thousand miles—ten millions ? " Away with your guessing ! Science says, I have measured that train, and it is one hundred and thirty-two millions of miles long. And are these the arrows with which the quiver of the Almighty is filled ? Can he strike with these terrible weapons ? The infidel says, " Ah, it's all——" and then he waves his hand as if that settled everything. Jesus tells you, it is a messenger of the Almighty that is running, along the breath of his own purpose ; and that finding its way through the universe it shall never stagger, it shall not disturb the tiniest asteroid in the great glory of the universe ! I prefer to believe Jesus. It is more in keeping with reason, sense, common judgment, to believe that great wise teacher. To him I have committed my soul. If he is wrong, I would rather be in his company—looking at all his life, the beauty of his character, the sublimity of his disposition—than I would be elsewhere. With him I live ; with him, if need be, I would choose to die ! Yet I think we are very mighty men in our own estimation, are we not ? We get up behind our little rail and we say, " Give up the idea of God ; give up the idea of the future, shut up your Bible, do not go to church any more, and do not listen to Christian teachers any more." And then we shake our heads as if we had settled the case. Who are we ? We are very mighty within our own sphere ; but an inch out of it and we are weakness itself !

I had a great difficulty to contend with the other morning. It was intended, indeed, to be the most serious difficulty of my life. Two enemies of mine had conspired to shut me within my dwelling place, so that I could not get out ; and they did their work in the night time, and when I came out in the morning I found it quite finished. There was a barricade before my door; it was a beautiful barricade; it must have taken a great deal of construction; I admired the thing. In the centre of it were two great spiders—mine enemies—who in the night-time contrived this wonderfully malicious scheme to shut me in. How could I get out? There it was. I just took a walking-stick, and with one or two aims destroyed the web which was to have shut me in as with iron. And what is this but the feeblest illustration of the power of the Almighty! When we have set against him our little reasonings, and have tried to put him out of his own universe, and have endeavoured to show our own power on a scale of stupendous magnificence,—what if he need not lift his finger, if he need but to blow upon our fortresses and our mighty works, to turn us into confusion and bring us to shame!

Is there any inquiring man who is giving his mind and earnest studies to any department of life? I thank God for his earnestness. Am I going to take the book away from the man who is deeply and truly studying, with a view to knowing more about human life? No! Am I going to reduce the school hours of any man, who gives himself zealously to learning? Not by a moment. What am I going to do then? I am going to say this: You are indeed doing well. You are thinking; and it is always healthful and beneficial in diverse ways for a man to exercise his intellectual faculties. But you are like the child who is finding his way home, and has got inside the king's palace. We are glad you are in the palace of your fathers; but at present you are lingering on the great staircase—a noble, wondrous structure— but there is your Father's door. Knock at that, and it shall be opened unto you! You are in the palace, on the staircase. Go into his sanctuary, lie at his feet and receive his blessing!

PRAYER.

Thou hast invited us to speak unto thee, our Father, in the name of thy Son Jesus Christ, our one and only Saviour. We cannot see thee, but we feel thy presence. We know how near thou art, because our hearts glow with a new sense of love, and because our minds are lifted up to new elevations of thought, and because we are sure that beyond all we see there lies the true reality.＊ Thus hast thou made us. We feel the greatness of our life even while we bemoan its littleness; we are of the earth, yet we are of heaven; we are dying, yet we die into immortality. Thou hast sent thy Son to tell us this, and he has told it to our hearts in music, he has expressed it in tears, he has symbolised it in the Cross. We know all that we do know of thyself through Jesus Christ thy Son. He called thee Father; he told us when we prayed to address thee as Our Father; he gave himself up to thy will, and he taught us to say in prayer, Thy will be done on earth as it is done in heaven. From our childhood we have said this, but we have rarely felt it in all its meaning, in all its pathos, in all the sublimity of its obedience. Teach us day by day, little by little, a lesson at a time; for we are poor scholars in thy school, not apt to learn, wishful to have our own way too much, blinded by pride and vanity and self-trust; yet thou art patient beyond all motherliness of waiting, thou art tender beyond all we ever know of love; so thou wilt not drive us away if we ourselves wish to remain in thy school and learn a little more. Help us to bear the burdens of life; we can count the few tears we have to shed; at the most they make but a little rill amid the green delights of our inheritance and our joys. Teach us that these tears have a ministry of purification; show us that thou dost not willingly afflict the children of men, and that no chastisement is by thy hand delivered but in the spirit and with the purpose of love; thus we shall glory in tribulation also, and shall be exceedingly glad in conditions which make other souls afraid. Work within us all thy ministry; show us what thou dost mean by it all, and teach us that if we be crucified with Christ no stone rolled to our sepulchre door by man or enemy of what name or grade soever shall keep us in the earth, but we shall rise with him, and with him see all thy glory. Amen.

Chapter vii. 1.

"The Jews sought to kill him."

THE EVER-LIVING CHRIST.

THEY could never do it. To the end their purpose was unchanging in its cruelty, but they could never bring it to consummation. We have forgotten who killed the Son of

138

God. It would be an infinite relief to us if we could charge this wholly upon the Jews, or upon some persons who lived twenty centuries ago. That would be unjust and unwise on our part. The one thing that is forgotten is the name of the murderer: his name is Man. The Jews did not murder Christ, nor the Gentiles, nor the heathen, nor any one geographical section of the world, except in some local and narrow sense: the Son of God was killed by Man. Until we realise that we can make no progress in Christian knowledge, we shall be blaming the wrong parties; our commiseration will take a false direction; men who are blaming others should be broken-hearted about themselves. The perpetual difficulty is how to get rid of Christ. We want his place, not his company. We can do with him as a religious luxury, but not as a religious discipline. We love to hear briefly about him, but were the word to be shot into our heart personally, we should call it an affront, and take care that the wound never healed. Hence the weakness and the vanity of the Church.

The possibility of vanity being the inspiration of beneficence is a painful and horrible thought. Can men do good through ostentation? Who can have any doubt as to the answer? Can men make apparent sacrifices under the inspiration of vanity? Who will not fear, though he may not reply? If any man accused some other man of working through vanity, he would be distinctively human in his criticism and in his ill-nature, and his criticism would amount to nothing, for all such criticism should be turned inward, and the question should be asked, as with a spear thrust, by every man of himself, What is the inspiration of all I professedly do and want to be done in the name of Christ? We think we have dismissed Christ from human history, when, lo, he reappears in an unexpected form. We can only change the aspects of his relation to any time: the relation itself is vital and eternal. There is more than a point of criticism in that suggestion; there is a revelation of all the hopes that can animate and sustain Christian activity. A proper understanding of that suggestion would bring us comfort in many a dreary hour. Christ never goes down: the sun never sets, though we have a time we call the going down of the sun; we look westward with enlarging eyes, because the vision is apocalyptic in glory and in colour, and we wonder as we should wonder at a king dying in a palace of gold. But there is in reality no setting of the sun. He sets to rise again. It is even so with this blessed Lord and Saviour Jesus Christ. His particular relation to a time may change, for a time he may even appear to withdraw altogether from our civilisation, but his is an eternal march, an ever-continuous evolution, a perpetual new-shaping of himself to the passing ages. Now he is a grand doctrine, and men say this shall be the abiding aspect of Christ; he is set forth in vivid dogmas, in what are called positive truths, in mechanically-shaped catechisms, and in stiff and orthodox standards.

Does it ever occur to the Church that sometimes Jesus Christ will come upon the ages other than as a doctrine? Such an idea never has occurred to the Church, but it has been thrust upon the consciousness of the Church by the undeniable providence of God. Sometimes Jesus Christ is in the world as an image of pity, a missionary of beneficence, an apostle of charity, touching the human heart with the sacred influence of clemency and tenderness, and making men's lives all tears. In such softening and bowing down of human obduracy there is a ministry of the Son of God. Such tears abide in fountains that are sealed to every hand but Christ's. Therefore, now Christ is a doctrine, and the age is theological; now he is a charity, and the age is benevolent; now he is an inspiration, and the Church is an aggressor, thundering at the gates of evil, cursing, with holy malediction, every form of wrong. What has changed? Christ? No; he is the same yesterday, to-day, and for ever; but his direction of movement or his aspect of revelation may have changed. What the Church has to believe is that Christ cannot die. Yet, unless Christ come in some particular aspect, we have groaning and complaining over the decadence of faith, and the eclipse of doctrine, and the retrogression of religious feeling. It is ignorance that rebukes; it is ignorance that despairs: true conceptions of Christ will sustain the Church, saying, Now my Lord is a summer sun; now he is the bright and morning star; now he is the root and the offspring of David, in whom all history culminates in its final glory; now he is an angel of pity, seeking the lost, blessing the unblest; and now a judge terrible in wrath, a lamb inflamed with judicial anger. Believe not those pessimists who think that Christ has been driven away, or that the Gospel is being no longer preached, or that faith is declining. Say the sun is exhausting his light, and the moon is losing her soft beauty, and the wind that brings freshness from southern lands and western climes is no longer equal to the task; say the ocean has lost its old throb of thunder;—these trifles may have occurred, but Christ can never yield his sovereignty. When an age is all controversy, when theology is turned upside down, when catechisms are sold for waste-paper, and orthodox standards are put in the fires as quickly as hands can put them in, is not Christ misunderstood and expelled? No; the door, perhaps, is the more widely opened that he may come unto his own home. We have papered him out of his own chamber; we have made it hard for him to climb up into his own palace;—if he had to climb up to it he would never get in; he descends upon it, and that way we cannot block, blessed be his grace, his tender, all-pitying love!

There is no spectacle to my own imagination more expressive of ignorance and unbelief than that of a Christian man who thinks that his Lord is getting the worst of the battle. Such a thing cannot be. Why throw your arms round an impossibility, and almost worship it as if it were a kind of idol? What we want strengthening in is the fundamental position that Jesus Christ must reign till he hath put all enemies under his feet. He will die upon a cross, but that will make no difference; he will be banished from this land or that, but such a policy has no effect upon the sum total of his purpose; he will himself change his aspect, but he will still be the Sun of Righteousness.

Yet a tremendous attack may be made upon the Son of God; but it cannot be made by the chief priests and scribes directly, it can only be made from the inside. This attack can only be conducted by a Judas. That is the most appalling of all thoughts. No man can injure you but one. Shall I name the man who can injure you? That man is yourself. Nobody can for a moment injure a true man in any vital sense; all criticism, all sneering, all caricature, all attempts even to defame him, end in smoke so thick that it cannot curl, and so foul that nobody wants to preserve it. One man can injure me fatally; that man is myself. No man can injure the Church; but the Church can injure itself. There are many forms of Judas. How eager we are to study the character of some ancient person called Iscariot; how eloquent we are in blame; how damnatory in criticism; oh, how expressive and noble in judgment! We know not that we are condemning ourselves, otherwise our eloquent tongue would cleave to the roof of our mouth, and our memory of words would become a blank. Judas is alive, and Judas is still selling his Lord. If any man tells you that God left you out of his love when he created the world, that man is Judas Iscariot, whatever land he may live in, and whatever language he may speak. Should he sit in his own retreat and muse upon the goodness of God in choosing him, and in the discriminating grace which left you out of the bundle of life, he is a liar, a blasphemer, and a thief; he is the man that is doing the Church injury. He may be elected, but he has no right to say you are reprobated. God neglecting you, and choosing Judas Iscariot, is a suggestion which might make the angels weep. Poor soul! God's love is greater than your sin, if you have broken all the commandments every day you have lived since your birth. Soul of man, God's love is not new to thee; it is an eternal solicitude. Any man who will tell you that Jesus Christ is come to seek and to save a few sour-visaged, impracticable bigots is a Judas. The Son of man is come to seek and to save that which was lost. Are you lost? For you he came. The difficulty we have to contend with in preaching this glorious gospel is that some persons have picked up names that they do not understand, but that worry them in a most awful manner. For example, there would be those who would tell you that this is Arminianism. They do not know whether Arminianism is a theorem in Euclid, or a puzzle in algebra, or a speculation in the navigation of the Atlantic. But they have heard about it, and it has somehow the effect upon them of naming a mad dog. Whatever it is, it is my hope and trust and joy and strength that God leaves out no poor child, no old woman, no self-condemned, broken-hearted sinner.

Another form of Iscariotism is only too strikingly found in those who, having convictions, keep them in a state of continual chloroform. There are persons living to-day who have convictions they never express. They are the dangerous people. We have nothing to fear from blatant infidelity or disbelief; but we have nothing to hope from those who say, We keep our Christianity quiet, and our convictions we only mumble to ourselves. We need not go to this heroic point in order to display the sad state of affairs. There are persons in Christ's Church who never lift a finger for their Lord. Ask them to take office, and they are instantly so overwhelmed with modesty, that they will not open a door for him, or light a lamp, or sit on a footstool that somebody else may sit in the upper position. Can such men pray? Never. Can such men be saved? Not in that way. Are not such men Christians? They are anything but Christians. Ask a man who has a gift of song to join the leaders of the public psalmody, and he cannot do so, because he does not like to make himself conspicuous. He would not stand up for his Lord; then let him know that he has no Lord to stand up for; we must uncloak him, and unmask him, and tell him that his name is Iscariot. Ask for any service from some professing Christians, and they are pre-engaged. As if any man should be pre-engaged when Christ wants him! The greater law should swallow up the lesser. Astronomy should regulate Geography. We must not forget the motion round the sun, whilst we are so careful about the rotation upon our own axis. This is the state of affairs. It is pitiable lying for persons to be talking about the amount of infidel literature which is being published when they are acting thus towards their nominal Lord. The Christian has only one engagement, and that is to serve Christ; all other so-called engagements are incidental, transient, superficial, without value, or are only permanent and valuable in so far as they are inspired by the spirit of a larger consecration.

As judgment begins in the house of the Lord, so in the house of the Lord must begin a true revival, a solid and permanent reconstruction of all best thought and all holiest endeavour. We should have a time for the renewal of vows, an hour should be appointed for the repetition of old wedding words: again we should accept the ring from the Lamb.   Lives of consecration can never be sneered at with any advantage on the side of unbelieving argument.   Sacrifice is its own eloquence ; self-denial, patience, love, the enduring things of the nature of affliction for others, that is a piety that cannot be talked down or exploded.   Have not our 'eachers been emphatic on the wrong words ?   Have not many of them been forcing us in wrong directions ?   There are some persons in an almost dying state of excitement to know what people did in the fourth century.   I have no very keen interest in what they did or did not do ; but there are minds so singularly constituted in the economy of God that they seem to have no relation to the century they live in.   What was done about the year one hundred and thirty-nine after Christ ? or what did Constantine think ?   I really do not know, and I do not care what he thought; it may be callous upon my part, but I have next to no interest in anything he ever did or said ; a glance will show me all I want to know : but the men that are round about me are dying men ; the masses are poor ; many of the people are the victims of public temptation and private snares, and they are being drawn to their destruction by many a wicked way ; the relations of class to class are wrong in many instances ; temptations are lighted up every night in every city for the allurement and destruction of souls.   To ask a man who realises these things what his sober opinion is about the Nicene Creed is to him intolerable ; he wants to save the drunkard, to gather the little children into school, to repress the oncoming of every form of wickedness.   He wants to be pure himself and to purify the State in which he lives.   Such a man, it appears to me, better represents the Church of Christ and the meaning of the Cross than some other man who is painfully and sleeplessly excited to know what was done about the year two hundred and seventeen after Christ.   Nor do I altogether depose such men from their amuse-ments and their luxuries.   Tastes differ, appetite has sometimes to be encouraged a little : I only wish to say that, personally, I am not akin to those men, though they may belong to a higher family. The relation of Jesus Christ to this age is a relation of sympathy, pity, beneficence.   Leave the word-mongers to wrangle over their controversies, and go ye and seek out that which is lost, distressed, and without hope.

What is the Church ?   It is a body of living men sustaining a living relation to living realities.   It is not a soft outline ; it is not an antiquated skeleton.   Whoever does Christ's work is Christ's kinsman.   No man can call Jesus Lord but by the Spirit ; no man can do a Christian work without Christ being in him.   It may be found some day that those who were discarded and cast out as not Christian have all the time been Christ's loving bondmen, doing all his will, without recognition by men ; yea, and without any right relation of their own consciousness to the solemn and glorious fact.   What we have to understand is the changing relation of Christ.   He is now a doctrine ; now a history ; now a mission ; now a pity ; now a manifold service, social, political, economical : but one eternal thought shoots through, and rules all the economies in which he enshrines and incarnates his glory.   Whatever changes, this never changes— namely, that he wants to save us, every one.   My creed is : God made us all ; God loves us all ; God wants to meet us all at Christ's dear Cross.   I cannot believe that the spirit of Judas is growing in the Church.   It is well to indicate what it is, and to point out the subtlety of its operation ; but he would be a poor observer of events, an ungenerous and unjust critic of human history, who did not recognise the fact that in the Church there is proportionately but one Judas.   There are men who really love the Saviour, and serve him, and who count not their lives dear unto them, that they may serve the blessed one of the Most High.   There are men who can say humbly and truly : " For me to live is Christ.   I am crucified with Christ, nevertheless I live ; yet not I, but Christ liveth in me, and the life which I now live in the flesh I live by the faith of the Son of God, who loved me, and gave himself for me."   "God forbid that I should glory, save in the cross of the Lord Jesus Christ."   Yes ; there has been a Judas in the Church ; there has been also an Apostle Paul.

Chapter vii. 15.

"And the Jews marvelled, saying, How knoweth this man letters, having never learned ?"

JEWS MARVELLING AT JESUS.

THEY thought there was only one way of learning. Jesus Christ committed the crime of irregularity. Propriety can never forgive that offence; it cannot in medicine, it cannot in commerce, above all it cannot in theology. There is a certain way in which things are to be done; if they are not done in that particular way they are not done at all. Jesus Christ was a thorn in the sides of the devotees of regularity. They did not know what to make of him : he was born at the wrong place, he associated with the wrong people, he supported the wrong cause —the cause of the ignorant, the poor, the blind, and the helpless; he turned upside down things that had for ages been regarded as sacred : he was not to be tolerated. The assault in this case is made upon his learning. There is no challenge addressed to his moral character; but the wonder is that a man who never went to school should be able to read, and especially a man who never went to their school. They reveal themselves herein. What can you expect from such minds? Narrowness, bigotry, sectarianism, littleness, incapacity to understand either night or day—for the night has its mystery of stars, and the day its pomp and apocalypse of light. Yet the mischief is, that these men have in all time undertaken to preserve the faith; have undertaken to patronise God and truth and eternity, and have specially registered themselves as the persons who know who is going up and who is going down. Until they and all belonging to them are swept out of the way, the kingdom of heaven, in all its ineffable blessedness, mercy, tenderness, compassion, love, can make no great progress. The kingdom of heaven suffers more from its nominal friends than it can suffer from its most hostile

opponents.   Jesus Christ has not been understood by the schools.
You cannot get at him through grammar.   He is not to be parsed
like a lesson in syntax; he is to be felt, touched, known by
the spirit which is akin to his own.   The mistake, we say,
which these men made was that they supposed there was only
one way of learning.   There was a curriculum; certain books
were to be read in a certain order, and certain examinations were
to proceed under the scrutiny of a competent examiner.   Any
one who had not passed through this course, no matter what he
said, what he sung, how much he knew, and touched and blessed
the human heart, was uncertificated, was without rabbinic and
official endorsement.   Blessed be God for irregularity; the
heavens be praised for the spirit that rises occasionally above all
mechanism, formality, and so-called propriety and conventional
limitation, and shows the spirit of liberty.   This can only be done
occasionally; there is a way that is prescribed, and that way
must often be trodden : the danger is that some should imagine
they can fall down upon learning as if making a great condescension, whereas they are the very people who ought to begin at the
first point, at the alphabetic origin, and work their way, letter by
letter, and syllable by syllable, until they are able to converse
with the Master on things concerning himself.   Instead of there
being only one way by which men can be learned, there are ways
innumerable; there are many schools and schoolmasters, many
severe-looking teachers, and many gentle patient monitors, and
many curious pedagogues who have undertaken by sharp instruments to lacerate men into knowledge, to flagellate them into
intelligence.   There are more schools than one.   The mountain
is not to be ascended by one path only; it may be climbed by
a great number of roads, beaten by the feet of eccentric travellers,
men of adventure and daring, who might have lost themselves,
but did not.

Some have learned by experience what they never could have
learned by lectures.   Experience is a costly teacher; experience
gives object lessons, and forces the truth home upon the mind
and the heart in many curious and urgent ways. . Parts of the
Bible can only be read through the eyes of experience.   Scholars
cannot read all the Bible ; they can parse it to a nicety, they can

correct its various readings with amazing erudition, they could die for a comma; but they do not know the Bible, necessarily, for all that. The broken heart knows what scholarship can never comprehend. Feeling has taught many men some of the higher and tenderer mysteries of the kingdom of God. It is the fashion to ridicule emotion; but without emotion what is human nature?—hard, narrow, austere, selfish. What garden can live in all its beautiful colour without the dew? We see oftentimes further through our tears than through our literary acquisition. There is a genius of feeling; there is an inspired emotion. Some parts of the Bible can only be read sympathetically; the grammar is all awry: some Biblical writers are here and there; they are desultors, now on this horse, now on that, but they never leave the horizon around which they were destined to ride with noble urgency. We must therefore know a good deal of the Bible by our feeling; it must show itself to us through our tears; it must come in through the rents and breaks and fissures which sorrow has made in the disappointed and wounded heart. There are men of such quick mind that they know the end from the beginning of every subject which they are capable of grasping; they are gifted with what is known as great intuitional power; they overleap processes. The anatomist boasted that if you gave him the bone of any animal that ever lived he could from that one bone construct the skeleton of the entire animal. Such genius is not given to all. There are those who, on hearing a proposition, know all the conclusions which are involved; we call them hot-headed, strong, impetuous, vehement, enthusiastic, wanting in that soul-patience which exhausts itself in the building up or finding out or putting together of processes. We are not all of one mould, one capacity, one temperament. When we learn this, and understand its meaning, we shall have less sectarianism, less bitterness, less mutual censoriousness, and a greater delight in the manifoldness of human things, seeing into the manifoldness of the giving God.

But "The Jews marvelled, saying, How knoweth this man letters, having never learned?" Now above all things it is pre-eminently true that religion is not learned by letters; it is a divine action in the soul; it is a divine communion; it is the claiming of a kinship long ignored or long misunderstood; it is the look of friend to friend; it is the recognition which comes into the eyes of the wandering child when through all his sin and sorrow and disablement he begins to trace the outline of a pursuing and loving father.   Then grammar would be out of place; only one eloquence is possible—the eloquence of sobbing, the eloquence that chokes the throat when it would talk, for talk in such circumstances approaches profanity.   Yet there are those who can give you all their reasons for being religious.   It would be harsh to condemn them.   There is a piety that goes by the calendar; there is a prayer appointed for to-day which must not be said to-morrow, and which would have been out of place yesterday; there is a mechanical, formal, and even disciplinary way of living, but there is a religion that cannot give any reasons for itself beyond the reasons which childhood suggests, which love breathes, which an ineffable confidence clings to.   We must make room for all these varieties.   Wherein a man can explain his second birth, by all means let him explain it; but another man says, The wind bloweth where it listeth, and thou hearest the sound thereof, but canst not tell whence it cometh, and whither it goeth.   So was I born of the Spirit : in my Christianity, such a voice might continue, there is only one logic, the logic of a persuasion which nothing can destroy.   Make room for all and every kind of learning.   Christianity is not a controversy; it is peace, it is a sacred gladness of the heart that dare sometimes scarcely allow itself to hear its own voice, lest it should lose a charm, a possession infinite.   There is a silence that is eloquent.   Being justified by faith through our Lord Jesus Christ, we have peace with God—a peace that passeth understanding, a joy unspeakable and full of glory.   There is a line beyond which language cannot go; it says to the mind, I must leave you at this point; we have had some sweet communion, but the next step you take will bring you into a region where I am not known.   Farewell.   Instead of speaking you must muse, burn with holy glowing, sing with immeasurable rapture.

Jesus Christ deigns to explain how it was that he had excited this marvel :—"Jesus answered them, and said, My doctrine is not mine, but his that sent me."   By "doctrine" understand teaching; not formal theology, not mechanical piety, not a thought shaped and thrust and consolidated in one form for ever, but teaching,—that endless process, that mystery of progress which claims eternity for its completion. "Not mine"; it is not an invention, not a theory, it is not something I have thought out and elaborated, and have brought to set before you in a given form; I am but a medium, I am but an errand-bearer. I do but speak the word I have heard and learned of my father; know that my incarnation is but the object on which the infinite silence breaks into the spray of speech. This was more marvellous than ever. Here is an inspired man. Behold a teacher who is teaching what he has heard in some other world! It is just there that so many teachers fail. They have only one world, and one world can hold nothing but its own grave. The teacher sent from God has all the worlds, he has the key of every mansion in his Father's house. What theories men have invented, what neat philosophies, what sublimities of impotence! Why? Because they have had no eternity, no infinity, no overshadowing greatness. So we have alphabet-makers and book-makers, and persons who have given us thinking in four-square form, beginning, continuing, and ending, measurable, estimable, for so much sold, for so much taken back again; where the ghost of eternity, everlastingness? They have not that spirit; what they say is their own, and therefore it can all be said. He who speaks from eternity halts, suddenly deflects, adapts himself to the capacities with which he has to deal; says, "I have many things to say unto you, but ye cannot bear them now." Know the Bible in a thousand ways, and no man ever had the Bible taken out of his hands. That is the mystery. He may have had a book taken out of his hands that he was making a fetish of, an idol, a vain thing; but no man who ever grasped the Bible with his soul had it plucked from him; he does not hold it syntactically, he holds it with his heart.

Yet this knowledge has a human aspect according to the teaching of Jesus Christ:—"If any man will do his will, he shall know of the doctrine, whether it be of God, or whether I speak of myself." The English does not give the full force of the expression; the "shall" or "will" is not an auxiliary, it is the word which carries the emphasis—if any man willeth to do his will, he must resolutely betake himself to it. Doing is learning. It is so in language. Speak the language if you would learn it. Your first utterances will be full of grotesque errors, and you will receive for replies things you never dreamed of; but continue, persevere, never mind even a sarcastic laugh; you are learning, and you want to learn, and you say, One day I will speak this language with precision and fluency and masterliness. Then do not turn back and take no more heed of it; go where the language is spoken, speak no other language, and soon by willing to do the will the language will become part of yourself, and you will not know you are speaking it. A man hardly knows that he breathes. It is so in athletics. No man ever learns to swim by standing on the shore. You have never known of an instance of a man becoming a great swimmer who always looked out of the window at the water and never went any nearer to it; we are not aware that history records a solitary instance of a man ever becoming an expert swimmer who never went into the water. If any man willeth to do the will, sets himself to do it, says, "In God's strength I will do this," he shall know the teaching, it will come to him little by little. Do not make the mistake of supposing that there is only one set or class of religious teachers. The Rabbis thought they only knew the law; the scribes thought they only knew what was written, and they alone could read it. There are a thousand teachers. Nature, Alma Mater, sweet old loving mother, says she will tell us a thousand things we never dreamed of if we will sit down and listen to her, or if we will accept her key and go into all the rooms she has, and study there; we shall come back with all the fresh winds blowing around us, with the light of the noonday in our eyes, with the fragrance of flowers. Little children are about the greatest theologians going, the greatest theological teachers. A prodigal son in a family helps the head of the house more than anything else to understand God. Many a man has been a sour-visaged predestinationist, handing men over to the devil in millions, until his own son broke his heart; then he began to read, "Like as a father pitieth his children, so the Lord pitieth." That made him a man,—a son of God; he could have answered any number of theological propositions, but when he heard the tap on the door at midnight, and the lump came into his throat because he thought it was the wanderer who had come back again, he understood the theology of sacrifice, of love, the theology that carries with it the gospel of redemption.

History is a teacher. So we have many teachers as well as many schools,—nature, and children, and history. Go to some of these schools; accept some teacher. Do not feel yourself in the darkness more and more; accept counsel, and cry mightily unto God to point out to you the teacher that will understand you best, and for you work the miracle of a new life. No matter what a man knows if it will not bear the stress of practical life. Test your religion in the market-place. Will your creed go down to the place where merchants most do congregate, and there talk righteousness, and deal honestly, and look fearlessly in the face of insincerity and fraud and dishonourableness? It is a good piety; do not give it up because some charmer who has nothing to give in exchange for it tells you that he has been looking into certain ancient documents and finds such and such things are not there. Cling to the spirit that is in you; it burns rottenness like fire, it disinfects a pestilential area. Will your piety go home and help the sick one, and sit up all night, and teach you the art of touching the pillow without making a noise, and bringing help to the sufferer without increasing his agony? and will you in the morning say nothing about sleeplessness or hunger or disquiet, but smile upon the sufferer as if he had done you a great favour? It is not a bad piety: keep it; will to do that will, and who knows but that some day you may see the meaning of the apocalypse, some day God will come to you and say, In reward for your obedience, patience, self-sacrifice, here is the key, open my kingdoms, and revel in them by divinely invested right. No matter what a man's religion is or profession is, if it will not bear the stress which daily life puts upon human experience, it is a misconception, it is a lie.

PRAYER.

ALMIGHTY GOD, we would be led by thy Spirit into all truth. He is the Paraclete, he can take of the things of Christ and show them unto us. This is his mission; we live under his dispensation; we continually await his incoming into our heart, that he may guide us into all the mystery of the divine kingdom. Great and marvellous are thy works, Lord God Almighty; but how much thou hast outdone all that we look upon when we turn in upon ourselves and see the mystery of manhood, the mystery of immortality. Thou hast in Christ Jesus thy Son shown us a light above the brightness of noontide; thou hast, in the words of Christ, brought us to listen to a music not otherwhere to be heard. We wonder at the gracious words which proceed out of his mouth: never man spake like this man. May we read his words not with wonder and admiration only, but with trust and thankfulness, and accept them in a spirit of obedience, that they may be turned into life and conduct and service. How great is the kingdom of God; yet how small are we, how unable to lay ourselves upon the infinite space covered by the purpose of God: may we therefore be humble, obedient, docile, expectant, always hoping for larger light and more room and better opportunity to work in. For this spirit we bless thee: this is none other itself than a miracle of grace. Thou hast subdued our rebellion and defiance and self-will, and hast brought us into an attitude of prostration; may our sincerity be without guile, may our faithfulness express the honesty of the soul, and may our hands go out to the living God in token of need and holy expectation. Satisfy us early with thy lovingkindness, and abundantly delight us with all thy goodness. We bow at the Cross, we name the only name by which men can be saved; we look at the Sufferer, we cannot understand the agony, but we know that he suffered for us, for our iniquities he was bruised. Whilst we look we pray, we wait, we say Amen.

Chapter viii. 3–11.

"And the scribes and Pharisees brought unto him a woman taken in adultery; and when they had set her in the midst, they say unto him, Master, this woman was taken in adultery, in the very act. Now Moses in the law commanded us, that such should be stoned: but what sayest thou? This they said, tempting him, that they might have to accuse him. But Jesus stooped down, and with his finger wrote on the ground, as though he heard them not. So when they continued asking him, he lifted up himself, and said unto them, He that is without sin among you, let him first cast a stone at her. And again he stooped down, and wrote on the ground. And they which heard it, being convicted by their own conscience, went out one by one, beginning at the eldest, even unto the last: and Jesus was left alone, and the woman standing in the midst. When Jesus had lifted up himself, and saw none but the woman, he said unto her, Woman, where are those thine accusers? hath no man condemned thee? She said, No man, Lord. And Jesus said unto her, Neither do I condemn thee; go, and sin no more."

THE CONVICTED WOMAN.

IN such an act did the power, the love, or the wisdom predominate? As well ask which colour predominates in the rainbow: they all blend into one arch of beauty.

Would we see Jesus in his most fascinating charms? Then we must look at him as he stands face to face with a notorious sinner. That face of his never lightens into such a glory as when it looks upon the darkness of penitent guilt.

This incident suggests four lessons:—

(1) It is possible to take an interest in social crime merely for the purposes of religious partisanship. Did these scribes and Pharisees care one tittle for the spirituality and sanctity of the law? When they found this poor unhappy creature, did their hearts bleed with pity, or their eyes dissolve in tenderness, or did they say with the sorrow of a great disappointment, Alas! our poor sister has been overmatched by the enemy of man, and we must save her from the pit on whose brink she lies? Not a word of it! Not a tear stained their eyes—not a pang of pity quivered in their steel breasts—their humanity was eaten up by their pompous and zealous bigotry. They looked at her through the medium of the stern law, on the one hand, and on the other regarded her as a practical puzzle for the revolutionary Teacher. They took an interest in criminals, indeed, but their interest was a stroke in business, a defence of policy, a blow at progress. I allude to this department of the story with special emphasis, in order to denounce a most pretentious and rotten philanthropy. There are men who find their meat and their drink in criminal statistics. They are most industrious in collecting facts—in visiting gaols, hospitals, workhouses, and penitentiaries—in cross-examining prisoners, paupers, and refugees—with what intent? What is the meaning of all this industry? I judge no man; but I do urge that it is perfectly possible to do all this, to earn the reputation of a great philanthropist, and yet all the while to be

using all the facts merely for the purpose of entangling and frustrating the representatives of a wider and diviner creed. These scribes and Pharisees acted as though they were glad of having found a rare example of crime, which they could use as a test of Messiah's morality. It was an opportunity not to be lost. It was a trap which must be skilfully set. It was an occasion which might lead on to victory. Now, it is worth while inquiring whether our interest in criminals and crime is really the expression of a piteous and yearning philanthropy, or whether we encourage it merely for the purpose of maintaining and illustrating some favourite theory? Are we naturalists, going forth to the mountains and dales for the purpose of collecting a museum of curiosities? Are we a kind of geologic moralists, digging into deep strata that we may find unusual specimens? Are we sportsmen who delight in capturing game, that we may nail to the hall door the memorials of our triumphs? Or do we, like the blessed Philanthropist, our Lord and Saviour, go forth "to seek and to save the lost," to lift up the downcast, and turn the wanderer into the right way? Let us guard against a lifeless and tearless philanthropy; let us dread the day when we can look on crime with eyes which glisten only because our favourite hypothesis is maintained; let us remember that it is one thing to be the policemen of the Church, bringing in poor prisoners for judgment, and another to be like him who wept and bled that prisoners might be free. Philanthropy may degenerate into mere formality. Men may be driven to any lengths in defending a sectarian idea. An anatomist may slash the dissecting knife through the heart of his own father for the purpose of establishing some favourite physiological dogma.

(2) The highest qualification for social judgment is personal innocence.—"He that is without sin among you, let him first cast a stone at her."—Jesus does not abrogate the law,—he does not set himself in opposition to Moses: the scribes and Pharisees desired to antagonise Moses and Jesus, but the answer which they received withered up their purposes, and gave their thoughts a turn which they regarded with supreme aversion. He shows, however, that the law is to be administered by clean hands; that the thunders of the law are to be articulated by pure lips; that

the stone of judgment is to be flung with the pity of holiness, and not with the wantonness of revenge.

I value this counsel for two reasons :—

First. It gives full scope to the faculty of conscience. Jesus did not accuse these men ; they accused themselves. He might have arraigned them one by one, and passed judgment on each, but he abbreviates the process by making each man judge himself. He did not say, "There is not a sinless man among you," but he asked the sinless man to step forward and cast the first stone at the erring sister. Conscience takes the candle into the inmost recesses of our being. Conscience holds up a mirror to the leprous soul. Conscience shows us the cracks in our porcelain respectability, and the specks upon our boasted morality. This dread agent of God in the human soul showed that the main difference between the accused and the accusers was that her sin was found out, and theirs was not ; the sun had got hold of her iniquity, while theirs lay rotting in the darkness. They wished to pass for respectable men—decent members of society—pillars in the temple of rectitude ; but when conscience, commissioned by divine authority, began to rifle their history, they fled from the sanctuary without daring to fling the stone of retribution.

Second. It reveals God's view of human society. The Lord seeth not as man seeth. Man saw these scribes and Pharisees in eager haste to honour the law, to brand crime, to maintain righteousness ; but God saw the under-lurking villainy, and marked every spring of poison which bubbled in the depraved heart, and bade them look at themselves before looking at and despising others. God sees the hidden chamber of imagery. His eye alights on the interior view, and it is by that view that all his judgments are regulated. Stripping society of its pompous garniture—laying off its gilded trinketry—he pours the sunlight into the caverns of the heart, and shows how the reptiles of iniquity are fattening there. God does not see us as we see each other as we sit in church ; his eye searches the very core and spring of our being. Personal innocence, then, is the highest qualification for social judgment. He is a daring or a wanton man who lightly assumes the functions of social magistracy. Where there is most holiness there is most pity. It was

God's own holiness that wept itself into mercy,—such mercy!— mercy that died and rose again that sinners might "sin no more." When we are under the full dominion of that mercy we shall need but the faintest breeze of appeal to shake the tears of pity from our melting eyes.

(3) Readiness to accuse another is no guarantee of personal rectitude. To have seen these men haling the poor woman and stating her crime so fully and emphatically, one might have concluded that they were themselves just men, who lived daily in the fear and love of the Most High; and yet such a conclusion would have been in utter antagonism to the melancholy reality of the case. We have all seen men who have gnashed their teeth with diabolic savageness through the quivering frame of a poor offender, and hung on to the swelling flesh with a pertinacity that would have done credit to the fiercest beast in the jungle; and these men all the while imagining that by dooming others to perdition they were proving their own meetness for the highest heaven. Alas! though such men may turn their red eyes to heaven as if in prayer, they have not the spirit of Jesus, who forgiveth and receiveth the world's worst sinners. The scribes and Pharisees were more ready to condemn than was Jesus Christ. The Saviour was not so intent upon condemning men as they were. Eagerness to hurry men off to perdition is but a poor pledge of piety. Many men would avoid this poor unhappy woman, who are themselves no paragons of excellence. I know not of a more distressing sight than to see one poor sinner dealing harshly and furiously with another. Each sinner seems to think his own sin less heinous than that of his neighbour. There, is a man who drinks himself into stupidity every night at his own fireside, and who renders himself disgusting to every member of his household,—yet that man turns scornfully away from this poor woman! There, is another, who is "such a son of Belial that a man cannot speak to him;" from whom his own children flee in terror; who cultivates the lowest and meanest of all tyrannies, tyranny in his own family,—yet that man turns scornfully away from this poor woman! There, is a stingy, shrivelled soul, that can hardly afford himself bread, who begrudges his family every article of apparel, who accounts himself clever if

he can cheat his tradesmen out of a shilling, who would grind
and crush the bones of his workmen, and could see every one of
them buried in a pauper's grave,—yet that man turns scornfully
away from this poor woman!   There, is a proud, haughty, glass-
eyed, hard-hearted man, who expects the poor to clear themselves
off before his imperial march, who never wept over weakness,
never shed a smile on the orphan's lonely way, who talks to the
poor of the parish laws, and points the breadless and homeless to
the workhouse,—yet that man turns scornfully away from this
poor woman!   There, is a man who can spend hours in slander,
who smacks his empoisoned lips like a debauchee, when he has
words of dishonour to speak about another, who can whisper
defamation, who can hiss syllables of cruelty,—yet that man can
present himself among the sons of God, and turn scornfully
away from this poor woman!   Oh, it makes one's heart sore and
sad to mark how one child of guilt can eagerly brand another,
and send him, amid frantic clapping of unclean hands, to the
fellowship of devils.

(4) True interest in social crime is best shown by saving the
criminal from despair.—" Go, and sin no more."   The good man
never ignores the presence of sin.   Jesus Christ, with all his
gentleness and mercy, did not tell the woman that she was
innocent, nor did he treat her as an innocent woman.   Christ
was ever forward to maintain the broad distinction between
right and wrong.   I believe that if we follow his example we
shall frown upon sin in all its aspects and tendencies, and never
cast the faintest smile upon its downward course.   We must
never treat the thief as though he were honest, or the liar as
though he were truthful, or the proud as though he were
humble, or the miser as though he were generous.   We owe
such distinctions to the dignity of virtue, and they must be
maintained for ever.   At the same time our lesson is this :
Never cast the penitent sinner into despair.   Jesus said, " Go,
and sin no more."   Take one more chance in life ; turn over a
page ; begin again ; treat this as a second birthday ; go, and
make the future better than the past.   Thank God for such
words of hope !   The beams of mercy shoot far across the gloom
of guilt ; the voice of hope falls on the ear of the remotest

wanderer! Christ here teaches us the true method of rescuing and restoring the criminal,—never cast him into despair.

> "Men might be better if we better deemed
> Of them. The worst way to improve the world
> Is to condemn it. Men may overget
> Delusion—not despair."

If you can say one gentle word, or give one hopeful glance, to the prisoner who is brought before you, I call upon you in the name of God to do it. The blessing of him who is ready to perish will come upon you, and in a recovered life you may find your ultimate reward. Would not this poor woman for ever feel a kindling love to him who spake this word of hope to her? Would she hesitate for a moment on whom to pour the benedictions of her glowing and expanding heart? The righteous Pharisees, the holy scribes, would have smitten her with death; but the divine Saviour spread a new page of life before her, and told her to begin again. A word of hope may strike a happy influence through an entire lifetime. Those of us who imagine that we have never sinned do not know the value of such a word; but those of us who have taken our sins into dark places, and wept over them, and then taken them to the Saviour's Cross, and heard his voice of mercy, know how the soul warms, and gladdens, and sings in reply to the word of liberty and love. "Deal gently with the erring one." To-morrow thou mayest thyself eat of the forbidden tree, and pine for some look of hope. The enemy may get a sudden advantage over thee, and if thou hast only scribes and Pharisees for friends, thine will be an unhappy lot. O pause, ere consigning a fellow-creature to the hell of despair! Arrest the harsh word which burns on thy tongue; consider thyself lest thou also be tempted. "With what measure ye mete, it shall be measured to you again." The voice of Jesus to every man is, "Go, and sin no more." Christ came into the world that he might make an everlasting end of sin. He is the sinner's only Saviour. "This is a faithful saying, and worthy of all acceptation, that Christ Jesus came into the world to save sinners." He not only bids us "sin no more," but he helps us to conquer every temptation Not only does he urge us to rise to heaven, but he puts forth his hand, and gives us the very power which he bids us employ.

Chapter viii. 39.

"If ye were Abraham's children, ye would do the works of Abraham."

HISTORICALLY TRUE, MORALLY FALSE.

THIS is an apparently novel test of kinship and pedigree. If a man is really in the line of Abraham, how can he be in any other line? or how can he be genealogically displaced? There are circumstances under which kinship is not a question of physical relation, but of mental and moral sympathy. Jesus Christ was always leading us out into wider and larger definitions. Presently, he will make us all, if we be obedient, into one family. He will begin where he can, or where we will allow him to begin: but judge not the Lord's end by the Lord's way of beginning; judge not the harvest by the handful of seed which is sown. "Abraham" is not the name of a mere individual. When it is pronounced by Jesus Christ it is the type of a special kind of life—the life Abrahamic, the faith-life; the life that takes its staff and goes out not knowing whither it goeth because a voice divine hath said, "I will give thee a land." When does Jesus Christ adopt a narrow signification? When does he lose an opportunity of amplifying words into their largest meaning? Thus may we know who are Christians, who have learned of Jesus, who have been steadfast and reverent scholars in his school; men who enlarge all things beautiful and true and good, and see in symbols whole heavens of beauty and rest. We speak of children in various senses ourselves; we say they are children of evil, or we say they are children of light. Sometimes we describe a man as a "child of genius," and there is a common phrase, namely, "children of grace." We must get this word "children" out of its narrow roots and small limitations, as if it were a mere term of animal life, and must set it in the true light, and in its proper spiritual relation.

The great law which Christ here lays down is, that that which is historically true may be morally false ; men may be genealogically akin, and spiritually alien ; natural relation may be forfeited by moral apostasy. On what great principles he bases his teaching ! He introduces into human thoughts a law which overturns all our little sophisms and illusions, and gives us a new conception of God and life and nature. Again and again he says, " Ye do err, not knowing the Scriptures " : you quote them, but do not cite their meaning ; you drag in the letter according to some old custom of interpretation, but you do not bring in the spirit with all its vitality and luminousness. Few men read the Bible ; the spirit of the Bible is not in them, and, therefore, they cannot read the Bible itself ; they pronounce the words, but they do not utter the thought. Nor is this peculiar to the Bible ; it is a law which applies to all human life. You cannot deliver the message of a man unless you are in sympathy with the man himself. You may deliver the very words he told you to deliver, and yet all the message may go out of them, and words which were intended as gracious salutations, and assurances of love and co-operation, may be no better than cold ashes. These men to whom Christ is now speaking said, We are Abraham's children ; and Christ said, No, there you are mistaken. They offered to produce the record, but he said the record was not a matter of paper-and-ink ; it is a matter of likeness, spiritual identity, soul kindred. If ye have not Abraham's faith, then you abuse Abraham's name by using it ; in justice to the dead let sacred names alone, unless in assuming them you fill them with the spirit by which they were first ennobled and consecrated. How Jesus Christ, then, dispossesses men of pedigree and claim and status and record, unless the men themselves are of the right bulk and colour and quality and force ! The Abrahamic dignity is not superimposed, or handed down like an heirloom ; every man must support his claim by his spirit and his action. " If ye were Abraham's children, ye would do the works of Abraham," but because ye do not the works of Abraham, you have no right to use the holy man's name. You do a certain kind of work and there is no mistake about its quality—there is devil in it at every point ; it throbs with devilism,—" Ye are of your father the devil." Let us, then, look at our records, and see how

ght it?—sleeping in church, never going out in foul weather,
forming opinions, but doing nothing to support or sustain them
that is of the nature of sacrifice. You, who never damped a foot
in God's service, a child of the old Covenanters! Do not dishonour the dead. If you want to tell lies, tell them in your
own name, limit them by your own personality, but do not bury
the Covenanters in the grave of falsehood. If ye were the
children of the Covenanters, ye would do the work of the
Covenanters,—you would know the truth, and love the truth,
and support the truth, and preach the truth, and no man would
be able to stop your mouth in the hour of testimony. How
stands the case now?

Here are more modern men who say, We are of a good old
Methodist stock. Are you? I doubt it. We have portraits of
old Methodists. Very likely. And what do they do for you?
It is a pity you have them; they ought to be in the hands of
better men. But if you are of a good old Methodist stock, then
you will be men of enthusiasm, passion; you will be "sensational" Christians; at uncalculated times you will be breaking
out into song, praising God, disturbing the decorum of too-dignified
ceremony in church; you will be rapturous Christians, your
voice will be heard in the psalm, you will love the exercise of
prayer. The old Methodists hazarded their lives for the Lord Jesus
Christ,—when did you ever hazard a meal? Do not dishonour

the dead; do not make conveniences of their names; do not try to acquire respectability by the use of their arms. If ye were the children of the Methodists, ye would do the work of the Methodists, and not allow some other section to leap up as if out of the dust to take your crown and leave you in the rear.

Others say, We are the children of gentlefolks. We can easily test that. You need not produce a single record. We have only to spend a day with you, and to see you under trying circumstances, to know your quality. What are gentlefolks? Just what the name implies—gentle, patient, large-minded, large-hearted; not impetuous, fierce, cruel, vengeful, but filled with the spirit of gentleness, taking the kindliest view of every action and every deed, and happiest when doing most to increase the happiness of others. If ye were the children of gentlefolks ye would be gentle yourselves. If you are gentle, then your pedigree is proved, and it ceases to be a mere genealogy, and becomes a life of sacred fellowship and brotherhood. How many a man would to-day be the owner of a title and an estate if, as he says, he could only find one piece of paper. What a pity that any man should be kept back from a title and an estate because he cannot find one piece of paper! Can nobody find a piece of paper for him? It is a marriage certificate, an entry in a parish register; he has nineteen proofs, but because he has not the twentieth he is going to the workhouse, and he is going to pass out of the world namelessly. It is just so with many persons who claim to be the descendants of gentlefolks. They have everything—but the gentleness. Up to that point all their proofs are valid; the shrewdest, keenest legal eyes can see no flaw whatever in all the yellow writing; but when it comes to the one question of gentleness, charity, great heart-sweep, proof there is none, except proof to the contrary. All who are of pure descent from a pure origin are known by instincts, sympathies, and fellowships, which no transient circumstances can conceal or destroy.

Jesus Christ showed the Jews, and therefore showed all men, what the test is by which a pure descent is known. They said they were not children of fornication, they had one father, even

God—as if to say, There we are strong; you may throw some
doubt upon our Abrahamic descent, but God made us. Jesus
said, There you are wrong once more; you are always wrong,
you wicked generation! I have never heard from your lips one
right word. If you quote the Scripture, you spoil it; if you enter
upon an argument, you fill it with sophisms; if you make a
statement, you simply invent a lie. Now, "if God were your
Father, ye would love me"—that is the test—because ye would
know me; my disguise would not conceal me; you would say,
Though he is in the flesh, he is not of the flesh; though he is
on the earth, yet he is in heaven; there is something about
him that there is about no other man. "Ye would love me,"
come to me, ask to be allowed to live with me; like would come
to like; you would be moved by a strange feeling of kinship;
you would say, Though we never saw this man before, he
belongs to us, and we belong to him; he comes locally from a
poor place, genealogically from a poor family, circumstantially
out of poor conditions, but we cannot do without him; in his
face is deity, in his voice is music, in his touch is resurrection:
we will take up our abode with him. If God were your Father,
you would rise above all local prejudice, and seize the essence
of the truth: you would know the divine through every disguise.

Do not boast that you are of God unless you love all that is
godly. God is not a name. Regarded as a name it becomes a
symbol, a symbol of all truth, purity, righteousness, goodness,
gentleness, charity, redeemingness. If God were your Father,
you would be godly. Jesus Christ has the best of the argument,
even if the dialogue be judged merely as a human composition.
What Jesus Christ says is fundamental, it involves the whole
question, he leaves nothing untouched and unrelated; the other
talkers are mere chatterers, gossips, men who relate the little
words of the little time without a philosophy that involves and
includes the universe. When Jesus Christ speaks he lays down
a law that crystallises everything that belongs to it; he speaks
like a philosopher—"Never man spake like this man." How
destructively he spoke upon this occasion! When the Jews
stood upon the Abrahamic pedestal, he swept them off, declaring
that they should not stand there, posing as liars and hypocrites;

when they claimed to be children of God he said that God knew nothing about them—ignored them : " I never knew you : depart from me, ye workers of iniquity." " Ye are of your father, the devil " : you have a pedigree, you have a father ; if you want to search into origins I can take you down a straight line, and your father will be found to be a murderer from the beginning, one who abode not in the truth, because there is no truth in him ; when he speaketh a lie, he speaketh of his own : for he is a liar, and the father of it.

Jesus Christ was not likely to make himself a popular preacher. He divided his congregation, he searched them with the candle of the Lord, he riddled them through the sieve of judgment and truth. What a great principle is this ! How it applies in all educational directions—namely, that if we are of a great teacher certain consequences will flow from that filial regard, and there will be no doubt whatever of the purity of our descent ; if we are of God, we shall know things godly, wherever we find them. Suppose we find some beautiful ethical principle in the writings of Confucius. What an awful thing to do ! Confucius actually wrote some proverbs as beautiful as those that are in the Bible ! What would Jesus Christ say to us when we came upon such proverbs ? He would say, If ye are the children of God, ye would know God's Word wherever you find it. When the Chinese philosopher wrote that beautiful sentence he wrote as he was moved by the Holy Ghost. Ye fools and blind ! can God's wisdom be bound up in any two covers made by human hands ? Why, if all that God had to say, Christ might have continued, were to be published, the whole world could not contain the books that would be issued. If, then, we are of God, and have the really godly spirit in us, wherever we find truth or beauty, or the beginning of the best life, we shall say, Lo, God is here, and I knew it not : this heathen book is, in respect of all these deep, true, pure words, none other than the house of God and the gate of heaven. Here is a flower growing in the fissures of a rock. Is it an orphan flower ? is it a self-made flower ? If it could come down from its rocky height and walk into the well-cultured garden, might it not say, We have all one father, and one gardener hath taken care of us

every one : I am glad to have come down from my stony isolation, and I am thankful to be able to join the floral brotherhood ?
What if the garden brotherhood should say, We do not know
thee ; we are of our father the gardener ?   Who art thou ? what
is thy pedigree ?   They would be foolish flowers, and not deserve
to live another year.   It is by the operation of this same law that
we know brotherhood.   Being of the same quality, we accost one
another in the same language.   That is the secret of the Church.
It is not a company of strangers; although the men may never
have seen one another before, yet they know one another by
the genius of the heart, by the masonry of sympathy and love.
Here, then, we have a permanent Church, because it is not built
upon changeable conditions, but it is founded upon instincts,
sympathies, impulses, aspirations—universal, profound, ineradi-
cable.   This is the brotherhood of man.   We are not akin
because we were born of the same parents, under the same
roof; we may be strangers at daggers drawn.   We shall know
to what family we belong as life evolves.   It is at the end that
men are born, not the beginning.   At the first, all is experiment, novelty, uncertainty, but as life evolves, and men come
and go, and the whole illusion of life expands, we begin to see
who is our father, and mother, and sister, and brother; then
will we understand the words of Jesus Christ himself—he that
doeth the will of my Father which is in heaven, the same is my
kinsman, kinswoman—here, there, now, and through eternal
duration.   If the Church were built upon arbitrary conditions,
the Church would be a merely political arrangement, which
could be changed by incoming or outgoing governments : the
Church is a brotherhood, built on instinct, on family impulse
and feeling, and therefore the gates of hell shall not prevail
against it.

    Is there not a completing truth ?   Must the preacher end
here ?   Nay, for then he would leave half his tale untold ;
he would not have begun to preach the larger gospel.   What
he has said may be true enough in all substance; whatever
re-adjustment of detail in argument or illustration might be
made, the preacher might be substantially sound and correct
up to this point : but is there not another word that needs to

be spoken ? Can any heart suggest it ? The intellect may not think of it, fancy may never direct her wing into that quarter, but may not the heart say that there is another truth to be told, and insist upon its being told ? Let us yield to the gracious insistence. The other truth is, that though we may have been children of evil, we may become children of Abraham ; though we may be by nature the children of wrath, even as others, yet we may become the children of God. If there is a way called apostasy by which man may lose his Abrahamic dignity and relation, there is also another way, upward, large, brighter than the sun at noonday, walking up which a man shakes off all that is impure, undivine, unholy, in his descent, and becomes an adopted child of God. Because we have been born in the family of the devil that is no reason why we should not belong to the family of the saints. " Ye must be born again." " Being born again, not of corruptible seed, but of incorruptible, by the word of God, which liveth and abideth for ever." We were as sheep going astray, but now we have returned unto the Shepherd and Bishop of our souls ; we had not Abraham to our father, but by the mercies of God we are able to call Abraham our father, as he was father of the faithful. We were not born children of God, but children of wrath and of judgment; but being born again God hath sent forth the Spirit of his Son into our hearts, whereby we cry, " Abba, Father ! " He comes upon us like a new sunlight, like a dawn we have never seen before—the very Light of Eternity.

PRAYER.

ALMIGHTY GOD, thou knowest us by name, and canst come to us according to our special wants. Thou hast treated us as if we alone were thy children, as if thou hadst not a whole universe beyond us to care for and bless; as the sun doth bathe the earth in light, as if it were the only world over which thou didst set it, so thou hast filled us with hope and glory, as if we were thine only begotten sons. We come to thee with overflowing hearts; our mouth is opened in renewed praise; we have made haste to appear in this thy house; thou hast given us so much; thou hast held back nothing from us; thou hast made us rich with thine own self. We have left the pursuits of the world for an hour, and we thank thee that we have hope of rest in thee whilst we abide here. Wilt thou not hasten to help us? Wilt thou not give us a reviving? Why should we thus question thee when thou hast already answered us—Lo, God is here, and this is a holy place. Let us now see the littleness of earth, and let us feel the infinite preciousness of heaven. Help us to be truthful, noble, courageous, and every way like Jesus Christ; may we do our worldly business in an unworldly spirit; may we perform all our pilgrimage in haste. This morning give us the bread which, being eaten in secret, shall be pleasant; and the waters which, being stolen from the time of the world, shall be sweet. In this hour we shall live long—these are the moments which deepen our vitality. Though we are in the midst of the week, yet do we anticipate the Sabbath; we hear its voices of music, we feel its hallowing and quieting spell. Lord, make our whole life as a Sabbath. Give us rest even in the midst of labour, and divine elevation even amidst the distractions of an uncertain and unsatisfactory world. God be merciful unto us sinners. We cannot cease this prayer whilst we are conscious of the presence of our sins in our life; yet do we utter it in assured confidence that it is thy delight to forgive. We think of the Cross, and remember that Jesus Christ came to take away sins; we think of the Resurrection, and enter into the spirit and rest of our Redeemer's triumph. We shall be delivered from all evil; thou wilt clothe us as with white linen, and there shall be no stain of sin upon us for ever. Amen.

Chapter viii. 42.

"Jesus said unto them, If God were your Father ye would love me."

SONSHIP.

THEN are not all men the children of God? It would seem, indeed, as if they surely were—as if, indeed, the necessity of the case excluded every other possibility. Did not God make

man in his own image and likeness? He did not make him as
the beasts that perish; but he breathed into his nostrils the
breath of life, and talked to him and confided to him high
responsibilities. It was not a mimic creation. God was not
playing at man-making when he fashioned Adam out of the dust
of the earth. What is the reality of the case? We could have
had no being but for God, and our being is of that particular
kind which points to child-like relation and child-like dependence
and service. How is it, then, that in the Scriptures we are
constantly coming upon a distinction which separates between
man and man, designating one man a child of light, another a
child of darkness—one a child of God and another a child of the
devil? We ought to be anxious to know the exact teaching of
Scripture upon this point. Our perplexity arises from the fact
that it looks, on the face of it, as if we must all be children of
the Highest. Why, then, this particular distinction? Why this
moral separation? These should be questions that give the
heart no rest until they are determined by the authority of Holy
Scripture itself. We read of Solomon these words, "I have
chosen him to be my son, and I will be his Father." Of Ephraim
we read, " I am a father to Israel, and Ephraim is my first-born."
So here is the doctrine of separation. Here is something that looks
like a law of discrimination and election. I want, so far as may
be possible, to grasp the underlying and all-explaining principle
of this pathetic and, in some respects, most mournful distinction.

There is a sense in which a man may not be the father of his
own child! Our conceptions of fatherhood may be too narrow,
so narrow indeed as to become really false in all higher aspects
and relations. Consider for one moment this extraordinary proposition—there is a sense in which a man is not the father of his
own child! We must appeal to facts in evidence, and in gathering those facts and sifting that evidence we shall be compelled to
own to a greater mystery on the ground of the man's fatherhood
than on the ground of his having no real relation to the child.
We are not animals only. In the true and complete idea of
fatherhood and sonship there must be the element of consent.
You do not want to live in such animal affection as may subsist
naturally between and amongst the beasts of the earth and their

offspring. That is not love in its divine significance and application. Here, for example, is a good man with a bad son. I say, they are not relations at all, in the higher sense. They are related physically, by the law of consanguinity ; there is a blood bond between them which neither of them could help, but they are not father and son in the enduring and complete sense of those terms. Take such a son and ask him where the bond of union is between himself and his father. Your father is a praying man ; he walks with God, his conversation, or conduct, is in heaven, he is filled with a godly and inspiring expectation which lifts him above the meanness and the bondage of time and earth ; he walks in company with the angels, every morning is to him a revelation and every eventide a benediction. What is your life ? Prayerless, thoughtless, godless, selfish, mean, sensual, self-indulgent, marked out upon the surface of time and without any settled and thoughtful relation to things unseen and eternal ! To tell me you are the son of such a man is in the deeper sense of the term a falsehood. Kinship is in the soul. Your kindred are not of your flesh, but of your mind, your heart, and sympathy. "Who is my mother? and who are my brethren? Whosoever shall do the will of my Father which is in heaven, the same is my brother, and sister, and mother." The case will bear to be inverted. Take a bad man with a good son. What a mystery is that ! Yet we have known it. We look upon some young persons and say, "How did they come to be what they are, considering the circumstances under which they were born and trained ? What refinement, what intelligence, what high sympathies, what noble purposes and impulses !" How can you account for these? By atmospheric laws? Why, this is a miracle! I know of no miracle of a superior kind. Do you tell me that that bad, self-indulgent man is the father of that godly, devoted, self-sacrificing youth ? But for merely animal considerations the youth might shake him off and disown him, with the contempt not of vulgarity but of refinement, as light shakes off darkness, and as that which is holy looks with repellent indignation upon everything that even appears to be of the nature of evil. What is it, then, that constitutes fatherhood ? Fatherliness. You are not a father if you are not fatherly. But is it possible for a man who is a father to be *un*fatherly ? Most certainly;

and therein is the plague of much home life. The man at the head of the home is no father. He is a governor, a leader, a paymaster, a tyrant, an overlooker; but he is not a father, full of love and wisdom and tenderness, strong in his sense of rectitude, yet beautiful in the dews of pity and compassion which make him charmful and approachable. Why did you go to your father, dear child ? Simply because of a physical relation between you ? Then all children would go to their father the same as you did, but they do not; then there must be some difference. What is that difference ? You went to your father because he was fatherly—a man of a great heart, into whose eyes the tears soon came, and into whose voice the tender tone leaped instantly when he saw you in weakness or fear. You went to him and prayed to him in an earthly, but very significant and beautiful, sense every day. Sometimes you made him do what you wanted him to do ! That is what God permits in his high court ! In common words he would say, " Tease, importune, give no rest, knock again and again ; come up seven times, and do not go away until both hands are full, and your heart is overflowing ! " " The kingdom of heaven suffereth violence, and the violent take it by force," that is, by the force of love and earnestness. You have not a God unless you yourselves are godly. Do not tell me of your intellectual and metaphysical god; he is vanity. Be mine a wooden Baal rather than a shape-less, intangible, mocking cloud. I will hug to my mocked heart some cold, deified stone rather than follow you in your meta-physical dreaming and God-planning and heaven-mapping. He has a God who is himself godly ; he is a father who is fatherly.

We must remember, too, that though God may be our Father we may not be his children. For example, take this passage, " That ye may be the children of your Father which is in heaven." Take another passage, " As many as received him, to them gave he power to become the sons of God, even to them that believe on his name." Now, it is in this inner sense that I want to be a child of God. Here comes the element, as we have already called it, of consent. I am not a mere creature which I cannot help being ; I am a willing child of God. I have said, " Abba ! " Father, my heart has said it. I love to say it. " Creator ! " So says the beast of the field. "Father!" So says the awakened, living, consenting heart. Do not, therefore, give way to the sentiment which tells you that all are God's children, irrespective of age, condition, moral aspiration, or moral behaviour. That is a sentiment which will not stand against the shock of the trying wind or the flood of testing waters. Such reasoning does not consult our humanity; leaves our reason out of the question; takes no account of our moral consent. Such a theology drags men at its chariot wheels willingly or unwillingly. It is not, therefore, a gospel of the heart; it is a mere exercise of iron strength, and in such so-called sonship there can be neither loyalty nor worship. The appeal, then, to us is this, Will you become the children of God by faith in Christ Jesus? That is Paul's expression, and it cannot be well amended. Paul makes the distinction very broad and very clear; his words are these, "They which are the children of the flesh, these are not the children of God." What is his idea? That a man must, as to his main purpose, be living either downwards or upwards. In other words, he is either a child of the flesh or a child of God. What is your dominating thought in life? There are some men that are verily flesh. With the full consent of everything that is within them they consent to the evil, they wallow in the mire, they find their enjoyment in the gratification of the flesh. It is not succumbing to a temptation. It is not being "overtaken in a fault." It is not an occasional slip or even sin, but a daily delight, a continual consent, a waking in the morning to repeat it, a sleeping at night to renew it in unholy dream, a turning of the earth into an incipient and preparatory hell; a joy, devil-born and devil-rewarded. Paul says of such people, "You are children of the flesh, and not the children of God." Let not my charity be evil spoken of, or perverted, if I say that I have great sympathy with men who may be suddenly ensnared by an evil, who may be overtaken in a fault, and who, now and again, maybe, depart a long way from the right course. I am not commending or approving them, nor am I holding them up as examples, and the solemn fear in uttering even one word of charity is, that some may eat the bread who are not entitled to it. Yet I cannot allow certain souls to be cast out of the sanctuary when I know that, how manifold soever their departures and

slips and sins, they can honestly say, " I hate them every one;
I will arise and go to my Father, and will say unto him, ' Father,
I have sinned; God be merciful to me a sinner.' " At the
risk of some dog eating the child's bread, I will not allow
such persons to be mixed up indiscriminately with the class I
have described who live on the brink of hell and enjoy the
sulphurous fumes of the pit of perdition.

Then there comes this difficulty—which will presently be
shot through and through with sunlight and become a golden
cloud—namely, If you are children of God how does it come
that you have so much sorrow and affliction? This is the seal
of sonship! " If ye endure chastening, God dealeth with you as
with sons; for what son is he whom the father chasteneth not? "
" If ye be without chastisement . . . then are ye bastards and not
sons." " My brethren, count it all joy when ye fall into divers
trials, knowing that the trial of your faith worketh patience,"
and to patience God grants the most vivid and beauteous revelations of his grace. From patience God keeps nothing of God.
" He that overcometh shall inherit all things; and I will be his
God, and he shall be my son." Who, then, would not love to
engage in a fight when the guerdon is so rich in the case of
overcoming? We must be tried in battle. God's is not a paper
army, but an army of living souls. We must be tried by fire.
God's gold is not to be mixed with dross. We must be chastened
in the furnace of affliction. Ours must not be a doubtful love;
it must be a love that goes up at the last, having fought well,
having come out of the fire unscathed, having passed through
affliction adorned with a more beautiful resignation, and inspired
by a more confident hope. Life is not a holiday. Life is a
discipline. " As many as are led by the Spirit of God, they are
the sons of God." " Ye have received the Spirit of adoption,
whereby we cry, Abba, Father. The Spirit itself beareth witness
with our spirit, that we are the children of God; and if children,
then heirs; heirs of God, and joint-heirs with Christ." Who will
set any affliction against that? Who will venture to utter his
little whimper of complaint against this great promise, spoken
with all the thunder of God's power, and yet whispered with all
the tenderness of God's love?

PRAYER.

ALMIGHTY GOD, all things are in thine hands. Even when we suppose ourselves free agents, behold we are but working out thy will. Thou dost cause the wrath of man to praise thee, and the remainder thereof thou dost restrain. Thou hast fixed the purpose and the scope of all things; it is ours to study, to obey, to suffer, to carry out all thy will, simply, lovingly, and hopefully. We have nothing that is our own; we are stewards and trustees of the living God; if we have wisdom, the lamp was lighted at the sun of thy throne; if we have power, it is borrowed from thine almightiness; every one of us shall give account of himself to God; we shall all stand before the judgment-seat of Christ. If we could believe that thou art governing us all, directing our steps, upholding our way, behold we should be calm, in the night-time we should have song, and every morning would be a new opportunity for generous action and heroic service. Lord, may our faith never fail; may we know that the furnace is thine as well as the fountain, that when we are condemned to suffer we are still under thy sceptre, and none can harm us; all things are measured out and determined by the sovereign, loving Lord. All this we have learned in the school of Jesus Christ, thy Son, our Saviour, Immanuel, God with us. He showed us the Father; he represented things eternal; he embodied the everlasting mysteries, and out of his words and actions, out of his example and sacrifice, we draw lessons which enlarge our understanding, and ennoble our life, and lift us to new hopes, and point us in the direction of greatest destiny. Lift us up with Jesus on the holy Cross; then we shall see what he saw, and in our measure feel what he felt, and despising the shame, we shall look onward to the final glory. May we have the seeing eye, the hearing ear, the understanding heart, lest we walk through life like fools, and have nothing to show at the end, being without noble recollection, and without solid thought, mere wrecks of manhood; but as we go through the devious paths of time may we gather what we can of knowledge and wisdom, history and thought, and be devout students of the mysterious providence of God. May we begin our journey at the Cross; may we conclude our travels at the Cross; may we never wander from the Cross; may we test everything by the Cross; and when we examine ourselves, whether we be in the faith, may we examine ourselves at the Cross. God forbid that we should glory, save in the Cross of our Lord Jesus Christ,—the mystery of law, the mystery of righteousness, the mystery of love, the mystery of mercy. There may we find all we need —pardon, purity, peace, heaven. Amen.

Chapter viii. 42.

"I proceeded forth and came from God."

JESUS CHRIST'S CLAIM FOR HIMSELF.

SHALL I startle you if I say, notwithstanding the multitude of books written upon the life of Christ, there is yet not only room but necessity for a volume to be written on that unexhausted theme ?   We have had outward lives of Christ enough, perhaps more than enough—lives that tell us about places and dates and occurrences ; books of beautiful colouring, high description of locality and scenery, and the like.   All the circumstantial occurrences of the life of the Son of God have been given us with tedious and painful minuteness and repetition by bookmakers of various degrees.   What then is this other book we want?   A complement, a completion, and an explanation of all other books, viz., " The Inner life of Jesus Christ, the Son of God."   Not a life of circumstances, but a life of thoughts, purposes, feelings, aspirations, desires ; the inward, spiritual, metaphysical, eternal life of Christ.   Can it ever be written ?   It will be often attempted—it will never be done, for no limited book can exhaust an illimitable subject.

Until we study this inner life of Christ deeply, all the outward life of Christ will be a plague to our intellect and a mortification to our heart ; we shall always be coming upon things we cannot understand and cannot explain ; not only so, we shall be coming upon things that seem to confront the understanding and to defy the intelligence of men.   But if we get into sympathy with the inward spiritual life of Christ, then we shall do what Christ did —move out upon these outward and visible things, and see them in their right relations and colours and proportions.   The inward always explains the outward ; why should it not be so in this greatest case of all ?   Come to the outward only, and you will have controversy, difficulty, discrepancy, intellectual annoyance, moral surprise, and perhaps spiritual disappointment.   But begin at the other end—get to know the man's soul, get into sympathy with his purpose, see somewhat of the scope and the outlook of his mental nature, and then you will take up the miracles as a very little thing.

Let me now give you, roughly, some hints of the kind of thing that is wanted. Suppose we saw one of the miracles of Christ. So far control your mind as actually to realise that you are present at what was called, in the days of Christ, the raising of the dead. Let us make this as realistic as we can : the dead man is here, the living Christ is here, the mourning friends are here— and presently the dead man rises and begins to speak to us, and we have seen what is called the miracle of resurrection. But now, is it trick or miracle you have seen ? Is it an illusion or a fact ? How am I to determine this question ? I cannot determine it in itself. Why ? Because my eyes have been so often deceived. I have seen what I could have declared to have been the most positive and absolute facts, and yet when the explanation has been given I have been obliged to confess that I was deceived and befooled by my own vision. If it has been so in a hundred cases, why not so in this ? At all events, there is that suggestion which may be pressed upon me until it becomes a temptation, and the temptation may be urged upon me so vehemently and persistently as almost to shake and destroy my faith. I can declare that I saw a man get up—but the conjurer comes to me and says, "I will show you something equally deceiving." I go, and I see his avowed trick : it does baffle me and surprise me exceedingly, and if he then shall follow up that conquest, and shall say, "It was just the same with what you thought the raising of the dead," he will leave me intellectually in a state of self-torment. I shall still think I saw the event, but he will continue to perplex my vision by a thousand tricks, and show me how impossible it is for any man to trust his eyesight.

Then what am I to do ? Leave the outward altogether. Watch the man who performed the miracle—listen to him : if his thoughts are deep and pure, if his mental triumphs are equal to his physical miracles, then admire and trust and love him. Take this same conjurer just referred to. When he is on the stage, and, so to speak, in character, he seems to be working miracles : they are miracles to me. Therefore, indeed, I go to see them, and have no other reason than to be baffled and surprised and confounded, and to have my keenest watchfulness returned to me without the prize which it coveted. His tricks outrun my vision—my eye cannot follow his supple hand. How then? When he comes off the stage and begins to talk on general subjects I begin to feel my equality with him rising and asserting itself. On the stage I could not touch him—watching his hand I could not follow its manipulations at all. But when he comes away from his official character and his professional region, and begins to speak upon subjects with which I am familiar, I sound the depths of his mind, and get the exact measure of his character, and then he becomes clever, artful, surprising, delightful—but only a wizard, only a conjurer: wonderful with his wand in his fingers, nothing without it.

So when I go to Christ as a mere stranger I see him raising the dead, opening the eyes of the blind, and I say, "We have seen these things attempted before, and very wonderful successes have followed the wand of the wizard and the word of the enchanter. This man may be but cleverest of the host, prince of princes, Beelzebub of the Beelzebubs. I will, therefore, not go further into this case; I have no time to examine this man's credentials, I must be about another and a higher order of business;" but when he begins to talk I am arrested as by unexpected music. I say to him, "Speak on." His words are equal to his works. He is the same off the platform as on it. Not only do I say, "I never saw it on this fashion before;" but I also say, "I never heard it on this fashion before." I listen to his thoughts, to his purposes, to his desires, and I find that he is as inimitable in his thinking as he is in his working and acting. What then? I am bound to account for this consistency. All other men have been manifest exemplifications of self-inequality. We know clever men who are fools, strong men who are weak, eloquent men who stammer, men who are great in this direction, small in some other, self-contradictions, self-anomalies; and this want of self-consistency and self-coherence is at once a proof of their being merely men. But if I find a man in whom this fact of inequality does not exist, who is as great in thinking as in working, who says that if I could follow him still higher I should find him greater in thinking than it is possible for any mere man to be in acting; then I have to account for that consistency which I have met nowhere else, and to listen to this Man's explanation of it: "I proceeded forth and came from God;" "I am from above;" that explanation alone will cover all the ground which he boldly and permanently occupies.

It will be infinitely interesting to study the inner life of Christ; to make ourselves, so far as possible, as familiar with his thoughts as we are with his works. And if we do this, we shall come to set the same value upon his miracles that he himself did. What value did he set upon his miracles for their own sake? None. When did he ever say, "Behold this mighty triumph of my power, ye sons of men"? Never. When did he sound a trumpet and convoke a mighty host to see the loosing of a dumb tongue, and the opening of a blind eye? Never. When did he ever make anything of his miracles other than something merely clementary and introductory, and of the nature of example and symbol? Never. How was this? Because he was so much greater within than he was without. If he had performed the miracles with his fingers only, he might have been proud of them; but when they fell out of the infinity of his thinking, they were mere drops trembling on the bucket: they were as nothing before him. We might as well follow some poor breathing of ours and say, "Behold, how wonderful was that sighing in the wind!" It is nothing to us, because of the greater life. And these miracles are puzzles, enigmas, confounding surprises to people who will come to Christ, along the line which begins in the outward, in the visible, in the circumstantial. If ever they can get hold of his heart, and speak to him face to face for five minutes, they will feel the heaving of his great sympathetic bosom; they will see the miracles as he saw them, then they will appear to be very little things, momentary spasms, examples to guide children through the grammar of a higher law, mere exemplifications, symbols, types of the infinite and the inexpressible.

It is very remarkable that this Man once said, "Greater works than these shall ye do;" but I will ask you to find a passage in which he ever said, "Greater thoughts than these shall ye think." I cannot find such a passage. You must not forget that in your argument about Christ's divinity when he piled up his miracles, raising the dead, opening the eyes of the blind, feeding the hungry miraculously, unloosing dumb tongues and unstopping deaf ears; when he aggregated them all into one sublime spectacle, he said, "Greater works than these shall ye do;" but never did he say, "Greater thoughts than these shall ye think; greater words than these shall ye speak; greater purposes than these shall ye conceive." There he touched the unsearchable riches of his own nature, as in the miracles he pointed to circumstances and to events which would receive larger unfoldment as the ages went on.

Now let us look at this inner life of Christ from two or three points. I watch this Man day by day, and I am struck with wonder at his amazing power, and the question arises, What is the impelling sense of his duty? Why does he do these things? And he answers, frankly, "Wist ye not that I must be about my Father's business?" Never did prophet give that explanation before. He is working from his Father's point of view, in the light of his Father's will; it is the paternal element that is moving him. He has given me that as his key; I will put it into every lock of his life to see whether he has entrusted me with the proper key or not. I defy the world to find him wrong as to the use of this key. Put it where you like, the lock answers it; and is no credit to be given to a Speaker who, at twelve years of age, took the key from off his girdle, put it into the hands of inquirers, and told them to go round the whole circle of his life with that key in their hands? He was but a boy when he gave up that key—he was but twelve years old—approaching manhood by Jewish reckoning, but merely a child in years. Can he keep up the high strain? Listen: "My Father worketh hitherto, and I work." "I and my Father are one." Can he sustain that high key when he is in trouble? Listen: "Father, if it be possible, let this cup pass from me." Can he go higher still? Listen: "Father, into thy hands I commend my spirit." O ye who know the modes of music, tell me, is this harmony? The key note is, "Father." Away the Anthem rolls, high as heaven, deep as hell, tortuous as the paths of the forked lightning, and yet with infinite precision it returns to its initial note. Give Christ credit for this. He was but a Galilean peasant ; give him what honour is due for preserving his rhythmic consistency through a course, not rugged only but most tragical and unparalleled.

Arguing from that point, another question suggests itself. If this Man is about his Father's business, what is his supreme feeling ? What answer would you expect to an inquiry like that, after the self-explanation which Jesus Christ has given ? Is his supreme feeling a concern for the dignity of the law ? Is he jealous with an infinite jealousy for the righteousness of God ? Does he come forth from his hiding-place saying, " I am jealous for the holiness of my God ; I must vindicate the righteousness of the Unseen and Eternal One " ? No. What is the dominant feeling of this Man Christ Jesus ? It is named again and again in the New Testament. No change ever occurs in the term, and I will ask you to say how far it corresponds with the first declaration, " Jesus was moved with compassion." Ye musicians, tell me if that be consonant and harmonious ? " Wist ye not that I must be about my Father's business ? Jesus was moved with compassion." It was always so ; the word " compassion " occurs in no solitary instance alone, though its occurrence in one instance would still have been argument enough. But from beginning to end of his life he is moved with compassion. " Jesus, here are some thousands of people that have been with thee three days and have nothing to eat." Does he wait for us to say that ? No. "But Jesus was moved with compassion when he remembered " that the multitudes were in that condition. Coming out once, and looking upon the crowds, " He was moved with compassion, for they were as sheep not having a shepherd." When he was walking to a grave, " Jesus wept." And when people came to him they seemed to know this sympathetically, for they said, " Jesus, Son of David, have mercy upon us, have compassion on us, thou Son of God." He speaks like a Son, and is thus faithful to a Father's message.

What explanation does he give of his own miracles ? Once he gave us an explanation, as it were, incidentally and unconsciously ; but we caught the word, and it saved us from unbelief and explained all mysteries. How was that long-ailing woman

cured ? " Virtue hath gone out of me." He did not say, " I
have performed this with my fingers; this is an act of manipulation which no other man ever learned to do; it was by swiftness
and suppleness and dexterity, and by a mysterious flashing of
the fingers over certain parts of the affected body." No, but he
perceived that virtue had gone out of him. No trickster, but a
mighty sympathiser,—no manipulator, but infinite in the exercise
and processes of his redeeming power. Whatever he did took
something out of him. Behold the difference between the
artificial and the real! What did our redemption cost? The
healing of one poor sufferer took " virtue " out of him. What
did the redemption of the world take out of him when he said,
" My God, my God, why hast thou forsaken me?" The last
pulse gone. Is he self-consistent still? Still!

And to what are all his triumphs eventually referred? To
his soul. Not to his intellectual ability—not to his skill of finger
—not to his physical endurance, but to his soul—an undefinable
term, the symbol of an infinite quantity. " He shall see of the
travail of his soul, and shall be satisfied." You know the meaning of the word in some degree. One man paints with paint—
another paints with his soul. One is a clever mechanic—another
an inborn and indestructible genius. One man speaks with his
teeth and tongue and palate—another speaks with his soul : they
use the same words, but not the same, as Hermon was not the
same with the dew off; as the bush was not the same before the
fire came into it. You say one man sings artificially, mechanically,
correctly—every tone is right; the proper balance, the proper
measure, the proper quantity : artificially the exercise is beyond
critisism, but still the people sit unmoved. Another man takes
up the same words and the same notes, and the people are
stirred like Lebanon by a wind, like Bashan when the storm
roars. How is it ? The one man is artificial, the other is real
—the one man has learned his lesson, the other man had the
lesson awakened in him—it was there before, and an angel passed
by and said, " It is morning : awake and sing." This Christ, this
dear Son of God, shall see of the travail of his soul, of the outgoing of his blood—he sows the earth with the red seed of his
blood, and he shall see the harvest and be satisfied. He was

often wearied with his journeying : when was he wearied with his miracles ? His bones were tired : when was his mind enfeebled ? The instruments of articulation might be exhausted, but when did the word ever come with less than the old emphasis —the fiat that made the sun ?

Let us now ask—What did this man claim for himself? It will assist us in our study if we hear from his own lips a distinct statement of what he does claim on his own account. Reading in the book of Exodus about the great God, I find that he gave his name as "I AM," that he amplified that name into "I AM THAT I AM." We could make nothing of that name ; it was too remote for us; our genius had never been in such high regions, never scaled altitudes so perilous. We could therefore but wonder. The name sounded grandly ; it had in it all the boom of an infinite mystery, and we were content with it because the condescensions which that same God made to this human life of ours were so mighty yet so pitiful, so wondrous in their sweep and yet so compassionate in their lingerings that we had begun to think, though the name was mysterious, the grace was familiar enough. A marvellous word was that spoken to Moses—" I AM ; " it seemed as if it were going to be a revelation, but suddenly it returned upon itself, came back to its centre, and finished with—"THAT I AM"! As if the sun were just about to come from behind a great cloud, and suddenly, after one dazzling gleam, hide itself behind a cloud denser still. The fulness of the time had not yet come. God's "hour" was not yet. He had said "I AM," but what he was he did not further say. By-and-by more will be said. It will be interesting, there-fore, to inquire whether Jesus Christ connects himself with that mysterious name, "I AM THAT I AM." If I can trace his talking, his thinking, his preaching, so as to find one point in connection between himself and that great name, then a new and large argument will take its inception, and a new and subtle evidence will be put in that this Man was more than man—as mysterious as the Name, perhaps as gracious. Let us see.

I cannot read the life of Christ without constantly coming upon the expression, "I AM." Reading it, I say, I have met these words before, and wonder where. My memory bethinks itself, and I hasten back into the grey old pages of the ancient time, and find that the Lord revealed himself unto Moses as " I AM THAT I AM." I want to know, therefore, if this great ladder, the top of which is in heaven, can by any means find a place upon the earth ; can it come down that I may touch it ? Yes. Jesus adds to the " I AM " little words, simple earthly words, nursery terms, school ideas—brings down the " I AM " so that we may touch its lower meaning, and hear its earthly messages. It will, then, be most interesting to see how this is done, and to listen to this modified music of the Eternal.

What does Jesus say after the words " I am " ? He says everything that human fancy ever conceived concerning strength and beauty, and sympathy, and tenderness, and redemption. He absorbs the whole. He leaves nothing for you and me except as secondary owners, except as those who derive their status and their lustre from himself. Thus, "I am . . . the Vine." What a stoop ! Could any but God have taken up that figure? Think it out. You have heard it until you have become familiar with it —forget your familiarity, think yourself back to the original line, and then consider that One has appeared in the human race who says, without reservation or qualification of any kind or degree, "I am the Vine." Thus is the mysterious simplified ; thus is the abstract turned into the concrete and the inner into the visible, the simple, and the approachable. Will he ever say "I am" again ? Many a time. Let us hear him. " I am the Light." Ah, we know what the light is ; it is here, and there, and every-where—takes up no room, yet fills all space ; warms the planets, yet does not crush a twig. The " I am " fell upon us like a mighty thundering. " I am the Light" came to us like a child's lesson in our mother's nursery. Thus does he incarnate or embody or personify himself; thus doth the ladder rest in the mean dust, whilst its head is lifted up above the pavilions of the stars.

Will he say " I am " any more ? Often. How ? Listen : " I am the Door." Dare any but himself have taken upon him so mean a figure ? " Ah," said he, " it is not a mean figure if you interpret it aright. A door is more than deal. A door is more

than an arrangement swinging upon hinges.   A door is Welcome,
Hospitality, Approach, Home, Warmth, Honour, Sonship—I am
the Door."   Still more: " I am the Bread, I am the Water, I am
the Good Shepherd, I am the Way, I am the Truth, I am the
Life."   When I see how this Man absorbs all beauteous figures,
all high and tender emblems, I begin to think that there is
nothing left for us by which to distinguish ourselves figura-
tively and typically.   If we take any of these words, they must
be taken as with his signature upon them, having a first lien and
a prior claim ; we are but intermediary and temporary, and
altogether subordinate in our stewardship and right of status.
How any man could be a man only, and yet take up these
figures, it is impossible for me to conceive.   It is easier for me
to say, " My Lord and my God," than to say, " Equal with me ;
better only in the accidents of the case."

Seeing that Christ claims so much for himself, it will be equally
interesting, and will be the complement of the same subject, to
start a second inquiry, namely, What does he claim from men ?
He claims everything.   Sometimes in mean mood of soul I have
wondered at his divine voracity.   For once, a woman came to
him who had only one box of spikenard, and he took it all.   I
was amazed—half distressed.   I never saw such impoverishment
made before.   He did not say, " Give me part of it," but took it
every whit, and the woman had no more left of that precious
nard.   Could you have done that ?   Would your humanity have
allowed you to do it ?   Surely you would have said, " Part of it
—just a little ; you are so kind as to offer me a donation out of
your one box of spikenard, let me take a little myself—I must
not have it all."   But this Man, what said he ?   He said, " Let
her do it—I will have it all, substance and fragrance too."   And
another woman—she might have touched his heart as she came
along, for she was poor and poorly clothed, and had on a widow's
weeds—I expected that he would have said, " Poor woman, we
cannot take anything from you."   No ; she came along, took out
her two mites, which make one farthing, put them in, and he
took them both !   Is he man ?   Is that humanity ?   Strange
man ; marvellous exceeding above all other men ; not only did
he take them, but he said, " She hath done more than anybody

else who came up to the treasury; she hath cast in all her living."

Is he doing the selfsame thing in our own day ?   Verily he is ! Look at this family, father and mother, with a boy and a girl as their sweet children.   How many things has that boy been in his father's hopeful dreams !   A lawyer and a judge; then a clergyman and a bishop; then a merchant, a politician, a states-man, and a prime minister !   But one day the mother says that she feels "something is going to happen"; a vague expression, but full of deep and sad meaning to her own soul.   She tells her husband that "something is going to happen," and he smiles at the shapeless and nameless fear.   And what does happen?   A proposal that the boy should become a missionary !   What ! the only son ?   Yes !   "It cannot be," says the stunned father; "no, no, it must not be !"   For many an hour there is silence; ay, for days next to nothing is said, but many a wistful look is exchanged.   At length the mother says, "I have been thinking and praying about this, and I remember that good Mr. Wesley used to open the Bible to see what answer God sent him to his prayers, and I have got my answer to-day.   After prayer I opened the Bible, and my eyes could see no words but these, 'Even so, Father, for so it seemeth good in thy sight.'   He must go."   The father is silent.   A great weight of grief burdens his heart.   He, too, goes to pray—goes a hale man under fifty—comes back in an hour an old man, crushed, blanched, withered, and grey, "but more than conqueror," and he, too, says the child —the one son, the heir, the first-born—must go.   And Christ takes him !   Humanity would have spared him when so many large families could have furnished a missionary, but God takes him ; the God that took the spikenard and the mites.

It will be curious and interesting now to start a third inquiry to this effect : How did the people who were round about, and who were not malignantly disposed, who constituted the better class of his contemporaries, regard Christ ?   Here is one typical man—a man of letters and of local renown, careful and exact in speech, somewhat timid in disposition, yet marked by that peculiar timidity which is capable of assuming the most startling boldness. He climbs his way up to Christ, opens the door in the dark, goes up to him, and says in an undertone, lest the enemy should hear—" Rabbi, thou art a teacher come from God." Evidence of that kind must not go for nothing. Send men of another type of mind to him—men of the world, shrewd, keen men. Here are several of them returning from an interview with the Son of God. I hail them in English terms, and say, " Gentlemen, what say you ? " " Never man spake like this Man." Add that to the evidence of Nicodemus. Here are women coming back from having seen the Lord ; tears are in their eyes. What will they say ? Never yet did woman speak one word against the Son of God ! Mothers, did you see any-thing to blame? " Nothing." Women of pure soul—sensitive as keenest life—what saw ye ? " The Holiness of God." Pass him on to a judge—cold, dispassionate, observant, not easily hoodwinked. What sayest thou, Roman judge ? " I find no fault in him." What is that coming to the man now, while he is talking ? A message. What saith the message ? It is a message from the judge's wife. " Have thou nothing to do with this just person, for I have suffered many things this day in a dream concerning him." Let him go—nail his right hand, nail his left hand, nail his feet, lift high the dreadful tree, crush it into the rock, shake every nerve and fibre of his poor body, let him writhe in his last agony, and will anybody speak about him then ? Yes. The centurion beholding this, accustomed to the sight of blood, knowing how men deport themselves in judgment halls and in prisons and in the supreme crisis ot existence, said— " Truly this Man was the Son of God." Observe what he claimed for himself—what he claimed from others. Put these testimonies of observers one after the other, accumulate them into a complete appeal, and then say whether it be not easier to the imagination and the heart and the judgment to say, " My Lord and my God," than to use meaner terms.

Another question arises : From such a Man what teaching may be expected ? Given, a man distinguished by such attributes and elements as I have endeavoured simply to indicate, to find out what kind or manner of teaching and public ministry we may expect from him. I shall first expect extemporaneousness. He cannot want time to make his sermons, or he is not the man he claims to be. He is not an essayist. He will not be a literary speaker; there will be a peculiarity, a uniqueness, a personality about him not to be found otherwhere. Does he retire to his study, that he may write out elaborate sentences full of nothing but ink? Will he come before me as a literary artist, with well-poised sentences, beautiful periods, sounding climaxes, leaving the impression that he has wasted the midnight oil, and taken infinite pains to please those who went to hear him? There is nothing literary about the style of Christ; it is simple, graphic talk, much broken to our minds, occasionally incoherent, rapid in transitions, utterly wanting in elaboration, and the balance prized by men who have nothing else to do than to live by their folly. I shall further expect instantaneousness of reply by Christ Jesus if he be God. God cannot want time to think what he will say. Does this Man ever ask for time; does he ever adjourn the interview? He answers immediately, and he answers finally. He never asks for time to bethink himself, to refer to the authorities, to consult and connote the precedents. He does not say, "You have posed me by an unexpected question; I must retire and give this inquiry my profoundest consideration." Never; and he was but a carpenter. He had just thrown the apron from his waist; he was but a peasant. Rabbinical culture he had none, high connection disdained the mention of his name, and yet there was an instantaneousness about him to which I can find no parallel but in the " Let there be light, and there was light." Give every man credit for his ability; give this Man, carpenter and peasant of Galilee, credit for having extorted from his enemies the acknowledgment, "Never man spake like this Man."

What do I find in this Man's teaching? High allegory, types of things unseen, incarnations of the spiritual, embodiments of the invisible, parables beautiful as pictures, wide as philosophies, lasting as essential truth. Strange man—marvellous productions of a barren soil. Why, he himself was an incarnation. What was his ministry? An incarnation too. What had he to do with the men who heard him, and all succeeding generations? He had to embody, to physicalise and bodily typify the kingdom

---

of God: hence he said, " It is like a grain of mustard seed ; like
a net cast into the sea ; like treasure hid in a field ; like leaven
hid in three measures of meal." " It is like unto——" when we
said that, what did he do ? He repeated his own birth. He
renewed his own incarnation, he was born again in every parable
that escaped his lips. To embody the bodiless, to typify in
allegory and figure the infinite and the inexpressible, was the
all-culminating miracle of this peasant of Galilee. Then I ask
myself, " Is it consistent with all I have heard about him ? "
And I am compelled to say it is exquisitely in consonance with
all we have yet seen of his character and studied of his speech.
A man like this coming up from unbeginning time must be ex-
temporaneous in his speech, instantaneous in his reply, and
allegorical and typical and symbolical in his method of presenting
truth, for he knows the essential, and alone can give it beauty
and expression, and movement and colour. Give him the credit
due to his power.

Jesus Christ's is the kind of teaching that survives all the
changes of time. It is seminal teaching : it is not like a full-blown
garden, it is like treasures of living seeds and roots, and therefore
it abides for ever. Where are the grand and stately and polished
sermons of the great doctors of the Church ? Do you know ? I
do not. But they were grand, were they not ? Why did not you
keep them then ? But they were stately, majestic, complete,
cathedral-like, strong in base, exquisite in pinnacle, almost
fluttering in the delicacy of their architecture ; indeed, why did not
you take better care of them ? Where are they ? Gone into a
stately past—majestic shadows of a majestic oblivion. What
lives ? Suggestiveness, what is called incoherence, want of finish,
want of polish ; the great mighty oak, the everlasting Bashan ;
not the cabinet-makers' pretty and expensive fabrication.

Now I will come to the final point, and it shall be of the utmost
severity in its relation to this argument. The question I put is
this : Did this Man Christ Jesus live up to his own principles?
I can imagine persons of a certain kind of mind suggesting that
the speeches and parables, and conversations generally of Jesus
Christ, conveyed very high theories, very sublime philosophies

of things, but were too romantic to be embodied in actual behaviour. The question I press upon you is this, so far as the evidence in the Book goes, Did this Man Christ Jesus embody his own doctrine? What said he? "Bless them that persecute you." Did he do it? Let one of his disciples answer. "When he was reviled, he reviled not again ; when he suffered, he threatened not." What said he? "Pray for them which despitefully use you, and persecute you." Did he do it? One of his historians says that in his last agony he prayed, when he had no hand to stretch out upward to his God, "Father, forgive them, for they know not what they do." Is this to go for nothing? Are we at liberty to dismiss this witness, and say he does not know of that which he testifies, or that which he affirms? Be careful, for if you cannot confer a character you have no right to take one away.

I call you to this living Christ; I will try to go nearer to him than ever I have been before ; I will call for him to come nearer to me, and I will press still nearer. He knows me, he speaks to me ; there is a masonry between us for which you have no word or symbol : a grip of the hand he only can give, a symbol that hath morning in it, and hope and immortality, secret messages, transmissions in cipher which he makes the devil himself bring. Can I give him up? Can I sell him for thirty pieces of silver? Can I exchange him for some other master? Oh, then the sun would bring no morning with it, midday would be but a great black cloud, and the summer a mocking promise without an answer. To whom, then, could I tell my sin ; to whom could I pray my prayers ; to whom could I empty my heart in darkness and in close and absolute solitude, after I have looked all round the horizon to see even if an angel be there to watch the secret interview? Nay, I must serve him still, preach him still, and if he say to me, "Wilt thou go away?" I will answer in words I cannot amend, "To whom can I go? Thou only hast the words of Eternal Life !"

Chapter viii. 43-59.

"Why do ye not understand my speech? even because ye cannot hear my word. Ye are of your father the devil, and the lusts of your father ye will do. He was a murderer from the beginning, and abode not in the truth, because there is no truth in him. When he speaketh a lie, he speaketh of his own: for he is a liar, and the father of it. And because I tell you the truth, ye believe me not. Which of you convinceth me of sin? And if I say the truth, why do ye not believe me? He that is of God heareth God's words: ye therefore hear them not, because ye are not of God. Then answered the Jews, and said unto him, Say we not well that thou art a Samaritan, and hast a devil? Jesus answered, I have not a devil; but I honour my Father, and ye do dishonour me. And I seek not mine own glory: there is one that seeketh and judgeth. Verily, verily, I say unto you, If a man keep my saying, he shall never see death. Then said the Jews unto him, Now we know that thou hast a devil. Abraham is dead, and the prophets; and thou sayest, If a man keep my saying, he shall never taste of death. Art thou greater than our father Abraham, which is dead? and the prophets are dead: whom makest thou thyself? Jesus answered, If I honour myself, my honour is nothing: it is my Father that honoureth me; of whom ye say, that he is your God: yet ye have not known him; but I know him: and if I should say, I know him not, I shall be a liar like unto you: but I know him, and keep his saying. Your father Abraham rejoiced to see my day: and he saw it, and was glad. Then said the Jews unto him, Thou art not yet fifty years old, and hast thou seen Abraham? Jesus said unto them, Verily, verily, I say unto you, Before Abraham was, I am. Then took they up stones to cast at him: but Jesus hid himself, and went out of the temple, going through the midst of them, and so passed by."

PLAIN SPEAKING.

THIS section of Holy Scripture contains a very vivid example or specimen of plain speaking. The frankness would necessitate one of two things: either revenge or submission. We need not tell the name of the speaker in this dialogue. There are no words like the words of Jesus. We might risk the whole Christian controversy upon the tone and scope of this conversation. Let any frank-minded man stand by and listen to the colloquy, and then let him say by the music only where the truth is. We never know what the words of Jesus Christ are until we have laid down our greatest author, and then opened the New Testament. Christ always sounds like a speaker of music, but he sounds the best always after the greatest man has finished ; he then proves his deity—not when answering some wild and embittered Jew only, but when following in succession earth's brightest speaker, earth's chiefest poet ; then do we see his stature. The sayings of Christ are unfathomable. How well he maintains his own if this be taken as merely a dramatic dialogue ! How calm he is ! How strong in positiveness, how clear in statement, how assured in the possession of every qualification that can dominate the history of men ! Yet he surprises us by the use of startling language. We speak of the meek and lowly Jesus ; but cannot that claim to meekness and lowliness now be set aside by quotations from Christ's own speeches ? Jesus Christ called the men who were looking at him—when did he speak to absentees like modern preachers ?— fools, hypocrites, liars, murderers, thieves, whited sepulchres, wolves in sheep's clothing, devourers, children of the devil. What wonder that he had not where to lay his head ? He might have had a downy pillow could he have talked the other way. Yet this is the meek and lowly Jesus ! What wonder that he sent a sword upon the earth, dividing whole families, and making relations strangers and aliens ? We have associated a tone of passion in connection with such words as fools, hypocrites, liars. Who could call another man a liar in cold blood, as if he were merely making a remark ? We have to be stung into the use of such descriptives. Jesus Christ had not. We should have heard the very tone in which he called men by these dishonouring but accurate names. He was not scolding, merely upbraiding, or trying to exasperate his hearers ; he was revealing spirit and character and purpose, and doing it with the calmness of philosophy. We could not call a man a child of the devil without being angry, and our anger would spoil the revelation. Never believe an angry man. It was the solemn, calm, serene manner of the speaker that made the terms so truly awful.

Is it not from the quietest that the severest always issues ? Does not lightning leap forth in a time of sullen silence ? We praise the majestic tranquillity of Science. Science, unlike

Theology, we say, is serene, never ruffled, most tranquil, lake-like in its sunny serenity. Is that true ? We might speak of the meek and lowly Science: but Science is the most desperate character that is now abroad. There is nothing so tremendous as the Science which you praise as tranquil, dispassionate, altogether devoid of the *odium theologicum* which embitters all religious fellowship. Science is very calm, but very murderous. Picture some ancient battle with bows and arrows, with catapults and stones, battering rams and huge cumbrous weapons of war ; picture a modern battle-field, with its arms of precision, with its devastating forces: what did it ? Calm, impartial, tranquil Science. Look at that ship—torn, shattered, started out of the water, as if a ghost had struck it : what did it ? Calm, impartial, tranquil Science concealed a torpedo, and went home to brood upon the ignorance of mankind, and retired to rest with the reputation of being so different from theology, so dispassionate, so tranquil, quite a meek and lowly thing. What tore the building in twain ? What frightened the Parliament ? What shook the bridge ? Science—by nitro-glycerine, by dynamite ; tranquil, dispassionate, lowly-minded Science, never agitated by her theological tumults, threw the Metropolis into a panic. Science is the greatest murderer known in history. Yet all done so tranquilly, leaving all fighting to be done in the Church.

We must look at this conversation, then, in another light. It comes up from behind Abraham's time ; it looks upon Abraham as a very modern instance. This speech is delivered from the platform of eternity. There is no modern word in it ; there is nothing of yesterday's paint or decoration or enamel about its high eloquence, its sharp glittering rhetoric ; it is calm as eternity is calm. Jesus Christ says—

"Ye are of your father the devil, and the lusts of your father ye will do. He was a murderer from the beginning, and abode not in the truth, because there is no truth in him. When he speaketh a lie, he speaketh of his own ; for he is a liar, and the father of it " (ver. 44).

This was not spoken in an excited tone. This is a philosophy, not an insult. That is the difference between a man who speaks superficially, and a man who speaks with the background of eternity. How familiarly he speaks of their father, who was a murderer from the beginning! How well he knew ancient history—because there was no history ancient to him. A man who is the contemporary of all ages knows nothing about the meaning, in a technical sense, of what to us is ancient history. He was present at the birth of the devil; he has watched all his tricks and policies ever since he was born,—nay, the devil claims a kind of grim eternity. Jesus Christ thus adopts the principle of heredity, and starts it from a new point, and traces it up with scientific precision. He says, You are not yourselves only, you are a progeny; you had fathers, ancestors, and he takes them into the college of heraldry, and he makes them find out their crest and their motto and their father's image. "The lusts of your father ye will do." He speaks calmly of this fate. He does not upbraid the men as if they themselves were so much to blame; they express a historical moral necessity. There is a kind of ghastly consistency in their malice and obstinacy and hatred of truth; they keep up the family name well; there is no bar sinister on this diabolical escutcheon unless it be altogether in its very self a bar sinister on the escutcheon of the universe. Would that good men were as consistent as bad men; their consistency might accumulate into a pleasing and conclusive argument. We are worsted by our inconsistency, though the term inconsistency itself is not always fully comprehended and justly applied. Christians can falter a good deal; they have the gift of hesitation, they have the genius of incertitude; they spoil their prayers for want of emphasis.

But if this reading of heredity be true on the one side it will be equally true on the other; hence we have this declaration, completing the former, and giving hope to men—

"He that is of God heareth God's words: ye therefore hear them not, because ye are not of God" (ver. 47).

Here is a mystery which cannot be explained, but it is a plain simple fact. There are some men who cannot be religious, from any point that is obvious to our thinking. There are some ministers who cannot pray; they are scholars, they are expositors, they are earnest men, but they do not know how to pray. "He that is of God heareth God's words": he that is of music knoweth music when he hears it; he that is a child of art knows the painter's touch from the daub of the unskilled hand. We are born what we are—musicians, poets, artists, housewives, merchants, lamplighters, journalists, leaders, heroes, cowards,—it is of birth, not of choice. This may seem to ruin a good deal of hope. It does nothing of the kind, properly accepted. Awaken yourselves; who can tell what angel sleeps in your dulness? Who knows what bright spirit has taken up its residence for a time in the hostelry of your soul? Arise, awake, put on thy strength! You cannot tell what you are, until all the awakening ministries have been brought to bear upon your indifference and your obstinacy.

When were deep sayings intelligible to corrupt hearts? The Jews did not understand this man's speech. They blundered in every remark they made upon it. They continually took it from the wrong end, and they so mingled the words that they lost all their philosophy and all their music. Blessed be God, therefore, that there are men who can teach alphabets. The Beatitudes are mysteries. "Blessed are the pure in heart: for they shall see God." The world heard and passed on to its merchandise, saying that some fanatic had taken possession of the mountain, and was raving there, harmlessly but most incoherently. "Blessed are the meek: for they shall inherit the earth." In that one sentence there is a whole library of the deepest, holiest thinking, an infinite philosophy of life. But the people who listened to Jesus knew absolutely nothing of what he was talking about. When he gave away loaves and fishes his congregation amounted to some thousands; when he began to give away his own flesh, and to hand out in cups of gold his heart blood, his congregation amounted to twelve persons, and even they stood with their backs half to him as if they would go away; in fact, he asked them if they were going. Blessed is he who can talk to men of his own kith—to poets who see a universe through the slot of a single proverb. Jesus Christ never had such hearers in his own day in the flesh, but they are gathering around him now, and calling his sayings ineffable in suggestiveness and sublimity.

The Jews thought they caught Jesus now and then. How little theybecame! How microscopically small!

"Then said the Jews unto him" (in a tone which can never be reported), "Now we know that thou hast a devil. Abraham is dead, and the prophets; and thou sayest, If a man keep my saying, he shall never taste of death" (ver. 52).

How can you talk to such men? What interest can you have in men who think that Abraham is dead? There is nobody dead. The Protestant says, What, worship a dead woman, the Virgin Mary! There is no dead woman. That is the mistake we make. Abraham is dead. No, he is not. You are wrong at the foundation. "I am the God of Abraham, and of Isaac, and of Jacob": God is not the God of the dead, but of the living. Who can teach this doctrine properly? Who can feel it in all its heavenliness? Who can find house-room in the heart for this immortality? We might dwell long upon this and find it nutritious. To the Jews, people did die. To fools, people die now. There are even people who are wearing mourning. It will be a long day before Christianity kills Paganism. There are Christians who are going out to-morrow to buy mourning. You would not think it possible, but it is a fact. "Abraham is dead, and the prophets": what an empty world they lived in who spake thus! How hollow their voices sounded in the chambers of the past! You can never teach such people anything. They think they are the only living people in the world. No man dies. The little child is not dead; it is like a dewdrop that has gone up to the sun to be used in the fashioning of a rainbow. The friend is not dead; he lives and waits; he is now half out of heaven looking for some of you: do not disappoint him.

"Jesus answered, If I honour myself"—if I have no water but that which flows on the surface, it can be scooped up with a cup and used, drunk at one meal, and there would be nothing afterwards but burning thirst; only that water is sure which comes up out of the rock—spring water, living water, water that the heat can never get at to dry it up. Then Jesus came upon them with a revelation which was too much for their ignorance :—

"Jesus said unto them, Verily, verily, I say unto you, Before Abraham was, I am" (ver. 58).

That is true. His words establish the truth of the declaration,

They are not dictionary words, they are not rhetorical terms, they are not sentences and phrases fashioned and carved in the schools, and beautifully enamelled, and ticketed in plain figures for sale in the market-place; they are weird words, ghostly, eternal words. He said, "Abraham rejoiced to see my day: and he saw it, and was glad" (ver. 56). Then the Jews perfectly revelled in contempt of the man : "Thou art not yet fifty years old, and hast thou seen Abraham ?" Who can reproduce the tone of their bitter speech ? Fact seemed to be so dead against this man. He has just turned thirty, but he looked fifty—he looked a thousand. It was a wondrous face. It might have been any age. Age seemed to have nothing to do with it. It was fifty faces. What sorrow it could wear ! What joy flashed from it now and then ! When nobody was supposed to be looking at him how far he went away from his face, and left himself physically a blank ! How the tears came into those eyes, and how heaven shone out of them ! When people said, What age is he ? nobody could tell for certain,—by the record, thirty; by the look, thirty centuries ; by the words, thirty millenniums. "Your father Abraham rejoiced to see my day : and he saw it, and was glad." Who could bear such talk ? Who could bear to have facts so trampled under foot ? Who could have statistics ignored in this reckless way ? What wonder that this man had not where to lay his head ? People were afraid to take him in ; he talked so incoherently, so insanely. Religion is always associated with insanity—and properly. There is no man religious who is not insane about it. To have been before Abraham was a necessity of making a true revelation. But when Jesus Christ made this revelation the people were moved to stone him— "Then took they up stones to cast at him." This also was natural logic ; a true and proper sequence of all that had gone before. If congregations were to act according to their own feeling to-day they would stone all the best preachers. Instead of that they make a collection to defray expenses; a weak exchange, and remarkably foolish. We shall never be right until our preachers are stoned and spat upon. At present they are criticised, and neat little opinions are expressed about them and they can go in and out of the temple as they please—and the sooner they go out the better. Jesus " went out of the temple, going through the midst of them," concluding his miracle of language with a miracle of disembodiment. Who can stone a ghost? Who can throw missiles at a spectre? Who would shoot with a cannon at the light of day? It will be even so in the end with this Jesus. He will arouse men, excite them, madden them, work them into a tempest of wrath and delirium, and when they are in their madness he will walk through them like a sunbeam, and pass on, until they become calm enough to hear him once more.

How good it is to come near this divine teacher! How he soothes us and blesses us, yet how he excites and inspires us! When did he say, All things are very little, and not worth looking at? Herein he taught from the other end than that which was adopted by Solomon, because Solomon had bought all his things and he became sick of them. They were connected with bills and invoices, and estimates and valuations and umpires, and final appeals, and when he paid for them he said in effect, Take them where you please ; I do not want them. Vanity of vanities, saith the preacher. Jesus did not buy them, he made them ; he valued them therefore differently. All things were to him suggestive, significant, symbolic. The sparrow, the lily, and the little child, and the ear of corn, and the fig-leaf,—all these were signs of a kingdom infinite. On the other hand, how pitiful it is to be associated with men who always take little views of things, who suppose that Abraham is dead, that Jeremiah is in the cemetery, and Isaiah is in the churchyard, and the minor prophets are all dead and forgotten. What is there, then? Beware of false teaching. But sometimes Jesus Christ could go no further than this ; he could only say, Beware of the leaven of the Pharisees, of the Herodians : take care how ye hear : many false Christs go about in the world, and many arise to say Christ is here, and Christ is there ; go not after them. Then saith an apostle, "Beloved, believe not every spirit, but try the spirits whether they be of God." Sometimes all the very best and bravest teacher can do is to warn his generation, and even sometimes that warning may not be put into words, because it is a warning that comes from the point of instinct, rather than from the point of logic. Do the children remember how this was said to have been proved by an instance in natural history? May we not read it in our children's books at home? The man you see before you is a king of Persia, and he is devotod to the sport of falconry. Who can tell how many falcons the king has? He has been indulging in this sport hour after hour, and now he is weary and thirsty, and he stands before a dripping rock with his cup in his hand and his falcon on his wrist. He holds the cup to the dripping rock, and slowly catches drip after drip of water that he may quench his thirst. There is a little water in the cup and he will drink it, but as he brings the vessel to his lips the falcon throws out its wings, flutters itself, upsets the cup; and the monarch is angry. He will hold his cup a second time to the dripping rock, and oh, how slowly does it drip, drip, drip! and how hot and burning is his thirst! He fills his cup again, and again applies it to his lips, and again the falcon flutters, and throws out the water; and the king is angry and takes the falcon and dashes it against the rock, and kills the falcon. Presently there comes a servant to the king of Persia, and the enraged king says, Take this cup and go up to where the water is fuller, and fill it for me, and haste back; I die of thirst. The servant climbed the rock, filled the cup; on returning found that the channel of the little stream was intercepted by the head of a great serpent, dead, the foam of whose mouth is carried away by the stream. What was then the monarch's sorrow! How, then, could the king atone to the dead? By an instinct, which science has not yet explained, the falcon knew that there was death in the pot; by an instinct more than human it ruffled its wings and dashèd the death-charged vessel from the king's hands. The falcon was not heeded, the falcon was slain; the falcon could not speak, could not explain; but the day of explanation came, and the king's heart grieved for the king's madness. There are men to-day who are stifling warning voices. They are thirsty, they must drink; the matter cannot be explained: but preacher, apostle, prophet, seer, poet,—these men are dashed to death or starved. But the day of explanation will surely come.

Chapter ix. 1.

" And as Jesus passed by, he saw a man which was blind from his birth. "

SINNER OR SAVIOUR ?

WHY did he pass that way ? Could he not have gone by some other path ? The answer is, No. Grace has its necessities; love has its predestinations. Jesus Christ always looked out for opportunities of doing good. He knew which road to take; he said, The blind man is down this road, therefore this is the road along which I am about to travel. This is how he came to find so many opportunities of doing good : he sought for them. We never see any openings for doing good : how can we ? we do not look for them. Jesus Christ made it his business to find out who wanted him. He even stands at the door sometimes, and knocks. In a sense, does he not thrust himself upon men who need him ? so graciously and quietly that it has no appearance of obtrusiveness or aggression ; still he makes himself felt by events, by appeals, by sudden recollections, by suggestions from friends, by Church service and sacrament,—yea, a thousand ways he sends us hints that he is there, and has with him all the resources which are needed for our redemption, purification, and final coronation in heaven. When you felt inclined to pray it was Jesus Christ who moved you in that direction. When you said, I think I see more clearly to-day ; truth seems to be enlarging,—it was Christ who was performing a miracle upon you. Trace all happy impulse, all sacred inspiration, all ennobling influence, to the touch, the glance, the benediction of Christ. He undertook work of the kind described in this chapter simply as introductory. Physical miracles were not worth doing if there had not been something more important to follow. The prologue was too sublime for the little drama if Christ came only to heal diseases, and to relocate broken joints, and to give eyes to the blind or hearing to the deaf. All this was symbolic, introductory, and was intended merely to secure a kind of foothold for him, standing on which he might do his larger, nobler work. That is the reason he gives us bread in the morning. The bread is nothing and the body is nothing. Bread is only a kind of bribe to hunger, at best a species of compromise or truce; for the wolf comes back again with wider mouth and sharper teeth. But he gives the bread that he may give his flesh himself.

What an advantage he had in performing physical miracles compared with the delivery of his profound—yea, his unfathomable—discourses. Everybody could see a miracle: only a man in a multitude of instances could understand a discourse. The vulgarest onlooker knew when a miracle was wrought: it took an almost-angel to catch the first hint of the meaning of the Beatitudes. This is Christ's opportunity, therefore; he says in effect, This man wants sight; having given him sight I shall call attention to the work, I shall start a process of inquiry and thought in this man's mind at least; and who can tell but that an opened eye may mean an opened soul? let me, therefore, continued the blessed tender-hearted Messiah, begin where men will allow me to begin: they want their bodies healed; perhaps having felt my touch in that direction they may ask me to heal their souls. A medicine man has an infinite advantage over a gospel speaker, if he succeed in his work; and he is more likely to succeed, in some degree at least, than is the spiritual thinker and reformer. Who cares for a thought? There are men who have succeeded in allowing ten thousand jewel sentences to pass before them without seizing any one of them and keeping it as property. There are men who have seen perfect Niagaras of jewels rolling over the cataract who have never yet seized any one of them and taken it home as a treasure and a pledge of better things. There are souls on which—I will not say on whom, for I will not put grammar to base uses—all Shakespeare and Milton would be lost; they would as soon hear some street ballad with nothing in it but a running jingle, as the music of Eternity. But because it is the music of Eternity it can wait. Its opportunity will come. There are some enjoyments we get through; they perish in the using; they amuse, they excite, they please, they gratify for the moment, but there is no wearing in them, they cannot bear stress; they are good as the climate is good, as the immediate health of the possessor is good; but they abide not day and night, ever and ever, in the soul, friends that can charm darkness and assure continual day and peace.

Christ excited surprise by his works more than by his thoughts, yea more than by his personality. The neighbours said, Is not this he that sat and begged? They would have cared nothing about him if he had received a new idea into his soul. The moment he began to worship he was forgotten. As long as he was a curiosity men came around him and asked him questions, and endeavoured to provoke and exasperate him, so that he might deny the very hand that had touched his sightless eyeballs. Providence excites more attention than theology. Understand by " providence" great historic movements, the events of the day, the miracles of the transient hour. Men make their fortunes by telling lies about these things. They publish in the evening what has to be contradicted in the morning; they misreport everything they hear in order that they may work out some ulterior purpose, as a felon only can work on stealthy feet and with velveted fingers. There are men who can create wars, who can bring messages from foreign courts without the slightest authority for doing so, and who can send the business of the world into tremor and panic by a lie. Men are more sensitive about their money than about their souls, their thoughts, their hopes of future life, their aspirations after God. You could take away any man's sleep to-night by telling him that by to-morrow morning all his property will have fled away like a frightened bird. Jesus Christ excited attention by his miracles, his works, his wonderful signs and tokens. The people ran away and talked about them. One woman left her water-pot and fled away in the greatest haste to say that she had met a man who had told her all the things she ever did in her life. We never heard of any one running down the mountain to report a single beatitude. It is infinitely difficult to get attention to spiritual thinking and spiritual inspiration. A story will scatter an argument. Yet Jesus Christ worked on, doing the miracles, and hoping that some opportunity would occur through them of doing his greater work.

We find Christ enriching the Sabbath with holiest memories. This was a complaint that was made against him: "And it was the Sabbath Day when Jesus made the clay, and opened his eyes,"—and gave him two Sabbaths for one, a whole heaven in exchange for a little cold earth. How many men can gratefully say, "and it was the Sabbath Day when Jesus——" then comes the particular incident, the personal recollection, the tender memory, the blessed thought! Who may not make music out of this or turn it into a refrain charged with pathos? It was the Sabbath Day—when Jesus touched my heart, opened the eyes of my soul, gave me a new view of truth, charmed me out of my despondency, lifted me out of the darkness and set me on a hill bathed in morning light. It was the Sabbath Day when Jesus opened heaven, so that I saw him standing at the right hand of God. This is the kind of Sabbath that legislation can never protect, and that iniquity can never put down. What is your Sabbath? If it is only a set of hours, then it may be handled by men, it may be ordered to begin at a certain time and close at a certain hour; the law may step in and meddle with it; but if it be a Sabbath of real piety, of real sympathy with goodness, an opportunity of prayer, an opportunity for deeper study of the Word,—if it be a time in which great miracles were wrought in the soul, a time when tears were dried, and bonds relaxed, and heavy burdens were lifted from the trembling back, then there is no need to protect this Sabbath; the heart knows when it comes, the heart knows how long it continues, the heart knows with what worship to mark the blessed gift. Entrust the keeping of religion to the heart of the people. It cannot be written in a statute book; it cannot be a supplement to an Act of Parliament; it cannot be regulated by men who know nothing about it: religion, true, pure, before God and the Father, undefiled as untrodden snow—this must be in the keeping of the renewed heart; and this must be the fountain of the Church, its daily inspiration and nourishment, its establishment and its endowment; and if there be not this to begin with, to

build upon, and to give assurance of security, then all patronage
is burdensome, all protection is but violent weakness. Religion
is of the heart, or it has no assured existence in the world.
Could the restored blind ever forget the Sabbath Day? It came
back week by week, and there needed no church bell to call the
man to the renewal of that sacred memory; he understood the
time; it quieted him like a mother's blessing; it opened some
unsuspected door in the sky, and brought the glory upon him
from uncalculated quarters. Never profess to keep the Sabbath
if you do not keep it in reality. If you have nothing to keep,
say so, and be good plain infidels, definite and estimable liars.
Those men who have memories of the Sabbath Day ought to
embalm those memories, sanctify them by enlargement of worship,
by increasing publicity, and ought to make the name of Jesus
known wherever there is another blind man. Tell who healed
—his address—his name in full—abbreviate it not. Let it be,
Jesus Christ of Nazareth, a Man of sorrows and acquainted with
grief, the Man of the Cross, the Conqueror of the tomb.

Here we have Jesus Christ dividing the thoughts of men :—

" Therefore said some of the Pharisees, This man is not of God, because
he keepeth not the sabbath day. Others said, How can a man that is
a sinner do such miracles? And there was a division among them "
(ver. 16)—

as there always must be. He is so great as to occasion controversy. There are those who would trace controversy to some
mean origin. Probably they understand not the philosophy of
the case. There is so much controversy in theology because
there is so much truth in it. There is next to no controversy
about a gatepost; the judgments of men are tolerably unanimous
upon that subject. But given a great truth that is at once a
commandment, a revelation, an inspiration, a discipline, a comfort,
a promise, a friend on earth, a companion in death, a joy eternal;
and probably you will find a good deal of discussion about it.
Find in the controversies of Christendom the grandeur of Christianity. It is true that the grandeur of Christianity may have
been debased, but that is not the blame of Christianity itself;
it is a reproach upon those who have not discussed Christian
subjects in a Christian spirit. Jesus Christ has a philosophy

with which to meet the world. It is not a theory, a conjecture, but a philosophy,—that is to say, it is based upon reason, it fits the universe, it harmonises all things, it is equally strong at every point. There be conjectures many, as who should say about the soul, It may be this way, It may be that way, It may be some other way. But Jesus Christ never changes; he lays down an infinite philosophy, and says he himself is the Light of the world, the Bread sent down from heaven, the Saviour of all men, and that without truth there can be no peace, and without purity there can be no rest, and without pardon there can be no heaven, and that without the shedding of blood nothing that stains the heart can be taken out of that seat of life. If we have debased a philosophy into a sectarian theology, let the reproach rest upon ourselves. Jesus Christ loved the world, and offered it healing for its soul There is all the difference between a philosophy and an experiment even in earthly things. We see this in statesmanship. Some statesmen are philosophers; others are ratcatchers. Some statesmen grasp the whole situation, and they are so profoundly philosophical as to be above the touch of panic, above the debasement of fear; they deal with vitalities, with far-reaching issues, with the heart and soul of things; their balm is for the wound that is within. There are other fussy little constables that are going about arresting everybody, and making no end of uproar and tumult and various noise, and doing nothing else; they cannot understand a philosophical statesmanship. So there be reformers who are endeavouring to do a good deal of really useful work on the surface, but there is one Christ only who says to men, " Ye must be born again." That is no trimming of the surface, no renewal of the enamel under which men hide their hypocrisies; it is a birth, a rebirth, a new manhood, a mighty miracle of God the Holy Ghost.

Here is Christ creating personal witnesses. The man said, " Whether he be a sinner or no, I know not,"—I am not a metaphysician,—" one thing I know, that, whereas I was blind, now I see,"—I—the very man—myself: look at me: I am not speaking about some man a thousand miles off. There are some persons who are very much afraid of egotism—they are

the greatest egotists in the world. You find a man who writes
in the newspaper about some other man that he is "awfully
egotistic," and you may be sure he dipped his pen in the inkhorn
of his own infirmity. This man said—"I was blind, now I see."
There is a heroic egotism, there is a grateful egotism, there is an
egotism of pure sincerest thankfulness for blessings received,
and if a man should prove himself to be awfully humble by
speaking of himself in the plural number, let him do it. It is a
singular pride that gives a man the right of plurality, talking
about himself under the nomenclature "we." A suspicious
humility! Suspicious? Let that word be withdrawn, and another
take its place—a proved hypocrisy!

Christ completes his own work :—"Jesus heard that they had
cast him out; and when he had found him"—how did he happen
to go that way? For the same reason that he went the way in
the first instance. He knows all the roads—the little cross-road
that runs up to yonder farm; that little well-hedged path in
which you walk at eventide to meditate; the back way, the front
way: he knows all the roads to human dwellings and human
halting-places. "Jesus heard that they had cast him out; and
when he had found him, he said unto him, Dost thou believe
on the Son of God?" He had a right to ask the question. He
who has done good to the body has established a right to ask
about the soul. He may do so without affront or roughness.
The largeness of the first miracle is an introduction to any
mind that remembers the wonder that was done. Now we
come to the real pith and purpose of Jesus Christ's mission—
"Dost thou believe on the Son of God?" Was it not enough
that the man could see, that one of the senses had been brought
back again or had actually been created for the occasion? Was
it not enough that the man had a sound body? He had eyes,
and ears, and hands; he could smell the flowers, he could touch
the very bloom of creation—was it not enough? Jesus Christ
must needs go to the inner man, and ask the all-involving
question—"Dost thou believe on the Son of God?" O man, if
thou dost not so believe thou art not a man in the full sense of
the term; thou hast not yet begun to live. It is in this belief
we see and feel and realise our life. Without faith we cannot

fly, we cannot be in heaven, we cannot get past the black horrible tomb, we cannot cope with death and throw the monster in the last wrestle. "Dost thou believe on the Son of God? He answered and said, Who is he, Lord, that I might believe on him?" We know some men by their tone, by their touch. This man seemed to realise already in whose presence he was. We sometimes speak with men from whom we expect the veil to fall any moment, that we may see the revealed angel. Sometimes we feel in talking to certain men that if they went one sentence further they would go beyond the common boundary and speak to us from another world. They are magnetic men, inspired men, men of sympathy and enthusiasm; men who know the mystery of the over-soul, and touch all other men as by a miracle of sympathy. "Jesus said unto him, Thou hast both seen,"—how appropriately that word occurs in this interview—"Thou hast both seen"—to this use have thine eyes been put; thou hast seen the figure, the body, the open and patent reality—"and it is he that talketh with thee." Oh, sweetest words! He might have known who it was: never man spake like this man. What a voice! what subdued thunder! what tender sympathy! what suggestion! what music about to utter itself! "it is he that talketh with thee. And he said, Lord, I believe,"—and he stood there—a man!

PRAYER.

ALMIGHTY GOD, do thou always show us to what higher height we may climb, in what brighter light we may live our day, and what purer joy we may realise in all the wondrous ways of life. Forbid that we should look down; enable us evermore to look unto the hills, whence cometh our help. Thou hast made the high places of the earth as altars; men worship there, they begin in wonder, they end in praise. They say, Lo, God is here; we knew it not. This is none other than the house of God, though in the open air, and this is the gate of heaven, made without hands. If thou wilt show us these higher heights and brighter glories, and fill our souls with the Holy Ghost, we shall go on from one degree to another of quality and of life, until we shall hardly regard heaven itself as a great surprise. Enoch walked with God, and he was not: without sound or violence or rush of whirlwind, he passed into his proper place. May we so live that we shall not die. When we come to what men call death may we know that it is but an ascension, a rising into the land of morning and the city of peace. We have learned these things at Bethlehem, we have seen Christ's star, and have been led to worship him; we have seen Christ's Cross, and have been led to cry out, God be merciful to me a sinner! May the star and the Cross always be before the vision of our hearts, then there shall be no darkness, and there shall be no despair. We bless thee every day and every moment for the Cross: it is heaven's gift, it is the gate of heaven, it is the answer of God to himself, it is eternity revealed in all its higher thought and issues. God forbid that we should glory, save in the Cross of our Lord Jesus Christ. We are there now; our arms are round about it in the embrace of love; our eyes are fixed upon the Victim and the Priest, and we find in the Lamb of God the Saviour that we need. Help us to be wise readers of all things; may we read one another clearly, may we read all nature and gather learning, may we read thy Book, and see that it is all good books in one. Help us to read Providence, and redemption, and inner ministries, and all the mysteries which make up the secret of life, and may we so read as to be masters of Israel. Pity the heavy laden; give the weary rest. That is all they ask for; they ask, not for riches, but for rest. Oh sweet, sweet rest! Not sleep, but rest; not unconsciousness, but rest. Give them such rest as Christ only can give. Amen.

Chapter ix. 1-38.

INDISPUTABLE CURES.

" AND as Jesus passed by." The eighth chapter closed with the words " and so passed by "; the ninth chapter, therefore, had better open with the expression—" And as Jesus was passing by." Was this a casualty, something that happened, but might not have happened; quite an uncalculated and incalculable event in life; what we should denominate a chance, a singular circumstance, or a peculiar coincidence? Nothing of the kind. That is vain talk; it is not so written in the books of heaven. Everything is foreseen, foreknown; no revelation can be made to God, no surprise can be inflicted upon God. Wherever Jesus Christ went he went on purpose; whenever Jesus Christ was found in difficulty it was not because of love of difficulty, but because there was some battle to be fought, some extrication to be completed, some act of mercy to be done. Why do we not rest in his peace? Why do we not say, The enemy can only come the length of his chain? Why should we fret ourselves in any wise to do evil? If we are poor, God knows it, and before the last piece of bread is swallowed another loaf will be provided; we do not know how, but there is the bread. Why go into the metaphysics of the theology, or into the mystery of the providence? Bless the bread, and eat it as God's gift. Jesus Christ went that way because there was a man born blind who was awaiting his ministry. Jesus Christ did not happen one day in the eternal duration to see the earth, and then form the idea that he would go down and heal the little wandering rebel. He came on purpose. He knew the whole case from eternity; yea, from eternity he himself was slain on account of this very earth. He was not passing by on some kingly procession through the constellations, and happened to see this little leper. Nothing happens to God in that accidental, riotous, shapeless way. The very hairs of your head are all numbered. God knows how many sparrows there are, and not one of them falleth to the ground without your Father. If we could seize this truth and live it, there would be no infidels.

The incident is infinitely significant, because it brings Jesus Christ face to face with a vital and positive necessity. We have some six instances of blindness recorded in the New Testament, but this is the only case in which the man was born blind. We wanted to see our Saviour face to face with a case of this particular sort; we should have been uneasy, because the evidence would have been incomplete without it. The other men might only have been partially blind ; very little assistance might have been needed in their case just to open the eyelids and restore vision to the fulness of its function and utility. What would he do if he met a man who was born blind ? When did Jesus ever shrink from the occasion because it was great ? Did he not, to our poor senses, enlarge himself as the occasion expanded ? He overtopped every stature. He overflowed every channel ; he "is able to do exceeding abundantly above "—how the language quakes under the apostolic assurance and under the apostolic inability to say the whole thought that glows in his imagination and in his recollection. It is recorded that Vespasian once cured a man who was born blind ; but there soon arose an historian of the very nation of Vespasian who said that the lives of the emperors were studied lies. We are born blind. Every man who to-day sees is a man who was blind from his birth. It would appear, difficult as explanation may be, as if sin did not come upon mankind after birth, inflicting its disadvantages and its penalties ; we feel that we are born disabled and mutilated ; that we are, so to say, born dead. "You hath he quickened, who were dead in trespasses and sins." This we cannot understand. If any man should ask us to explain human depravity or original sin, we can no more explain it fully than we can explain the origin of evil. We must deal with facts. If any man was not born spiritually blind let him rise and say so. If any man was born wholly morally beautiful, stainless, pure, let us see him. The world awaits great sights, and will pay for great shows : what could be more attractive than the spectacle of a man who was born as good as God ? There is an argument of consciousness, as well as a declaration of revealed truth. Men can go into their own innermost heart, and settle this vital question for themselves.

Why is it so ? The answer is given, " That the works of God should be made manifest in him "—that God may have all the field to himself. God addresses himself to this disastrous condition of affairs, that he has only to deal with men who are born blind. If there are any cases of temporary blindness, accidental loss of vision, let the empirics get what fame and money they can from these. God addresses himself to the born blind, where he cannot have any help, where the work must be his alone, where the action must be sovereign, undivided, and the glory incommunicable. There are some things we can do, and some that it would be folly to attempt. We cannot light the sun, but we can go forth into the meadows when the sunshine glorifies them, or we can accept the light as an opportunity for service. We cannot control the sea; no man has the key of the Atlantic; the Pacific is not locked up in some man's iron safe; yet there are uses to which the sea may be put. We cannot hasten the summer. We complain of the late snow; we speak with significant tone and expression of face about the biting wind : why not change it ? There would be an opportunity for genius ? Why not attemper the wind? Why not melt the snow ? Why not kindle an artificial fire and warm the landscape ? Able men, with a peculiar bent of mind, can calculate an eclipse, but not one of them can create one. Let us see what we can do; for the moment we step beyond the line we become trespassers or spies : within our limit we are giants ; beyond it our iron muscles melt and our tones of thunder are choked into whispers of feebleness and humiliation. God himself alone will heal the born-blind. If any man is going to any other to have his born-blindness cured he will never see the light of day.

We see Jesus Christ working from the consciousness of his own authority : "As long as I am in the world, I am the Light of the world." That is not the word of a weak man ; that is not the word of a man who is going to fail in a miracle. Men ought to be very careful how they address themselves to great events, because they may fail in the very middle of the process, and their boasting will be reckoned against them, and will increase the completeness of their humiliation. But Omniscience need not calculate, for it knows all things ; Omnipotence need not pause, for it can do all things. He speaks himself God. Why did not some other man arise and say, "No; I equally with thyself am the light of the world"? These words cannot be interpreted on the theory that Jesus Christ was only an excellent young man. He would have destroyed his own excellence by his blasphemy. In the fourth verse he says, " I must work the works of him that sent me." It is singular to notice that all the best manuscripts have a change of grammar in this verse; for they read thus, according to the most established criticism : " We must work the works of him that sent me," as if there were co-operation, fellowship, in these processes that lie round about us as indicative of our sphere of labour. Some other manuscripts read, " We must work the works of him that sent us." But no manuscript ever changes the singularity of the fifth verse: " As long as I am in the world, I am the light of the world." What is this claim, being interpreted in plain terms ? It is this : All blind men are in my charge; they are my parishioners ; they are the souls that I must look after. If any men say they see, I have nothing to do with them. The Son of man is not come to call the righteous, but sinners to repentance: all the hungry people are mine ; make them sit down, the feast shall be spread, this miracle shall certainly be wrought. All the ignorant are mine ; enlarge the school, make it a night school as well as a day school, bring the most backward scholar in, yea, the man who is no scholar, not having seen one little letter in all his life ; he belongs to me by the right of ignorance." It is our weakness that gives us our right to pray ; it is our sin, rightly comprehended, that is our letter of introduction to the Cross. Righteous men, snow-covered men, away! ye have no invitation to Calvary. All the lost are mine. How he flushes with a consciousness of power when he is face to face with a case of indisputable necessity! He is as a warrior who sees the victory ere the battle is begun. This is precisely what the Church ought to do and ought to say. Here comes in the operation of the plural term : " We must work the works of him that sent us, while it is day." There may be both a singularity and a plurality of action in this divine beneficence. If we are called to partnership in the divine mystery of sacrifice, it is of God that we are called ; he permits us to glorify ourselves through suffering. The Church should say, My programme is this : wherever there is a blind man, I claim him ; a hungry man, he is mine ; a poor child, that child belongs to me ; a poor lost wandering one, that creature, homeless, destitute, friendless, is mine. If the Church could speak so, there would be nobody to speak against it. It is when the Church speaks metaphysics that the infidel has his turn. It is when the Church becomes inexplicably profound that the sceptic gets up a rival institution. That is his only chance. Let the Church talk polysyllables, and infidelity will have a field-day ; but let the Church do good, and talk sense, and claim the poor, the lost, the blind, the hungry, and insist upon having them, and treat them as nobody else can treat them ; then might the Church extend her space, because her hospitality is good, large as the need of life.

Jesus Christ next comes face to face with popular judgment. The miracle has been wrought : now comes the criticism that was passed upon it. " Is not this he that sat and begged ? " Otherwise, " Is not this he that sits and begs ? " " Some said, This is he : others said, He is like him : but he said, I am he." Thus we have the criticism of the world to deal with. We cannot have an honest judgment pronounced, because of infinite and unmanageable prejudices. We do not like to confess the supernatural. It pleases us, because we are sensuous and vulgar, to say that the house was actually built with our own hands ; the king likes to say, " Is not this great Babylon, that I have built ? " But when a thing is done without us, done whilst we are asleep or abroad, actually accomplished in all its fulness and utility without our being consulted, our pride does not like it. So we cast about upon the identity of the man, upon the reality of the work, upon the accuracy of the report ; we are prepared to say that by-and-by the whole thing will be explained upon another basis : instead of simply and directly accepting the miracle, and blessing God for his interposition in life. The Pharisees proceeded upon another line. They began by taking away the character of the man who had done the miracle. " This man is not of God, because he keepeth not the Sabbath day." They will start their argument from the doctrinal point. Why not start it from the beneficent side, and say—This man must be of God, because he heals other men ? Some minds cannot be taken away from the metaphysical centre. Only say the very words they say, and you are right, no matter if you pass all the blind men in creation seven times a week, and never speak to one of them. Other men will start their whole thinking from the beneficent side, and say, That Church must be good, there must be a blessed spirit in it, because she is always doing good, feeding the hungry, clothing the naked, teaching the ignorant, blessing the unblessed, and turning human houses into human homes. These latter are not metaphysical, therefore it is impossible for them to be orthodox; their words are too short for their doctrines to be right; they go too immediately to the mark to be really what they ought to be. The Pharisees denied his power; they did not believe concerning the man that he had been blind and that he had received his sight. Not only did they take away the character of the Healer, they took away the character of the healed, and practically they called that man a false witness. He had distinctly said, " I am he," but they would not believe it. What said they then, those pious men ? They said, " Give God the praise : we know that this man is a sinner." Often this passage is misunderstood. We should collate it with the words which were addressed to Achan, who had stolen the garment and the wedge. The leader said to him, " My son, give, I pray thee, glory to the Lord God of Israel, and make confession unto him ; " a form of objurgation which meant : Confess, speak the truth to God, forget all popular impression, and all selfish prejudice, and give God the praise ; stand up and confess that you have been telling lies, and be faithful to God. Thus we make hypocrisy.

Here we have Jesus Christ in the hands of an honest straight-forward man. What does the man say ? " I am he." That is what we will not say. "Let bygones be bygones " is our poor proverb, our mean and ungrateful policy. Once a man forgets the hole out of which he was dug, all his testimony evaporates. We are only right in our elevation in proportion as we remember the degradation out of which we came. Keep the pit in view ; keep the hole in sight ; then go up to heaven, and your foothold is perfectly secure. "I am he." We want the reformed drunkard to stand up and say, "I am a sober man, by the grace of our Lord Jesus Christ." We want the worldly man to say, " I am he " : once I was a miser, a worldling, a mere grubber in the earth, piling soil and stones, and glorying in the accumulation ; now I see that the world is nothing, that time is nothing, that the reality is to come; I seek a country out of sight : I am he. We do not want indirect witness; oblique testimony is of very little consequence in this great argument: produce the living man, the actual soul. But there were metaphysical difficulties about it. The Pharisees knew that the Healer was a sinner. The man said, " Whether he be a sinner or no, I know not "—I cannot go into those questions—" one thing I know, that, whereas I was blind, now I see." That settles the whole case. Produce one converted man, and Christ has won the battle. Has there ever been one genuine conversion? Do you know of any man who once was as bad as he could be, and who is now by the power of God endeavouring with an honest heart to lead a better life? That miracle is the miracle of God the Holy Ghost. But why seek these miracles in reports of other men? Why not be the miracle yourself? If you are building your theology upon anecdotes, your theology will be consumed and destroyed. If you are building your confidence upon the reality of your own consciousness and experience, no man can take away from you the testimony of your own heart. The man might have been born blind, but he certainly was not born dumb. He was a man who was on every side of the case too strong for his antagonists. He was a witty man; he had a shrewd, keen, piercing tongue; his voice no doubt was resilient, telling, carrying its emphasis right through to the last syllable and breath. "Why, herein," said he, "is a marvellous thing, that ye know not from whence he is, and yet he hath opened mine eyes." You ought to have known about a man of this quality; this is not a mere cipher that society could do without : "we know that God heareth not sinners"; that is acknowledged on every hand—"The prayer of the wicked is an abomination unto the Lord"—"but if any man be a worshipper of God, and doeth his will, him he heareth. Since the world began was it not heard that any man opened the eyes of one that was born blind. If this man were not of God, he could do nothing." So the man added to a fact an argument; but the fact came first, then the argument. Do not lie your facts on your arguments; lie your arguments on your facts, and then build up heaven-high.

How did the Pharisees answer him? As honest, straightforward men are always answered—they abused him. That is the trick of all time ; that is the unchangeable ingenuity of moral insanity. Sometimes it is done in Parliament ; it has been done in the Church ; but it is a continual fact in history—abuse the man you cannot answer. "They answered and said unto him, Thou wast altogether born in sins, and dost thou teach us ? " Impertinent fool ! Who art thou ? We had to call thy parents to identify thee, and now there is a mystery about thy birth ! "They cast him out." "Jesus heard that they had cast him out." When did he not hear that ? He has heard that about us all. He heard that they had cast him out ; he was watching the case ; he did not complete the miracle and then leave it ; he knew that certain issues would flow from this interposition. "And when he had found him,"—for he knew exactly where he was, and went immediately to the spot,—"he said unto him, Dost thou believe on the Son of God ? He answered and said, Who is he, Lord, that I might believe on him ? And Jesus said unto him, Thou hast both seen him,"—he first gives the faculty, then the vision ; the eye, then the landscape ; the power of sight, and then the beautiful picture,—"Thou hast both seen him, and it is he that talketh with thee ;" thou knowest his voice, thou hast not forgotten the music. "And he said, Lord, I believe," that is the sentence that makes history ; that is the declaration that indicates regeneration. "I believe" ; then there is no more selfishness, no more self-trust, but a continual outgoing towards the object of faith. This was clear. "And he worshipped him" —went out to him, in trust, and homage, and love. It is in vain that we say we believe Jesus if we do not worship him. This is the testimony we want to-day. This man is a model witness. He spoke for himself ; he went to the point ; he stood by the history ; he planted himself on the fact. "And they cast him out "—just what should and must happen to us if we would be really found of God. God will not find us until we are cast out. So long as we have one foot in the house of our respectability he does not know us, but as soon as we are "cast out" we are taken in, received, and welcomed.

PRAYER.

ALMIGHTY GOD, we bless thee for Jesus Christ as a Teacher sent from heaven. His words are words of life and power; they search the heart, they try the reins, of the children of men; they are sharper than a two-edged sword. We rejoice that thou dost enable us to submit ourselves to the searching criticism of Jesus Christ's word. We have been false to ourselves; we have concealed our true nature even from our own eyes; we have looked on the outside only; we have forgotten our inner life, the life of motive, of secret impulse, of purposes we dare not explain; we have looked only to our hand, when we ought to have examined the very life of our heart. But Jesus Christ, thy Son, doth not spare us; he searcheth us as with a candle; he kindleth upon us the flame of the Lord, and in the light of that fire he searches and tries us, and sees if there be any wicked way in us. We rejoice in the plainness and the vigour of his speech. We thank thee that Jesus Christ layeth the axe to the root of the tree; we bless thee for his radical teaching, for his going to the roots of all evil things, for his making the tree good that the fruit may be good, for his purifying the fountain that the stream may be pure. May we learn of Jesus Christ in these things, and seek to do thy will, not as man-pleasers, not with eye-service, but with all the simplicity of love, with all the strength of entire trust, honouring goodness for its own sake, and loving truth because it is the speech of God! Deliver us from all deceitfulness, all falsehood, all pretence, and enable us to serve thee in spirit and in truth; and out of a life based on godly sincerity, may there come works of love, pity, charity, and beneficence which shall bless all with whom we come in contact! Have mercy upon us wherein we have sinned. We have done the things we ought not to have done; we have left undone the things that we ought to have done. We accuse ourselves. If the surface has been right the motive has been wrong if our hand has been clean our heart has been leprous. Do thou wash us in the blood of Jesus Christ, shed for the sins of men,—the sacrificial blood which is our propitiation, our plea, and our answer before God! Let thine own people glory in the truth, feel its power, acknowledge its sovereignty, bless its giver. If there be before thee, or shall come within the influence of our word, any man who is hypocritical, who seeks to cover up his real state from the eye of society and from the eye of his own conscience, apply thy word to such as a flame of fire, finding its way into the secret chambers of the soul and lighting up the darkest recesses of the life. Make us glad in the Lord! In the world we have mortification, disappointment, tears, broken staves piercing our hands, much sorrow, great difficulty. But in God's house, on God's day, gathered as we are around God's book, surely thy children shall not plead in vain for the gladness which comes of thy presence! Amen.

Chapter x. 19.

"There was a division therefore again among the Jews for these sayings."

DIVISION OF OPINION.

THE last thing we should have expected about the sayings of Christ is division of opinion. Having proceeded forth and come from God, one would suppose that every word he spoke would be instantly recognised as divine, and accepted as wise and beneficent. This was not the case. Whenever Jesus Christ addressed men he provoked inquiry, controversy, sometimes direct and bitter hostility ; his ministers do not accomplish this miracle—at least, not intentionally. What do they love so much as that all men should instantly applaud them? We deprecate controversy in the Church. There would be better and larger church-life if there were more controversy amongst us, were that controversy conducted in a benign, patient, forbearing, and intelligent spirit. How was it that Jesus Christ provoked such division of opinion? Let us hear him for ourselves :—

"Verily, verily, I say unto you, He that entereth not by the door into the sheepfold, but climbeth up some other way, the same is a thief and a robber. But he that entereth in by the door is the shepherd of the sheep. To him the porter openeth ; and the sheep hear his voice : and he calleth his own sheep by name, and leadeth them out. And when he putteth forth his own sheep, he goeth before them, and the sheep follow him : for they know his voice. And a stranger will they not follow, but will flee from him : for they know not the voice of strangers " (vers. 1-5).

What could be more beautiful? This is the very beginning of poetry. What could be sweeter, lovelier? So the people imagined, for they took no heed of it :—

"This parable spake Jesus unto them: but they understood not what things they were which he spake unto them " (ver. 6).

He was making new clouds, and showing those clouds in new lights. They were very beautiful clouds, but they seemed to have no direct relation to human life. He was rewarded therefore with the applause of silence. There could not be any controversy about a beautiful parabolical statement like that. Nor was there any controversy. Then where is the point of anger? You find the explanation in verses 7-18, which must be read in their entirety.

"Then said Jesus unto them again, Verily, verily, I say unto you, I am the door of the sheep. All that ever came before me are thieves and robbers: but the sheep did not hear them. I am the door: by me if any man enter in, he shall be saved, and shall go in and out, and find pasture. The thief cometh not, but for to steal, and to kill, and to destroy: I am come that they might have life, and that they might have it more abundantly. I am the good Shepherd: the good Shepherd giveth his life for the sheep. But he that is an hireling, and not the shepherd, whose own the sheep are not, seeth the wolf coming, and leaveth the sheep, and fleeth: and the wolf catcheth them, and scattereth the sheep. The hireling fleeth, because he is an hireling, and careth not for the sheep. I am the good Shepherd, and know my sheep, and am known of mine. As the Father knoweth me, even so know I the Father: and I lay down my life for the sheep. And other sheep I have, which are not of this fold: them also I must bring, and they shall hear my voice; and there shall be one fold, and one shepherd. Therefore doth my Father love me, because I lay down my life, that I might take it again. No man taketh it from me, but I lay it down of myself. I have power to lay it down, and I have power to take it again. This commandment have I received of my Father."

How personal does the statement become now! It is no longer a parable; it is a direct personal application and claim. Now the tone of the assembly will change. Jesus talks about himself; instead of talking about some abstract or imaginary shepherd he speaks of himself as "the good Shepherd"; he says, "I am the Door," "I am the good Shepherd"; "The thief cometh not, but for to steal, and to kill, and to destroy: I am come that they might have life, and that they might have it more abundantly. . . . I am the good Shepherd, and know my sheep, and am known of mine"; "I lay down my life for the sheep." We shall have controversy now. The moment the preacher leaves the realm of parable and begins to talk personalities, himself or the people being the personal quantity, we shall have a new temper in the meeting. The original parable passed by as a gilded cloud might pass in the soft wind; now that the preacher begins to talk directly, now that he clothes himself with all the meaning of the parable, men will look at him from a different standpoint, and he who was once a dreamy, poetical fanatic, uttering very highly coloured and beautiful things, becomes a claimant of deity—a blasphemer, a man who is demented. That is the point of hostility through all time. When Christians make a personality of their Christianity they will have to fight for their standing-ground. Unhappily, some of them have learned the art of parable-making; but they have not learned the art of turning the parable to concrete uses. The people who listen to sermons love to have it so. There is nothing so much dreaded as a personal sermon; there is no congregation on earth that could not be scattered in an hour if the preacher were faithful. But what love of poetry there is! When a climax closes with a jingling rhyme, how beautiful it is! Clouds in infinite number and infinite variety—how charming the upward look! But let a man attack the crimes of his day, the false weights and the false measures, and the false politics, and the false philosophies, and the hypocrisies that are to be found in places of fashion, and in places of poverty as well, and he will soon have to go a-begging. Congregations have an infinite voracity for beautiful parables; they can eat up endless parables at a meal; but applications are not popular. Instantly a man would say, That was meant for me—that was a personal appeal. Certainly; and that is the only preaching worth hearing —a preaching that comes down to you and says, Thou art the man! But who can afford, financially, to preach so? It costs a Cross. O thou popular talker, applauded idol, with an infinite genius for bubble-making and bubble-gilding, thou shalt have a hot place in hell!

But the matter does not end with the preacher; it has a large application. Let any man stand up to-day in the market-place and say about himself, "I am a Christian," and he will have a hard time of it from that hour,—the meaning not being, I am a Christian believer, a believer in certain ecclesiastical dogmas and theological positions; but, I am a Christ-man—my badge a cross!—and he will not be invited again to that company. This is how we kill Christ. Let a man say, "I lay down my life for the world," and he will be avoided as a leper, or a madman. Yet this is what every Christian is called upon to do in his own degree and in his own way,—not in the degree and way in which Jesus Christ laid down his life for the sin of the world; we do not lay down our life as an expiation as he did, but we lay down our life as a service, a devotion, a consecration. No man ever yet said, "For me to live is Christ; this one thing I do: God forbid that I should glory, save in the Cross of Christ. I am determined not to know anything among you save Jesus Christ and him crucified," without driving the fashion, the pretension, and the hypocrisy of his day miles from the place of his feet. Let any man say, "I am a believer, I am a child of God, I embody, God helping me, all the truth of Christ's Cross," and no body of men will want to see him. If he could make blank verse he would be popular ; if he could speak parables without applications he would be invited evening after evening to delight the minds that never think. Who wonders, then, that Christ was in critical controversy ? Seize the meaning of this exposition, and keep vividly before the mind the fact that whilst Jesus Christ was speaking the parable the people were apparently quiet, even attentive; they did not know what he was saying, yet it sounded well: but the moment that Jesus Christ came to represent the parable in actual life and embodiment, the whole disposition of the auditory underwent a marked and undesirable change. Men are leaving the Church quickly now in many directions. Some are abbreviating the Church ; many have a small pocket edition of the Church—which they often forget to take with them. Why ? Because Christianity will, even in the most indifferent hands, give some indication of its anti-worldliness, anti-selfishness, its love of truth and fairness and justice and honour and progress. We do not like this. Sing some lullaby, O thou Son of man, and rock us to sleep by the plash of thy liquid music. Send no sword, no fire, no controversy : we want to be let alone.

The judgment that was pronounced upon Christ will be pronounced upon Christians also if they take Christ's course :—

"And many of them said, He hath a devil, and is mad ; why hear ye him ?" (ver. 20.)

That is popularity of the right sort. There is meaning in that. Have people really opposed to you in some desperate way, and you may convert them. Some men have never been so near crying bitterly as just after they have been cursing and swearing, and denying that they ever saw the man Christ Jesus. Indifference is eating out the life of the Church; tepid applause directed to so-called beautiful sentences is taking the place of enthusiasm that was willing to be burned and the sacrifice that counted the stake one of the thousand ways to heaven. No preacher can ever make himself felt for good throughout the whole world and through all time until he has been denominated mad. Trace the history of all the great pulpit reputations, to go no further, and you will find that there is not one of them that has not at the root of it a charge of insanity. Sometimes the charge is not made in definite terms; it is hinted at as eccentricity, peculiarity, love of notoriety, self-consciousness, and twenty other euphemisms, which, being correctly translated, mean—insanity. It was so with Christ; it was so with Paul; it was so with Wesley; it was so with Whitefield; it is so in many modern instances. On the other hand, there are more discriminating people now, as there were in the days of Christ, who say, "These are not the words of him that hath a devil. Can a devil open the eyes of the blind?" Ay, that is the question. The works must be our vindication; the good that is done must be our one argument.

So there was a division among the Jews, a sharp division; one party saying, "He hath a devil, and is mad"; another party saying, "These are not the words of him that hath a devil. Can a devil open the eyes of the blind?"—there is a wonderful background to this man's words; he does not reveal all his meaning at once; we come upon some of his significations suddenly; we are surprised by them; his words bear thinking about; they come into our dreaming, they follow us in the day-time, they whisper to us at unexpected hours and sometimes at inopportune seasons. No, this is a wonderful talker; never man spake like this man; and I know that he opened the eyes of one who was born blind. So Christianity must stand upon its effects. The men who have realised those effects must be bold enough—that is to say, must be grateful enough—to say that they have seen Jesus, and have learned of him.

This controversy led to a demand that appears to be very simple on the surface :—

"Then came the Jews round about him, and said unto him, How long

dost thou make us to doubt? If thou be the Christ, tell us plainly"
(ver. 24).

What is "plainly"?   There are persons who think that all
human conversation is divisible into Yes and No : the lawyers
are addicted to that view of human intercourse. What is plainly ?
If the question were, Are you going east or west? a plain answer
could be returned ; if the question were, Did you put out the
right hand or the left ? there could be no difficulty in replying
plainly : but the questions that gather around the name of Christ,
that are summed up in his marvellous character, are not questions
that admit of easy, plain, superficial, and conclusive answers.
We must live with Christ to know him ; we must love him to
understand anything he says. To have said plainly, " I am the
Christ," would have been to trifle with the infinity of his
personality, his sovereignty, and his claim. Great subjects
cannot be dealt with in this particular way, each wrapped up,
and put on a place by itself, and appraised in plain figures.
You cannot snap off an inch or two of infinity and say, That is
a sample of it. Infinity has no samples. You cannot snip three
inches out of the wind and say, This is a sample of the tempest.
As soon might you take one little stone out of a palace and say,
This will give you an idea of the royal residence. Christianity
is a whole ; Christ is Three-in-One, One-in-Three ; a contradiction
in number ; he is here, and not here ; he is a root out of dry
ground, he is a plant of renown. Herein is the difficulty of what
is called plain preaching. All plain preaching may be suspected ;
all preaching that goes from one to two, and from two to three,
as if they included the universe, is mischievous. The plainer the
preaching the more suggestive will it be of infinity. There will
be plain points ; there must be plain points, plain charges, plain
declarations of divine love, plain welcomes to Christ's heart;
but even these shall be so spoken as to be felt to be connected
with eternity. The atmosphere of the discourse is an important
quantity in the estimate of its value. There is perspective as
well as straight line, and unless we have the perspective as well
as the straight course we shall miss the wondrous power that is
of the nature of spirituality. Jesus Christ spoke plainly enough.
The Jews never asked Jesus Christ clearly to tell them their duty.
We want plainness at the wrong point. When men come to

Christ and say, Lord, what shall   do with these scales, they
are unequal? he says, Burn them.   There is no mistake about
that answer.   Lord, what shall I do, for I am addicted to drunkenness? Give up your wine and strong drink, and never touch them
more.   That answer could not be well improved in plainness and
directness.

Who asks Christ to be plain about duty?   Who does not ask
him to be confidential about speculation, imagination, and things
eternal, without the being plain about Christian practice and
discipline?   Ask for plainness at the right point, and Christ will
accommodate you : ask him for another miracle, and he will turn
round upon you and leave you in the darkness of sevenfold night.
The mystery of Christianity is in its infinity.   It is because it is
so great that it cannot be reduced to the comprehension of men
who have no heart for its study.   Hence we say that Jesus Christ
told the people distinctly that they could not understand him
because they were not of his sheep—" I told you, and ye believed
not."   They had a plain answer, and did not understand it to be
plain.   They kept it outside of them, and therefore they could
not comprehend it.   There are many persons coming to Christ
when they understand all about him, when they can meet him
upon equal terms, and say they completely comprehend all his
meaning, and now they have no objection to admit him to their
society.   That is not the way of salvation.   Many men are going
to believe the Bible when they know who wrote it, when it was
written, who signed it, who has seen the manuscripts, where is
the Hebrew text of the Old Testament, where is the original copy
of the Greek New Testament, where are the signatures of the
prophets and the apostles,—then they will come in.   It is much
like men saying, regarding an empty house when they are in
search of a dwelling, Who built that house? who planned it?
where is the signature of the architect? name the forest where
the wood grew.   Other people say, Well, with regard to these
questions, they are very important, no doubt ; at the same time
we are going into this house, and we will find these things out
from the inside.   They are the wise men.   Come into the Bible ;
begin where you can ; take up such portions of it as are applicable
to your own case ; find your way from point to point ; and the

time will come when you will care nothing about Hebrew manuscripts and Greek autographs. You will say, This is none other than the house of God and the gate of heaven : this book talks to me, knows me, loves me ; I cannot do without it now. There are two ways of coming to the book or of coming to Jesus Christ : one the outside way that will do nothing until certain long lists of questions are answered one by one ; and the other by coming into the offered light and the offered blessing, and beginning where we can, and going on little by little, until we feel the inspiration of the book, until we get into touch with the heart of Christ, and thus become enabled to say, when he asks us, Who am I ? Thou art the Christ of God. Let us beware of terminating with mere parables ; let us be thankful to the men who have sacrificed themselves for our spiritual advantage ; let us bless God for such men as Paul, to whom we can do no favour that he might lay down what he knew of the riches of the knowledge and wisdom of God for our using. Let us also hold in reverent and grateful remembrance the noble men who died for their faith that they might show us how to live. Christians can get through the world very easily by being only nominal professors, by loving parables and poetry, blank verse and rhyme ; we can get through to the other end without much ado : but the other end is not worth going to. What we have to do as Christians is to begin where Christ began, walk where Christ walked, follow him in all things, take up his Cross daily ; practise the mysterious art of self-denial, and thus through the Cross find our way to the crown. Jesus calls us in that direction. This would seem to be an age of intermission of Christian inspiration, but Christian inspiration is not therefore dead. There are times when the tide ebbs, and men say in ignorance, The sea is fleeing away : but the sea recedes only that it may flow in fulness of power upon the shore. So it is with Christian influence. To-day is the ebb time. To-day men are giving up Christian thinking and Christian worship to a large extent. To-day men are making a name stand for a reality, a profession is taking the place of a sacrifice. But this is only a question of time. He will come whose right it is. He will overturn, overturn, overturn ; and after devastation he will bring in paradise and summer and peace.

Chapter x. 41.

"John did no miracle."

LIFE WITHOUT MIRACLES.

[AN OUTLINE.]

LET us inquire how far it is possible to build up a really good and strong character without doing any works that are miraculous, romantic, or merely sensational. The life of John the Baptist furnishes us with an admirable study upon this subject. "Among them that are born of women there hath not risen a greater than John the Baptist"; yet John did no miracle. He was "a burning and a shining light"; yet John did no miracle. "He was a prophet, yea," etc.; yet John did no miracle. "All that John spake of this man is true"; yet John did no miracle. Now, how far is it possible for us to win the Master's approbation, and to come into a great estate of honour and joy, without having any power in things miraculous? Some of us may think we are living a monotonous and profitless sort of life, remarkable for nothing but sameness and insipidity; morning, noon, night coming round and round without our ever doing anything that strikes observers with amazement; always working in the same place, always surrounded by the same faces, always tethered by the same short string. If I can send one word of comfort into any heart that is mourning the narrowness of its sphere and the monotony of its pursuits, my object will be answered. Human life needs some such cheering. No doubt many people are without ambition or aspiration, and they need no help; but there are others to whom a word of interpretation and comfort will be as refreshing water in the tiresome journey of commonplace life. Some of us, too, seem always on the very point of really doing something worth doing. It seems as if a miracle were the very next thing to be done, and that we only miss the doing of it by a hair's breadth.

We shall get some help in the direction of our study if we answer this question—Upon what kind of life did Jesus Christ set the seal of his blessing?

(1) He specially blessed the spirit and ministry of John the Baptist; and yet John did no miracle: (*a*) It is possible to be true; (*b*) courageous; (*c*) self-controlled; (*d*) illustrious; and yet to do no miracle.

(2) That this approval was in no sense exceptional is made plain by other parts of Jesus Christ's recognition of man's life and work: (*a*) Seventy returned; (*b*) cup of cold water; (*c*) employment of talents.

All this is made the clearer by a case on the other side—"In thy name done many wonderful works," etc.

When did Jesus Christ ever set a man in higher honour in his kingdom simply because the man was a worker of miracles?

What, then, are the qualities which God most esteems in us? "A meek and a quiet spirit, which in the sight," etc. "The Lord loveth a cheerful giver," etc.

Nowhere is the brilliant man singled out, etc. "Many that are first," etc.

(1) A word to the poor; (2) women; (3) nobodies.

What doth the Lord thy God require of thee? Miracles? "To do justly," etc. Covet earnestly the best gifts, and yet charity above all!

Chapter xi.

CHRISTIANITY IN FAMILIES.

"Now a certain man was sick, named Lazarus, of Bethany, the town of Mary and her sister Martha" (ver. 1).

W E can sometimes better understand Jesus Christ's character and spirit when they are brought to bear upon a comparatively small space, than when they are so enlarged as to embrace the universe. Let us, then, study the relationship which Jesus Christ appeared to sustain to this family at Bethany. Let us see how Jesus Christ stands in relation to this family. From what we can learn of his relationship to one household, we may be able to infer something of the spirit in which he administers the affairs of the larger family of mankind. The family was in peculiar circumstances, as we gather from the third verse—

"Therefore his sisters sent unto him, saying, Lord, behold, he whom thou lovest is sick."

The family is in distress, and the family, in the midst of its pain and sorrow, sends for Jesus Christ, the one Healer and eternal Friend. There is something very pathetic as well as most instructive in the message which is thus delivered: "Behold, he whom thou lovest is sick." It is no stranger's name that is spoken to Jesus Christ. I am not sure that the name of Lazarus was pronounced at all. Sometimes it is better simply to indicate the character, and to leave the proper name out of the question ltogether. The reverence of the man's disposition will identify him at once. So the sisters, gathering up all the affection and desires which Lazarus entertained towards the Son of God, described their brother as "He whom thou lovest." Sometimes people do not send unto Jesus Christ until they are sick. It would appear, from the very construction of this message, that Jesus Christ was on familiar terms with the family at Bethany

227

___

long before the event described in this verse occurred. Jesus Christ often has a stranger's name handed to him. He has, as it were, to look at the card again and again, and to say—(if I may attribute to him aught of the limitation of human ignorance) —" Who is this ? I have not seen this name before. Who calls upon me now ?" And he finds that it is a worn-out old life ; a shattered manhood, which being unable longer to enjoy the things of time and sense, begs an interview with One who is supposed to have healing and comfort at his disposal. It was not so in this case : " He whom thou lovest is sick. The man thou knowest so well, to whom thou hast spoken so many tender words, whose spirit is dear to thee, lies now at the very gate of death." How is it going to be in our own case ? Are we going to defer our religion until the end of our life, and call in Jesus Christ when we have darkened the windows, and have made up our minds that it is a case of extremity ? or, are we going at the very commencement of our life to say, "Now, in the very midst of sunshine and prosperity and great progress, join us, O Son of God, and be our companion during the remainder of our days"? Our years are going ; they seem to steal away, they fly off, and if some of us be not very prompt in our dealings, behold we shall be old men presently, and our great account to the Living One will yet be to determine! My hope is, that in studying a subject of this kind—so tender and so pathetic, and so calculated to appeal to the best sensibilities of our nature—some will yield themselves to Jesus the Saviour of families, the Healer of the sick, the Redeemer of the world !

Look at the words again, for they are full of meaning as the grape is full of juice. "He whom thou lovest is sick." Would the text not have read much better had it been worded thus : Lord, "He whom thou abhorrest is sick ; he who has offended thy law and violated thy commandments and dishonoured thy spirit is in the grip of death " ? We think there would have been a natural rhythm in a sentence of that kind. Yet the text reads just contrariwise, "Lord, he whom thou lovest is sick,"—the man whose eyes ought to have stood out with fatness, upon whose cheek ought to have been the ruddiness of health, whose blood ought to have been without taint or stain, because of his

love of them and their love of him. This, however, is God's way
with men. "Whom the Lord loveth he chasteneth, and scourgeth
every son whom he receiveth." If ye endure chastening, God
dealeth with you as with sons; for what son is he whom the
father chasteneth not? "Now no affliction for the present
seemeth to be joyous but grievous; nevertheless, afterward it
yieldeth the peaceable fruit of righteousness unto them which are
exercised thereby." One can understand a bad man rejoicing
over this; pointing out the case with a finger of suspicion and
scorn, and saying, as he points it out, " See, I should have thought
that if any man loved Jesus Christ he would have been spared
the ills of this life! Behold, the loved one is afflicted like other
men, and he who honours the name of Christ pines and dies like
the blackest atheist amongst us." Men who only see a little of
the case may talk in that way. Men who look at the outside
only have a very short way to take in order to get at such conclusions as please their own imperfectly trained judgments.
When, however, we come to look at circumferences rather than
at mere points, to put to-day and to-morrow and the next day
together, and to sphere off divine movement and divine purpose,
we come to modify some of our conclusions, and to find that
some of our reasonings have been immoral; and we have, with
prostration of heart, to cry to God to pardon inferences we have
falsely drawn regarding his spirit and his government. Do you
know good men who are sick? Can you point to your friend in
a given street in London or elsewhere, and say of him, "That
man is a Christian; yet everything he touches seems to go to ashes
at once"? Are you able to point out case after case of good
men, who are always in the dust, who have their breath half
taken from them and who are weary of this life? Are you sometimes inclined to jeer over them, to talk flippantly about their
piety, and to trace their sufferings to their religion? Beware
what you are doing; be careful how you draw your inferences.
If we lived altogether upon the space of a finger-nail, you might
have some right to your conclusions; because a sense of the
divine presence in the soul does keep men back from certain
kinds of prosperity. Some of us might have been in better health
if we could have trifled with our spirits more. Some men might
have been riding in their carriages if they had shut their eyes

when they saw wrong, instead of turning aside that they might
escape the temptations of the evil one.   I repeat, therefore, if the
whole case rested upon the space of a finger-nail, some of your
conclusions might be right enough.   But to time add eternity, to
man add God, and wait, for the time of drawing conclusions is
not yet.   It may be that weakness will turn out to be the highest
strength, and some kinds of poverty may prove to be the only
enduring wealth.   I only ask for a pause; I only beg that men
be not rash.   We shall have time, by-and-by, to say how things
have been managed.   The people in Christ's day, who waited
and saw his processes and kept themselves in restraint until those
processes were completed, said in a shout, in a song, at last,
" He hath done all things well ! "   It shall be so with those who
keep a strong and loving faith constantly in exercise in the Son
of God.   Let us, however, proceed to see how Jesus Christ seems
to dally with this case.   But before doing so, we shall find one
utterance of his that ought to be engraven upon every memory

"When Jesus heard that, he said, This sickness is not unto death, but for
the glory of God, that the Son of God might be glorified thereby " (ver. 4).

Is it not truly beautiful to find that Jesus Christ knows the
purpose of every event in our individual and family life ?   Many
a messenger of providence comes to our door, and we are at a
loss to see what that messenger signifies.   Is it not a comfort to
the heart to believe that there is One who knows why he caused
our door to be opened, that the strange, mysterious, and oftentimes unwelcome visitor might be admitted ?   Jesus knew exactly
why the sickness had fallen upon Lazarus.   "This sickness is
not unto death."   It is not that death may finish the process that
sin began in the history of mankind.   But you shall see that in
this case circumstances shall so conspire that the result of the
whole will be an additional glory given to the Lord of Hosts and
to his Son Jesus Christ.   The earth and the heavens work
together.   Things below and things above come into strange union
and combinations, and sometimes things have to be broken down
that they may be lifted up.   Oftentimes, indeed, God comes to
us along a path which is strewn with wrecks, with blighted
hopes, with thrown-down towers, and plans and projects of
divers kinds; and we say when the wind rages very highly, and

when things are toppled over into confusion, " Behold, this is
death ! "—not knowing that in this way, strange though it may
appear beyond all other mystery, God is working a way upon
which his own foot shall pass. Is there not joy, peculiar and
oftentimes intense, in the companionship of a man who has the
gift of interpretation ? Is it nothing to have at hand a man who
can tell you what your dream means, what your pains signify,
and what that great loss, which has so impoverished you, was
intended to speak to your heart ? There are some men amongst
us who are gifted with the faculty, if I may so call it, of interpreting things. When they come into a family afflicted and
deserted, they can speak so wisely and so sweetly about the
affair, as if God had passed down the key of the lock to them and
said, " Take that ; turn it just so, and behold, you will open it,
and bring light and comfort to those who sit in darkness and
captivity." If it be so amongst ourselves ; if a friend can revive
us by suggesting a reasonable interpretation of certain things in
our life ; what of him who knows the secret of God, who holds
that secret in his own right hand, and who can whisper to us
amid all suffering and all loss, " The meaning of this, my
brother, is that God intends to work out in your life a higher
refinement and a nobler strength, a more dignified patience, and
to perfect you by trial severe as fire " ? This is what Jesus Christ
does for men. He tells them the purpose of their sickness, he
tells them the meaning of the brevity of time ; he explains to
them how it is that they have only a certain degree of strength,
and why they are kept short of a higher degree still. He interprets
things ; he gives them their right meanings ; he stops men from
imperfect, and especially from godless, conclusions. In this way
he enriches our life continually. I have taken many a hard case
to him. There is not a man who has had harder cases to deal
with in life than I have had to encounter ; and this I know—
and no man shall take away my boasting from me or my joy—
that not until I have gone and told Jesus, and explained the
thing from my point of view to him, has there come into my
understanding and my heart such a sense of the rightness of
things as has comforted me, and lifted up my soul from the midst
of the lions that had assailed it and the darkness that was
gathered around it. It is a great thing, amid misinterpretations,

and prayerlessness, and worldliness, to hear a man say that, in plain simple English, who affixes his own signature to it, and does not send men into dusty libraries to exhume antiquities to prove it, but who says in his own proper person, "I have received from communion with the Son of God interpretations of sickness and loss and hardship and loneliness and bitterness, which have cheered me and made me young again ; and what I have received I wish to give,—having found out a well-head in the wilderness, I wish to tell every thirsty traveller about it. I do not wish, such is the effect of the living water upon a man, to run away and say, I shall keep the secret to myself, for I may want that well again ! Contrariwise, I would proclaim that there is in Christ Jesus water for us all to quench the burning thirst of the life, to satisfy the necessities of the spirit and the understanding and the heart." The more we drink it, the more there seems to be. More than that. I wish to say, in English equally simple and direct, that every other well is poisoned, every other well is shallow, and every other invitation is a lie !

"Now Jesus loved Martha, and her sister, and Lazarus" (ver. 5).

Every member of the family,—there was nobody shivering in the cold outside who was not embraced in this all-redeeming and all-comforting love. There are sad hearts in many homes,—because there is one wanting who ought to be in the company ; one young man not in the household who ought to be there,—a very genial, open-hearted, kind, noble young man in some aspects, but drawn off by the insidious tempter, and made corrupt and evil-minded ; so much so, that it would not be safe to admit him into the presence of little children, or into the presence of persons who have any sense of purity or right. Nothing is said about him, but the heart goes out after him, sadly, moaningly, and would gladly bring him back again. Do we know a family that is complete in Jesus ? We may know more than one such—a family in which we find the father and the mother, and all the children, loving the same Saviour and loved of the same Christ ! Is there any picture on earth to be compared with that for simplicity, for beauty, for pathos, and for all the qualities that touch the deepest sensibilities of our nature ? Alas, there are other families that are not complete, and you are the absentee, perhaps! I call you home. Your father waits, and your mother and your sisters, and you only are absent, and they cannot be at rest until you come in. They have joy—great joy, that wells over the very sides of their hearts; but what an addition to their joy would come from the fact that you have said, openly and firmly, "I will arise and go to my Father, and will say unto him, Father, I have sinned!" The joy, which is now very deep and intense, would then be completed,—nought would excel it but the rapture of heaven itself!

" Now Jesus loved Martha, and her sister, and Lazarus ;" and they were all different. Martha was busy, anxious, fretful, industrious, a housewife from her birth, elect to have the control of household affairs ; her sister was quiet and thoughtful, contemplative, pensive, silent ; and Lazarus represented another side of human character altogether. Jesus loved them all. Oh, wondrous love ! Our artificial lights can only give a little relief to the darkness of particular places ; but the great sun in the heavens lightens, with impartial glory, the palace and the cot, the great landscape and the poor man's little garden,—it enters every garret and window, as well as penetrates all the sumptuousness of palaces. It is even so with the love of Christ. Some of us can only love particular kinds of character. We feel that we must draw a line when certain persons come into connection with us, for we really cannot understand them, or appreciate them, and therefore our love becomes cramped, and says, " I cannot go any farther on." But Jesus can love us all. He knoweth our frame, he remembereth that we are but dust ; he understands our peculiarities ; he knows through what processes we have passed—processes that have roughened us and made us unlovely ; processes that have gone far to break down our very spirit. Yet he sees what is left in us, and with impartial benediction he would bless us all. As the great firmament holds the mighty sun and the tiny asteroid, so that greater heart of Christ folds in its infinite embrace all mankind. Why, then, should one of us—the obscurest, the poorest, the roughest, the worst—stand back, as though he had no God, as though his name had not been thought of when Calvary was made the centre of the universe !

"When he had heard therefore that he was sick, he abode two days still in the same place where he was" (ver. 6).

This is an aspect of the divine government which we have great difficulty in understanding. Would not the sentence have read much better thus: "When Jesus had heard that Lazarus was sick, though he had a great deal of very urgent business on hand, yet he left the whole instantaneously, and sped to Bethany as quickly as he could possibly proceed"? There, we should have said, is the outworking of love; that is precisely how affection shows its genuineness and its depth. Yet we read that Jesus Christ, having heard that his loved friend was sick, remained two days longer in the very place where he received the intelligence. God does appear sometimes to be slow in his movements. Our impatience cries for him, as he sits still, as if we were but noisy children, not knowing what we were talking about. We say, "Speak to us, Lord, or it will be too late," because we measure time by a local standard ; we call it astronomical time— time taken from the sun ;—but God takes his times from something higher than our standards. We now and again wonder, and sometimes our reverence threatens to break down in the process of our wondering, that God does not make more haste than he appears. to do. At such times there comes in this solemn, majestic sound, "A thousand years are in thy sight but as one day, and one day as a thousand years !" A sentence which means that God does not measure himself or his movements by our idea of time. He takes the beat of his step from another standard altogether, and at last he will show that he is not slack concerning his promises, as some men count slackness. Is God delaying? With whom is he delaying? "He is delaying with me," says some poor, fainting heart. Do I doubt it? Far from it. Has he not delayed with myself many a time? Do I not want him now, instantaneously, to come down to my relief? I do. Yet he sits yonder above the sun and stars, away on that great burning effulgent throne, and my prayers seem unable to hasten him in any one movement. I own it; I do not attempt to modify it ; I accept it as a solemn and instructive fact. What then? This: Wherever I have been privileged to see anything of the meaning of his delay, I have always found that he has been delaying not for his benefit but for ours ; and that when he does come he will bring with him some greater blessing than we had ventured either to hope or expect. Let God be Judge. There can be but one Lord. The child is impatient with you because you do not move so actively as he would like you to move; but you, in your maturer wisdom and deeper love, are acting upon a principle which he cannot understand; and the child will come to know and learn that any impatience on your part, equal to his own, would mean the destruction of your family and the utter ruin of your peace. You must pause; you must be restful; you must be tranquil when others would like to see you excited. You must hasten slowly in some things, for your intent is to complete your work and rest it upon a basis which cannot easily be shaken. There are many mysteries about this side of the divine government. There are mysteries about every side of the divine administration, and we glory in this mystery. To-morrow is the mystery of to-day; night is the mystery of noon-tide; immortality is the mystery of death; heaven is the mystery of earth. I would not care to live if all mystery were taken away. It is in the exercise of a deep, tender, loving faith in the Unseen and the Unlimited that I find joy which animates my suffering and wounded heart! In the twentieth verse we reach the point at which Martha and Jesus meet:—

"Then Martha, as soon as she heard that Jesus was coming, went and met him: but Mary sat still in the house."

They both loved the Saviour. Martha went out; Mary remained at home. Such is the difference of method by which we show our quality and our nature. Martha was restless, unquiet, anxious; she found consolation in activity; so long as she could be moving about she felt a kind of relief in the very change of position. Mary sat still; she found rest in wonder, in contemplation, in silent sorrow; if you moved her you discomforted and disquieted her. So do not let us say that Martha was more anxious about Lazarus than Mary was, or that Mary had a deeper love than Martha. We are made differently. We are the same, yet we are not the same. We may be born in the same house, and so far as difference of character is concerned we might have been born in different zones. What then? Let us be gentle in our judgment of one another. Do not let Martha, as she hastens fretfully down the road, say, "Mary does not love her brother so much as I do, or she could not sit still as she is now doing,—she would come out and meet the Master." And do not let Mary say, "Oh, that fretful, restless, anxious sister of mine, there is no peace wherever she is! If she had more piety she would have more composure." Nothing of the kind. We are made, I repeat, differently. It is difficult to understand one another. Blessed be God, we can get enough of mutual appreciation, if we be in Christ Jesus, to enable us to take the most favourable view of circumstances and of movements which we cannot fully understand.

"Then said Martha unto Jesus, Lord, if thou hadst been here, my brother had not died" (ver. 21).

It is just the speech that Martha would make. We find—so true is it that extremes meet—that when Jesus came into the house Mary made precisely the same speech to him. It was a speech of love, yet of ignorance. It was a speech of trust, and yet a speech that arose from the want of a right understanding of divine power and divine relationship. Hear the words: "If thou hadst been here." She limited the Holy One of Israel; she assigned locality to the Saviour. As yet she had not entered into the meaning of the words, "Lo, I am with you always!" Nor do I wonder at her not doing so. The full revelation of the Spirit had not been given; the entire purpose of the scheme of mediation had not been revealed and applied. Martha did just what we ourselves, under similar circumstances, would have done. What have we now to do? To learn this: That presence is not bodily; that presence is not formal; that the Son of God is here, though I see him not. "For wherever two or three are gathered together in my name, there am I." May two or three not be gathered together in his name in the house of affliction? Yea, verily so. The afflicted ones are standing by the bed-side, and they are one in their earnest desire that Christ would interpose— and Christ is there, if the desire arise from a penitent and believing heart. Then why does he not heal the sick one? Healing! Knowest thou what thou sayest when that word escapes thy tongue? What is healing? He is healed who dies. He who lives is patched up for a moment. Death is healing. We do so suffer by the narrowness of our interpretations. We put such small meanings upon words. When your dear little child was breathing its last you said, "Oh, that it might be healed!" And when the last breath went out of it, it was healed! You said, "Dead"; the angels said, "Born." You said,—

> "It was our home's undoing,
> Oh, the ruin!"

Jesus said, "Let the little ones come unto me." "Healed! Plagued, you mean; more keenly tried, you mean; tossed about more violently in the world, you mean." They are healed whom he takes. "They shall hunger no more, neither thirst any more; neither shall the sun light on them, nor any heat; and the Lamb that is in the midst of the throne shall feed them, and lead them unto living fountains of water; and God shall wipe away all tears from their eyes."

"If thou hadst been here." This was an expression on the part of Martha that arose from great love, great trust, but void of a true understanding of the meaning of Christ's presence. What, then, have we to preach? This. We shall all die! Do not let us postpone the intimation of our need of the Son of God until we are so faint that we can only receive him at the side of our death-bed. Do let us be more decent, more courteous, more civil. We shall all die! That is a fact that men have never been able to reason out of human history. If they could come to me and say, "We will guarantee you shall never die, you shall always be as you are—young and strong and active and prosperous," then I might incline an ear to their reasonings more deferentially than I am disposed to do at present. But when they are talking to me against religion and against the deeper life, against faith and spiritual love and service of the unseen, what do I behold? Oh! this: Over their shoulder, a grim, ghastly spectre called Death! Do not let us postpone our prayers until Death knocks at the door, because when he knocks we cannot send him away and tell him to come another time. "Now is the accepted time; behold, now is the day of salvation."

Chapter xi.

"IF."

IN selecting this word we are struck with the frequency of its occurrence in this chapter. This would seem to be the field in which the word grows. Some soils suit certain plants; this soil would seem to suit the word "if" admirably. I know not of any other chapter in which it occurs so frequently, so variously, and so instructively. It is not legitimate to choose the word "if" for a text if the meaning be to hang upon it whatever may first occur to an unlicensed imagination. The word "if" is not fantastically chosen, but is chosen from the point of view of an expositor. It is not a little word to be trifled with, a cherry-stone to have an image engraved upon it; it is a keyword, solemn, indicative of serious thinking, and of the philosophies of life. Keep within the bounds of this chapter, and say if this be not so. The word is used by everybody—by Jesus, by the disciples, by Martha, by Mary, and by the chief priests and the Pharisees.

First of all, here is the "if" of wisdom :—

"Jesus answered, . . . If any man walk in the day, he stumbleth not, because he seeth the light of this world " (ver. 9).

From Jesus himself we first receive the word. Then he gives us an instance of the "if" of otherwise unimaginable folly :—

"But if a man walk in the night, he stumbleth, because there is no light in him " (ver. 10).

But will any man be such a fool as to walk in the night when he cannot see his own hand before him? Is not this a dream bordering upon romance, and not far away from insanity? No man will walk in the night. So we should certainly have said ; but Jesus Christ points to a different possibility. Who can tell the limits of insanity? Who knows the boundaries within which

238

the evil heart exercises itself in all iniquity ? There are men
that love the darkness. They wait for it as you would linger for
a chosen companion. They look round and say, Would the
darkness were here! They cannot stir but in the darkness ;
they are not children of the light or of the day or of the morning
or of the summer ; but owls and bats—evil men that work in
the darkness with faithful industry. The word " if" as thus used
is not indicative of many of those possible actions which are
usually associated with the term : the Lord is laying down a
great philosophy of work ; he is indicating that there are times
and seasons for labour, and that not only is work to be done, but
done at the proper time—the light for labour, the darkness for
rest. " The light he called Day, and the darkness he called
Night ;" and each has its needful opportunity that will not
exchange places. If an irregularity is set up in nature, so that
night becomes day, until that irregularity has become custom it
disturbs and upsets, and creates painful tumult.

Then here is the " if " of human hope shadowed by fear :—
" Then said his disciples, Lord, if he sleep, he shall do well " (ver. 12).

We know how that "if"was spoken. We know how many ways
there are of passing a lie. We know what it is to give consent
with reservation, to yield acquiescence with unspoken reluctance.
The disciples seem to have felt that Lazarus was dead, but
hearing Jesus say that he slept, the disciples said, " Lord, if he
sleep." Who does not know what it is to have a mocking
doubter in the heart whilst the tongue is confessing all manner
of theologies and orthodoxies? Who does not know what it is
to have a spectre overlooking him, even in the middle of prayer,
and to hear that spectre whisper with cold breath, Thou liar ?
Who does not know what it is to say to the sick one, You are
better to-day ? It was not the heart that spoke ; the visitor or
the friend thought it would be well to cheer the sufferer, and
therefore said, You look better. How could you say so ? You
knew that the cheek was whiter than yesterday, the lips more
livid, the eyes more lifeless : how could you say so ? And yet
it seemed to be right to say just that at that time. We cannot
be kept back by cold fact, judicial impartial reason ; sometimes
the heart leaps and outruns the head, and is at the sepulchre

before the lumbering Peter can come up. Who would have himself tried by arithmetical rules and geometrical figures? Who would not have many sides to his nature, so that his imagination may be miles ahead whilst his limping reason—poor, shuffling, ambling cripple—is looking round for staff or crutch? Does not a blessing come with those whose ministry is such as to enable them to speak words of hope when their hearts are cold with fear? Do we not sometimes say, It is so,—when we mean, We wish it were so? Do we not play false with grammatical forms, and change moods and tenses at will, coming with holy violence against the custom of speech in order to tell a gospel or sing a line that will cheer the fainthearted? Sometimes we have said, Lord, if there is another world,—if there is a resurrection,—if there is a Judgment Day. We put the case as if we were stating a creed and stating a doubt in the same breath; so it is a troubled utterance, a most tumultuous expression, understood in heaven, and there only can any creed be understood. We do not believe the less because of this shadowing " if " ; yea, we would seem to believe the more,—that is to say, we would take more blessing " if " we could, or might. Lord, help our incapacity !

Now we come to another " if," uttered by the two sisters, in almost identical words, probably with identical meaning ; but it is the " if " of ignorance :—

"Then said Martha unto Jesus, Lord, if thou hadst been here, my brother had not died " (ver. 21).

They conversed together, and to that woman Jesus revealed some aspects of his personality and ministry that might have been revealed to an attentive universe. Then Mary comes upon the scene :—

"Then when Mary was come where Jesus was, and saw him, she fell down at his feet, saying unto him, Lord, if thou hadst been here, my brother had not died " (ver. 32).

Is there a tone of reproach in that statement? Does it mean, It thou hadst come, instead of abiding two days still in the same place, our brother would still have been with us, and the little house at Bethany would have been as bright and cheery as ever? Or does it involve a philosophy? Does it say, Lord, where thou art no death can be : death and Jesus cannot be in the same chamber long ?   Probably the meaning was exhausted by the first view, namely, that Jesus Christ came too late; if he had come earlier the event would not have occurred : the two sisters agreed in that ; activity and contemplation found a common resting-place in the assurance that if Jesus Christ had not been in the house death dare not have come in at the front door.   This is a beautiful " if," without doubt.   It is employed for the purpose of increasing emphasis, deepening and enlarging spiritual certitude, "Lord, if thou hadst been here, my brother had not died" : thou didst love him, and though death stood at his bedside ready to leap upon him as a conqueror might leap upon an overthrown foe, yet thou wouldst have kept him back, and my brother had been alive to-day, leading the household psalm, and distributing the household bread.   Yet this is a doctrine marked by ignorance.   For death is the servant of God—the black, grim, weird servant who finds his wages in his work; he eats millions a day, and hungers for millions more.   Why do we separate the devil as if he had a little universe of his own in which he was sole king, constituting a court that owed allegiance to no sceptre ?   Why do we think of death as something wholly apart from God ? As an enemy that has taken advantage of God's absence from the household of creation ?   The devil is a chained dog; a beast capable of infinite barking, but the chain is on his throat.   And Death—old, old Death—thriving these countless ages upon beast and bird and fish, and then leaping upon man and overthrowing him,—this monster is a servant of the court of heaven.   The Lord reigneth! Has not the Lord a right to send for those whom he will, for those who are ready, for those whose mischief upon earth must come to an end?   What could the Lord do without death when he has so little space to work upon on the face of the globe ?   Death is a necessity.   If emigration relieves the congestion of nations, so death relieves the congestion of the globe.   Death is servant, not master.   Yet, a beautiful thought is it that where Jesus is there can be no death.

"I am the resurrection, and the life : he that believeth in me, though he were dead, yet shall he live: and whosoever liveth and believeth in me shall never die" (vers. 25, 26).

Men do not die when Christ is in the house ; they ascend

Let Pagans die; Christians must languish into life. Let beasts die; but men must be liberated, must accept the word of emancipation and receive the crown of freedom. With Jesus in the house there can be no death; the little child will not die, but go up like a dewdrop, called for by the warm sun. In the house of the saint bereavement itself becomes a sacrament. Death doth but enlarge the horizon, and show the greater width of the universe.

Then here is the " if " that calls to faith. Only Jesus Christ himself could speak this " if."

"Jesus saith unto her, Said I not unto thee, that, if thou wouldest believe, thou shouldest see the glory of God ? " (ver. 40.)

Could she not see the glory of God without believing? No. Can you see the stars without the telescope? What can you see with the naked eye ? You have invented lenses that can search a leaf, a grass-blade, or a water-drop, and that can search the infinite spaces of the heavens,—here is a lens called Faith by which we see the glory of God. If men will not use the microscope, do you say that the microscope is useless, and that there is no under-world to be discovered? If men will not use the telescope, do you proclaim the universe a blank, saying, Even the street lamps have been put out, and death reigns in all the arch of the sky ? You say to such people, You ought to use the means. But when the theologian or the Christian or the apostle says, "You ought to use the means," he is called a fanatic. People who distrust the naked eye in everything want the naked reason to discover the metaphysics of the universe. This cannot be done. Lord, increase our faith! God holds nothing back from faith. He would give us a brighter summer if we had more faith ; he would send us brighter mornings if we had larger faith capacity to receive them. We could frighten death away if we had faith ; we could create harvests anywhere if we had faith. We should have plenty of bread if we had plenty of faith. When we hear that a man has discovered a new star, we never find it added that he discovered it with the naked eye. Sometimes men say to amateurs, "Get the focus right." What has the focus to do with it ? Can I not see ? Have I not eyes? No, you cannot see, and what eyes you have want assistance,—get the focus right. So say those who teach the inner and upper mysteries of the kingdom eternal : Brother, get the focus right ; see that the glass suits your eye ; see that you are on the line of vision ; see that no hindrance is in the way intercepting the revelation,—" Said I not unto thee, that, if thou wouldest believe, thou shouldest see the glory of God ? " We cannot have this great telescopic faith all at once : we may have it little by little. Sometimes we begin at a very humble point. Who has not in his childhood smoked a piece of glass rather than not have some medium through which to look at the sun, at an eclipse, at some peculiar view, or some startling pheno-menon of the heavens ? Some of us are no farther on religiously. Understand that a kaleidoscope is not a telescope. There be many who have theological kaleidoscopes : looking through the kaleidoscope they see Methodism—all the Methodist preachers that ever lived ; another turn, Congregationalism—all the Con-gregationalists. You are only looking at pieces of glass ; the stars—cold, bright, glorious—are away yonder, and you must have another instrument by which to scan their glory. One man was no farther on than this—it was a poor telescope, but he saw a good deal through it. He said, " Lord, I believe ; help thou mine unbelief." There is a cloud on the glass,—O Blessed One, take it away, then I shall see thee in thy beauty !

Now we come to the " if " of human despair :—

"Then gathered the chief priests and the Pharisees a council, and said, What do we ? for this man doeth many miracles. If we let him thus alone, all men will believe on him" (vers. 47, 48).

Even the Pharisees must have an " if "—" If we let him thus alone." There are some men who must do mischief, who must circulate evil reports, who must pass narrow criticisms, who must write stinging articles in journals that have small enough circulation to take them in, in the hope that they may sell an extra copy. There are people who must run down other people, depreciate them, who say, " There are spots on the sun,"—there will be spots on the earth as long as they live ! So the Phari-sees get into a council. There are some men never strong except when they are on a committee. Meet such men one by one, and they are deferential ; let them get together on a committee, a council, or a board of directors, and perhaps a finer set of cowards could hardly be met.   They assist public deliberations by crying, "Vote, vote!" "Hear, hear!"   That is the sum total of their contribution to the illumination and advancement of great questions.   The Pharisees must get into council.   One will speak and another will say, "Hear, hear!" and the rest will applaud, and nobody can tell exactly who said it.   When did a Pharisee boldly and frankly come up to Jesus Christ and face him as man faces man in singularity?   Oh, when the pack of hounds met how the hounds barked and yelled!   Some men have been killed by councils, killed by committees, killed by numbers of persons who have absorbed their own personality in the troubled existence of other and indescribable lives.   This matter is a personal one.   We cannot be saved by councils, nor ought we to fear being condemned by them.   We cannot be saved by committees; why should we wait for them as if they had it in their power to pervert our judgment or trouble our conscience?   Be right, and go on; be sure of your ground, and then stand still, and advance, pray, and consider as the circumstances which come and go may determine.

Were we not right in saying this chapter is fruitful in "ifs"?   If I might go beyond the chapter it would be to quote two other "ifs" full of meaning : "If we say we have no sin, we deceive ourselves, and the truth is not in us."   Is it possible for a man to say he has no sin?   So it would seem, because the supposition is here affirmed.   There are people who believe in their own respectability—"not that they wish to be proud," when they are so proud that the universe can hardly find a throne high enough for them to sit down upon.   "If we say we have no sin, we deceive ourselves"—we deceive nobody else.   We are liars, and the truth is not in us.   We must make acquaintance with our own sin ; we must face it, name it, weigh it, measure it, and call it ours.   This may begin the reckoning.   But you cannot reckon upon your soul's destiny in the dark.   Men must be faithful to themselves, right-down frank with their own spirits.

Now comes that second "if"—a gospel, an opening heaven—"If we confess our sins, he is faithful and just to forgive us our sins,

and to cleanse us from all unrighteousness." How admirably is
the statement put in both aspects ! " If we say we have no sin,
we deceive ourselves,"—If we confess our sin God will follow
confession by absolution. Thus stands the matter. Let no man
trifle with it. For ages men have lived upon these truths :
hence the Church ; hence all evangelistic effort ; hence all holy
doctrine ; hence all comforting proclamation. There are times
when men need precisely such words as these, " If we confess
our sins." We are not always in a mood to receive that exhortation : sometimes it comes to us weakly, most feebly ; so much so
that we resent it, and say that preaching is for churches on
Sundays, and not for market-places and the common thoroughfares of life. But, sometimes, even in the city, a man would be
glad if he could hear a voice behind him saying, " If we confess
our sins, he is faithful and just to forgive us our sins, and to
cleanse us from all unrighteousness." He would account the
market-place a church if he could hear that sacred word. When
he has been robbing his employers ; when he has been playing
false with sacred oath and vow ; when he has been doing the
things he ought not to have done ; when he is living in fear of
detection because to-morrow the audit will take place and the day
after judgment will be delivered ; when every wind that blows
around him is a breath from perdition, a blast from hell ; when
every step he takes is a step into a quaking bog ; when every
voice he hears may be the voice of judgment final and irrevocable ;
then if some one could say to him, " If we confess our sins, he is
faithful and just to forgive us our sins," he might be turned to
better thoughts ; it might soon be said of him, " Behold, he
prayeth !"

Chapter xi. 7, 8.

"Then after that saith he to his disciples, Let us go into Judæa again. His disciples say unto him, Master, the Jews of late sought to stone thee and goest thou thither again?"

CHRIST'S COURAGE.

[AN OUTLINE.]

"THE Jews sought to stone me" would be, for certain natures, a sufficient reason for not again venturing into their presence. Christ teaches us one divine lesson by this act of fortitude, viz., to go wherever there is work to be done. In Judæa there was a sleeper who could be awakened by his power alone; hence he returned to Judæa, in spite of the malignity which he had recently endured. Christ was called, by the sympathy of his own heart, to remove the sorrow which threatened to engulf two bereaved sisters, and to prove his divinity by a miraculous exertion of his power. He knew that in Judæa there were multitudes ready to put him to death; yet his own convictions overbalanced the fury of his enemies, and brought him to the graveside of his beloved Lazarus.

Christianity develops true fortitude. There is a bravery which results from animal passion, there is a courage which arises from ambition, pride, love of applause; but these must be distinguished from Christian heroism. The valour of a Christian is the result of regnant conviction : he is heroic because he is right; he fights to prove his loyalty to divine principles. Can your faith bear stoning? Dare you venture into Judæa when every hand is ready to smite you? These are test-questions. It is but a lean, shivering, pitiable faith that dreads any form of reproach or chastisement.

Clamour is not necessary to the exhibition of true fortitude.

246

Some men cannot fight without acquainting the public with their battles. Christ was often dumb in his sufferings ; he had not always the relief which speech or groan often insures, " he opened not his mouth." His was true endurance ; his deepest sufferings secretly exhausted themselves. Christ endured many stonings of which history is ignorant. The severest trials of fortitude are not necessarily visible : the deadliest blows are aimed in the sacred hours when eye and pen are excluded.

The Church that fears stoning is useless for practical purposes ; it may be ornamental, but its beauty is perishable. It will make no vital impression on a neighbourhood ; it is a delicate hot-house plant, that cannot bear the climate of an unsympathetic and ruthless world. Christ in a Church will lift that Church above the fear of stoning ; for Christ transforms the churches into his own nature. We shall be surrounded by weaklings and cowards, until the fellowship of professors be entirely impregnated by the spirit of him who never quaked in the presence of danger, or blushed in the enunciation of the principles on which his life was founded.

PRAYER.

ALMIGHTY GOD, we would see Jesus as we have never seen him befoi e. This is the glory of the Lord, that he shines with different lights, that his glory varies as we look upon him, heightens as we adore him, and encompasses us round and round like a divine defence. We have seen Jesus at Bethlehem, we have heard his teaching in the Word and somewhat of it in the spirit; we have seen him upon the Cross, and we have seen him ascending into glory; still we want another vision, a brighter, fuller, tenderer disclosure of Jesus Christ's presence and ministry. We have heard that he prayeth for us in daily intercession, taking up our poor cries of need, and magnifying them into prevailing prayer. Give us faith to hold fast by this sweet doctrine, then we shall have more faith in our prayers, because they are taken up by him and made availing through his Cross and blood, and ascension and intercession; yea, they become his prayers uttered from his heart and by his lips, and they must elicit answers that will satisfy our poverty and all our desires. When we read the Holy Book may a new light shine upon it from above, and a fuller glory rise from within itself; then in thy light shall we see light, and there shall be in our souls light above the brightness of the sun. Thine is a marvellous light, O Son of man, O Son of God! We cannot imagine it, we cannot forecast it, we cannot say, It shall be thus; for we know not how great is thy power, how gracious thy purpose of self-disclosure. Surprise us with new light: at midnight may there be a shining as of the dawn, and at noonday may the sun be sevenfold in strength. May we look at everything from the standpoint of Jesus Christ's ministry, specially from Jesus Christ's Cross; then shall we see meanings otherwise undiscoverable, then shall we see the unfolding of purpose, passing the discernment of human sagacity: we shall see God working out his plan of love, caring for all, caring most for the least, mighty in all, but omnipotent in the uttermost weakness. Thus shall we have great content- ment of heart, deep tender peace of mind; we shall hail death as a friend, we shall say the garden is not complete until a grave has been dug in it, and we shall know that life is nothing till it is thrilled with the agony of heavenly expectation. We bless thee that we see life's meaning somewhat: it is a poor life in itself, it is a glorious life in its indications and possibilities. Now it is a pain, but by-and-by it will be a joy, and the joy will be greater because of the preceding pain. Enable us to stand upright in the strongest wind, and to look straightforwardly, even though the darkness challenge our vision. May we say, There is no darkness with God; this poor cloud is transient, easily punctured; it may be gone in a moment. Thus in thy strength, thou mighty Bearer of the Cross, may we carry our life with all its burden and all its pain. Grant unto aged servants renewal of youth; grant unto thy youngest children sense of thy nearness, the responsibility and solemnity which come of conscious nearness to God, and to all thy servants who are busy here and there teaching the lesson that they have nothing that is certain except that which they have given away; and thus may all life be blessed, and every day become a gate opening upon heaven. Cheer the despondent; thou knowest how sad the life is and weary: oh for one breath of summer wind, one look of summer light! Guide the perplexed and the bewildered, and lift up the stumbling lest they totter to their fall; and as for those who are weak enough to vow and break the vow, the Lord give them strength from on high, and make the most infantile the most gigantic. Spare us yet a little while, that we may recover ourselves, and smite us not down in wrath; when thou dost call for us let it be by some angel's whisper, not by some great storm. Amen.

Chapter xii. 20-29.

"And there were certain Greeks among them that came up to worship at the feast: the same came therefore to Philip, which was of Bethsaida of Galilee, and desired him, saying, Sir, we would see Jesus. Philip cometh and telleth Andrew: and again Andrew and Philip tell Jesus. And Jesus answered them, saying, The hour is come, that the Son of man should be glorified. Verily, verily, I say unto you, Except a corn of wheat fall into the ground and die, it abideth alone: but if it die, it bringeth forth much fruit. He that loveth his life shall lose it; and he that hateth his life in this world shall keep it unto life eternal. If any man serve me, let him follow me; and where I am, there shall also my servant be: if any man serve me, him will my Father honour. Now is my soul troubled; and what shall I say? Father, save me from this hour: but for this cause came I unto this hour. Father, glorify thy name. Then came there a voice from heaven, saying, I have both glorified it, and will glorify it again. The people therefore, that stood by, and heard it, said that it thundered: others said, An angel spake to him."

CERTAIN GREEKS.

THESE were not Greek Jews; they were simple Greeks: otherwise translated "Gentiles"; real, indisputable outsiders. That was the thing that made Jesus so glad. There were Greek Jews; but we must not confuse the one class with the other. The whole point of this glowing interview will be lost if we fail to fix our minds upon the one instructive fact that the Greeks were Gentiles, in the simplest, broadest sense of that term. And when Jesus heard of them he said, This is glory, this is daylight, this is the meaning of it all; and such a radiance overspread that face as well-nigh put out the sun. "Certain Greeks": only a few, but not a few to Christ; because Jesus

Christ does not reckon by our arithmetic. That is an invention of our own. Without the faintest authority we have said that two and two are four. That is a purely human supposition, and altogether questionable, except on the ground of convenience. "Certain Greeks" : quite a handful ; perhaps two, perhaps five. But the light must strike some point first : what if it struck these few Gentile wanderers in the first instance ? What do we mean by the word "few"? Sometimes we have a contemptuous significance ; but if we looked at things really as they ought to be looked at we should regard a few as equivalent to a pledge, the first drops that precede the rich rain. What about the first blade that pierces the dull earth and stands up in green beauty : is it a favourite ? No : it is better ; it is a harbinger ; it says, I have only come first ; they are all coming. It is not elected in the sense of other green blades having been blighted underground : it is elected in some sense of precedence ; it outran the others ; they all started together, but this little one came up first, elected to preach the harvest, called, not to singularity, but to expressiveness, to algebraic suggestiveness, saying, This is the indication that you must presently get your sickles ready, for we are all alive and all unfolding and all coming ; to-morrow the land will be green, and the day following it will be yellow with corn. The blade is only first, because there are more to follow. It would be neither first nor last if there were no succession ; it would stand alone, it would be without an arithmetical indication at all, except there be some word that signifies loneliness, some figure that typifies isolation ; it is either first or last, because there are more.

"The same came therefore to Philip," and "Philip cometh and telleth Andrew." Why that "therefore"? Read : "There were certain Greeks among them that came up to worship at the feast : the same came therefore——" That is not evident. "The same came to Philip," possibly : but why "therefore"? What is this unexpressed logic ? What is this subtle ministry that urges a man to watch, to sleep ; that bids him sit down and wait till the traveller comes up who will tell him all the rest ? There is a "therefore" that seems to have no antecedent ; there is a conclusion which seems to be without premise, major or minor. Poor man-made logic! It touches scarcely anything, and is rich only in principal blunders. Why not live upon this larger "therefore"? Why not avail ourselves of what the logicians call the *enthymeme*, in a far larger sense, feeling that everything is unexpressed but the conclusion? Why did you call upon me? I do not know. But you had to do it. Why did you not go next door? I could not : I was brought to your door, and you have an answer to my question, and you will give it. There were certain Greeks, and they came to Philip, and Philip to Andrew. Very singular that these are the only two disciples that have Greek names. "Philip" is Greek, "Andrew" is Greek, and "they" were Greek, and they got together : how? We cannot tell. Why did we go? We do not know why we went. Why did we not go? We cannot tell why we did not go. Are there ghosts in the air? Yea, verily. The universe is a ghost : we have made it into something vulgar. How does like come to like? How does the magnet attract its own metal? Why this stirring among all the filings? Is some one breathing upon them? No. Is some one touching them? No. How they move! What is it? A magnet held over them, or under them, or at some little distance from them. It is singular that the Greeks should find the Greeks, and that the Greeks who were found should be only Greek in name. Who can write the history of love, of sympathy, of friendship, of congeniality, of masonry that has no banqueting-table but at the heart? They are the mysteries of life. In old times names had significations; now they have none. A man will call his son "Philip" or "Apollos" without the slightest reason for doing so. Heathenism has given us our names, and yet we are Christians. We owe the name of every day of the week to pagan mythology, and yet we are followers of Christ. We call a man jovial, jolly, jubilant, not knowing that we are talking astrology, that we are going back to the time when the astrologist found in Jupiter the origin and fountain of all these names. We describe a man as "Mercurial," never thinking that the astrologer gave us that name ; and we speak of "Saturnine," and "Saturnalia," the dark revel, not knowing that we are talking paganism. Yet we call ourselves a Christian nation. There is a law, inscrutable, indisputable, immeasurable, that brings us together. Every preacher has his own audience.

They are all alike, if you could see the right line or stand at the
right point of view ; their heads are all alike, and their shoulders,
and their purpose. We do not see it, because we see nothing,
poor moles; but as seen in the right line the preacher and the
congregation are one, all moving in the same direction, all excited
by the same appetences, all stirred by the same aspiration : the
differences are external, superficial, transient ; the likeness is a
likeness of soul. Why does not a certain preacher get a larger
congregation than he does ? Because there are not so many
people of his sort. He cannot get a larger congregation than he
has ; all that is settled. Why not have gone to some other
disciples ? Simply because they could not.

What was the appeal, so tender, and so simple, and almost
childlike ?—"Sir, we would see Jesus." Perhaps it was unconscious, certainly it was imperfect ; they did not know what
they were going to see, and yet they must see the object of their
search. When we come to understand that inquiry the Christian
Church will be much enlarged. We cannot all see the same
aspect of Jesus ; we cannot all take in the same quantity of Christ.
One man takes in the good-doer, and follows the Good Shepherd,
the good Samaritan, the child-nurse ; he cannot go away from him.
Another man of another quality and range of imagination takes in
all the miracles; he has no doubt about curing the eyes of the
blind, unstopping the ears of the deaf, unloosing the tongues of
the dumb, and raising the dead, and quieting the seas ; he has
all that quality of imagination that can take in the whole series ;
he cannot give up the miracles, the other mind never took them up.
A third will find out all the theology, and construct a system for
himself, and will put other people in jail who do not adopt what
he has written,—he is a broadminded bigot. See as much of
Christ as you can. What do you see of him ? That is enough ;
certainly enough to begin with. Have you touched the hem of
his garment ? By-and-by you shall rest your head upon his
beating heart. Did you see him take up a little child and bless
it ? Hereafter ye shall see heaven opened, and the angels of
God ascending and descending upon the Son of man. Do you
say you can understand little parts of the New Testament but
not all ? Then walk by the light you have, and the light will

come more largely as you obey more implicitly. Above all things, do not argue. Obey, serve, sacrifice yourselves ; keep close to what little you do see, and ere you are quite aware of it the sun will be in the zenith and you will have as much daylight as you need. Who knows how far his questions reach when they come out of the heart ? Blessed be God that we know so little, not because it is little in itself, but because everything we can know is as nothing compared with that which remains to be known. Avoid the men who say they know all things that can be known here and now; and follow implicitly, and honour as with a crown of love, the man who tells you that we know nothing yet as it is and as it will one day be seen, but who charges you with loving exhortation to follow on, to pursue, to press forward. There is life in his voice ; it is a resurrection trumpet.

What was the effect of the appeal upon Jesus Christ when Andrew and Philip told him ? What did they tell him ? See how they went to him and said : " Jesus, there are some Greeks who want to see thee." See the effect. How Jesus Christ erects himself, takes on him the port of a conqueror, and says, Already the fields are white unto the harvest. He did not say, They are only two or three little green blades ; we must not make too much of these, presently I will attend to these Greek inquirers. No : he saw in their coming the fulfilment of prophecy, the coronation of his own wounded head, the uplifting which meant the elevation of the world. In effect he said, They are coming, they were promised to me ; I am to have the heathen for mine inheritance and the uttermost parts of the earth for my possession, and here I see the beginning of the great promise· He says, The rain is ceasing, the storm is crying itself to res*, and out of these black clouds that are left the sun will make a thousand rainbows, and presently you will hear the voice of the turtle in the land. How much good it did him ! Christ needed encouragement ; the cup was heavy, the darkness was dense, the Cross was a great burden ; to have whispered in his ear by two friends that certain Gentiles wanted to see him was to have heaven opened and the earth turned into one grand cornfield, requiring all the angels for its reaping. To Christ this was not a mere inquiry; it was a revelation. Another quality of mind would have limited it to an inquiry, but Jesus Christ's quality of mind enabled him to multiply it into a revelation. Do not despise small numbers. Certain events are to be weighed; for others it will do to number them. Look at events typically: what do they mean? What do they portend? They are index-fingers; they do not terminate in themselves; they say, The meaning of all this is presently to be seen. The proverb declares that one swallow does not make a summer; but the proverb is wrong, as most proverbs of man's making are; they are only clever, they are not inspired; they are only sharp, they are not philosophical. One swallow does make a summer, typically viewed, rightly understood. No swallow was fool enough to mistake winter for summer; when that swallow came, it said, You may think I have made a mistake, I have made none; mine is an exact calculation; whilst you are making your poor little proverb over me I will be joined by a thousand other swallows, and then away goes your proverb, and a dozen more, and the summer will be here presently. Thus Jesus Christ judged of events. Does one man pray? If so, the whole world will presently be on its knees. That one man is the pledge of all men. Christians must take this view of events, otherwise they will often be discouraged. If there has been one man saved, that means the salvation of the whole world, if the world will receive the Son of God. What then becomes of your statistical inquiries? What do they amount to? They amount to arithmetic, not to philosophy, certainly not to revelation. What is the right way of looking at circumstances? To look at them in their typical significance, in their symbolical suggestiveness; not to say, Here is one green blade, but, Here is the beginning of harvest; not, Here is one poor man praying, but, Here is the first man, and the others will presently join him. All events are related, and interrelated, and a mysterious "therefore" connects all the so-called accidents of time.

How Jesus Christ always rejoiced when any outsider came to him! It is most instructive to notice the difference in Jesus Christ's mental mood when any heathen came and wanted to speak to him. Said he on one occasion, "Verily I say unto you, I have not found so great faith, no, not in Israel." On another occasion he said, " There hath not returned to give glory to God, save this stranger." On another occasion he said that a Samaritan came where the dying man was. Thus he rebuked the Jew ; he would not accord to the Jews, locally and temporarily his own nation, the honour of having cured or helped the wounded man ; it was upon the head of a Samaritan, a stranger, an outsider, that he put his crown. And the Syrophenician woman overthrew him in the friendly wrestle, lifted him up and threw him by the might of love. He wished to be so overthrown ; he loves to be beaten in a controversy when he tries our faith, and momentarily obscures our hope that afterwards he may fill it with a brighter light ; he loves to give way under the pressure of that gracious violence which takes the kingdom of heaven as if by storm. How his heart glowed ! How he leaped beyond the Cross and entered into his glory ! How eloquently he talked when he heard of these Greeks asking about him ! Said he,—

"The hour is come, that the Son of man should be glorified. Verily, verily, I say unto you, Except a corn of wheat fall into the ground and die, it abideth alone : but if it die, it bringeth forth much fruit. He that loveth his life shall lose it ; and he that hateth his life in this world shall keep it unto life eternal. If any man serve me, let him follow me ; and where I am, there shall also my servant be : if any man serve me, him will my Father honour."

How little these Greeks knew what they were doing ! How little you know what you would do if you were to return to your human father to-night and say to him, " Father, I have sinned." It would make the old man young again ; the midnight would be as the midday, and there would be no fire hot enough in the house to cook the smoking feast. A question may revive and reconstruct a life. Are men to remain outside us always ? Is there to be no time of dawn-breaking, heart-yielding, hand-uplifting ? You will not always be an outsider. The outside is cold ; the inside is home and love and safety. To Jesus Christ all nature was full of symbols : " Lift up your eyes, and look on the fields ; for they are white already to harvest." There comes a time when it is difficult to distinguish between the spring and the harvest. There may be four months according to the almanac, but there are not four moments according to the spiritualised imagination, the fancy fired from the holy altar ; then the spring is the harvest, the seed-time is the gathering time, the outgoing is the home-coming, and the field is but the road to the granary.

Then he knew there was something to be done. For a moment the depression returned; the Cross had yet to be carried —"Now is my soul troubled; and what shall I say?" Note the punctuation of this verse, for everything depends upon that, "Now is my soul troubled; shall I say, Father, save me from this hour?" Put the mark of interrogation after the word "hour"; then you have the whole meaning,—"Now is my soul troubled; shall I say, Father, save me from this hour?" Then he answers himself: "For this cause came I into the world; for this cause came I unto this hour"; I will not say, Save me from this hour: I will say, Father, glorify thy name. Then there came a voice from heaven, saying, "I have both glorified it, and will glorify it again. The people therefore, that stood by, and heard it, said that it thundered: others said, An angel spake to him." Thus it always is: there are always two explanations of events: the vulgar will call the explanation thunder, and the spiritually refined will call it an angel. Would we see Jesus? Then say so. The very saying of it will be the realisation of it. Say so to the right people. The unbeliever can never show you Jesus. The man who lectures against the Cross can never expound it. Say so with the right spirit; mean it, insist upon it, and there is no cloud in heaven that will not shake out of it the stars that belong to your faith. To have seen everything but Jesus is to have seen nothing. Where can we see Jesus? Really only in one place. We say of certain men, You have never seen them until you have seen them in debate; you have never heard certain men speak until you have heard them in high argument; you have never seen certain other men until you have seen them at home, in the midst of domestic surroundings; other men you have never seen till you have beheld them under some strain that developed their quality and tried their temper. Of Christ we may say we have never seen him until we have seen him on Calvary.

PRAYER.

ALMIGHTY GOD, we know thee through thy Son. We see not God, but we see Jesus: it is enough. He fills our vision with glory; his presence is an overflowing blessing in the soul. Lord, abide with us. There is no darkness where thou art; thou art the Light of the world; there is no need of the sun in thy heaven; thou art the light thereof, none other is needed. If we be in thee, thou Light of the world, we ourselves shall become children of light; then shall we let our light so shine before men, that they, seeing our good works, may glorify our Father which is in heaven. May we understand somewhat of the ministry of light, may we in very deed be children of the day; let us say to our souls, The night is over and gone, we now stand in heaven's eternal dawn. May we live in the morning of thy love; may our path be as the shining light, shining more and more unto the perfect day, because in our hearts we are just. Help us to obey thee more and more, with a tenderer love, a fuller obedience, a more persistent constancy: in obedience is growing life, and in growing life is growing light: leave us not, thou Light of the universe. We pray for light whilst kneeling at the Cross; there is no other altar for sinners that are lost. All we like sheep have gone astray, we have turned every one to his own way, and we are now found at the foot of the Cross by no will or motion of our own, but by the overflowing and ineffable grace of Christ. There is room for all at the Cross; may the worst know that the Cross was set up most of all for him. May the prodigal return, may the backslider retrace his steps, may the cold in heart be warmed this day; inflame us with heavenly zeal, thou God the Holy Ghost. Amen.

Chapter xii. 35.

"Walk while ye have the light, lest darkness come upon you."

WALKING IN THE LIGHT.

ACCORDING to the Revised Version the text reads, "Walk while ye have the light, that darkness overtake you not." This word "while" is full of significance and energy. Christ used it more than once. It indicates opportunity, chance, occasion. It is as if one should say, Now is the time: be no longer languid, reluctant, dull of heart; now, behold, this is the day: arise, know the light, and receive it with thankfulness. Jesus Christ himself said, "I must work while it is called day." "While"— the same word again. So he was constantly saying to those round about him, Now is the time : watch, be ready: me ye have not always. You have me to-day, make the most of me ; to-morrow I shall be gone. There should be no to-morrow in Christian love and Christian service. There is only one time to the Christian, and that is To-day. We do not realise this with sufficient clearness ; we still think that to-morrow will come. It may come and bring with it darkness ; we have nothing to do with any time that is future, however near that future may be. We are so constituted that there is but a step between us and death. Our breath is in our nostrils ; we are as a flying shadow ; therefore, said Christ, Work whilst ye have the light : I must work while it is called day. "Lest darkness come upon you" is a tame expression ; it is not kindred in energy to the earlier part of the statement ; there must be some better word. The Revised Version says "overcome." But what does "overcome" mean ? Does it mean that there will be more darkness than light ? It may mean that, but it means much more. Set forth in its literal graphic meaning, the text would read thus : Walk while ye have the light, lest darkness tear you down.

We have no particular objection to darkness overtaking us, coming upon us ; it may come quietly, silently, inoffensively ; we may hardly know it until the twilight has deepened into sevenfold darkness. But that is not the figure. It is the figure of being pulled down, torn down, arrested, collared, seized, and humiliated. That is what happens in life. We are not dealing with trifling issues, we are not face to face with momentary inconveniences ; as who should say, If you do not make the most of to-day you will have an opportunity to-morrow of recovering your ground. Do not be unduly in haste ; the darkness will come, then you will rest. That is not the tone of the text at all. Shall we put it in an image ? Imagine a man going on a journey. He is travelling along a road known to be frequented by robbers or known to be frequented by ravenous beasts ; it is altogether a dangerous road. Then the idea is, Get on as fast as you can, make the most of the morning, the danger is least whilst the light is brightest : do not tarry for the afternoon, for the lengthening of the shadow. There are on that road beasts that prowl by night, robbers that live by the darkness ; make all the haste you can ;

it is morning.   Up! and be well on your road by twelve o'clock
in the day, lest ye be pulled down, lest the tiger spring upon
your shoulder and bring you to the dust, lest the robber lay his
strong hands upon you and throttle you, or cast you down and
violently assail you.   Make haste!   Thus   said   our   blessed
Teacher and Lord.   While ye have the light, walk—walk quickly
—make the most of it; because after a certain part of the day
who knows what evil ones may break out upon your road and
tear you down ?   That was the practice as well as the doctrine of
Christ.   He said, " I must work while it is called day ; the night
cometh when no man can work."   I must make the best of my
opportunities, I must not fritter away the light ; light is dowry,
fortune, opportunity, responsibility : all I have to do is to watch
the light and make the most of it.   And if he must work while it
is called day, how much more we, poor, infirm, imperfect creatures,
who can at the best do so little, who seem to need an eternity to
make a mere beginning.   How ardent should be our zeal, how
industrious our hands, lest the darkness tear us down.

This idea admits of large application to Christian thought
and life and progress.   In fact, this text supplies a doctrine of
philosophy for the whole development and education of life.   The
Bible is not only a theological book ; it is the best book upon
every subject.   It may not go into detail, but it lays hold of the
principle, the essential thought; it connects everything with
the fountain of being.   There is little need therefore that the
teacher of youth or the guide of life should go otherwhere for
a text than to the one that is now before us.   " Walk while
ve have the light, lest darkness come upon you "—overtake you,
overpower you, spring upon you, and drag you down.   Here is
an encouragement ; here is a warning ; here is an inspiration.
What darkness can come upon us ?   All our life is exposed to
this overpowering darkness,—the darkness, for example, of
impaired faculties.   Read whilst your eyesight lasts ; get all the
books you can into you.   Do not put off your reading until you
cannot read.   Your eyes can only work for a certain time ; they
want to work, they were made to work, now use them and take
in all knowledge and beauty, all spectacle and all event, that
thus you may carry your library for ever.   What are you wasting

your eyes upon, man of business, young man, worldling, pleasure-seeker? Are you using your eyes by way of abusing them? or are you reading the prophets and the seers, the teachers and the poets, and the mighty suppliants who have the gift of prayer, and have written for you words that will make you calm and wise and triumphant in all times of danger and perplexity and battle? " Walk while you have the light": read whilst you have your eyes; be active while your limbs are supple. You know nothing to-day, you stalwart youth, of rising ground; all ground is on a level to you. You have the full use of your limbs, you can go where you please; you would as soon walk five miles as one; you do not know the meaning of weariness. How are you using that gift of physical suppleness and activity? Are you going about doing good? or are you putting off going about to do good until you cannot walk? God doth not want your cripplehood; he says, I give you youth, energy, light of a physical kind,—walk while you have the light, lest darkness come and tear you down, and you cannot call upon your next door neighbour. Now—this day—nay, this day?—this breath, this flashing moment; now, do right, be good, serve the Lord.

We might go into the school with the text and talk to our little ones, and to the academy and talk to our elder pupils, and say, Store the memory while the memory is plastic. There comes a time when we have no memory. We read over the sweet hymn and think we will remember its beginning, its continuation, and its conclusion; but we cannot do so. When we were five years old we could have committed a hymn to memory in a few minutes; when we were at school we had quite a quick, sensitive, receptive memory; what we learned then we cannot forget. We can repeat whole lists of words that have no connection or cohesion. We can recite now in advanced years the whole list of adverbs, prepositions, words that have no meaning in them, simple arbitrary tokens and signs of language. There comes a time in life when we can commit nothing to memory. What saith the text? Speaking academically or educationally, it says the very same thing that it says theologically and spiritually. This New Testament is the world's book, spreading its instruction over the whole area of human want and human power. Store the memory, saith Christ, while it is young. What you are treasuring up now will be your companions in old age ; the little Sunday School hymns will come back upon you, and your earliest prayers and memories will revive within you, and in old age you will re-live your youth. This is one passport to a not insubstantial immortality.

There is darkness yet to come upon all of us and tear us down if we have not made a right use of the light. There is the darkness of affliction and sorrow. That will try our quality. A man is in reality what he is in his deepest affliction or his most poignant agonies. Pain gets at a man's faith. Even atheists have been known to cry mightily towards an empty heaven for help in the time of their distress. Do not hand me some written creed made in a time of health and fatness and wealth and prosperity ; that creed is but so much paper and ink. Tell me what you said when the teeth of the enemy closed upon themselves through your heart; tell me what you said when the night was very dark, when the firstborn died, and with it died every bird in the forest and every sunbeam in the sky. What did you say then ? Had you made any preparation for that downtearing ? Men should lay up in store ; they should know there will come a time when they will be arrested, sprung upon, torn, and overpowered, if they themselves have not strength to overpower. It comes to one of two things : we must be overpowered, or we ourselves must overpower the assailant. In order to overpower the assailant what shall we do ? Walk while we have the light. We cannot carry the light into midnight. Midnight and midday each has its own place. Be minute, observant, jealous, miserly. Know this, that the light is for a time, and that time is Now.

Darkness sometimes comes suddenly. Sometimes it is dark at noonday. Do not call any man strong or rich ; there is no such man in the world, except for the passing and uncertain moment. Let not the rich man boast of his wealth. When he opens the lid of his treasure-box to-morrow morning he will find that place of treasure empty in all the four corners. Let not the strong man boast of his strength ; whilst yet the boast is upon

his lips the marrow in his bones may be turned to ice. Let us
have no boasting, and let us have no atheistic or selfish calcu.a-
tion about the downcoming of darkness. You left your friend
yesterday hale and strong, and with many kindly words you
promised to meet to-morrow. He died last night. Quite suddenly?
Yes: he was boasting so much that the Lord said to him, Thou
fool! Are we prepared for this sudden darkness? How can
we be prepared? Only by laying in the light. Walk in the
light, receive the light, store up the light. What shall be the
issue of it? Christ tells us. He tells us that if we walk in
the light we ourselves may be the children of the light; that is
to say, not have the light outside us but within us. That is the
test of spiritual progress. Christ is here that he may be within
us. He does not want to stand in front of us historically, the
finest spectacle on the landscape. He wants to come to us, and
take up his abode with us, and be part of us, and live with us,
and never go away from us. Oh, whilst he tarries be you up and
doing! Let me seize the moment of his presence that I may
receive him into my heart. I do not want to make an external
study of him; he is not a forest to be painted, a landscape to be
sketched, a lamp to be gazed upon: he is a Life, a Light to
be received within, that he may shine forth from my heart.
Herein is that saying true, "Ye are the light of the worla."
Walk with the light, that ye may become light; walk with
Christ, that ye may become Christ's; so company with the
Saviour that others shall say of us, As he was, so are ye in
the world. A gentle kindly word, a sweet gracious possibility,
is set before us. While ye have light, believe in the light
of God, that ye may be the children of light, that ye may be
fountains of glory, centres of splendour, out of your life going
forth an irradiating illumination that shall make your families,
your neighbourhoods, and your several countries glad with
your brightness. Perhaps you thought that the light was
always to be outside of you; it is to be an internal or spiritual
light. This is what the Saviour is himself, and what he is
so would he have his servants be. This growth into light may
become so perfect, as it has done in himself, that in heaven
there is no need of the sun; the old servant is dismissed. He
has done well; he was made to rule the day, but there is no

heaven for the sun because there is no need of him there. How is the place lighted ? By the Lamb, by life. Light is fire ; life is light. Why have we been living the beast's life ? Why have we been alway in the dust and at the trough, and sleeping deep sleeps, made wild by nightmare, when we might have been living up towards the light ; having shed off the crust of the body our souls might have blinded the sun with superior splendour. Walk while ye have the light.

There is a darkness that will come—come upon all—must come. Men call it night, men call it death. Death is night; death is darkness. We must all die. That sentence is now called commonplace—to such vulgarity have we grown ! If a preacher should stand up and say, " Man is mortal," he would be said to have uttered a platitude,—so have we fooled ourselves away ! Yet we speak of spendthrifts and prodigals and persons who do not take hold of life by the right end, but prosper at the bank, in the shambles, in the marketplace. Why, we are spendthrifts who have got through these elementary truths that ought to constitute the very capital of Christian meditation and practice. We must—I repeat it at the risk of uttering a commonplace— we must all face the darkness of death one by one. We have wronged ourselves by living much in crowds. It is well for us now and then to know that each for himself alone—ALONE— must die. What preparation have we made for death ? There is only one rational and sufficient preparation, and that is walking while we have the light. Christ is the Light of the world. Walking whilst we have Christ—an opportunity of studying Christ; an opportunity of receiving Christ into the heart; an opportunity of serving Christ by all good deeds. If you have made any other preparation for death you are foolish ; and the very wisdom you have shown in making other preparation aggravates your folly. You have insured your life—you have let your soul go without defence. You have barred all the upper windows against the thief—you have left the front door of the house wide open. Sevenfold in folly are they who have made every possible preparation for death, except walking in that light which sends a glorifying beam through the whole valley of its shadow.

We have the same word in other places. For instance, we have in chapter i. 5—" The light shineth in darkness; and the darkness comprehended it not "; in the Revised Version, " overcame it not "—in the margin, " overpowered it not." There is the idea, the idea of overpowering; the Light was in the world, the Christ-light, and the darkness did not pull it down, the light remained; the storm came, the wind blew, the rains descended, and the whole heaven seemed to be angry, and yet the light outshone the darkness. We are to be as Christ was in the world. John speaks of Christ as of a Light that shone in darkness, and the darkness did not pull it down, tear it towards the earth; the light remained, nothing could extinguish it. Atheism as a doctrine cannot extinguish God as a fact. This is our supreme comfort. There is only one darkness we may fear, the darkness of being separated from God by sin. Can the worldling hear all this and make no answer? Thou wicked and slothful servant, out of thine own mouth will I condemn thee. Thou hast a perverted version of this very text. Show me that Bible, I will read it to thee. Why, here in the worldling's own book is this text in other words. What saith it? Why, these are the very words, " Make hay while the sun shines." O soul, is life to be a question of haymaking, money-making, worldly progress, body-feeding? Is that life? Exalt your own proverb, carry it on to its noblest expansions and applications, and you will find it consummated and glorified in the text, " Work while ye have the light, lest darkness come upon you." This is no haymaking, no secular life merely, but a great salvation of the whole nature. Herein is the beauty of Christ's religion : it comprehends all, includes all that is good; it sends men away to the hayfield, saying, " Make hay while the sun shines "; it sends men away to thrift and economy, saying, " Gather up the broken portions, that nothing be lost "; it sends men away upon industrial pursuits saying, " Work while it is called day, for the night cometh wherein no man can work." Christ heals the body that he may get at the soul. He is no doctor of the bones, no surgeon of the joints; he will undertake that minor practice that he may get at the immortality that is being ruined. All the bread he gives you is sacramental. There are some men who never get beyond eating and drinking. They are feeding a body, they are slaking a thirst. But when Christ gave me the bread he said, "Son, this is my body"; when he gave me the water, he said, "This is my blood."

And then the text occurs again, and this is final, in the awful sentence "Be sure your sin will find you out." Be sure your sin will overtake you, overpower you, pull you down. Let that be a warning to hearts that keep a private hell; let those words sink into souls that have consecrated darkness as the sanctuary of the devil. Be sure your sin will find you out. You say "find you out" is a tame expression; so it is in English, but as originally written or spoken it means just what the text means— tear you down, pull off the straw garland, tear away the sheep's clothing and show the wolf; pull you down from your pride, your titles, and your distinctions, your local fame and your national influence; pull you down, and send you out into the world a leper white as snow, naked, without a fig-leaf to cover your shame. O earth, earth, earth! hear the word of the Lord! But I could not end with these words of thunder and darkness and terrible night; if our sin is sure to tear us down, so, if we confess our sins, God is faithful and just to forgive us our sins, and to cleanse us from all unrighteousness. "There is a fountain filled with blood." It is opened in the house of David for sin and for uncleanness. "If we say that we have no sin, we deceive ourselves, and the truth is not in us." Do not therefore say we are waiting to be torn down by the wolves of a just retribution. No man need be torn down if he will first tear himself down, if he will pull his heart to pieces and go to Christ, to God in Christ, and say, "Father, I have sinned!" The wolf of law will be ordered away. There will come into the soul the experience of a great release. All over the life there will shine a new morning—let us call it Heaven!

PRAYER.

ALMIGHTY GOD, we know thee in all ways, some by this, and some by that; but we all know that behind what is seen is the unseen, the eternal, the all-shaping, and the all-ruling power. Thou hast made us variously, yet are we one; herein is the mystery of our nature, and herein is the mystery of thine own being. We see without looking, we look without seeing; we feel without reasoning, we reason without feeling: in the dark we see; when there is no one present we lay the hand of our love upon a life that cares for us and redeems us. It is all mystery, radiant mystery, tender, enlarging, ennobling mystery; verily this night is full of stars. Come to us, thou Son of God, and make us feel that thy chariots are twenty thousand in number, and that thou dost ride forth in each as it doth please thee, and blessed is the man who sees thee in some aspect, in some light, in any way, for he too is caught by the beauty of the vision of God. Saviour wounded, Saviour crowned, hear us now, and alway hear us, for thy hearing is an answer. Amen.

Chaper xii. 43.

"For they loved the praise of men more than the praise of God."

THE FALSE ESTIMATE.

WHO were the people spoken of? Had this declaration been made of some persons we should not have wondered; we should have been surprised indeed if any contrary declaration had been made. We must turn to the context to make ourselves acquainted with the character of those who are thus characterised : " Among the chief rulers also many believed on him; but because of the Pharisees they did not confess him, lest they should be put out of the synagogue: for they loved the praise of men more than the praise of God."

This is the fatal calamity. They were believers, not confessors. In their own hearts they said all the while, Truly this man is the Son of God : never man spake like this man. We have been accustomed to look at men and form an estimate of their capacity and their purpose, but we never saw a man like this before.

Why did they not say so audibly, publicly ?   Why did they not make confession, and follow the man in whom they believed ? To that inquiry the text is a reply—frank, complete, humiliating —" for they loved the praise of men more than the praise of God." Is this the reason why many do not confess Jesus Christ to-day. Is there a good deal of secret belief, unspoken wonder difficult to distinguish from faith ?   Do some hearts go to Jesus stealthily, and look on until they burn ? and does the glow become so intense that the tongue almost speaks ?   How we are conquered by immediate circumstances !   The future, the larger, can have but little effect upon men who are thrust down by that which is p sent, immediate, and overshadowing.   A most startling revelation is this from another point of view.   Ought not the praise of men and the praise of God to mean the same thing ? Is it possible that the Creator is praising one thing and the creatures another ?   What is the meaning of this ?   Was it so at the beginning ?   One would have thought, and justified the thought by high reasoning, that what God approved man would instantly accept, and that he would be ashamed to put his opinion in opposition to the judgment of heaven.

Men got wrong when they threw off the theocracy. Demo-cracy, poorly defined, is a lie and a blasphemy ; so is every other human ocracy.   There is but one rule that can touch all time and hold beneficent dominion over all forces and ministries, and that is the theocracy, the rule of God, undisputed, lovingly accepted, loyally obeyed, longed for.   Yet this is not conformable to fact.   What wonder, therefore, if serious questions have been asked by philosophers and theologians ?   What wonder if various theories have been propounded to account for this?   Is it any comfort to us to know that we have grown up from a plasm almost imperceptible to the microscope itself, and have struggled thus far in a process of development, evolution, and that therefore we are not to be judged as if we had been guilty personally or ancestrally of an original apostasy ?   That would be a comforting doctrine up to a given point.   But every man must be his own accuser in this matter.   He says, Whatever others may accept I cannot accept that explanation, for I have known the right and yet the wrong pursued ; I could have done the right, and I neglected to do it. In instance after instance a thousand strong I could have been true, righteous, noble, kind, and I failed ; if I had been asked to do something which I could not now do, then I might promise myself that by an elaborate evolution I might in a century be able to accomplish it ; but I have seen things that I could do and I did not do,—nay, I purposely neglected,—nay, I thrust them behind me, and said, I will have my own way, I will play the God to myself. So this balsam does not heal this wound ; this proposition will amuse me in my hours of leisure, and enlarge the margin with which my speculation takes its nocturnal walks in the infinite darkness of the unknown ; but when I come to think of it all, and to know what I could have done and what I have not done, I feel that philosophy daubs the wall with untempered mortar, and cries, Peace, peace, when there is no peace. What wonder if theologians have begun the argument from the other point, and have said, " God made man upright, but man sought out many inventions. All men like sheep have gone astray ; they have turned every one to his own way : there is none righteous, no, not one " ? It is not a comfortable doctrine ; yet sometimes it feels as if it were true. It is incredible surely that men of intelligence, such as chief rulers, men of education, should love social praise more than divine commendation. There is no music in that statement. It rolls backward. We long to contradict it. Given God and man to judge a case, and what can occur but that man shall be silent until God has pronounced ; and then man shall take up divine conclusion, and hold to it, so that none shall modify the tenacity of the faith ? The facts are against that theory. We are afraid of one another. Society victimises itself. Yet where is society ? Who can arraign it, cross-examine it, disprove its positions, inflict upon it adequate penalties ? It is here, yet there ; there, yet yonder, farther on—near—distant ; a tremendous burden, an impenetrable presence. But what a tyrant it is !

Moreover, to accept social praise rather than divine commendation is the most shortsighted policy. But men are shortsighted. Their proverbs are often manufactured by their shortsightedness. Their very wisdom is folly, when they detach themselves from the currents that are spiritual and unseen, and set up intellectual and moral action, rising from themselves as from the point of origin. Who does not like to be satisfied with to-day ? If we could take into our purview to-day, to-morrow, and the third day, the whole policy of our life would be changed ; we should do things which to the shortsighted would be foolish ; we should take seed, and throw it away, and men who know not the chemistry of agriculture would say, Fools are they who waste their bread-corn. Nay, we should reply, this is wisdom, this is the longsighted course and policy, this is the very philosophy of life ; we must give if we would get, we must reason in harmony with all the ministry of nature if by-and-by we would put in our gleaming sickles and cut down the golden grain, and enlarge our barns to hold the largess of heaven.

Not only is it incredible and shortsighted—it is servile. See man looking out to see what his brother man is going to do before he himself will take a definite position. Moreover he does not remember with vividness sufficient to make an impression upon him that his brother man is at this moment watching him to see what he will do. This is what we call servility, walking softly where we should walk straightly ; peeping where we should look squarely and directly ; muttering where we ought to speak like thunder. How often has this been proved to be servility, because when a heroic soul has arisen, how many has he drawn forth from their obscurity and attached to himself, and how they thanked him for his paternity, for in very deed he became their father, their leader and king. It would be so in many quarters now.

We want the loud voice. Many are prepared to sing who are not prepared to begin the tune ; some could join a little who would be almost ashamed to be heard singly ; and oftentimes when the multitude is great even a harsh voice is softened and fined by being overpowered and mellowed by the mightier strain. If the father in the family could speak one decisive word, he might turn a whole household round, and stand up in a new sovereignty, and finally be blessed for a most sacred influence. If a young man in the city warehouse could with modest boldness say that he is a Christian, without any ostentation or impious consciousness of vanity, others might come and thank him for making that bold and simple declaration; and out of that declaration might come additions to numbers and to influence, and there might be originated periods and exercises of prayer and praise and godly activity—all coming through the influence of the one man who dared to say, "As for others, I will serve the Lord, whatever they do." This would be longsightedness, this would be genius, because it takes in such a large view. All great life must have a great sky to live under. This little earth needs every inch of sky that you can see, and every little flower needs the whole solar system for its growth and nourishment. He who lives in God wants all God's creation-temple to offer his homage in. We are ennobled by the vastness of the space which we claim, and intellectually and morally occupy. Who will consecrate himself to the service of the living God by simple, bold, and emphatic testimony as to the effect of Christianity upon his own soul? Let a man come forward and say he has thought of Christianity as a controversy, and he will awaken responsive debate; his words will be argued down by greater speakers than he is himself, by masters of sentences, and masters of quotation, and by casuists of every degree and calibre; but let a man come forward and say, "Once I was blind, and now I see; once I was wandering from the light, and now I have my face straight to it, and my very vision is warmed by its tender glow;" let him make a personal testimony of it, and it will be difficult to answer that testimony, because the character of the man is the invincible defence of the argument.

What does God praise? Wherein does he separate himself from the judgment of his creatures, or wherein do they separate themselves from his criticism? Search the Scriptures, and see what God actually praises. If we cannot find out the Almighty to perfection in this matter, we may make companionship with Christ, and watch him in his distributions of judgment. Upon whom is his praise pronounced? "Except ye be converted, and become as little children." Does he praise little children? Always: he makes them types of the kingdom of heaven; he says unless we become like little children we cannot see the kingdom of God Whom does he praise? Hear this word:

" Verily I say unto you, This man went down to his house justified rather than the other." Who was " this man " ? The man who had been in the temple, and had said with broken-heartedness, " God be merciful to me a sinner." Whom else does he praise ? He says, " She hath done more than they all." Who ? The widow who gave the two mites ; but they were her last, nothing in a series, but everything in a single point. Two mites out of two thousand would have been a calculated insult to the majesty of heaven, but the last two outshone the diamonds of the skies. Whom does God praise ? Whom does he commend ? Along what line does his criticism operate favourably ? Along the line of moral beauty : " I was an hungred, and ye gave me meat." Go to heaven ! He cannot speak sparingly when he commends ; he would seem to have nothing less than heaven to give. " I was thirsty, and ye gave me drink "—pass on to the eternal summer where the fountains never cease, and throw up their living water to the higher sky. God praises good character, simple purpose, religious zeal, self-abnegation, spiritual consecration ; along that line God comes to crown the workers, and to entrust them with his heaven.

Whoso would secure the praise of God must be prepared for temporary sacrifice. " Thou fool, that which thou sowest is not quickened, except it die," has a bearing upon this philosophy of life. If a man will save his life, he shall lose it ; if a man is prepared to lose his life for Christ's sake, he shall find it. God tests men. He sees what they will do when the immediate blessing is taken away : sometimes it is a child, sometimes it is a fortune, sometimes health, always it is a depletion that makes the heart momentarily sore. God does not take away a little thing, for then no man might miss it ; but he takes away something that really interests the affections, involves the deepest solicitudes, and thus he tries the constancy and the faith of men. The praise of men can bear no strain. What is it that men praise ? " Men will praise thee when thou doest well to thyself." Men praise the skilful trick, the act that is agile and successful ; men applaud that which is immediate, momentary, an advantage that can be realised instantaneously. But the praise of men will bear no stress upon it. You must not rely upon that commenda-

tion; there is no wine in those waxen grapes of human praise
and applause and caress. If you live upon human praise your
encomiasts will leave you the moment they feel the sting of fire;
they will not know you; they can turn their once beaming faces
into the uttermost blank; they can pass you on the street, and
they would not drop a crust for your eating, lest some man should
see the crust that was dropped and mistake it as a sign of friendship. It is written of one man, having left his father's house
and gone into a far country, and spent his living, "There arose
a mighty famine in that land, and he began to be in want, and
no man gave unto him." Human eulogists can disappear. The
praise of men is a flying wind, a kindly breeze when the sun
shines upon it; but it can soon cease, or fly away, or deepen into
a groan, or heighten into a storm under change of circumstances.
To be commended of the good is desirable beyond all rubies,
because the good man values no commendation that is not deeply
religious. The good man cannot praise bad character. No flower
will he plant in the accursed soil of mere ambition, pretence, or
hypocrisy. Where the good man sets his seal it is immediately
under the sign-manual of God. When, therefore, we speak
against the praise of men, it is against the praise of selfish,
worldly, little-minded, prejudiced, self-loving men; we speak not
of encomiums which are pronounced upon good men by good
men; we long to hear their kind word. We live in the sunshine
of encouragement. We read of children who plucked the good
man's gown that they might share the good man's smile. Without such mutual recognition life would not be worth living. In
denouncing, therefore, the praise of men, it is to be understood
that it is a certain kind of men whose praise is accounted worthless and is despised.

Look at the effect of this miserable servility upon public men.
The temptation in this direction is severe. By taking a certain
course you can win a hundred votes. You know that course is
wrong, but how the mind reasons, how it sways to and fro, how
on the whole it grasps the votes! It says, If I had those votes
I could make good use of them in another way; perhaps I had
better secure them; for the moment I know I should be doing
wrong, but I should bury the moment in oblivion and retain the

instrument for a great work. So the poor fool commits the act of self-dementation, the act of moral suicide. See how hard a position is that of the public man who dares to defy worthless praise. How bitterly he is detested! How ardently is he persecuted! How mockingly is he sneered at! How he is charged with all meanness! How his very goodness is turned into an argument against him, as who should say, He plays his goodness like a trump, that he may take the trick; this is calculation, this reckoning; all this is part of the manipulation; his prayers are tesselated into his policies, that he may carry them with the more effect and certainty. What a temptation it is to a man to go on the side where the praise is flowing abundantly, and is distributed lavishly! A young man coming into society says, If I adopt a certain course, social or political, there is nothing to hinder me from going straight to the throne. There is a great want of talent on that side; the men upon that side are poor thinkers and poor speakers, and they would covet a man who had a certain faculty and power: if I go on the other side there is a plethora of talent: I shall count for nothing, I shall be a secondary man there. I think I will go into the paper sky, where I shall be a planet of the first order. These temptations do assail men, and there have been men, blessed be God, who have resisted them, who have chosen rather to suffer affliction with the people of God than to enjoy the pleasures of self-suffocation as to moral principle and purpose for a season. There have been men who have said, Whether it be right in the sight of God to obey man rather than God, judge ye, but we cannot but speak. That was divine impulse; that was heavenly inspiration. "Whosoever is ashamed of me and of my words," said Jesus Christ, "of him shall the Son of man be ashamed, when he cometh in his glory." Who, then, will testify for Christ? Only they can testify for him soberly, modestly, and successfully who are living in Christ, who are, so to say, absorbed in Christ, who have found joy in agony, triumph in humiliation, the root of heaven in Golgotha.

Chapter xiii. 15.

"I have given you an example, that ye should do as I have done to you."

CHRIST'S EXAMPLE.

THE incident recorded in this chapter is made the more beautiful by certain features of surpassing grandeur which are found in immediate connection with it. There seems, indeed, at first an inequality between the majesty of the mountain and the value of the frail flower which blooms on its sunny height. We are startled by the difference between the introduction and the progress of the narrative. It is as if God had called attention by great thunderings, and when he had excited the expectation of the universe, introduced, not a burning seraph—who might have maintained the high tone of the introduction—but a quiet little child, a miniature of his own gentleness and purity. This is the introduction, hear it, and say whether the representation now given be correct. "Jesus knowing that the Father had given all things into his hands, and that he was come from God, and went to God——" At this point wonder is excited. We inquire what will he do now, at this critical and trying juncture of his life? Jesus knows the fulness of the mystery set forth in his incarnation; he sees the beginning in the light of the end; he knows all; he sees God behind him sending him into the world,—sees God before him welcoming him after the completion of his earthly ministry. What will he do now? Jesus has come within sight of the end; all the fragments of his life are gathering themselves together and taking wondrous shape, as he beholds them coming into union and forming themselves into their hidden meanings,—what will he do now? We wait almost breathlessly for the next sentence. Let us read it as our imagination might dictate it. Jesus knowing that the Father had given all things into his hands, and that he was come from God and went to God, unfolded secret wings and went up into the light;

274

unveiled splendours which had been conce aled under the guise
of his flesh ; called angels—host upon host, a dazzling throng—
to bring the crown he had left in heaven. This is our notion
of greatness, of pomp, of circumstance. But, just as when
the disciples asked who is greatest in the kingdom of heaven,
Jesus set a little child in the midst of them,—so when we ask,
What will he do when the great mystery is revealing itself to
him ? he does not any one of the supposed wonderful things
which he might have done, but, knowing that the Father had
given all things into his hands, he began to wash the disciples'
feet! Who but himself could have afforded such an apparent
anti-climax ?   Where is there any creation of your romance that
can play so with the public ? What man can afford in one moment
to affect sublimity and grandeur and majesty, and in the next
ask to wash your feet?   It seems as if Jesus Christ might have
washed the disciples' feet in the midst of his most obvious
humiliation.   He need not have reserved that display of his
humility for the supreme moment of consciousness, when God's
eternity was round about him, beating in waves of immortal
blessedness upon the earthliest and poorest aspects of his mission.
Yet it was then, when the whole thing, in all the brightness
of its glory, showed itself to his inmost heart, that he stooped
to wash the feet of the men who had followed him!

Consider this attentively.   We ourselves, creatures redeemed
and sanctified, sometimes have moments of special spiritual
vividness.   Now and then we see our grandeur as sons of God.
In such moments we get views of ourselves as seen in Christ
Jesus which bless us with divine elevation and peace.   Now,
what is the social expression which we give to such sublime
consciousness ?   How is that consciousness made to tell upon
the people who are round about us ?   The consciousness will
surely perish, leaving no heart-blessing behind it, unless under
its inspiration we do deeds of nobleness, compassion, charity,
which shows how even the commonest and poorest side of life
may be lifted up and made beautiful.   This was how Jesus Christ
turned to practical account his highest consciousness of Sonship :
knowing that the Father had given all things into his hands, and
that he was come from God, and went to God, he began to wash

the disciples' feet! Sublime consciousness was thus turned into condescending service; high spiritual dominion and joy found expression in a deed of humility without which even the greatest revelation of majesty, the revelation of the Son of God, would have been incomplete. The deed was simultaneous with the consciousness. Jesus did not wait until the keenness of his joy had abated a little. In the very fulness and glory of his power he laid aside his garments, took a towel, girded himself, and began to wash the disciples' feet. Do not let that picture pass away from your minds as if it were nothing. He laid aside his garments, took a towel, girded himself, and began to wash the disciples' feet. If that picture will not melt men and make them solemn, it can do them no good. It was in the highest moment of his consciousness that he did this. We are to do even little things when we are at the highest stretch of our strength. All the work of life should be done under inspiration. Not only the greatest things; not only the fine carving, but the mortar-mixing; not only the fighting of splendid battles, but the taking home of straying lambs and the gathering up of fallen fragments. So, if we catch aright the meaning of Christ, the elevation of our consciousness is to express itself in the beauty of social charity and service. It is not to consume itself in beatific quietism and sentimental contemplation; it is to prove itself divine by embodiment in visible and useful labour. The apostle says, "We know that we have passed from death unto life." Pause a moment, then, and let us try to find out the reason. Because we feel very comfortable in our hearts, because we like to sit very closely to the fire and read a favourite author, because we have occasional gushings of very tender feeling, is that how we know we have passed from death unto life? The apostle says, No. His argument is this: We know—the same word that we have in the text, Jesus knowing—that we have passed from death unto life because we love the brethren. Alas! there is this danger about our religious life to-day: We think, when we get hold of a favourite book, and repeat certain familiar hymns, and look upon ourselves, in relation to the social blessings with which God has gifted us, that we are doing everything that is needful to show our relationship, to prove our redemption by Christ. The Saviour, knowing the full mystery of God's purpose concerning his ministry in this world, seeing his hands filled with the gifts of God, opened those hands that he might wash the feet of the disciples. There is a contemplation of which I am afraid. There is a species of spiritual luxury which amounts to the most terrible temptation and snare. Do you say there are times when you feel as if you could wash the feet of the poorest disciple of Christ? Then why do you not do it? You wear away your feeling, and incapacitate yourself for its recurrence in all its finest sensibility, by allowing it to reach the highest point without turning it into the most condescending service.

In the course of his attention to the disciples Jesus came to Simon Peter. We are entitled, are we not, from the structure of the sentence, to infer that Simon Peter was not taken first? We do not stop to debate the question. The point is of little importance except as bearing upon those who draw mischievous lessons from the supposed supremacy of Peter. The principal point is found in the conversation which passed between the wondering disciple and his condescending Lord When Jesus Christ came to Peter that disciple spoke to him. "Dost thou wash my feet?" "Yes." "Lord, thou shalt never wash my feet." Peter reasoned from a much lower consciousness than Christ s. Peter saw nothing beyond the mere fact of washing the disciples' feet. To him it was only a fact; it was not an emblem. It lost its meaning because he did not look at it in a spiritual light. It was only something done; it was not a parable full of secret meaning, palpitating with divine mystery. How true it is that to the wise man, whose eyes are in his head and whose heart has any sympathy with God, "things are not what they seem." Now, in Jesus Christ's answer to Peter we find the other half of the gracious truth on which we have been insisting. It has been said that consciousness is to express itself in service. We now see that, as consciousness sometimes precedes service and dictates it, so occasionally facts prepare the way for consciousness. There is a kind of reciprocal action. Some men can work from consciousness best; can work from the intuitive, the subjective, the internal, the spiritual. Other men can only work from the point of information, from the point of mere fact; they must see something, handle something, and work their way from the visible to the unseen.   It was so in the case of Peter : hence Jesus Christ said, " What thou knowest not now thou shalt know hereafter."   We are not always to work from the point of knowledge, observe.   We are not always to work from the point of understanding.   There are occasions in life when our highest powers of reasoning are to be set aside, and we are to become little children, creatures of yesterday, receivers only. Those who are blind are invited to put their little hands into the great hand of God.   It is as if Christ had said to Peter : " Let the thing be done.   Do what I wish,   Do the will, and afterwards thou shalt know the doctrine,—that external thing which occasions nothing but wonder now, which seems a mere waste of power on my part, shall in due time be seen to have deep meaning, shall become a precious emblem and an inspiring example."

Illustrations of this are not wanting in daily life.   You may find one in the ordinance of infant baptism.   To each infant it may be said, " What thou knowest not now thou shalt know hereafter."   This baptism is a fact of which the spiritual meaning and spiritual blessedness will come by-and-by.   Let it stand at the very beginning of thy life, and God will tell thee all the intent of it when thou shalt be able to hear him in thy heart.   Ordinances are not to wait for reason.   There are persons who affect to find amusement in observing the ordinance of infant baptism. They talk about the crying little children, and they quite shake themselves with a species of inexplicable fun as they look upon half a dozen poor trembling little things brought up to a basin of water.   They say, " What do they know about it, and what can they understand about it ? " as if we understood anything,—forgetful that the old man is a young being!   When shall we give over looking at our ages according to the returns of registrars and the calculations of actuaries ?   The oldest man amongst us is old and venerable as a man within the limits of this earthly discipline and pilgrimage ; but manhood is only a fraction of being, and ten thousand ages are nothing when set against the eternity of God.   We know nothing.   We understand in its fulness and perfectness nothing.   What if we should be pushed aside, and Jesus should take up one of those sweet little infants, and say, This is the greatest in the kingdom of heaven ?   It would be very humiliating to us,—because we know and we understand, and we snatch a moment's vulgar sniffling from seeing little children baptised in God's house.

Sometimes things are to be done, and the explanation is to come after the fact. Our first question must always be, Is this the will of God? If so, we shall find the explanation of the mystery in God's way and God's time. I planted a little seed, and, as I was hiding it away in the dark ground, it asked me why I did not let it lie in the sunshine, where it could see the bright blue day and hear the singing birds. I answered, "What thou knowest not now thou shalt know hereafter." The sun came and the dew and the living air, and for awhile they tarried at the prison-door of the seed. By-and-by the prisoner came forth, beautiful in form and exquisite in colour; day by day it grew in strength and increased in loveliness; and in the fulness of the summer time it knew, without asking me, why I had hidden it in the earth. It is even so with children whose minds and memories are stored with the truths of God's Word. At first they know but the letter. The knowledge of the letter may come through strife and pain. For long years it may lie dead in the heart; but in some season of special sorrow, in the day of trouble and sore distress, when heart and flesh do fail, it may arise and bring deliverance, and lead away the soul into the very presence of God. Believe, then, in the mysteries of life; believe in facts, ordinances, means. The intent and purpose of each do not lie upon the surface. Wheresoever God may bid us go let us hasten to the place, for there we shall find his blessing.

I have said that the explanation of a fact may come by-and-by. In the case before us the explanation came immediately after the event. After he had washed their feet, and taken his garments, and was set down again, he said unto them, " Know ye what I have done to you? Ye call me Master and Lord : and ye say well; for so I am. If I then, your Lord and Master, have washed your feet ; ye also ought to wash one another's feet." Suppose that Jesus Christ had laid down the abstract doctrine,— Christians, ye ought to wash one another's feet. What would have been the result? Who would have believed him? We should have found in that an instance of mistranslation; there would have been great hunting up of grammars and lexicons upon that point, because it stands to reason that the thing is utterly absurd. There is a missing letter; there is a wrong punctuation; there is a great difference of opinion between critics, we should have said, as to the meaning of this. But what does Jesus Christ do? Instead of merely laying down the doctrine, he gave the example. This shows how teaching may start from either of two points,—from philosophy or from life. It may be based upon a course of reasoning; it may express itself in example, in service, in deed. Some teaching must, from the necessity of the case, be purely intellectual; it does not admit of incarnation. Other teaching may at once be practical; it may rise out of the life, and prove by positive demonstration the practicability and beneficence of its philosophy. Christ's method did not admit of debate. It was not a theory, it was a fact. There it was,—a stoop that could never be forgotten, an argument which no ingenuity could ever impair. It was practicable; the Lord and Master had done it. It was worth doing, or he who never trifled with life would not have set the example. This shows in a wonderful manner the vocation of men to whom God has assigned positions of lordship and mastery in life. What is our business in proportion as God has set us in eminent places, given us great talent or great wealth, or great position of any kind? Our duty is to set examples of lowliness and charity,—the lowliness which comes out of righteousness, the charity which stands upon law. We require all the stimulus of illustrious precedent in order to do some things which are unwelcome in life. We have not courage to do some things solely on their own merits. Even if we could see them to be duties we could never bring ourselves to discharge them. We want somebody else to do it first. We want to hide ourselves under a great name. Christ provides for this peculiarity of our nature. He allows us to use his name and example. "You may say that I did it. If ever you are caught in the humiliating act of washing your brother's feet, and there should come into your cheek a tingling of shame, you may say that I did it." You will in life—such are the combinations of society—occasionally **want precedent.** You cannot always work upon the abstract and the right. Sometimes you will want the defence of a name; you will occasionally want to be able to point to somebody behind you and say, "He did it first." "Now take my name, I have given you an example." So we get out of a splendid precedent what we never could have got out of an abstract command. We all know well what this is in life. The young man who wants to try some new plan of doing his work, trembles a little before doing so, and then he says, "I will do it." And when he has been brought to book about it, it has been an encouragement to him when he could point to some older man and say, "He does it." We thus live in one another, and the Past becomes the inspiration of the Present; and precedents and examples are vitalised into the living influential forces of to-day. This is how our greatest work has been done.

[*See another treatment of this subject in the discourse which follows.*]

PRAYER.

ALMIGHTY GOD, we draw near to thy throne without fear or trembling, because thou hast exhorted us to come boldly unto the throne of grace. We come that we may obtain mercy, and find grace to help us in time of need. Our life is one crying want. We have nothing that we have not received; thou art the Giver of every good gift and every perfect gift. We humbly desire, therefore, to thank thee for all the mercies we enjoy, and all the grace which has strengthened and soothed our life; for all the hope which has inspired us in the dark and cloudy day; and for the manifold comforts which hath healed our diseases and consoled us when the help of man was vain. We have come up from our households that we may bless God in his own house. We have come to speak the praises of the Most High God, for thy mercy, O King of saints, endureth for ever! We have not forsaken the assembling of ourselves together, as the manner of some is; but with one accord are found in one place, and we lift up our hearts with one consent. Each worshipper brings his own tribute, each heart has its own song, each hand its own gift. Yet have we common mercies, for which we can find common praises. We can all unite in praising thee for the light of the heavens, the air on which we live. Thou hast spread our table in the wilderness; when we had no bread thou didst multiply the crumbs that were left; when the cruse of oil did fail, thou didst cause it to flow on; when the staff broke in our hands, thou didst give unto us thy rod and thy staff, and they comforted us; when the road was hilly and stony and difficult, thou didst uphold us with strength unfailing, thou didst bring us to the mountain top; when the wind was cold, thou didst shield us from its blast; when the dark night came suddenly down upon us, thou didst set thine eye in the darkness, and behold, it was bright as day beneath our feet! What shall we render unto the Lord for all his benefits towards us? Some have come from the toils of business, the anxieties of earthly life, and are hardly able to emancipate themselves from recollections and apprehensions, from fears and suggestions, which are unfavourable to worship, and which mar the continuity of their contemplation and interfere with the stream of their devotional love. Do thou grant them release from all worldly torments, from all earthly cares, and give thy people to feel the liberty of heaven, the joy of the presence of God! Some have returned to thy house after long absence; thou hast seen fit to lay them aside from the busy crowd, to give them hours of pain, days of restlessness, and nights of weariness. Now that they have returned to public worship, they desire to speak of the goodness of God, his peace, his healing power, and to be thankful for his sustaining grace. Lord, hear the grateful psalm of such, and abundantly sustain and comfort them, now that they have formed resolutions of intenser devotion and more constant love. Most of us have brought sorrow with us;

some little shadow or dark cloud, some wearing grief, some tormenting, oppressive burden,—sorrows we cannot tell, we dare not sigh, lest listeners should suspect the hidden grief. We can only bow down ourselves before God, praying that the sorrows of our life may be sources of joy; that out of our very grief we may be able to extract honey which shall refresh the strength of our souls. Do thou sanctify the discipline of life to us; give us control over events and circumstances, so far as to enable us to feel that thy shaping hand is moving amid all the chaos of life, and that thou art working out thine own wondrous order and beauty. It will be enough for us if we know thou art near, and that thy throne absorbs all other powers. The stranger is here, far away from home; the young man is here, far from early association and restraint of home love; the wanderer is here, not knowing why he was born, surrounded by difficulties, depressed, almost despairing; the unsuccessful man, who has knocked at a thousand doors, and no kindly hand has opened one to him that he might have hospitality; the hypocrite, with well-set visor, with double-painted mask, well fitted to his face, the man who can say words with his lips which were never dictated by his heart; the inquirer is here, tossed about by doubt and difficulty and perplexity, sincere in his heart, yet there is a heavy mist upon all his thinking, and he is groping his way towards God, towards life; the little child is here—the summer bud, the June flower—and even the parent's eye cannot foresee altogether the development and destiny. Look upon us as we are before thee! Lift up those that be bowed down. Strike the visor from the false face. Soothe the sorrowing; dry the tears of grief. Give stimulus and strength to every man in whom there is high aspiration, to every heart in which there is a noble purpose. Enable us all, whether tottering on the brink of the grave, or looking out from earliest life upon all the wonders of existence, to know that thou art our Father, our Redeemer, our Sanctifier, and in God may we have our being! Have mercy upon us, thou loving One! Thou delightest to forgive; we all need thy forgiveness. Help us from our heart of hearts to confess our sins. May we show how truly we confess it by the intensity of our hatred of it. When we own our guilt, may we tremble and be in despair, until we see the Cross, the light of the advancing Saviour, the Lamb of God, which taketh away the sin of the world. Wash us, and we shall be clean. Let thy blessing now go from congregation to congregation, from minister to minister, until all who are engaged in worship feel the fire of devotion glowing in their hearts. May souls to-day be reclaimed, be re-established, be edified, be comforted. Thus at eventide we shall be a Sabbath day's journey nearer home! Amen.

Chapter xiii. 15.

"For I have given you an example, that ye should do as I have done to you."

WASHING DISCIPLES' FEET.

TO know the full force and value of those words we should connect them with the third verse of the same chapter, which reads thus: "Jesus, knowing that the Father had given all things into his hands, and that he was come from God, and went to God." That is the introduction. It excites expectation that amounts almost to intolerable rapture. What will he do now, in this supreme consciousness, in this hour of the resurrection before the time, the Cross behind, the resurrection past, the whole meaning of the divine sovereignty in the incarnation of Jesus Christ revealed in cloudless, dazzling light? Now he will take wing and flee away! He knows now who he is, what he is, what God's meaning in his incarnation and whole ministry is; he sees, from the human standpoint, the beginning and the end; he lays his hands, so to say, on both ends of the chain. What will he do in the moment of supreme consciousness? He will show his diadem now; with his right hand he will take away the cloud which veiled it, and the shining of that diadem shall put out the sun. What will he do in this summer time? We have analogous times in our own consciousness, when we feel what we are, when the divinity stirs within us, when we feel the blood of a hundred kings burning in our veins. What is our wish under the pressure of such heroic and tempting consciousness? Surely to do some great thing; surely to vindicate our right to be called by brilliant names. What did Jesus Christ do? Mark the time: the whole pith of this part of the discourse is in the point of time—" Jesus knowing "—in modern words, the consciousness of Jesus urged to its highest point, realising its utmost sensitiveness, receiving into itself the full revelation of the divine meaning. " Jesus knowing "—that his right hand was full, and his left hand—yea, " that the Father had given all things into his hands "—what did he do? He arose from supper, he laid aside his garments, he took a towel and girded himself, he poured water into a basin, "and began to wash the disciples' feet." Surely this is madness; surely the sentence frays out here into feebleness. That is our way of looking at all things. We do not know the meaning of what is taking place around us; we do not see that the circle is always bending, and that things made of God are in circles. That is the simple geometry. We cannot tell the meaning of condescension in the divine economy; we do not see that God is always stooping; we do not see that the Infinite is always doing this very self-same thing, and that suspension of such service would mean the ruin of all finite things. This is what God is doing: he is always washing the feet of angels and men, and the whole universe. God is love; love lives to serve; love does not want to sit down in stately ease—sweet angel! she is only happy when she is busy and cumbered about many things.

Let us look at the matter from the human standpoint first of all. Says Jesus: "I have given you an example." Bold—how dare he speak so? "Is not this the carpenter's Son?" Do we not know his father and his mother and his sisters? Are they not all with us—common folks, like ourselves? But he was both. Compared with his audacity, the boldness of Isaiah was blushing modesty. When did Jesus Christ ever copy an example? Never. These circumstances constitute, to my mind, the most connected and cogent argument in proof of Jesus Christ's deity. Never did Jesus Christ ask for time that he might put his thoughts together; never did Jesus Christ withdraw a speech and ask to be allowed to substitute another in its place; never did the Saviour amend a solitary sentence that he once delivered; in no instance did Jesus Christ say, "This is an example which I myself must copy." Trace him from beginning to end, and he owes no man anything. He gives; if he receives it is to return in ampler love. He never learned letters, yet he was never second in conversation. He was always in himself above his age. He said: "I have given you an example." Many can give advice, many can administer rebukes--many can offer all these, but few can set examples towards which they challenge the criticism of all time; yes—that is the point—all time. It were not difficult to set an example that might live through one cloudy day—a day so cloudy as to make it almost impossible to distinguish between one colour and another; but to set an example that should hold its own against all the coming and going of time—brighten and shine over all the days of tumultuous life—surely the good of such an example, if it stand the test of time, is the quietest and completest miracle ever wrought by the Son of God. We must find the universal element in the teaching of Jesus Christ, or it was only a lesson for a day—a transient speech to an assembly which dissolved in the very act of listening to it. We must have nothing local in Jesus Christ's teaching.

Whatever he says must spread itself over all time, all space; must be equally at home at the north pole and the south pole, in the tropics and in the coldest regions of the earth; must have the faculty of entering into all languages, tabernacling in all symbols, and looking out with bright, angel-like hospitality from every tribe, and kindred, and people. In the moment of supreme consciousness Jesus Christ did something that can be done seven days a week on every habitable line of latitude and longitude through all the ages of time; and in this universality and adaptation I find a subtle but invincible testimony to the completeness of the mind, the dignity of the character, the deity of the personality of Jesus Christ.

Being about to leave the world, as we call leaving, what will Jesus Christ do? Look at the disciples as they had never been looked at before, with a countenance whose revelation would mark the critical point in their personal consciousness and history? No. Order them off to some mountain solitude, where, as hermits, they might wait for death? That is not the course which Jesus Christ pursued; he simply—we should say he profoundly—adopted the course of washing the disciples' feet. That is the unfathomable simplicity of Christ—the thing which appears to be so intelligible, and yet that carries with it all philosophies, theologies, and possibilities of thinking worthy of reference. Where is there a man who does not suppose that he instantly sees the whole meaning of an incident of this kind? Yet the angels desire to look into it. We lose so much by dismissing so many things as merely simple. The simplicity of Christ was the profundity of God. There is nothing simple in Jesus Christ. The cry—the fool's cry—"the simple gospel"— it is an affront to heaven! There is no "simple" gospel, except in the sense that simplicity is the last result of omniscience and omnipotence—not a simplicity at the beginning, but at the end: the outflow and last miracle of the divine mind and power. I wonder not that believers in the simple gospel—vulgarly and mistakenly so-called—reel, and totter, and abolish themselves.

The eternal meaning of the text is: that humility is to be a social advantage. There are many humble speakers who ought never to open their mouths in the cause of humility. There are many speakers whose hearts are humble, but whose mouths were not made for mincing. We must leave the inner and complete judgment to him who made us. Criticism of others is not humility ; inverted pride is not humility ; the confession of some barren sentiment is not humility. Humility is dumb ; humility keeps no looking-glass ; humility is unconscious of its own blushing; humility wists not that its face, having been turned towards God in long fellowship, burns with the reflected glory of the Image it has gazed upon. Humility has to be an active power in life. The greater we know ourselves to be, the humbler will be the service we shall render, without knowing that it is a service of humiliation—not self-display. There is a way of washing feet which says in the doing of it, " Your feet do very much need to be washed, therefore I am washing them." No ; the feet will be the viler for the touch. Do not say how servile is the work you are doing, how menial the service you are discharging, and, therefore, how humble you are in endeavouring to carry out the word and wish of the Son of God. Service of this particular kind can only be done in Christ's spirit. It can be done otherwise in the letter ; but done in the letter it is not done at all ; going to church because you must go—you do not go. Washing feet, or doing any service symbolised by that phrase, cannot be done—let me repeat—except in the spirit of Christ ; but being done in that spirit, it is no longer the service of humiliation, because it is balanced by the consciousness out of which it came. In Christ's own instance : " Jesus knowing— Jesus washed." If we do the washing without the spiritual consciousness, it is menial service, it is a slave's reluctant obla- tion on the altar of obedience ; but coming out of great prayer, out of something like complete vision of God, it is done as if it were not done, and in the doing of it we do but add to the consciousness which was its first inspiration ; and thus whilst we are on earth we are in heaven, and being in heaven we stoop to take dear little earth up and cleanse it, and lift it back into its Maker's smile.

This is Christianity—not letter worship, not eye service, but the unconscious doing of works of humiliation through the higher consciousness that there is nothing mean that is done for Christ's sake. When this spirit is in us we shall have no dainty dislike for certain kinds of service in the Church. We do now sometimes pick and choose. We have no objection to high office, but we are not going to do certain things which other people of smaller income might very properly do. We are not going to keep the church door, or light the church lamp, but let us pay a man a few pence to do it—a man we can order about, a handy man, who can be here and there and everywhere, and dare not answer us again. O wounded One, Man of the five mortal wounds! Thou washer of the disciples' feet! this is what we have done. Wilt thou look on us? We dare not look at thee. In thine eye is not anger—that we might for a moment bear—but pity, weeping pity, divine pity, that we dare not look at; it hurts us by its pathos. We cannot do service in the Church, men and brethren, except in the Spirit of Christ—by that I mean service that shall have in it the true quality of Christian sacrifice and oblation on the one altar of the Cross. We cannot preach except in that spirit. To preach without great hot tears is not to preach; if there be not times when the heart says, " I cannot bear it any longer! O this pity for human souls!" there is no preaching. We may preach sentences we have made, phrases we have measured off mechanically; but preaching that shall be a washing of men, a cleansing of their lives, a going down to them and lifting them up, is the very gift of God; there is nothing like it, though men do not acknowledge that—the painter first, or the poet, or the politician, or the entertainer, or the man of musical genius; but if we knew it, there is but one great man in all creation—he who does not know he is great, but who is swallowed up in the love of God and the consequent desire to cleanse the lives of men. In what spirit are we working? Are we willing to be anything or nothing? Is our Christianity: "Lord, what wilt thou have me to do?" Are we willing to be London ministers, but not African missionaries? Do we covet the honours, but leave other people to do the drudgery? Or is the drudgery the honour, the deeper the higher, the meaner the diviner? Dost thou so reckon? No man then shall take thy crown.

PRAYER.

ALMIGHTY God our Father, made known to us in Jesus Christ thy Son, we will open the day in thy name and in thy love. We would begin it in thy fear, and in confident hope in thy mercy because thy mercy endureth for ever. We can have no fear if we fear God; we are rich if we live in him; we shall be filled with a sacred contentment if we tarry alway at the foot of the Cross. Help us to bring forth abundant fruit to the honour of thy name; may we now be mindful of ourselves more than ever : may we hear the apostle saying unto us, " Look unto yourselves," that in education and discipline and refinement we may make great advance in the things pertaining to the life that is in God. Thou canst do great things for us, yea, thou canst do exceeding abundantly above all that we ask or think. We bless thee that thine answers are not limited by our prayers. Thou knowest what we need, thou knowest what is best for us; keep back what would please us and yet harm us, and give us that which we dread if in its use we shall find ourselves nearer God. We bless thee for all the past. It has been wondrous music; thou hast done great things for us whereof we are glad. We have changed our way of life, we have gone from house to house, we have seen all the varieties of business life; we have known what it is to be at school, to be suffering from bodily disease, to be rejoicing in abundant health; we have walked in the summer garden, and we have seen the winter snow : and through all the varied way thy hand has led us and thy right hand has upheld us. We will therefore not be silent in thine house, we will make a joyful noise unto the Rock of our salvation, yea with loud songs and psalms will we praise the right hand of the Most High. We thank thee above all other thanks for the gift of thy Son by whom alone we know or can know the Father. He has spoken gently to our listening souls, he has fed us with the bread of life, he has not kept back from us any visions that our eyes could endure; he has saved us from our sin, he has led us to higher character and to more wondrous destiny. Blessed be the Son of God who is to us God the Son, who loved us and gave himself for us. We leave ourselves under thy care, thou loving One, Father and Mother of us all, the great Creator, the tender Redeemer, the wondrous Sanctifier : God the Father, God the Son, and God the Holy Ghost. We rest in thy hands, thou mighty One, eternal in majesty and eternal in love. Thou knowest what our purposes are; help us to realise them in so far as they are good. Thou hast made us after a wonderful fashion : we do not know ourselves, we are surprised at our own littleness and at our own greatness ; we are amazed by sudden visions that lighten the whole heaven as by a flash from thy throne, and we are amazed that we are so soon overthrown and made to fear and tremble as if we were in the hands of chance and not in the hands of God. Enable us, at home, in business, in the Church, on the highway, at school, in the sick-chamber, everywhere, to know that things are meted, we are in the hands of a watchful gracious Father, and that not a sparrow can fall to the ground without his knowledge. May we live and move and have our being in these great principles; then we shall be calm, restful, contented, and our life shall be as the outgoing of solemn yet tender music. Amen.

John xiii. 18-35.

18. I speak not of you all: I know whom I have chosen: but that the Scripture may be fulfilled, He that eateth bread with me hath lifted up his heel against me. [The impossibilities of history; the ironies and contradictions of things; the ghastliest ingratitude; the thing that never could have been imagined,—' He that eateth bread with me hath lifted up his heel against me"; the bread must have turned to poison.]

19. Now I tell you before it come, that, when it is come to pass, ye may believe that I am he. [We vindicate our prophetic function by tokens. The historian reviews, the prophet foretells. Remember what I said to you: It is about to take place; watch events, and be just to the prophet.]

20. Verily, verily [Assuredly, assuredly], I say unto you, He that receiveth whomsoever I send receiveth me; and he that receiveth me receiveth him that sent me. [Lives are related to one another. All human life is a marvellous tessellation. There is no individuality in any sense of absolute isolation. The father means the child, and the child the father, and man may mean God.]

21. When Jesus had thus said, he was troubled in spirit, and testified, and said Verily, verily [Assuredly, assuredly], I say unto you, That one of you shall betray me. [Yet not necessarily be worse than the rest. There is a transmigration, there is also a transformation, of souls. We represent one another. When Adam fell, all that is Adamic fell. Every man is a Judas, an Iscariot; every man has put in his pocket the price of Christ's blood: there is none righteous.]

22. Then the disciples looked one on another, doubting of whom he spake. [Their characteristic ignorance; their affected simplicity: yet every heart was quickened. The accent might fall upon any syllable, but the word would be one, the deed would be unbroken.]

23. Now there was leaning on Jesus' bosom one of his disciples, whom Jesus loved. [Loved in spite of what was wicked in him; not in consequence of it, but in spite of it.]

24. Simon Peter therefore beckoned to him, that he should ask who it should be of whom he spake. [Beckoning and whispering. There are times when it is profanity to speak aloud. The eye must speak, the hand must signify; a whisper must convey the tremendous question. Find out for us, thou loved One, the meaning of this foretelling.]

25. He then lying on Jesus' breast saith unto him, Lord, who is it? [Who is it that shall act for us all? Who is it that shall seem to be the worst? He will not act for himself alone : a great tragedy is involved here, and it cannot be limited by Iscariot's individuality,—who is it?]

26. Jesus answered, He it is, to whom I shall give a sop, when I have dipped it. And when he had dipped the sop, he gave it to Judas Iscariot, the son of Simon. [That was Iscariot's cross. There are men who feel the heavy weights of the world. There are burden-bearers as well as singers.]

27. And after the sop Satan entered into him. [Satan took more full possession of him; Satan lighted every piece of fuel that had been brought from hell; Satan fired him through and through; Satan leaped upon him, drove him to madness.] Then said Jesus unto him, That thou doest, do quickly. [Through no fear on the part of Christ, through no wish for mere haste, but to express detestation. Do not roll thy hands in blood—dip them and be gone; do not linger in murder; take no holiday in crime; let it be done shortly, sharply, almost imperceptibly as to time.]

28. Now no man at the table knew for what intent he spake this unto him [Thus meanings are lost, or are half-caught and are misreported, and the speaker is misjudged, and the reporter is the unfaithful witness.]

29. For some of them thought, because Judas had the bag, that Jesus had said unto him, Buy those things that we have need of against the feast; or, that he should give something to the poor. [Thus attaching false meanings to the deepest words; thus using the sun as a light to pass up and down in paths of frivolity.]

30. He then having received the sop went immediately out: and it was night. [What unconscious poetry! What a marvellous coincidence! What a background! "It was night." No other word would have fitted that frame of things; any other picture would have been out of place there. "It was night": sevenfold night, midnight, darkness that might be felt, a night in which a man might commit suicide.]

31. Therefore, when he was gone out [A wonderful change took place in the atmosphere: it was all over; the bitterness of death was passed], Jesus said, Now is the Son of man glorified, and God is glorified in him.

32. If God be glorified in him, God shall also glorify him in himself, and shall straightway glorify him.

33. Little children, yet a little while I am with you. Ye shall seek me: and as I said unto the Jews, Whither I go, ye cannot come; so now I say to you.

34. A new commandment I give unto you, That ye love one another; as I have loved you, that ye also love one another.

35. By this shall all men know that ye are my disciples, if ye have love one to another.

Chapter xiii. 26.

"Judas Iscariot, the son of Simon."

JUDAS ISCARIOT: A STUDY OF CHARACTER.

IT will help me very greatly in my delicate work of examining the character of the betrayer of our Lord if there be an understanding between us, that it is not presumptuously supposed on either side that every difficulty can be explained, and that perfect unanimity can be secured on every point; and especially if it be further understood that my object is not to set up or defend any theory about Judas Iscariot, but solemnly to inquire whether his character was so absolutely unlike everything we know of human nature as to give us no help in the deeper understanding of our own; or whether there was not even in Judas something that, at its very worst, was only an exaggeration of elements or forces that may possibly be in every one of us. We always think of him as a monster; but what if we ourselves be —at least in possibility—as monstrous and as vile? Let us go carefully through his history, and see. My purpose is to cut a path as straight as I may be able to go, through the entangled and thorny jungle of texts which make up the history of Iscariot. I propose to stop here and there on the road, that we may get new views and breathe, perhaps, an uncongenial air; and though we may differ somewhat as to the distance and form of passing objects, I am quite sure that when we get out again into the common highways we shall resume our unanimity, and find it none the less entire and cordial because of what we have seen on the unaccustomed and perilous way. First of all, then, let us try to get a clear knowledge of the character of Judas Iscariot, the disciple, and apostle, and betrayer of the Son of God.

I. EXPOSITORY.

"Have not I chosen you twelve, and one of you is a devil?" (John vi. 70.)—Who, then, will say that the men with whom Christ began his new kingdom were more than men,—not bone of our bone and flesh of our flesh, but a princely sort, specially created and quite away from the common herd in sympathy and aim? He chose twelve men who fairly represented human nature in its best and worst aspects,—they represented gentleness, ardour, domesticity, enterprise, timidity, courage,—and one of them is a devil. Not a devil in the sense of being something else than human. Judas was a man like the others, but in him there was a pre-eminent capacity for plotting and attempting the foulest mischief. We are certainly not to understand that our Lord chose twelve men who, with one exception, were converted, intelligent, sanctified, and perfect ; nor is it by any means certain that our Lord chose even the most intellectual and influential men that it was possible for him to draw into his service. I do not know that we are entitled to regard the apostles as in all respects the twelve best men of their day ; but I think we may justly look upon them as an almost complete representation of all sides of human nature. And as such they utterly destroy the theory that they were but a coterie,—men of one mean stamp, without individuality, force, emphasis, or self-assertion ; padding, not men ; mere shadows of a crafty empiric, and not to be counted as men. On the contrary, this was a representative discipleship ; we were all in that elect band ; the kingdom of God, as declared in Christ Jesus, would work upon each according to his own nature, and would reveal every man to himself. A very wonderful and instructive thing is this, that Jesus Christ did not point out the supremely wicked man, but merely said, " One of you is a devil." Thus a spirit of self-suspicion was excited in the whole number, culminating in the mournful " Is it I ? " of the Last Supper ; and truly it is better for us not to know which is the worst man in the church,—to know only that judgment will begin at the house of God, and to be wondering whether that judgment will take most effect upon ourselves. No man fully knows himself. Jesus Christ would seem to be saying to us, At this moment you appear to be a child of God : you are reverent, charitable, well-disposed ; you have a place in my visible kingdom,—even a prominent place in the pulpit, on the platform, at the desk, in the office ; appearances are wholly and strongly in your favour, yet, little as you suspect it, deep under all these things lies an undiscovered self—a very devil, it may be; so that even you, now loud in your loyalty and zealous beyond all others in pompous diligence, may in the long run turn round upon your Lord and thrust a spear into his heart ! Can it be that the foremost some-

times stumble ? Do the strong cedars fall ? May the very star
of the morning drop from the gate of heaven ? Let the veteran,
the leader, the hoary Nestor, the soldier valiant beyond all others,
say, "Lord, is it I?" Which of us can positively separate
himself from Judas Iscariot and honestly say, His was a kind of
human nature different from mine ? I dare not do so. In the
betrayer I would have every man see a possibility of himself,—
himself, it may be, magnified in hideous and revolting exaggeration, yet part of the same earth heaved, in the case of Judas, into
a great hill by fierce heat, but on exactly the same plane as the
coldest dust that lies miles below its elevation. Iscariot's was a
human sin rather than a merely personal crime. Individually I
did not sin in Eden, but humanly I did ; personally I did not
covenant for the betrayal of my Lord, but morally I did,—I
denied him, and betrayed him, and spat upon him, and pierced
him, and he loved me and gave himself for me !

Of course the question will arise, Why did our Lord choose a
man whom he knew to be a devil ? A hard question ; but there
is a harder one still, Why did Jesus choose you ? Could you ever
make out that mystery ? Was it because of your respectability ?
Was it because of the desirableness of your companionship ?
Was it because of the utter absence of all devilishness in your
nature ? What if Judas did for you what you were only too
timid to do for yourself ? The incarnation with a view to human
redemption is the supreme mystery ; in comparison with that,
every other difficulty is as a molehill to a mountain. In your
heart of hearts are you saying, "If this man were a prophet, he
would know what manner of man this Judas is, for he is a
sinner" ? O thou self-contented Simon, presently the Lord will
have somewhat to say unto thee, and his parable will smite thee
like a sword.

"The Son of man goeth as it is written of him : but woe unto
that man by whom he is betrayed."—I think we shall miss the
true meaning and pathos of this passage if we regard it merely as
the exclamation of a man who was worsted for the moment by
superior strength, but who would get the upper hand by-and-by,
and then avenge his humiliation. These words might have been

uttered with tears of the heart, Woe will be the portion of that man who betrays me ; yea, woe upon woe, even unto remorse and agony and death ; the chief of sinners, he will also be chief of sufferers ; when he sees the full meaning of what he has done, he will sink under the intolerable shame, he will give blood for blood, and be glad to find solace in death.

And if our hearts be moved at all to pitifulness in the review of this case, may we not find somewhat of a redeeming feature in the capacity for suffering so deep and terrible ? Shall we be stretching the law of mercy unduly if we see in this self-torment a faint light on the skirts of an appalling cloud ? I do not find that Judas professed or manifested any joy in his grim labour ; there is no sound of revel or mad hilarity in all the tragic movement ; on the contrary, there is a significant absence, so far as we can judge from the narrative, of all the excitement needful for nerving the mischievous man to work out purposes which he knows to be wholly evil. All the while Judas would seem to be under a cloud, to be advancing stealthily rather than boisterously ; he was no excited Belshazzar whose brain was aflame with excess of wine—though he, too, trembled as if the mystic hand were writing letters of doom upon the old familiar scenes. So excited is he that a word will send him reeling backward to the ground, and if he do not his work "quickly" he will become sick with fear and be incapable of action ; as it is, he has only bargained to "kiss" the Victim, not to clutch him with a ruffian's grasp. Then came the intolerable woe !

This great law is at work upon our lives to-day. Woe unto the unfaithful pastor ; woe unto the negligent steward ; woe unto the betrayer of sacred interests ; woe unto them that call evil good and good evil ;—to all such be woe ; not only the woe of outward judgment—divine and inexorable—but that, it may be, still keener, sadder woe of self-contempt and self-damnation. With such sorrow no stranger may intermeddle. The lesson to ourselves would seem to be this, Do not regard divine judgment merely as measure for measure in relation to your sin, —that is to say, so much penalty for so much guilt ; it is more than that—it is a quickening of the man into holy resentment against himself, an arming of the conscience against the whole life, a subjective controversy which will not be lulled into unrighteous peace, but will rage wrathfully and implacably until there shall come repentance unto life or remorse unto death. Shall I startle you if I say that there is a still more terrible state than that of such anguish as Iscariot's? To have worn out the moral sense, to have become incapable of pain, to have the conscience seared as with a hot iron, to be " past feeling,"—that is the consummation of wickedness. That there is a judicial and outward infliction of pain on account of sin, is of course undoubted ; but whilst that outward judgment may actually harden the sinner, the bitter woe which comes of a true estimate of sin and of genuine contrition for its enormity may work out a repentance not to be repented of. If, then, any man is suffering the pain of just self-condemnation on account of sin ; if any man's conscience is now rising mightily against him and threatening to tear him in pieces before the Lord, because of secret lapses or unholy betrayals, because of long-sustained hypocrisy or self-seeking faithlessness, I will not hurriedly seek to ease the healthy pain—the fire will work to his purification, and the Refiner will lose nothing of the gold ;—but if any man, how eminent soever in ecclesiastical position, knows that he has betrayed the Lord, and conceals under a fair exterior all that Ezekiel saw in the chamber of imagery, and is as a brazen wall against every appeal—hard, tearless, impenetrable, unresponsive—I do not hesitate to say that I would rather be numbered with Judas than with that man.

"It had been good for that man if he had not been born."— Then why was he born? is the question, not of impatient ignorance only, but of a certain moral instinct which God never fails to respect throughout the whole of his intercourse with mankind, and which he will undoubtedly honour in this instance. Take the case as it is ordinarily put : Judas, like the rest of us, had no control over his own birth ; he found himself in a world in whose formation he had no share ; he was born under circumstances which, as to their literal and local bearing, can never be repeated in all the ages of time. So far as we can gather from the narrative, Jesus spoke to him no word of sympathy, never drew him aside, as he drew Peter, to tell him of preventing prayer, but to all appearance left him to be the blind and helpless

instrument of the devil, and then said, " It had been good for
that man if he had not been born." This cannot be the full
meaning of the words.   Instantly we repeat the profound inquiry
of Abraham, " Shall not the Judge of all the earth do right ? "   He
may, and must, transcend our understanding ; he will, by the
very nature of the case, dazzle and confound our imagination by
the unsuspected riches and glory of his many mansions ; but he
must not trouble our sense of right if he would retain our homage
and our love.   Personally, I can have no share in the piety that
can see any man condemned under such circumstances as have
just been described ; it is not enough to tell me that it is some
other man and not myself who suffers,—a suggestion ineffably
mean even if it were true ; but it is not true ; I do suffer : a
tremendous strain is put upon my sensibilities, and I cannot,
without anguish, see any man arbitrarily driven into hell.   Upon
his face, writhing in unutterable torture, is written this appeal,
" Can you see me, bone of your bone and flesh of your flesh, thus
treated, weighed down, crushed, damned, by a power I am utterly
unable either to placate or resist ? "   That man may be my own
father, my own child, my most familiar friend ; and though he be
a stranger, of name unknown, he has at all events the claim of
our common humanity upon me.   I have purposely put the case
in this strong way, that I may say with the more emphasis that I
see no such method of government revealed in the narrative now
under consideration.   If I saw anything like it in any part of the
Word of God, I should say, " My understanding is at fault, not
God's justice ; from what I know of his method within the scope
of my own life, I know and am sure that righteousness and
judgment are the habitation of his throne, and that his mercy
endureth for ever."   I see things that are mysterious, incom-
prehensible, baffling ; I come upon scriptures which utterly defy
all scholars and interpreters ; but this is the confidence that I
have—"The Judge of all the earth will do right."   As to the
particular expression in the text, two things may be said : first, it
is well known that the Jews were in the habit of saying, " It had
been good for that man had he not been born,"—it was a common
expression of the day, in speaking of transgressors, and did not
by any means imply a belief in the final destruction or damnation
of the person spoken of ; and secondly, this passage has again

and again exactly expressed our own feeling in many crises of
our own life : it must be for ever true that non-existence is better
than sinfulness. When the lie was on our lips, when part of
the price was laid down as the whole, when we dishonoured the
vow we made in secret with God, when we rolled iniquity under
our tongue as a sweet morsel,—at that time it had been good
for us if we had not been born. Such, indeed, is the only form
of words equal to the gravity of the occasion ;—better we say,
again and again, not to have been born than to have done this ;
if this be the end of our being, then has our life been a great
failure and a mortal pain. I hold that these words were spoken
not so much of Judas the man as of Judas the sinner, and that
consequently they apply to all evil-doers throughout all generations, and are in reality the most tender and pathetic admonition
which even Christ could address to the slaves of sin.

We may get some light upon this expression by considering
the fact that " it repented the Lord that he had made man." In
studying all such passages we must have regard to the order of
time. St. Paul said, " If in this life only we have hope, we are
of all men most miserable ; "—so, if we break off our own life
at certain points, we shall say the same thing of ourselves, and
if we interrupt human history, so that one fact shall not be
allowed to explain another, it would be easy to find sections
which would prove alike the disorder and malignity of the divine
government. We know what this means in some of the works
of our own hands. Thus, for example : You undertook to build
a house for the Lord, and your heart was full of joy as you saw
the sacred walls rising in your hopeful dreams ; but when you
came to work out your purpose you came upon difficulty after
difficulty,—promises were broken, contracts were trifled with,
the very stars in their courses seemed to fight against you, and
at length, after many disappointments and exasperations, you
said, " It repents me ; it gives me pain, it grieves me, that I
began this house." Such is the exact state of your feeling at
that particular moment. But other influences were brought to
bear upon the situation, resources equal to the difficulty were
developed, and when the roof covered the walls, and the spire
shot up into the clouds, you forgot your pains and tears in a

great satisfaction. You will say that God foresaw all the difficulty of building the living temple of manhood, that the whole case was clearly before him from eternity ; that is, of course, true, but the pain of ingratitude is none the less keen because the ingratitude itself was foreknown.   Take the case of Jesus Christ, God manifest in the flesh, as an illustration ; he foresaw all the triumphs of his Cross—all heaven thronged with innumerable multitudes out of every kindred and people and tongue—yet he prayed that the cup might pass from him, and he needed an angel to help him in the time of his soul's sorrow.   In magnifying God's omniscience we must not overlook God's love ; nothing, indeed, could surprise his foreknowledge, yet it grieved him at the heart that he had made man ; and he called upon the heavens to hear, and upon the earth to be astonished, because his children had rebelled against him !

"This he said, not that he cared for the poor, but because he was a thief, and had the bag, and bare what was put therein."— It is more to the credit of the apostles themselves that this should be regarded as an after-thought than as an undoubted conviction, or an established fact, at the time that Judas sat with them at the Paschal Supper, or even at the time that he asked why the ointment was not sold for the benefit of the poor.   This is the more evident from the fact that the writer indicates Judas as the betrayer, whereas at the moment of the test his identity was not established.   There is no mystery about the insertion of this explanatory suggestion, for we all know how easy it is after a character has fully revealed itself to go back upon its separate acts and account for them by their proper motives— motives unknown at the time of the action, but plainly proved by subsequent revelations of character.   This was probably the case in the instance before us, else why did the disciples allow Judas to keep the bag ?   Why did they not humble and exhaust him by an incessant protest against his dishonesty ?   And why did not our Lord, instead of mildly expostulating, say to Judas as he once said to Peter, "Get thee behind me, Satan " ?   Here, then, is a great law within whose operation we ourselves may be brought,—the law of reading the part in the light of the whole, and of judging the isolated act by the standard of the complete character. Illustrations of the working of this law will occur to you instantly. Let a man eventually reveal himself as having unworthily filled prominent positions in the Church—let his character be proved to have been corrupt, and then see what light is thrown upon words and deeds which at the time were not fully understood. How abundant then will be such expressions as these in recounting his utterances :—

" He advised prudence and care and very great caution in working out Church plans; he counselled concentration; he deprecated romantic schemes : this he did (as we now can see), not that he was a lover of Prudence or a worshipper of Wisdom, but because he was a thief, and he feared that bold and noble schemes would shame him into reluctant generosity."

" He urged that the church should be built with the least possible decoration or ornament; he spoke strongly against coloured glass and elaborate enrichment : and this he did (as we can now see), not that he was devoted to Simplicity or absorbed in spiritual aspiration, but because he was a thief, and feared that every block of polished marble would increase the sum which his respectability would be expected to subscribe."

" He denounced all heretical tendencies in the Christian ministry; he knew heterodoxy afar off; he never ceased to declare himself in favour of what he supposed to be the Puritan theology : and this he did, not that in his heart of hearts he cared for the conservation of orthodoxy, but because he was a thief, and had a felonious intent upon the reputation of independent thinkers whose shoe's latchet he was not worthy to unloose."

All this comes out after a man has revealed himself as Judas did. But let me also say that the " thief " may be dictating our speech even when we least suspect it, certainly where there may never be such a disclosure as there was in the case of Judas. There are conditions under which we hardly know what influence it is that colours our judgment and suggests our course,—may it not be the " thief " thus underlies our consciousness, and so cunningly touches our life as never to excite our suspicion or our fear ? We know how subtle are the workings of self-deception, and perhaps even the godliest of us would be surprised to know exactly the inspiration of some of our most fervent speeches,— surprised to find that though the outward orator seemed to be an earnest man, the inner and invisible speaker is the "thief" that prompted Judas! Who, then, can stand before the Lord, or be easy in the presence of his holy law? It is under such inquiries that the strongest man quails, and that the swiftest of God's messengers humbly prays, "Enter not into judgment with thy servant, O Lord; for in thy sight shall no flesh living be justified."

"Then one of the twelve, called Judas Iscariot, went unto the chief priests, and said unto them, What will ye give me, and I will deliver him unto you?" (Matt. xxvi. 14, 15.) Why should there have been any bargaining, or why should there have been any difficulty, about the arrest of Christ? We must look to an earlier verse for the solution. The chief priests, the scribes, and the elders, had met for consultation in the palace of the high priest, Caiaphas, and the principal question was, not how they might take Jesus, but how they might take him "by subtilty," by craft, deceit, guile, as if they would have secretly murdered him if they could,—murdered him in the darkness, and in the morning have wiped their mouths as innocent men! Judas would appear to have gone to them secretly, and offered himself as one who knew the haunts and times and methods of Christ; and in doing so he showed the weak and vicious side of his nature, his covetousness, his greed, his love of money,—and herein his guilt seems to culminate in an aggravation infernal and unpardonable. But are we ourselves verily clear in this matter? Are we not every day selling Christ to the highest bidder? When we stifle our convictions lest we should lose a morsel of bread; when we are dumb in the presence of the enemy lest our words should be followed by loss of domestic comfort or personal honour; when we soften our speech, or hide the Cross, or join in ungodly laughter that we may avoid an ungodly sneer, we are doing in our own way the very thing which we rightly condemn in the character of Judas.

"Then Judas which had betrayed him, when he saw that he

was condemned, repented himself, and brought again the thirty pieces of silver to the chief priests and elders, saying, I have sinned in that I have betrayed the innocent blood : and he cast down the silver pieces in the temple, and departed, and went and hanged himself" (Matt. xxvii. 3-5). Is there not a tone in these words with which we are familiar? Is there not, indeed, something of our own voice in this mournful story? Let us look at it carefully :—

"When he saw,"—that, at least, is familiar! Not until our actions are set a little off do we see all their relations and all their meaning; in their progress we are too near them to get their full effect; if we take but one step back we shall be affrighted by the very actions of which. the doing gave us a kind of frenzied joy. We make our own ghosts. We shut the eyes of our minds whilst we are doing certain things; and when the last touch is given to the deed, we are taught by the bitterness of experience that Temptation destroys our sight and that Guilt restores it. Recall the case of Adam and Eve,—"And the eyes of them both were opened!" Very short and cloudy is the sight of the body : how keen, how piercing, is the sight of a self-convicted soul! Before that discerning vision the air is full of eyes, and the clearest of all days is dark with menaces and gathering thunders.

"When he saw that he was condemned."—At that moment the surprise of Judas himself was supreme and unutterable : evidently he did not expect that this catastrophe would supervene ; he may, indeed, have said to himself—as a man of inventive and daring mind would be likely to say—I am quite sure, from what I have seen of his miracles, that he will prove himself more than a match for all his enemies ; he has done so before, and he will do it again. They said they would cast him down from the brow of the hill, but he went through the midst of them like a beam of light, and when they took up stones to stone him their hands were held fast by that strong will of his. He has provoked them to their face, heaped up all their sins before them, taunted and goaded them to madness, and yet he held them in check and played with them as he listed. It will be so again ; besides, he may just want a plan like mine to bring things to a point ; I will put him into the hands of these men, then will he shake them off, proclaim his kingdom, drive away the spoiler from the land of the Hebrews, and we shall come into the enjoyment of our promised reward. Judas may not have used these words, but in effect they are being used by sinners every day! This is the universal tongue of self-deception, varying a little, it may be, in the accent, but in substance the same all the world over; a putting of one thing against another, a balancing of probabilities, an exercise of self-outwitting cunning; a secret hope that something can be snatched out of the fire, and that the flames can be subdued without undue damage,—this is the method of sinfulness of heart, a method confounded every day by the hand of God, yet every day coming up again to fresh attempts and renewed humiliations.

"When he saw that he was condemned he repented himself."— Is there not hope of a man who is capable of any degree of repentance, even when repentance takes upon itself the darker shade of horror and remorse? I know what the word is which is translated "repented," and I remember with joy that it is the word which is used of the son who said he would not go, and afterwards repented and went; it is the word which Paul used of himself on one occasion in writing to the Corinthians. But even if the word be rendered "was filled with remorse and shame and despair," I should say, "So much the better for Judas." Under such circumstances I should have more hope of a man who had absolutely no hope of himself, than of a man who could sufficiently control himself to think that even such a sin—infinite in wickedness as it must have appeared to his own mind—could ever be forgiven. It is easy for us who never experienced the agony to say what Judas ought to have done: how he ought to have wept and prayed and sought forgiveness as we now should seek it. We cannot intermeddle with his sorrow, nor ought we harshly to judge the method of his vengeance.

"I have sinned in that I have betrayed the innocent blood."— Not, "I was hurried into this by others"; not, "Others are as much to blame as I am"; but, "I did it, and I alone." Not, "I have made a mistake"; not, "This is a great error on my part"; but, "I have sinned,"—the very word which he might have heard in his Lord's parable of the Prodigal Son,—the word which our Father in heaven delights to hear! "If we confess our sins, he is faithful and just to forgive us our sins, for his mercy endureth for ever." "If thy brother turn again, saying, I repent, forgive him;"—Judas repented himself! "How often shall I forgive him? Seven times. Seventy times seven!" And shall I forgive him the less because his repentance has deepened into remorse, and he has lost all hope of himself? Surely the more on that very account. And if he slay himself because of his sin against me? Then must I think of him with still tenderer pity, nor cloud his memory with a single suspicion. And here let me say, as to the spiritual application of this matter, I have no faith in the moral value of fine-drawn distinctions between repentance and despair; my belief is that until we reach the point of self-despair as to our sin against Christ, we can never know the true meaning or realise the true joy of repentance. That Judas should have slain himself with his own hand is, in my view of the case, wholly in his favour. It must have appeared to him, indeed, to be the only course open to him; floods of tears he could never set against the blood of an innocent man; to cry and moan and weep bitterly, would be just to aggravate the appalling crime. With a stronger light beating on our life than ever Judas was permitted to enjoy, guarded by all the restraints of Christian civilisation, living under the ministry of the Holy Ghost, we are by so much unable to sympathise with the intolerant horror which destroyed the self-control of the betrayer of our Lord. So far as I can think myself back into the mental condition of Judas, his suicide seems to me to be the proper completion of his insufferable self-reproach. And yet that self-control was preserved long enough to enable Judas Iscariot to utter the most effective and precious eulogium ever pronounced upon the character of Jesus Christ. How brief, how simple, how complete —"innocent blood"! If the proper interpretation of words is to be found, as it undoubtedly is, in circumstances, then these two words are fuller in meaning and tenderer in pathos than the most laboured encomium could possibly be. Consider the life which preceded these words, and you will see that they may be amplified thus: "I know Jesus better than any of you can know him. You have only seen him in public, I have lived with him in private; I have watched his words as words of man were never

watched before ; I have heard his speeches meant for his disciples alone ; I have seen him in poverty, weariness, and pain of
heart ; I have heard his prayers at home ; I trusted that it had
been he who would have redeemed Israel from patriotic servility ;
I curse myself, I exonerate him,—his is innocent blood ! " How
glad would the Jews have been if Christ had been witnessed
against by one of his own disciples ! They would have welcomed
his evidence ; no gold could have adequately paid for testimony
so direct and important ; and Judas loved gold. Yet the holy truth
came uppermost ; Judas died, not with a lie in his right hand,
but with the word of truth upon his lips, and the name of Christ
was thus saved from what might have been its deepest wound.

"Those that thou gavest me I have kept, and none of them
is lost, but the son of perdition."—At the first glance these words
would seem to put the fate of Judas Iscariot beyond all controversy, yet further consideration may show how mercy may
magnify itself even in this cloud. Judas is called "the son of
perdition" ; true, and Peter himself was called Satan by the same
Lord. And if Judas was "the son of perdition," what does
Paul say of all mankind ? Does he not say, "We are by nature
the children of wrath, even as others"? But in this case "the
son of perdition" is said to be "lost"; but does the word "lost"
necessarily imply that he was in hell ? "We have all erred and
strayed like lost sheep"; "The Son of man came to seek and
to save that which was lost"; and, "There is joy in the presence
of the angels of God over one sinner that repenteth [Judas repented himself], more than over ninety and nine just persons,
which need no repentance." It is our joy to believe that wherever repentance is possible, mercy is possible ; and it is heaven
to us to know that where sin abounded, grace did much more
abound. And are we quite sure that there is no ray of hope
falling upon the repentant and remorseful Judas from such words
as these, "And this is the Father's will which hath sent me,
that of all which he hath given me [and that he gave him Iscariot
is clear from the very passage we are now considering] I should
lose nothing, but should raise it up again at the last day" (John
vi. 39) ? But there is still more light to be thrown on this great
gloom. Take this passage (John xviii. 8, 9), "Jesus answered,

I have told you that I am he: if therefore ye seek me, let these go their way; that the saying might be fulfilled which he spake, Of them which thou gavest me I have lost none." Now suppose that the ruffians had answered, "No, we will not let these go their way; we will slay them with the sword at once,"— would it follow that Jesus Christ had lost his disciples in the sense of their having been destroyed in unquenchable fire? The suggestion is not to be entertained for a moment; yet this is the very "saying" which is supposed to determine the damnation of Judas! As I read the whole history I cannot but feel that our Lord was specially wishful that his disciples should continue with him throughout his temptation, should watch with him, that in some way, hardly to be expressed in words, they should help him by the sympathy of their presence,—in this sense he was anxious to "lose none"; but he did lose the one into whom Satan had entered, and he refers to him not so much for his own sake as that he may rejoice the more in the constancy of those who remained. But the whole reference, as it seems to me, is not to the final and eternal state of men in the unseen world, but to continuance and steadfastness in relation to a given crisis.

"This ministry and apostleship from which Judas by transgression fell, that he might go to his own place" (Acts i. 25). —One reputable scholar has suggested that the words "go to his own place" may refer to Matthias, and not to Judas; but the suggestion does not commend itself to my judgment. I think we should lose a good deal by accepting this interpretation. I hold that this is an instance of exquisite delicacy on the part of Peter: no judgment is pronounced; the fall is spoken of only as official and as involving official results, and the sinner himself is left in the hands of God. It is in this spirit that Peter speaks of Judas,—

> ' Owning his weakness,
>   His evil behaviour,
> And leaving, with meekness,
>   His sins to his Saviour."

II. Practical.

Such a study as this can hardly fail to be fruitful of suggestion to the nominal followers of Christ in all ages. What are its lessons to ourselves,—to ourselves as Christians, ministers office-bearers, and stewards of heavenly mysteries?

(1) Our first lesson will be found in the fact that when our Lord said to his disciples, " One of you shall betray me," every one of them began to say " Is it I ? " Instead of being shocked even to indignation, each of the disciples put it to himself as, a possibility ; " It may be I. Lord, is it I ? " This is the right spirit in which to hold all our privileges. We should regard it as a possibility that the strongest may fail, and even the oldest may betray his trust. " Let him that thinketh he standeth take heed lest he fall." Do you suppose that there was but one betrayal of the Lord once for all, and that the infamous crime can never be repeated ? " I tell you, nay ! " There are predictions yet to be realised—" There shall be false teachers among you, who privily shall bring in damnable heresies, even denying the Lord that bought them ;"—" Lord, is it I ? " It shall surely be more tolerable for Judas Iscariot in the day of judgment than for that man ! Living in the light of gospel day ; professing to have received the Holy Ghost ; ordained as a minister of the Cross ; holding office in the Christian Church—is it impossible for those who were once enlightened, and have tasted of the heavenly gift, and were made partakers of the Holy Ghost, and have tasted the good word of God, and the powers of the world to come, if they shall fall away, to renew them again unto repentance, seeing that they crucify to themselves the Son of God afresh, and put him to an open shame ? " Lord, is it I ? " " In the last days perilous times shall come : men shall be traitors ;"—" Lord, is it I ? " Governing our life by this self-misgiving spirit, not thinking all men sinful but ourselves, we shall be saved from the boastfulness which is practical blasphemy, and our energy shall be kept from fanaticism by the chastening influence of self-doubt. Looking upon all the mighty men who have made shipwreck of faith and a good conscience— Adam, Saul, Solomon, Judas—let us be careful lest after having preached to others we ourselves should be cast away. It is true that we cannot repeat the literal crime of Judas ; but there are greater enormities than his ! We can outdo Judas in sin ! " Whosoever speaketh a word against the Son of man, it shall be forgiven

him : but whosoever speaketh against the Holy Ghost, it shall not
be forgiven him, neither in this world, neither in the world to come"
(Matt. xii. 32). We cannot sell the body, but we can grieve the
Spirit. There can be no more covenanting over the Lord's bones,
but we can plunge a keener spear into his heart than that which
drew forth blood and water from his side ; we cannot nail him
to the accursed tree, but we can pierce him through with many
sorrows. Judas died by the vengeance of his own hand ; of
how much sorer punishment, suppose ye, shall he be thought
worthy who hath done despite unto the Spirit of Grace ? Judas
shall rise in judgment with this generation, and shall condemn
it, because when he saw the error of his ways he repented himself, and made restitution of his unholy gains ; but we have rolled
iniquity under our tongue as a sweet morsel, we have held our
places in the sanctuary while our heart has been the habitation
of the enemy !

(2) Our second lesson is a caution against mere intellectual
sagacity in directing the affairs of the Christian kingdom. It is
admitted on all hands that Judas Iscariot was far ahead of the
other apostles in many intellectual qualities, yet " Judas by transgression fell." How self-controlled he was ; how stealthy was his
step ; how lingering and watchful his cunning ! And if Whately
and De Quincey be right in the suggestion that he merely wanted
to force the Lord to declare himself the Prince of princes and
make Israel glad by despoiling the oppressor, it discovers the
instinct of statesmanship, and shows how his strategic ambition
sought to ensnare the Roman fowler in his own net. Judas is
supposed to have reasoned thus with himself : This Jesus is he
who will redeem Israel ; the whole twelve of us think so ; yet
he hesitates, for some reason we cannot understand. His power
is astounding, his life is noble. This will I do, I will bring things
to a crisis by going to the authorities and making them an offer.
I believe they will snatch at my proposition, and when they come
to work it out he will smite them with his great power, and will
avenge the insult by establishing his supremacy as King and
Lord of Israel. As a matter of fact we know that this kind of
reasoning has played no small part in the history of the Church.
The spiritual kingdom of Christ has suffered severely at the hands

of men who have been proud of their own diplomacy and general-
ship ; men fond of elaborating intricate organisations, of playing
one influence against another, and of making up for the slowness
of time by dramatic surprises alike of sympathy and collision.   It
is for this reason that I cannot view without alarm the possible
misuse of congresses, conferences, unions, and councils : these
institutions will only be of real service to the cause of the Cross
in proportion as spiritual influence is supreme.   Once let political
sagacity, diplomatic ingenuity, and official adroitness in the management of details become unduly valued, and you change the
centre of gravity, and bring the Church into imminent peril.
Unquestionably human nature loves dexterity, and will pay high
prices for all kinds of conjuring, and loudly applaud the hero who
does apparent impossibilities ; and from this innate love of mere
cleverness may come betrayals, compromises, and casuistries,
which crucify the Son of God afresh.   Judas looked to the end
to vindicate if not to sanctify the means ; and this is the policy
of all dexterous managers, the very soul of Jesuitry, and a chosen
instrument of the devil.   I do not pray for a leader, fertile in
resource, supple and prompt in movement ; my prayer is for
a man of another stamp, even for an Inspirer, who, by the ardour
of his holiness, the keenness of his spiritual insight, and the
unction of his prayer, shall help us truthward and heavenward ;
and under his leadership we shall hear no more about secularities
and temporalities, but every action—the opening of the doors
and the lighting of the lamps of the sanctuary—shall be done
by hands which were first outstretched in prayer.   Not the crafty
Judas, but the loving John will help us best in all our work ;
not the man inexhaustible in tricks of management, but the man
of spiritual intelligence and fervour, will deliver us most successfully in the time of straits and dangers.   Managers, leaders,
draughtsmen, and pioneers, we shall of course never cease to
want, and their abilities will always be of high value to every good
cause ; yet one thing is needful above all others—closeness to
the dear Lord, and daily continuance in prayer.

PRAYER.

ALMIGHTY GOD, we are gathered around thy Son in his humblest form, and we wish to hear every word that may be spoken by the voice of his heart. The traitor has gone out, so now we may hear the music of love—the inner word which traitors may not hear. They have gone out into the night to be lost in the darkness they love; but here we tarry in the morning, in the summer glow, and we are all bending forward to listen to the sweet Gospel voice, full of love, full of hope,—so gentle a voice, hastening, as it were, to its own death to rise again in trumpets and thunders of sovereignty and power. But we will hear its lesser tone, we will listen to the gentler speech; we will listen with our hearts. Speak, Lord, for thy servants hear! We are tired of all other voices; we would purge our ears of all inferior sounds; and if thou wilt circumcise our ears, we shall hear, and nothing shall escape our adoring and grateful attention. Our hearts need thy voice: they are lone and weary and full of troubling wonder; yea, they are often sore afraid. They need to hear the voice from the great light, saying, "Let not your heart be troubled, neither let it be afraid." The voice is comfort, the call brings with it great strength in every tone, the battle is already won; whilst our Master speaks to us we rise like men enriched with answered prayer. We love thy tabernacles, thou God of Zion; our souls have a desire and longing to enter into the courts of the Lord. There we find great liberty; there we spread out our whole strength—no fold that is not rolled out to its fullest length; there we eat and drink abundantly; there the high festival of thy love makes us forget all weight, all burden. We are thine, bought with blood, sanctified by the Holy Ghost, made meet by thy grace to be partakers of the inheritance of life. We would know to whom we belong: we would see thy signature written upon our life, we would feel thy claim in our hearts urging us by sweetest persuasion of love to do some nobler deed. Thou hast led us to despise time and the earth, and all things we can see, when compared with the eternity of heaven and invisible realities. Thou dost train us by our impatience; our being kept so long outside the door that opens back upon the heavens is itself an education. We knock, and are not answered; we wait, and there is no reply; we linger through the night and are wet with heavy dews, still the door is not opened from within; but we wait, we still continue, we cannot go away; our standing at heaven's gate helps us to do earth's weary work. We have come to make many speeches to thee, because our hearts are many and our histories a great number. Hear the plaint of the sad and those who are ill at ease—disappointed men, vexed and troubled hearts, souls that love right, and wish evermore to walk in the light, and yet are hindered by those who ought to help them; men of feeble will, whose prayers break right off in the middle and fall down to earth again, who wish to do right and feel as if they could not, who put out their hand to the altar and quickly let it fall; men who are full of concern about health and business and domestic affairs and success and ability to live honestly in the sight of all men—things will not come right; if they are put right overnight, they are all wrong in the morning. These men are full of trouble, and they are like to fret themselves to do evil. The Lord have pity upon them and put an end to their vexation, lest it become a stumbling-block over which they fall and never can rise again. Thou dost train us by a way that is often weary. Our eyes are vexed by the prosperity of the wicked; our souls are full of wonder because they are not in trouble like other men. We cannot understand their fatness, their abundance of gold, and the innumerableness of their cattle; but thou hast surely set them in slippery places, and presently the tremendous solution will begin. We commit one another to thy care. Draw us closer to thyself; speak as we are able to bear it; adapt the light to our vision, and when we would pray, let thy Spirit work mightily within us; teach the heart great words to express great desires. Qualify us every day for broader service, for more patient suffering, for deeper and more loving obedience; and when the little flame of life's short day dies down and goes from human eyes quite spark out, may our souls hail thee in heaven's eternal morning! Amen.

NOT NOW, BUT AFTERWARDS.

"Not now, but afterwards."—JOHN xiii. 36.

THE whole verse reads thus :—" Simon Peter said unto him, Lord, whither goest thou? Jesus answered him, Whither I go thou canst not follow me now; but thou shalt follow me afterwards." Children will have everything now : " afterwards " is a word that plagues them. It is a most mocking word : it points to a time that can never come : it may be to-morrow, or next year; but whether to-morrow or next year, it lies beyond the vision and beyond the range of the little grasping hand. As life advances we become more intimately acquainted with the word "afterwards," and, indeed, we come to like it. As for time, it is nothing : we begin to touch the meaning of the august expression, " A thousand years are as one day." We know that nothing is so near as the future; we know that yesterday is gone beyond recall, and that to-morrow is always coming and is always available. It is the mystery and the charm of this little life. How throughout the whole of this chapter Jesus Christ is

Lord and Master ! The title fills the whole chapter, gives nobleness to all the Divine speeches, covers with tender radiance all the
interviews which Jesus Christ conducts on this day of shadows
with his wonder-struck and fear-troubled disciples. It is a
master's tone delivered with a brother's heart and voice which
says, " Not now, but afterwards." This is the second time in
the chapter that Jesus Christ has said the same thing to the
same man. Simon Peter was never more impatient than within
the lines of this chapter. Said he, " What is the meaning of this
feet-washing ? I do not know what thou doest " ; and the answer
was : " What I do thou knowest not now ; but thou shalt know
hereafter." Then again he comes before us : " Simon Peter said
unto him, Lord, whither goest thou ? Jesus answered him,
Whither I go thou canst not follow me now ; but thou shalt
follow me afterwards." So this child-man was constantly put
back and told to wait till the clock struck and the hour had come
when he should have the keener vision, the more sensitive heart,
the more receptive spirit and understanding mind. This was the
training Peter needed : Peter was a man who wanted everything
to be done instantaneously ; there must be no waiting ; to-morrow
must contrive to push itself into this day, and everything which
the impatient heart desired must be supplied the moment the
desire was expressed. The Lord, knowing this, always said to
him, " Not now," that most vexing and teasing word. We want
it now ; we could do well with it now ; it seems to us as if this
were the very time to have it ; and when we are in that high
blood—mad with impatience—he quietly, with sovereignly tone,
says, " Not now." He says it as from a throne, there is no halting or incertitude in his way of saying it ; at first he taught with
authority, and not as the scribes, and now, the shadows gathering
around him quickly into darkest night, he still speaks with the
authority which at first made him conspicuous. This is a grand
doctrine ; who can receive it ? We have to be drilled into it ;
patience of this kind is not born in us. Blessed be God, we can
be chastened and mellowed into the reception of the doctrine that
afterwards is greater than now, and that not to have an afterwards is to be imprisoned and impoverished. Jesus Christ
lived in to-morrow ; early in his ministry he said, " Hereafter
ye shall see."

Look at this in the direction of revelation. We cannot follow any great Scriptural doctrine now in all the range of its thought, in all the scope of its imagination, in all the possibilities of its issues. Who can explain the Atonement? The angels desire to look into it; the Voice from above says, " Not now, but afterward." We begin in the right spirit when we begin in the spirit of waiting. Personally, I accept the Cross, but cannot explain it; personally, I need the Atonement by a necessity for which there are no words, but which presses upon my heart with all the gnawing agony of hunger. It cannot tell the quality of the blood, the measure of the oblation, the efficacy of the sacrifice. It is called " precious blood," it is called " self-sacrifice " : the words dimly hint to me a meaning very gracious and comforting; what they imply in all the compass of their thought I know not now, but shall know afterwards. Is there then an afterwards for me, a higher school, a brighter day, additional facilities, closer intercourse with things and spirits and forces Divine? To be assured of that is to know the meaning of the mystery, " Death is abolished."

Or look at the same doctrine in relation to the mysteries of daily providence. " Thou canst not follow me now; but thou shalt follow me afterwards," the direction not being from one locality to another, from one point of space to another, but a following in thought, purpose, meaning, and sovereign decree— a mighty flying after God, a keeping up *pari passu* with the great Leader, whose way is in the whirlwind and in the cloud. I limp now, halt and stagger and fall and half rise again and am down before I can straighten myself; I cannot follow, except in the dim far distance now, but afterward ——. We want to know why we were made as we are—so singular, constituted so mysteriously, with a will so easily led, with passions so instantly ignited, with dispositions now rising upwards, now flinging downwards, with a life that seems all forms ; why not have been made otherwise, dear Lord,—with stronger wills, with tenderer hearts, without perversity, without selfishness? And the Voice says, " Not now, but afterwards shalt thou know." This individuality is a heavy burden; this personal secret of the Almighty, which every man carries in his heart, is a most tormenting fire. An explanation would help us to bear it. To think that if we had been just otherwise made, in some line or curve of being, with an additional element, with a certain quality that is omitted from our constitution, we should have prayed ourselves into answers and have lifted ourselves by the power of intercession into the temple where there are no clouds, no nights, but where the interviews are face to face with hand locked in hand. We want to know why ; it would comfort us to have some hint of meaning, and the only reply we can elicit is—" Not now, but afterwards." Why this suffering ? Who did sin, I or my parents, that this burden is laid upon me—a burden for which I have certainly no light and certainly no strength ? But for it, I could fly ; with it, I am buried every day. What a life would yours be but for the one thing in it that enters the soul like iron ! Old age could never touch you but for that one thing. It is that one thing that takes the erectness out of your figure, and makes your hair white in a night, and ploughs your cheeks into great furrows through which the tear rivers roll. A hundred times have I heard you say, " But for that I could sleep soundly all night, and be cheerful all day ; the eating of bread would be a sacrament and the going out of the house an eager hastening to fight for God and the truth ; why should I have had this chain upon my feet, this manacle upon my hand, this black night shadow bound round my poor eyes ? Why ? " And the answer is : " Not now, but afterwards." " No chastening for the present seemeth to be joyous, but grievous : nevertheless afterward it yieldeth the peaceable fruit of righteousness unto them which are exercised thereby."

There cannot be an afterwards of revelation unless there is a now of obedience. The now is not evacuated of all meaning, stripped of all urgency, and turned into a blank nothing ; now has its agony, now has its immediate fight. To obey in the darkness is the great thing. Were I to say, " I will trust God in the seventh trouble because he has delivered me in six," I should be saying something hardly worth saying. There is a subtle selfishness in that verbal piety ; there is a most suspicious selfishness about that reasoning, though it sounds so holy. Hear it : " He hath delivered me in six troubles, and in seven he will be with me." The testimony in itself is good, and is sincere, because it is historically true and is meant to be full of solace from the historical side; but do not make too much of it as a test of growth in grace. Who then has grown in grace? This man who says, "Though he slay me, yet will I put my trust in him." That is faith. If you tell me that you have been so reduced, that you knew not how to turn, and at the very moment of extremity light appeared and deliverance was wrought out, and therefore you intend to hope even under similar circumstances, your speech within narrow limits is perfectly good; it is a most valid testimony, but it is no necessary sign of growth in grace. This I want to be able to say: "I have nothing, I know not in what direction to turn, and if nothing should remain nothing, my hymn shall still be sung; though the fig tree shall not blossom—I don't say, though there be a late harvest of figs, but though the fig tree shall not blossom—I will be as pious as ever." That is growing in grace, that is maturity in the life Divine, and that is the lesson which we learn now; the afterwards is not in that particular lesson: it is the agony, the stinging fire of the immediate moment. How many persons make a deep mistake here! They think they are pious because, having been delivered out of six troubles, they feel sure they will be delivered out of the seventh. That may be a species of profanity; on the other hand, it may be the testimony of a grateful heart. But this is piety—to have nothing in the right hand, nothing in the left, nothing in the world, and then not to pray, which is a beggar's attitude, but to sing, which is a child's and a prince's posture. This is the miracle of God; this is the ideal attainment. We are bound to keep it steadily before our dazzling eyes; we count not ourselves to have attained: far from it; but this one thing we do—we press toward the mark. We know our selfishness better than any other men know it, and we mourn it, but seem as if we could not get rid of it; yet the grace of God is equal even to this miracle. So, whilst we pray, we will sing; and whilst we mourn, we will also hope.

Obedience now is revelation afterward. We shall know if we follow on to know. He that doeth the will shall know of the doctrine. Obedience is preparation for revelation. Blessed is that servant who shall be found watching, waiting, when his Lord cometh; verily, I say unto you, he will put keys into that servant's hand, and call him to honour, and sit him in inner

places, and make a son of him. " Mine, then, is a drudging life."
Be it so. " I have to keep beating at this door so—no sign of
opening." No matter. "The Lord told me to knock, and
here I am knocking, knocking, knocking; I want to fly, but he
says, ' Knock '; I want to go inside, and hold festival with the
angels, but he tells me to knock." Obedience prepares the mind
for revelation, takes out of that revelation the light that would
dazzle the spirit's vision, and prepares the heart to receive wider
demonstrations of the sovereignty and grace of God. We must
be blind three days before we begin to see the outline of things ;
we must lie down as blind, helpless creatures, simply and
lovingly waiting for any prophet God may send to us to open
our eyes and teach us our first lesson in the higher alphabet.
This does not suit us : we want to walk more quickly, pass on,
because we are measuring time by a false chronometer. We do
not know the joy which is laid up for us in complete obedience
to the word, "Stand still and see the salvation of God." There
is marvellous graciousness in a gradual revelation. If " the path
of the just is as the shining light, that shineth more and more
unto the perfect day," it is because his spiritual education is
imaged by that same fair symbol. The next piece of knowledge
comes easily. Were the child to be compelled to overleap seven
years of the process of education, and to commence a lesson
which lies seven years ahead of the page he is reading to-day, he
would be overcome with fear, and no strength would be left in
him. What the child has to do is to read the next line, and then
to turn over the next page. What we, as Christian students,
have to do is to keep to the present truth, obey the immediate
duty, do the work that lies next and easily to hand ; and then
the revelation will, so to say, steal upon us, and then encompass
us without the violence of haste and without the unrest of
surprise. We cannot tell how the light grows in the heavens.
In the morning it is seed-time, and at noon-day the harvest fields
of the firmament are white with an abundance of result ; hardly
is the morning seed-time past than the noontide harvest is
ripe. So in mental illumination and in spiritual culture and
growth. We shall know when we receive our last accession
of truth. God's accessions are known by various names—sometimes by the starting up in the mind of a distinct fact ; sometimes

by the gift of an impression; sometimes by the prick of a new impulse; sometimes by the glow of a new ambition; sometimes by a mysterious, profound, all-calming peace. But when the accession comes—be it under this name or under that, the great fire, shocks of whirlwind, tumults of thunder, or a still small voice—we shall have no doubt about its identity. Divinity cannot be successfully imitated.

NOTE.

"Towards the close of our Lord's ministry St. Peter's characteristics become especially prominent. Together with his brother, and the two sons of Zebedee, he listened to the last awful predictions and warnings delivered to the disciples in reference to the second advent (Matt. xxiv. 3; Mark xiii. 3, who alone mentions these names; Luke xxi. 7). At the Last Supper Peter seems to have been particularly earnest in the request that the traitor might be pointed out, expressing of course a general feeling, to which some inward consciousness of infirmity may have added force. After the supper his words drew out the meaning of the significant, almost sacramental, act of our Lord in washing his disciples' feet; an occasion on which we find the same mixture of goodness and frailty, humility and deep affection, with a certain taint of self-will, which was at once hushed into submissive reverence by the voice of Jesus. Then too it was that he made those repeated protestations of unalterable fidelity, so soon to be falsified by his miserable fall. . . .

" Judas had left the guest-chamber when St. Peter put the question, Lord, whither goest thou? words which modern theologians generally represent as savouring of idle curiosity, or presumption, but in which the early Fathers (as Chrysostom and Augustine) recognised the utterance of love and devotion. The answer was a promise that Peter should follow his Master, but accompanied with an intimation of present unfitness in the disciple. Then came the first protestation, which elicited the sharp and stern rebuke, and distinct prediction of Peter's denial (John xiii. 36-38). From comparing this account with those of the other evangelists (Matt. xxvi. 33-35; Mark xiv. 29-31; Luke xxii. 33, 34), it seems evident that with some diversity of circumstances both the protestation and warning were thrice repeated. The tempter was to sift all the disciples, our apostle's faith was to be preserved from failing by the special intercession of Christ, he being thus singled out either as the representative of the whole body, or, as seems more probable, because his character was one which had special need of supernatural aid. . . .

" After the agony of Gethsemane, when the three, Peter, James, and John, were, as on former occasions, selected to be with our Lord, the only witnesses of his passion, where also all three had alike failed to prepare themselves by prayer and watching, the arrest of Jesus took place. Peter did not shrink from the danger. . . . Thrice, each time with greater vehemence, the last time with blasphemous asseveration, he denied his Master. The triumph of Satan seemed complete. Yet it is evident that it was an obscuration of faith, not an extinction. It needed but a glance of his Lord's eye to bring him to himself. His repentance was instantaneous, and effectual. The light in which he himself regarded his conduct is clearly shown by the terms in which it is related by St. Mark."—Smith's *Dictionary of the Bible.*

Chapter xiv.

THE REVELATION OF THE FATHER.

[AN OUTLINE.]

THE testimony of Scripture upon this point is most explicit. Thus : " No man hath seen God at any time; the only-begotten Son, which is in the bosom of the Father, he hath declared him." "No man knoweth the Son, but the Father; neither knoweth any man the Father, save the Son, and he to whomsoever the Son will reveal him." This, then, is one answer to the inquiry, What has Christ done for men that men could not have done for themselves? Namely, he has revealed the Father.

What does this expression mean? Three things are clearly excluded : (1) Christ did not reveal the existence of God; (2) he did not reveal the Fatherhood of God, for God is repeatedly called Father in the Old Testament; (3) he did not reveal the mercifulness of God, for God himself revealed this to Moses. In what sense, then, did Christ reveal the Father? Clearly in the sense that, as far as human conditions made it possible, (1) he visibly embodied the Father,—" He that hath seen me hath seen the Father"; (2) he made the Father universally intelligible,— " My doctrine is not mine, but his that sent me"; "Go ye into all the world and preach the gospel to every creature"; (3) he made the Father universally accessible,—" For through him we both have access by One Spirit unto the Father." The first revelation carries with it the remaining two, for if Christ made the Father visible, it follows from the necessity of the terms that he also made the Father intelligible and accessible in exactly the degree in which he himself could be understood and approached. We are not to insist on a literal visibleness, for that is impossible; but on a manifestation so unique and distinct as to justify the declaration, " He that hath seen me hath seen the Father." I propose a new use of these words, as elucidatory of the whole life of Christ. Thus :—

" He that hath seen me healing the sick and feeding the hungry hath seen the Father doing these things; the invisible care of God has been exercised from the beginning, but now is made manifest, and ye see it in this action of mine,—what you now see is but a revelation of that which God in secret has never ceased to do! He that hath seen me teaching the ignorant and offering the weary rest, hath seen the Father doing these very things; from his habitation in eternity he has been doing even so ever since he made man to possess the earth ; this, therefore, is no new act, no new love, no changed affection, it is the invisible revealed to your eyes! He that hath seen me seeking and saving the lost, receiving sinners and forgiving sins, hath seen the Father so doing; and he that hath seen me sorrowful unto death, surrendering my own will, taking upon me the form of a servant and becoming obedient unto death, even the death of the Cross, hath seen what the Father has been and has done through all time; he has always been pitiful and forgiving, always sorrowful and self-sacrificing, always on the Cross! This is a great mystery, and only to be seen in those occasional moments which surprise the soul into a consciousness of its own grandeur and value. He that hath seen me rising from the dead, and ascending high above all heavens, that I may fill all things, hath seen the Father in those invisible processes by which he turns the death and corruption of buried seed into the life and fruitfulness of golden harvests. The things which have been hidden from eternity, and which have been the secret and mystery of the universe, have thus been revealed in my earthly ministry : ye believe in God, believe also in me."

Or take the same truth in another form :—

(1) He that hath seen me hath seen the Father, accepting humiliation yet escaping indignity. No man suffered as Christ did ; yet whilst he was on earth he was in heaven. Such was the dignity that could never be impaired. So God has been mocked, defied, grieved, disowned by his children, distrusted by his saints, abandoned by his worshippers; yet he has fed the sun with fire, and sent abroad the arrows of his lightning, he has weighed the mountains in scales and the hills in a balance ; in all his humiliation he has never been less than God.

(2) He that hath seen me hath seen the Father, offering sympathy, yet escaping defilement. This was what man could never do. Man could pity the leper, but Christ could touch him.

This power of God was the divine gift to man; to ancient priest, and modern apostle: "I give unto you power to tread on scorpions and serpents, and over all the power of the enemy; and nothing shall by any means hurt you." "They shall take up serpents, and if they drink any deadly thing it shall not hurt them." "And Paul shook off the beast into the fire, and felt no harm." From the beginning God has been in the midst of the wickedness of those who have forsaken him, yet the contagious corruption has had no effect upon his holiness. Who can touch pitch and not be defiled? None but God.

(3) He that hath seen me hath seen the Father, stooping to death, yet escaping annihilation. He that hath seen me die, hath seen the Father die. You think of death as extinction, and therefore you shudder at the thought of God dying. But see how I die! My enemies kill the body, and after that have no more that they can do; I allow the body to die; I enter the grave; but at the appointed time I rise again and spoil the power of the enemy. It is so that the Father dies. He is grieved, disappointed, and his voice is lifted up in lamentation; yet he will overthrow the evil one and turn again the captivity of his own distress,— I have come to show you that that which you sow is not quickened, except it die.

How, then, is it true that they who have seen Christ have seen the Father, and yet only they have seen the Father to whom Christ has revealed him? This reminds us that there is seeing and seeing; every one knows that there is a seeing which sees nothing;—"Eyes have they but they see not; ears have they but they hear not; and hearts have they but they do not understand." Seeing is truly the gift of God. "But their eyes were holden that they should not know him." "Mary saw Jesus standing, and knew not that it was Jesus." "Jesus stood on the shore, but the disciples knew not that it was Jesus." Clearly, then, something more is meant than the mere sight of the body; to see the Bible is not to see a revelation; so to see the form of Christ is not to see "the image of the invisible God." To whom, then, will the Son reveal the Father? To the man who is humble and of a contrite heart; not to the wise and prudent, but unto babes.

Chapters xiv., xv.

THE SELF-REVELATION OF CHRIST.

WE cannot understand the opening of the fourteenth chapter unless we read it in immediate connection with the close of the thirteenth. "Peter said unto him, Lord, why cannot I follow thee now? I will lay down my life for thy sake. Jesus answered him, Wilt thou lay down thy life for my sake? Verily, verily, I say unto thee, The cock shall not crow, till thou hast denied me thrice." "Let"—notwithstanding all cowardice and recession and loneliness—"not your heart be troubled": life does not end in a cloud; all appearances will be against me and against you, but the issue will be right. "Ye believe in God, believe also in me," and wait with sweet prayerful patience until the dawn; when the light comes all things will be seen as they are. There are many imperatives in the speeches of Christ which do not instantly appear. It is better that this verse, so full of comfort, should be read with three imperatives, thus: Let not your heart be troubled; believe in God; believe also in me. It is singular that in this gospel, which is supposed to be the very gospel of life, Jesus Christ should be delivering commandments in the voice of Sinai, yet with a subtle and suggestive accent of Zion. Again and again he uses the words "command," and "commandment." Has it come to this? Does history thus recur upon itself? and is there an all but impalpable line connecting Sinai and Zion, the mountain of thunder with the mountain of peace?

In these chapters Jesus Christ speaks pastorally; so to say, he excludes all who cannot understand him, and reducing the number of those to whom he will speak to a minimum, he says even to them, Come nearer: I do not want to lift up my voice above a whisper. A tone might destroy this music; it needs the finest whisper; if we increase the volume of sound beyond that, we shall lose much. Let none stand away; let each come closely to me. This is the pastoral relation, when the voice of the teacher is lowered, when he does not want the misunderstanding public to hear him, but only those who are in closest fellowship with his soul; the very attitude is pastoral, the very voice is charged with solace. Yet there will be more than sentiment; even in the impartation of this comfort there shall be rousing appeals, great promises, somewhat now and then of military strain; for the disciples are not about to be lulled to rest, to be put to bed at an untimely hour; they are to be fed with comfort, and then sent out to fight life's great battle. We have seen in our expositions that the word "comfort" in the New Testament is a singular word, often misunderstood or too narrowly applied; we have resisted the notion that it simply means soothing, lulling, caressing. We have seen that when Barnabas was called a " son of consolation," he was really designated a rousing preacher. That is an idea which is seldom attached to the word. Hence many men are called sons of consolation who know nothing about comfort; they have no power to sustain the human heart by the right quality and range of solace; they think if they say nothing, if they put out the hand in a patting and caressing manner, if they sigh, if they aspire, that they are comforting the heart. There is nothing which a man in grief dreads so much as uncomforting comfort; he cannot bear to be spoken to by those who do not know what comfort really is. He comforts who rouses; makes life more conscious of itself and its powers; enlarges the scope of vitality; brings up in a man the self that was going down in sleep. An awakening is a comforting teacher. We shall find as Christ reveals himself that he means out of all this consolation to make an army invincible.

Look at the twelfth verse as a proof—

"Verily, verily, I say unto you, He that believeth on me, the works that I do shall he do also; and greater works than these shall he do; because I go unto my Father."

Jesus Christ thus indicated a period of working. He never made anything of his miracles. Other people were surprised at them, he was never amazed; beholders exclaimed, What a worker of wonders!—Jesus went out that he might pray. To pray is the greatest wonder of all; to touch heaven by right of love and faith is the supreme token of filial fellowship with God. As to quieting storms, and soothing seas, and raising dead bones, these are infantalities, trifles, things hardly to be accounted of at all; but to hold God by the violence of prayer is the great end and aim of spiritual education, to be consummated in the other world by an exchange of prayer for the delight and the satisfaction of praise. When did Jesus Christ ever call his Church to less and less work? When did he say, By-and-by, all this necessity will cease, and then the whole week will be be one hymn-singing Sabbath day? Never. He said, You have worked well to-day, but to-morrow with what sinew, with what strength, will you ply the vocation of God! You have done well this week, but next week you will not know your former selves; you will be giants refreshed, you will have new programmes, new enterprises; you will see new heavens, new earth, new possibilities, and there will be no holding you back. This is the mission I open to you, this is the reason why I comfort you; if I give you a moment's sleep it is that when you are waken out of it you may be the better qualified to prosecute your noble toil.

"Greater works than these" there are always to be done. Work begins on a small scale, enlarges, increases, develops, and you enlarge and consolidate along with your service, and thus you are proceeding upon an ever-enlarging line of service. There is no end to Christian culture; there is no period in the literature of sacrifice; whilst anything has been withheld nothing has been given; whilst one pulse has been kept back from God's altar the whole life has also been kept back. Never believe any men who think their work is done; even if they think their own personal work is done, the work is being carried on by braver men, keener minds, larger hearts, and more perfect fidelity. No man has ever imagined with any approach to completeness what God means humanity to be. This word must always resound in our soul, "Greater works than these." What we do is nothing compared to what we shall yet do. Is there not need, then, after such a revelation of the future, of a word of special comfort and encouragement? Trust the divine artist; he knows where the light should be, and where the shadow should fall.

Having thus called his disciples to greater labour, Christ says:—

"And whatsoever ye shall ask in my name, that will I do, that the Father may be glorified in the Son. If ye shall ask anything in my name, I will do it" (xiv. 13, 14).

They might well wonder how the greater works were to be done. Here is the answer. Ask, and ye shall receive. What a marvellous combination of limitation and illimitableness we find in these words! Never man spake like this man! "And whatsoever,"—that is bold, almost to recklessness. Who can tell what human fancy may crave, what human imagination may suggest? But the word does not end with "whatsoever," but proceeds thus—"ye shall ask in my name." Everything must be sanctified by the name, limited by the name, defined and designated by the spirit of Christ. Here, then, you have obedience, surrender to God, confidence in the divine wisdom, an asking that is not bold, but that is made humble and reverent by the completing expression—"Not my will, but thine, be done."

Again the revelation comes. The disciples had to receive "the Spirit of truth; whom the world cannot receive, because it seeth him not, neither knoweth him: but ye know him; for he dwelleth with you, and shall be in you." They are to become new men, under new dominion, the subjects of new impulses; they are to be controlled, and yet to be emancipated; to have an enlarged liberty, and yet an ennobled discipline. Is not another word of comfort there specially needed? It is; and it is given—"I will not leave you comfortless." This is an unfortunate translation, because it seems to connect the word "comfortless" with the word "Comforter"; whereas, there is no connection between them in the thought of Christ. The tenderer translation is this: "I will not leave you orphans." In an ancient translation of the Bible into English the quaint translator says, "I will not leave you faderless"—without a father. This connects the thought of Christ with the words, "He that hath seen me hath seen the Father." I will not leave you orphans or fatherless: I am your Father; but you did not know it. All definitions of family relationship are merged in the supreme relation fatherhood and sonship. I will not leave you fatherless—"I will come to you"; and when I come the Father comes : " I and my Father are one ; in my Father's house are many mansions : I go to prepare a place for you " : I am always engaged upon your service; wherever I am, I am doing something for the redeemed humanity: you shall never know the cold, the loneliness, the sorrow of orphanhood.

So Christ proceeds to speak to the heart, quietly, whisperingly, sympathetically, culminating in this benediction, " Peace I leave with you, my peace I give unto you : not as the world giveth, give I unto you "—an expression that is rarely properly understood. " Not as the world giveth " is not a reflection upon the manner in which the world gives, but a characteristic of the kind of things the world gives. " Not as the world giveth "—gold, and silver, and horses, and chariots, and estates, and social status ; in this line of bequest I do nothing ; I will not operate as the world operates ; I give what the world cannot give—heart-calm, the balm of tranquillity, the jewel of peace, the eternal Sabbath Day. Thus he always separates himself from, the world, and from all rivalry, and all attempt to approach him along his own line ; whenever men think they are going to do what Christ does, he steps away to the invisible height, and leaves them grovelling in the valley of darkness below. He will have no rivalry ; he will not pluralise himself, and be like other redeemers and gods ; he is Christ by virtue of his uniqueness ; " only begotten " marks him off from all the tribes and families of men, but never prevents his coming down to them with fruit plucked from heaven's trees and water drawn from the river of God. When, therefore, we read about his not giving as the world giveth, we are to understand that he is speaking not of manner but of quality, not of limitation but of contrast : the world can give gold, but not wisdom ; the world can give estate, but not peace. The devoutest father that ever died never gave his son one atom of his reverence that could be accounted his in addition to those things which were comprehended within his own personal responsibility. Thus Christ gives as the world cannot give, and the world can never be a substitute for Christ; and the things the world gives can never make up for the things which Christ gives. It is not in number to touch the region of quality. The worldling and the Christian live in different universes.

Drawing nearer to the disciples by way of figure and emblem—
for they still needed the miracle of symbol in order to make them
understand even in an approximate degree the deeper mysteries
of this new life—he said,—

"I am the true vine, and my Father is the husbandman" (**xv. 1**).

Is it not important in all life to know who is the principal, the
head man, the lord of the occasion? We make much of this in
our business; why should we make little of it in our religion?
Why should we be content to talk to a servant when we can talk
to the Lord? We say in business, with some show of shrewdness, Let me see the chief man; I do not want to deal with
intermediaries; I want to see the head of the firm. A man will
say that with some pride of a commercial kind, as if he were not
easily to be put off; yet that same man plays false with his own
reasoning when he comes into the highest matters of all. The
contention of the Christian teacher is this, that men ought to
inquire who is the principal, who is Lord, where is the fountain,
the origin, the secret spring of all vitality? Jesus Christ addresses
himself to this question, and answers it by anticipation, "I am
the true vine"; "I am the vine, ye are the branches."

"If a man abide not in me, he is cast forth as a branch, and is withered;
and men gather them, and cast them into the fire, and they are burned. If
ye abide in me, and my words abide in you, ye shall ask what ye will, and
it shall be done unto you" (xv. 6, 7).

Is there anything unreasonable, then, in Christianity, when its
principal quest is to know the head and origin, the fountain and
spring, of things? This is indeed Christianity. It will not be
content with minor explanations, with any work of men's hands;
it cannot sit down at the outer line of phenomena and say, These
will do: they are very wonderful! Christianity does not send us
to create a museum of specimens of curiosities, oddities, and
eccentricities; Christianity says, To the fountain, to the origin,
to the all-supplying force of things—where is that? Having
found that all the rest will come, by naturalness of development;
but until you have found the well-head, the spring, and the
fountain, you have found nothing that may not perish in your
hand, and disappoint you even in the moment when you thought
you had touched the height of victory. This is the supreme
characteristic of the New Testament; this is the supreme

characteristic of Christianity. Christ reveals the Father: "No man hath seen God at any time ; the only begotten Son, which is in the bosom of the Father, he hath declared him." Jesus Christ proceeded forth, and came from God : hence the mysteriousness of his speech, hence the uniqueness of his personality, hence the unapproachableness of his morality. It is not an affair that springs out of the earth, and is to be tested by geometric appliances ; it is a revelation from heaven, a descent of the Holy Ghost, and is only to be understood even in a partial degree by those who walk with God. Here, then, at once we find an encouragement and a standard.

What will be the reward of this, the faithful prosecution of Christ's commandment? The answer is given in verse 15— " Henceforth I call you not servants," but " friends." That is the line of promotion. We shall know when we are called friends by Christ; a new consciousness will dawn within, a larger sense of life will possess us; we shall know, when the lifetide rises, when a nobler enthusiasm inflames our nature, when mightier impulses stir within us,—we shall know that we have gone up in the grade of Christian relationship, and that we who began as slaves have been promoted to the rank of friends. In this school we must graduate. Herein we may all take the honours of the school, and the meekest will take the most. We have read in Isaiah that Abraham was called by Jehovah, " my friend." When Augustus called Virgil his friend it was thought he had conferred an honour upon the singer—as if an emperor could confer an honour on a poet! Jesus Christ calls us friends. Why does he change the designations—" for the servant knoweth not what his Lord doeth "--is not in the innermost secret of things ; he only waits at the door, and beholds from afar—" but I have called you friends ; for all things that I have heard of my Father I have made known unto you." I have created you trustees, I have invested you with the dignity and the responsibility of stewards ; you have in you, did you but know it, the manifold wisdom of God ; so then, ye are no more your own souls. This is the reasoning of the Apostle Paul—" If any man be in Christ, he is a new creature ": he has not got some new faculties, aptitudes, opportunities, but he himself is a new man, a new soul. " Old things have passed away, all things have become new," and amongst the new things are the new and abiding honours : the lesser name has been exchanged for the greater name ; the servant has blossomed into the friend. This honour is open to all who love the Saviour. Say, is there any honour compared with that when a man can truly say to himself, I am the friend of Christ ? Once I beheld him afar off; I was once in the infantile region of wonder, open-eyed amazement, uninstructed surprise and astonishment, always admiring him, but never really approaching him in any sense of kinship ; but now I have laid my head upon his shoulder, and have wept myself into a new relationship. I understand things now I never understood before ; I do not want to hear now about miracles, signs, tokens ; I want nothing but to feel him breathe. This is the ecstasy so transcendent as to be calm ; this is the peace of God.

Then Christ changes his tone, and begins to " command " the disciples and say,—

" Ye are my friends, if ye do whatsoever I command you ; . . . These things I command you, that ye love one another " (xv. 14, 17).

He is Lord as well as Paraclete ; he is Sovereign, as well as Redeemer ; he is Lord of all. Yet, who thinks of Jesus Christ giving commands ? We often think of him as the Creator of the beatitudes, the Poet of benefaction, the Man who had fine fancy enough almost to invent characteristics for separate qualities ; we read his beatitudes, and bless him for his gentle words ; but the Author of the beatitudes is the Author of the Christian commandments : Follow me ; believe God ; believe me ; love one another. These are not proposals that may be modified ; these are not suggestions that are open to compromise ; these are the living commandments of the living Christ. We bless this mighty speaker for his eloquence on the mountain which all men might hear, but with a tenderer praise we thank him for these other words, spoken in the privacy of love, uttered in the secrecy of heart-to-heart intercourse. We might know more of Christ if we loved him more. To love he will ever manifest himself—to criticism he will seldom speak. From love he will never withdraw.

Chapter xiv. 2.

"I go to prepare a place for you."

THE PREPARED PLACE.

THERE are two remarkable things about this statement. First of all, that the master should prepare for the servant. This upsets the ordinary course of procedure. You are expecting to entertain some chosen friends. All your appointments are made; you have sent before your face servants in whom you have confidence, and have told them to do as you have commanded, that all things may be in readiness for the invited guests. This is customary; this is considered right. But Jesus Christ says to his servants—such poor, incomplete, and blundering servants too—"I, your Lord and Master, go to prepare a place for you." This is quite in keeping with the method which Jesus Christ adopted in his ministry. This is no exceptional instance of condescension, self-ignoring, self-humiliation. "He took a towel, girded himself, and began to wash his disciples' feet." And having finished this lowly exhibition, he said, "If I, then, your Lord and Master, have washed your feet, ye ought also to wash one another's feet. I have given you an example." So his whole life was a humiliation. Wherever he was on earth he was, so to speak, out of place; if his method be measured by his original and essential dignity, his whole life was a stoop, his whole ministry a Godlike condescension. So, why did we begin our discourse by saying it was a remarkable thing that the servant should be prepared for by the Master? Only remarkable when looked at in the light of our little standards and false relations; but quite in keeping, perfectly and purely in harmony, with that divine condescension which marked, ruled, and glorified our dear Christ's ministry.

The second remarkable thing about the text is,—That the

329

divine Being, God the Son, should ever have occasion to "prepare" anything. To prepare may signify to get ready, to put
things in order, to look after arrangements, appointments, and
the like, so as to have all things in due proportion and relation,
that the eye may be pleased, that the ear may be satisfied, and
that all our desires may be met and fulfilled. Why, Jesus Christ
talks in the text as if there was a great deal of work for him to
do somewhere, and he must make haste and get it done. Go to
prepare ? Can he who fills infinitude and breathes eternity have
anything to do in the way of arranging and ordering and getting
things ready for his servants ? He accommodates himself to our
modes of thinking. He does not always throw the infinite at us.
He often steps out of his tabernacle of glory and talks our own
speech,—makes a child of himself that he may be understood in
this little rickety nursery of a world. He knows we are all in
the cradle still ; that the mightiest speaker amongst us is only a
lisping babbler, and that he must continually break up his words
and turn himself downwards, in order that he may convey the
very dimmest hint of his unutterable meaning !

There are some things which the Master only can do. Will
you go and prepare summer for us ? You might try. You have
seen half a hundred summers : now you go, and try to make the
fifty-first ! Come ! You are an artificer ; you have the organ
of form largely developed ; you have an eye for beauty ; you can
buy oils and paints and colours and canvas and brushes of all
kinds. Why do you not go and prepare summer for us ? The
great Master, looking down upon this little under-world of his—
this basement story of his great building—says, " I am going
to prepare the summer for you." And he makes no noise,
he makes no mistake in his colours, never gets things into
discord. He continually renews the face of the earth, and not
a man in all the busy boastful world can do it ! If the servant
cannot prepare the summer, how could he prepare heaven ? If
the saint exhausts himself when he lights a candle, how could he
fill the great heavens with the morning that should never melt
into sunset ?

Observe, therefore, that always the servant has to wait for

the master. He can only go as he has example set before him.
The servant has no original ideas.   The servant is not a voice,—
only an echo, muddled, indistinct.   I would that we could reflect
very deeply on that point,—that every now and then in life we
have to stand back, and let the Master go out before us.   We
can do a hundred and fifty little things, and multiply the hundred
and fifty by ten, and double that number, and we actually get
into the notion at last that we can do anything.   When you have
made one little rosebud, advertise it, and we will come and look
at it.   When you have made one new plant, let us hear where
it is to be seen, and we shall examine it.   "Canst thou command
the morning ? "   " Canst loose the bands of Orion ? "   Art thou
known by the Pleiades ?   Canst thou open the gate of the Milky
Way ?   What art thou ?

   This text gives three intensely gratifying, comforting, and
inspiring views of the Christian believer's position and destiny.
The Christian believer is the object of Jesus Christ's zealous and
tender care.   When Jesus Christ was going away he said to his
wondering disciples, " It is expedient for you that I go."   When he
addressed them on the occasion of the text he said, " I go to prepare
a place for myself " ?   No !   " For you."   And the Apostle Paul,
catching his Master's sublime tone, said, " All things are yours."
And Peter, thunder-tongued, cried out, " Blessed be the God
and Father of our Lord Jesus Christ, which according to his
abundant mercy hath begotten us again unto a lively hope by
the resurrection of Jesus Christ from the dead, to an inheritance
incorruptible and undefiled, and that fadeth not away, reserved
in heaven for you ! "   Yet we hang our heads, and moan and
cry and fret and chafe as if we had nothing, not knowing that a
man's life consisteth not in the abundance of the things which
he possesseth.

   Wherever you find Jesus Christ you find him working for his
people,—doing something for those who believe in him and love
him.   " He ever liveth to make intercession for us."   There is
a beautiful necessity of love about this arrangement.   For if he
were to fail here,—fail in training, educating, sanctifying the
Church,—he would fail altogether.   What if he has made countless millions of stars : can the stars talk to him ?   Can he get

back the idea which he gave? Can he have sympathy with
form, substance, glory, majesty, as found in mere matter? If
he does not get us—poor, broken things—right into his blue,
glad heaven, he has failed! That is the one work which he set
himself to do. If he drops one poor little child out of his great
arms because he has not capacity and strength, he could never
be happy in his heaven. Think of this: Christ always thinking
for us, caring for us, going out in all the passion of his love
after us, and then say whether the Church ought always to have
tears in her eyes and never to have peace in her heart?

Not only are Christian believers constant objects of Jesus
Christ's most zealous and tender care, but they are to be eternally
his joy. " I go to prepare a place for you." The plain meaning
of that is,—Fellowship, residence together in common. He said
afterwards, " And if I go and prepare a place for you, I will come
again, and receive you unto myself; that where I am, there ye
may be also "—giving us the idea of permanence, continuity of
residence, and fellowship. We do some things for the moment.
It is enough for God if he limits April to thirty days; he does
not want it on the thirty-first day; it ceases, and goes back into
his great heaven, and May begins. He does not bring back
any one year that has passed, and say, " There, I have brushed
it up for you, and made the best of it I can: you must try it
again." No. He takes the years, blows them away; creates
new ones; never gives you an old leaf, or tells you to put a
faded flower into water and try to restore its colours and its
fragrance again. " He is able to do exceeding abundantly above
all that we ask or think." " He fainteth not, neither is weary."
As for these heavens, he will one day dismiss them. He will
create a new heaven and a new earth. He will burn up and
utterly destroy what he has made. He makes some things for
the time being; but wherever we read of the place prepared for
Christian believers, we have the idea of continuous, enduring
time—never-ending fellowship. All true life is in the heart.
Love alone is immortal. " God is love." We shall drop argument, logic, controversy, letters, technicalities, pedantries of all
sorts, tongues, prophecies, hope, faith itself, and only Love shall
live for ever!

The world is made poor whenever it loses pathos. Whenever the emotional goes down, man goes down. Logic is but intermediate help ; it is but a poor ladder compared to heart, love, pathos, sensibility. Love must endure as God endureth. This is it which binds Christ and Christians—love. Love is knowledge. Love hath the key of interpretation. Love can explain what learning can never fathom. Love knoweth the Lord afar off,—beyond the stormy deep, in the far-away desert, in the night-time dark and cold. Love can see the invisible, and touch the distant. Do we love Christ, or are we still in the beggarly region of mere controversy and cold intellectual inquiry ? If we love him we shall be with him for ever.

Seeing that Christ makes the Christian believer the object of his constant and zealous care, and that the Christian believer shall be for ever with his Lord, the Christian is entitled to look at the present through the medium of the future. The more we can bring the power of this love to bear upon the passing moments, we can look into the things which are seen and at the things which are not seen, and step out of eternity morning by morning, do our little paltry day's work, and go back again into God's pavilion. If in this life only we have hope, we are of all men most miserable. For we know that if our earthly house of this tabernacle were dissolved, we have a building of God, an house not made with hands, eternal in the heavens.} Moses endured as seeing the invisible. Jesus Christ teaches this most beautiful doctrine : That the Christian heart is not to be troubled, because in his Father's house are many mansions. So he brings down heaven to help up earth. He says, " When you are weary of the present, look forward to the future ; when the road is steep and difficult and tortuous, think of the end and be thankful and glad." It is by this power we draw ourselves onward. We lay the hands of our expectant love on the golden bars of heaven and draw ourselves forward thereby. Some will know what I mean by that expression. You who have been in sickness and sorrow and loss—you who have been tired of looking downwards, and feel the very heart dying within you, when you saw nothing but this earth's narrow circumference, and then have had sudden visions of God's eternity and Christ's blessed immortality, you draw on yourself through all the care and sorrow and bitterness and unrest of time by loving, intelligent anticipation of eternity.

Now, if Christ has gone to prepare a place for the Christian believer—what then? The place will be worthy of himself. Send a poor creature to prepare a place for you against to-morrow, and the place will be prepared according to the capacity and resources of the messenger. It is a poor person who has gone to prepare a place for you, therefore you will not see gold and silver, you will not have a sumptuous reception; but if the poor person has done all that she could, it is enough. You will see the intent of the preparation everywhere; every speck of dust that has been removed means, "I would put down gold there if I could." Every little thing, even a wild flower out of the hedgerow, put into a little glass that can hardly stand, means, "I would give you paradise, if I could." Every little deed that is done ought to be amplified by your grateful love, because it means so much more than it looks. But Jesus Christ says, "I go to prepare a place for you. I have made worlds, stars, planets, comets; I have sent forth the lightning and uttered the thunder. Now I am going to do my greatest deed of all. I am going to get a place ready for those whom I have bought with my blood and glorified by my Spirit." What kind of place will he get ready for us, who has all things at command,—when the silver and the gold are his, when he can speak light and command worlds to fashion themselves and shine upon his children? What kind of place will he get ready? You like to be prepared for. If the person preparing for you is poor, you take every little deed as a great deed. If the person preparing for you has ample resources and receives you as if—"Really, well, you have come after all; but, at the same time, it would have been quite as well if you had lost your way,"—you naturally feel indignant, dissatisfied, resentful, because it might have been done nobly. Jesus Christ has gone to prepare a place. We judge men by the capacity of their resources. We have seen what he has done. If he has loved us with unutterable love, he will enrich us with inconceivable glory. The riches which he has are called "the unsearchable riches of Christ." "Eye hath not seen, ear hath not heard, nor hath it entered into the heart of man to conceive, what God hath prepared." "Come, ye blessed of my Father, inherit the kingdom prepared for you."

Preparation implies an interest in us, an expectation of us. He is waiting for his guests; he will open the door presently, and we shall go straight in. God has prepared nothing for the bad man. There is a place,—the pit of damnation, the worm that dieth not, and the fire that is not quenched ! But it was not prepared for him. It was prepared, Christ says, for " the devil and his angels." That is the only place he has for the bad man ! He made no preparation for him,—thought, perhaps, that at the very last moment he might turn and say, " God be merciful to me a sinner!" Christ did not get anything ready for you ! All that there is is the devil's pit—never, never got ready for man—man who was redeemed by the precious blood of Christ !

Chapter xiv. 21.

"He that loveth me . . . . I will love him, and will manifest myself to him."

ON CHRIST MANIFESTING HIMSELF.

HERE is a promise of divine manifestation to the human mind, and of divine indwelling in the human heart. "He that loveth me shall be loved of my Father." "If a man love me, he will keep my words : and my Father will love him, and we will come unto him, and make our abode with him." So, then, God need not be unto the human soul as a far-off and unapproachable King—he may be in the heart as a gracious Father ; his presence need not be as a coldly glittering star away in the inaccessible heights, but as a summer filling the heart with fire, working in the life all the strange enchantments of inter-mingling colours, and covering the soul with abundant fruitfulness. Thus we have distinctly set before us the highest possibility in spiritual life—the possibility of being temples of the Holy Ghost, of having fellowship with the Father and with his Son Jesus Christ, and of being made partakers of the divine nature. This thought should silence the clamour of all earthly appeal to our affections, and give us the true idea of our susceptibilities as children of God. We can do the daily business of life, yet through it all can have shining upon us the most holy and transfiguring image of the Son of man ; we can be in the city of men, yet hidden in the sanctuary of God ; our feet may be in the dust, but our heads among those who worship day and night ; we may carry with us him whose name is Wonderful, Counsellor, Mighty God. So being and so doing we are no longer of the world ; we are only waiting to pay it back the dust it lent us, and then we shall be free of it for ever ; our true life is hidden ; it is in God's keeping ; it is never seen drawing water from this world's muddy wells, nor eating the base food of the beasts that perish; it lives on the living word, it draws water from the wells of salvation ; it has meat to eat that the world knoweth not of. " This is a great mystery, but I speak concerning Christ and his Church "—and I invite you to follow me, in a prayerful and quiet spirit, in an endeavour to show first the condition on which divine manifestation is granted ; and, secondly, some of the blessed evidences by which we may know that such manifestation has been realised in our own experience. O Spirit of Light, shine upon us, that we may see every step of the ascending and glorious way !

(1) The condition on which divine manifestation is granted to man.—That condition is distinctly asserted in the text, and in other Scriptures, to be love. " The Father himself loveth you, because ye have loved me." " If any man love me, I will manifest myself unto him." Where love is wanting, all is wanting; there may be rough interpretations of the divine presence as seen in the wonders of creation; for he would be a fool who could mistake the sun as having been written by any other hand than God's; he who reads only the writing on the face of nature is as the letter-carrier, who reads only the outward address, not the wise and tender words written for the heart. Love is, so to speak, the faculty by which we apprehend God, without which we can never know more of him than that he is a dread mystery. Love is the fulfilling of the law: thou shalt love the Lord thy God with all thy strength. Nor need it appear strange that love is the only interpreter of God. In all our education and inter-course we find again and again that love sees farthest, hears quickest, feels deepest. God has not set up an arbitrary test of manifestation, he has taken the common course of our life, and given it applications to himself. I might challenge the worshipper of Nature to say whether his god does not demand precisely the same condition of manifestation ? The mountain is saying, If any man love me, I will manifest myself unto him ; the sun holds the same language, so does the sea, so does every leaf of the forest. Two men shall walk along the same road ; the one shall see nothing of beauty, and hear nothing of music. When he reaches his journey's end he may, perhaps, have a dim impres-sion that there was a hedge on one side of him and that there

was garden land on the other; he may not be prepared absolutely to deny that a bird or two might have been singing in the air as he came along; he may not be ready to take an oath that now and again he passed a wayside flower; but he knows nothing, he is not in the slightest degree enriched by reason of his walk through the enchanting scenery. To such an eye as his Nature refuses to reveal herself in any but her most outward forms, and even they are misunderstood by so blind a reader. The companion who walked with him has, on the contrary, enriched his mind with many a picture; he has heard voices which will linger in his ear for many a day; the wayside flower has spoken to him some tender message, and the whole scene has been to him as the distinct handwriting of the great Creator. How are we to account for the difference? The road was the same, the two men travelled the same path at the same moment; yet the one was poor at his journey's end, and the other was filled with a sweet delight. The explanation is easy: the one loved Nature, and therefore Nature manifested herself to his admiring eye; the other cared nothing for Nature, and Nature in return cared nothing for him. What I wish to insist upon is, that even in your sanctuary, O worshipper of Nature, the same law holds good as in the sanctuary of the living God; in both we hear the words, " If any man love me, I will manifest myself unto him."

The same rule holds good with Art. Every great picture is saying to those who look upon it, If any man love me, I will manifest myself unto him. It is not every man who can read a picture. To some men a picture is only so much canvas and so much paint, without life, without idea, without poetry; there the great work hangs, having no message to those who look upon it with unappreciative eyes. You have heard persons who knew nothing of works of art, who, in passing great pictures, have said, "That is not so bad," or, "What a glorious frame that is!" but into the soul of the painter they have not seen at all; they have not appreciated the expenditure of mind which has been lavished on that costly work. On the other hand, there have been men who have stood before a great picture dumb with amazement, quivering with inexpressible delight, moved to the very depths of their being! The picture is the same, the light

in which it is viewed by both parties is the same ; yet to the one
mind the picture is representing truths too deep for utterance,
and to the other nothing but the coarsest exterior. Here again,
therefore, we are thrown back upon the law of the text, and are
shown that it is no arbitrary law which Almighty God has set
up. Art unites with Nature in saying in the most distinct
manner, If any man love me, I will manifest myself unto him.
Nor do we come to a change of this law if we enter into the
circle in which human nature is most deeply studied. You can
never know a man deeply until you love him. If you wish to
know what is in your friend, sound his depths by entrusting
him with more and more of your friendship. As flowers expand
in the sunshine, so character discloses itself under the genial
radiance of trustful affection. All character, indeed, does not
reveal itself in the same way, but some men, and probably the
grandest men, do not show themselves fully except under the
influence of love. We may make many happy conjectures concerning the disposition of men. By putting one thing and another
together which we may have seen in their character, we may
come to some tolerably correct conclusion regarding the life of
those whom we carefully study ; but to know a man deeply and
truly, to know him as he knows himself, we must test him by
our own love, we must develop him by the fulness and reality
of our special trust. The mother often knows more about the
child than the father does. You may remember that in your
childish days you were able to go to your mother with a very
broken story, and she was patient and wise enough to put it
together for you and make something of it ; but you did not care
to go to your father until you had a straightforward story to tell,
and were prepared to stand a close cross-examination upon it.
Perhaps some little girl may say that in her case it was precisely
the contrary, for she could go to her father better than to her
mother. I am glad to know it ; such an instance does not at all
destroy the validity of my position ; it still remains true that
where there is the most love there will be the highest power of
interpretation, and that love will draw from its object most
surely all that it requires. What we have found in Nature,
in art, and in the family circle, we find in the whole course of
our general study. The poet is saying, If any man love me,

I will manifest myself to him. He will not speak to the prosaic reader. His poem will be but so many lines to the man who has no poetic faculty. The poet will only speak to the poet. Two men shall read the same poem—one will feel it tedious and wearisome exceedingly ; the other will feel as if it ended too soon, so rich, so inspiring, so grand he felt it to be. What is this but the application of the principle of the text ? So with the musician : to some men (men, indeed, who are to be sincerely pitied) music is nothing ; it does not come to them with inter-pretations which could never be expressed in common words ; they are lost in what, to them, is a terrible discord—the clash of instruments, the throbbing of great drums, the roll of stupendous organs, the blending of many voices—to them it is all confusion, without spirit, without figure, without signification. To others, music is as a voice from heaven : in the grand compositions of the masters they see, as it were, the very spirit of music walking upon the wings of the tuneful wind, and beckoning them away to higher scenes and nobler delights than earth can afford. How is this ? Music will not visit the silent chambers of the soul that gives it no loving invitation ; music, on the contrary, will never cease to sound in the hearing of those who pray that her voice may continue to soothe and inspire them.

We come, therefore, again and again upon the principle of the text. Whatever be your god—be it Nature, be it Art, be it humanity—you will find in it the same law that you find in the text, namely, that without love there can be no true manifestation. It is the same with reading books. All authors are not the same to us ; we must take something to an author before we can get from him all that he will give. The "Stones of Venice" must be hard reading to a man who cares nothing for Gothic, Byzantine, bases, jambs, and archivolts ; Shakespeare is uninteresting to the man who brings nothing of the dramatic in his own nature to the interpretation of the great poet ; such a man will flee to Euclid's Geometry, as to an ark of refuge. Yes, even geometry itself insists upon the application of the law which we find in the text. Euclid is dull reading to the man who does not love mathematics ; but to him who has, so to speak, a geometrical mind, even straight lines and circles are apt to become things of beauty. You will not regard these illustrations as tedious if they help you in any degree to realise the principle, that love is the secret of manifestation. In setting up love as the condition of divine fellowship, God does not set up an arbitrary law. This, indeed, is the common law of the universe. Like ever goes to like. He who loves the devil most, knows most of the devil. To love vice is to be a learned scholar in the school of the infernal spirit; is to be really clever at wickedness, to be refined in iniquity, to be a genius in abomination. Some men are so little learned in the arts of the devil as to expose themselves to the interference of the policeman and the magistrate; they are such clumsy servants of their bad master as actually to be imprisoned, and to be otherwise punished by the laws of their country; others, again, are such adepts in the art of doing that which is forbidden, that they can manage to build up a reputation for respectability while they are actually engaged in practices which cannot bear the light of day,—so silent are they, so skilful, so deeply do they love the devil, that they receive from him the most secret manifestations, whilst they can look abroad upon the world with a face which simulates the appearance of innocence. The law is impartial. To love is to know; to love is to have; to love is strength; to love is life.

(2) I intended to say something about the blessed evidences that we have realised this divine manifestation; but why attempt to explain what must of necessity be too great for utterance in words? When God is showing himself in the heart, there are many signs of his presence. In our deepest intercourse with the Father our souls enter into an ecstasy in which language is felt to be powerless. You cannot have God in your heart without knowing that he is there. You cannot always explain, in common language, how it is that you are assured of his presence; yet there are flashes of light upon your mind, there are surgings of love in your heart, which tell you most unmistakably that you are enjoying immediate fellowship with the Father and his Christ. If I were to enter into an enumeration of the evidences by which any man can be assured that God is manifesting himself to the human heart, I should put, first and foremost, this—namely, where God dwells there will be increasing hatred of sin as sin.

I do not say that there will be mere dr ad of consequences; I do not teach that men will avoid sin simply because they fear the terrible rod which never fails to follow the evil-doer. I insist rather, that where God is reigning in the heart there will be an ever-deepening detestation of sin on its own account; of sin because it is sin, because it is so infinitely hateful to God himself. Where the spirit of order is in a man, he does not require to go with a square and compasses, and other mathematical instruments, in order to test whether this or that is out of order, or out of proportion; he detects it instantly, by reason of the very spirit that is in him. Where the spirit of honesty is in a man, he does not retire in order to consult an Act of Parliament before he completes his transactions with those who have entered into business relations with him. He does not say, "If the Act will allow me to get off for elevenpence three-farthings, certainly I shall not pay one shilling." He is himself an Act of Parliament; he is the incarnation of the spirit of honesty—he represents the great law of divine righteousness, and, because of the spirit of integrity which is in him, it is utterly impossible for him to go astray from the path of rectitude. And even thus it is with regard to the very highest attainments of the divine life. When the spirit of holiness is in a man, his whole life will be made holy thereby; he will not care to consult rules and codes as determined by human critics; the spirit of holiness that is in him will lead him into truth, into purity, into the very holiness of the all-holy God. Let us then put ourselves to the test on this point: if we would really know whether God is manifesting himself to us, let us each say, Do I hate sin as sin, or would I roll it under my tongue as a sweet morsel if I could do so without suffering evil consequences for it? Do I abominate sin because it is opposed to the nature of God, or do I profess to hate it merely because such profession will secure for me a better standing in society? Would I sin if I were left alone, or if the most perfect secrecy could be granted to me? These are the piercing questions by which a man may test whether he is really enjoying divine manifestation, or is living a superficial and perhaps a hypocritical life.

Next to insisting upon this proof of divine manifestation to the human heart, I should point out that where God really dwells with men there will be on the part of men supremacy of the spiritual over the material. The flesh will be servant, not master. Christianity indeed does not destroy human passions, but gives them a higher direction. Where God dwells in the soul, and fills the mind with heavenly light, and stirs the heart with blessed expectation, the passions will, of necessity, take their order from reason. As the material universe is under God's control, so will the human body be under the control of the human spirit, where God dwells in the heart. As in nature we find occasional outbreakings of storm—as the winds now and again threaten to rock the world and shake it out of its place— as the volcano bursts forth in devastating fire—as the sea roars tumultuously, so there may be in our bodily experiences proofs that we are yet in a region where the enemy has some power over us; yet as God sits above the floods, and controls all the forces of creation, so will he give our spirit ability to overmaster all the agitation and turbulence which show that even yet we are more or less strangers in a strange land. Out of this hatred of sin and this spiritual supremacy there will, of course, come perfect trust in God's government of the world. The world becomes quite a new study when the heart is renewed in Christ's love. The world is no longer a threatening mystery; it is still, indeed, a problem, but there is the most perfect assurance in the heart that the solution will bring nothing but glory to the divine name. When God manifests himself to man, man is delivered from the terrors of the present world; he ceases to see mere accident in the courses of daily life that perplex him and distress him. He says, I do but see part of the divine movement in this; so far as these events that appear to be disastrous are concerned, I see that which is fragmentary, and I must patiently and confidently wait until God has completed his whole purpose. This is a sure sign that God is in the heart, for the world is displaced, its power is thrown down, and, even in the most threatening circumstances, there is a calmness which was never wrought in the human mind by carnal philosophy or unassisted reasoning. The world becomes less and less to a man who enjoys divine fellowship. To some men the world is, of course, everything; they have but one little world in their tiny universe—of course they are bound to make the most of it; to the man who is the temple of the Holy Ghost there is a great and indeed immeasurable universe, in view of which this speck of dust, on which some men would live for ever, dwindles into its proper insignificance. The Christian and the worldling are not, as they ought not to be, able to look upon the events of life with the same composure. The worldling must, of necessity, live in a constant state of alarm, because he is exposed to the mercy of what he calls accident, chance, misfortune. The Christian, on the other hand, by reason of taking wide views of things, by reason of associating himself with that which is infinite and absolute, enters into a profound and imperturbable peace. Yes, this peace is a sure sign that God is revealing himself to the heart. Where grace is, there will be the most blessed peace. "Great peace have they that love thy law." The Lord will bless his people with peace.

Is any man in search of the Holy Grail? Here it is. "If any man love me, I will manifest myself unto him." Hast thou been on the holy quest in many countries? Pause. The answer is here, "If any man love me, I will manifest myself unto him." After many heartaches, many blighting disappointments, many cruel mockings, art thou still sighing for the Holy Sangreal? I have the answer, "If any man love me, I will manifest myself unto him." We must begin with love, the love which comes of earnest desire to know that which is heavenly, and then, in due time, will come a still tenderer affection. We must get to the point of love. All our self-sufficiency, all our high notions, and mighty imaginings, must be cast away as things unclean and unsatisfying, and then we shall see the Father. "Blessed are the pure in heart, for they shall see God." Love is the brightest purity. Purity is the divinest love. I cannot tell you how wondrously God reveals himself to love! He can never do enough for it. It moves him to lavish upon us unsearchable riches. Nor is love on our part a fixed quantity; we may grow in love for ever, constantly going out after God, never exhausting his grace, yet ever increasing in capacity to receive it. As for your god, O ye idolaters of Mammon, your love is a vanishing quantity, though it may appear to increase; you are daily impairing your very power of love; you are letting your greedy god eat up your hearts, and yet suffering him to delude you with the notion that you are independent and high-minded thinkers. Mammon! accursed god! never satisfied, never thankful, never beneficent, thou dost slay all to whom thou dost reveal thyself! Men of business, let me warn you against this flattering and mocking money-god; he will deceive you at last; he will stir you with most exciting promises—he will show you the kingdoms of this world, and the glory of them; he will throw open the doors of enchanting palaces, and give you visions of temples in which all is golden—but at last he will laugh you to scorn! Yes! he will surely reveal himself to you; he will grin as devils only can grin; and when you see him as he is you shall be like him. Blessed are they who have turned with loathing from his jewelled altars, and sought the Sangreal in the blessed Cross! Blessed is their life—blessed is their peace—blessed is their hope. Daily they draw themselves through the discipline of earth, by the inspiring expectation of heaven, and by the sweetness of grace they overcome the bitterness of sin.

Chapter xvi. 7.

"It is expedient for you that I go away."

BLESSINGS IN UNEXPECTED WAYS.

THE text calls us to meditate upon some of the sudden and unexpected changes in divine movements. Sometimes heavenly blessings come to us, so to speak, by steps so clearly marked, so orderly, and so natural, that we can almost calculate how and in what measure they will descend upon us. Sometimes God gives us blessings to our reason; we have thought about them, prepared for them, felt assured that by a kind of gracious necessity they must be ours, and sometimes he has given us blessings in sudden and startling ways. We have been in a position, again and again, to expect our blessings. We have looked for them as for friends that were pledged to come; and we have been able to say, almost with positive certainty, when they would come, and how they would come, because God has appointed channels of communication with his creatures. There is, then, if I may say so, a division in the divine government about which men can calculate, and reason, and foretell with almost perfect certainty; and there is another division in the divine government about which we know nothing—sudden breakings out upon us, startling innovations upon our life, voices that we never heard before, and manifestations for which we were entirely unprepared. So I am not going to look at the commonplace and ordinary method of the divine movement, but to turn aside, and look at some of what are to us God's sudden, unexpected, mysterious visitations, in ways that we never thought of as being accessible, except in the way of judgment and retribution. Sometimes you can say in the morning that it will rain to-day. You say that the wind is in this quarter, or in that, and the clouds are gathering, and there are evident signs that we shall have rain; and sometimes we say, "Oh that rain would come!" "Oh that out of this great Arch of Summer a baptism

346

of rain would come!" but there is no sign of any such blessing. And perhaps quite suddenly, baffling all the speculations and calculations of the meteorologist, as if out of the very fire of the scorching summer, there has come down upon us an unexpected and gracious rain. So it is in the divine movement. Sometimes we are enabled to say, We shall have a blessing to-day. Such and such preparation has been made; such and such endeavours have been maintained, and the natural result of this process is blessing, grace, peace, triumph. And then, again, on the other hand, we have said, "There shall be nothing to-day." "The heart is barren, the inner voice is smitten with sudden dumbness; there will be nothing for us to-day but stony silence. It will be a day of fasting and sorrow." And, quite unexpectedly, God has sent his angel with blessings we had never thought of; and when we looked for a dreary day, a day of fasting and gloom, God has opened the windows of heaven for us, and given us blessings that it had never entered into our calculations to imagine. It is so with many of the divine movements; and yet we often vex God when he comes to us by unwonted ways. Though he has come to us through the pathway of a thousand storms, yet we still tremble before the gathering gloom, as if God had forgotten to be gracious. Though he has come to us with the wings of many a fire, we have still dreaded the flame, as if it tabernacled no God. Have you thought about that depart- ment of your sins I have thought of it many a time. We will not let God have any extraordinary methods of manifestation to us. We will have yesterday repeated to-day, and to-day is to be the image and prophecy of the morrow. And yet God will not have it so. He will come to us, not always by the great grand staircase of his daily providence, when we can see him as it were descending in all the pomp of his infiniteness; but he will come to us along passages, and down by-lanes, and will start up before us suddenly and unexpectedly; and it is then we become so weak as oftentimes to grieve him, as if he had not ten thousand ways into his universe beside the one way that we speak of as his peculiar path.

Now, here is one of the instances of unexpected blessing, of unexpected movements, of movements that escape all calculation, and set aside all that the heart would have predicted. I propose, therefore, to look at this text in the first instance as reversing our own notions of the divine movement. " It is expedient for you that I go away." We cannot see that. It does not look so to us. Let us, therefore, be fair and candid with the spirit of the text. It looks to us exactly the contrary of that ; and we should therefore say it is inexpedient for us that Christ should go away. It is the blackest and direst calamity that can befall us that Christ should go away ; and yet he says expressly, in words that a little child may understand, It is expedient for you that I go away. Here, then, is an upset of our ordinary notions. We should have said this, viz., " Jesus Christ must remain upon the earth until the very last soul is saved. He must be the last to go away. He must stand by the grave until he sees every saint pass through it—until the last little child is winged as a cherub—and then, when he has seen all this done, let him go." That is how we should have talked ; and not, I think, without common-sense, viewing the subject in a purely earthly light. Walking in the light of our own understanding—in the light of daily fears, in the light of what is called prudence and discretion—we should have said, Blessed Saviour, thou must remain until the very last gleam of day, and when thou hast seen the very last of thy recovered lambs enfolded in the high mountains of Israel, then thou must also come and complete the great assembly in heaven. Instead of that he says, I must go first; I must go now, and it is expedient for you that I go away. And so God is constantly, in all the processes of our daily life, upsetting our notions ; this we do not like, and it takes a great deal of hard and terrible drill to bring a man to this point, viz., " God is King, let him do what seemeth good in his sight." It would appear that God will not have our calculations. It would appear as if he took special delight in proving our calculations to be mistakes. So we can never get on two days at a time. We say, To-morrow shall be as this day, and more abundant, and the third day we shall go into this and yonder city ; and God says, No, I will break your days in two, and where you expect prosperity you shall find a grave. So God will not have our long-headed calculations, and he will not have our deluded predictions as to this event and that. It would seem, I repeat, as if he took special delight in reversing all our ordinary methods, and training us to wisdom by first convicting us of folly. It is so, for example, in our social life. We should have said this, " God will never take away the head of a house until all the children have been trained, educated, and established in life. God will certainly see that the father of the family remain until his last little child leaves his roof a man, a woman." And yet God says, " No, the head of the family must go first; " and he says this also, " It is expedient for you that your father go ; " and the heart cannot say, " It is well." No, that cannot be. But God is always doing that; always turning our ideas upside down, and appointing us bless- ings where we expected despair. We should have said that God will allow every man to bring his work to something like completion ; he will never go and break the little bud off the stem ; he will never allow a man to work up his column, and not to put the capital on ; he will never allow an author to begin a volume without allowing him also to finish it, to revise it, to attach his signature to it by way of endorsement, and to hand it to society as a complete thing. And yet he is doing exactly the opposite of this. You say, Here is a beautiful little bud, and it shall be nourished with light and with dew, and become the best flower in the garden ; and God comes in at night, and nips it off, and in the morning we have tears and sorrow. We begin to build our pillar, and it is growing under our touch, and we say, This shall be a beautiful column, a noble pillar ; it shall be capped in the most elaborate style of sculpture ; and God takes us away just as we are putting on the head, and our purposes are broken off. And as for the author, poor man ! just as he dips his pen to finish a sentence, God says, That will do ; and he punctuates the paragraph with Death. That is a fact ; but this is what we are perplexed by, viz., when God takes away the little blushing bud, and breaks the column in twain, and arrests the hand of genius in its wondrous fabrications, and then says, It is expedient for you that it be so. And it is at this point that we either become strong men by the triumph of faith, or we succumb as the captives of unbelief.

Let us look at the text, then, in another light, viz., as showing the superiority of the spiritual over the material. It was a great thing to have the visible Christ; it is a greater to have the spiritual Christ. This is a most difficult point in human education, viz., to proceed from the letter to the spirit—from the material to the immaterial. And this is the difference in scholarship—one man is learned in the letter, another is learned in the spirit; the one is a reader, the other is a genius. In proportion as we get spiritual power are we rich for ever. You lose your friend, but you never lose his friendship. Death breaks up the assembly, but he never impairs the fellowship. Death hushes the communications of the lips; he cannot silence the more eloquent interchanges of the heart. Those whom we truly love are always with us—not always audible, but always present. You have not lost that child of yours you buried years ago. The little creature is still with you. And oh, what talks you have together now! When you go out alone, the little one seems to know where you are and to come to you; and your face does so brighten, and your breast does so heave with unwonted and blessed emotion, as you talk over the days that are gone. And even that prodigal child of yours is with you to-day. You cannot see him—you may not, perhaps, know his address—you may be unable to write to him, yet the lad is close to your heart. You see him when you retire to rest; you look at him in the morning as he is standing by your bedside; and he is with you all the day, notwithstanding his sin, and perhaps (so wonderful are the mysteries of the heart) the nearer because of his sin. There seems to go out after him a realising love, deep and agonising; and if he would but come back again, there would be more joy in your heart over that recovered one than over all the family that never gave you a moment's pain. But I want to fix the mind upon this point, viz., the realising power of love. My friend has gone away from me over the sea and beyond the mountain, but I have him in my heart; his thoughts, his views of life, his behaviour under given circumstances, his noble impatience, magnanimous scorn of all that is low and mean, never leave me; they will mould my life, they will save me in many a temptation. He is with me always because of the realising power of love. And this that we know something about in friendship, in the family circle, in literature, reaches its highest consummation in Jesus Christ; for though he has gone away from us, he says, " I am

with you always, even unto the end of the world." Though we
cannot see him, yet he says, "I will never leave thee nor forsake
thee." Though we would gladly lay hold of his wounded hand,
he says it is better not. It is expedient for you that fleshly
contact cease, and that you lay hold of him by the tendrils of
your love. For what if we did grasp hands, Death would break
up our union; but if we grasp hearts, we are one for ever.

Now, do not expect young Christian people at once to get up
into that high line of Christian experience. I am not unwilling
that you should continue the child's song,—

> "I think, when I read that sweet story of old,
> When Jesus was here among men,
> How he called little children as lambs to his fold,
> I should like to have been with them then."

It is a poor prayer that you will come to dislike more and
more the longer you live, though it is a beautiful song for children.
You will come to know what it is to say you are glad that Christ
is known to you no more after the flesh, but now is known to
you through the hunger of eager love, through the thirst of your
heart, through the desires of an unquenchable life.

Then let us look at this text in the third place, as conveying
blessing to us through the medium of a trial. It must have been
a trial for these simple, unlettered men to lose the presence of
the visible, personal Jesus Christ. It could not have been an
easy thing for such men. Try to realise their circumstances,
if you would get really into the spirit of the text. It could not
have been an easy thing for them to acquiesce in this bereavement, and yet Jesus Christ distinctly points out that he was
going away for their sakes, and not for his own. He did not say,
"My brethren, I am weary; this world is too heavy a load for
me; I have seen you for a little while, and my heart is sickened
and sore and weary, and I must go away again." He did not
speak about himself at all. He said, "It is expedient for you
that I go away." And do not let us think this strange, because
we ourselves have had experience that may help to illuminate
the mystery of this separation. For example, here is a mother
who is teaching her little child to walk. You know what a

pleasure it is to see a little creature taking its first walk from one chair to another! I do not think I shall ever forget the first time I taught a little child to walk, and the joy I had in seeing the little toddling creature manage to go three steps without my help. There came to me a sense of triumph, a sense of something done. Well, here is a mother teaching her child to walk from one chair to another, and she begins by holding the child's waist gently with both hands, and as the little thing steadies itself, and seems to have found its feet, she just takes away her hands little by little. Why does she take away her hands? Does she say, " I am tired; I do not like this posture of embracing thee, or of holding thee"? No, but she says in effect, "It is expedient for thee, my little child, that I take away this motherly support; thou must learn to walk by thyself;" and so the hands go away, not because the mother is weary, but because the child must be taught, sooner or later, self-reliance.

Here is a father sending his boy to school, and there is such a dreary night before he must go. The father and the mother half think they may never see him again. He has never been out of their sight for twenty-four hours, and now they are going to send him away to a distant school, and the mother hardly sleeps all night, and the father gets up at an unusually early hour, and altogether there is a general sense of a sort of domestic earthquake in the house, because the youth is going to be sent to school. Now, why all this discomfort? Why do they not keep him at home? Why do they not keep him constantly in their sight? They say it is expedient for him that our presence be withdrawn; it is expedient that he escape the temptations of home; it is expedient for him that he undergo drill and discipline; it is expedient for him that he meet his equals in the great scholarly contest; it is expedient for him, and on that principle the father strengthens himself, and the mother makes herself a strong woman, and they bid him good-bye, not with delight, and yet with a secret comforting conviction that it is for the youth's good that he should undergo this separation. So then we know something of this—we know something of trial in this direction; and this kind of trial reaches the perfection of its meaning in Jesus Christ's bodily separation from his Church. He says, It is expedient for you that I go away ; I shall always be with you, nevertheless ; yet by my bodily absence you will be trained to thought, you will be trained to spiritual realisation ; the highest faculties of your nature will be called into exercise ; and in order that this may be so, I shall no sooner go away than I shall send down upon you the Holy Ghost, for the Holy Ghost is better than the dying body ; the Holy Spirit of God better than these pierced feet and these wounded hands.

We shall have a poor notion of life if we regard it as being a blessing only in proportion as it is a succession of sunny scenes. That is not life ; it is but one aspect of it. No great life is made up of all sunshine ; we get strong by discipline, we grow by strife. The great storm rocks us into rugged power, and by this power of endurance we come into the grace of gentleness. Great sorrows make tender hearts. We are softened and refreshed by the dew of tears. When we are weak, then are we strong. You never can be great and reliable, full-grown men, till your hearts have been crushed within you, and God has taught you in the gloomy school of a thousand disappointments.

This leads me to say, no true manhood can be trained by a merely intellectual process. You cannot train men by the intellect alone ; you must train them by the heart ; and this shows the fundamental mistake which is being made by some modern teachers. You can never train a Church out of the head ; you may have a Church so-called, and you may open halls and bring to them the most scientific men in Europe, and you may lecture on all scientific topics, yet you can never make a Church out of the head. You must take hold of manhood by the heart, if you would train it into strength and dignity and usefulness. A Church, then, can only come out of the heart. So, if you have been training yourselves only by the intellect, I do not wonder at your being a poor and shrivelled Church. I never find a Church that takes hold of the head alone going forward, I find it progressing backwards ; and I thank God that I see it shrivelling out of existence. But in a Church whose fundamental principle is this, With the heart man believeth unto righteousness, I find ʲty, tenderness, nobleness, benevolence, and divinity ; and

23

this is the secret of Christ's power over man. He does not come to discuss with them some empty conundrum, some wretched enigma, that challenges only the intellect; he sets himself down in the heart, and trains that, brings that, into the liberty of his blessed captivity, and out of the heart there comes his kingdom, which never can be moved. So I have no fear about people who are setting up Churches of Progress, and Churches of Science, and Churches of Literature; I have no fear of them emptying Christian sanctuaries, because a man is not all head. If he is, he is not all man. You must lay hold of his heart, and by his affections and by all his moral sympathies you must train him, and then he will be ready to receive all the light, all the knowledge you can possibly convey to him; but if you train only his intellect, you do but plant flowers upon a ghastly tomb.

One word, finally. The text may be regarded as giving the proper explanation of Jesus Christ's bodily absence—I go away. The words must be regarded as revealing part of a plan—I go away; I am not sent, I am not surprised away; I am moving according to a scheme, a plan. There are no unexpected thoughts in the mind of God. The changes that are strange and startling to us are links in the chain of God's own fashioning. Lay hold of this, and you escape the atheism of chance, and come into the peaceful region of familiar trust. Therefore, in proportion as I think of God's government as a plan am I at rest. In proportion as I take it to pieces and discuss it in detail am I vexed, and troubled, and disappointed. When I think of God building a great temple, I say, Give him time till he brings the topstone on, and says it is finished. And be careful, too, lest you mistake the scaffolding for the temple. God often requires, as it were, laborious scaffolding; and when I come to look at his unfinished temple and see nothing but these great beams, and posts, and planks, I say, "There is no temple here; there is nothing but confusion;" but God says to me "Wait, wait." And I come back and back; and when I return on the last day to look at it, all the scaffolding is gone. Then shall I find the floor laid with fine gold, and the roof lighted with such beauty as was never painted by the brush of the artist.

Some need this lesson. I speak in the presence ot some among us who are mourners, and they need to be gently reminded that God is working out a plan—one thing belongs to another—that there is nothing fragmentary and detached and isolated in God's movement. Where we see confusion, he sees a plan, and he is working it out. You need that gentle hint. May it fall like morning-light on your troubled hearts !

Though the Saviour has gone away, he has made a path into the heavenly kingdom for us. He will not suffer us to rest short of his own Throne. " Where I am, there shall ye be also." Could we but see things as they are, we should see the whole Church all over the world move in one grand procession towards the gate of the Upper City, a band of freemen, an army of conquerors, having banners dipped in light, and singing of the Cross that gives them the right of way to their Father's house. We cannot see things as they are. This is the day of cloud and gloom ; the full brightness is not yet.

"And when he is come, he will reprove the world of sin."

THE CONVICTION OF SIN.

WHEN he, that is the Spirit of truth, is come, he will reprove, he will convince the world of sin. He will show the sinfulness of sin ; he will work in every sinner's heart the torment of self-conviction. He will accuse the world of sin, and will prove the accusation. The work of the Holy Ghost, in reference to sin, is first a work of revelation and then a work of conviction. He will show sin to the sinner—show it until the sinner is startled, ashamed, self-pierced, self-condemned. The Holy Ghost will reveal the unholy man. The revelation of sin is distinctly and specially a spiritual act. It can be done completely, with all necessary clearness and terribleness, only by a Ghost, and only by a Ghost that is Holy, and only by a holiness that is perfect as God. The Ghost of God sees things as they are ; sees essences, realities, hidden tendencies, remote possibilities ; sees the soul in its nakedness, and knows the thought of man afar off. When that Ghost comes into any heart, he will reprove, convince that heart of sin.

Let us try to work our way to some approximate idea at least of the intensity and agony of that conviction. Take the case of a man who is reeling in the streets under the influence of strong drink. That man does not require the Holy Ghost to convince him of sin. There is no common man on the road side that would not instantly turn upon him and say, " That is a sinner." No ghost is needed to make such a revelation. Every child, seeing the reeling man coming near, will instantly feel that he is in the presence of a sinner. God is not required to come down to the earth and say to the drunkard in his drunkenness, " You are a sinner ; " to the blasphemer in the madness of his

356

profanity, " You are a sinner ; " to the adulterer in his uncleanness, " You are a sinner." All these things are known by the
common morality, the non-christian instinct which is in every
man, and which teaches him to distinguish—though not always
minutely and spiritually—between right and wrong.

Let us dismiss all those foul and vicious characters whose
moral nature is plainly written on their foreheads, and look in
the next place at a person of the utmost social respectability.
Examine his conduct from week to week in the market-place, and
there is not a man who comes in contact with him who can justly
bring any charge against his behaviour. The man is diligent in
business, punctual in his appointments, straightforward in all
his dealings ; a man who, by the continuousness of his probity,
has earned for himself a position of confidence in the commercial
world ; his speech is the speech of an honourable man, so far
as all the affairs of this world are concerned, and so far as his
intercourse on matters of business is concerned. He is a member
of a Christian church ; he sometimes engages in prayer ; he
contributes to charitable objects. Altogether, I repeat, he is a
man of the utmost social respectability. What is required to
convince that man of the real state of his heart ? A ghost ! If
you and I were to speak to him, taking cognisance of his character,
he might resent the intrusion, and dare comparison of our own
life with his daily conduct and behaviour. The Holy Ghost
enters him, and finds in him a faint trace of lust, evil desire,
having reference to some forbidden object or other. The man
never named it, never confessed it to himself, never ventured
to whisper it in the most subdued breath ; but there it is, in
the depths of his nature ; and the Ghost of God works upon that,
reveals it, develops it, shows what it really is, expands it in all
its horribleness—until the man whose outward character was
irreproachable, whose behaviour could challenge comparison with
the average behaviour of the world, trembles, burns under the
influence of an internal fire, and dare hardly fall down upon his
knees to ask God to forgive an enormity so great ! He never
would have known what that faint, hardly describable vein of
evil desire was but for the ministry of the Holy Ghost. He
would shrink from the presence of an unclean person ; he would

denounce in the most emphatic terms the irregularities of the drunkard ; he would shudder when he heard the profanities of the blasphemer. But the Ghost of God cut him in twain, and pierced even to the dividing asunder of all within him that was secret and most compact, and took up this vein and said, " That is you ! " until a speck became a mountain, until a single speck, an atomic, microscopic speck—nay, such a microscopic speck as the eye of God alone could discern—grew into proportions over-shadowing and overwhelming. And the man, outwardly so respected, praying in prayer-meetings and giving to charities, cried out, " O wretched man that I am ! who shall deliver me from the body of this death ? " No man can come to that experience—can know anything at all about it in its torment, in its killing agony—until the Holy Ghost has been at work upon his heart.

Here is a man who is equally respectable—a man of excellent standing, a man against whom nobody can utter a single reproach justly, a man equally honourable and upright and straightforward with the man whom we have just delineated. The Holy Ghost comes into him and shows in him a secret, subtle, unexpressed selfishness, in ways that the world cannot take note of. Remote acts of selfishness ? Nay, not acts ; when it comes to acts then anybody can sit in judgment upon them. But thoughts of selfishness,—little, tormenting, urging, importuning dreams of selfishness,—something between a thought and a thing, trem-bling, hovering in that border-land,—sometimes almost personify-ing itself, then shrinking back again into impalpability ! The Holy Ghost shows him what he would be under certain cir-cumstances, if certain fears could be taken away, if certain possibilities could be set aside,—all that unspeakable atmospheric spiritual pressure which never can be defined and only can be felt. And when he sees the thing in its reality, as illuminated and expanded by God the Holy Ghost, all his cry is, " God be merciful to me a sinner ! Nobody thinks me a sinner. I can walk up the main aisle of the church to-morrow and there would be subdued applause at my presence. Many a man would speak well of me if called to testify in open court concerning my standing. But oh ! thou God the Holy Ghost—thou piercing,

cleaving Spirit—thou hast shown in me one hidden vein that I
never knew of, and I see it in the blaze of thy fire! God be
merciful to me a sinner!"

The great difficulty in conducting spiritual education in our own
hearts, and in the hearts of those who wait upon our ministry, is
this: To see the difference between sin and phases of sin; between wickedness in the heart, in the thought, unexpressed and
unconfessed to ourselves, and the mere accidents of wickedness
which relate to time, place, or form. There are many men to
be found who would condemn worldliness of spirit, so-called;
condemn, perhaps, certain amusements which other people
accept with all innocence and with legitimate enjoyment. There
are those who say the Church is fast becoming like the world;
men who will not play at this game, or go to that amusement, or
sit in this society, or identify themselves with yonder movement,
because they suppose that all these things savour more or less
of worldliness. Very well. One of these men who is so
unworldly and so exemplary shall be heard in his tea-table talk.
He says unkind words about his neighbour; slanders his minister,
is a sneak when sneaking will win him what he calls success; he
is a traitor when treachery will bring him thirty pieces of silver,
more or less; there is no meanness he would not stoop to; there
is no length of censure and censoriousness to which he will not go.
Yet that man condemns another who rides on a fine horse and
goes to find some of his amusement in a painted house! What is
required to show the man what he really is? The Ghost of God,
to show him that an unkind whisper may be murder; that a
shrug of the shoulder may be incipient assassination; to take
him by the hand, and condemn him in the sight of God, for a
villainy too refined for common morality and too subtle to be
taken note of by any of the magisterial tribunals of the land!
Only the Holy Ghost can pierce a man with such reflections and
convictions as these. It is not the profane oath, it is the profane
heart; it is not the open, overt, deadly deed, it is the feeling of
needless, exaggerated, unrighteous anger; it is not the hand wet
with blood, it is the spirit that longs for some measure of revenge
and some degree of retaliation. It is when we get into these
essences of thought that the Holy Ghost alone can be our perfect

teacher, showing us what sin is without its accidents of time, place, and form,—the wickedness of sin in the sight of the holiness of God.

We have to guard against seeing the sinfulness of other people without seeing the beam that is in our own eye. We need the Holy Ghost to enlighten us on these matters. We are so sensitive in some particulars, we shudder so revoltingly in the presence of certain forms of sin, without perhaps feeling that sin, if it never took form at all, or was never heard in speech at all, is as hateful in the sight of God as if it came out in the blaze of day and defied the judgment of nations. The religion of Christ is spiritual, the religion of Christ is intense; the word of God searches the heart, and tries the reins of the children of men. Who then can be saved? If the blink of an eye may mean profanity, uncleanness, rebellion against law, determination of secret enjoyment of sin; if the holding up of a finger be in God's estimation, under some circumstances, terrible as the drawing out of a sword and the defiance of the Most High; if he searches our thoughts, if he reveals the secrets of our hearts,—who then can be saved? " I never oppressed the poor; but I once had a thought which must have broken the heart of God. I never uttered a profane word; but once I gave a look that was blasphemy! I have prayed long vehement prayers; in my heart I have had desires I dare not name to woman, priest, or God." If a man's experience be anything like that, and that experience be illuminated by the Holy Ghost, and forced back again upon the man,—oh! how terrible the accusation,—how heart-breaking! Who then can be saved?

Now, if this doctrine be laid down, and in the heart be deeply and intensely realised, four consequences will follow. All attempts to establish life upon a basis of mere morality will be abandoned. Morality is impossible apart from theology. Theology is impossible apart from the direct spiritual continuous teaching of God the Holy Ghost. You say, " I challenge you to criticise my deeds." I reply, " Sir, it is not first and last a question of deeds: it is a question of motive, intent, impulse, secret desire." "Have not I given fifty pounds to this charity?" You have with your hand, but not a penny with your heart : it is what is given with the heart God accepts. " Have not I prayed often and long ? " Yes ; but never a word went beyond the roof under which you uttered your empty mocking words, because whilst your lips were eloquent your heart was dumb. The Lord seeth not as man seeth. Man looketh on the outward appearance ; the Lord looketh on the heart. Where, then, is our morality ? which, being interpreted, is our system of manners, our way— often, indeed, a skilful and artistic way—of putting our life into certain angles and showing it under given lights. Morality is often but an effort of art. Morality is often a study of the way of putting things. But the sincere man—the man who lives in the tabernacle and sanctuary of God—never says, " How will this look ? " His life gushes out of him into activity and form and service ; and knowing that his spirit and motive are right, he says, " It is a small thing to be judged of man's judgment."

Some of us have taken a long time to be persuaded that our morality is less than nothing and vanity,—our chief sin. Not until we get rid of our morality can we be made moral. It is that overweening conceit about our own nice way of doing things that keeps us back from the Cross of Christ, from the mystery of the Atonement. " If the light that is in us be darkness, how great is that darkness ! " If our very morality be our curse, how ponderous is the millstone which will drag us into the depths of the sea ! Not until a man comes without price in his hand, without self-hope in his heart, without self-praise in his mind and says, " God be merciful to me a sinner," can he ever know how worthless is his own morality, how despicable and vain are his noblest deeds.

> "In my hand no price I bring,
> Simply to Thy Cross I cling."

The man confesses himself a sinner—not much of a sinner ; not a sinner in certain lights and in certain degrees ; not a sinner hardly so sinful as other people—but a sinner ! Vast in its concentration is that confession. Overwhelming is that utterance in its very simplicity. When men feel themselves to be what the Spirit of God describes them as being, they want no epithet, no qualifying adjective, to define their position. " A sinner " expresses more in its simplicity and concentration than could be said by the minutest elaboration of speech.

Where the true idea ot sin is realised under the ministry of God the Holy Ghost, the necessity of the sacrificial work of Jesus Christ will be understood, realised, and will form the one foundation of human hope. I have much to say on this point and I cannot say it. The idea has long been floating before my mind, and I have found no words to speak it to others; but it is the stay of my life, it is the strength of my ministry, it is the secret of any earnestness I may feel in preaching the ever-lasting gospel, namely this: The Atonement I do not receive merely as a grammarian, logician, metaphysician, theologian. I cannot understand that Cross—great, rugged, melancholy Cross—if I look at it only from the eminence occupied by the scholar, the philosopher, the theologian. But when I feel myself in my heart of hearts a sinner, a trespasser of God's law and God's love; when I feel that a thought may consign me to everlasting destruc-tion, that a secret unexpressed desire may shut me out of heaven and make me glad to go to hell to be out of the way of God's shining face,—and some man tells me that Jesus Christ was wounded for my transgressions, bruised for my iniquities, that the chastisement of my peace was laid upon him; I press my way through all the grammarians, logicians, philosophers, theologians, saying, "If I perish I will pray, and perish only at the foot of the Cross; for if this be not sufficient, it hath not entered into the heart of man to solve the problem of human depravity and human consciousness of sin."

The sinner does not ask for explanation—minute, critical, and technical—when he comes into that state of heart before the dear bleeding Christ. He leaves all questions of criticism, technical and formal theology, to be settled by-and-by. In the meantime he feels this: That if the blood of the Son of God cannot reach those secret sins, those unexpressed desires, then no river that flows through the earth can wash him clean, no detergent dis-covered by industrious morality can ever take out of him the deep stain and taint! Sometimes we look at the work of the Lamb of God without feeling that we are sinners. Then we have a thousand difficult questions to put about it. At other times the burden of our sin is so heavy upon us, we see the sinfulness of sin so clearly, we get away so entirely from all mere accident of time, place, and shape, so far as they relate to sin,—we see sin as God saw it and as God ever must see it, then we say, "O Lamb of God, thou didst not shed one drop too much of thy precious blood ; thou didst not endure one needless pang ! We see sin now in some measure as thou didst see it. We understand what thou meanest when thou didst say, 'My soul is exceeding sorrowful, even unto death.' We know what is meant by the glorious gospel that Jesus Christ came into the world to save sinners ! "

If I might address brethren in the ministry, students of letters, grammars, philosophers, theorists, and speculators, I would venture to say, that there is much in such studies that may be fruitful of good ; they are not to be contemned and passed by as utterly valueless. At the same time we ourselves as preachers cannot understand the Cross of Christ till we understand ourselves as sinners. No man can be led to the Cross by the hand of mere philosophy. He must go up the dolorous way, with his eyes blinded with penitential tears, his heart choked and suffocated by inexpressible emotion, then there will be a writing above the superscription of Pilate ; " This is the Son of God. Whoso cometh unto me, I will in no wise cast out."

Wherever this view of sin is truly realised and received in all its simplicity, an intense earnestness for the world's salvation will be excited. Do you ask, " Are the Chinese not happy without your gospel ? " I say, Probably they are happy without the gospel, so far as they understand happiness. " Are the people of India not rich and prosperous without the gospel ? " Probably they are. Why should you go and break up households and separate the father from the son, and the mother from the daughter, and the daughter-in-law from the mother-in-law ? Why should you send fire upon the earth and a sword through the nations of mankind ? I tell you, because of what the Holy Ghost has taught us about sin. It is not a question of civilisation, of a gilded surface, of a material prosperity and of a so-called social happiness. If the Holy Ghost has correctly revealed to us the nature of sin, then I must go ; I cannot rest until I have taught other people what has been communicated to me of the spiritual, not of a terrible enormity, not of a bloody deed, not of an outspoken blasphemer, but of secret thoughts and unexpressed desires which are foreign to the nature of God.

This is the secret of our missionary enterprise,—this is the inspiration of our moral service. If it were a question of this world only, let the Chinese alone ! They enjoy themselves after a certain fashion ; they have their own notions of civilisation and success. Do not trouble them. The same with Africa and India ; the same with the most distant portions of the globe. Let them alone ! But when we know, by the teaching of the Holy Ghost, what sin is, a responsibility comes along with the revelation ; and in proportion as we realise it, that responsibility will never tire of breaking up households if need be, of sending a sword into families, and kindling fires upon the earth !

Then, last of all, if we had truly spiritual notions about sin, we should regard one another with a gentler charity. You do not sin as I sin. Shall I therefore vehemently condemn you, and seek a character for my own morality by the urgency and impetuosity of my condemnation of your particular sin ? I do not do as you do when you criticise worldliness, but I may speak an unkind word about a brother minister. I will not speak an unkind word about a brother minister, but I may stoop to any ignoble deed in order to realise my own schemes. I will not stoop to any sneaking, underhand method of doing things ; but I may never forgive an enemy ; I may pursue him to the death, and half a century after the deed my anger shall burn as on the first day. Is it so with us ? You would not go to a theatre, but you are vain as a peacock. I am not vain, but I will do things in secret that I would not like my dearest, truest earthly friend to know. So indeed it is. We must get to know what sin is, not the accident of sin ! We must not be vehement about the accident when we are comparatively indifferent about the essence. When we feel sin to be what it is, our mouths will be shut ; there will never be an hour of unkind judgment in our whole lives ; we shall all be in the same condemnation. Who art thou that speakest against another man ? will be a sore question that will pierce us and cut us in two whenever words censorious and slanderous shall rise to our lips.

May God the Holy Ghost show us sin till we hate it,—show us the reality of sin until we feel our need of the Cross! May he show us the fulness of the love of Christ, until we know what is meant by Christ's ability to take up our sin, our secret sin,—take it up in his pierced bleeding hands and cast it away for ever, and present us unto himself a glorious Church! This is a great mystery, but in Christ all such mysteries are solved. He is, in very deed, the Light of the World!

NOTE.

"The third example of our Lord's discourses is that which closes his ministry—'Now is the Son of man glorified, and God is glorified in him. If God be glorified in him, God shall also glorify him in himself, and shall straightway glorify him' (John xiii. 31, 32). This great discourse, recorded only by St. John, extends from the thirteenth to the end of the seventeenth chapter. It hardly admits of analysis. It announces the Saviour's departure in the fulfilment of his mission; it imposes the new commandment on the disciples of a special love towards each other which should be the outward token to the world of their Christian profession; it consoles them with the promise of the Comforter who should be to them instead of the Saviour; it tells them all that he should do for them, teaching them, reminding them, reproving the world, and guiding the disciples into all truth. It offers them, instead of the bodily presence of their beloved Master, free access to the throne of his Father, and spiritual blessings such as they had not known before. Finally, it culminates in that sublime prayer (ch. xvii.) by which the High Priest as it were consecrates himself the victim; and so doing, prays for those who shall hold fast and keep the benefits of that sacrifice, offered for the whole world, whether his disciples already, or to be brought to him thereafter by the ministry of apostles. He wills that they shall be with him and behold his glory. He recognises the righteousness of the Father in the plan of salvation, and in the result produced to the disciples; in whom that highest and purest love wherewith the Father loved the Son shall be present, and with and in that love the Son himself shall be present with them. 'With this elevated thought,' says Olshausen, 'the Redeemer concludes his prayer for the disciples, and in them for the Church through all ages. He has compressed into the last moments given him for intercourse with his own the most sublime and glorious sentiments ever uttered by human lips. Hardly has the sound of the last word died away when Jesus passes with his disciples over the brook Kedron to Gethsemane; and the bitter conflict draws on. The seed of the new world must be sown in death, that thence life may spring up.'"—SMITH's *Dictionary of the Bible.*

Chapter xvi. 15-33.

THE DIFFERENCE BETWEEN CHRIST AND CHRISTIANS.

" ALL things that the Father hath are mine." We often speak of the union between Christ and his disciples, as if these terms were mutually equivalent. It may be well to look upon the distinctions which separate Christ from his disciples, in order that we may learn our true relation to the Son of God. This may turn out to be but another aspect of union, though at first sight the discourse will seem to be one upon the divisions and contrasts which separate so widely the Lord and his followers. We must not get into that easy way of thinking that Jesus Christ and his people are practically one, in any sense which denotes equality as between them ; as if a Christian were a Christ, and as if Christ were but a Christian, differing in some sense in degree, it may be, but identical in quality. All that line of thought needs sifting, defining, and guarding, lest we lose reverence, and loyalty, and sense of what is due in worship, and trust, and sacrifice. Jesus Christ was very condescending, but in his condescension there was a majesty, unequalled and uncomprehended. The very stoop of Christ was more majestic than the enthroned attitude of any monarch. We should therefore dwell now and again, yea, frequently, upon the contrast which is established between Christ and his supreme apostle ; we should, as it were, calculate the difference, which is really incalculable in degree and in quality, between the Son of God and those whom he has saved by the shedding of his blood. His words are full of significant accent and meaning when he dwells upon this subject. He, himself, is indeed now and again most frank about it ; if he should appear to come near to us, and associate with us on terms of equality, he suddenly rises from the feast, and leaves us to feel for a moment what we should be were he to withdraw altogether. We become so accustomed to the light that we take no heed of it: we expect it; we reckon upon it, as one of the certain quantities in the whole arithmetic of life; but the sun has only to hide himself for a few moments, and he stops the traffic of the world.

Let us hear some words of Jesus Christ bearing upon this matter, in which he will not allow any one to share his glory; in which his personality shall stand out in its singular and un-approachable solitude. We think so often of Jesus Christ as meek, and lowly, and condescending, that we are apt to forget his majesty. The sight of the noonday sun may be instructive and gladdening.

"I am the Vine, ye are the branches." There is no identity there in the sense of equality. The vine can do without the branches, but the branches cannot do without the vine. "Without me ye can do nothing." It is as if a unit were talking to all the ciphers in creation; the unit says to the assembly of ciphers, "With-out me ye can do nothing": you may put yourselves into a great line, and you will signify at the end what you signified at the beginning, and that is nothing; but when I stand at your head my relation to you fires you every one, gives you personality and value and meaning. This was the speech of the meek and lowly in heart, the poor in spirit, the Man of sorrows, the Man acquainted with grief. He would not have shed tears with us upon an equality, saying, Your sorrow is great, and so is mine, and we are found in a world of woe together, and therefore together we must mourn and weep. In his tears he was alone; when his soul was sorrowful he threw into nothingness the grief of all other life.

"I am the good Shepherd." Is there only one? Jesus Christ assures us that there is only one Shepherd, and that he is the one himself. Then all the apostles and martyrs, apologists and missionaries, preachers, teachers, Christians—what are they? They are the flock, the sheep, under his care. Is the flock equal to the Shepherd? Can any sheep in all the flock say to the Shepherd, I will take thy place, and thou mayest rest awhile?

Is there a more pitiable spectacle upon the earth than sheep without a shepherd? Are not sheep chosen as the very image of silliness, helplessness, imbecility, when God describes his people after they have detached themselves from his government and shepherdliness? Observe always that this was the speech of him who was meek and lowly in heart. Yet never does he allow his singularity to be pluralised.

"I am the Way, the Truth, and the Life." There again Christ stands alone. There is none to divide his honour; there is none even to reflect his glory in some of these higher ranges of his personality and priesthood. Where now the thought of condescension, lowliness, abjectness, self-immolation, in the sense of putting away crown and sceptre and throne, and being only a man? These terms are not permissible in any one who is in any sense only equal to his brethren. They cannot be passed by without notice, or regarded as hyperbolical, or as being coloured with a poetical imagination; they are too distinct and graphic and practical. They are only to be accepted on one of two theories: either the man was mad, or he was God. When a man describes himself saying, "I am the Light of the World; I am the Vine; I am the good Shepherd; I am the Way, the Truth, and the Life," he does not offend against modesty; he violates truth, and he violates the reverence which is due from the finite to the infinite. We ourselves have no difficulty about going up to him and saying, My Lord and my God, if I have any crown I will take it and cast it at thy feet, for thou only art worthy of the honours of infinite and eternal sovereignty."

Hear, however, how he speaks: "All things that the Father hath are mine." No man must be allowed to talk that language without rebuke. If there is some hidden sense in which it may be made to appear to be true, that hidden sense must be revealed and defined; otherwise we shall have spreading amongst us the very spirit of presumption, infallibility, and mock divinity. Who can claim to hold in his hands what God holds? Who dare say, "All things that the Father hath are mine," without qualification, and yet only be meaning in some far-off and semi-spiritual sense that he is part-proprietor of the universe? There is a morality of language. Men ought not to be allowed to speak hyperbole which is falsehood. Within the acknowledged limits of rhetoric, they may take what figures of speech they like, but they must declare them to be figures of speech, that we may distinguish between truth and falsehood. " Therefore said I, that he [the Paraclete] shall take of mine, and shall show it unto you." Even the Holy Spirit is here represented as the minister of Christ. Ask for the text upon which the Holy Spirit discourses, and the answer is, he speaks evermore upon one text, namely, Jesus Christ. When he speaks of doctrine, it is the doctrine of Christ ; of righteousness, it is the righteousness of Christ ; of sin, it is the sin for which Christ died. Ought we to allow a man to speak so, with no other than a merely rhetorical meaning ? A book, part of a larger volume, containing such words ought to be torn out of the volume of which it is a part, and burned with unquenchable fire. If we admit a rhetorical criticism we may have to admit by-and-by a rhetorical Christianity, which means a rhetorical morality : words will be emptied of their meaning, and all speech will become but sounding brass or a tinkling cymbal. According to the twenty-third verse, prayer is to be offered in Christ's name. " Verily, verily, I say unto you, Whatsoever ye shall ask the Father in my name, he will give it you."

Where is meekness and lowliness of heart in any sense which means simple equality with human nature ? Observe what Jesus Christ does in these words : he pledges the Father. The words are most emphatic, " Whatsoever ye shall ask the Father in my name, he will give it you ": I pledge his existence, and his honour, and his throne. Again and again we must remark, This is not the language which any man must be allowed to use unless he can vindicate its use by qualities so sublime as to make the use of that language obviously appropriate. The language must fit him like a robe ; there must be no discrepancy between the word and the thing, the symbol and the substance ; here and there in this life there must be an outshining of glory which justifies the use of language so sublime—nay more, which shows that even language so sublime pitifully fails of its object in expressing a dignity ineffable. Jesus Christ guarantees the

answer.   He speaks as the inhabitant of eternity, as the custodian
of the riches of the universe, as one who lays his hand familiarly
upon everything and says, Ask for it, and the Father, through
me, will give it; I will take it up with my own hand and pass
it down until it reaches your hand.   This is not the language of
a mere man; it must not be admitted as such.   We must not get
into the frame of mind which will allow us to pass a man like
this, saying, He does not mean what he says, or he has some
signification far short of the obvious interpretation of the common
language.   Then we could only retain our religion at the expense
of our morality ; we could only cling to Christ by giving up the
first principles of honesty.

Then, again, he declares a divine descent for himself.   " I
came forth from the Father, and am come into the world."   This
cannot be a mere commonplace.   If there is a sense in which
every man may be said to have come from the Father, then the
words of Jesus Christ lose all their special significance.   He does
not say, Brethren, we all came forth from the same Father, and
we are all returning to him.   He speaks in his own name, and
speaks of a common human nature, and declares that he " came
forth from the Father, and am come into the world "—implying a
kind of accommodation to the smallness of the space, as if he
should say, I have so related myself to the world that I can find
room enough in it for the little time that I shall be here.   Having
built the world, I have built a door into it, through which I have
passed through momentarily visible ministry, and presently I shall
be gone again, and leave what little room there is to be occupied
by yourselves.   This is blasphemy if it is not divinity.   This
is rant if it is not infinite reason.   The Church will lose all
vigour when it comes to the paring down of words so as to
rid them of their rhetoric, in order to give them commonplace
meanings.

The weak-minded disciples thought their opportunity had come.
They were but children—half-grown, untaught, inexperienced.
What faces they wore when the Master talked to them!   They
wanted to appear to be intelligent when they were not fully
comprehending the meaning of the speaker; they loved him with

strange admiration and passion; they were quite sure he was right, though they could not follow his high strain of thought and speech—looking as they might have looked upon an eagle gradually mounting into the dim air, keeping sight of him for awhile, and now the great black wings passing away from the visual line; they are quite sure he is flying, and the moment they see the reappearing wing they will exclaim as children utter their delight. So in this case. Jesus Christ has been taking a flight into the highest regions of spiritual thought, and his disciples have been looking on with awed amazement, and half-anticipation that they might never see him any more; but now he is coming within their horizon, and when he says, "I leave the world, and go to the Father," they exclaim, " Lo, now thou speakest plainly "—now we know what thou dost mean ; now we are quite sure about thee ; now we feel as if upon a measured equality with thee : remain on that plane of thought, and never leave us alone any more. It was a momentary bubble on the river of their life. They looked at one another with a kind of vacant delight. They could only exclaim; they could not explain. Jesus—piteous, tender, compassionate—descended to their level, and said, "Do ye now believe?" You think you do : poor souls, you cannot understand a word I have spoken to you. God's method is to lay up a great deal in the mind which history has to explain in due time; so that the Old Testament is searched by the New Testament, and is read in the illuminating glory of the latter days. You think you understand me, and I see your childish pleasure. Now listen, "The hour cometh, yea, is now come, that ye shall be scattered, every man to his own, and shall leave me alone." You will know whether you understand me or not when you have to suffer for me. Do not imagine that heaven has begun; I observe your delight, I cannot but feel sympathetically with you. It is no pleasure of mine to rid you of your immediate joys, but as I look upon you I see you already being driven forth into desert places. I observe your condition, and it is that of sheep being pursued by wolves ; in the dark night you must receive explanation of all this mystery.

So the contrast remains as broad at the end as at the beginning. Jesus Christ never mingles with others as an equal,

When he is counted one of a number, he is the one, the others are the unmeaning ciphers. This being the case, some practical questions immediately rush upon the mind, and some fears, indeed, threaten to leap upon the spirit and quench its trembling hope. There need not be any alarm of that kind. Though the difference between Christ and his disciples is the difference between infinity and infiniteness, there need be no hindrances to communion. The little earth communes with the great sun : the earth never found room for the sun, or hospitality, or entertainment, for one brief day. The difference between them is an abiding distinction which can never be lessened ; they never change places. The earth is always little, and cold, and naked, and the sun is always what he is in the summer-time and in the winter, the origin of such heat as the earth receives and utilises, and such light as makes earth's poor little grey day. The earth might say, were we to personalise it and give it faculty, and reason, and speech, "I am so little and can do nothing. I will take myself away, and fall into the oblivion which best becomes my insignificance." But the earth makes no such speech ; rather does it say, "I am little and the sun is great ; the sun might do without me, but I cannot do without the sun. O thou great Light, let me see thee every morning ; let me feel thee when I cannot see thee ; warm me, cheer me, enlighten me, bless me, and make me fruitful, that I may grow all that is needful for the hunger of man and beast. I am but little, spurn me not, but rather fill me with thy light, and make me do my duty in my little sphere with gladsomeness and music and gratitude." It has pleased Christ to make his people the light of the world, but only in some reflective sense. The moon is the light of the world, but only at night. She knows the time and the limit of her shining, and sweetly does she run the round of her gentle ministry. "Let your light so shine before men, that they may see your good works, and glorify your Father which is in heaven."

Not only is this distinction no hindrance to communion, it is a positive guarantee of blessing—"These things I have spoken unto you, that in me ye might have peace." I have not shown you my majesty that I might dazzle you, but that I might comfort you; I have not blazed and burned upon you from heavenly heights that you might close your eyes and run away into the congenial and healing darkness, but to show you that whatever may come of you, in me ye shall have day and summer, and light and beauty, riches unsearchable. When the rich man displays his wealth to the poor man it may be to keep the poor man at arm's length, saying, Who are you? for you have no wealth to compare with this. Be satisfied with your situation, and keep at the other end of the staff, nor venture to look upon me as an equal. But when Jesus Christ displays his riches he says, These are yours because ye are mine; and because of your faith and love, your trust and service, my wealth shall be at your disposal, and you can never be really poor whilst I live. Some such word as this was needed at the end of such a discourse. Having companied with Christ so long, if we put ourselves into the place of the disciples, we may say we had become almost familiar with him: we have seen him when he was weary and weak; we have seen the great tears standing unshed in his gentle eyes; many a time we have helped him and done our best to comfort him amid the woes darkening upon his life, and so accustomed have we been to his coming and his going that we have looked upon ourselves as in some sense his equals and fellow-labourers. But now, suddenly, he has become a strange man to us; he has changed the whole tone and scale of his speech; he does not even use the common simple little words that used to pass between us as the currency of love. He seems to be seated upon a throne, and to be talking from heaven to earth, and gradually separating himself from us, and we cannot bear it. Whilst such hearing overpowers the listener, the great divine Speaker says, These things I have spoken unto you, that in me ye might have peace, assurance of plenty, confidence of unexhausted spirit, and the tranquillity which arises from these profound assurances. Say now, Christ is mine, and I am his; and because of the union between us, all that he has I have, and so long as he can lift an arm no foe shall overwhelm me. I have no confidence in myself, in my poor little strength, in my mean resources, but I live in Christ; I am crucified with Christ; nevertheless I live; yet not I, but Christ liveth in me; and the life which I now live in the flesh, I live by the faith of the Son of God, who loved me, and gave himself for me. I can do all things through Christ which strengtheneth me. If we make that reply to the sermon which Christ delivered, we shall understand what he meant when he said, " These things I have spoken unto you, that in me ye might have peace."

Then he concludes with an assurance that the conquest is already won. " Be of good cheer ; I have overcome the world." Why should we be of good cheer on that account ? Have we ourselves not yet to overcome the world ? Why should we joy in another's gladness because he has triumphed when we ourselves are left in the thick of the fight? Therein we reason erroneously, and altogether mistake the real condition of the case. When Jesus Christ says that he has overcome the world, he means that his conquest is the pledge of ours. If he had failed we could not have succeeded. It is because he has succeeded that we cannot fail. These are Christian promises; these are Christian delights ; these are the joys of the sanctuary. My soul, when thou art afraid because of the war, put thyself into the keeping of the all-conquering Lord; when the chariots against thee are a million, and are all made of iron, and when the horses are down upon thee like lightning, hide thyself in the Rock of Ages, draw upon the stock of the infinite store. " What time I am afraid I will trust in God." I know by this meditation how vast is the difference between Jesus Christ and myself. If I had been guilty of the presumption of thinking that he had made me an equal, I feel that the mistake has been entirely on my own side. He has not made me an equal, nor can omnipotence do so. There is but one infinity. The difference between the creature and the Creator can never be reduced to nothingness. But this can be made of it : a means of communion, a fountain of blessing, an assurance of protection. That is enough ! Poor little earth, do not distract thyself because thou canst not be the great sun. Keep in thy place; roll on in thy peaceful course, and keep thyself open to receive morning messages of light and evening assurances of defence.

Chapter xvii. 20-32.

"Neither pray I for these alone, but for them also which shall believe on me through their word; that they all may be one; as thou, Father, art in me, and I in thee, that they also may be one in us: that the world may believe that thou hast sent me. And the glory which thou gavest me I have given them; that they may be one, even as we are one: I in them, and thou in me, that they may be made perfect in one; and that the world may know that thou hast sent me, and hast loved them, as thou hast loved me."

UNITY IN CHRIST.

WHAT is Christian unity? Is it an affair of regulation, compromise, concession, toleration, for the sake of good neighbourhood, and easy social and ecclesiastical movement? That view of Christian unity certainly receives no support from the Lord's intercessory prayer. The deepest meaning of Christian unity is union with Christ, oneness with the Son of God, identification with Christ in spirit, purpose, and labour; and coming out of that, as a cause and an inspiration, union of Christians, genuine brotherly love and trust, a love that sees the Christian in the man and that sees Christ in the Christian. Christian unity is living sympathy with Christ; it is being so like Christ as to be almost himself; it is to be under the sweet dominion of passionate devotion to the blessed and all-blessing Cross of Christ. How strange it is that Christian unity should now need to be defined and to be guarded by most careful safeguard! Has Christian unity been interfered with, simulated, perverted, tampered with? Surely a relation so simple needs no definition, unless wicked hands have been laid upon it to force it into unholy and inadequate uses. In endeavouring to promote the cause of Christian unity, let us get rid of all the simulations and mockeries which have gathered around it; let us go back to that which is fundamental and biblically authoritative, and take our quiet stand there, and judge everything by the standard of the written Word. Suppose any man, or any body of men, should attempt to set up

375

a doctrinal standard, saying, By this alone can unity be determined. Such men would assume a tremendous responsibility. Who are they ? By what authority do they erect this standard ? What are their credentials ? How does it come that they claim to have a right to say for unborn generations, what is formally and dogmatically correct and orthodox ? Are we quite sure that we do not inflict injustice upon such men by imagining that they would never have changed their view of things, and never have modernised their speech, and never have taken any account of progressive civilisation, science, and spiritual thought ? Do we not ourselves overburden those whom we almost adore as fathers ? Might not they in face of such a claim start up as schismatics, secessionists, protestants, saying that they never meant so to throw their thought over all the ages as to bind men ; they merely adopted what, according to the light of their time, were the best definitions possible, and they only intended those definitions of doctrine to be accepted as the best expressions of the day ? Suppose any man should now set up such a standard, he would make heretics ; and no man has a right to make unbelievers. No man has a right to put up any such standard and claim for it finality. There can be but one final book, and that book is never final,—namely, the Book written by the finger of God ; and it is never final, because it holds within itself the very seed of truth, and is always expressing itself in new leaf and bud and blossom, and gracious fruitfulness ; the same, yet not the same ; always in substance and in grace, and in eternal gift, immutable, but as to its forms, phases, revelations, always part of the very time we live in, part of the very breath we breathe. So it is the ancient of days, and it is the gospel of this very hour ; old as God's eternity, new as our present progress and immediate necessity.

Suppose any man should erect an ecclesiastical standard, saying, This is the Church, and outside of it there is no Church. That man also would assume a very onerous responsibility—a responsibility which no man has the right to assume. A man should not attempt to go beyond his strength ; his arm is so many inches long, and he must accept the length of it, and work accordingly. Who made us Church-makers ? By what patent or authority do we say, This is the Church, or that, and there is none other ?   That we are at liberty to organise ourselves into companies and fellowships for mutual edification, instruction, and comfort, is (I was about to say) more than true,—that is to say, it is a necessity of grace, the very sweetness of life, the gracious compulsion of sympathy and love ; but having so gathered ourselves into companies of men who agree substantially, and see things from the same point of view, what right have we to say that we take in the whole horizon of truth, and that there is nothing hidden from us in all the counsel and way of God ?   We should hold a very different language.   Our communion should be thankful for the truth which it believes itself to hold, and should always be on the outlook for more light, vision into further distances, and grasp of treasure hitherto unpossessed. What if it should take all Christian communions to constitute the Church ?   What if even some forms of superstition and even idolatry might claim a place just inside the boundary line ?   Who expects that we can all see everything in the same atmosphere, the same distance, in the same perspective, under the same colour, and can utter ourselves sufficiently and finally in one form of expression ?   There is no such monotony in God's kingdom. We have no right to create monotony, and call it peace ; we have no right to create uniformity, and baptise it with the sacred name of union.   Christian unity is broken by the very existence of such standards.   In our attempts to unite, we actually disintegrate.   Our idea of union, if founded upon doctrinal standards and ecclesiastical standards, prevents union.   It does not begin with a right conception of the human mind ; it is psychologically wrong, though it may be mechanically not without some superficial beauty.   Minds differ—differ in capacity, in temper, in training, in opportunity of development; and for all these psychological differences provision must be made ; and they are made in the great prayer of Christ, in the sublime conception of the Son of God, when he founded the Church against which the gates of hell shall not prevail.

Christian unity, therefore, is not formal but spiritual.   If we are looking for formal union we are looking in the wrong direction, and we are looking for the wrong thing.   It is as if we should

ask the question, Are men alive ? and should then determine the
answer to the inquiry by stature, complexion, accent, or by any
other accident attaching to the individual. Who would assent
to the doctrine that it is right to determine living humanity by
such incidents or accidents ? We should protest against the
judgment ; we should say, We are looking in the wrong direction,
we are in quest of the wrong test and standaids : life is wholly
different from stature, complexion, or local position and attitude.
Human love is not formal, it is spiritual. What is its shape,
what its colour, what its bulk in plain ounce weight? Where
is it ? Yet we all know it, we all feel it ; life would be poor
without it : yet it resists organisation beyond a given point ; it
believes in organisation also up to that point, and most fully and
sacredly.   Love claims united love ; love is the genius that
presides over household life ; love will unite even national life
when political instinct fails to touch the necessity of the hour.
Still, love is more than organisation. Love is always surprising
us with new revelations of its beauty and goodness ; love is
always revealing to us some hitherto unknown or unrealised
aspect of God. Human life is not formal, it is spiritual. Who
has seen life ? Where does life reside in the body ? Put a
finger upon the residence of life, saying, Here you will find it,
and nowhere else. No man has seen life. Yet life is organised ;
life has its body, its tabernacle, its system of nerves, and its
wondrous incarnation ; it presses itself against these forms in
palpitation that means that it is greater than can be confined
within physical boundaries. Life, like love, is always surprising
us by new energy, new passion, new capacities. Who can throw
a line upon life and say, We will keep thee here, and bind thee
like a beast of burden ? The very life that could purpose to deal
so with other life gives itself the lie ; its own energy, its own
aspiration after primacy, declares that it has miscalculated the
quality and the quantity of that supreme mystery which we call
Life. So it is with the Church of Christ. It has organisation ;
without organisation it could not live : but it has more than
organisation. Emerson speaks of some men who are blessed
with " over-soul "—soul enough and to spare ; soul that goes
out in evangelistic yearning and solicitude after other souls less
favoured, pining away in the desert or in the darkness. So

with the Church of Christ. Its organisations are valuable ; up
to a given point those organisations are sacred : but whose house
has out-built all other houses and made them nothing but huts not
worth living in ?   The house is sacred, yet there is a house next
door, there is a house behind, there is a house opposite ; the
whole place is covered with joyous habitations lighted early in
the winter-time, rich with flowers all the summer-time, and
the children are so like one another in their laughter, in their
innocent glee, that only their mothers can tell which is which. Is
there not some analogy, or at least dim hint of meaning, as to
ecclesiastical and religious life to be gathered from the life of
the household and of the neighbourhood ?   When we lose the
spiritual conception of unity, then the mechanical conception is
exaggerated ; it is set in false proportions and in misleading
cross-lights ; we have lost the meridian, and men are keeping
their time by their own guesses and their own wild conjectures
and speculations. The moment we lose hold, so to say, of Christ's
hand, we are the prey of the enemy, we are lost ; we are like
planets loosed from their centres ; we plunge where we ought to
shine ; we dash against other parts of the universe where we
ought to revolve in silent rhythm around the governing Flame.
Men become controversial when they become unspiritual. When
men cease to pray, they begin to argue and to fight. How
wonderful it is that men are usually one in prayer ! but the
moment they rise from their knees and begin to state their
opinions, the Church becomes a battle : pray, then, without
ceasing.

Spiritual unity is the only unity that can permit and control
honest diversity.   That is my fundamental point.   Spiritual
union is so large, so energetic, so divine, that it can permit, and
in permitting control, the widest divergences—so wide as to
amount to contradictions ; yet they are all held in leash by a great
spiritual ministry, and the men who are thus held say, One star
differeth from another star in glory, but the heavens are one ; no
star holds any other star in contempt ; differences in glory do not
disturb the unity of the stellar Church.   If we had more of the
spirit of Christ we might even rejoice in the differences which
prevail amongst us, saying, How large is the kingdom of heaven,

how wondrous is human nature in its possibility of development
and spiritual action ! Behold in this diversity another miracle of
him who is wonderful in counsel and excellent in working. All
denominations may be right, and all denominations are right in
the proportion in which they love and serve the Son of God.
Why may not our creed be substantially reduced to one line—
"I believe in Christ Jesus, the Son of God, the Saviour of the
world"? After that we might welcome differences, we might
be pleased to hear diversity of speech and accent; and things
hitherto called heterodoxies, scepticisms, infidelities, might be
brought within the great astronomic action and made parts of the
redeemed universe. Philanthropy sees the man through all ethnic
differences. Philanthropy is not a geographical term; it has
nothing to do with lines of latitude and lines of longitude; it asks
not upon what river the city is built; as philanthropy sees the
man through all ethnic differences, so Christianity sees the Christ
through all creeds and forms and organisations, if the Christ is
there. Christianity goes in search of the Christ. Christianity does
not start out saying, I will number all the infidels that live to-day.
I am not aware that Christianity ever made itself the statistician
of infidelity, or ever went out for the purpose of taking a census
of non-believers. It takes account of excellences, virtues, aspirations, prayers, sacrifices, and it gives back the cup of cold
water with all heaven added. So gracious, so divine, is the
spirit that breathes and burns in Christian thought and love !
The cure of disunion is not in the abolition of sects, but in the
abolition of sectarianism. Every man has a right to choose his
companions, his spiritual fellowships, to work where he can be
most at home, where all his faculties can be best developed,
where all his spiritual hunger can be most healthily satisfied;
but having entered into such relations as are involved in these
inquiries he is not to enclose himself within impenetrable walls,
saying that he alone has the key of the door, and they who are
outside his door are in outer darkness. Astronomic action, as
we have just said, levels the mountains. They are very huge
from a geographical point of view, great overshadowing hills and
crags, habitations of eagles: how stupendous they look ! But
caught in the action of the astronomic movement, where are
they, and where the seas so turbulent, so tempestuous, so

wrathful, so boundary-hating? where are they? The high places are low, and the tempestuous elements are quiet, and the great globe itself swings like a censer before the altar of God. Have we lost the astronomic action? Are we but geographers when we ought to be astronomers? Speaking of the Lord's Table, the late Dean Stanley has expressed the whole idea with his wonted sweetness and music,—

> "When diverging creeds shall learn
> Towards their central source to turn,
> When contending churches tire
> Of the earthquake, wind, and fire,
> Here [the Lord's Table] let strife and clamour cease
> At that still small voice of peace—
> 'May they all united be
> In the Father and in Me.'"

Whatever hinders or jeopardises Christian unity thus understood seems to me by so much to be condemned as wrong. Suppose it is an Act of Parliament that hinders unity. An Act of Parliament may be repealed in one of two ways. If we have thought that an Act of Parliament can only be repealed in one way, probably we may have been mistaken. An Act of Parliament may be repealed formally; we know what that is: or an Act of Parliament may be repealed by the growth of public opinion which makes the Act an anachronism, throws it behind, and leaves it there to find its way into still deeper obscurity and oblivion. An Act of Parliament may be obeyed in one of two ways. We speak much of law; but who distinguishes as to the scope and action of law? Is law but a solitary term? Is all law alike? Is all law of one value? Is there not a law which is simply measured by the word "regulation," and is there not a law which is measured by the word "right"? The regulation may be modified, adapted, changed, abolished, but the right is as everlasting as God himself. When, therefore, men talk about "law," I must know what they mean by law in the connection in which they use it. But a law may be obeyed in one of two ways: first, it may be obeyed sympathetically; then the man who obeys it will say, This is the law, I adopt it, I re-enact it, I assume the responsibility of its correctness and goodness. I obey it because I accept it, and honour it, and love it,—that is one form of obedience : but a law may also be obeyed regretfully, as when a man shall say, This is the law, and I am sorry for it ; it is a very old law and not altogether a good law, but there it is, and I must now fulfil its letter, but believe me I do so with reluctance.   I would it were out of the way as a thing too old for the present time, a thing too old for the progress which nineteen centuries of Christian civilisation have made. Understand, there- fore, that a man in obeying a law is not shut up to one way of obeying it.   He can obey it so as to modernise it and make it offensive : he can obey it so as to make it truly venerable and truly irksome. Everything, therefore, in my judgment, depends upon the way in which any law is obeyed. When Christians wish to come together, any man who hinders the approach on any plea or any ground whatever incurs a tremendous respon- sibility. Go and tell the Son of God that you wanted to come together, but were hindered by an Act of Parliament ; you longed to mingle your prayers and to unite in a common testimony in relation to the Cross and the salvation of the world, but you were obliged to speak to one another through the dividing wall of an Act of Parliament. I will not go with any deputation that proceeds to report so to Jesus Christ of his Church on the earth.

Christian unity is not a mere sentiment, it is a gracious and operative ministry.   It tells the world that they may be one, all one,—"That the world may believe that thou hast sent me." Union is not argumentative.   Union is not sentimental ; it is practical. Who can answer a united Church ? When internecine war ceases, when all domestic troubles are calmed by the genius and spirit of love, when the Church presents a united front as to its real trust in Christ and therefore trust in one another, the voice of unbelief will not be heard. What can speak like love ? We have never yet heard the true music of love's voice, because the voice of love has been broken, strained, discordant ; the voices have been answering one another instead of blending into one harmonious tone charged with the deliverance of a gospel to a benighted world. If any man should ask which of the divided parties is to blame, I will answer him. That party is to blame which will not follow the spirit of union. When men have asked me in family quarrels which of the two combatants is to begin the process of reconciliation, I have said—You ! Were I asked who is to blame I should say, Is there any attempt whatever at intelligent, reasonable, and honest approach ? If there is, the people who resist that approach are, in my judgment, wrong. These matters will never be settled until we have more of the spirit of Christ, more of the love of God. I do not ask for ecclesiastical uniformity, for we can never have it, though we may claim it. I would have many regiments, one army ; many folds, one flock ; many waves, one sea ; many stars, one great radiant sky. He who would understand union must often read the Lord's intercessory prayer. He who would obey the spirit of that prayer must make many a personal sacrifice. Let there be no misunderstanding about unity meaning monotony. Union means diversity ruled by substantial unity of thought and feeling. Unity means many people, but one human family ; many accents, but a common language ; many ways of doing things, but only one motive—to serve God, to please the Lord Jesus Christ, and to answer the ministry of God the Holy Ghost.

Chapter xviii. 36.

"My kingdom is not of this world."

THE TRUE KINGDOM.

JESUS CHRIST was now approaching the termination of his earthly ministry. He who came to bear witness of the truth was standing for judgment at a human tribunal: the Judge of universal man stood as a criminal before Caiaphas, Herod, and Pilate ! Society had mistaken its best friend for an impostor— and had thrown out of its breast the Being who alone could ensure its purity and repose. But had he not disciples ? Why did not these men take up arms in their Master's service ? Would not steel do much towards a settlement of the controversy ? Undoubtedly the peacefulness of Christ and his disciples excited the amazement of contemporaries, forasmuch as the sword has ever been called into requisition by the founders of empires, and yet here is a Being who attempts to establish a kingdom without shedding the blood of a single foe ! To the perplexity of Pilate, Christ makes this reply : " My kingdom is not of this world : if my kingdom were of this world, then would my servants fight, that I should not be delivered to the Jews: but now is my kingdom not from hence." Words indicative of so much spirituality could hardly be understood and appreciated by a man who knew nothing of any throne, or crown, or sceptre, except that which is "of the earth, earthy." It will be necessary to guard this declaration from two misconstructions.

First : It does not imply indifference to the political government of this world. Society must have government, and government involves governors ; but governors exist for the good of society, and not society for the benefit of governors. Christians must not imagine themselves exempt from responsibility in the matter of national condition and progress ;—it is true that they may not

384

all be intellectually or constitutionally fitted to take any prominent position in the direction of political affairs, yet such may be intercessors at his throne before whom all kings must bow, and in that capacity may manifest the most vital interest in the temporary affairs of this fast-dissolving scene.

Secondly : It does not imply monastic seclusion from the engagements of the world. In becoming Christians we are not to betake ourselves to " a lodge in some vast wilderness." We become light for the express purpose of shining in a dark place— we are made free, to the end that we may proclaim the opening of prison doors to them that are bound—we are made children of God that we may teach the self-alienated the way of return to filial loyalty and service. Christ's own example is all-determining on this point : he sat with publicans and sinners that he might call them to repentance, and never sat at the board of hospitality without spreading the festival of sovereign grace and infinite love. I do not object to Christians going into " the world "—technically so called—provided they take their Christianity along with them ; but I do, in the Saviour's name, protest against any disrobing, or any diminution of light—when you go, wear your beautiful garments, and " let your light so shine before men, that they, seeing your good works, may glorify your Father which is in heaven."

What, then, is the Saviour's meaning ? I answer—Christ's kingdom is a purely spiritual constitution—he came not to found a physical empire, but to establish the sovereignty of great and holy principles—his mission was not to dispute the title of mere earthly governors to their several thrones, but to lay the foundation of a kingdom whose royalty will survive the splendour of material pomp. He unsheathed no sword but the " sword of the Spirit."—He marshalled no army except the army of divine doctrines and precepts.—He created no treason against political monarchs.—He breathed no inflammatory speeches against governments, as such. When he spoke, as in syllables of lightning, it was against the monarchy of hell—when he sought the overthrow of a sovereign, it was the prince of the power of the air whose throne he shook. When, therefore, Christ declares that his "kingdom is not of this world," we are to infer the pure spirituality of the Christian Church. My special purpose is not so much to follow out this declaration in its special relation to Christ, as in its applicability to man. The first question, therefore, which I propose is—When may it be justly said that a man's kingdom is of this world ?   I answer—

(1) When man's energies are exclusively devoted to the accumulation of earthly treasure.—There are men whose creed may be condensed into one word—Gold!   Such men invariably prove their faith by their works—their creed controls and sustains their life.   Their motto is, "With all thy gettings, get gold"— their business is with "getting"—they have a certain goal to attain, and no matter how filthy or dangerous may be the road, they start on their journey, animated with the hope of securing the golden prize.   Such men's kingdom is of this world—these men look at all nature and institutions through this medium— Gold.   When they gaze upon the landscape, it is not to admire the undulation of hill and dale, the stately wood or swelling river, but to speculate upon its properties as a farm ; when they turn their cold eye to the nocturnal fires kindled by the hand of Deity, it is not to praise the wisdom and power to which they unceasingly testify, but rather to speculate as to the probability of having fine weather on which to prosecute their business-journey. Such men's kingdom is of this world.   When they rise from their bed, they have no time to consult him to whom the silver and gold belong ; they are in too eager haste to join the race—when they retire to rest they are too weary to acknowledge the dread Power that has given them "life and breath."   Their laugh is merry in proportion as their gains are heavy.   Their face is a commercial barometer; by appealing to it you may learn the condition of the business-atmosphere.   When they use the words "all right," they mean that their coffers are healthy, and their highest idea of happiness is to receive a smile from the fickle goddess of Fortune !   Such men's kingdom is of this world.   We cannot, surely, be told that such men do not exist.   When we see men too miserly to give their children a good education—so miserly as to begrudge even medical aid to those whom they profess to love—ever ready to take advantage of the ignorance of

the novice—stealing a portion of God's sacred day on which to examine their accounts, or write their letters of business—when such things confront us, it is too late to deny the truthfulness of the portraitures now delineated. I may not now address such men as are under review, but knowing that prevention is better than cure, I may appeal to the young to beware lest they should become so wedded to the temporal as to forget the eternal. Man! created originally in the image of God, let me reason with thee by the way : Is it right that powers so noble—that faculties so divine, should be exclusively devoted to the piling of dust ? Is it even good policy to spend your energies on the accumulation of that which can be of no service in any other world than the present ? We know it is quite possible for men who set their hearts on accumulation to amass immense sums, but when their accretive work is accomplished how much that is really noble has been done ? Look at the picture until your eye affects your heart : every energy has been consecrated to the service of self— all the pages of time have been stitched into a ledger—all that wit could suggest, or fancy contrive, or muscle perform, has been pressed into the service, and now that the labour is finished, and the labourer dead, what epitaph shall we inscribe on the stone which marks his resting-place ? Ask justice to dictate the inscription, and words of the severest condemnation will be furnished ; and even if gentle charity herself be consulted, she would say, write—" He had his kingdom of this world."

(2) When man fails to exert any effort for the moral elevation of his race —Some men profess that their benefactions are known to none but God and the recipients. Others determine not to let the left hand know what the right hand doeth ; and this is by no means an unwise policy where the right hand is doing nothing, and therefore has no tidings to communicate. What fearful disclosures will that text make in the great audit day ! Thousands of do-nothings have hidden themselves behind that divinely-woven veil, and have thus evaded the powerful appeals of religion and general benevolence ; but a day is approaching on which the veil will be uplifted, and then the universe will know how far it has been abused by the hypocritical and ungenerous. It is an appalling fact that the vast preponderance of effort made for the

moral elevation of the race represents a small section of professing Christians. To some men all appeal for moral labour is
entirely in vain. Ask them to contribute to the missionary fund,
and they will instantly become so sensitively patriotic as to demand that more should be done for the benefit of our own country.
They blunt every appeal—they would fail to shed a tear on the
corpse of the Saviour, or to feel a single pang were all moral
instrumentality paralysed beyond resuscitation! But such conduct is strictly consistent with their creed—their kingdom is of
this world, hence they practically ignore every movement which
contemplates the unalterable destiny of the soul. Show me a
man destitute of sympathy with moral movements—a man who
has consciously done nothing to lessen the sum of human misery,
or to swell the currents of human joy—a man whom every
supporter of gospel institutions shuns—and you have shown a
man whose kingdom is built upon the sand, and which the
boisterous storm shall shiver into irreparable ruin!

(3) When man draws his highest joys from the fascinations
of this life.—The carnal mind knows nothing of any joy but that
which flows through earthly channels. His highest study is the
promotion of self-comfort. He has no internal sources of pleasure;
while "the good man is satisfied from himself," the wicked is
as a fountain dried up. The thorough worldling is ever dependent on excitement. The ball-room, the theatre, the gay saloon,
have irresistible charms for him. The word of God or the sober
treatise are to him intolerably dull—he is happy only amid the
"voluptuous swell" of music and the incessant stream of
sensuous amusements. Such a man's kingdom is emphatically
and exclusively of this world. Can you imagine degradation
more abject than that of an intellectual being seeking his joys
amid the purely material? A being capable of holding fellowship
with Godhead, enslaved to the charms of earth! A being to
whom the fountains of most exquisite joy are accessible, crawling
to the broken cisterns that can hold no water! A being that
might eat the richest viands which the universe can supply,
directing a hungry look to the table of ragged and shivering
beggary! I ask in all solemnity whether you know of any
degradation more pitiable and appalling? You mourn the broken

fortunes of the aristocrat who has been driven from the ancestral hall into some lowly and obscure home, but that man may be pure and happy in his poverty—his conscience may kindle glory in his humble hut ; but what say ye to a man who is self-expelled from the holiest and loftiest society, and who prefers the gross enjoyments of animal existence to the inexhaustible pleasures of spiritual life ! Take from such men the toys with which their fancy is dazzled—deprive them of the glittering dust which is the only object of their worship—stand at the threshold of their dwelling and forbid pollution again to enter—and by so doing you visit them with the most afflictive bereavement which can wither the human heart ! You have shaken their kingdom to its foundation—you have burnt their monarchy to ashes !

We need not roam far in search of the men now under description. In our midst there are men who are immeasurably more interested in securing for a county an additional member of parliament than in sending forth the messengers of salvation into the midst of domestic or foreign heathenism ! There are many more who may possibly be more anxious to promote universal suffrage than universal salvation ; and thousands there may be who have been more agitated and sorrowful at having been out-voted at a political meeting than ever they were at the untold and inconceivable sufferings of the Redeemer. Such men's kingdom is of this world. To them everything is little in comparison with political reform ; the greatest of achievements is the passing of their resolutions, and the defeat of an opposing ministry is to them a greater historical fact than that uttered by the Saviour, "I beheld Satan as lightning fall from heaven." Let me be clearly understood on this point : let no man misquote or distort my language : I confess the great importance of political purity and freedom ;—the desirableness of every intelligent man being fully represented ;—the necessity of out-rooting parliamentary corruption, and promoting merit to its rightful supremacy : but while attaching due weight to all such reforms, my spirit cannot be content with them as a " kingdom "—my spirit aspires to a loftier and a sublimer royalty ! I would remind the enthusiastic politician of the possibility of making a kingdom of politics—of mistaking the triumph of an hour as the source of enduring satisfaction—and of building a mansion which the first moral tempest will utterly destroy.

Having thus endeavoured to answer the inquiry, when may it be justly said that a man's kingdom is of this world? Let us proceed to the discussion of a question of equal importance, namely, when can it be truly affirmed that a man's kingdom is not of this world? I answer—

(1) When man regards the world as a means rather than as an end.—The watchword of the Christian is, "Here we have no continuing city." He uses this world as the builder uses scaffolding, merely for temporary purposes—or as a waiting-room in which he tarries till the chariot of death shall bear him home—or as a school in which he prosecutes his rudimentary studies, with a view to the engagements of a higher academy—he never looks upon this world as a final resting-place. If he has wealth, it is to him a means of usefulness; if he has influence, he employs it in the promotion of the highest good: he is too wise to expect satisfaction in the merely temporal— things are great to him just in proportion as they rightly affect his eternal well-being. Assure me beyond all doubt that there is no world but this; satisfy my judgment and appease my conscience beyond the remotest possibility of reversal; convince me that my duty is to abandon the holy Book; outroot all instincts and longings for immortality; thrust forth your hand and convince me that you touch the very extremity of being; tear asunder the veil beyond which I am imagining there is a glorious heaven or a terrible hell, and prove to me that all beyond is an infinite blank—and then I may be glad to find a kingdom in this world—my affections will entwine around the charms of the present—and though I may bitterly weep over the grave of my hopes, I shall honestly toil in the perishing vineyard of earth! But, while I am persuaded that we are but in the porch of a palace, vast as infinitude—while my spirit is satisfied of being an heir of immortality, it is impossible to engage in the service of the transient hour with all the earnestness that is due to the claims of eternity!

(2) When man regards the evangelisation of the world as of supreme importance.—In proportion as man attains this spirit does he approach the likeness of Christ. Christ came for the express purpose of seeking and saving the lost. He only sought political reform in so far as the greater comprehends the less. His method of cleansing the stream was by purifying the fountain —he healed the leprosy of governments by curing the moral diseases of individuals. This is the philosophy of permanent cure. When men understand and discharge their duty towards God, they will not be slow in adjusting their relationships to each other. The Christian's highest ambition should be the enlightenment and salvation of souls. In bringing men to the Cross, we are indirectly aiding the true progress of nations; principles are there imbibed which sanctify social bonds and consolidate social interests. While, therefore, the Christian's kingdom is not of this world, yet this world is unspeakably benefited by the Christian's kingdom. As the sun is not of this world yet sheds upon it life-giving light and heat, so the Christian's kingdom is infinitely higher than the monarchies of earth, yet exerts upon them the most inspiring and sublimating influence.

The history of martyrdom is a glorious illustration of the text. The martyrs were men of whom the world was not worthy. Through the force of their loyalty to a spiritual king they forfeited the smile of their earthly sovereign; they endured as seeing the invisible; the sensual and the grovelling failed to understand their spirituality, and laughed to scorn their dreamy visions of a distant but imperishable kingdom. Every man as he was bound to the stake practically exclaimed, " My kingdom is not of this world." Every man as he ascended the scaffold practically averred that the day of his murder was the day of his moral majority, on which he entered into the inheritance of divine sonship. The day of martyrdom was the day of coronation, the day on which the temporary hut was exchanged for the mansion of light.

The history of foreign missions, too, affords a brilliant exemplification of the text. However much some evil-disposed persons may question the motives of the missionary, there is a nobility about his work which distinguishes its celestial nativity. You have seen a young man whose spirit yearns for the salvation of his race: he is educated and mentally strong; his home is a scene of happiness, parents and relatives hold him in highest regard; were he to employ his talents in his fatherland they might ensure him competence, and perhaps renown; but he is determined to realise his convictions of duty; he is ready to sever the strong attachments which bind him to the land of his birth, and brave the innumerable perils which may beset his enterprise—forasmuch as his kingdom is not of this world. You find in such a youth an illustration of a principle already enunciated; he is not destitute of interest in the political progress of his nation, far less is he wanting in affection to those who gave him life—but he cannot make a kingdom of such considerations; he renders to them the attention due to their respective merits, but in his estimation there are claims whose importance is infinitely greater. His life-cry is, "For me to live is Christ, everything must subordinate itself to Christ. Christ is the fairest among ten thousand, and altogether lovely; he redeemed me with his blood, and shall be served with undivided energy, for, in serving him, I am most effectually promoting the well-being of all the objects of my love."

(3) When man can cheerfully relinquish his earthly possessions.—It is hard work for a monarch to abandon his kingdom. Into whatever region he may pass he feels himself an exile; however far into distant realms he may travel, he can never find a throne; his kingdom is behind him, and must remain there for ever. Not so with the Christian. He has not entered upon his kingdom yet; he is born to it, but at present is journeying towards the land in which he shall reign as king and serve as son. Under these circumstances he cannot feel the strong attachment to the charms of this world which binds the hearts of those who are without hope as to the mysterious future. The man whose kingdom is of this world is sorely tried when death demands a separation. You must observe that such a man is actually leaving his kingdom; and if he is leaving his kingdom, to what is death about to hasten him? Death makes his unwelcome appearance at the worldling's throne, and asserts his determina-

tion to overthrow it, and conduct its occupant into scenes unlighted by a solitary ray. The occupant protests his unwillingness to forego his kingdom, but death is stern and cruel, and interrupts the protestation by thrusting his dart into the heaving breast. There is no appeal—the earthly king dies, and dies without a title to a throne anywhere in the boundless universe. Your imagination may follow the departed spirit—that spirit is now an exile, mark its horrors—its subjects of conversation are gone; once it expatiated with ardour on its possessions, its vast estates, its countless luxuries, its prolific soil, its social influence, but now it gazes on a dreary blank, and a voice, sounding from an inaccessible region, deepens its already insufferable horror by these simple words, " Son, remember that thou in thy lifetime receivedst thy good things."

Behold, in glorious contrast, the condition of the Christian. Though surrounded with many comforts, and it may be not a few luxuries, yet he is their master not their serf. He can look upon the splendid mass, and truly aver his independence of its enslaving power! Death sounds his warning, and the good man is ready! He has been awaiting the final message—sometimes, indeed, he has even had a "desire to depart and be with Christ," —so that when death demands a pause in the throbbings of his heart, he knows that the time of coronation is at hand! As a child rejoices to return to its paternal home after a prolonged absence, so the soul of the Christian rises into rapture as he steps into the valley of the shadow of death! Your imagination may follow this departed spirit, too. He has not gone from a kingdom, but to a kingdom; his subjects of conversation are not exhausted—he spoke of God while on earth, now he gazes on the splendours of Deity; those who remember his conversation know that the name of Jesus was often on his tongue; now he sings, "Worthy is the Lamb that was slain"—he was wont to declare that he sought a city which hath foundations, whose builder and maker is God, now he walks its golden streets, and breathes its untainted air!

Distinguish, then, I beseech you, between having your kingdom in this world and having it in that which is to come. Far be it from any minister of the gospel to contend that the very highest state of secular comfort and elegance is incompatible with the spirit of Christianity : were any bold enough to make the assertion, thousands of brilliant instances would rebuke and disprove the allegation. Let it, therefore, be clearly understood that all my argument has been directed against the iniquity of making your kingdom in this world. " Where your treasure is, there will your heart be also." Amidst all your accumulations, I entreat you to "lay up treasures in heaven, where neither moth nor rust doth corrupt, and where thieves do not break through nor steal ;" amid all your endeavours to prepare for the day of commercial panic or physical decrepitude, I entreat you to anticipate the day of death, and make provision for the well-being of your undying spirits.

Young man ! that which engages most of your affections is your kingdom. The question, therefore, must be entirely determined by yourself. You may, to a large extent, discard all gross and debasing pursuits, and yet your kingdom may be of this world ; you may take little or no interest in political agitation, and yet your kingdom may be of this world ; you may despise the miser who hoards his dust with an energy that never tires, and yet your kingdom may be of this world ! I repeat, therefore, that in order to ascertain what your kingdom is, you must analyse your affections—you must track their course, and mark where they rest. One young man is an eager devotee at the shrine of fashion ; another is ambitiously aiming at fame ; a third is unceasing in his merely intellectual pursuits ; a fourth is totally indifferent to the appeals and claims of religion : yet all agree in having their kingdom of this world ! I would to God that all young men could be driven to earnest self-scrutiny, that thus they might determine whether their kingdom be present or to come. The young man described in the gospel had reached a high standard of character by keeping all the commandments from his youth ; yet he lacked one thing, and that solitary deficiency was as a gulf separating the dominion of earth from the kingdom of heaven !

I have only a word of pity for you who confess that your

kingdom is of this world.   Every night that draws its sable
curtain silently attests the shortness of your reign ; every grey
hair and incipient wrinkle or deep furrow indicate that your
monarchy is perishing ; every storm that rages threatens to
destroy some portion of your territory.   Time is eating into
your crown ; the moth is doing its deadly work on your throne,
and you who are known as kings on earth will be branded as
paupers throughout eternity !   You have made a fearful mis-
calculation—you are involved in a terrible embarrassment, and
standing at the mouth of the pit into which you have fallen, I
proclaim not your degradation only, but the infallible method of
restoration !   Blessed be God ! you may now become sovereigns
of a moral kingdom.   Jesus Christ lived a life and died a death,
the object of which was that men might be made kings and
priests unto God !   You, O sinner, are not ignorant of his
beneficent life, of his atoning death ; nor are you ignorant of
the terms on which you may appropriate all the blessings which
he purchased by his blood.   If you pursue the wrong, it is not
because you are ignorant of the right ; if you imagine that your
possessions are the true gold of heaven, it is in spite of ten
thousand demonstrations that they are lies and vanity !   We have
walked through your kingdom and exposed its corruptions ; we
have handled your treasures and shown you their rottenness ;
you yourselves have even confessed their ephemeral nature, so
that if you longer attempt to solace yourselves with a known
poison, be prepared for a holy universe to shudder as it pronounces you a desperate suicide !

You will never make a proper use of the life that now is until
you regard it in connection with that which is to come.   Standing
at the Saviour's Cross you will be able to take a right view of
both worlds.   You will see earth in all its littleness and tumult,
and heaven in all its magnitude and peacefulness ; and, while
rendering to the one the attention which its transient importance
demands, you will reserve the fulness of your energy for the
momentous claims of the other.   I make no apology for asking
whether you are making a kingdom of your politics, and whether
you have begun at the true source of all genuine and permanent
reformation ?   My firm conviction being that Christianity will

adjust the relationships of individuals, and consolidate the liberty of empires, my life is consecrated to its explanation and enforcement. When the heart is right with God there will be little difficulty in arranging political details; but while the heart is swollen with passion—while selfishness holds out her greedy hand, and party spirit rends the air with her clamorous cry—while Pride looks disdainfully on the poor, and Rank draws its invidious boundaries—while Capital is regardless of the true interests of Labour, and Merit must give place to Patronage, there can be no lasting reformation. We must strike the Upas at its roots. If you, as political reformers, can amputate any of the deadly branches, you will indeed earn the gratitude of your race —far be it from me to question the utility of your labour; but, again I tell you we must strike the Upas at its root! Church of the living God, this is your business! It is for you to lift the axe and smite the deadly tree! You have a tremendous power which you can bring to bear, not only on the spiritual, but on the civil interests of man; every prayer you breathe may exert influence on the political destiny of the nation! I call upon you, therefore, to do your utmost in the propagation of the Christian faith; in the name of God I forbid you to relax any spiritual effort. Toil on, and in due time there shall be but one kingdom and one King; he shall come, whose right is to reign—on his head shall the crown flourish. Freedom and Peace shall unfurl their banners; Brotherhood and Charity shall wake their sweetest music : then shall a cry be heard, loud as the roar of the thunder, the rush of the whirlwind, and the anthem of the sea—Alleluia! the kingdoms of this world have become the kingdoms of our God and of his Christ.

Chapter xix. 1.

"Then Pilate therefore took Jesus, and scourged him."

SCOURGING JESUS.

WE know this to be historical. We read of this in otner books than the New Testament. Some of us, therefore, who are so much afraid of superstition as to look with some wonder if not doubt upon lines that are found in the New Testament, or Old Testament alone, may feel ourselves to be upon solid ground. Jesus loved, taught, was scourged, crowned with thorns, clothed with purple, killed. For this information we are not dependent upon evangelists; for this assurance we have the authority of men who never prayed,—who, therefore, can doubt their word?

"Pilate therefore took Jesus, and scourged him,"—literally, flagellated him. We cannot tell what that Roman punishment was. We read about it in the olden books, but men do not understand what they read so much as what they feel. The victim was tied by the hands to a post or standard; he was compelled to assume a stooping position; the knotted thong was in the hands of a Roman executioner, and he administered the punishment largely according to his own will or passion. It was not so in the Jewish law. Always have we found some touch of grace, some hint of gospel, even in Jewish sternness. In the law there is a shadow of good things to come. The Jewish law was that "forty stripes, save one" should be administered. There was no corresponding reservation in the Roman law; the judge or the executioner might administer punishment according to personal disposition; there was no restraint as to the number of the stripes. We have heard of the knout in Russia; in our own land we have the "cat," so feared by felons; in the Roman law there was this arrangement for scourging, that men might be humbled as well as punished, that the truth might be extorted from them as well as a penalty inflicted, that they might be brought into lowliness of mind and submissiveness of temper, so that the judge could do with them what he pleased. The hands of Christ were tied to the stake, the flagellum was used upon his naked back; he was scourged by Roman hands.

"Pilate therefore." That word "therefore" has a wondrous surrounding. It is a logical term, and it is a term that expresses a force more than logical, for pressure was put upon Pilate. To find the full force of this "therefore" we must go back to the other gospels, called the synoptic gospels, where more detail is given, and there we shall find the people pressing upon Pilate, insisting that such and such a course be taken, driving him to his wits' ends, not allowing him to hesitate more than a moment, bearing away all his protestation in a storm of anger. "Pilate therefore": the storm was upon him, the tempest was beating upon his head; all the ministries that made up the momentary experience were ministries of anger, and Pilate was the victim of popular clamour. He did not know what to do. He knew what he wanted to do. A wonderful face had Pilate—rocky, rugged, cavernous face, but a whole fountain of tenderness behind it all; he could have cried like a woman. He was over-borne; crosslights perplexed his vision: it was right,—it was wrong; he would be tender,—he must not be disloyal; he would be gracious,—he must not be treasonable:—"Pilate therefore." In some senses a lame and impotent "therefore," but not an inhuman one, not out of keeping with the proportion of our own action, the mystery of our own policy. We are often glad of any "therefore" that will help us not to inflict punishment but to escape perplexity. Many men are more afraid of perplexity than they are of an army. Courage often breaks down at unexpected places: who would be afraid of mental bewilderment, of ambiguous thinking, of the double intentions and purposes of life? Yet some men are so constituted that a perplexity has frightened them more than a lion would. "Pilate therefore." Where is there a man who has not his reason for action? Because they are reasons they are not necessarily valid; they may belong to that multitudinous array of reasons which may be safely denominated excuses. Still, where is there a drunkard, foul-mouthed liar, thief with a hundred stealing hands, that has not his miserable "therefore" out of which to extract illicit but transitory comfort?

Let us meditate now rather than analyse. "Pilate took Jesus, and scourged him." Let us lay the emphasis upon the supplied word "him." The word is not in the original; yet there could be no sense in the history without it. Sometimes an element is present without being avowedly and nominally present; it is there in all the ghostliness of suggestion and necessity; it may not stoop to adopt the costume of grammar, but it is there, pulsing, throbbing, palpitating with infiniteness of energy. Let us dwell upon that sublime word—and verily write it in italics. Written in italic because it is not there,—now let us write it in italic because there is nothing else there. "Scourged him"— who spoke the beatitudes! It is impossible! Surely a mistake has been made in the writing. The man who is now bent, and on whose bared back the knout falls, said, "Blessed are the poor in spirit: for theirs is the kingdom of heaven. Blessed are they that mourn: for they shall be comforted. Blessed are the meek: for they shall inherit the earth. Blessed are they which do hunger and thirst after righteousness: for they shall be filled. Blessed are the merciful: for they shall obtain mercy. Blessed are the pure in heart: for they shall see God. Blessed are the peacemakers: for they shall be called the children of God." Can he now extract any comfort from these words? Has this preacher to live his own sermon? Is his unfathomable and ineffable eloquence to be applied to and by himself? Did he see further than all these beauteous flowers? So far we might accompany him, saying, This is poetical, most rhythmical, wondrously complete and morally harmonious. Can he go further? Beatitudes could not end with peacemakers. There would have been a great omission if only the poor in spirit, the mourning, the meek, the righteous, the merciful, the pure in heart, and the peacemaking had been included; verily a hiatus all but infinite in human history would have been left if the beatitudes had ended there. But they do not there terminate. Hear what Jesus said, "Blessed are they which are persecuted

for righteousness' sake: for theirs is the kingdom of heaven."
A beatitude like that might sing to a man when he was bound to
the standard, the stake. "Blessed are ye, when men shall revile
you, and persecute you, and shall say all manner of evil against
you falsely, for my sake. Rejoice, and be exceeding glad; for
great is your reward in heaven: for so persecuted they the
prophets which were before you." Now what omission is there?
None. No flower is unblessed by this gracious dew; not one
could lift up its drooping, fainting head and say, The Lord hath
forgotten to be gracious to me. Every flower-cup is filled with
this wine of blessing. But do men who speak beatitudes come
to flagellation? They do, if they speak beatitudes with the
right scope. If they limit their beatifications to certain negative
qualities, and certain pointless amiabilities, they may escape
scourging; but if they reserve their blessing for virtue as well
as grace, for energy as well as patience, for the reforming spirit
as well as for the acquiescing temper, then they may come to
find their way to heaven through much tribulation.

"Took Jesus and scourged him"—scourged him who blessed
little children! This is impossible! But the Latin historians
say it was real. The disciples did not dream this. This is
written in Latin as well as in Greek, and is written in common
Greek as well as in scriptural Greek. There is no doubt about
it. We are now on flatly historical ground. You remember the
incident? Mothers brought their children to Jesus that he
would bless them; the disciples drove them away; but the
Master said, "Suffer little children to come unto me, and forbid
them not, for of such is the kingdom of heaven." What a
kingdom he made! There was not a king in it; there was no
decorated person in all the empire, there were no so-called
"solid corner stones" about it; the kingdom was made up of
little children, of men who had the child-spirit; made up of
pureness, meekness, tenderness. These are moral qualities
that the wind cannot blow down nor the tempest shake, and
the lightning plays on them like any other blessing. Jesus
took little children into his arms and blessed them. To have
been in those arms—what a heaven was that: what a caress!
A caress which only a child could feel: and this was the Man—

speaker of the beatitudes and lover of little children—who was scourged, flagellated and lacerated, till the thick seams rose on his quivering back ! If the apostles had said this we might have doubted it, but it is declared as if on oath by men who never cared for the God of heaven.

"Then Pilate took Jesus, and scourged him "—him who had fed the multitude, and not only fed the multitude as a necessity, but fed the multitude as a prevention. Here was the statesman's act as well as the redeemer's pity. Said Christ, " They have been with me now three days ; I will not send them away hungry, lest "—in that lest you find his deity. Many a man will give bread when dead, grim, ghastly hunger is looking at him ; he pays to get rid of the ghost. But here is a man who says, "I will not send them away empty, lest "—lest what ? " Lest they should die by the way." Though they were out of sight they would still be fainting, and blessed be his name—oh, blessed be his heart !—no man faints without his beholding it.

Let us dwell upon these points, because they all help us to understand the scourging. What a pain it must have been to such a nature ! " Pilate took Jesus, and scourged him "— scourged him who spake parables !—the Parable of the Prodigal Son that set the home-door open and kept it open all night, because the fool might return at any moment ragged and hunger-bitten ; spake the Parable of the Good Samaritan, wherein, though Jews were looking at him angrily, he painted the Samaritan as the true redeemer of that man,—a parable that had in it poetry and judgment. Only he dare have set up a Samaritan in that position. Now he was scourged !

Does the whole truth lie within the limits of a local incident ? No. There is an Old Testament as well as a New, and in a scourging of this kind the Old Testament becomes alive again ; it is no longer archaic but modern ; it brings up its prophecies and says, Seal us, for now we are fulfilled; subscribe this prophecy with your hand, and let it pass as a letter that has been glorified. All this was foretold. The fifty-third chapter of Isaiah would make an excellent introduction to these closing chapters of the evangelic story. Jesus gave his back to the smiters, and his cheeks to them that plucked off the hair, in the Old Testament—the same Jesus, not then manifest in the flesh, but still there. He has never been out of the world; he made it. He did not come into the world in any sense that indicates his ever having been separated from it; he came into it by vividness of manifestation, by showing himself. Historically, there was birth, there was circumcision, there was baptism; but morally, spiritually, there was a personal presence in the world that only needed disclosure. He was in the world, and the world knew him not. Not only was all this foretold, it was voluntarily accepted. No word does Jesus utter, no protest; he does not argue with Roman procurator, or with Jewish rabble. He speaks mysterious words; he evidently supports himself by eternity. He is well-backed; it is an invisible support, because so great. Had it been less, say a pair of human hands, the support might have been seen. But who has eyes to see eternity? He was led as a lamb to the slaughter, and as a sheep before her shearers is dumb, so he opened not his mouth; when he was reviled, he reviled not again; when he was insulted, he threatened not. Why that peace? It is not indifference, it is not even resignation, it is not an acceptance of grim fatality; it is a peace that shines, it is peace with radiance, it is peace with subdued joy. The explanation is, "I lay down my life; no man taketh it from me; I lay it down of myself. I have power to lay it down, and I have power to take it again." When did Jesus Christ take a low and narrow view of any case or any situation? He did not feel himself to be murdered; he accepted the act as a sacrifice. " He was wounded for our trangressions, he was bruised for our iniquities; the chastisement of our peace was upon him, and by his stripes "—a still larger flagellation—" we are healed." What do these words mean? We cannot tell. Whoever took the sun into his own little house to examine it and tell what it was made of? We can only say that the sun gives light, and we can only say that Jesus makes us see, gives us life and hope and immortality, and has so wrought upon us that we can say to death, " Where is thy sting? and grave— black, grim, tremendous grave—where is thy victory?" Any man that has wrought this miracle in us is worthy of all the

crowns that make heaven royal.   We stand to say that Jesus
has done this for us.

May we change the tone of the meditation ?   Shall we be no
longer quiet, almost silent,—shall we accept another spirit, and
giving way to its inspiration shall we become violent in denunciation ?   We might, and still be in harmony with the spirit of
the text.   Let us beware lest we waste our sentiment on historical
humiliation.   It is not enough to weep because a Man was
flagellated twenty centuries ago.   That Man is flagellated to-day ;
the knout still seams his quivering flesh, still makes it start up
in red scars ; he is still tied to the scourging post.   That is the
terrible truth ; but for that we might paint the picture, and sell
it ; but it is too modern to trifle with.   How is the process of
scourging still going on ?   Pilate is dead.   Certainly : the Roman
Pilate is dead ; but they scourge Jesus who nominally profess
to serve him, and do not serve him with all their mind, and heart,
and soul, and strength.   That is a flagellation which is terrible
to him.   He was no coward under the knout, but he quails with
anger-grief when he is used as a mere decoration, when his Cross
is worn as an ornament and not felt as a burden.   They scourge
Christ who are silent when hostile attacks are made upon him.
He feels our silence more than he feels the attack.   Where does
he suffer—in the flesh ?   No more.   What is a flesh wound,
a flesh sorrow ?   Flesh and sorrow of that kind are but for
a moment.   He now feels everything upon his naked heart.   The
slightest puncture is as a great wound.   Who has not stood back
and heard Jesus attacked and reviled and dishonoured, and never
spoken a word for his Friend ?   In that case what did Jesus
Christ feel ?   Not the attack at all ; but how his eyes reddened
with tears when he marked the silence !   What, said he, will ye
also go away ? have you nothing to say ? does no holy memory
awaken within ? does no tender association enlarge your love
and stimulate your courage with a noble inspiration ? have I not
visited you in sorrow, in contrition, at home, at midnight, when
the child lay ill, when the new grave was dug, when all life
darkened into a frown and threatened you as with a tempest of
thunderbolts ?   What do we ourselves feel ?   Some men feel an
insult more than a wound.   In proportion to the spirituality

of the relation is the sensitiveness as between the parties, as between the disciple and the Lord. Our relation to Christ is nothing if it be not one of love. It is not an intellectual relation, as who should say,—Lord, I had mind enough to understand all about thy kingdom ; dolts and dunces I have left behind,—I had the genius that caught thy meaning; I am the clever member of the household. There is no such relation with Christ. He does not acknowledge it. He knows nothing about cleverness, except to contemn it. He puts cleverness under his feet as an enemy. It is simplicity, docility, felt necessity, rising love, answering sympathy, the intuition that will never allow itself to be iron-bound by empiricism or logic in any form. There the relation begins and operates. He feels it, therefore, when any man who has been healed by him dare not say to hissing and mocking Pharisees, "Whether he be a sinner or no, I know not : one thing I know, that whereas I was blind, now I see." If every cured blind man would speak there would be eloquence enough.

They scourge Jesus who use his name for unworthy purposes, as a social key, as an answer to many inquiries. There are men who pay more for their atheism than others pay for their Christianity. There are atheists who if they were not honest could not be in society to-day. There are nominally professing Christians who because they are dishonest have the *entrée* to all saloons and gathering-places, and the rendezvous of the great and empurpled and titled. Better be an honest atheist than a dishonest professor of Christianity. The atheist will have more chance at the last; in fact, he only will have a chance as compared with those who dishonestly or only nominally profess Christ. It is quite imaginable that at the last some poor blind atheist may have his eyes opened and may begin to pray, and may pray more in one cry than many nominal Christians have prayed in a lifetime. It is not for us to limit the kingdom, nor is it for us with licentiousness of sentiment to proclaim that they may disobey Christ, and yet be found at last in the company of those who loved him. Let every statement be made clear, definite, simple, and let the maker of the statement feel that he himself will have to answer for it at the last ; then let him leave heaven to make what margin can be made by love.

They scourge Jesus who think more of bodily pain than of spiritual cruelty. There are men who would have released Jesus from the bodily pain, and yet never have taken notice of his heart wound. We are of course limited by our senses, and with a meaning that is obvious we are the victims of our senses. A blow to some people would seem to be more than neglect. There are houses of baptised people in which there is more suffering by neglect than there is by violence; indeed, violence there is none. Violence would give hope, because wherever there is passion there may by-and-by be devotion. The man who curses and swears and denies with oaths that he never knew Christ will be found in a day or two breaking his heart and calling back all his oaths and curses, and burning himself with them. But neglect, coldness, studied respectability, calculated forbearance and gentility,—coldness that freezes love, —these are the deadly enemies of household trust and progress; so they are the deadly enemies of ecclesiastical brotherhood and advancement. We must account the body nothing, and the soul everything; we must feel neglect more than we feel a sword-cut; we must feel the oozing of the heart's love more than the out-bursting of the heart's blood. Jews were guiltless as compared with Christians. Jesus Christ said so; he said in his last prayer, "Father, forgive them, for they know not what they do." We know what we do. We do it on purpose; we do it by calcula-tion; we make a study of it. They crown Jesus who obey him. Do not let us imagine that by singing about crowning Jesus we are going to do some wonderful work in coronation. We could crown him now. We speak of by-and-by casting our crowns before him, being lost in wonder, love, and praise. That is perfectly right; there is a holy meaning attached to such sacred words. But all who would crown Jesus now may do so by saying, and meaning, " Lord, what wilt thou have me to do?"

Chapter xix. 4.

"Behold, I bring him forth to you, that ye may know that I find no fault in him."

NO FAULT FOUND.

[AN OUTLINE.]

PROBABLY there is not, in the whole compass of history, a more vivid illustration of hesitancy and instability than that afforded by the conduct of Pilate immediately prior to the crucifixion. In the outset Pilate was reluctant to undertake the judgment of the case ; hence he said to the Jews, "Take ye him, and judge him according to your law." Being compelled to ascend the judgment-seat, he held a private interview with Jesus, and then uttered the memorable declaration, "I find in him no fault at all." Again did the implacable Jews treat the Saviour with the most studied indignity, crowning him with thorns, and putting on him a purple robe, exclaiming, "Hail, King of the Jews!" and smiting him with their hands. Pilate again protested, saying, "Behold, I bring him forth to you, that ye may know that I find no fault in him." Hardly had the utterance fallen, when the rabble thundered out, "Crucify him, crucify him!" The hesitant judge interposed, saying, "Take ye him, and crucify him : for I find no fault in him,"—the savage reply was instantaneous, "We have a law, and by our law he ought to die, because he made himself the Son of God." This was as an arrow shot into the heart of Pilate, for "when Pilate therefore heard that saying, he was the more afraid." Again did he confer with Jesus, and again was he impressed with the Saviour's innocence; for, according to John, "from thenceforth Pilate sought to release him." Vainly, however, did he plead ; the omnipotent appeal now rang from the maddened mob, "If thou let this man go, thou art not Cæsar's friend : whosoever maketh himself a king, speaketh against Cæsar." 'Twas enough ; Pilate could stand no longer : " Then delivered he him therefore unto them to be crucified. And they took Jesus, and led him away."

Such are the circumstances. Pilate was destitute of strong conviction, and was consequently weak in the presence of a determined opposition. Pilate had not learned the majesty of that most majestic word—ought ! That word is as a consuming fire, devouring all pleas and subterfuges : it is the watchword of the absolute in truth, purity, and freedom ; it is the embodiment of God ; it is the summary of the universe ; it is the sentinel of heaven ; it is the summary and memorial of Sinai ; it is the immutable standard to which all loyal spirits will eternally aspire. Men are nothing if devoid of intelligent and all-daring convictions. Such convictions will infallibly insure three results :—

First. Such convictions will deliver men from the despotism of popular fury.—Is any position more unenviable than that of a Pilate between two great billows of passion ? See an un-decided official in church or senate called upon to determine a disputed question ! He is the butt of every witling : he would vote on both sides ; if his opinions venture the slightest disclosure, he trembles when the storm utters its voice ; he is as helpless as the *débris* on the impetuous river, or the dust scattered by the whirlwind. A man of strong conviction in such a position would abide in perfect calm until the storm cried itself to sleep ; then would he ascend the throne, and show that Right has patience to wait and power to conquer.

Second. Such convictions enable men to sacrifice the highest human patronage.—To be " Cæsar's friend " is an object in whose attainment the sublimest principles are often trodden in the dust. There are men who can see no higher than Cæsar. Their feeble vision is so dazzled by the light of earthly pomp that they cannot see the "glory which excelleth." The true-born son of thought and feeling looks through the mock-splendour of earthly jets to the palace where reigns the King Eternal, whose garment is light, and whose throne is built of the riches of the universe ;

and beholding the Majesty of heaven, he scorns the patronage of any Cæsar for which he must pay his blood or mortgage his eternity!

Third. Such convictions enable men to serve the truth in the most perilous circumstances.—" Perfect love " of principle will " cast out fear " of personal injury. He is the truly royal man who, in divine strength, "plants his footsteps on the sea, and rides upon the storm." Ornamental men may be applauded in seasons of calm, but they are useless when fire-bolts are flying, and foundations shaking, and thunders rolling ; then we require men who can front frowning senates, and abash them with the regal decree, " We ought to obey God rather than men ! "

Let us be strong,—"strong in the grace that is in Christ Jesus." Being found mighty in faith, " rooted and grounded in love," invincible in argument, and unimpeachable in life, we shall be the faithful servants of all the principles which can inspire and ennoble the race. We shall be firm as the eternal granite, and gentle as the harmless dove. When the enemy demands our crucifixion of the truth, instead of being Pilate-like, we shall reply by a louder utterance of its praise, and a profounder reverence at its throne !

Chapter xix. 37.

WHAT SCRIPTURE SAITH.

YOU will infer from the text that I want to insist upon a right way of reading the Bible. Our prayer, therefore, has been, Open thou our eyes, that we may behold wondrous things out of thy law; open thou our understanding, that we may understand the Scriptures! In my judgment, I know of hardly anything that has been so mischievous in what is termed Christian education as the tearing away of little pieces of Scripture under the name of texts. Portions of Scripture so treated have been made to represent false meanings, and have gone up and down the ages of the Church doing all sorts of spiritual harm. There ought to be no texts in any partial sense, or in any sense which mangles and mutilates the integrity of Holy Writ. The subject is never in the text, it is always in the context. If any man take a text, he should take all the texts bearing upon the subject, so that we may know the exact evidence of Scripture in its volume and weight and applicableness. An error may be sealed by a text; a denomination may be falsely based upon a portion of Scripture torn from the current in which it is found. We ought not to want little mottoes and short maxims; we ought to have grown out of the childishness of wanting a text; we should now want the Scriptures, a thousand texts, or all the texts that can be found bearing upon the subject that is to be elucidated. But herein the pulpit is dragged down. There are persons who will always insist upon having a text, one text, a little verse; they like to be surprised by it. They are not students of the divine word; they are the victims of their own foolish curiosity. We ought to say, What does the whole Bible declare upon a given subject? Let us have all the evidence carefully and luminously put before us, then by the aid of the Spirit of God who wrote the testimony we may be able to come to broad and intelligible and useful conclusions.

Consider how far this involves your own spiritual misadventures. How many little torn texts have you in your memory? What do you know about the Book as a structure, a unity, a complete figure and integer? Have you ever really read the Bible? I know you have read the Gospels, you have also perused many of the Psalms : what do you know about the Book of Numbers, Deuteronomy, the Judges, the Chronicles? If you do not know them all, almost by heart, how can ye understand the Scriptures? A few instances will show more precisely the meaning of the expression "Again another Scripture saith." It is that "other Scripture" we want, that supplementing, completing, and illuminating Scripture. Many of us have the one text but not the other. The devil had a set of texts. The devil saith unto him, "It is written"; and Christ answered, "Yes, and it is written again." It is that "again" that explains the quotation. We must therefore have regard to the proportion of faith, or the analogy of faith, or the general balance and drift of scriptural testimony; in this way we shall clear out many denominations, sects, eccentric communions of people who build themselves on rags and patches of divine testimony.

How many persons there are who say, when they are asked to join some great philanthropic or benevolent movement, that they prefer to work secretly, and not to let the left hand know what the right hand doeth. They justify themselves by a text; they forget that "another Scripture saith," "Let your light so shine before men, that they may see your good works, and glorify your Father which is in heaven." How now? Why do you not quote the "other Scripture"? Why do you not say with Jesus Christ in the time of temptation, "It is written again"? What becomes now of your little selfish secrecy? You might say, "Let your light so shine before men, that they may see your good works, and glorify your Father which is in heaven," and then having accomplished that good, you might go out and do no end of useful service, and say nothing about it. The first text would come in admirably after you had attended to the duty or fulfilled

the opportunity created by the second. Is it true what I hear
that you never allow the right hand to speak to the left, because
the right hand has nothing to report ?

How many persons excuse themselves from public worship on
the ground of a text ! They say, in a tone that is itself not only
weak but impious, " Thou, when thou prayest, enter into thy
closet, and pray to thy Father which is in secret." That is
beautiful, that is perfectly right ; but " again another Scripture
saith," " Forsake not the assembling of yourselves together, as
the manner of some is." Now how long will you remain in cold
and isolated secrecy ? Not only are we to attend to God in the
closet, we are to worship him in the public assembly ; we can
get something in the assembly we cannot get in the closet, as truly
as we can get something in the closet that we cannot get in the
public assembly. Public worship ought to be a grand opportunity
for the highest education and stimulus of our minds and hearts.
We complete each other ; we get in the commonwealth what we
cannot get in the individual. We should hear each other's voices,
study each other's method, commingle with each other's aspirations, and enter into all the mystery so far as is practicable of one
another's agonies and burdens and miseries. We were not made
to live alone, we were made for society. On the other hand, if
any man shall say, " Forsake not the assembling of yourselves
together," and be always in the public thoroughfare or always in
the huge assembly, then he should remember that " another
Scripture saith," " Thou, when thou prayest, enter into thy
closet." Thus the one Scripture supplements the other, completes
it, or explains it. If any man shall vaingloriously go about
saying, " I have been doing good all day long ; I am weary in the
service of humanity ; if any man has seen me to-day he has seen
a very busy man in the cause of Christ,"—then he should
remember that " another Scripture saith," " Let not your left hand
know what your right hand doeth." Remember always that
" other Scripture."

How often we hear persons delight in calling Christ, in the
words of the prophet, " The Prince of Peace." They stand upon
that text, they seem to know no other. That expression exactly

represents the purpose of Christ's advent and priesthood in the universe. He is the Prince of Peace; when he was born the angels said, "Peace on earth and goodwill toward men." So they did; Isaiah did call the coming One the Prince of Peace. We would not detract from the glory of that light; not one tiniest jewel would we take out of that diadem. But "another Scripture saith," "I have come to send a sword upon the earth." Jesus Christ was the greatest fighter; no warrior was ever so deeply engaged in battle as was the Prince of Peace. He had not a day's rest in all his brief ministry. By reason of his strenuous efforts, his continued controversies, his unceasing conflicts, his three years were three generations,—the longest ministry ever exercised by man. Yet how prone are we to forget the sword element! We conceal from ourselves the sterner and severer aspects of Christ's ministry. No man can know what peace is who does not know the meaning of the sword. There can be no peace until there is righteousness; and righteousness comes by many a conflict, many a fierce—thank God, by many a bloodless!—controversy. Have you ever fought for the Master? not querulously, or resentfully, sharply; but enduringly, patiently, argumentatively, and, above all, by that great logic and eloquence of exemplification? A Christian man cannot be silent in the presence of wrong. When the Church becomes dumb in the sight of oppression and injustice, the Church is no other than a dumb dog that cannot even bark. So let us always balance one text with another. If any man shall be furiously controversial, needlessly combative, if he be always fighting the wind and raising up little figures that he may break them down again, then let him remember that "another Scripture saith," "The name of your Master is Prince of Peace." Thus we find in Scripture a self-emendation or a self-completion, and unless we get into the rhythm of this music we shall, even as preachers, totally misrepresent the testimony of divine revelation. The text has ruined many a preacher; it has actually made a fool of him, has almost lured him into blasphemy, for he has been building upon a point when he ought to have been building upon a line; he has been endeavouring to set a kingdom upon an apothegm, instead of on a wide and immovable philosophy.

A poor soul is fond of quoting, "Bear ye one another's

burdens." Is that a text? Yes, it is. He says, I am burdened, help me to carry my load. Every charitable institution borrows the motto; every begging letter is full of it; every complaint suggests it. It is a sweet Scripture; there is no denying its divine authority; without it the Bible would be incomplete. Yet "another Scripture saith," "Every man shall bear his own burden." We must have no burden-bearing that means a premium upon incapacity or laziness. There is only one way of teaching the indolent man, and that is by letting him hunger. "If a man will not work," saith the apostle, "he ought not to eat." That may bring him to his senses. Has every man to fight his own battles? Yes, certainly. Have we to bear one another's burdens? Yes, undoubtedly. It is for wisdom to reconcile the paradox, if it need reconciliation. There are persons carrying burdens who ought not to carry them one inch farther—honest, noble, good souls that in human estimation have never done anything really wrong or vicious. They are overburdened, and it becomes us well to help them at least one finger, if not a whole hand, in bearing the burden ; they would assist if they could, and we must assist them because we can. On the other hand, there are persons who will never let you alone; they have always a new request, a new necessity, and they are always proving their own incapacity and worthlessness. If you give them money they put it into bags, as Haggai says, that have holes in them ; you are endeavouring to give them water in a sieve, and you cannot do so, because the water runs away. I do not know why such people were created, unless it be to try the patience and perfect the temper of other people. To such we must preach a rather stern doctrine—every man must bear his own burden. How to carry both these great principles is often a great difficulty Better to err a little in helping than in not helping. Adam Clarke said, if in a hundred cases that came before him there were ninety-nine impostures, he would rather reply to the whole hundred and be imposed upon ninety-nine times than reject the one really genuine case. Believe me, you will be forgiven if you do more good. I think I am entitled now to write you a certificate and sign it, which you can show anywhere, to the effect that if you will go on doubling all your good, no ill will befall you at the last. The angels will not spite you by saying that you have been doing far too much good. They will not say to you, Poor soul, you have been working too hard down in the little dark earth; you should not have done one tenth of what you have done. Why, you have quite exhausted yourself in the service of charity; you have ceased to win our respect because you have been so easily imposed upon. There are no idiot angels. You go on doing the good, and I will answer for the consequences.

We come now to the most sacred ground of all—to the great mystery of the universe. Read the text; these are the pathetic words—" They led him away to a place called Calvary." *They* did it? Yes: they led him away, arrestingly; they took him into custody, they laid strong hands upon him and led him away? So the text says. But "another Scripture saith," "I lay down my life: no man taketh it from me, but I lay it down of myself." Then he led them away? Yes; that is the higher meaning. Viewed within the darkness of this twilight world, Christ was led like a lamb to the slaughter, Christ was led away; but read in the light of heaven's eternal noon, it was the Saviour who led *them* away, that they might witness the tragedy and the mystery of his self-sacrifice. Thus it is written, man murdered the Son of God; the apostle said, and said truly, in his great speech, "Ye killed the Prince of life; him have ye taken and by wicked hands have crucified." That is right, within its own limits; yet Jesus Christ himself rises and says, O fools, and slow of heart to believe all the deeper meaning of my history and revelation to mankind! You are right in the letter, they did lead me away, and yet I led myself away. I went voluntarily to the Cross. This commandment did I receive of my Father, that I might lay down my life and take it again; I was not killed in the higher sense, I gave my life for every man.

Thus we bring within our purview this Scripture and that, the first text and the second, the devil's quotation and Christ's, "It is written again." John's first text, and John's second, wherein he says, "And again another Scripture saith." Why not read this book in all its parts? Why not bring those parts together, and constitute the radiant and glorious unity of the divine thought? When will men read the Bible—lovingly, sympathetically, spiritually?

They would then see that those men who are said to spiritualise Scripture are not often so far wrong as they appear to be.   There is a spiritualisation that is objectionable; but there is a materialisation which is more objectionable still, a literalisation that tends to weakness and poverty and nothingness.   When I read, "In the beginning God created the heaven and the earth," and preach a gospel sermon from it, I am not so far wrong as I at first sight may appear, for, "another Scripture saith," "Without him [that is, without Christ] was not anything made that was made." So in Genesis we find John, in Leviticus we find Calvary, in Creation we find the Saviour, in Providence we find the Cross. O remember, lest you get wrong by taking out some little line and saying, This is God's book, and this is God's testimony. Say, I will find out what the other Scripture saith; I will compare Scripture with Scripture.   I will go a second time to the Book as Christ went a second time to the altar, and in going the second time I may find the completing text, I may bring on the topstone with shoutings of "Grace, grace unto it!" for the building is beauteous; it is of fair aspect, it is hospitably roomy; it is the home of the soul.

John xx. 1-18.

1. The first day of the week cometh Mary Magdalene early, when it was yet dark, unto the sepulchre, and seeth the stone taken away from the sepulchre. ["First," and "early," and "dark," and "sepulchre,"—what a crowd of terms! Out of this warp and woof comes life's mixed and tangled web. There is a solitary woman in this verse.]

2. Then she runneth, and cometh to Simon Peter, and to the other disciple, whom Jesus loved [With what frank delicacy he indicates himself!], and saith unto them [Breathlessly; she had been running. How quickly bad news flies! they run to tell it], They have taken away the Lord out of the sepulchre, and we know not where they have laid him. [Where they have laid him is heaven, if we could but find out the place. The sepulchre without the Lord chills those who go near it.]

3. Peter therefore went forth [A quick and ardent logic is involved in that *therefore*], and that other disciple, and came to the sepulchre.

4. So they ran both together: and the other disciple did outrun Peter [How he sustains the delicateness of his own references!], and came first to the sepulchre.

5. And he stooping down, and looking in, saw the linen clothes lying; yet went he not in. [He had his first place. Every man has his unique position in the Church, if he could discover it; he may not have been first called, he may not be senior in time, prior chronologically; yet at some point he was first: let no man take his crown.]

6. Then cometh Simon Peter following him [Was it a calculated second place? Was he a coward still? Did he allow himself to be beaten? how could he? when it is said], and went into the sepulchre [The one *looked* and the other *went in*: that is the difference of men to the end of time], and seeth the linen clothes lie,

7. And the napkin, that was about his head, not lying with the linen clothes, but wrapped together in a place by itself. [He was self-possessed; he had the full use of all his faculties, he noted and remembered.]

8. Then [Some emphasis should be laid on that word, as indicating a peculiar moment in time] went in also that other disciple, who came first to the sepulchre [came first, went in second], and he saw, and [here he recovers priority] believed. [Some men seem to have only to open their

416

eyes to believe—to go one step further, and to be in heaven; and other men have to be scourged into a kind of barren belief.]

9. For as yet they knew not the scripture, that he must rise again from the dead. [And yet they did know it: it had been spoken to them often enough; it was the one thing Christ dwelt upon in his later ministry. Again and again he told them that the Son of man should be raised from the dead: they knew it in the letter, they knew it in the ear of the body, but the music never got down into the ear of the soul. We know things variously—we know, and do not know; we do not know, and yet we know: for want of right definitions of the word " know " we flounder and blunder in our highest thinking.]

10. Then the disciples went away again unto their own home. [They were soon thrust back; they accepted the intermediate for the final.]

11. But [Indicating a difference of character] Mary stood without at the sepulchre weeping [That was her home; the men could find a home without Christ, but she could not: where the love is, the home is]: and as she wept, she stooped down, and looked into the sepulchre [through the telescope of tears],

12. And seeth two angels in white sitting, the one at the head, and the other at the feet, where the body of Jesus had lain. [If the men had wept they would have seen the angels. You see nothing with dry eyes: the naked eye has but a sky of gilded points; the clothed and assisted eye rolls through all the universe of suns. The New Testament should be read through tears, then Jesus would be seen everywhere; and if the Old Testament could be read with the same help, he would be found in Moses, and in the prophets, and in the Psalms.]

13. And they say unto her [for they speak all languages], Woman [Not a harsh term, but full of gentleness as spoken by angels' lips], why weepest thou? She saith unto them, Because they have taken away my Lord, and I know not where they have laid him. [Her tears were rational: like all Christian sentiment, they could be vindicated by reason.]

14. And when she had thus said, she turned herself back, and saw Jesus standing, and knew not that it was Jesus. [This is a mystery in divine providence. God concealeth himself, but he is not the less there: he conceals himself for a purpose; he thus educates men.]

15. Jesus saith unto her, Woman [How strange he can be, how like a foreigner he can look! How he can put a space between himself and his dearest ones,—always for a purpose, and always that he may come the nearer], why weepest thou? whom seekest thou? [What is wanting in thy life? where is the circle broken?] She, supposing him to be the gardener [and to be inspired merely by a spirit of civility], saith unto him, Sir, if thou have borne him hence [Did she whisper this, as if she would

extract a secret from him under seal of confidence?], tell me where thou hast laid him, and I will take him away. [I will play the honest thief. I am but a woman, but I can carry him: the spirit is strength: we can carry what we like.]

16. Jesus saith unto her, Mary. [We live in tones, in glances, in touches, in little things.] She turned herself, and saith unto him, Rabboni; which is to say, Master. [If there was the faintest incredulity in her tone, the incredulity was but momentary: she would have sprung upon him, but]

17. Jesus saith unto her, Touch me not; for I am not yet ascended to my Father [I am on my way: there is a time for everything: touching would mean arresting, detention upon the earth, interruption of a great purpose]: but go to my brethren, and say unto them, I ascend unto my Father, and your Father; and to my God, and your God. [And I make the worlds one, the family complete: I set up the magnetic communication, and none can destroy it; henceforth earth is hardly distinguishable from heaven.]

18. Mary Magdalene came and told the disciples that she had seen the Lord [That is the only gospel worth preaching], and that he had spoken these things unto her. [That is the true proof of what is said: if we had not seen the Lord we should not talk about him, and if he has not spoken to us we should not speak to others. Tell what he has given in thine heart.]

PRAYER.

ALMIGHTY GOD, may a man speak unto thee face to face, uttering the thanks-givings of many hearts, the confessions of the sins of the people, and a cry for thy pardoning mercy, without which we cannot live? Wilt thou so reveal thyself unto us as to leave no doubt of thy presence, giving us such drawing, such enlightening of mind, such enlargement and quickening of our affections, as shall constrain us to say, This is the Lord's doing, this is the Lord's house, and this is the gate of heaven? We have had familiar intercourse with our Father; we have felt his nearness; our hearts have leaped for joy at his drawing nigh. Why not repeat the visit of thy grace, now that on the morning of thy holy day, in the midst of the great city, we may feel that thou art near our hearts with infinite blessing and love? We praise thee for thy marvellous works towards us as creatures of thine hand. Thou hast preserved our life, and given us in continuance of days a new song. Thou hast spread our table in the wilderness, in the presence of our enemies, and so thou hast given us renewed cause to adore thy goodness and trust thy power. Thou hast sent a plentiful rain upon thine inheritance, and caused us to enjoy the odours of the garden of the Lord. Thou hast given us an interest in things not seen. Thou hast called us unto eternal life. Thou hast put death under our feet. Thou hast come to us in unexpected ways; not always along the highroad of thy daily providence, where we have expected to meet thee—where we have prepared for thy coming, and waited confidently for thine appearing. Thou hast come to us in many of the incidents of life, when we did not expect thee. Thou hast given us blessings out of the cloud. Thou hast turned the darkness into sudden light. Thou hast given us a goodly heritage in places where we expected to mourn and die. So that, altogether, thou hast been gracious unto us with exceeding favour. Thy great daily gifts have not been with-held, and other gifts thou hast given with them, so that our cup runneth over. Our hands are full of the blessings of the Lord, and our hearts have been made as the treasure-house of his grace. We live in God. We have no life but in thy light. It is enough. We are immortal in our God; we are everlasting in the everlasting Father. We beseech thee, therefore, that we may be enabled to bring the power of an endless life to bear upon the concerns of the present time. May we deal with the affairs of earth as those whose conversation is in heaven. May we descend upon the concerns of time with the lofty dignity and the impatient urgency of those who would quickly return unto the higher places, in which their souls delight. Keep us from long-tarrying in the market-places of the world. Keep us from long-lingering in the highways and streets of commerce and pleasure and self-promotion. While we are there, may we ever be in haste. May we ever be looking forward and aspiring towards the highest service and joy of thy children. May men take knowledge of our impatience. May men wonder concerning our hurry in the world, and be led to know that our citizenship is in heaven, that here we have no continuing city, and that, by our impatient haste, we are declaring plainly that we seek a country. Oh that we may so live as to think of death only as a step over a shadow into the infinite brightness and the unending peace! We bless thee, that we have known distaste for the things of the world. We have seen their vanity, we have sounded their hollowness. We have left the altar of the world with a sickened heart, and thou hast drawn us into the sanctuary, and thrown before our wondering vision the things that are not seen and eternal, and filled us with a holy desire to go and be for ever with thee. And yet thou hast enabled us to do what we have had to do upon the earth with fidelity and earnestness and success. Such is the mystery of thy government; for when we are most heavenly, then do we triumph most entirely over the trifles of time; when we are most in the sanctuary of the skies, we are most masters of the things that lie round about us in this poor, gloomy, dying scene. Hence have we known that "godliness is profitable unto all things"; and when we have been seeking first the kingdom of God, and his righteousness, thou hast added unto us all other things. We have sinned before the Lord. God be merciful unto us sinners. If we have escaped public accusation, yet do our own hearts convict us of a thousand transgressions. If our hand cannot be impeached by the social justice of the world, yet in our spirit have we hidden sin. We have gone astray from God in our hearts; our motives have often been mixed, and often impure. And if thou wert strict to mark it, if thou didst take hold of thy sword when we gave the occasion for judgment, behold we had not lived in thy sight to-day. But thou art merciful; thou hast sent thy Son Jesus Christ, equal with thyself in Godhead, to be our Saviour, to offer a sacrifice for sins, and because of his work we have hope in God that our sins shall be remembered no more. Lord, help us, in the delight of pardon, to triumph over the tormenting memory of our conscience, and to have peace through our Lord Jesus Christ. Amen.

Chapter xx. 13.

"They have taken away my Lord, and I know not where they have laid him."

MARY: NEEDLESS TROUBLE.

THIS weeping woman, standing beside the empty tomb of Jesus Christ, is a typical rather than a unique character in human history. Specially is she typical of those people who are always missing the point in Christian narrative and Christian doctrine. They are faithful, kind, intelligent, deeply and richly sympathetic, but they miss the point. They go long journeys in order to get wisdom, but they always leave the principal thing behind them; they put away the key so carefully that they never know where to find it again, and their minds, though filled with conflicting thoughts, have lost all power of grouping events and shaping them into order and meaning. Mary rushed into the details of a controversy instead of standing a little way from it and catching its outlines and its general bearings. There is very much practical atheism in this devoted woman's talk. Though she is speaking to angels, she has left God out of her sobbing and tearful speech, and consequently the words which ought to have glowed with a sublime faith are only feverish with personal disappointment, and more or less of peevish complaint. She speaks as if the whole question lay between certain other people and herself; thus, "They have taken" and "I know not." She is lost where millions of other people have been lost; that is to say, in the murky and noisy region of second causes. She was calculating time by her own ill-going clock, and not taking the hour from the unchanging and truth-telling sun; just what we are all doing—and in the doing of which we bring ourselves to disappointment and tears.

Many of us ought to take our stand beside Mary. Those, for example, who are unable to see the divine hand far above all human meddling and strife. To many of us human history is but a disorderly and haphazard movement, an undisciplined and scrambling race, a neck-or-nothing race, enlivened with rude wit or degraded by ruder pleasures. Where is the religious eye that sees God above it all, and that can trace his hand in all the grotesque and riotous features of the course? Mary said that somebody had done mischief—had taken away her Lord; the idea never occurring to her that her Lord might have taken himself away; and thus she missed the point. She saw the Jews, the Romans, the mad rabble, the cruel and hilarious executors, clearly enough; but the divine hand was hidden from her eyes. And what is human history without that hand? A piece of mischief, truly—a gambling speculation or a murderous fight; but when that hand is seen the whole spectacle is changed—it is a chaos out of which order will come, and music and peace that will last for ever. In the meantime we are victimised by our own senses; our eyes deceive us, and our ears and our hearts have lost the power of completely trusting God; and so life has become an enigma without an answer, and a fight in which the strong man wins all, and that all is less than nothing and vanity. That heart-broken, crying woman is this day the centre of a vast multitude of people, all of whom are equally blind to the supreme Presence, though but few of them express their deprivation in tears of helplessness and sorrow.

The great company thus gathered around Mary may be increased by the addition of the innumerable host who in all ages have given themselves up to unnecessary grief. Truly there was no occasion for Mary's tears. The angels said unto her, "Woman, why weepest thou?" Mary had her answer ready, but it was an answer founded upon a mistake. So we, too, have doubtless some explanation of our grief, but our explanation may be but a fool's answer, or a blind man's guess as to the things that are round about him. Are not God's angels often asking why men weep and mourn and pine in heaviness of heart? The angels see the things that are hidden from us. In the dead seed they see the coming harvest. Behind the bleak east wind they see the fair spring ready to spread her flowers at our feet when the unbidden and unwelcome visitor is gone. We see the underside of the pattern which God is weaving; they see the upper side in all the charm of its celestial colour and all the beauty of its infinite perfection. Over sin we may weep night and day, but over God's providence no tear of grief is either pious or reasonable. No doubt it is a providence full of mystery, a road of deep declivities and sharp curves, with many a jungle and many a den where beasts may lurk in cruel patience for their prey; yet there is a foot-track through it all onward to the summer landscape and the harvest plain. Why weepest thou? Surely not over the child who has gone to the care of the angels and the sweet rest of the pure skies? Surely not over the disappointment whose sharpness has taught thee thy best prayers and mellowed thy voice to the tenderest music? Why weepest thou? If for sin, weep on; if for God, your tears are not vain only, but unnatural and impious. When Mary knew but part of the case, she wept over it; when she knew it all, her joy became almost a pain by its very keenness. So shall it be with ourselves in the revelations which are to come. We cannot stop the tears now—they will come—they must come ; but out of every tear shed over the unknown or misknown way of God there will come a new and surprising joy.

The company round about Mary may be increased by another large accession ; those, namely, who can only recognise Christ under certain forms and in certain places. If Mary had seen the dead Christ in the grave, probably she would have felt a sad satisfaction ; to look at the face cold and pain-stricken, but still sweet with ineffable tenderness, would have brought a comfort welcome to the bereaved heart. But the idea of death having been turned to life never occurred to her. She little thought that this water could be turned into wine, and that all the signs and wonders of Christ's ministry could culminate and be repeated in the magnificent miracle of his resurrection. Christ was infinitely larger in spiritual influence than Mary had imagined, and he is infinitely larger and grander than any Church has conceived him to be. I would to God I could adequately rebuke all theological and ecclesiastical narrowness. There are people who would rather have a dead Christ in their own sect and ritual than a living Saviour outside of their own approved boundaries. There are others who care more for their own idealised pictures of Christ than they would for the living man himself, were he to look upon them face to face. Now, upon this matter we may all have much to learn. For my own part, I find Christ in all Churches where the Christly spirit is. Christ is not a theory ; he is a divine and infinite life, infusing himself into our spirit and history in innumerable and unnamable ways, covering and absorbing all theories, and honouring all honest thought, and reverent doubt, and pure aspiration. The people who mistake a crucifix for a cross are not unlikely to mistake a dead dogma for a living faith. Christ lives in Unitarianism and in Trinitarianism, in the expiatory atonement and in the sympathetic reconciliation, in the resonant Christian anthem and in the sweet children's song ; and until this fact is recognised, and not merely recognised but illuminated and glorified, Christendom will be rather a congeries of squabbling sects than a living and indissoluble

Church. But the devil of sectarianism can only be expelled by prayer and fasting. As a Protestant, I wish I loved Christ as some Papists have loved him. As a deeply convinced believer in the Godhead of Jesus Christ, I wish I could know him, and preach him as some believers in his simple humanity have done ; and as one who subscribes with his whole heart the evangelical creed, I wish I could get views of truth which have opened upon men who have stood on the bare rocks and slippery places of speculative doubt, or even of intellectual antagonism. What man has seen all the truth of God ? In what single pulse throbs the solemn eternity ? Into what sectarian hut has God crowded all the riches of heaven ? You may find Christ everywhere if you seek him with a true heart ; not, perhaps, just in the way you expected, not nominally, not formally, but in all the subtlety of his spiritual power, and all the tenderness of his recovering and comforting grace. You will not suppose that we are to be blind to each other's errors, real or fancied ; on the contrary, we are bound to detect and expose those errors, but we are to look for them with the eye of love, and to refute them with the tongue of charity. Controversy may be elevated into an instrument of high spiritual education, or it may be degraded into a weapon for fighting rude and godless battles.

Another addition may be made to the great crowd already gathered around Mary ; those, namely, who are always talking about Christ as if he were absent : it is a historical Christ they refer to—a Christ that once was, but no longer is—a Christ taken away, hidden, or otherwise lost. Now, at the very moment of Mary's complaint, the Lord was looking at her and listening to her ! She thought he was the gardener ! How clearly this shows that though we may think we know Christ, yet we know him only in one aspect, and if we happen to see him in any other we actually know nothing about him. This selfsame thing is occurring every day, infinitely to the disadvantage of our Christian education and to the sad disproof of our supposed growth in spiritual perception and sympathy. We only know Christ in one place, in one ritual, in one theology, in one Church. Take him out of these, and he becomes a common man, unknown, and suspected of stealing Christ, stealing himself ! Lord, pity our ignorance, and save it from becoming sin, and save thy preachers from the infinite disgrace of speaking to their Lord as a suspected stranger! Probably there is not in all history so striking an illustration of not knowing Christ except in one particular form and guise. Some persons do not know Christ except from the lips of their favourite preachers. Others do not think they have kept Sunday properly unless they have attended a particular place of worship. Some people can only see Christ in church. I would see him and hear him everywhere: in all history, in all communions, in commerce, in art, in all the endeavours and enterprises of civilisation. Ye fools and blind, ye can read the face of the sky—can you not discern the signs of the times?

Chapter xx. 21-23.

"Then said Jesus to them again, Peace be unto you : as my Father hath sent me, even so send I you. And when he had said this, he breathed on them, and saith unto them, Receive ye the Holy Ghost : whose soever sins ye remit they are remitted unto them ; and whose soever sins ye retain they are retained."

THE CONFESSION AND REMISSION OF SINS.

THE time at which these words were spoken should be considered in attempting to estimate their meaning and their value. Jesus Christ had risen from the dead, and was rapidly drawing to a close his personal ministry upon earth. It was consequently time to disclose the very highest phases of the great work which he came to accomplish. The relations subsisting between the Father and himself, and between himself and the disciples, were now formally specified ; the method by which the Christian economy was to be extended was particularly declared ; and the divine Agent under whose direction that method was to be carried out was directly given by Jesus Christ himself. Now that their Lord was about to ascend to the Father, it was natural that the disciples should wish to be instructed and empowered as to the future. Jesus Christ's personal ministry had been brief ; viewed within a limited range, it had been marked by much failure ; his miracles had been traced to the devil ; his doctrines had been pronounced heretical and blasphemous ; his Cross had been the laughing-stock of a ribald mob. What, then, was the future to be ? Was the future to be a repetition of the past, or by a transition from the bodily to the spiritual was truth to find its way to the innermost heart of man, until that derided Cross should be everywhere confessed as the only way to heaven ? On the termination of his personal ministry Jesus Christ had to provide for the future. He had cast the grain of corn into the ground : how was it to germinate and fructify until the whole world should be covered with the fruitfulness of harvest ? The answer to all such inquiries will be found in the last addresses which Jesus Christ delivered to his disciples. One of those addresses is before us, and we can reach its deep meaning only by the aid of that spirit which it bestows. Holy Spirit, commune with us and teach us all we ought to know !

This address, it must be borne in mind, was delivered to the disciples in their corporate capacity. The disciples, with the exception of Thomas, were assembled on the first day of the week, with closed doors for fear of the Jews, when Jesus presented himself amongst them, and spake the words which are before us. They were not spoken to one disciple, but to all; we have no reason to infer that any one of the disciples received a larger measure of the Holy Spirit than his brethren. It may be assumed, then, that the Holy Ghost was given to the disciples as a body, and to each of them according to his capacity. They were sent forth by Jesus Christ, as Jesus Christ had been sent by the Father. Here is the divine commission of the Church. The Church is of God, not remotely or collaterally, but immediately and positively. The terms of the commission are most precise and emphatic—" As my Father hath sent me, even so send I you." The question then arises, How did the Father send Jesus Christ ? He himself says, "I came down from heaven not to do mine own will, but the will of him that sent me." This answer comprehends all details ; the Church is sent to do God's will, not its own ; the Church is not upon its own errand, it is upon God's ; it is God's servant, God's representative, God's light in a dark world. If it has proceeded upon the divine law, it is all this to-day ; for it will be observed that Jesus Christ lays down the principle of transmission of authority—the Father hath sent me, I send you, and you must send others. If we have any doubt as to the propriety of this enlargement of Jesus Christ's commission, it will be removed by Paul's words to Timothy—" The things that thou hast heard of me among many witnesses, the same commit thou to faithful men, who shall be able to teach others also." It will be seen that the transmission is not one of doctrine, but that it proceeds upon personal qualification ; the men to whom the doctrine is committed are to be "faithful" and "able," and their faithfulness and ability can be known truly only by the spirit which God has committed to his people. Keeping, however, on the main line laid down by Jesus Christ himself, it appears perfectly plain that the disciples were divinely commissioned; that they were something more than zealous propagandists; that, in short, they held their authority from God. This would be evident even if the commission ended with the words—" As my Father hath sent me, even so send I you." To these words, however, is added a special gift—" Receive ye the Holy Ghost." The possession of the Holy Ghost separated and contra-distinguished the disciples from all other men. It was distinctively a Christian gift; it was given to all who received the faith of Jesus Christ,—not confined to an official body, but conferred upon all believers. Events recorded in the Acts of the Apostles leave no doubt upon this point. For example, on the day of Pentecost " the disciples were all with one accord in one place, and were all filled with the Holy Ghost, and began to speak with other tongues as the Spirit gave them utterance." While Peter addresses Cornelius and his household, " The Holy Ghost fell on all them that heard the word," and Peter asked, " Can any man forbid water, that these should not be baptized, which have received the Holy Ghost as well as we ? " No words can more clearly show that the gift of the Holy Ghost was not confined to the apostles. Afterwards, when " the apostles and brethren that were in Judæa " contended with Peter about his going to the Gentiles, he answered, " Forasmuch then as God gave them the like gift as he did unto us, who believed on the Lord Jesus Christ ; what was I, that I could withstand God ? " And on the same subject he afterwards said,—" God which knoweth the hearts, bare them witness, giving them the Holy Ghost, even as he did unto us, and put no difference between us and them, purifying their hearts by faith." These passages are enough to show that the Holy Ghost was not confined to the apostles, nor do we anywhere find a hint that the apostles claim to have the Holy Spirit in any degree superior to all believers in Jesus Christ.

So far, there can be no doubt of two things : first, that the Church is divinely commissioned, and second, that its divine commission is attested by the personal presence and power of

the Holy Ghost. We now come to a third point,—"Whose soever sins ye remit, they are remitted unto them ; and whose
soever sins ye retain, they are retained." This power, it would
appear, is not separate from the Holy Ghost, but identical with it ;
apart from the Holy Ghost, it could not have any existence. It
was given to the disciples as a body ; and though the disciples of
course received it as individuals, yet there is no hint that it was to
be exercised by particular individuals in any secret or confidential
manner ; on the other hand, the terms are open, general, ecclesiastical, addressed to the disciples in their plurality. So far as the
practice of confession of sin can be ascertained from the inspired
writings, it was public, never confidential, except where the sin lay
strictly between two individuals. In ancient Israel, for example,
confession was made publicly. In the fourth chapter of Leviticus we
find the elaborate law respecting sins of ignorance ; and all that was
to be done by the priest, the congregation, the ruler, or the common
people, was to be done openly. In subsequent chapters we find
confession and restitution referred to, but not in a single instance
is there any trace of secret confidential confession. Even where
special cases arose, as between a man and his wife, the priest
was referred to by the party who had been aggrieved, not by the
party who had done the wrong, and then not for confession, but
for the administration of such tests as God himself had provided.
Leaving the Old Testament and coming to the baptism of John,
we find this statement—"Then went out to him Jerusalem and
all Judæa, and all the region round about Jordan, confessing their
sins,"—the baptism and the confession being spoken of as equally
public. It is not necessary to the elucidation of the text to enter
upon a minute discussion of the particular manner of the confession made by the Jews ; the point to be noted is that nowhere
is secret or confidential confession referred to, or secret absolution
permitted. We do find open confession, open penitence, open
sacrifice, together with a continual illustration of the principle
laid down in the Book of Proverbs—"He that covereth his sins
shall not prosper : but whoso confesseth and forsaketh them shall
have mercy."

The principle of confession is implied in the very terms of the
commission. Sins cannot be remitted unless they are known,

and they cannot be known except they are confessed. It will be found, too, in the teaching of Christ and the apostles that confession is always made an indispensable condition of forgiveness. It is so spiritually, it is so individually, it is so ecclesiastically, One passage will show that it is so spiritually : "If we confess our sins, he is faithful and just to forgive us our sins, and to cleanse us from all unrighteousness." Observe that the forgiveness depends upon the confession, for "if we say we have no sin we deceive ourselves, and the truth is not in us." Jesus Christ lays down the law of confession between individual and individual most explicitly. He says, "If thy brother trespass against thee, rebuke him; and if he repent, forgive him." There can be no forgiveness where there is no repentance ; and where repentance is expressed, confession is made. Jesus Christ adds, "And if he trespass against thee seven times in a day, and seven times in a day turn again to thee, saying, I repent ; thou shalt forgive him." Still, repentance, or confession, precedes forgiveness. On another occasion, also, Jesus Christ provided for the treatment of individual offences. He said, "If thy brother shall trespass against thee, go and tell him his fault between thee and him alone : if he shall hear thee, thou hast gained thy brother." Here the offended party is to give an opportunity of confession,—if he shall hear thee, shall accept thy arguments, respond to thy entreaties, confess his offence, thou hast gained him. These instances elucidate the law which is to govern individual confession and forgiveness. The text now before us relates to a case not provided for in the law relating to spiritual offences or individual trespasses. The disciples were addressed as a body. Jesus Christ distinctly recognised the power of the Church when he made it the ultimate appeal in individual cases: "Tell it unto the Church, but if he neglect to hear the Church, let him be unto thee as an heathen man and a publican." Paul recognised the same authority ; for when a case of discipline arose in the Church at Corinth, he wrote, "For I verily, as absent in body, but present in spirit, have judged already, as though I were present, concerning him that hath so done this deed, in the name of our Lord Jesus Christ, when ye are gathered together, and my spirit, with the power of our Lord Jesus Christ, to deliver such an one unto Satan for the destruction of the flesh, that the spirit may be saved in the day of the Lord Jesus." The Church in its corporate capacity ("when ye are gathered together") is here called to the exercise of extreme discipline. Addressing the same Church, the apostle gives, in a subsequent portion of the epistle, another view of Church discipline. "Sufficient to such a man is this punishment which was inflicted of many; so that contrariwise ye ought rather to forgive him and comfort him, lest perhaps such an one should be swallowed up with over much sorrow," the "sorrow" showing that the man was in a fit spiritual state (amounting to confession) to receive the forgiveness and comfort of the Church.

From the structure of the passage more immediately under consideration, it is inferred that as the commission respecting the remission and retaining of sin was given to the disciples in their public and corporate capacity, so it refers only to sins which relate to the corporate and public aspect and jurisdiction of the Church. This inference is confirmed by passages already cited which provide for individual trespasses, and purely spiritual offences against God.

This construction of the passage illustrates the deeply spiritual nature of the Christian Church. That Church is not a miscellaneous gathering of people; it is a confraternity of souls under the dominion of him who bought them with his blood, and under the personal guidance of the Holy Ghost. No man is truly identified with the Church who is not first identified in all his deepest affections and sympathies with Jesus Christ. He who is so identified with Jesus Christ has received the Holy Ghost; "Know ye not that ye are the temple of God, and that the Spirit of God dwelleth in you?" "Ye are the temple of the living God, as God hath said, I will dwell in them and walk in them." He is no longer a common man; he is a new creature; the spirit of wisdom and of a sound mind is put within him. It is true, indeed, that he may grieve or even quench the Holy Spirit, but "if any man defile the temple of God, him shall God destroy."

Not only does the passage illustrate the deeply spiritual character of the Christian Church, it invests the Church with high spiritual authority. Members of the Church are keepers of one another; they are called to a common sympathy alike in sorrow and in joy; they are bound to deliver some men to Satan, that they may learn not to blaspheme; they are called upon to note others and to have no company with them, that offenders may be ashamed; and they are authorised to reject the man who is "an heretic after the first and second admonition." And Jesus Christ, who in the gift of the Holy Ghost gave them this authority, says that he will ratify their decisions.   The Apostle Paul claimed that cases of dispute should be settled "before the saints," and asks, "Do ye not know that the saints shall judge the world? and if the world shall be judged by you, are ye unworthy to judge the smallest matters?   Know ye not that we shall judge angels? how much more things that pertain to this life?"   Let the Church take heed lest its heavenly vocation be exchanged for a technical and worthless formalism.   If it is to realise Jesus Christ's idea of being the light of the world, the salt of the earth, and the city on a hill, it must claim all the powers and privileges which its Founder put within its reach.

Let us now look at a few inquiries and objections.

First of all, it may be asked, Where is the Church?   The Church is where two or three are gathered together in Christ's name.   They indeed are not the whole Church; but in a mystical sense, which unregenerated men cannot appreciate, they are the Church.   Where is the sunlight?   Is any man at liberty to confine himself in darkness because he cannot admit all the sunlight?   The whole earth itself on the longest summer day receives but a small portion of that light; rays of the great glory strike other worlds, and carry morning and noon and summer to distant spheres; what then?   The child can still play in the sunshine, and the weakest floweret claim to have been painted by the sun.   So the Church is not wholly to be found in this place or in that; there may be a Church at Philadelphia, a Church at Smyrna, a Church at Thyatira, and at Jerusalem, at Antioch, at Laodicea, at Pergamos, at Rome: where two or three are gathered together in Christ's name, Christ himself is, and that union makes the Church.

It may be objected that the Church is fallible, and consequently its remissions and retentions of sin may be mistaken. True, the Church is fallible; but the Holy Ghost is infallible, and it is the Holy Ghost who directs the Church to remit or retain sins. It is impossible for a man to sin against his neighbour or against the Church without at the same time sinning against God. The true confession, either to the individual or to the Church, is that which comes after confession to God; the truly penitent offender does not come first to the human side of his offence but to the divine side, and having poured out his contrition before God he is impelled to abase himself before the offended individual or the dishonoured Church. But may not an offender make an insincere confession of sin? True; but rules cannot be made for hypocrites, the gracious provision can be made only for sincere men. The Church is bound to deal with each case upon its merits; to make the most searching inquiry; to put all doubtful men to the most exacting tests; and, having satisfied the spirit of wisdom, it must exercise the spirit of righteousness and charity. Jesus Christ says, "Whosoever believeth shall be saved." An insincere man may profess belief,—will he therefore be saved? In all such cases (and they are many in spiritual life) there is necessarily an assumption of conditions. When Jesus Christ says, "Ask and ye shall receive," the implied condition is that he who asks is sincere, and that his petitions are confined within a legitimate bound; when he says, "He that believeth shall be saved," the implied condition is that the man believes with his heart; so when he says, "Whose soever sins ye remit they are remitted," the implied condition is that the offending man has made a candid and contrite confession of his guilt.

"But," it may be urged, "the apostles had the power of discerning spirits; we have not this power." We may exagger-ate the gift of discerning spirits as possessed by the apostles. For example, when they wished to ordain one to be a witness with them of the resurrection, they did not discern between Joseph and Matthias; on the contrary, "They prayed and said, Thou Lord, which knowest the hearts of all men, show whether of these two thou hast chosen." Will the Church proceed either to remission or retention of sins without prayer? Will it be an

off-handed exercise, making no demand upon the highest sensibilities, no strain upon the very heart of hearts? Will it not, on
the contrary, lead the Church to a deeper spiritual abasement,
bring it into the most entire sympathy with the pure and merciful
spirit of Jesus Christ? and if it must needs fast and pray, even
through many days, who dare say that God will not openly
smite the liar with vengeance, and give the true penitent a new
hope in life?

And even with regard to discerning spirits, dare we say that
we have exhausted the measure of the Holy Ghost which Jesus
Christ intended his Church to receive? If we surrendered ourselves entirely to God's will; it we knew nothing among men but
Jesus Christ and him crucified; if by giving our days to study
and our nights to prayer we did really and truly "prove" the
God of heaven, who dare say that he would not open the
windows of heaven and pour out his Spirit upon all flesh, that
their sons and their daughters should prophesy, their old men
dream dreams, and their young men see visions? If we were
charged with presumption or blasphemy we could answer with
Jesus Christ who sent us as he himself was sent of the Father,—
"The words that I speak unto you I speak not of myself: but the
Father that dwelleth in me, he doeth the works."

No doubt that in the application of these principles some
practical difficulties will arise, but not one that cannot be overcome by ordinary sagacity and care. When is it that we pronounce the application of such principles impracticable? Is it
when we have been living a most worldly life, or when we have
spent much time in fellowship with God? Everything, so far as
difficulty is concerned, depends upon the spiritual mood in which
we consider the question. When the heart is most deeply conscious of Jesus Christ's excellence; when it gets farthest away
from the debasing influences of its worldly associations, and by
so much nearer to the great light which spreads eternal morning
upon the sphere into which Jesus Christ has entered, then all
difficulty is scattered, all doubt is cleared off. This, I am persuaded, is one of the truths which can be apprehended only when
the soul is in its very highest moods. It belongs emphatically to

the sphere of inspiration. Jesus Christ placed it there; he breathed, or, as Tyndale translates it, he blew, upon the disciples, —he inspired them, that they might accept and adopt an inspired truth.

There is a touching incident in ancient history which throws light upon several points of this argument. The incident will be found in the first book of the Anabasis of Xenophon. Cyrus summoned a council of his fellow-soldiers and friends to confer with them as to a just sentence to be pronounced upon the arch-traitor Orontas. Cyrus told the court-martial that his father had placed Orontas under his command, yet that the traitor had made war upon him but was compelled to succumb, and then he took the hand which Cyrus generously offered him. In the presence of the court-martial, under the cross-examination of Cyrus, Orontas confessed that Cyrus had done him no injury; he further confessed that after this he went over, without any provocation, to the Mysians and depopulated the lands of Cyrus. Orontas further confessed that as soon as he found his own weakness he fled to the altar of Diana, professed repentance, induced Cyrus to think him sincere, and once more succeeded in receiving the confidence of the magnanimous soldier. "What injury, then," said Cyrus, "have I done you, that you should have been induced the third time to betray my confidence?" Orontas denied that Cyrus had done him any injury. "Then," said Cyrus, "you admit that you have done me an unprovoked injury?" "That," said Orontas, "I am under the necessity of confessing." Then the noble Cyrus, with more than soldierly grace, with a dignity indeed that would adorn a Christian, asked him, "Can you, O Orontas, on my forgiving you, be an enemy to my brother and a friend to me?" To which the wretched man, stung by the recollections of his repeated treachery, answered, "Were I to say so, O Cyrus, neither you nor any other person would believe me." Cyrus then put the case to Clearchus, his first general, who gave a verdict of condemnation; the whole camp coincided, even the traitor's relations united in the opinion, and the oft-forgiven but incurable traitor was led forth to death. Truly there is a spirit in man, and the inspiration of the Almighty giveth him understanding. In this narrative we have a sin committed against the individual, and condoned, upon confession, by the individual; we have also a sin against the army, tried and condemned by the army ; and we have an appeal to the deep moral sense that is in all human hearts ; and we have that outraged moral sense justly demanding the life of a man who employed repentance as an ally of villainy, and made confession the password to a confidence which he plotted to betray.

It is upon this moral sense that the Holy Ghost descends in all-quickening, enlightening, and sanctifying power. The Church should present the only true example of a refined and thoroughly educated moral sense. Its spirit should be quick in judgment. By profound study of Jesus Christ it should come to hate sin, to know it afar off, yet to have all the pity of the heart turned upon the repentant sinner. It may be, and do, all this ! Why does it tarry behind, when it might be the terror of all evil, and the refuge and joy of everything that is good in heaven and on earth ?

The result of a careful examination into biblical teaching upon this subject is the acceptance of the following propositions :—

(1) That the power of forgiving sins is divinely bestowed upon the disciples of Jesus Christ in their corporate capacity, and that such power is in harmony with the purpose of Jesus Christ's mediation and the genius of the religious epoch in which we live.

(2) That Jesus Christ taught the doctrine of individual confession to the offended individual, and called upon the offended individual to forgive the offender upon receiving such confession.

(3) That nowhere in the sacred Scriptures is forgiveness promised apart from confession and restitution,—whether the sin lie between man and man, or between man and God.

(4) That nowhere in the sacred Scriptures is there any authority given to any official person, bishop, priest, minister, or deacon, to receive secretly and confidentially a confession of sins.

(5) That the confession of sins is too sacred a duty, involving consequences too many and important, to be reduced to a system and presided over by any single human being.

(6) That all overt sin has a human as well as a divine aspect,

and that the Church, inspired and sanctified by the Holy Ghost, has power to deal with the human aspect, according to the nature of the confession which the sinner may make.

(7) That to shrink from receiving confession of sin, and dealing with it according to its merits, may have the appearance of great reverence and humility, without the reality,—may show that the Church has part in the first baptism only, and not in the baptism of fire.

(8) That to avoid all priestly pretension and destroy the confessional, that infinitely hateful institution which has degraded and oppressed every nation in which it has found an existence, and further to show that all who have the Holy Ghost are kings and priests unto God, the sinner should openly confess his overt sins in the presence of the Church (which could be done by writing, or before such a number of witnesses as the Church itself might appoint), and receive from the Church such comfort as can never be refused to those who truly confess and heartily repent their sins.

We cannot be unaware that other interpretations than that which is now before us have been given, nor should we deny that much deference is due to those who with patient devotion have endeavoured to discover the mind of the Spirit. The most generally received interpretation is, that in preaching the gospel the disciples declared the principles upon which sins were either remitted or retained,—he that believeth shall be saved, he that believeth not shall be damned. This interpretation appears to me to be utterly inadequate; entirely opposed to the grammatical construction of the text; and a weak dilution of the wholesome spirit of its doctrine. Such an interpretation limits the function of the Church to a mere preaching ministry. One of the principal objections urged against the view presented in this discourse may be urged against this interpretation. There may be insincere believers as well as insincere confessors; if you tell a man who insincerely believes the gospel that his sins are remitted, are they therefore remitted? The commission merely says, "he that believeth," not he that truly believeth; yet who would found any argument upon that? It is enough to repeat that terms can be offered only to sincere men; hypocrites can evade or resist anything. The view suggested in this discourse honours the Church by honouring the Holy Ghost, and gives the sinner to feel the moral influence of men who live constantly in the fellowship of Christ. Of course the Church upon earth has its imperfections; but the imperfections are felt in the preaching of the gospel as much as in any other department of Christian service, so that if they invalidate confession they invalidate the whole ministry. Bad men preach the gospel; is the preaching of the gospel therefore opposed to the will of God? Imperfect men preach the gospel; is there therefore no Christian truth?

Believing that God's gifts increase rather than decrease, that his plan is progressive not retrogressive, I see no reason why the first disciples of the Lord should have greater spiritual privileges than those of the present age; but I do see that if the Church will magnify its office, and show a disposition to possess the best gifts,—if it will seek to know more thoroughly the will of Jesus Christ, it will attain an exaltation compared with which all its former eminence shall be unworthy of remembrance.

PRAYER.

ALMIGHTY GOD, thou hast surrounded us with mercy upon mercy, countless and precious. What shall we render unto the Lord for all his benefits towards us? Receive our thanksgiving, so far as words can express our gratitude, and cause us to feel the inexpressible thankfulness which never can be uttered in mortal speech,—the thankfulness of our whole heart, expressed in the consecration of our whole life. We are sinners. God be merciful unto us! We come to the Saviour's Cross; we look unto the Lamb of God; we lay our hand upon the one Sacrifice. God be merciful unto us! We cannot justify our ways before God. We have no reasons to set in order before thee to vindicate our conduct wherein it has been contrary to thy most holy Word. We shut our mouth, we lay our hand upon it, we bow ourselves down into the dust. If we might say ought before thee, we would say, Unclean, unclean! But if we confess our sins, thou art faithful and just to forgive us our sins, and to cleanse us from all unrighteousness. Undertake that work. Sanctify us, body, soul, and spirit. May our whole nature be pure. May every aspiration, affection, desire, be sanctified by the Holy Ghost. May our whole strength be an offering unto the Lord's service, accepted because offered on the Cross of the Lord Jesus. Thou hast added another week unto our years; thou hast taken another week from our life upon the earth. Help us to live in Christ, then our life cannot be measured by time. May our heart be in Christ's keeping. May our whole life be hidden with Christ in God, then eternity itself can never waste our energy or impair our perfect beauty. Come to us now according to our want. To the hunger of our soul do thou apply the bread of heaven. To the burning, consuming thirst of our love and highest nature do thou apply the water of the river of life. Revive the drooping. May they look up where they cannot stand up. May they feel thy presence and submit to thy rule. Dry the tears of our sorrow. Explain thou to us, if so be we may thereby be stronger in the Lord and in the power of his might; if not, help us to believe in the future, where there is no sorrow because no sin, where there is complete ever-enduring rest. Look upon thy servants who have to face the world day by day,—whose life is often a battle; whose battle is often a failing strife; whose hearts are discouraged, and whose strength is wasted. Give them thy grace, work in them thy peace, and give them hope. Look upon thy servants who seem to carry everything before them; who speak, and it is done; who command, and it stands fast; who dream themselves into success; who put forth the finger, and carry all things as they will. This is a great temptation: who can bear it? Our

439

success endangers us, if our roots be not fixed in God, if our love and our faith be not established in Jesus Christ. Teach thy servants that all this world can give is but a splendid nothing. Show them that if the whole world were at their feet it would ultimately fall away and leave them without possession and without rest. May we set our affections on things above. May we look at things not seen. May we dominate over time and sense, and even now sit down in the kingdom of Jesus Christ. Amen.

Chapter xx. 25.

" Except I shall see in his hands the print of the nails, and put my finger into the print of the nails, and thrust my hand into his side, I will not believe."

DOUBTING THOMAS.

WE call this man "Doubting Thomas"—as if there were only one man who had ever doubted. He does not deserve this speciality of distinction. It is possible that there may be some Christians who think they advance themselves a step in their reputation with God in talking about an old disciple as "Doubting Thomas." The actual Thomas has become a kind of proverb in the English tongue. There is nothing so remarkable or special about Thomas's doubt. What did Thomas want? He wanted simply to be put upon a level with the other disciples. And imagine the other disciples getting around this unhappy man and pointing him out as "Doubting Thomas." They had forgotten all the circumstances of their own experience. That is just what men always do: they forget their own spiritual history, and then they begin to wonder at the doubts and difficulties, the troubles and the conflicts, which gather themselves up in the experience of other men. Jesus came into the midst of the disciples, and "showed unto them his hands and his side." We do not know whether they made any demand in that direction; the gospel history is elliptical, and it is often wanting in those parentheses which would explain circumstances. Here may be an ellipsis which leaves us in ignorance whether the disciples said, "Show us thy hands and thy feet, and then we will believe." As a matter of fact, Jesus Christ did show them his hands and his feet; and how do we know but that they had told Thomas, and Thomas may have said, Very well; you say it is thus and so: now, except I do just what you have done, I will not believe. I must put my finger upon the print of the nails, and thrust my own hand into the side, then I will believe; if I cannot do that I will not believe. What right, then, had these disciples to gather around this one brother, and describe him as " Doubting Thomas " ? They themselves had been satisfied by the very thing that he wanted done; they therefore had no right to look upon Thomas as if he were hardhearted or criminally obstinate.

Yet Thomas made a vital mistake. What was the mistake made by this man ? It is the mistake of the world. Everybody is making it. The mistake which Thomas made was to lay down the one and only way in which Christ should come to him : " Except . . . I will not believe." That is to say, I must have it my way, not God's way; I must appoint the gate through which the Lord must come into my life, and if he attempt to come by any other way, I will not receive him. If I may stand at that gate and watch it, and keep the key of it, and see the Lord when he comes, and open the gate for him, then I will believe. That is the mistake of the world. We do not allow room for God ; we watch him as if he were an enemy; we never allow Providence scope enough. We might be saved in the wildest seas if we would let the ship alone, but we cannot keep our meddling fingers still. We must help ; we must eke out Omnipotence. The sea would rock you and nurse you with musical undulation, only you will plunge, you will not lie still. We who were born yesterday, and know nothing, say that the Bible ought to consist of so many books, written at such and such times and by such and such men, and all the pieces should dovetail into one another in such and such a way, or we will not believe. And what does our not believing amount to ? Is our infidelity a fist that can smite God's face ? Is our infidelity a circumstance worth noting in the development of the universe ? A man will say, Except every comma and semicolon written in the Bible be inspired, I will give up the whole thing. What will happen if he gives up the whole thing ? Nothing. But thus we magnify ourselves, thus we make a great figure of " I will not believe": there shall be one infidel in the universe unless I can have my own way. This is what men are doing to-day, and are always doing, and this is how they shut out God from their lives; whereas we ought to say, Lord, come in any way thou wilt, all the ways are

thine; come to us through sweet blossoming vernal nature, just
opening its young heart to tell us secrets of beauty and secrets
of growth and strength; come to us through what is called by
man natural theology—forgive the offensive term, for we map
thee out into little sections; or come to us through whispered
love, or deep conviction, or strange stirring of the soul, or weird
figures at midnight, or through a mother's lullaby, or some great
song of victory, or through conspicuous events in daily story:—
come in thine own way, and may we be found ready when thou
dost stand at the door and knock. Men cannot grow up into this
great all-conquering faith at once. Pity, therefore, rather than
scorn, the men who want God to come along little private roads.
It is natural. There is about it a selfishness that may be chastened
and sanctified; it is not the worst kind of selfishness: yet there
are souls that would like to entertain God with private hospitality, and would not allow others to come and join the banqueting-
board but by special invitation or permission. There are those
who would keep the Atlantic in their back-garden if they could,
just that they might have a sea breeze all to themselves; but the
Atlantic is a little too large for that species of accommodation.
There are those who would like to lock up theology, keeping
it as a private interpretation and a personal possession, and
measuring all other people by standards which these private
custodians have elected and pronounced authoritative; but
theology cannot find room enough for itself in heaven, much
less in our strong-boxes of which we keep the keys. Theology
fills heaven and the heaven of heavens, and asks, Where is the
trust deed that ye have written out at so many pence per folio?
Theology is God struggling into words, and the struggle never
comes to anything but a struggle.

   This would be the one error, then, that Thomas fell into,
namely, establishing a private road by which the Lord is to come,
and an apparent determination not to see the Lord except he
come along that private path. Take care that ye limit not the
Holy One of Israel! There are men who come to pastors and
say, We do not belong to the Church, we belong to Nature.
Should the pastor stand up and rebuke such, as if they had
no relation to the kingdom of God? Verily no: say, Who made

Nature? whence did Nature come? what does Nature mean? what is the signification of all its parabolism, its wizardry of flower and bird and song and star and morning and summer? What is the meaning of this eternal procession that has about it the completeness of a circle, and the dignity and weirdness of an uncontrollable and inexplicable miracle? You cannot get out of your Father's grounds. What of the young man who lives always in the garden, and will never come in to the fireside? What of the youth who will always hold confidential intercourse with the gardener but never speak to his father? The fact that there is a house might suggest a tenant; the fact that there is such a house might suggest a God. There are persons who do not delight in our ordinances and institutions, in our rites and ceremonies, and therefore they think themselves exiled from God's great home. Nothing of the kind. Do you really and truly love music? You are not far from the kingdom of God. Would you stop to talk to a flower, to wonder about it, to pat it with the finger of love, to ask it questions addressed to its innermost heart? you are not an infidel. Wherever there is any longing for fuller light, more exquisite beauty, grandeur, profounder harmony amid all the relations of life and duty, there should be a consciousness on the part of others that they who so struggle and wonder, and almost pray, will one day find that the thing they have been really looking for but they did not know it was the Cross. Let us have no more excommunication than can possibly be helped; let the priest choke himself so that he cannot pronounce the words of excommunication; let him strain himself to find redeeming points, and not endeavour to show his priestly cleverness by finding out reasons why men should be exiled and damned.

There are points at which men may demand, legitimately, certain kinds of evidence. For example, it would be legitimate to say, Except I see that Christ can do more than any other man can do, I will not believe. There you assign breadth, you create an occasion worthy the event which you seek to establish. Can Christ do more for men than any other man ever did? If so, is not this man the Son of God? How long will he stay with a man? When does Jesus Christ turn round, saying,

I cannot go any farther with you? When does Jesus Christ say, If you commit one more sin, I will leave you? When does Jesus Christ say, This soul-leprosy is too inveterate for my touch : I can cure very much leprosy, but not of this kind ; this is a disease that goes through and through the soul, and I cannot do anything with it, I cannot relieve the sufferer? When? Never! I think men are entitled to say, Except I see that Christianity produces a higher quality of character than any other religion, I will not believe it. Men have a right to insist upon character being of the very highest quality. Here is the responsibility of Christians ; here is the terrible impossible task of representing Christ to other people. Yet people have a right to expect that if Christ be in us there shall be about our character a bloom, a fine quality that cannot be found under any other circumstances. There we all fail, the preacher more than any. What should be the quality of that man who professes to be a temple of the Holy Ghost, and to have Christ dwelling in him? what his temper, his chivalry, his love, his self-sacrifice, his nobleness? There "I the chief of sinners am" each may say. Yet even along that line there is some encouragement, for Christ says if we want to love him ; we do love him ; if we want to be like him we are like him ; if we are struggling we are succeeding; if we are fighting we are winning. It pleaseth the Lord thus by his redeeming love to multiply our little struggles and deeds and purposes into great realities, and to regard beginnings as consummations ; such is his love. Were we to be judged by our own character there is no pit deep enough for the best of us, but if we are to be judged by what Christ sees in us, motive within motive, purpose higher than purpose expressed in words, who can tell what his eye sees in our poor souls? By what he sees he judges.

What did Thomas want really and truly? He wanted what everybody must have : Thomas wanted personal contact. Of course he happened to take the very lowest point ; the contact which Thomas desired was physical or bodily. But personal contact is larger than can be defined by any one instance. Thomas wanted what we need, I repeat, namely, personal touch. The youngest must know what "contact" means—*con*, together ;

tact, touching, together. A great grasp is contact; so is a gentle touch, as of the finger-tips, a touch that dare not attempt the larger contact of hug and grasp and assured possession. This we must have in some form. If any have this in a low form, so be it; that is all they can do at present; they may believe in the letter, especially in the letter when it is a capital letter, and almost forces itself upon the dull vision. Some people can believe in the nouns or substantives, and the more striking and aggressive verbs, who cannot read all the little words in between. Let them read what they can; you may be saved by a very few letters, if you get the right hold of them. There is, however, this larger truth that there may be contact of spirit with spirit, soul with soul. Speculation is worthless, historical certainty is worthless, negative opinion is worthless; the only thing that has any value in it is the consciousness of contact with God, with the spirit-world, with the ghostly awful realities of the universe. There be those who have no Bible except the Bible they can carry in their hands; that will do them no good. By-and-by they will want a Bible that their souls will be too small and too weak to carry; meanwhile do not rebuke them, they want the revelation in ink, in visible letter, and they must have it so because it is adapted to their age and to their capacity. By-and-by they will read without reading, they will have a revelation larger than any book can ever be, they will have a consciousness from which God can never be excluded, they will live and move and have their being in God; now they must pray morning, noon, and night; now they cannot pray except they be on their bended knees, and except they close their eyes and fold their hands, and fall into a child's attitude of prayer. So be it; the time will come when they will pray all the day. Have they therefore abandoned form, and scorned rite and ceremony, and poured contempt upon their weaker brethren? Nothing of the kind; they have grown into a larger manhood, they have by the spirit of the indwelling God developed a more sensitive and responsive consciousness.

Christ himself believed in touch. He touched the blind man's eyes. Oh, it was worth being blind to feel that touch! The blind man had the advantage over us in his very blindness. Nor can we tell whether all infirmity shall not prove to be an advantage by-and-by. We can never know health as the leper knew it; he was cleansed, and his flesh became as the flesh of a little child. We accept our health as a commonplace, but to be redeemed from the very grave and made to feel all nature in every pulse, who can describe the very passion of such health? And so the blind man has been going through the earth without ever seeing it, and the first object he beholds is God. What a contrast is that! What a vision of glory! In that revealed beauty the blankness of a lifetime is forgotten. We, too, believe in touch. The poor woman said—and she spoke for us all—" If I may but touch his garment, I shall be whole."

Sometimes we have personal contact with God without that contact assuming what may be called a theological form. Sometimes it comes to us through great emotions, through new solicitudes, through pantings and yearnings we cannot express in words. Why this concern for others? why this pity for those who are in great sorrow? why this sense of victory, this mounting above death and the grave, this shouting of conscious triumph, this almost heaven? What is the meaning of it? It may be the action of God in the soul. Why this holy peace, this deep tranquillity, this profound calm that nothing can ruffle, and which when it speaks says, "God is our refuge and strength, a very present help in trouble. Therefore will not we fear, though the earth be removed, and though the mountains be carried intc the midst of the sea"? The swelling of the ocean shall not cause tumult in our soul, if we live and move and have our being in God.

We cannot have personal contact with Christ without other people knowing it. Once there were some very poor crude unlettered men—men that might have been taken from the fishing boat or even from the plough or from some ordinary avocation of life, and they went before very great magistrates whose fingers were unsullied with labour, and these magistrates looked at them and said, How singular these men are! how rude in outline! what disadvantages they must have undergone! and yet what is that about them that makes them singular ? There is a kind of radiance on all that roughness of exterior: what is it?— " And they took knowledge of them that they had been with Jesus." To be with Jesus is an education ; to be closeted with Christ is a refining process. When Moses came down from the mountain his face was like a sun ; he had been with God : and the rude fishermen, with all their roughness, clumsiness, with all their want of pomp and form, had something about them that impressed the magistracy of the day, and the great priests took knowledge of them that there was a refinement not taught in the schools, a singular beauty, a fascination suggestive of the highest spiritual culture. We ask no other distinction, we pant for no greater fame than to be taken knowledge of that we have been with Jesus.

PRAYER

Oh, thou who art merciful and gracious, full of compassion and long-suffering and tenderness; thou art kind to the unthankful and to the evil! We hasten to thee with our offering of praise, inasmuch as thou hast crowned our life with lovingkindness and tender mercy, and made it beautiful with continual love. We praise thee; we magnify thee; we offer thee the whole strength of our heart. We hasten to thee as men who have been mocked by the promises of the world, and who long to find satisfaction in thine infinite and unspeakable peace. We have been disappointed. The staff has been broken in our hand and pierced us. We mistook the scorpion for an egg. We have hewn unto ourselves cisterns; they are broken cisterns, which can hold no water. Foiled, smitten, wounded, humiliated, and disgraced we come into thy presence, knowing that in God, as revealed in the person and doctrine of Jesus Christ, and made known unto us by the ministry of the Holy Ghost, we can find rest which our souls could not find elsewhere. All our springs are in thee. Thou givest us what we need. They who are in thy presence, who live in thy light and thy love, hunger no more, neither thirst any more, neither are subjected to weariness or decay. We would live in God. We would have our being in the Eternal. We would know nothing among men but Jesus, and him crucified; and by the mystery of pain and the mystery of love, symbolised by Christ's Cross, we would endure the trials of the world, and discharge the whole service of life. Meet us as sinners, and pardon us. The blood of Jesus Christ, thy Son, cleanseth from all sin. May we know its cleansing, healing power. We have done the things we ought not to have done; we have withheld the testimony which it became us to deliver; we have often been timid and unfaithful; we have hesitated when we ought to have gone forward; we have compromised where we ought to have died; we have become self-seekers where we ought to have sought the crown of martyrdom; we have kept an unjust balance and an untrue weight; our measure has been false; our word has been untrue; our spirit has been worldly; our very prayers have been selfish. All this we say when we truly know ourselves, as we are revealed to ourselves by the in-dwelling, all-disclosing Spirit. God be merciful unto us sinners, and cleanse us from all unrighteousness! Give us the hearing ear and the understanding heart, the obedient will, the ever-industrious hand in the service of Jesus Christ. When we have done our best to serve our day and generation, and the time of reckoning has come, may we find all our worth in the worthiness of the Lamb, and be accounted fit to sit with him on his throne, because in our degree we have shared the pain and shame of his crucifixion. Amen.

448

Chapter xxi. 10-25.

"Jesus saith unto them, Bring of the fish which ye have **now** caught. Simon Peter went up, and drew the net to land full of great fishes, an hundred and fifty and three : and for all there were so many, yet was not the net broken. Jesus saith unto them, Come and dine. And none of the disciples durst ask him, Who art thou ? knowing that it was the Lord. Jesus then cometh, and taketh bread, and giveth them, and fish likewise. This is now the third time that Jesus shewed himself to his disciples, after that he was risen from the dead. So when they had dined, Jesus saith to Simon Peter, Simon, son of Jonas, lovest thou me more than these? He saith unto him, Yea, Lord ; thou knowest that I love thee. He saith unto him, Feed my lambs. He saith to him again the second time, Simon, son of Jonas, lovest thou me ? He saith unto him, Yea, Lord ; thou knowest that I love thee. He saith unto him, Feed my sheep. He saith unto him the third time, Simon, son of Jonas, lovest thou me ? Peter was grieved because he said unto him the third time, Lovest thou me ? And he said unto him, Lord, thou knowest all things ; thou knowest that I love thee. Jesus saith unto him, Feed my sheep. Verily, verily, I say unto thee, When thou wast young, thou girdest thyself, and walkedst whither thou wouldest : but when thou shalt be old, thou shalt stretch forth thy hands, and another shall gird thee, and carry thee whither thou wouldest not. This spake he, signifying by what death he should glorify God. And when he had spoken this, he saith unto him, Follow me. Then Peter, turning about, seeth the disciple whom Jesus loved following; which also leaned on his breast at supper, and said, Lord, which is he that betrayeth thee ? Peter seeing him saith to Jesus, Lord, and what shall this man do? Jesus saith unto him, If I will that he tarry till I come, what is that to thee? follow thou me. Then went this saying abroad among the brethren, that that disciple should not die: yet Jesus said not unto him, He shall not die; but, If I will that he tarry till I come, what is that to thee ? This is the disciple which testifieth of these things, and wrote these things : and we know that his testimony is true. And there are also many other things which Jesus did, the which, if they should be written every one, I suppose that even the world itself could not contain the books that should be written. Amen."

A PATHETIC INTERVIEW.

WE cannot tell what happened at the interview between Jesus Christ and his penitent disciple. We remember how Peter denied his Lord : we have rejoiced to find him reappearing in the sacred story, and we have been made aware that when Peter was given to understand that Jesus was standing upon the shore, he went out to him—he "did cast himself into the sea," and he was the first to see Jesus, and he saw the Saviour alone. What happened at that interview we shall never know. We do not know the secret interviews which men have with their Lord;

we hear somewhat of their public prayer, but what they say
when they are quite alone we may never understand.   Blessed
be God, there are such interviews, occurring daily, and feeding
the soul with grace most secretly; and all that aspect of worship
must for ever remain known only to those who take part in the
sacred exercise.   Yet we have opportunity of drawing inferences
so far as this narrative is concerned.   One word is uttered by
Peter which enables us to penetrate in some permissible degree
the interview between Jesus and Simon.   That explanatory or
suggestive word is "knowest."   In the first answer we find this
—"Yea, Lord; thou knowest"; in the second answer it returns
—"Yea, Lord; thou knowest"; in the third answer it appears
again—"Lord, thou knowest all things; thou knowest."   How
did Jesus know that Peter loved him?   So far as the open
history is concerned, the last incident points to Peter's denial of
Jesus Christ; but we have not to deal with the open history
alone, but with the secret and unreported interview: in that
solemn colloquy it was made clear to Jesus Christ that under all
the blasphemy there lay an affectionate heart, under all the lapse,
and shame, and treason there throbbed an immortal love.   So
in the speech of men we hear words now and then full of significance; they are to be interpreted in their larger relations.   We
are surprised when we hear such words, and we try to fit them
into the current and open story of the lives of the speakers, and
we cannot do so; and then the mind is thrown back upon the
fact that the minutest history contains only occasional references,
points here and there; the line as it is written is full of lacunæ,
great open gaps which we cannot supply: but the words which
have surprised us and affected us enable the reader to fill up
these vacancies with some degree of intelligibleness and adequacy.

How wise was Jesus, Son of man, Son of God!   He instantly
set the disciples to work : "Jesus saith unto them, Bring of the
fish which ye have now caught.   Simon Peter went up."   It was
the very word he wanted.   Contemplation was not his forte; to
sit still and engage in an exercise of self-introspection—to read
the black book of his heart—was not Peter's delight; but to be
called to activity, to have something to do, to have all his faculties
called into exercise,—that was the medicine he needed for his

heart's healing in that hour of poignant and humiliating memory. We have been in the same condition,—oh for something to do ! This perpetual contemplation of life, this looking into it with an analytical vision, this taking it to pieces in order that we may examine its motive and the quality of its fibre, this we cannot endure. Oh that God would call upon us to plunge into the sea, to run across a continent, to carry a message for him to persons thousands of miles away—anything to awaken us out of this contemplative mood ; because in service, in energy, we should find healing and comfort, and in the open air we should throw off much of that which now oppresses us with the burden of a mystery.

This work having been done, a very singular incident occurred —" None of the disciples durst ask him, Who art thou ? " If we may invent a word, we should say there are unaskable questions in human life—questions we dare not ask, and other questions we may not ask, and burning questions to which we know the answer without putting the inquiry.; so that the heart is full of dumb questioning. A sacred fear kept the disciples quiet : they knew, and yet they did not know ; they were perfectly assured, and yet far away ; almost beneath their consciousness there lay a wonder as to the personality of this most distinguished presence. Do we not all know what it is to want to ask a question, and yet to feel the needlessness of asking it because there can be only one answer to the inquiry ? We dare not ask, Who made the world ? knowing that it was the Lord : it looks so like him ; it is as to bulk and range and lustre worthy of him. Even if we dissect it and take up one speck of it we know that only the Lord could have made the microscopic atom, for it is as beautiful as ever the great sun could be, and, indeed, the sun himself only exceeds the atom in mere bulk and size and weight ; the atom and the sun are one in quality, in make, in insignificance, in suggestiveness. Sometimes we do ask the question ; but why we ask it we cannot explain, because we know all the time that it was the Lord who made it. We dare not ask, Who made man ? knowing that it was the Lord. Verily, he looks as if he were God-made ! Sometimes he is common enough in his aspect ; sometimes he shows that he was made of the dust of the ground ; but now and again there flames within him a fire which has never been found in the dust; now and again there issues from him a tone of which it might be said that it came from heaven. Man is so mysterious, so complicated, altogether so marvellous in his constitution, structure, energy, inspiration, that we feel that it was the Lord that made him. We durst not ask, Who made history? knowing that it was the Lord. The workers never saw one another; they were, so to say, carrying on their manufactures in different factories or places of work: one was making part of the machine, and another was making another part of the same machine, and not until long years transpired did the parts come together and begin to show their relation one to another, and to something yet larger than themselves. Were any man to ask for a proof of God's existence, I should refer him to human history. Some one was asked to give a concise proof of the inspiration of the Bible, and he answered, " The Jews." It was a full reply. Who has read the history of the Jews? So, were any now to ask, " Give us a concise proof of the existence of God," the answer might well be —Human history, not of to-day, or yesterday, or any one day or decade or century, but the whole quantity comprised by the human story, in all its varieties, undulations, in all its transitory aspects and flashing phases, in all its rises, lapses, recoveries. Understand that, then no man durst ask, Who made human history? knowing that it was the Lord. There is a half-concealed God; there is a half-disclosed Omnipotence, bright to dazzling at points here and there, and quite clouded almost to concealment in vast sections of its infinity.

How shall we know that it was the Lord? The answer is in the 13th verse, " Jesus then cometh . . . and giveth." That is the proof. It is an eternal proof. When did Jesus do otherwise than give? He said of his Father in this very Gospel, " God so loved the world, that he gave." This is the proof of Christ's deity. He is the eternal Giver. He " giveth to all men liberally, and upbraideth not." He giveth to men in their need; when the poor and needy seek water, and there is none, and their tongue faileth for thirst, he hears them, and he opens a fountain in the sand, or makes the rocks pour water upon the parched ones. Read the history of the blessed Christ of God,

and you will find it is a history of Giving. What did Jesus do
in this instance? He performed a miracle of healing. How
do we know that it was a miracle of healing that he performed?
What was the disease? The disease was the double disease of
fatigue and hunger. Why talk of disease as if it were limited to
only one manifestation or form of suffering? Disease is a large
term; it includes weariness. What ails thee, O thou throbbing,
energetic life? and the answer is, Nothing positive, but I am
weary. Thy Lord will heal thee. Hunger is a disease. Only
Christ can appease it. This is the daily miracle of the world.
We look for miracles amongst the diseases which are familiar to
us by ghastly names; we speak of "all the ills that flesh is heir
to"; and probably there is hardly a man who could not write
out a list of ailments or diseases,—but who would put into that
list, sorrow of heart, tears unseen, hunger, thirst? Yet it is in
that region that Christ performs his most gracious wonders. He
heals the hunger that kills, and the weariness that gives sense
of exhaustion even in the presence of the tempting and exciting
universe. We should need no proofs of Providence if we opened
our eyes. Men are always looking in the distance for proofs of
God. We have already seen that about the time of our Lord's
coming, when it was already announced in the land, people
looked far away, as if they were searching the horizon for his
figure; and behold a voice was heard saying, "There standeth
one among you." Why do we omit the God that is near and
distract ourselves by seeking for a God afar off? He is nigh
thee, in thee, nearer than ever thy dearest friend could be to
thee; he burns in thy life-blood, he glows within thy garments.
Find the sacramental bread upon your table; find the wine of
God's love in all the succour of daily life.

How wise is Christ, we have said: and is there not a proof
of his wisdom in that he first healed the fatigue and hunger of
his disciples, and then began the spiritual examinations? "When
they had dined, Jesus saith." That is his plan on earth: first
heal the hunger of the hearer, then ask him spiritual questions;
first show your beneficent regard for his bodily needs, and then
begin to address his higher nature. "So when they had dined."
The dinner should never end in itself; the meal should open the

way for the Sacrament. After supper he took the same bread
and made new meanings of it. So when our daily meal is ended
are we to end our thought concerning it, as if we were but
animals made to consume? Shall we not after dinner think and
inquire, and wonder and pray, and pour out the heart in
acknowledgment and love and thankfulness? What questions
Christ might have asked! Simon Peter, hast thou repented?
Simon Peter, hast thou humbled thyself? Simon Peter, hast thou
told the disciples whom thou didst desert that thou art a wicked
man? Nothing of that kind was said by the gentle Jesus; he
uses the word which is chief in that Christian vocabulary,—
"Simon, son of Jonas, lovest thou me?"—a question you might
put to a child; the deepest question of all. This was profound,
because love carries everything; it is a fire that burns up all the
roots; it is a furnace that purges the gold of all its dross; it is
an enthusiasm which means prophetic insight, and sympathetic
identification with all things pure, true, and lovely. This is the
question which ought to be put to men in connection with Church
life—Lovest thou the Son of God? We are not made theologians.
The theologians can be but few in number, as the poets are, and
the philosophers, but we can answer the question as to our love.
Where there is love there will be no difficulty in the progress
of the Christian life: love sees in the darkness, walks on the
water, turns the wilderness into a glowing garden burning with
flowers that are not consumed; love is cast down, but not
destroyed, persecuted but not forsaken, in continual peril and
yet in continual security. When there is more love there will
be more progress. Love opens the door of every difficulty, and
love makes Christian education a daily delight.

This was gracious as well as profound, because it excited hope.
We sometimes ask a question, and convey the answer in the very
tone of the inquiry, so that the interrogation becomes its own
affirmative. Everything depends upon the tone in which a
question is asked. Who can tell the music of the inquiry as
addressed to Peter, "Lovest thou me?" Hidden in that inquiry
was the answer—I know what the reply will be, for thy great
heart is just a child's simple honest love. To say to a man,
"Understandest thou what thou readest?" is to excite the hope

that he may possibly understand it. Lovest thou the Church of the living God ? I have seen thee in the sanctuary sometimes : did thy being there signify that in thy poor heart there is some flame of love towards the Father ? The very inquiry stirred the spirit into hopefulness. Give a man to understand that you despair of him, and he may despair of himself; but ask him a question which has the effect of opening a door, and he might rise to the inquiry with a new energy and a new confidence.

This was practical as well as gracious and profound, because love is the true qualification for labour. A man cannot labour for Christ if he does not love Christ. It is love that fails, and therefore service goes down. But the heart will not confess this ; the heart is fertile in inventions and excuses for the lapses of life. Why do you forsake the sanctuary now ? Then will come a list of lies—accursed, unpardonable lies. Why do you not give so liberally now as you used to give ? Then will come anything but a confession of the truth. What is the truth ?—that love has gone down, the temperature of affection has rushed on its zero way. When we fail in love we cannot attain to service; we cannot reply to Christian appeals ; we cannot co-operate with energetic men,—we complain that they are too enthusiastic, and wish to go too quickly for us, and we begin to think that something of another kind is needed : and thus we lie, not unto man, but unto God. Could we say, " Our love has changed: we do not love the Cross as we did, we are not drawn towards the Son of God as we once were," we should have at least a statement made credible by its obvious truth. Peter gave a great heart-answer at the last, " Lord, thou knowest all things; thou knowest that I love thee," and his voice trembled when he said this. It was a noble voice, was Peter's, accustomed to speak out in the open sea, and to give orders whilst the wind was raging; but when this inquiry touched his heart all that great voice shrank into a tearful whisper, and he said, " Lord, thou knowest all things; thou knowest that I love thee." Right away down in the soul there is a true affection for thee; outwardly there are many things to disprove my affection, but in the centre and the heart of things there is a real loyalty to thee which I never felt to another. Christ, I love thee ! Until we get a heart-testimony like that, the Church will hesitate and flounder, will aim at nothing, and will beat the air.

Now then, said Christ, If you love me "feed my lambs," "feed my sheep," and again, "feed my sheep." They were all, too, the little sheep; even the sheep were lambs, and the lambs were lambkins; the terms are diminutive, so that we are taken down to the very first germs of love as well as of life. We need the love if we have to do the work; we cannot keep up the process of feeding, or succour, or education, or consolation, unless the love is in excess of the service. A man cannot go beyond his inspiration. He may attempt to do so, he may appear to do so; but by his languor, his reluctance, his half-heartedness, we should know that the life has gone out of him and all that is left is the flutter of an expiring pulse. And Jesus said, This feeding of the lambs, O Simon Peter, is only preparation for another form of service—thou shalt have thy love tested. There is a cross in every life, a place of crucifixion on every path: our love shall not be allowed to go forth merely as a verbal testimony, it shall be crucified, head downwards; it shall be tried as by fire.

John drops his pen here; he says, Many other things did Jesus do, but these can never be told—"If they should be written every one, I suppose that even the world itself could not contain the books that should be written." What a beautiful climax! Yet without any rhetorical artifice. What is the climax?—An *et cetera.* No artist could have ended with more consummate skill. We expect the rhetorician to climb the lofty steep and wave his triumphant flag upon the summit. But John, whose rhetoric was one of love, said, Now that I read what I have written I feel that I have written nothing worthy of the occasion; as I begin to think, the vision begins to grow. Miracle upon miracle did Jesus do of which no record is to be found; yea, if all he did were written the world itself could hardly contain the literature. That is true, because the world could not contain himself; he overflowed the empty space. It is the experience of all who follow Jesus that he never can be fully told. A man shall undertake to read the Bible through from end to end, and in proportion as he reads it minutely, will he say at the close, Let us begin again, for we have not begun at all.

INDEX.